XML

Al McKinnon and Linda McKinnon

Australia • Canada • Mexico • Singapore • Spain • United Kingdom • United States

XML

by Al McKinnon and Linda McKinnon

Product Manager:
Tricia Boyle

Managing Editor:
Jennifer Locke

Acquisitions Editor:
Bill Larkin

Development Editors:
David George
Lisa Ruffolo

Associate Product Manager:
Janet Aras

Editorial Assistant:
Christy Urban

Associate Marketing Manager:
Angela Laughlin

Production Editor:
Elena Montillo

Cover Designer:
Joseph Lee, Black Fish Design

Compositor:
GEX Publishing Services

Manufacturing Coordinator:
Denise Powers

Contributing Authors:
David Crewson
Arif Boga

Printed in Canada

1 2 3 4 5 6 7 8 9 WC 05 04 03 02

For more information, contact Course Technology, 25 Thomson Place, Boston, Massachusetts, 02210.

Or find us on the World Wide Web at: www.course.com

ISBN 0-619-03514-5

BRIEF

Contents

PREFACE xi

CHAPTER ONE
What is Extensible Markup Language (XML)? 1

CHAPTER TWO
XML Components 29

CHAPTER THREE
XML Creation and Editing Software 69

CHAPTER FOUR
Creating Document Type Definitions 105

CHAPTER FIVE
Creating XML Schemas 157

CHAPTER SIX
Creating XML Transformations 197

CHAPTER SEVEN
Linking in XML 235

CHAPTER EIGHT
Introduction to XHTML 287

CHAPTER NINE
Introduction to Vector Markup Language (VML) 325

CHAPTER TEN
Introduction to the Synchronized Multimedia Integration
Language (SMIL) 383

CHAPTER ELEVEN
Introduction to Cascading Style Sheets (CSS) 425

CHAPTER TWELVE
XML Data Binding Basics 471

CHAPTER THIRTEEN
Introduction to MathML 515

CHAPTER FOURTEEN
Introduction to the Channel Definition Format 571

INDEX 631

TABLE OF

Contents

PREFACE **xi**

CHAPTER ONE
What is Extensible Markup Language (XML)? **1**
XML Defined 2
XML as a Metalanguage 2
XML as a Markup Language 3
The Evolution of GML, SGML, and HTML 4
The Need for Standards 7
SGML 8
HTML 10
The Evolution of XML 13
XML is and is Not SGML 13
XML is Not HTML 14
Why is XML Such an Important Development? 16
The World Wide Web Consortium and XML 19
Chapter Summary 20
Review Questions 21
Hands-on Projects 25

CHAPTER TWO
XML Components **29**
Defining an XML Document 30
Document Components 31
The Prolog 31
The Element Hierarchy 37
Element Components and Properties 40
CDATA Sections 53
Well-Formed XML Documents 53
Valid XML Documents 55
Chapter Summary 58
Review Questions 59
Hands-on Projects 62
Case Projects 67

CHAPTER THREE
XML Creation and Editing Software **69**
Simple Text Editors 70
Graphical Text Editors 72
Microsoft XML Notepad 73
XAE 74
XML Pro 74
Peter's XML Editor 75
Adobe FrameMaker + SGML 76
SoftQuad XMetaL 77

Conglomerate 77
Microsoft Word and XML Creation 77
Integrated Development Environments 81
Xeena 83
XML Spy 84
Turbo XML 85
Integrating XML with Your Existing Document or Knowledge Management System 87
Initial Considerations 88
Business and Technology Considerations 89
Chapter Summary 91
Review Questions 92
Hands-on Projects 95
Case Projects 102

CHAPTER FOUR
Creating Document Type Definitions 105
Document Modeling and DTDs 107
When Document Type Declarations and DTDs Are Necessary 109
Internal Versus External DTDs 110
Internal DTDs 110
Private External DTDs 110
External DTDs with Different URLs 111
External DTDs for Public Access 112
Internal DTDs and External DTDs 113
DTDs and Valid XML Languages and Documents 114
Element Declarations 114
Element Names 114
The Content Model 115
Attribute List Declarations 123
Syntax for Attribute List Declarations in a DTD 123
Attribute Types and Default Values 124
Handling White Space 126
Language Identification 126
Attribute Value Normalization 127
Entity Declarations 127
Internal Parameter Entity 128
External Parameter Entity 130
Notation Declarations 130
DTDs and Namespace Declarations 132
Default Namespace Declarations 134
Prefix Namespace Declarations 135
Declaring Namespaces in the DTD 135
Limitations of DTDs with Respect to Namespace Declarations 137
Document Analysis and Testing 137
Documentation 138
Chapter Summary 139
Review Questions 140
Hands-on Projects 143
Case Projects 154

CHAPTER FIVE
Creating XML Schemas 157
Understanding Some Disadvantages of Using DTDs 158
The W3C XML Schema Recommendations 159
Schema Description 160

Schema Components 162
The Prolog 162
The Schema Element: Namespaces and Qualified/ Unqualified Locals 163
The <CONTACTS> Element: Element Types and Compositors 169
The <DEPT> Element: Attributes and Cardinality 170
The <NAME>, <EMAIL>, and <PHONE> Subelements: Simple Types and Schema Structures 171
The DEPTType Complex Type Declaration: Simple Content Types and Inheritance 175
Globally Referenced Simple Types (Archetypes) 178
Mixed Content Elements 178
Empty Element Content 179
Using Facets to Define Data More Precisely 179
Chapter Summary 182
Review Questions 183
Hands-on Projects 186
Case Projects 195

CHAPTER SIX
Creating XML Transformations 197
Why Transform XML Data? 198
Transforming XML Documents 198
XSL 199
XPath 201
XSLT 201
Sample Transformation—the TLSales Contacts List 202
Acquiring XSL Parsers 203
Examining the XML Source Document 204
Interpreting the DTD 205
Examining the Source Tree 206
Examining the XSLT Stylesheet 207
Chapter Summary 220
Review Questions 221
Hands-on Projects 224
Case Project 234

CHAPTER SEVEN
Linking in XML 235
Understanding the XML Linking Language (XLink) 236
Types of XLinks 237
Using Resources 239
Traversing Links 240
Applying XLink to Create Links in XML 240
Declaring An XLink Namespace Is Required 241
Using the XLink's Global Attributes in XLink 241
Restrictions on XLink Types and Attributes 244
A Simple-Type XLink Example 245
An Extended-Type XLink Example 246
Validating XLinks 249
Example 1: Employee Information with a Resource-type Linking Element 249
Example 2: Remote Employee Information with a Locator-type Linking Element 249
Example 3: Remote Employee Information Using Inbound Link Arcs 250
Example 4: Extended-type Linking Element 250
Validating Simple Links 255

Using the XML Pointer Language (XPointer) 255
Addressing a Document's Internal Structure with a Universal Resource Identifier (URI) 257
Fragment Identifier Components: Location Steps and Location Paths 259
XPointer Axes 261
XPointer Node Tests 262
XPointer Predicates 263
XPointer Location Set Functions 264
XPointer Examples 265
Understanding XPointer Points and Ranges 266
XPointer Points 267
XPointer Ranges 268
XPointer Abbreviations 269
Selecting an Implementation 270
Chapter Summary 271
Review Questions 272
Hands-on Projects 275
Case Project 286

CHAPTER EIGHT
Introduction to XHTML 287
Understanding XHTML 288
A Brief History of HTML and XHTML 289
Advantages of XHTML 292
XHTML Resembles HTML 292
XHTML Must Meet XML-compliant Coding Standards 292
XHTML is Extensible 292
XHTML is Modular 293
XHTML is Portable 293
XHTML is Backward and Future Compatible 293
XHTML Variants and DTDs 293
The XHTML 1.0 Strict Variant 294
The XHTML 1.0 Transitional Variant 295
The XHTML 1.0 Frameset Variant 296
Understanding the Difference Between XHTML Syntax and HTML Syntax 296
The Prolog and Basic Elements 297
Well-formedness 298
Element Names Must Be Lowercase 299
XHTML Elements Must Be Properly Closed 299
Extending an XHTML 1.0 Document 303
Converting Web Sites to XHTML 305
XHTML Utilities and Services Provided by W3C 305
W3C's HTML Validation Service 306
HTML TIDY 307
Amaya: W3C's Editor/Browser 308
Chapter Summary 309
Review Questions 310
Hands-on Projects 314
Case Project 324

CHAPTER NINE
Introduction to Vector Markup Language (VML) 325
Understanding Digital Imaging Technologies 326
Bitmap Graphics 326
Vector Graphic Images 328

Understanding the Vector Markup Language (VML) 331
History of VML 332
Other Vector Graphics Specifications 333
VML Advantages 336
Creating and Viewing VML Documents 337
VML Document Creation: Syntax and Features 338
VML Templates 343
The <shape> Element 343
Creating Paths: The path Attribute and <path> Element 345
Using Predefined Shapes 347
The <shapetype> Element 351
Placement of VML Figures 351
Altering Images 357
Adding Color to Shapes 357
Changing the Fill of VML Figures with the <fill> Element 358
Increasing or Decreasing Scale 362
Using the <group> Element 362
Chapter Summary 364
Review Questions 366
Hands-on Projects 369
Case Project 381

CHAPTER TEN
Introduction to the Synchronized Multimedia Integration Language (SMIL) 383
What is the Synchronized Multimedia Integrated Language? 384
SMIL 1.0 385
SMIL 2.0 385
Creating a SMIL Document 387
The Prolog 387
The <smil> Element 388
The <head> Element 389
The <layout> Element 389
The <meta> Element 394
The <switch> Element 395
The <body> Element 395
Synchronizing Media Objects 395
Using the <seq> Element for Synchronization 396
Using the <par> Element for Synchronization 398
Understanding the SMIL Media Object Elements 399
Hyperlinking Elements 404
Viewing and Preparing SMIL Documents 408
Chapter Summary 409
Review Questions 410
Hands-on Projects 413
Case Project 423

CHAPTER ELEVEN
Introduction to Cascading Style Sheets (CSS) 425
An Overview of Cascading Style Sheets 426
The World Wide Web Consortium and Cascading Style Sheets 426
Levels of Cascading Style Sheets 426
Support for Cascading Style Sheets 427

Specifying Styles for XML Documents 428
Affiliating External Style Sheets With XML Documents 428
Specifying an Internal Style Sheet 430
Specifying Inline Styles 431
Creating Style Rules 432
Understanding Selectors and Inheritance 434
Using Declarations, Properties, and Values 435
Displaying Inline and Block Elements 436
Using Selectors with Pseudo-Elements 437
Grouping Selectors by Classes 439
Grouping Selectors by Pseudo-Classes 443
Grouping Selectors by ID 447
Inserting Images With CSS Style Rules 449
Inserting Images as Backgrounds 450
Inserting Images as Discrete Elements 451
Other Introductory Style Specifications 452
Drawing Borders Around Elements 452
Text Alignment, Margins, and Indentations 453
Absolute and Relative Positioning 454
Why and How Style Sheets Cascade 456
Chapter Summary 457
Review Questions 458
Hands-on Projects 460
Case Project 470

CHAPTER TWELVE
XML Data Binding Basics 471
Data Binding Fundamentals 472
Data Consumer Elements 473
Using Extended Attributes to Retrieve Data 475
Using the <div> and <span> Elements 476
Using the <table> Element for Data Set Binding 478
Integrating XML Data Sources with XHTML Documents 479
Using Internal Data Islands 480
Using External Data Islands 481
Pairing Data Sources and Data Fields 483
Using Data Binding Agents and Table Repetition Agents 485
Working with Data Source Objects (DSOs) 486
Understanding How the DSO Returns Data 487
Data Nesting and the Two-Level Rule 489
Navigating Recordsets 491
Special Situation—Using the dataPageSize Attribute 495
Special Situation—Using Single-Valued Elements Instead of Tabular Elements 495
Chapter Summary 498
Review Questions 499
Hands-on Projects 504
Case Project 514

CHAPTER THIRTEEN
Introduction to MathML 515
Understanding Mathematical Expression Issues 516
The W3C and MathML 519
MathML Design Goals 521
MathML as Part of a Layered Software Architecture 521

Understanding MathML 523
MathML General Markup Specifications 524
MathML Presentation Markup Specifications 526
MathML Content Markup Specifications 528
Considerations for Using MathML on Web Pages 534
MathML and Namespaces 535
MathML DTDs and Validation 535
Using Tools to Create Math Expressions 535
Abstract Expression Trees 535
Layout Boxes 536
Exploring Examples of Math Editors and Presenters 537
Exploring EzMath 538
Exploring MathType 543
Exploring MathPlayer 544
Chapter Summary 544
Review Questions 545
Hands-on Projects 549
Case Projects 570

CHAPTER FOURTEEN
Introduction to the Channel Definition Format 571
Pushing, Pulling, and Webcasting 572
Basic Webcasting, Managed Webcasting, and Active Channels 574
Understanding the Channel Definition Format 576
CDF As an XML-Related Language 576
CDF, the W3C, and RDF 577
Using Channels 579
Investigating the Channels Already Available to You 580
Adding a Web Site to Your Channel List 581
Making a Channel Available for Offline Viewing 586
Viewing a Channel Offline 587
Creating a CDF Channel 589
Design the Channel 590
Create the Logo Images 592
Create the CDF File 593
Post the CDF File to Your Web Server 593
Provide Access to the Channel 593
Creating a CDF File 595
The Prolog 595
The <channel> Element: Root Element and Channel Identifier 595
Other CDF Elements 599
No Official DTD for CDF 608
Special Characters and Character Encoding 609
Sample CDF File and Description 610
CDF Resources 616
Chapter Summary 617
Review Questions 618
Hands-on Projects 621
Case Projects 630

INDEX 631

Preface

Knowing how to create and work with XML documents is becoming a required skill set for anyone who works with either Web design or database content. Files formatted using XML are found in all aspects of computing now from application configuration files to Web pages and data exchange.

Because XML is platform independent, most operating systems support it, including Windows, OS/2, UNIX, NetWare, and OS390, to name a few. Excellent XML tools are available for all these operating systems. Some XML tools require that you have installed a Java Software Developers Kit (SDK) on your system.

The Intended Audience

The book is intended to provide an introduction to what XML is and how it can be used. Prerequisites include only some basic knowledge of World Wide Web (WWW) services and HTML coding. No previous experience with XML is necessary.

The Approach

This book explains how to create XML documents to describe data ranging from simple headings and body text to mathematical formulas, music, and parts lists. This book also discusses XML-based markup languages, such as XHTML for Web pages, MathML for mathematic information, and SMIL for multimedia presentations. Whenever possible, the chapters use conceptual diagrams as well as coding samples to explain and illustrate XML concepts. Each chapter also includes the following features:

- **Chapter Objectives**: Each chapter in this book begins with a list of the important concepts to be mastered within the chapter. This list provides you with a quick reference to the contents of the chapter as well as a useful study aid.
- **Figures and Tables**: Figures and tables provide visual reinforcement of concepts covered and outline information in an easily readable format.
- **Notes**: Chapters contain Notes designed to provide additional information such as further resources and useful Web sites.
- **Chapter Summaries**: Each chapter's text is followed by a summary of chapter concepts. These summaries provide a helpful way to recap and revisit the ideas covered in each chapter.

- **Review Questions**: End-of-chapter assessment begins with a set of 20-25 review questions that reinforce the main ideas introduced in each chapter. These questions ensure that you have mastered the concepts and understand the information you have learned.
- **Hands-on Projects**: The Hands-on Projects provide the opportunity to practice the skills and concepts learned in each chapter. They include step-by-step instructions for installing and configuring software tools and for developing XML documents.
- **Case Projects**: Approximately two cases are presented at the end of each chapter. These cases are designed to help you apply what you have learned in each chapter to real-world situations. They provide the opportunity to independently synthesize and evaluate information, examine potential solutions, and make recommendations, much as you would in an actual business situation.

TEACHING TOOLS

The following supplemental materials are available when this book is used in a classroom setting. All of the teaching tools available with this book are provided to the instructor on a single CD-ROM.

Electronic Instructor's Manual. The Instructor's Manual helps you identify areas that are more difficult to teach, and provides you with ideas of how to present the material in an easier fashion. The Instructor's Manual that accompanies this textbook contains a variety of features, including the following:

- Additional instructional material to assist in class preparation, such as suggestions for lecture topics.
- A sample course syllabus.
- Solutions to end-of-chapter Review Questions.

ExamView®. This textbook is accompanied by ExamView, a powerful testing software package that allows instructors to create and administer printed, computer (LAN-based), and Internet exams. ExamView includes hundreds of questions that correspond to the topics covered in this text, enabling students to generate detailed study guides that include page references for further review. The computer-based and Internet testing components allow students to take exams at their computers, and also save the instructor time by grading each exam automatically.

PowerPoint Presentations. This book comes with Microsoft PowerPoint slides for each chapter. These are included as a teaching aid for classroom presentation, to make available to students on the network for chapter review, or to be printed for classroom distribution. Instructors can add their own slides for additional topics they introduce to the class.

Data Files. Files that contain all of the data necessary for the Hands-on Projects and Case Projects are provided through the Course Technology Web site at **www.course.com**, and are also available on the Teaching Tools CD-ROM.

Solution Files. Solutions to end-of-chapter Review Questions, Hands-on Projects, and Case Projects are provided on the Teaching Tools CD-ROM and may also be found on the Course Technology Web site at **www.course.com**. The solutions are password protected.

Distance Learning. Course Technology is proud to present online test banks in WebCT and Blackboard, as well as MyCourse 2.0, Course Technology's own course enhancement tool, to provide the most complete and dynamic learning experience possible. Instructors are encouraged to make the most of your course, both online and offline. For more information on how to access your online test bank, contact your local Course Technology sales representative.

ACKNOWLEDGMENTS

We'd really like to thank Tricia Boyle for shepherding XML from its very inception. We're also very grateful to Lisa Ruffolo and David George, our Development Editors, for their advice, hard work, and encouragement, and for explaining and coordinating the many and varied aspects of this project. A special thanks also goes out to Elena Montillo for her efforts toward keeping this book on schedule and making it a success. We're also grateful to Dave Brownfield, PhD, Mount St. Clare College; Linda Hemenway, Santa Rosa Junior College; DeeDee Herrera, Dodge City Community College; Bobbie Hyndman, Amarillo College; Lisa Macon, Valencia Community College; Jerry Mikulski, DeVry Institute – Pomona; Allen Schmidt, Madison Area Technical College; Jeff Snyder, Computer Learning Network; Michael B. Spring, University of Pittsburgh; and Jim Thomas, Ohlone College for reviewing each chapter of this book and providing constructive criticism and comments. Thanks to Mark Goodin, our copy editor, whose tolerance, attention to detail, and sense of humor were invaluable. Thank you also to Harris Bierhoff, Shawn Day, and other members of the Quality Assurance staff who spent long hours checking and re-checking the text and exercises.

Al and Linda McKinnon

Read This Before You Begin

The following information will help you as you prepare to use this textbook.

To the User of the Data Files

To complete the steps and projects in this book, you will need data files that have been created specifically for this book. Your instructor will provide the data files to you. You also can obtain the files electronically from the Course Technology Web site by connecting to *www.course.com* and then searching for this book title. Note that you can use a computer in your school lab or your own computer to complete the Hands-on Projects in this book.

Each chapter in this book has its own set of data files that typically include HTML and XML files. These data files are stored on a Data Disk. Throughout this book, you will be instructed to copy files from a folder on your Data Disk to a particular folder on your hard disk. Be sure to set up and use the specified folder structure to organize your Web projects and XML documents.

Using Your Own Computer

You can use a computer in your school lab or your own computer to complete the chapters, Hands-on Projects, and Case Projects in this book. Your computer setup should meet the following requirements:

- **Computer**. A personal computer with a Pentium II-class processor or higher.
- **Windows**. Microsoft Windows 2000 Professional or Microsoft Windows XP Professional.

The chapters, Hands-on Projects, and Case Projects were written using Microsoft Windows 2000 Professional (with SP2 "w2ksp2.exe"), and tested using Microsoft Windows 2000 Professional and Windows XP Professional.

- **Other software**. XML Spy 4.3 Suite, Internet Explorer 5.50 (with SP2) or later, and Netscape 6.1 or later.

A 120-day version of XML Spy 4.3 comes packaged with this book. You can also download a complimentary 30-day evaluation copy of the XML Spy Suite from *www.xmlspy.com*. When you open an XML document, XML Spy uses its built-in parser to check the document for well-formedness and to validate it against any specified DTD, DCD, XDR, BizTalk, or XSD Schema. For processing XSLT, you must download the Microsoft XML Parser 3.0 (msxml3.exe) from *www.microsoft.com*.

Some Hands-on Projects use additional software, which you can download from the Web sites listed in the following table. Download the latest version of the software.

Software	Web site location
Amaya	www.w3.org/amaya/
EzMath	www.w3.org/People/Raggett/ezmath1_1.zip
Java 1.4	http://java.sun.com/j2se/1.4/download/html
MathType	www.dessci.com
RealOne Player	www.real.com
Tidy	www.sourceforge.net/projects/tidy
Winzip	www.winzip.com
Xeena	www.alphaworks.ibm.com/tech/xeena
XML Notepad	http://msdn.microsoft.com/xml/notepad/intro.asp
XML Pro	www.vervet.com/demo.html

Preparing for the XML Projects

Before you work with the XML Spy Suite to create XML projects, you must create the home folder you will use for the Hands-on Projects and Case Projects.

To create the home folder:

1. Use My Computer or Windows Explorer to create a folder named **home** on your hard disk, such as drive C.
2. Open the **home** folder, and then create a subfolder within it. Use your name as the name of the folder. For example, a user named Linda would use home/linda as the folder names.

Visit Our World Wide Web Site

Additional materials designed especially for this book might be available for your course. Periodically search *www.course.com* for more information and materials to accompany this text.

To the Instructor

To complete all the exercises and chapters in this book, your users must work with a set of user files, called a Data Disk, and download software from Web sites. The data files are included on the Teaching Tools CD. They may also be obtained electronically through the Course Technology Web site at www.course.com. Follow the instructions in the Help file to copy the user files to your server or standalone computer. You can view the Help file using a text editor, such as WordPad or Notepad.

After the files are copied, you can make Data Disks for the users yourself, or tell them where to find the files so they can make their own Data Disks. Make sure the files are set up correctly by having students follow the instructions in the "To the User of the Data Files" section.

Course Technology Data Files

You are granted a license to copy the data files to any computer or computer network used by individuals who have purchased this book.

CHAPTER

1

WHAT IS EXTENSIBLE MARKUP LANGUAGE (XML)?

In this chapter, you will learn:

- How XML relates to other computer languages
- About the evolution of text markup technologies, including XML and its predecessors
- To identify the basic features of XML
- About the similarities and differences among GML, SGML, HTML, and XML
- About several individuals and organizations that have influenced, facilitated, and standardized XML and related technologies

Since 1997, XML-based languages have become essential technology. They provide the standard for the structure of data and for its transmission across a variety of networks, most notably the World Wide Web. XML has matured quickly as a metalanguage. Related standards are being developed constantly and hundreds of XML-related languages have proliferated through many organizations and industries around the world. Despite its strengths, however, XML is not intended to replace existing technologies, but to complement them in this increasingly connected, fast-paced, data-dependent world of international commerce and research.

Chapter 1 introduces XML in the context of its heritage. In this chapter, you review generic encoding and markup from its birth in the 1960s to the latest standards. You learn where XML is from, what it is, and what it is not. You also learn where to go to find additional resources to expand on the concepts introduced here.

XML DEFINED

XML is an abbreviation for **Extensible Markup Language**. You have probably heard of computer language categories like assembly languages, fourth-generation languages, machine languages, object-oriented languages, programming languages, or others. In fact, there are approximately two dozen such categories. Some are separate and discrete and dedicated to specific functions. Some are almost identical to others. Some are subsets of others, and some are actually hybrids of others, born out of the need for a language that performs more than one function simultaneously.

XML authors and developers are generally split into two camps: those who state that XML is a **markup language**, and those who state that XML is a **metalanguage**. Both camps are correct. Despite its name, XML is really two languages in one: XML can be categorized as both a metalanguage and a markup language. The function of a markup language (or **markup specification language**) is to design ways to describe information, usually for storage, transmission, or processing by a program. The function of a metalanguage is to create a formal description of another language. How each developer categorizes XML depends on what that developer uses it for. XML also has a formal definition, as stated in the **World Wide Web Consortium's** Extensible Markup Language (XML) 1.0 Recommendation:

"The Extensible Markup Language (XML) is a subset of SGML ... [the goal of which] is to enable generic SGML to be served, received, and processed on the Web in the way that is now possible with HTML. XML has been designed for ease of implementation and for interoperability with both SGML and HTML."

Further explanations of the Standard Generalized Markup Language (SGML), the Hypertext Markup Language (HTML), and the World Wide Web Consortium are found later in this chapter.

XML as a Metalanguage

While programming languages like Fortran, Basic, C++, or Java are used to create programs for conducting specific calculations, actions, and decisions, XML is used to create XML-based languages which, in turn, are used to create specific **documents** (or files) for use by the developer, their organization, or their industry.

XML allows developers to create their own specific customized collections of components (for example, tags, elements, and attributes, all of which are defined in Chapter 2) that accurately describe the physical contents of their documents. In this capacity, XML acts like an alphabet combined with its punctuation and other semantic symbols. XML doesn't make any sense alone; you have to create appropriate meaningful combinations with it.

As with standard documents, an XML document cannot do anything by itself. A specific program must be developed that interacts with it.

Documents created with XML-based languages can contain many types of information or data, including text, graphics, object metadata, e-commerce transactions, Application Program Interfaces (APIs), equations, and multimedia, among others. All documents contain one or more of these types of information according to a predetermined and deliberate structure. Structured information also indicates what role the content plays. For example, ordinary content in a document differs from header or footer content, which, in turn, differs from content found in a figure or a table. XML indicates what the content is, as well as how it should look.

Later in this chapter, a list is provided that describes a few of the hundreds of XML-based languages that have been developed by individual organizations or among organizations in various industries for in-house or industry-wide use.

XML as a Markup Language

XML is also a markup language and, as such, it is used to mark up text. Markup refers to the insertion of characters or symbols to indicate how the information in a document should appear when it is printed or displayed, or to describe a document's logical structure. Marking up text is a way to add information about your data to the data itself. Consider these real world examples of how you may already be marking up documents:

- Have you ever underlined words or passages, or used a highlighter pen, to indicate their importance?
- Have you ever marked up a rough draft of a report with symbols indicating "new paragraph here", or "bold this", or "remove this"?
- Have you ever made marks on a map indicating where you want to turn left, or hazards to avoid?
- Have you ever numbered bits of information, or steps, in an otherwise unnumbered procedure?

If you have ever performed any of those activities, you were marking up data. Your margin symbols, notes, or highlights indicated the relative importance, order, or other emphasis of the data at hand. Perhaps you were using some sort of standard marks or comments so that if anyone else looked at the markup, they could instantly identify the emphasis or order you were conveying.

In earlier days, markup was (and still is) used as a shorthand between authors and printers, editors, or artists to indicate how a manuscript should be formatted, and was actually written or typed onto the page. Since the widespread proliferation of information technology over the past several decades, markup has been adopted and used extensively by the information technology world. You might have seen "revealed codes", to borrow from a famous, word processing program. Those codes were markup that was inserted into a text document by its creator and they specified paper types, margins, the end of paragraphs, font type and size specifications, symbol insertions, etc.

With the proliferation of the Internet, intranets, extranets, enterprise networks, and home networks, the data transmitted over the wire, through the air, and through space must include all the information necessary for the computers, routers, firewalls, hubs, and other network components to deal with it. The recipient needs to be able to interpret the essence of the communication, whether it is the format and content of database data, multimedia graphic files or audio files, credit card authorizations, or any other of various document types.

The primary goal of markup is to separate the description of document logic, structure, data, and other content from the description of the final display. In addition, documents that use markup are ASCII (text-based), so they remain independent of platforms and operating systems.

Markup indicators are called **tags** or tag names. An XML document designer concentrates primarily on using tags to describe a document's contents as accurately as possible. Formatting is an automated process that occurs later. For example, a paragraph tag precedes all the paragraphs presented here so they are separated by an empty line from the preceding line. That tag is read and processed by XML-enabled Web browsers or by desktop publishing programs, depending on the medium and whether you're reading this on someone's web site, in a book, or projected on a screen.

Markup can be inserted by the document creator in many ways, including:

- Typing all the tag names using a simple text editor (e.g., MS Notepad)
- Using a more advanced text editor and prepackaged markup symbols to save keystrokes (e.g., MS Word)
- Using an integrated development environment editor (IDE) that lets you create the document as you want it to appear (e.g., XML Spy).

The Hands-on Projects at the end of this chapter present examples of XML files. In later chapters, you examine and create others.

THE EVOLUTION OF GML, SGML, AND HTML

The evolution from basic, text description languages to XML has taken almost forty years. A brief review of the evolution of XML and its predecessors can help you understand the principles of XML, and the context and rationale of its development.

More than 30 years ago (that is, up to the late 1960s), computer text processing applications were not designed to work together, or even on the same systems. They used proprietary coding, and their formatting instructions were combined with the body of the text in a document. For example, take a look at the various procedural markups shown in Figure 1-1.

```
\document class[legalpaper, 14pt]{article}
\begin{document}
\section{simple text}%The Inn He supposed to be a Castle
\begin{enumerate}
\item/textbf{Whereon he spied an inn}
\item/textbf{Which to his grief and Don Quixote's joy}
\item/textbf{Must needs be a Castle}
\end{enumerate}
```

Figure 1-1 Sample of an early text processing document

In September 1967, Mr. William Tunnicliffe, of the Graphic Communications Association (GCA), made a presentation during a meeting at the Canadian Government Printing Office. One topic covered was the separation of content information in documents from their format information. That presentation is considered to be a sort of flashpoint, because it is credited with initiating the evolution of generic coding, which ultimately formed the basis for XML.

In 1973, IBM released their **Generalized Markup Language (GML)**, a product that had been in development since 1969 (when it had first been called Text Description Language). Prior to GML, each of the separate functions (that is: text composition and editing, data-retrieval, and page composition) required separate and different applications of function-specific markup instructions (that is, each required its own distinct and different procedural markup). Further, those instructions would sometimes have to be changed according to the applications used to ultimately process the documents. For example, in Figure 1-1, at the beginning of every line there are at least two instructions, one for each applicable function. Plus, enclosing the "list" text in parentheses indicates yet another kind of instruction. The challenge faced by the GML developers was to integrate all the functions, to create a common set of markup instructions that they all could interpret.

With GML, IBM separated the specific formatting instructions from the content of the document itself. The markup was based only on the identification of the different types of structural components in a document (for example, heading styles, font treatments, bullet lists, paragraphs, etc.). Using GML, an author could assign various tag names to respective sections of text. The tag names came from a predetermined set of symbols available with GML. Once the various sections of text were identified, then any application could be provided with a separate set of instructions on how to process those sections. This was the beginning of generic (or descriptive) encoding, furthering the vision expressed earlier by Mr. Tunnicliffe. Figure 1-2 illustrates a sample of GML markup.

```
:h2.The Inn He Supposed to be a Castle
:01.
:li.Whereon he spied an :hp2.inn:ehp2.
:li.Which to his grief and Don Quixote's joy
:li.Must needs be a :hp2.castle:ehp2
:eol.
:hp1.Cervantes
```

Figure 1-2 Sample of a markup done with IBM's Generalized Markup Language

In Figure 1-3, a sample tag name is dissected. As you can see, a tag name in GML was preceded by a delimiter (the colon), which instructed the text formatter to begin processing the tag. Then the tag name itself appeared. It was followed by a content separator (the period), which told the processor to stop processing the tag, and then to process the text that followed according to the specification found in the tag name.

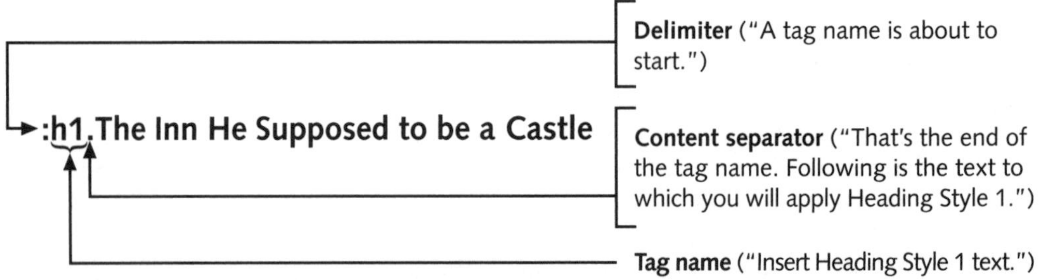

Figure 1-3 Sample of a GML tag name

The advantage to GML's generic encoding was that the document became **transportable**. It could be reprinted in different styles or processed in different ways without making any changes to the original document (i.e., to the original file), and the author did not have to set up the format details for displaying the document. Similar to the process used in the publication of these materials, the authors only have to be concerned with providing content and suggestions for general formatting. The rest of the development team takes care of all the subsequent publishing functions, such as choosing the fonts and formatting to associate with each code. Figure 1-4 illustrates the advantage of generic encoding. The document has been coded with components such as a basic font, a distinct title/heading, a list of numbered items, bolded text, italicized text, etc. The document displayed on the left indicates that its application interpreted the font code, for example, in one way: as Helvetica or Arial or similar. The document on the right has been processed by an application that interpreted the same code in a different base font: Gill Sans or similar. The point here is that the document has two different appearances, but each creates an impact similar to the other. However, the differences in appearance did not happen as a result of differences in the document's code. They happened as a result of the differences between the two applications, when each interpreted the coding in the document in their own distinct ways.

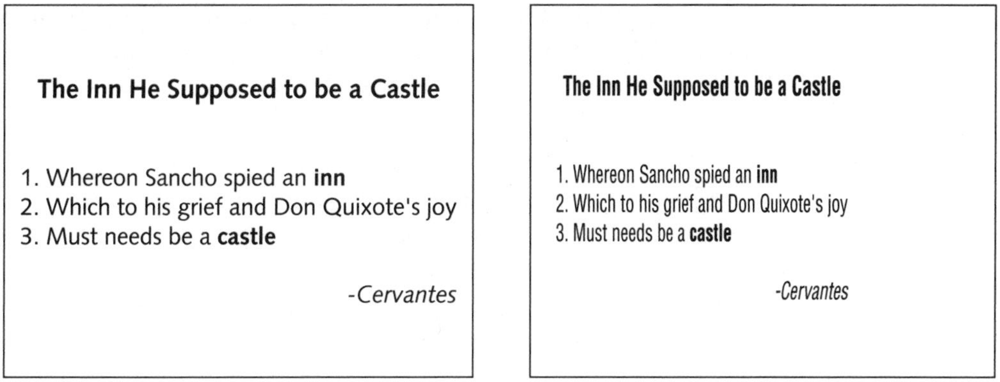

The Inn He Supposed to be a Castle	**The Inn He Supposed to be a Castle**
1. Whereon Sancho spied an **inn** 2. Which to his grief and Don Quixote's joy 3. Must needs be a **castle**	1. Whereon Sancho spied an **inn** 2. Which to his grief and Don Quixote's joy 3. Must needs be a **castle**
-Cervantes	*-Cervantes*

Figure 1-4 Generic encoding: one document, two different appearances

The Need for Standards

The development of GML indicated that there was potential value in creating a universal, machine-independent system of encoding documents. However, as development continued, it became clear that there were other document creation tools being developed by other organizations, and each of those tools had their own respective components and elements—some even included markup principles like GML. Two crucial points became apparent: for markup languages to be truly useful to many users in several display environments (e.g., hard copy, on screen, etc.) a standard must be developed to list the accepted, valid markup tags, and that such a standard must define what each markup tag means.

Each tag communicates its own specific layout to its respective display environment. In Figure 1-2, these cases, the :h2. tags render a Heading Style 2 (i.e., same font, larger font size, bolded, and centered on the line) and the now obsolete :hp2. tags render a highlighted phrase (in this case, "same font, same size, but bolded"). Notice that, in Figure 1-4, two different display environments (for example, a terminal screen versus a printer) might display the marked up content differently.

The principles behind standard development also included the following assumptions:

- Networks connected many different types of computers, and the information passed among them had to be usable on all of them.
- Information intended for public use could not be restricted to one technology and certainly not to one make, model, or manufacturer of such technology. (That would be the same as giving control of data format to private individuals or organizations, which would be unacceptable.)
- Such information should be in a form that could be reused in many different ways, to optimize time and effort.

Thus, proprietary data formats, no matter how well documented or publicized, would simply not be an option due to issues about loss of control, unexpected and unannounced changes, or the institution of exorbitant fees.

SGML

In 1978, the **American National Standards Institute (ANSI)** committee on Information Processing established the Computer Languages for the Processing of Text committee. That committee then undertook a project whose objective was the development of a standard, based on GML principles, for text description languages. The GenCode committee of the Graphic Communications Association (GCA)—dedicated, among other things, to advancing the cause of information interoperability—supported the effort, providing a nucleus of people dedicated to the task of developing the **Standardized General Markup Language (SGML)** standard. The first working draft of the SGML standard was published in 1980. Major adopters included the U.S. Internal Revenue Service (IRS) and the U.S. Department of Defense. By 1984, the project had also been authorized by the **International Organization for Standardization (ISO)** as well as ANSI. The ISO team was called ISO/IEC JTC1/SC18/WG8; the ANSI committee was called X3V1.8. Alignment between the two teams was maintained by IBM's Charles Goldfarb, the original inventor of GML, who served as project editor for both groups.

Finally, in 1986, after eight years of development, the Standard Generalized Markup Language (ISO 8879:1986) was approved. It is still recognized as the overarching, comprehensive international standard metalanguage. Its development was a watershed event in the evolution of markup languages, because it is not simply a document encoding language unto itself, but it facilitates the creation of any number of additional markup/metalanguages. These languages can then be tailored to the specific requirements of any organization or industry, as well as the creation of the respective electronic, machine-readable documents related to those languages.

SGML is an extremely powerful and extensible tool, and has led to the cataloging and indexing of data in many fields—medical, financial, technical, aerospace, telecommunications, and even the entertainment industry, among others. Table 1-1 lists just a few of the hundreds of SGML-based languages developed over the past 15 years.

Table 1-1 Examples of SGML-based languages

Language	Description
Extensible Markup Language (XML)	An SGML-based language used to create other industry-specific or organization-specific languages that can be served, received, and processed on the Internet
Hypertext Markup Language (HTML)	An SGML-based markup language used to create hypertext documents; it has been in use over the World Wide Web since 1990

Table 1-1 Examples of SGML-based languages (continued)

Language	Description
Formalized Exchange of Electronic Publications (FORMEX)	A European SGML-based standard developed by the Office for Official Publications of the European Communities; it is used for the exchange of electronic publications in the European Union
Text Encoding Initiative (TEI)	An SGML-based international standard that helps libraries, museums, publishers, scholars, etc., represent texts for online research and teaching
Air Transport Association (ATA)	Chiefly ATA Spec 2100, an SGML-based specification for the development of manuals and other documents by manufacturers (since 1989)
Telecommunications Industry Markup (TIM)	SGML-based specification for describing information in telecommunications documents

SGML uses generic descriptive markup, so that the content of a document may be defined in terms that are entirely separate from its processing. The structural basis of SGML is the division of information in a document into useful pieces—titles, paragraphs, part numbers, person names, text, graphics, hypertext links, etc.,—called **elements**, which can then be formatted, sorted, or searched in a consistent fashion.

Using SGML, an author can specifically and arbitrarily identify and name the elements so they can be managed and manipulated in specific ways. The element names (i.e., tags) are embedded in the data to identify the beginning and the end of the elements. The resulting tagged data makes the file usable with any conforming software tool running on any operating system platform. Please refer to the sample of SGML markup in Figure 1-5. Note that everything from the start tag <title> to the end tag </title>, including those tags, is part of the title element

```
<chapter><title>Sancho's Complaint</title>
<list>
<item>...it has been nothing but
<item>cudgels and more cudgels,
<item>blows and more blows;
<item>then, as an extra, I get tossed in a blanket...
</list>
<author>Cervantes</author>
```

Figure 1-5 Sample of SGML markup

Further, SGML formalizes the concept of a **document type** and provides for a separate file called a **Document Type Definition (DTD)**, which identifies all of the elements in its respective document(s), and indicates the structural relationships among them. A simple DTD is illustrated in Figure 1-6.

```
<!Doctype mybook_1.dtd [
<!ELEMENT chapter (title?,item+,author)>
<!ELEMENT title (#pcdata)>
<!ELEMENT item (#pcdata)>
<!ELEMENT author (#pcdata)>
]</mybook_1.dtd>
```

Figure 1-6 Sample of a simple DTD

SGML is used in this manner for activities as diverse as typesetting, indexing, CD-ROM distribution, World Wide Web hypertext creation, and translation into foreign languages.

The major advantage to SGML is that any SGML-related language—and the documents created according to the SGML-related language—may be customized according to the needs of an individual organization and even across organizations within an industry, provided the organizations cooperate in the development. The language and its documents may then be processed by all participants, without changes or losses, for different purposes and in different forms, through the use of any relevant application that understands SGML. Plus, the relevant documents can be developed for manipulation and display on a variety of platforms: on handheld or laptop computers, on personal computers at work or at home, on more powerful workstations, in print, or via projection without fear of inadvertent loss of information.

In spite of its considerable extensibility, which comes from its flexible tagging capability, there are disadvantages to SGML, especially with respect to its application across the World Wide Web. If you were to examine the SGML ISO standard, the pages of which number in the hundreds, you would quickly and correctly conclude that fully SGML-compliant languages would likely be large, expend a large amount of resources to implement, and be too cumbersome for Web browser-related duties. Therefore, using full SGML to create or view the much smaller and simpler World Wide Web documents is difficult to justify. And the commercial browser manufacturers, who are just now including XML capability, have indicated they do not intend to ever support full SGML. Full SGML systems, therefore, are better suited for large, complex data/document environments that justify the development expense and the installation and administration of the systems needed for development or processing. You are likely to find SGML systems serving very well within the internal structures of larger organizations with high speed intranets.

HTML

Hypertext Markup Language (HTML) is an **application profile** of the SGML ISO Standard 8879:1986. Thus, HTML, like XML, is one of the SGML document types: one of many dialects of the SGML "mother tongue". Any fully conformant SGML system should be able to read HTML documents.

HTML was originally designed at the **European Organization for Nuclear Research (CERN)**, original home of the Web, around 1990, to provide a very simple version of SGML that could be implemented by ordinary users.

At that point, the Internet was already well established as a technology, supporting a community of researchers and developers around the world. HTML, therefore, was designed to provide a universal means to present and link basic business-type documents around the Internet.

HTML combined the advantages of an SGML-based markup with hypertext technologies—those well-known links that provide quick connections between documents. Since HTML was free, simple, and widely supported, its use spread widely and quickly. It became one of the more famous—maybe the most famous—of the computer markup systems. Now, it is the document type most frequently used on the Web.

Web page developers have been working with markup languages since the late 1980s. They have predominantly used HTML to create hypertext documents that are platform independent. HTML markup can represent hypertext news, mail, documentation, and hypermedia; menus of options; database query results; simple structured documents with in-line graphics; and hypertext views of existing bodies of information. HTML defines a simple, fixed type of document with markup designed for common office correspondence or technical reports (e.g., headings, paragraphs, lists, illustrations, etc., and some provision for hypertext and multimedia).

HTML documents are SGML documents with predefined generic markup tags/symbols (i.e., predefined semantics) that are appropriate for representing information from a wide range of domains. Documents that have been marked up, that contain plain text as well as the tags that specify the rules for formatting that text, are read by an HTML processing application (e.g., a Web browser) that conforms to the display rules of HTML.

Unfortunately, since the inception of HTML, most Web page designers who use it have been concerned only with what the documents look like when displayed on the screen, inside the browser window. So, although HTML stands for Hypertext Markup Language, it has been applied mostly as a "Hypertext Formatting Language."

In addition, the elements and attributes of HTML use a limited and restricted (nonarbitrary) set of document structures. All HTML document developers can only draw from the same limited set of elements. For example, the <ul> tag specifies a rule that instructs an HTML processing application to begin an unnumbered list. Similarly, the <li> tag instructs the HTML processing application to treat the following text as an item in the list. The <b> tag tells the application to bold the text. Meanwhile, to end the respective elements, the tag names similar to the start tag names are used, but the end tag names are preceded by a forward slash " / ", like this: </ul>. There is only one exception to that rule: the <li> markup tag does not require such an end tag. Look at the example in Figure 1-7.

```
<html>
  <head>
    <title>Wit of Groucho Marx</title>
  </head>
  <body bgcolor="#ffffff">
    <h1><center><u><bold>Groucho Speaks!</h1></center></u></bold>
    <ul>
    <li>A child of five could understand this. Fetch me a child of five.
    <li>Outside of a dog, a book is man's best friend. Inside of a dog, it's too dark to read.
    <li>Time wounds all heels.
    </ul>
    Return to the <a href="marxpage.html">Philosophy Page </a><br>
    <hr>
    Created and maintained by XYZ Inc. <i><a href="mailto:DSMITH@XYZ.com">DSMITH@XYZ.com<br>
    </a></i>Last Updated: 10/05/02 <br>
  </body>
</html>
```

Figure 1-7 Sample of HTML markup

Now look at Figure 1-8 to see the rendered version of the markup in Figure 1-7. This rendering is typical of what any browser would return for such simple markup tags.

```
                    Groucho Speaks!

A child of five could understand this. Fetch me a child of five.
Outside of a dog, a book is man's best friend. Inside of a dog,
  it's too dark to read.
Time wounds all heels.
Return to the Philosophy Page
--------------------------------------------------------------
Created and maintained by XYZ Inc.    DSMITH@XYZ.com

Last Updated: 10/05/02
```

Figure 1-8 Rendering of HTML markup

Even though revised versions of HTML were released in 1994, 1996, and 1997, and individual browser manufacturers augmented HTML with the addition of style sheets and other proprietary extensions, they could not meet the functionality demands of an ever expanding Internet clientele.

The need for greater power and flexibility in markup languages used on the Internet led to a return to the SGML drawing board and to the development of XML. In later chapters, you are also introduced to an XML-related language called XHTML, the new generation of HTML with the extensibility of XML.

THE EVOLUTION OF XML

In 1996, as a result of discussions about developing a markup language with the power and extensibility of SGML but with the simplicity of HTML, the World Wide Web Consortium (W3C) decided to sponsor a team of SGML experts to try to do just that. That team pared away what they considered to be the nonessential, unused, cryptic parts of SGML to leave a smaller, more easily, and simply implemented markup metalanguage, which they named the Extensible Markup Language.

XML, like HTML, is an application profile of SGML (some call it an abbreviated version, a restricted form, or a distillation). Thus, any fully conformant SGML system is able to read XML documents, too. Like SGML, XML was developed as a public format: it is not a proprietary development of any company.

XML evolved quickly, drawing from the work of its sponsors and the work of other developers who were seeking to solve similar problems (such as Peter Murray-Rust, Director of the Virtual School of Molecular Sciences at the University of Nottingham, who had been working on the Chemical Markup Language and with the W3C Math Working Group, which was working on MathML). By mid 1997, the W3C's XML Linking Language XLL project was underway, and by the summer of 1997, Microsoft had launched the Channel Definition Format (CDF) as one of the first real-world applications of XML.

The Extensible Markup Language (XML) 1.0 (First Edition) specification was accepted by the W3C as a formal Recommendation on Feb 10, 1998. The XML specification (written mostly by Tim Bray of Textuality Services, Vancouver, Canada, and C.M. Sperberg-McQueen of the University of Illinois at Chicago) was only a couple of dozen pages long, compared to the ISO SGML standard, which was some 200 pages. Nevertheless, all the useful Internet and World Wide Web SGML functionality remained in XML.

Development continues today. In fact, Extensible Markup Language (XML) 1.0 (Second Edition) was accepted as a W3C Recommendation on October 6, 2000. Further information regarding XML development activity is found in the World Wide Web Consortium (W3C) discussion later in this chapter.

XML is and is Not SGML

As stated previously, XML is an application profile, or Internet/intranet-related, abbreviated version of SGML. XML is designed to make it easier to define XML-related languages for a specific organization or industry. XML was also designed to help programmers create specific document types for those XML-related languages and to help them write applications to handle those documents. By design, XML omits the more complex and less-used parts of SGML, and in return is an easier language in which to write applications, is easier to understand, and is more suited to delivery and interoperability over the Web.

SGML and XML are useful because SGML- and XML-tagged data can be used for the creation, management, and maintenance of large collections of complex information. SGML and XML are independent of platforms and software, so the same source files may be used with a wide variety of operating systems, and authoring and publishing environments. Because SGML and XML are platform-independent, they are considered by many to be the data format of choice for information with a long life.

A major advantage of XML is that it does not require a system that is capable of understanding full SGML. Nevertheless, XML is still SGML-related, and XML files may still be parsed and validated (those concepts are discussed in Chapter 2) the same as any other SGML file. Think of XML as being "SGML minus", not "HTML plus".

XML, like SGML before it, is a vendor- and technology-independent metalanguage. Users need to create XML-based languages and documents—and then the specific programs to read them—to make it all work. XML is like an alphabet and its related semantic tools: it is not useful until it is used to create messages.

XML is not expected to, nor intended to, completely replace SGML. XML is designed to deliver structured content over the Web. So, in many organizations, filtering SGML to XML (that is, using XML as an output format for an SGML installation) would be the standard procedure for Web-based delivery. But XML lacks several features that make SGML a more satisfactory solution for the creation and long-term storage of complex documents or for the use of high-end typesetting applications.

Fortunately, SGML can be designed to be compatible with XML, so their corporate or organizational environments need not be mutually exclusive. In this way, occasionally the advantages of both can be provided. However, there may also be subtle differences between some XML and SGML documents (for example, the treatment of white space immediately adjacent to tags may be different), so caution should be exercised in some instances.

XML is Not HTML

Certainly, there are similarities between XML and HTML. They are both derived from SGML. Both are text based, and both use tags, elements, and attributes. So they appear very similar.

However, XML is not like HTML at all and was never meant to replace HTML. The two languages were designed with different goals. The key concept to remember is that XML was designed to describe data and to focus on what the data actually *is*. HTML, on the other hand, was designed to display content and to focus on how the content *looks*. In other words, HTML is about displaying information, XML is about describing information. XML was created so that richly structured electronic documents could be easily shared, especially over the World Wide Web, no matter what software or hardware may be used to access it. The only viable alternatives, HTML and SGML, are not practical for this purpose, although for different reasons.

While XML and HTML tags look similar, the HTML tags are predefined in the HTML standard. An HTML author can only use tags that are found in the latest HTML standard. So, for example, a <b> means "bold this text", and it is difficult to change that meaning. Meanwhile, the customized meaning of an XML-related tag like <mompop.chocbar.sku> would elude HTML.

Over the past few years, the World Wide Web Consortium (W3C), in conjunction with browser vendors and the WWW community, has worked constantly to extend the definition of HTML to allow new tags. Admittedly, that strategy represents one way for HTML to keep pace with changing technology and to bring variations in presentation to the Web. But these new features and changes are confined by and depend on what the browser vendors have implemented. If you want to disseminate information widely, the latest HTML features may or may not be supported by the latest releases of the various Web browsers (usually Netscape and Internet Explorer, but there are others, like those developed for Linux).

Unlike HTML with its finite number of tags with their predefined semantics, XML allows users to arbitrarily create their own specific tags to meet their own specific requirements (thereby, providing XML's extensibility). Further, unlike HTML, XML allows users to structure and define the information in their documents.

Since XML doesn't predefine or specify tags and their semantics, it can function as a complement to HTML. Used correctly, XML makes developing and using HTML/XML pages easier and more efficient. XML provides a facility to define tags and the structural relationships between them. As stated before, XML is really a metalanguage for describing other markup languages. All of the semantics of the XML document are either defined by the applications that process it or by style sheets.

As the World Wide Web continues to develop, it is most likely that XML will be used to structure and describe the Web data, while HTML will still be used to format and display data. So XML would not replace HTML; it would coexist with and complement HTML in many environments.

Chapter 8 discusses the XHTML language, which has been developed as an XML application. While XML is not intended to replace HTML, XHTML *is indeed* intended to replace HTML by providing better data description, retrieval, and reuse capabilities. However, all that is explained in due course.

Figure 1-9 illustrates the difference between two documents: one created in HTML and the other created in XML. You can see how the second document, using tag names like <client>, <invamt>, and <remark>, is potentially more flexible and reusable.

```
<p>

ABC Co. owes us <strong>
3517.89 dollars.</strong>. This
account should be monitored.
```

HTML version

```
<text><client>ABC Co.</client>
owes us <invamt>3517.89 dollars.
</invamt><remark>This account
should be monitored.</remark>
</text>
```

XML version

Figure 1-9 Comparison of HTML and XML documents

Why is XML Such an Important Development?

XML is used in business by companies that need to share high volumes of information, especially over the Internet and World Wide Web, and that want to facilitate that process. Many industries (e.g., academia, insurance, aerospace, etc.) and organizations are writing XML-based languages and standards that everyone in their specific community can use, so that sharing data becomes easy and fast. To illustrate, look at Table 1-2, which lists some of the hundreds of XML-based languages that have been developed in recent years.

Table 1-2 Examples of XML-based languages

Language Abbreviation or Acronym	Language Name/Description
CDF	Channel Definition Format, one of the first real-world applications of XML, is an open specification that permits automatic delivery of updated web information (or channels) to compatible receiver programs, (developed by Microsoft).
CML	Chemical Markup Language allows for the conversion of current files into structured documents, including chemical publications, and provides for the precise location of information within files
EIL	Extensible Indexing Language looks for a particular tag in a document and assigns the content between the tags to a searchable field

Table 1-2 Examples of XML-based languages (continued)

Language Abbreviation or Acronym	Language Name/Description
ETD-ML	Electronic Thesis & Dissertation Markup Language converts theses from MS Word, for example, into SGML/XML
FlowML	XML-based format for musical notation; a format for storing audio synthesis diagrams for synthesizers
ITML	Information Technology Markup Language is a set of specifications for protocols, message formats, and best practices
MathML	Mathematical Markup Language is a methodology for describing mathematical notations
SMIL	Synchronized Multimedia Integration Language was designed to integrate multimedia objects into a synchronized presentation
VXML	Voice Extensible Markup Language allows interaction with the Internet through voice-recognition technology
XHTML	Basically, HTML 4.01 written as an XML application (to be discussed later in this book)
XSL	Extensible Stylesheet Language is the style standard for XML; it specifies the presentation and appearance of an XML document
XSLT	Extensible Stylesheet Language Transformation Language is used to transform (i.e., reformat) XML documents into other types of XML documents

XML was developed to overcome the shortcomings of its two predecessors: its parent, SGML, and its sibling, HTML. Although both were successful and popular markup languages, both were flawed in certain ways.

XML removes two constraints related to those languages:

- Dependence on a single, inflexible, document markup language (HTML) with a restrictive set of predefined tags and semantics that does not provide for arbitrary structure or tags
- The complexity of full SGML, the syntax of which allows many powerful but hard to program options, and which requires higher-powered technologies and is not browser-friendly

XML overcomes the major shortcoming of HTML with its extensibility properties; it allows a more arbitrary structure and provides the ability to develop specific and unique tags. On the other hand, SGML provides arbitrary structure, but is too complex to implement just for Web browser-related functions. Full SGML systems are still valuable, because they provide solutions for large, complex problems that justify their expense. XML reduces the options available in SGML to those most applicable to the Web, and allows the development of user-defined document types on the Web.

When should you use XML? XML-tagged data can provide high-precision searching in Web environments, and allow users to interchange reusable text over the Internet and through intranets. XML is preferable in environments where the advantages of SGML and XML are desired, but where the features of full SGML that are not supported in XML are unnecessary.

Prior to the advent of XML, developers in various fields had to manipulate their data to fit into the HTML document model, even when there was almost no fit at all. Because XML is a metalanguage and can be used to describe other XML-based markup languages (called **XML vocabularies** or **XML applications**), you can create your own sets of markup tags specifically tailored to fit your unique needs and to speak reliably and predictably to your specialized community. This ability is augmented by the ability to develop specific Document Type Definitions (DTD) or XML schemas that work with the XML documents. However, even though each XML vocabulary can be completely defined by its own unique Document Type Description or schema, you must play by the rules of the schema or DTD to create documents for its vocabulary.

Although each XML vocabulary is unique and varies widely from others in scope and intent, all vocabularies have two important things in common. First, each is written according to the same XML standards and rules, which makes them members of the same extended markup family and is therefore readable by any XML-compliant browser. Second, each vocabulary represents a markup language designed to describe content specific to an organization or industry.

After all this, you need to bear in mind XML's notable weaknesses:

- XML is a rapidly growing technology, but browser technology is still slightly behind it. The latest versions of Microsoft Internet Explorer, for example, generally appear to be the most XML-compatible of the consumer browsers. However, the latest versions of Netscape occasionally surpass IE with respect to compatibility, as you will discover in later chapters of this book.
- Your specific organizational or industrial needs may not be met by XML, perhaps because of the complexity of your data. You might, as an alternative, consider moving to SGML. Even then, you still might be able to use an XML vocabulary for output.
- XML is not as forgiving as HTML when it comes to syntax and structure. However, this is considered a strength by some.
- The development of XML documents and, especially, languages generally requires more careful planning, because they may be reused by others. Again, some consider this to actually be a strength.

The World Wide Web Consortium and XML

In October 1994, Tim Berners-Lee, inventor and architect of the World Wide Web (mentioned previously as the author of the HTML RFC), founded the World Wide Web Consortium (W3C) at the Massachusetts Institute of Technology, Laboratory for Computer Science [MIT/LCS], in collaboration with funding from the United States Defense Advanced Research Project Agency (DARPA) and the European Union.

Membership in the W3C has grown to more than 500 organizations from around the world, and the W3C is hosted by three organizations: MIT in the U.S., the French National Institute for Research in Computer Science and Control (INRIA) in France, and Keio University in Japan.

The purpose of the W3C is to develop interoperable technologies (specification, guidelines, software, and tools) to promote the Web as a forum for information, commerce, communication, and collective understanding. Further, as seen in several of the upcoming chapters, the W3C also acts as a referee or even arbiter between or among those who propose or develop standards in the rapidly changing and expanding Web universe. The actions and decisions of W3C are always guided by the principles, goals, and approaches listed on their Web site.

The first phase of the W3C's XML activity started in June 1996 and culminated in the February 1998 Recommendation "Extensible Markup Language (XML) 1.0." That Recommendation was revised in October 2000. However, since the first Recommendation appeared in 1998, there have been second (namespace, style sheet linking), third (XML query), and more (XML network protocol) development phases, resulting in the production of many W3C Recommendations and other documents. Several W3C Working Groups constantly conduct XML development work in parallel. Almost every day, the W3C announces progress on one XML front or another on their Web site at *http://www.w3c.org*.

Over the years, additional requirements have been addressed by other specifications; for example, the XML Pointer Language (XPointer) and XML Linking Language (XLink) standards have specified methods to represent links between resources. As stated above, several W3C Working Groups are actively pursuing and frequently publishing additional XML standards.

For the most part, reading and understanding the XML standards and specifications does not require extensive knowledge of SGML or any of the related technologies. Here are some XML-related goals and best practices as set out by the W3C in the W3C Recommendation "Extensible Markup Language (XML) 1.0." You can obtain more detail by reviewing the actual Recommendation.

1. It shall be straightforward to use XML over the Internet. Users must be able to view XML documents as quickly and easily as HTML documents. XML shall support a wide variety of applications: authoring, browsing, content analysis, etc.

2. XML shall be compatible with SGML. XML was designed pragmatically, to be compatible with existing standards while solving the relatively new problem of sending richly structured documents over the Web.
3. It shall be easy to write programs that process XML documents. They promote this "first glance" measure: it ought to take about two weeks for a competent computer science graduate student to build a program that can process XML documents.
4. The number of optional features in XML is to be kept to an absolute minimum, ideally zero. Optional features can lead to compatibility problems, confusion, and frustration.
5. XML documents should be legible to humans and reasonably clear. If you don't have an XML browser, you should be able use a text editor to examine XML content.
6. XML design should be prepared quickly. As evidenced by several of these goals, with respect to XML documents and languages, the emphasis is on quicker solutions to problems. Although the final product may be complex, the design stage should proceed with little delay.
7. The design of XML shall be formal and concise.
8. XML documents shall be easy to create. Sophisticated editors are available to create and edit XML content, but it must be possible to create XML documents in other ways, as with a text editor, or with simple scripts, etc.
9. Terseness in XML markup is of minimal importance. While several SGML language features were designed to minimize the amount of typing required, these features are not supported in XML.

CHAPTER SUMMARY

- From the two dozen or so categories of computer languages, XML fits into both the metalanguage and the markup specification language categories.
- XML is used to create XML-based languages, which are used to create specific documents for use by the developer, their organization, or their industry.
- The evolution from basic text description languages to XML has taken almost 40 years, and can be traced from a generic encoding presentation made by William Tunnicliffe of the Graphic Communications Association (GCA) in 1967, all the way to the latest XML-related vocabularies (i.e., specific languages created according to XML standards).
- In October 1994, the World Wide Web Consortium (W3C) was founded at the Massachusetts Institute of Technology, Laboratory for Computer Science [MIT/LCS], in collaboration with and funding from, DARPA and the European Union.

- After eight years of development, the Standard Generalized Markup Language (ISO 8879:1986)—the international standard describing markup for the structure and content of different types of electronic, machine-readable documents—was approved in 1986. SGML became the overarching standard metalanguage.
- The basis of SGML is the division of information in a document into elements, which can then be formatted, sorted, or searched in a consistent fashion.
- HTML is an application profile of the SGML ISO Standard 8879:1986. Thus, HTML is one of the many dialects of the SGML "mother tongue". Any fully conformant SGML system should be able to read HTML documents.
- HTML was originally designed at the European Organization for Nuclear Research (CERN), original home of the Web, around 1990, to provide a very simple version of SGML that could be implemented by ordinary users. At that point, the Internet was already well established. Because it was free, simple, and widely supported, the popularity of HTML grew quickly. It is now the document type most frequently used on the Web.
- Over the past few years, the World Wide Web Consortium (W3C), in conjunction with browser vendors and the WWW community, has worked constantly to extend the definition of HTML. At best, this is a stopgap strategy to allow HTML to keep pace as much as possible with changing Web technology.
- In 1996, a W3C-sponsored team of SGML experts took the parts of SEML that weren't related to the Web and pared them down to create the Extensible Markup Language (XML). Thus, XML, like HTML, is also an application profile of SGML.
- XML development is coordinated by the W3C. The Extensible Markup Language (XML) 1.0 (First Edition) specification was accepted by the W3C as a Recommendation on Feb 10, 1998. A second revision was accepted in October 2000.
- As the World Wide Web continues to develop, XML will complement HTML by structuring and describing data, while HTML will still be used to format and display that same data. So XML will not replace HTML, but will coexist with it.
- XML is used by those who need to share high volumes of information, especially over the Internet and World Wide Web. Many industries (e.g., academia, insurance, aerospace, etc.) and organizations are writing XML-based languages and standards to expedite data sharing. Hundreds of XML-based languages have been developed in recent years.

Review Questions

1. To which of the following computer language categories does XML belong?
   a. markup language
   b. assembly language
   c. fourth generation language
   d. metalanguage

2. A ________________ is used for the formal description of another language.
3. Before it can be effective, each XML-related document needs a specific program that does something with it. True or False?
4. All XML documents contain one or more types of information (e.g., text, graphics, etc.) according to some predetermined and deliberate ________________.
5. Which of the following could be called real-world examples of markup?
   a. highlighted words or passages in a book
   b. a marked up draft report with symbols indicating "new paragraph here," or "bold this," etc.
   c. marks on a map indicating where you will want to turn, stop, etc.
   d. numbers inserted into an otherwise un-numbered procedure
   e. all of the above
6. The primary goal of markup is to combine the description of document logic, structure, data, and other content with the description of the final display. True or False?
7. What are the names given to markup indicators?
   a. tags
   b. elements
   c. attributes
   d. tag names
   e. all of the above
8. With the development of ________________, IBM separated the specific formatting instructions from the content of the document itself.
9. Which of the following are principles underlying the development of standards?
   a. Networks connect many different types of computers; the information passed among them has to be usable on all of them.
   b. Information intended for public use should be restricted to as few technologies as possible.
   c. Only standards-related organizations or, if there are no such organizations, national governments should control data formats.
   d. Data should be in a form that can be reused in many different ways to optimize time and effort.
   e. all of the above
10. Who first undertook the development of a comprehensive international standard based on GML?
    a. ISO
    b. W3C

c. GCA

d. ANSI

e. none of the above

11. _______________ is the name of the official international standard describing markup for the structure and content of different types of electronic, machine-readable documents.

12. The standard mentioned in the previous question uses _______________ descriptive markup.

13. A _______________ is a separate file, formalized by SGML, that identifies all of the elements in its respective document, and indicates the structural relationships among those elements.

    a. schema

    b. Generalized Markup Language

    c. Document Type Definition

    d. XML Document

    e. none of the above

14. What is another name for XML-based markup languages?

    a. XML vocabularies

    b. XML parsers

    c. XML applications

    d. XML documents

    e. all of the above

15. Two types of documents that can be used to augment XML documents are _______________ and XML schemas.

16. Although (or because) XML is a rapidly growing technology, the development of _______________ still lags slightly behind it.

17. All XML vocabularies have two important things in common: they are written according to the same XML standards and rules; and each represents a markup language designed to describe content specific to an organization or industry. True or False?

18. Which of the following is *not* a host for the W3C?

    a. INRIA

    b. MIT

    c. Keio University

    d. ISO

19. What is the official name of the W3C XML standard? When was it first endorsed? When was it revised?

20. Which of the following are XML-related goals and best practices as set out by the W3C in the Recommendation "Extensible Markup Language (XML) 1.0"?
    a. XML documents should be legible by humans.
    b. It shall be straightforward to use XML over the Internet.
    c. The design of XML shall be informal.
    d. Terseness in XML markup is very important.
21. XML was designed to describe data and to focus on what the data actually is, while HTML was designed to display content and to focus on how the content looks. True or False?
22. Which of the following is true? (Choose all that apply.)
    a. HTML has only a finite number of tags.
    b. XML allows users to arbitrarily create their own specific tags.
    c. HTML tags have predefined semantics.
    d. XML tags allow users to meet their own specific requirements.
    e. all of the above
23. Which of the following is a drawback to using SGML for data transmission over the Web?
    a. SGML is an older language.
    b. SGML is compatible with HTML.
    c. SGML is powerful but complex.
    d. SGML is browser friendly.
    e. all of the above
24. Which of the following may be considered by some to be a drawback to using XML?
    a. XML tags describe data but not formatting.
    b. The grammar rules of XML must be strictly followed.
    c. XML is not as complex as SGML.
    d. XML documents are not as valid as HTML documents.
    e. all of the above
25. SGML and XML are ________________- independent and ________________- independent, so the same source files may be used with a wide variety of operating systems, and authoring and publishing environments.

Hands-on Projects

Hands-on Projects 1-1 through 1-4 are presented as your first introduction to actual XML coding. Don't worry if the coding seems unfamiliar to you now. After you have completed several chapters, you will be much more comfortable reading these and other examples. It is suggested that you relax and have some fun by doing the following for each Hands-on Project:

- Cover up the introduction to each project, and go immediately to the XML coding.
- Try to determine the purpose for which the coding is intended.
- Uncover and read the explanation in the introduction.
- Revisit the coding and see if it is any clearer, now that you have read the explanation.

Project 1-1

Take some time to examine this very simple, but still viable, XML file. It contains some basic greeting information that could be accessed by other programs. For example, the information might be displayed in a browser, integrated into a word processing document, or integrated into a database. Because the document is in this generic XML format, any program that needs this information could easily access it.

```
<?xml version="1.0"?>
<!-- edited with XML Spy v4.1 by User Name  -->
<message>
     <saying>
          <friendly>How are you?</friendly>
          <improper>Hey!You!</improper>
     </saying>
</message>
```

Project 1-2

Here's a slightly more complicated XML file. Examine it for a few minutes while covering up the explanation in the next paragraph, and see if you can determine where such a file might be used.

The file was copied directly out of an Internet e-commerce application. It is a "store archive tools" file that is utilized by the installation script to find out what the install path is, where the help files are located, and what the supported browser and language support requirements are. This file on its own is out of context, but it shows how such an XML file can be used to store information that is later used by software upgrade or update routines.

```
<?xml version="1.0"?>
<!DOCTYPE sartools-config []>
<sartools-config>
     <devtools>
          <config
```

```
InstallPath="C:\IBM\CommerceStudio"
HelpSystemPath="C:\IBM\CommerceStudio\web\doc\en_US\F1"
Browser="C:\Program Files\Plus!\Microsoft
Internet\Iexplore.exe"
Lang="en_US"
          />
     </devtools>
</sartools-config>
```

Project 1-3

These sample XML files are increasing in their complexity. Here is a more involved example. Like the previous two examples, please examine this one while covering up the explanation below, and see if you can determine where this file might be used.

This is a file that holds information that the e-commerce application uses to link the correct logon command with its contextual information. You might surmise that this is a logon command for store system administrators (and not ordinary shoppers) that has been coded as a Java servlet. Its web path has been set to *webapp/wcs/tools/servlet*. This file is used by the e-commerce application to locate the correct logon resources for the SARAdmin users.

```
<?xml version="1.0"?>
<!DOCTYPE sarsys [ ]>
<sarsys>
     <devtools>
          <config
               SARControllerCmd="SARAdmin"
               LogonCmd="Logon"
               WebAppPath="webapp/wcs/tools/servlet"
          />
     </devtools>
</sarsys>
```

Project 1-4

Here is another example of an XML file that is used by an e-commerce Web application. Notice it is much larger than the previous three files. Examine it, too, while covering up the explanation in the paragraph below. In particular, look at the Java servlets—they begin with "<servlet>," especially. What do you think the e-commerce application does with them?

Each servlet has its name, description, code locations, and specific loading characteristics defined inside this file. This particular Web application service reads this file when it is initialized, and then loads each individual servlet according to the information defined in the file. If a programmer was to write a new servlet, the code for the servlet would have to be copied into the respective directory with the other servlets, and then another element describing the new servlet would have to be defined in this file.

```
<?xml version="1.0"?>
<webapp>
   <name>default</name>
   <description>default application</description>
   <error-page>/ErrorReporter</error-page>

   <servlet>
      <name>snoop</name>
      <description>snoop servlet</description>
      <code>SnoopServlet</code>
      <servlet-path>/servlet/snoop/*</servlet-path>
      <servlet-path>/servlet/snoop2/*</servlet-path>
      <init-parameter>
         <name>param1</name>
         <value>test-value1</value>
      </init-parameter>
      <autostart>false</autostart>
   </servlet>

   <servlet>
      <name>hello</name>
      <description>hello servlet</description>
      <code>HelloServlet</code>
      <servlet-path>/servlet/hello</servlet-path>
      <autostart>false</autostart>
   </servlet>

   <servlet>
      <name>ErrorReporter</name>
      <description>Default error reporter
servlet</description>

<code>com.ibm.servlet.engine.webapp.DefaultErrorReporter
</code>
      <servlet-path>/ErrorReporter</servlet-path>
      <autostart>true</autostart>
   </servlet>

   <servlet>
      <name>invoker</name>
      <description>Auto-registration servlet</description>

<code>com.ibm.servlet.engine.webapp.InvokerServlet</code>
      <servlet-path>/servlet/*</servlet-path>
      <autostart>true</autostart>
   </servlet>
```

```
    <servlet>
       <name>jsp</name>
       <description>JSP support servlet</description>
       <code>com.sun.jsp.runtime.JspServlet</code>
       <autostart>true</autostart>
       <servlet-path>*.jsp</servlet-path>
    </servlet>
</webapp>
```

Project 1-5

The objective of this project is to ensure that you become familiar with the W3C Web site as well as their Recommendation "Extensible Markup Language (XML) 1.0 (Second Edition)."

If you have an Internet connection, start your browser application (for example, Microsoft Internet Explorer, Netscape Navigator, or similar), and go to the W3C's Web site where they keep the "Extensible Markup Language (XML) 1.0 (Second Edition)" Recommendation and take a look at it. The URL is *http://www.w3c.org /TR/REC-xml#sec-intro*. Here are the steps:

1. Click **Start**, point to **All Programs**, and click **Internet Explorer**.
2. When the browser window appears, enter the following location into the location bar: *http://www.w3c.org /TR/REC-xml#sec-intro*. Then click **Go**.
3. Scroll through and read the Recommendation. Look at the Table of Contents. There are six major headings and nine appendices. If you study and learn the contents of this Recommendation, it will not only benefit you in this course but also elsewhere in the "XML world", too.

CHAPTER

2

XML COMPONENTS

In this chapter, you will learn:

- To identify the different components of an XML document
- About XML parsers, applications, and errors
- How to recognize the basic logical structure of an XML document
- About XML's basic well-formedness and validity requirements
- How to build and modify XML documents

In this chapter you learn about XML's basic building blocks. You are shown some basic XML documents, learn what well-formedness requirements are, and see how these XML documents conform to the well-formedness requirements of the W3C's "Extensible Markup Language 1.0 Recommendation." That Recommendation contains extensive information about XML, since it is the "all things to all people" XML definition, but it also contains extensive detail and cross-referencing, as well as some rather disjointed-looking examples.

Also in this chapter we strip away some of the details and cross-references and provide simple examples to help you build your XML documents properly. Specifically, you learn how to declare your documents as XML, how to send instructions to applications processing the XML document, how to create XML elements using start tags and end tags, how to further describe elements with attributes, and how to enter certain characters into XML documents correctly so that the processor does not misinterpret them.

Finally, you are introduced to TL Sales, Inc., a small, fictitious retail merchandising company that is just starting to sell merchandise and services over the Internet. You monitor and contribute to their progress.

Defining an XML Document

Numerous XML-based languages and applications have been developed since XML first appeared in 1996. All of these products require proper and appropriate XML documents. The W3C XML 1.0 Recommendation defines XML documents as a class of data objects. It goes on to say that, since XML is an application profile (or a restricted form) of SGML, XML documents must also be conforming SGML documents.

In contrast to that definition, some users and developers tend to think of XML documents simply as text documents. However, that is too limiting and draws attention away from XML's major features: its extensibility with respect to data, its straightforward structure, and its human legibility. For our purposes, the word "document" refers to textual data documents like this book, and also to many other data formats such as vector graphics, e-commerce transactions, mathematical equations, and many other kinds of structured information.

The following terms are mentioned throughout this chapter and this book, and are essential to your understanding of the basic concepts of XML components.

- ***XML processor*** (*also called an* **XML parser**)—A piece of software that reads XML documents, does front-end screening of the documents on behalf of the application, and then provides access to their content and structure. Many parsers are available, including AlphaWorks XML for Java, which is used by IBM, Microsoft XML Parser, which is used in Microsoft Internet Explorer, and a parser called expat, which is used in the Netscape Navigator 6 browser application.
- ***Application***—The major processing software module(s)—in other words, a program or group of programs—intended for the end users and designers to access and manipulate XML documents. Do not confuse this term with an "XML application," which, as discussed previously in Chapter 1, is a term indicating another markup language that has been created according to XML Recommendation 1.0 concepts and requirements. For example, the well-known Microsoft browser Internet Explorer is an "application" that accesses and displays XML documents. On the other hand, XSLT (which is discussed in detail in Chapter 6), is an XML-related language—that is, an "XML application"—in that it has been developed using XML 1.0 constructs.
- ***Fatal error***—An error in the document that the XML processor must detect and then report to the application. Once a fatal error is detected, the processor may continue processing, but only in order to search for further errors, which it also must report to the application. When a fatal error occurs, a processor does not continue normal processing.

DOCUMENT COMPONENTS

The W3C Recommendation states that XML documents have a **physical structure**, made up of storage units called **entities**, which are fragments of an XML document and range in type and scope from single characters to entire outside documents identified by their respective entity reference names. Entities can contain either parsed or unparsed data. Although they are discussed in detail later, **parsed entities** contain text—a sequence of characters—that may represent markup or content data. An **unparsed entity** is a resource whose contents may or may not be text, and which may be in formats other than XML. It is generally intended that an XML processor check and manipulate parsed entities, while passing unparsed entities directly to the application as is.

The W3C also states that XML documents must have a **logical structure**. That is, each document contains one or more **elements**, or containers of document information, that can be nested within other elements. The boundaries of each element are delimited by start tags and end tags or, for empty elements, by an empty-element tag. A document author may also give each element a **type**, also occasionally referred to as its **generic identifier (GI)**, as well as one or more attribute specifications, which are special labels to further describe the contents of the element.

There are other viewpoints with respect to describing XML documents, however. Some developers and authors do not dissect XML documents according to structures or components; they state simply that XML documents are textual data objects. Others expand on that approach slightly by saying XML documents are made up of content and markup. Still others define document components in terms of the markup types found within them. The approach followed in this and all subsequent chapters reflects the logical structure discussed in the W3C XML Recommendation. Thus, whether the discussion addresses basic XML documents—as it does here in Chapter 2—or whether the subject is XSLT (Chapter 6), XHTML (Chapter 8), or the other XML-related languages, you will be introduced to, at some point the major components, as well as their subcomponents. The major components are:

- The prolog
- The root element and other elements

This way, you are given a common basis for understanding, comparing and even combining XML-based concepts, languages, and documents. Meanwhile, in addition to these components, other document component concepts and definitions are covered as they are encountered (in fact, here in Chapter 2, you can read about various "entities," important concepts even though their impact on the logical structure is not always apparent).

The Prolog

You may already be familiar with the word **prolog** as a preface or introduction to an event, a work, or some other form of development. XML document prologs are true to those definitions. The XML prolog is the first major logical component of an XML document and, because of its content, must be inserted prior to the next major logical component, the root element (also called the document element), discussed later in this chapter.

An XML document's prolog may comprise up to five possible components:

- An XML declaration
- Processing instruction(s)
- A Document type declaration
- Comment(s)
- White space

The five prolog components facilitate the passing of data and other information to the parser and, thereafter, to the application. The components provide instruction or explanation to the reader, and, in the case of white space, which can be single or more spaces, tabs and end-of-line indicators, help to organize the prolog and to facilitate human legibility. Please refer to the very simple XML document example in Figure 2-1. As you can see, it has a three-line prolog, consisting of an XML declaration, a processing instruction, and a comment. Later in this chapter and throughout this book you encounter other XML documents with usually more and occasionally less statements in their prologs.

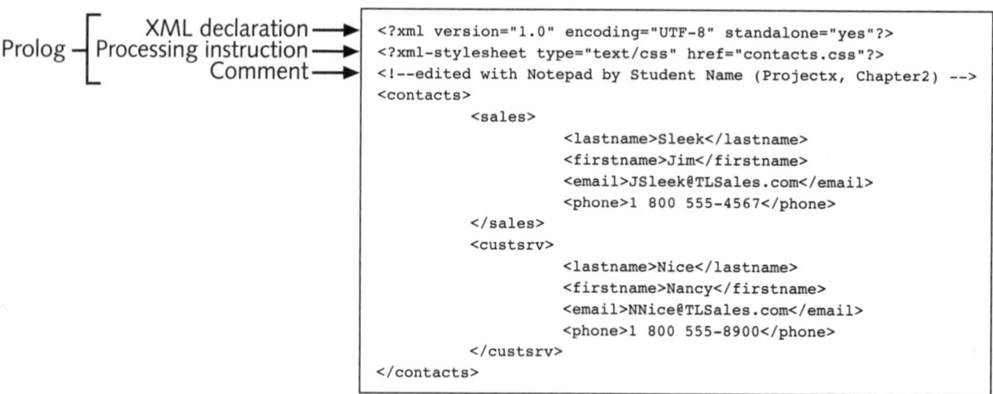


```
<?xml version="1.0" encoding="UTF-8" standalone="yes"?>
<?xml-stylesheet type="text/css" href="contacts.css"?>
<!--edited with Notepad by Student Name (Projectx, Chapter2) -->
<contacts>
        <sales>
                <lastname>Sleek</lastname>
                <firstname>Jim</firstname>
                <email>JSleek@TLSales.com</email>
                <phone>1 800 555-4567</phone>
        </sales>
        <custsrv>
                <lastname>Nice</lastname>
                <firstname>Nancy</firstname>
                <email>NNice@TLSales.com</email>
                <phone>1 800 555-8900</phone>
        </custsrv>
</contacts>
```

Figure 2-1 XML document prolog

The W3C XML Recommendation has been criticized for not being clear regarding prologs. It states that a well-formed XML document should begin with an XML declaration, but then it goes on to indicate, basically, that all prolog components are optional. It is recommended that if you want to ensure that your XML documents are always well-formed you should begin them with an XML declaration at the very least.

The following sections each discuss an individual prolog component.

The XML Declaration

As mentioned earlier, the W3C recommends that an XML document should begin with the declaration that states that the document is written in XML. That **XML declaration** (also called the **header**) should be on the document's first line, and nothing should precede it. Look closely at the first line in the XML document in Figure 2-1, which is reproduced below:

```
<?xml version="1.0" encoding="UTF-8" standalone="yes"?>
```

Notice that the basic syntax of the declaration (i.e., of its tag) is <?xml ?>. The "xml" is lowercase. Although some browsers permit both uppercase and lowercase, the W3C Recommendation specifies lowercase. There are three attributes defined in the XML declaration: the XML version number ("1.0"), the document's language encoding designation ("UTF-8"), and the standalone specification ("yes"). Attributes are discussed in detail later in this chapter. In the meantime, please remember to enclose the prescribed values of these and all XML attributes in double quotation marks.

In the XML declaration, the attribute prescribing the XML version refers to the most recent version of the XML Recommendation endorsed by the W3C. It is mandatory to state the current version if you provide an XML declaration statement. Currently, there is only version 1.0, corresponding to the W3C XML Recommendation 1.0.

The second part of the XML declaration is the encoding attribute, which is optional. The choices available to you are: UTF-8, Unicode, UCS-2, UCS-4, and several other character sets. If you do not specify an encoding attribute, the processor uses the UTF-8 by default. The following paragraphs provide some background information.

In the field of information technology, ISO and the **International Electrotechnical Commission (IEC)** established a joint technical committee and prepared International Standard ISO/IEC 10646. This standard defines the Universal Multiple-Octet Coded Character Set (UCS), which applies to the representation, transmission, interchange, processing, storage, input, and presentation of the written form of the languages and symbols of the world. At the same time, a consortium of manufacturers of multilingual software organized another standards project, the Unicode Project. In 1991, the participants of both projects began to work together to create a single code table. Although both projects still exist and their respective proponents still publish their standards independently, they have agreed to keep the code tables of the Unicode and ISO 10646 standards compatible. Not only that, but they also coordinate extensions to both standards. For example, Unicode 3.0 corresponds to ISO 10646-1:2000.

The code tables assign integer number values to characters, and there are several alternatives for representing a sequence of characters, or their respective integer values, as a sequence of bytes. Two popular encodings store Unicode text as either 2-byte sequences (Universal Character System-2, for up to 65,535 different characters) or 4-byte sequences (UCS-4, for approximately two billion characters!). Compare that capacity to the traditional and simpler English language-based ASCII encoding, which only allows up to 256 characters. UTF-8 is another alternative coded representation form for all of the characters of the UCS. It can be used to transmit text data through communication systems operating under specific assumptions regarding certain number ranges, control functions, etc.

Further information regarding character set encoding is readily available on the Internet at *www.unicode.org*, or at *www.cl.cam.ac.uk/~mgk25/ucs/ISO-10646-UTF-8.html*.

The third part of the XML declaration, the standalone attribute, is also optional. If the document exists alone—that is, if there is no need to refer to any external physical entities such as DTDs or schemas—the attribute value should be set to "yes." "Yes" is also the default value if the attribute is not specified. However, if external entities are enlisted by the XML document, then specify "no." As you can see, the simple XML document in Figure 2-1 specifies "yes." Later, you will see other documents that specify "no."

The Document Type Declaration

Unlike its predecessor SGML, XML does not absolutely require a **document type declaration** (also called a DOCTYPE definition) in all circumstances. However, when you want to include one, here is the basic syntax for a document type declaration:

```
<!DOCTYPE rootname options>
```

DOCTYPE tells the XML processor that the statement is a document type declaration. The **rootname** (or **class**) indicates the type of document according to the author's own specification. In Figure 2-2, the rootname specified by the document's author is "contacts," because it was the author's intention that the document contain a list of company contacts plus their respective contact information.

The "options" include other specifications, for example, an indication of where DTDs or schemas are located, their own types, etc. Thus, this type of declaration states what type the XML document is and to which DTD the document conforms. The declaration may list several elements, attributes, entities or other types of declarations within its own confines (thereby creating an internal DTD), or it may provide the name of an external DTD. Although document type declarations are considered optional, one is required if the author intends to refer to an external DTD or schema. So, to avoid ambiguity, it is suggested that a document type declaration always be included.

Notice that, in Figure 2-2, because the value of the standalone attribute has been set to "no" in the XML version statement, an external DTD named "contacts.dtd" is designated in the document type declaration statement. The W3C Recommendation addresses the reference to the DTD or schema slightly differently: "The document type declaration…points to markup declarations that provide a grammar for (the) class of documents." They then state that the "markup declarations" they refer to can be one of four possible types:

- Element-type declaration
- Attribute-list declaration

- Entity declaration
- Notation declaration

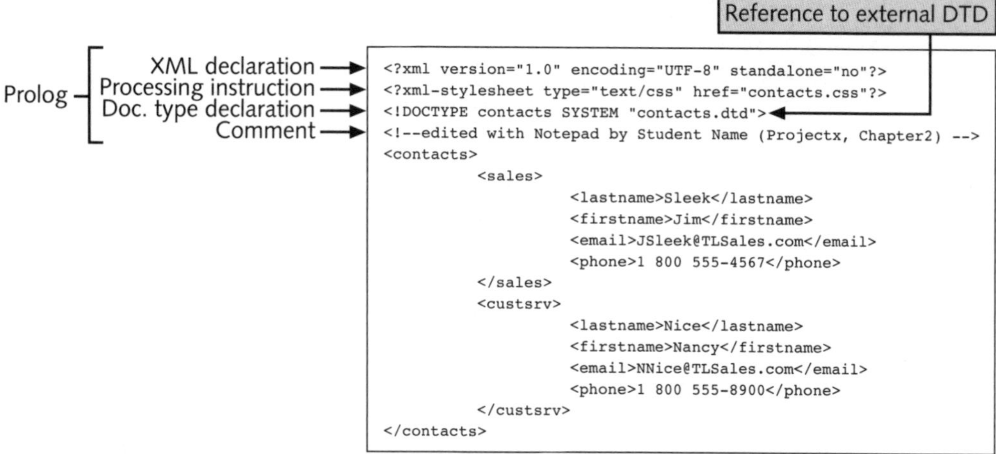

Figure 2-2 External document type declaration (DTD)

Their reference, although somewhat oblique in nature (referring to DTDs or schemas as "markup declarations"), is nonetheless correct: DTDs and schemas do contain those markup declarations (as you will see in Chapters 4 and 5). The upshot to this is that this XML document should follow the syntax and structure rules found in the DTD called "contacts.dtd" which, because the keyword SYSTEM also appears in the statement, is presumed to be found locally on the server.

In Figure 2-3, the value of the standalone attribute is set to "yes" and the XML document contains its own DTD (the DTD, therefore, is called an internal DTD). Please notice, in fact, that the DTD is contained entirely within the DOCTYPE declaration statement, and consists of an opening square bracket, several ELEMENT declaration statements, and a closing square bracket.

DTD keywords, ELEMENT statements, and other specifications are discussed in detail in Chapter 4.

Processing Instructions

Processing instructions (**PI**s) are not textually part of the XML document, but are instructions passed by the XML processor to the application. Processing instruction syntax looks like the following:

```
<?piname pidata?>
```

Notice that a single question mark appears at the beginning and at the end of the processing instruction. The piname, also called the **PI name** or **PI target**, identifies the PI to the application. Applications should process only the targets they recognize and ignore all other PIs. PI names beginning with the characters XML, xml, or something similar are reserved for future XML standardization by the W3C.

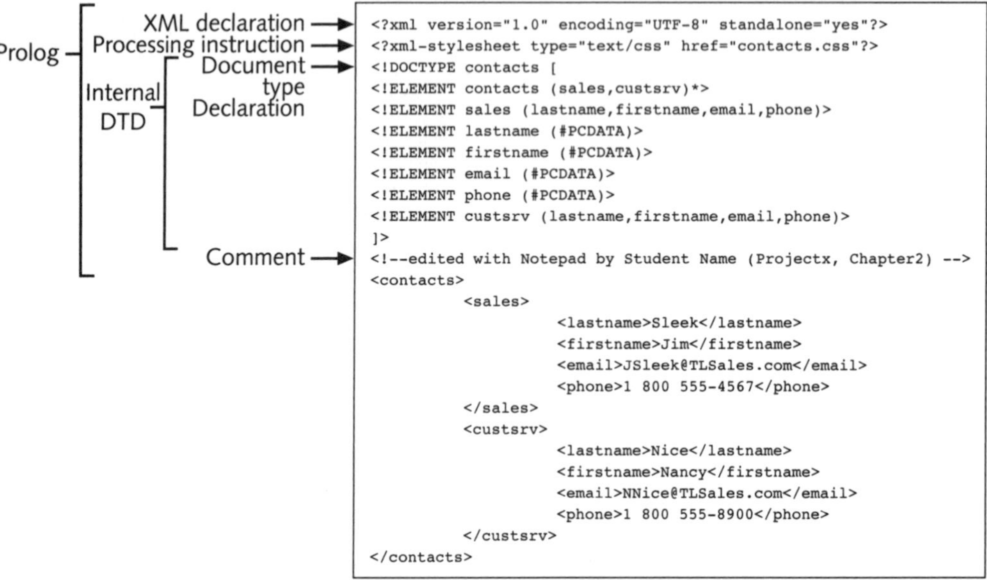


```
<?xml version="1.0" encoding="UTF-8" standalone="yes"?>
<?xml-stylesheet type="text/css" href="contacts.css"?>
<!DOCTYPE contacts [
<!ELEMENT contacts (sales,custsrv)*>
<!ELEMENT sales (lastname,firstname,email,phone)>
<!ELEMENT lastname (#PCDATA)>
<!ELEMENT firstname (#PCDATA)>
<!ELEMENT email (#PCDATA)>
<!ELEMENT phone (#PCDATA)>
<!ELEMENT custsrv (lastname,firstname,email,phone)>
]>
<!--edited with Notepad by Student Name (Projectx, Chapter2) -->
<contacts>
        <sales>
                <lastname>Sleek</lastname>
                <firstname>Jim</firstname>
                <email>JSleek@TLSales.com</email>
                <phone>1 800 555-4567</phone>
        </sales>
        <custsrv>
                <lastname>Nice</lastname>
                <firstname>Nancy</firstname>
                <email>NNice@TLSales.com</email>
                <phone>1 800 555-8900</phone>
        </custsrv>
</contacts>
```

Figure 2-3 Internal document type declaration (DTD)

Any pidata options following the PI name facilitate processing by the application. For example, in Figures 2-1, 2-2 and 2-3, the processing instruction has been:

```
<?xml-stylesheet type="text/css" href="contacts.css"?>
```

This is a common processing instruction, recognized by MS Internet Explorer and Netscape Navigator, that connects the XML document with a stylesheet; in these examples, it is a cascading stylesheet called "contacts.css". Styles and cascading style sheets will be discussed later in this book. For now, it should suffice to say that "contacts.css" contains all the instructions for the presentation—on the screen, for example—of the XML data that follows in the XML document.

Comments

There are two reasons you might want to add comments: to provide information to someone working on the XML document (i.e., chronicling, modifying, or fixing it), or to temporarily disable sections of markup and content. XML uses the same comment syntax as HTML. Any text or markup located between <!- - and - -> is invisible to the application processing the document but is visible to any person reading the document. Remember that comments are not considered part of the textual content of an XML document. The XML processor is not required to pass them along to an application. Do not confuse comments with processing instructions.

Here are a few rules to remember about comments:

- Although it is commonly believed that comments can be placed anywhere in a document, it is bad form to place a comment before the first XML declaration statement (the one containing the XML version, the language encoding, or the standalone designation).
- Do not place a comment inside actual markup statements.
- Do not use the literal string " - - " anywhere in the comment except at the end of it. Otherwise, the XML processor will misinterpret it, thinking that the comment has ended, and will then create errors based on the remaining characters.

In Figures 2-1, 2-2 and 2-3, the comment indicates who worked on the XML document, at what stage the document was created, and the application used to create it.

The Element Hierarchy

Elements are considered to be the basic building blocks of XML and, as such, they have specific properties and functions, and must be combined according to a specific structure. This section briefly discusses four methods of displaying XML documents, and then examines how elements are combined to create the basic structure of a simple XML document. The next section discusses the components and properties of elements themselves.

Displaying XML Documents

At the top of Figure 2-4 is a small XML document named contacts.xml. Although it is small, contacts.xml is typical with respect to basic XML structure. It consists of a prolog and 11 elements arranged in a prescribed manner to store—for provision to one or more applications that may store them in a database, perhaps, or display them on a Web site—the names of staff members who function, among other things, as contacts for their organization.

Figure 2-4 illustrates three different methods for depicting the structure of XML documents for purposes of design, analysis, or troubleshooting. There is no best style for depicting every document. Sometimes, one or another style suffices; sometimes one might be used in combination with another. The choice of style(s) depends on the task at hand and also on personal preference.

The top diagram is a listing of the document contents as you might see them in most typical text editors. Element sequence numbers have been added and indicate the order in which the elements would eventually be encountered and processed by the parser and application. This style of display is likely sufficient for designing and analyzing simple documents. The advantage to this style is that you can actually see the contents of each element.

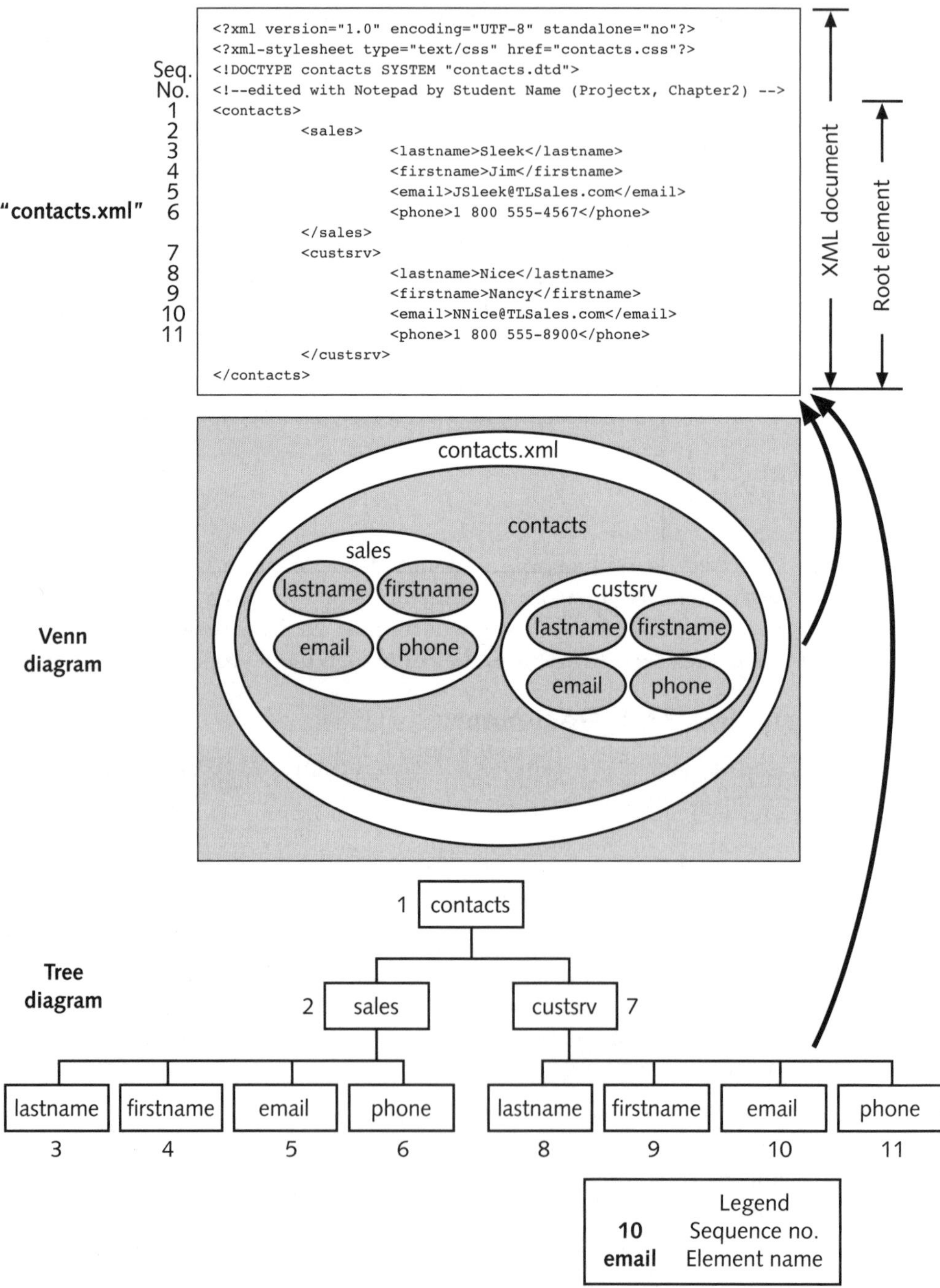

Figure 2-4 XML element hierarchy

The middle diagram is a Venn diagram, consisting of a number of oval and round shapes, one or more within others. Each of the shapes represents a part, usually an element, of the XML document. The largest, all-encompassing oval shape (called contacts.xml) contains the whole of the document: the prolog plus all the elements. Within the contacts.xml oval is another one which represents the document's root element, called <contacts>. It, in turn, contains all the rest of the elements, the names of which correspond to the names listed in the top diagram. Venn diagrams are handy for designing and analyzing fairly simple documents or parts of documents, especially if you need to show relationships between elements. Sequencing may not be easily demonstrated, though. As far as being able to see the document's actual contents, you generally can't, but that usually isn't the function of Venn diagrams.

The bottom diagram is a tree diagram of the elements in the same XML document. Tree diagrams are better for displaying whole or parts of larger, more complicated documents. Sequencing is generally indicated left to right and from the top down. However, it is still recommended that you place sequence numbers in or near the element names. As with Venn diagrams, tree diagrams are not usually used to display actual element contents. One style of diagram not shown in Figure 2-4 is the typical flow chart, which can also be used. A flow chart is used later in this chapter to illustrate the relationships among XML documents, parsers, and applications.

XML Document Structure

As mentioned previously, contacts.xml is a small document, but its structure is typical of XML documents. It stores the names of two staff members who act as contacts for their organization, along with their respective information.

It has already been mentioned that the root element of contacts.xml is named <contacts>. The **root element** is the **parent element** of all other elements, since all the elements in the XML document are contained within it. The concept of placing one element within another is called **nesting**. Use Figure 2-5 to follow this discussion.

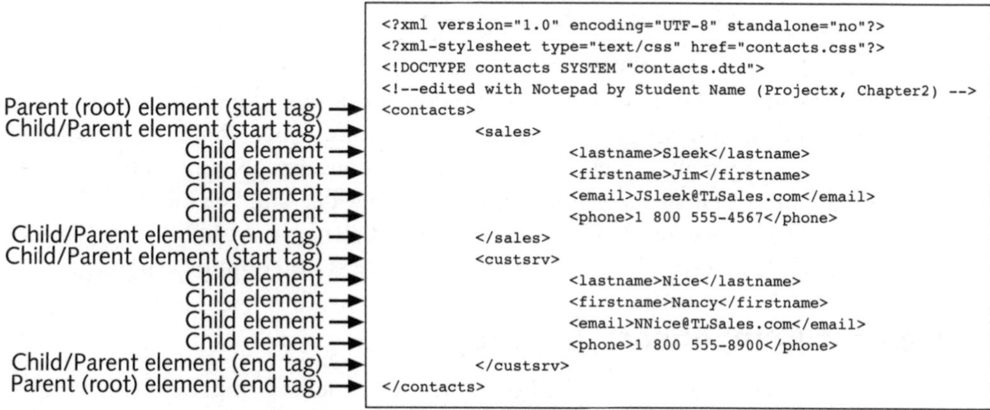


```
<?xml version="1.0" encoding="UTF-8" standalone="no"?>
<?xml-stylesheet type="text/css" href="contacts.css"?>
<!DOCTYPE contacts SYSTEM "contacts.dtd">
<!--edited with Notepad by Student Name (Projectx, Chapter2) -->
<contacts>
        <sales>
                <lastname>Sleek</lastname>
                <firstname>Jim</firstname>
                <email>JSleek@TLSales.com</email>
                <phone>1 800 555-4567</phone>
        </sales>
        <custsrv>
                <lastname>Nice</lastname>
                <firstname>Nancy</firstname>
                <email>NNice@TLSales.com</email>
                <phone>1 800 555-8900</phone>
        </custsrv>
</contacts>
```

Figure 2-5 Parent and child elements

In contacts. xml, <contacts> is the direct parent of two specific child elements: <sales> and <custsrv>, representing the Sales and Customer Service Departments, respectively. In other words, <sales> and <custsrv> are nested within <contacts>. The root element is not considered to *have* a parent, though it almost always *is* a parent. If the root element contains only data and no other elements, then the question of whether it is a parent or not becomes irrelevant.

Meanwhile, each non-root element in the document has one parent element. As illustrated in Figure 2-5, each child element must be wholly contained within the content of its own parent element, and must not be contained within any other child element that is in the content of the same or any other parent. The latter part of that sentence seems convoluted, but is vitally important with respect to the concepts of well-formedness and validity, which are discussed later in this chapter. To explain the statement by example, look at the <sales> element. From beginning to end, <sales> is contained within <contacts> only. No part of <sales> appears outside of <contacts> and no part of <sales> appears within <custsrv>. Thus, <sales> does not overlap with other elements; its start and end tags cannot be nested within another element (tags and overlapping are also discussed later in this chapter). Further, as another example, if you look at the <lastname> element within <sales>, no part of it appears within <firstname> or within <custsrv>. So <lastname> does not overlap, either.

Continuing, then, the <sales> and <custsrv> elements are each termed to be **child elements** (also called **subelements**), because each is contained within a parent element (coincidentally, here they share the same parent, <contacts>). However, in this case, <sales> and <custsrv> are also considered to be parent elements because they, in turn, contain their own respective child elements.

The <sales> and <custsrv> elements are also called **siblings** (some information sources refer to this type of relationship as **sisters**), because they are at the same level and share a parent element (in this case, as stated before, they share the parent element <contacts>). Tree diagrams usually illustrate sibling relationships best. As mentioned previously, siblings cannot overlap. Thus, any parent element can have more than one child element within it, but any child can have only one parent and cannot overlap with its sibling element(s).

Now, please note that <sales> contains four child elements: <lastname>, <firstname>, <email>, and <phone>. <custsrv> also contains four children, with identical names to the ones found within <sales>. As mentioned previously, child elements are considered siblings if they share a parent. If they don't, they are not considered siblings. Thus, the child elements found within <sales> are siblings to one another. The child elements within <custsrv> are also siblings to one another. However, the child elements within <sales> are not siblings to the child elements within <custsrv>, since there is no common parentage.

Element Components and Properties

The previous section discussed how XML documents comprise elements in a prescribed structure. This section examines the components that go into the elements, and also discusses some of the element properties that result from those components. You will see that there are rules for the creation of elements—rules that are absolutely fundamental and integral to building and understanding XML.

Tags and Tag Names

Each element begins and ends with its element name (usually referred to as a **tag**). There are two types of tags: each element begins with what is commonly called a **start tag** or an **opening tag** and, generally, each element ends with an **end tag** (also called a **closing tag**). Notice that each tag name is delimited by angle brackets (< indicates the beginning of the tag name; > indicates its end). In the end tag, the element name is always preceded by a slash (/). Figure 2-6 illustrates a typical generic element.

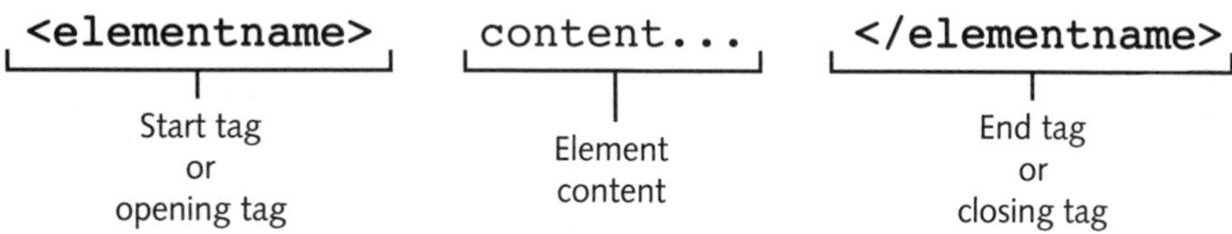

Figure 2-6 Generic element

The exception to this rule is the declared empty element (to be discussed later in this chapter), which does not have an end tag, but does have a special start tag. Figure 2-7 illustrates a typical declared empty element.

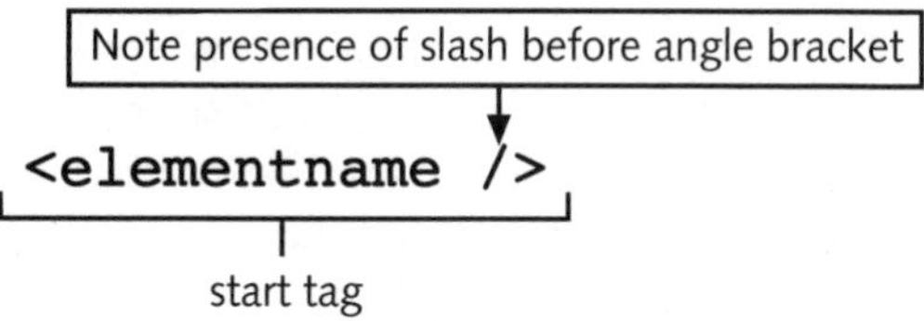

Figure 2-7 Generic declared empty element

If attribute specifications are to appear in the tag name, they appear in the start tag, as shown in Figure 2-8 (attributes are discussed later in this section).

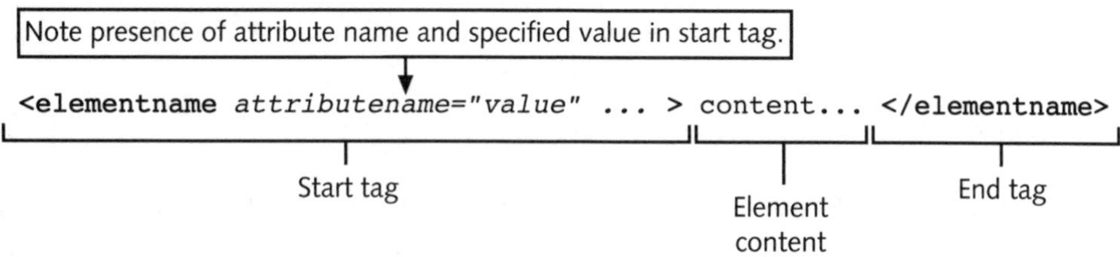

Figure 2-8 Generic start tag with attribute (name-value pair)

Here are some rules for element tag names:

- Element tag names can begin with a letter, a colon, or an underscore (but not numbers).
- Subsequent characters may include alphanumerics, underscores, hyphens, colons, and periods.
- Element tag names cannot contain certain XML-specific symbols, like the ampersand (&), the "at" symbol (@), or the "less than" symbol (<).
- Element tag names cannot contain white space.
- Element tag names cannot contain parenthetic statements.

It is recommended that when devising element names, authors should remember to make them somehow identify or describe the nature of their contents. This practice facilitates the human legibility aspect of XML as well as future searchability.

The name found in the element's start and end tags is said to specify the **element type**. As you will see in Chapters 4 and 5, the declaration of these element types—for example, the <!ELEMENT email (#PCDATA) > and other similar specifications listed in Figure 2-3—play a significant role in DTDs and schemas.

The Extent of an Element

Figure 2-9 illustrates the syntax of a typical generic element. As you can see from Figure 2-9, an element extends from the first angle bracket in its start tag through the start tag itself and then through the element's content (that is, through the text between the start tag and the end tag), then through the end tag and, right to the last angle bracket in the end tag.

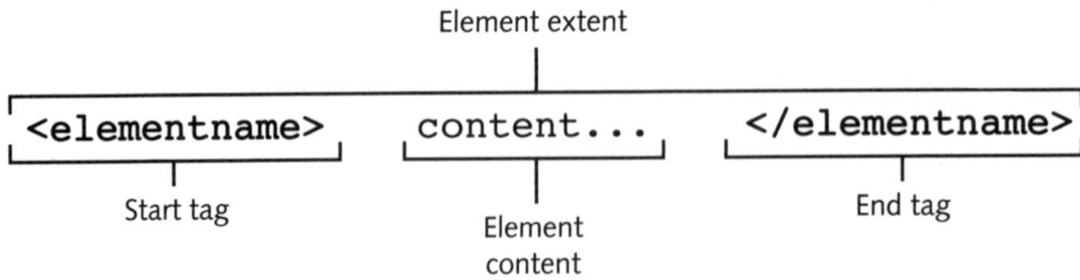

Figure 2-9 Extent of a generic element

As mentioned in the previous section, elements can be nested within one another. In those cases, each parent element extends from the first angle bracket in its start tag and continues through the child element(s), too, until the parent element ends with the last angle bracket in its end tag. See the illustration of this principle in Figure 2-10.

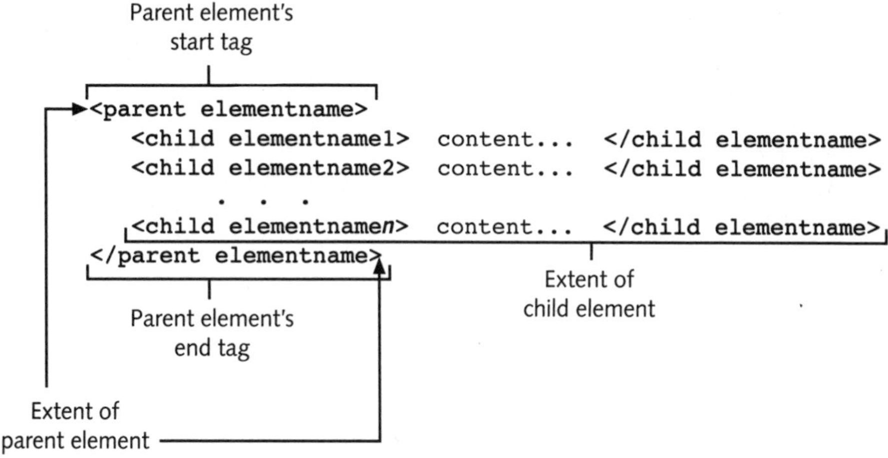

Figure 2-10 Extent of a generic parent element

Types of Element Content

It has been stated previously that the <contacts> element is the root element of the contacts.xml document, *and* the direct parent of two child elements: <sales> and <custsrv>. Because <contacts> contains the <sales> and <custsrv> elements, but no actual data of its own, it is said to have **element content**. The root element is not the only one that can have element content: any element that contains other elements is considered to have element content. The siblings <sales> and <custsrv>, like the root element <contacts>, also have element content, since they each contain child elements of their own.

Notice, however, that the child elements <lastname>, <firstname>, <email>, and <phone> do not have element content. Because they contain character strings (e.g., names, phone numbers, email addresses), they are said to have **data content** (not element content). Further, the data characters are capable of being parsed (that is, checked and appropriately manipulated prior to passing them to the application) by the XML parser. That's why, in the DTD-like !ELEMENT declarations seen earlier, elements like these are shown to have **#PCDATA** (**parsed character data** or **parseable character data**) in them. The discussion of DTDs and schemas in later chapters expands upon these descriptions.

It is also possible for elements to have **mixed content**. That is, it is possible for an element to contain both elements and data. Although mixed content and element declarations are not dealt with in detail in this chapter, here is an example of an !ELEMENT declaration specifying an element with mixed content (compare it with the syntax of other !ELEMENT declarations in Figure 2-3, for example):

```
<!ELEMENT outst_bal (#PCDATA | WARNING)*>
```

This sample declaration specifies properties for an element called outst_bal (in this case, that is intended to mean "outstanding balance on account") that may contain character data *or* a child element called WARNING. The vertical bar between #PCDATA and WARNING indicates an "or" relationship among the content types, and the asterisk indicates that they are all optional. (They must all be optional in these cases, according to XML rules.)

Use of a mixed content element like this is fairly common and, in fact, is termed a WARNING tag. It is used in those cases when a customer, supplier or other party has exceeded some dollar limit, payment period limit, etc.

Elements can not only contain element, data, and mixed content, but they can also be empty. In fact, the W3C XML Recommendation states that an element with no content is said to be **empty**. But empty elements are just a little more complicated than that somewhat simplified statement indicates.

In fact, there are two types of empty elements:

- Those elements that, in their respective DTDs or schemas, are declared to be empty
- Those elements that are declared to be eligible to contain content but, for whatever reasons, do not

Occasionally, there is confusion about the definitions, the respective syntax, and when each type of empty element should be used.

With respect to syntax, you have already seen how most elements in a document use start tags and end tags as wrappers around their content. However, as illustrated in Figure 2-7, elements that have been declared empty in their respective DTD or schema have a slightly different tag syntax. The different syntax stems from the fact that these declared empty elements *are* different: they are never intended to contain data content. They are intended to function as a kind of marker, to indicate a point where, during the course of the execution of the application in question, something specific is supposed to happen. (For example, in HTML, the insertion of a horizontal line when the application encounters an <hr> tag, is equivalent.) Figure 2-11 illustrates an example of a declared empty element that has been added to the contacts.xml document.

In Figure 2-11, you can see that Mr. Sleek and Ms. Nice have been appointed to be the heads of their respective departments, perhaps in anticipation of expanding the staff in those departments. The declared empty element is <head/>. When the XML parser encounters a tag with that syntax, it recognizes that tag and does not bother searching for an end tag like </head>, because it knows that no such end tag exists. The <element-name/> tag indicates that the application eventually deals with that element in its own way.

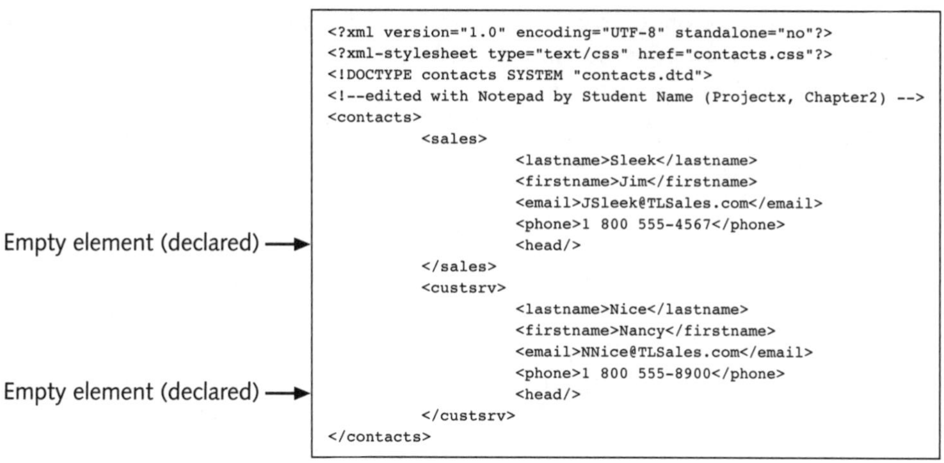

```
<?xml version="1.0" encoding="UTF-8" standalone="no"?>
<?xml-stylesheet type="text/css" href="contacts.css"?>
<!DOCTYPE contacts SYSTEM "contacts.dtd">
<!--edited with Notepad by Student Name (Projectx, Chapter2) -->
<contacts>
        <sales>
                <lastname>Sleek</lastname>
                <firstname>Jim</firstname>
                <email>JSleek@TLSales.com</email>
                <phone>1 800 555-4567</phone>
                <head/>
        </sales>
        <custsrv>
                <lastname>Nice</lastname>
                <firstname>Nancy</firstname>
                <email>NNice@TLSales.com</email>
                <phone>1 800 555-8900</phone>
                <head/>
        </custsrv>
</contacts>
```


Figure 2-11 Declared empty elements

Meanwhile, in the contacts.dtd file, there has to be an element declaration similar to the following in order for the document with the <head/> tag in it to be considered valid:

```
<!ELEMENT head (EMPTY)>
```

The fact that such a declaration exists is the reason that such elements are termed "declared" empty. Meanwhile, since XML documents do not absolutely require a DTD, without a clue like the modified <head/> tag, it could be impossible for an XML parser to determine whether a tag has deliberately been left empty or whether a mistake has been made.

Consequently, it has become legal in XML to use empty-element tag syntax, such as the following, for elements declared to be empty, as well as for those elements that are eligible to contain data, but that have no content at the time:

```
<head></head>
```

However, if interoperability is a concern, then, to avoid confusion the best approach is still to reserve empty-element tag syntax (e.g., <head/>) for elements that are declared to be empty, and to only use start tag and end tag pairs (e.g., <head></head>) for those elements that may not have any content.

Those elements that start with a start tag (<elementname>) and end with an end tag (</elementname>), but that have no content in them, are termed **elements with no content**, as opposed to declared empty elements. In their respective DTDs, they would be declared as ordinary elements and not as intentionally empty elements.

For example, you may have seen electronic forms requesting Social Security Numbers, email addresses, or annual income information. Often those fields are optional and a person may not need to insert any information into them. As a result, the form's <ann_income></ann_income> elements become, simply, elements with no content. If the elements are optional on the electronic form, then no error occurs when the application eventually processes the XML document containing the information that you have supplied on the form.

At this point, you can see how the declared empty syntax (like <ann_income/>) would be inappropriate for this situation.

Attributes

Elements may or may not include **attributes** (also called **attribute specifications**). They are a type of data that you can specify for your elements, and they appear in the form of name-value pairs. Applications can be programmed to look for them in data documents, and then to manipulate the elements in which the attributes appear. Attributes are inserted into start tags and placed immediately after the element name. If you wish to include them, you are certainly not limited to just one. You have already seen the generic syntax for an attribute in Figure 2-8. Now, for a more concrete example, look at the <contacts> element start tag in Figure 2-12.

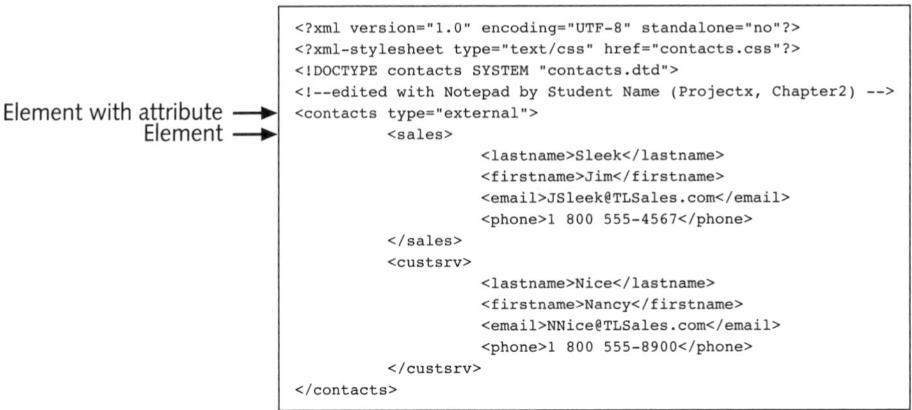


```
<?xml version="1.0" encoding="UTF-8" standalone="no"?>
<?xml-stylesheet type="text/css" href="contacts.css"?>
<!DOCTYPE contacts SYSTEM "contacts.dtd">
<!--edited with Notepad by Student Name (Projectx, Chapter2) -->
<contacts type="external">
        <sales>
                <lastname>Sleek</lastname>
                <firstname>Jim</firstname>
                <email>JSleek@TLSales.com</email>
                <phone>1 800 555-4567</phone>
        </sales>
        <custsrv>
                <lastname>Nice</lastname>
                <firstname>Nancy</firstname>
                <email>NNice@TLSales.com</email>
                <phone>1 800 555-8900</phone>
        </custsrv>
</contacts>
```

Figure 2-12 Element with attribute

The contacts start tag is also reproduced below:

```
<contacts type="external">
```

Notice how the start tag includes the attribute specification: the attribute's name is type and its value is set to "external" to indicate, in this case, that the elements within <contacts> contain the names and other details pertaining to company staff who can be contacted from outside the company.

During initial processing, the XML parser reads the attribute specification and passes the data along to the application. If, at some point in the application, there is a need for contact information to be made available to the public, then this element and its attribute specification type="external" is useful.

In this case, you may ask, "Instead of this attribute, why not just add another child element called <external>—which would also contain <sales> and <custsrv> and their respective child elements—instead of using an attribute specification?" That's a good question. It could be done. The choice of whether and when to use attributes versus elements is up to the developer, depending on other factors, including the flexibility of the structure needed, the processor power available, and the ability of a developer or other user to examine, modify, and fix the logical structure.

2

Be aware that the parser used for the XML document may impose a limit on the length of the attributes given to an element (check with the online documentation and reviews), thus requiring you to break the document or one of its elements into smaller elements.

Attribute names follow element tag name rules. Attribute names:

- Can begin with a letter, a colon, or an underscore (but not numbers)
- Can have subsequent characters that may be alphanumerics, underscores, hyphens, colons, and periods
- Cannot contain certain XML-specific symbols, like the ampersand (&), the at symbol (@), or the less than symbol (<)
- Cannot contain white space, since white space is used to separate the name-value pairs themselves and would cause confusion
- Cannot contain parenthetic statements (words enclosed in parentheses or brackets)

In addition, in any element, attribute names must be unique. If there are similar attributes to be listed, then remember that XML is case sensitive. If you are listing products from the fall fashion collection, for example, then an attribute named "SUBCATEGORY" is not considered the same as ones named "subcategory", "Subcategory", or even "SuBcAtEgOrY".

If you're going to create attributes, then you must assign **values** to them. If you don't—that is, if you try to create standalone attributes like those occasionally seen in HTML—then the XML parser treats them as errors (again, XML's well-formedness constraints, which are discussed near the end of the chapter, are violated).

In XML, all attribute values must be quoted (i.e., surrounded by quotation marks). The process of quoting can be complicated at times. First, here's the typical example used before, which is straightforward:

```
<CONTACTS type="external">
```

A complication might arise if the value itself were to include quotation marks, because the processor would not know where the value ended, or might not know what to do with characters following its perceived end of value. Consider the following:

```
<WARNING text='From AcctRcv: "Do not extend any more
credit to this customer!"'/>
```

In this case, using single quotes preserves the value of the attribute, which is a message from Accounts Receivable.

In the odd cases where the value contains both single and double quotes already, there is still an alternative: the use of XML-defined entity references. Consider this:

```
<DIMENSIONS length="1&apos;3.5&quot">
```

The translation? The length is 1' 3.5" (i.e., 1 foot, three-and-a-half inches).

XML and White Space

Developers often use white space (i.e., spaces, tabs, carriage returns, and blank lines) to organize a document or for better legibility. Beyond that, they don't care how XML parsers deal with white space. And it doesn't ordinarily matter to the parser if and when it may encounter white space; it usually does not apply any errors when it does.

Consider the following excerpt from the contacts.xml document:

```
<contacts type="external">
     <sales>
          <lastname>Sleek</lastname>
          <firstname>Jim</firstname>
          <email>JSleek@TLSales.com</email>
          <phone>1 800 555-4567</phone>
          <head/>
     </sales>
</contacts>
```

The XML parser would process the document as though it was:

```
<contacts type="external"><sales><lastname>Sleek
</lastname>
<firstname>Jim</firstname><email>JSleek@TLSales.com
</email>
<phone>1 800 555-4567</phone><head/></sales></contacts>
```

For elements with strictly element content or for data destined for storage, the previous examples may be quite acceptable. However, it may be important to preserve whitespace for other types of documents (e.g., performance scripts, meeting minute translations, long product descriptions, poetry and song writing, etc.). On those occasions, such "significant" white space should be preserved in the delivered version of the document. But how do you ensure that the significant white space is preserved?

There is a special attribute, named "xml:space", which can be used on the significant elements as follows:

```
<COLOR type="tvsets" xml:space="preserve">Black and White
</COLOR>
```

There are only two values for xml:space. The first is default (let the application do what it does normally), and the second is preserve.

Entities

There are two ways to look at entities. First, entities can be considered to be **text entities**, which are physical storage units that can hold parseable strings or blocks of text or non-parseable (i.e., non-XML data-like graphics), audio files, and video files. Alternatively, some think of entities as a way of referring to the physical data items. To keep things separate and clear in your mind, think of the **entities** as the physical storage unit for data, and then think of **entity references** as the method for referring to them. If you keep the terms separated, then you'll come to agree that entities are powerful content management structures.

Some characters have been reserved by XML for use with markup, which refers to instructions or codes embedded in text to indicate how the text should be processed or to specify what the text represents. Here are some examples of reserved characters in XML:

- The left angle bracket, or "less than" symbol (<)
- The right angle bracket, or "greater than" symbol (>)
- The double quotation mark (")
- The apostrophe, or single quotation mark (')
- The ampersand (&)

If you want to insert these characters into an XML document as content, an alternate way to represent them must be found to prevent the XML parser from trying to parse them. If an alternative isn't found, then either the XML parser always treats them as errors, or you cannot use them as content. Neither situation is acceptable.

To resolve this difficulty, XML provides five predefined general entities, one for each of those symbols. Respectively, they are: **lt**, **gt**, **quot**, **apos**, and **amp**. Entities are also used for two additional reasons:

- To refer to often repeated or varying text
- To include the content of external files

XML also provides entity approaches to cope with these situations. During the parsing process, the XML parser substitutes the actual data or text into the XML document in the place of the entity reference.

There are two kinds of entities: **general entities**, which can be used in the content of an XML document; and **parameter entities**, which can be used in a document's DTD.

Entities can also be categorized as follows:

- *Internal*—Those entities that are defined completely within the XML document that references them (in which case, the document itself is considered to become an entity)
- *External*—Entities whose content is found in an external source (e.g., a file); the reference to them usually includes the uniform resource identifier (URI) that points to their location
- *Parsed*—Entities whose content is well-formed XML text
- *Unparsed*—Entities whose content is simple text, binary data, or any other form of data you don't want the XML parser to interpret

General entities are discussed in this chapter. Parameter entities, which deal with DTDs and schemas, are dealt with in Chapters 4 and 5.

Most entities—there are a few notable exceptions—used in an XML document must first be defined with an entity declaration that assigns a unique name to the entity. Then the entity is referenced by that name in the XML document (for general entities) or in a DTD or schema (for parameter entities).

The five predefined general entities have already been mentioned; they are the exceptions to the declaration rule. Their specific entity references are similar to their names. Respectively, they are: < > " ' &. Since these are general entities, their references begin with the ampersand (&) and end with a semicolon. And since they are predefined, you don't need to define them in your document or in a DTD or schema. The XML parsers automatically recognize them and treat them accordingly.

Meanwhile, declaration syntax looks like the following:

```
<!ENTITY entityname entitydefinition>
```

Here is a simple and classic example. It is a substitution of the current date in a general internal entity named TODAY.

```
<!ENTITY TODAY "December 21, 2003">
```

Look at Figure 2-13 to see it in action.

Consider the following external variation of the above example. Suppose a file named date.xml exists that contains the current date. Look at Figure 2-14 to see how it can be accessed and used by the XML document. Notice how standalone has been set to "no", in the XML declaration statement, too.

"contacts" element modified
"date" element declared
General entity "TODAY" declared
General entity "TODAY" in use

```
<?xml version="1.0" encoding="UTF-8" standalone="yes"?>
<?xml-stylesheet type="text/css" href="contacts.css"?>
<!DOCTYPE contacts [
<!ELEMENT contacts (date,sales,custsrv)*>
<!ELEMENT date (#PCDATA)>
<!ELEMENT sales (lastname,firstname,email,phone)>
<!ELEMENT lastname (#PCDATA)>
<!ELEMENT firstname (#PCDATA)>
<!ELEMENT email (#PCDATA)>
<!ELEMENT phone (#PCDATA)>
<!ELEMENT custsrv (lastname,firstname,email,phone)>
<!ELEMENT lastname (#PCDATA)>
<!ELEMENT firstname (#PCDATA)>
<!ELEMENT email (#PCDATA)>
<!ELEMENT phone (#PCDATA)>
<!ENTITY TODAY "December 21, 2003">
]>
<!--edited with Notepad by Student Name (Projectx, Chapter2) -->
<contacts>
          <date>&TODAY;</date>
          <sales>
                    <lastname>Sleek</lastname>
                    <firstname>Jim</firstname>
                    <email>JSleek@TLSales.com</email>
                    <phone>1 800 555-4567</phone>
          </sales>
          <custsrv>
                    <lastname>Nice</lastname>
                    <firstname>Nancy</firstname>
                    <email>NNice@TLSales.com</email>
                    <phone>1 800 555-8900</phone>
          </custsrv>
</contacts>
```

Figure 2-13 Internal general entity

You have seen how a general parameter entity reference begins with an ampersand and ends with a semicolon. Parameter entity references begin with a percent sign (%) and end with a semicolon. Because parameter entities are used with DTDs and schemas, their references are discussed in Chapters 4 and 5.

Character references are a special kind of entity reference. They can be used to insert arbitrary Unicode characters from the ISO/IEC 10646 character set—ones that cannot be typed directly on your keyboard—into your document. Characters in the character set can be represented by numeric character references, which may be either decimal or hexadecimal.

Decimal references take the following form:

```
&#nnn
```

General entity "TODAY" declared →

General entity "TODAY" in use →

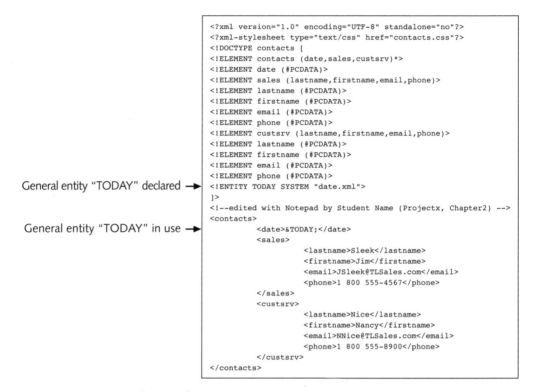

```
<?xml version="1.0" encoding="UTF-8" standalone="no"?>
<?xml-stylesheet type="text/css" href="contacts.css"?>
<!DOCTYPE contacts [
<!ELEMENT contacts (date,sales,custsrv)*>
<!ELEMENT date (#PCDATA)>
<!ELEMENT sales (lastname,firstname,email,phone)>
<!ELEMENT lastname (#PCDATA)>
<!ELEMENT firstname (#PCDATA)>
<!ELEMENT email (#PCDATA)>
<!ELEMENT phone (#PCDATA)>
<!ELEMENT custsrv (lastname,firstname,email,phone)>
<!ELEMENT lastname (#PCDATA)>
<!ELEMENT firstname (#PCDATA)>
<!ELEMENT email (#PCDATA)>
<!ELEMENT phone (#PCDATA)>
<!ENTITY TODAY SYSTEM "date.xml">
]>
<!--edited with Notepad by Student Name (Projectx, Chapter2) -->
<contacts>
        <date>&TODAY;</date>
        <sales>
                <lastname>Sleek</lastname>
                <firstname>Jim</firstname>
                <email>JSleek@TLSales.com</email>
                <phone>1 800 555-4567</phone>
        </sales>
        <custsrv>
                <lastname>Nice</lastname>
                <firstname>Nancy</firstname>
                <email>NNice@TLSales.com</email>
                <phone>1 800 555-8900</phone>
        </custsrv>
</contacts>
```

Figure 2-14 External general entity

In the hexadecimal reference form, *nnn* is the decimal number assigned to the character. For example, the decimal character reference for the copyright symbol is ©. The decimal character reference for the prescription (Rx) symbol is ℞.

Hexadecimal references take the following form:

```
&#xhhh (or &#Xhhh)
```

In the hexadecimal reference form, *hhh* is the appropriate hexadecimal number. For example, the hexadecimal reference for the copyright symbol is ©. The hexadecimal reference for the prescription symbol is ℞.

Notice that the examples above all show the character reference ending with a semicolon. This semicolon can be omitted in some circumstances (e.g., when the character reference is followed by a space), but you should always use it anyway, as a best practice. Currently, there is still somewhat limited support for hexadecimal references in the common browsers.

Further information regarding character references and for conversion charts can be found at the Unicode Consortium Web site at *www.unicode.org/charts/*.

CDATA Sections

There are occasions when characters that XML normally recognizes only as markup characters (again, the classic examples are <, >, “, ‘, and &) are intended to be passed directly to the application. Such a situation might arise when a description is passed along in an XML document:

```
<COLORS>
     Our <B> BRAND NEW </B>
     TV Sets are available in
     <I>COLOR</I> and <I>BLACK & WHITE</I>!
</COLORS>
```

Normally, the XML parser would encounter the &, consider it to be a markup signal, and then interpret it. If the parser did not create an error, then the application would likely create faulty output. To tell the parser to ignore the character and to simply pass it and the other characters on to the application, a **CDATA** section (for **character data** section) could be constructed, as follows:

```
<COLORS>
<![CDATA[
     Our <B> BRAND NEW </B>
     TV Sets are available in
     <I>COLOR</I> and <I>BLACK & WHITE</I>!
]]>
</COLORS>
```

There are a few things to remember about CDATA sections:

- They retain information about white space, so they are useful for creating and maintaining areas of program code.
- You cannot nest them. Once the parser finds one set of]]> indicators, it considers the CDATA section to be ended.
- You must be careful with the syntax. More than one otherwise reputable source has made mistakes.
- Any additional XML markup instructions between the <![CDATA and the]]>—such as elements, comments, processing instructions, etc.,—are not recognized by the parser. These characters pass directly to the application.

Such a construct may confuse most browsers until the manufacturers become more familiar and alter the code in the product to accommodate CDATA sections.

WELL-FORMED XML DOCUMENTS

So far in this chapter, several references have been made to well-formed XML documents. For example, it was stated at least twice that elements should not overlap one another, because that would cause the document to violate XML's well-formedness criteria. Now that several XML component topics have been discussed, it is easier to discuss those criteria and to define **well-formed documents**.

Well-formed XML documents are those that meet the following grammatical, logical, and structural rules, as outlined in the W3C's XML 1.0 Recommendation:

- An XML document meets all the well-formedness constraints given in the XML 1.0 Recommendation.
- The document contains one or more elements.
- Each of the parsed entities that is referenced directly or indirectly within the document is (also) well formed.
- An XML document can have only one root element, and all other elements fall within it. No part of the root element (also called a document element) appears in the content of any other element.
- For all the other elements in the document, if the element's start tag is in the content of one element, then the end tag must (also) be within the content of the same element. In other words, the elements, delimited by their respective start and end tags, must nest properly within each other. (Tags cannot overlap, and one element cannot fall within more than one parent.)
- Every start tag must have a matching end tag.
- Element names must obey XML naming conventions.

An example of a well-formed document is shown in Figure 2-15.

```
<?xml version="1.0" encoding="UTF-8" standalone="yes"?>
<?xml-stylesheet type="text/css" href="contacts.css"?>
<!--edited with Notepad by Student Name (Projectx, Ch. 2) -->
<contacts>
         <sales>
                  <lastname>Sleek</lastname>
                  <firstname>Jim</firstname>
                  <email>JSleek@TLSales.com</email>
                  <phone>1 800 555-4567</phone>
         </sales>
         <custsrv>
                  <lastname>Nice</lastname>
                  <firstname>Nancy</firstname>
                  <email>NNice@TLSales.com</email>
                  <phone>1 800 555-8900</phone>
         </custsrv>
</contacts>
```

Figure 2-15 Well-formed XML document

Notice how the root element is called <contacts> and how proper nesting occurs within it, and within and among the other elements. Now look at Figure 2-16, which is the same document with some changes deliberately inserted for illustration.

```
<?xml version="1.0" encoding="UTF-8" standalone="yes"?>
<?xml-stylesheet type="text/css" href="contacts.css"?>
<!--edited with Notepad by Student Name (Projectx, Ch. 2) -->
<contacts>
        <sales>
                <lastname>Sleek</lastname>Jim</firstname>
                <email>JSleek@TLSales.com<phone>1 800 555-4567</phone></email>
        </sales>
        <custsrv>
                <lastname>Nice<firstname></lastname>Nancy</firstname>
                <email>NNice@TLSales.com<phone>1 800 555-8900</phone></email>
        </custsrv>
</contacts>
```

Figure 2-16 Overlapping elements ("freeform XML")

Note, first, that it is acceptable to put more than one element on one line, since XML parsers, unless specifically instructed, are not concerned with the use of white space in this manner. However, within both the <sales> and <custsrv> elements, there are elements that violate one or more of the well-formedness rules (also called well-formedness constraints) listed above. First, there is a clear overlap in the <lastname> and <firstname> elements: the start tag of the second element is encountered before the end tag of the first element. Then, in the <email> and <phone> elements, it appears that the <phone> element content has, in effect, two parents (<email> and <phone>), another violation.

These practices reflect what is occasionally called freeform XML. In the past especially, such freeform practices may have been considered bad practice, but they were not considered fatal errors. However, more and more XML processors are being developed that conform to the W3C well-formedness constraints, so freeform approaches such as these have become grounds for fatal error, in accordance with the W3C's intent. It is recommended that freeform XML be avoided entirely.

Valid XML Documents

A **valid** XML document is a well-formed XML document that also conforms to the declarations, structures, and other rules defined in the document's respective DTD or schema. Validity, DTDs, and schemas are discussed in detail in later chapters. For now, consider the examples in Figure 2-17.

The version of contacts.xml on the left is a well-formed XML document. Next to it on the right is another well-formed version of contacts.xml, containing the same contact information, but also containing a document type declaration that specifies an external DTD (the document type declaration appears in bold print in Figure 2-17 only for illustrative purposes). If the right hand document conforms to its external DTD, then that document is a valid XML document.

```
<?xml version="1.0" encoding="UTF-8" standalone="yes"?>
<?xml-stylesheet type="text/css" href="contacts.css"?>
<!--edited with Notepad by Student Name (Projectx, Ch. 2) -->
<contacts>
        <sales>
                <lastname>Sleek</lastname>
                <firstname>Jim</firstname>
                <email>JSleek@TLSales.com</email>
                <phone>1 800 555-4567</phone>
        </sales>
        <custsrv>
                <lastname>Nice</lastname>
                <firstname>Nancy</firstname>
                <email>NNice@TLSales.com</email>
                <phone>1 800 555-8900</phone>
        </custsrv>
</contacts>
```

Well-formed XML document

```
<?xml version="1.0" encoding="UTF-8" standalone="no"?>
<?xml-stylesheet type="text/css" href="contacts.css"?>
<!DOCTYPE contacts SYSTEM "contacts.dtd">
<!--edited with Notepad by Student Name (Projectx, Ch. 2) -->
<contacts>
        <sales>
                <lastname>Sleek</lastname>
                <firstname>Jim</firstname>
                <email>JSleek@TLSales.com</email>
                <phone>1 800 555-4567</phone>
        </sales>
        <custsrv>
                <lastname>Nice</lastname>
                <firstname>Nancy</firstname>
                <email>NNice@TLSales.com</email>
                <phone>1 800 555-8900</phone>
        </custsrv>
</contacts>
```

Valid XML document

Figure 2-17 Comparison: well-formed vs valid documents

Now, take a look at Figure 2-18, which illustrates the processing of an XML data object.

Note how an XML document, in its most raw form, is referred to as a data object. The XML data object is considered a well-formed XML document once it has been checked by the XML parser and is deemed to have met the W3C's well-formedness constraints. The XML parser then checks the XML document for validity (by examining its components and structure against the declarations in its DTD or schema). If the XML document proves to be valid, then it is made available for processing by the application. Note also, however, that, depending on the application, an XML document need not be valid to be passed for further processing. However, generally, XML documents need to be well formed.

2

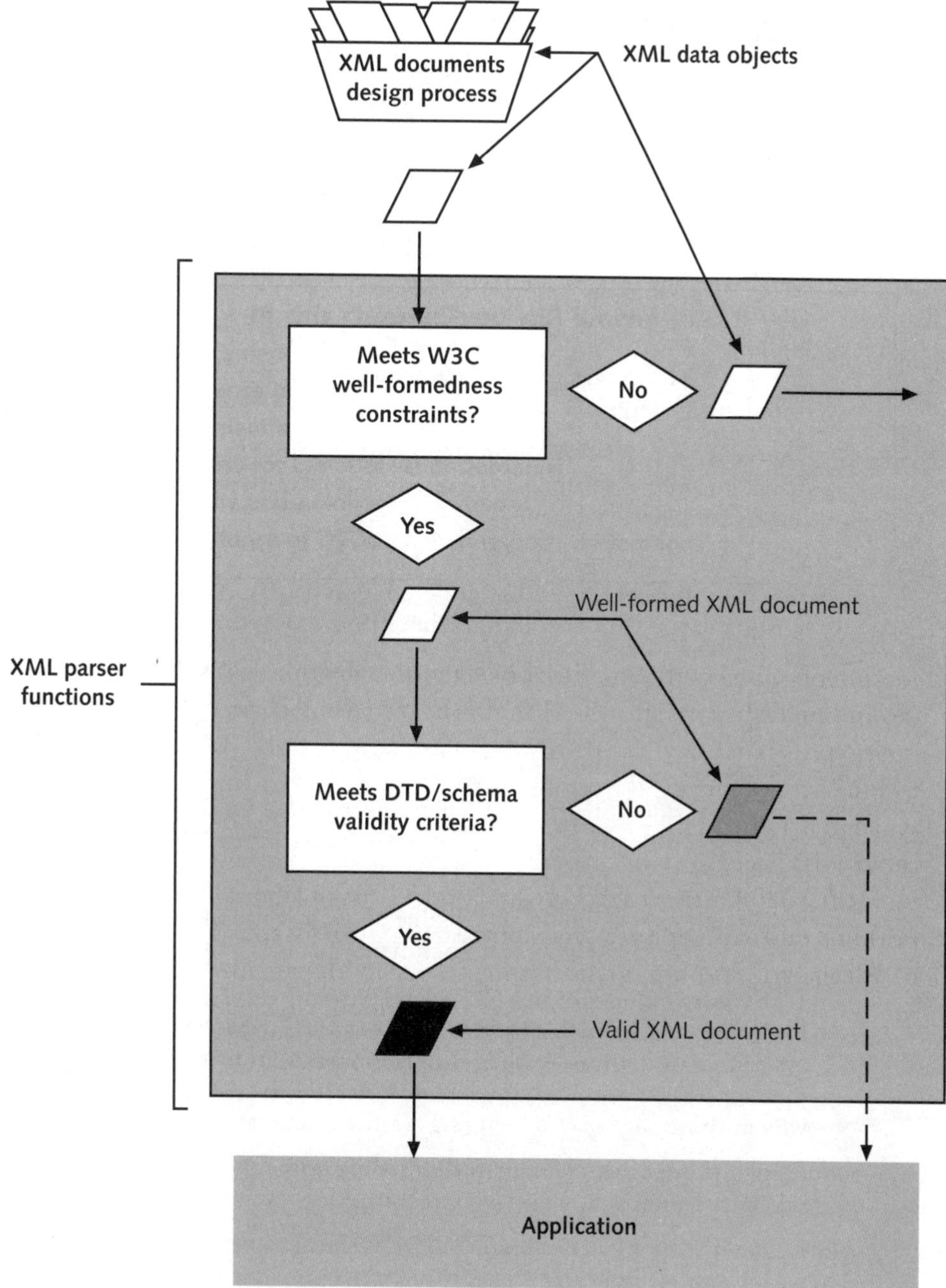

Figure 2-18 Process schematic: well-formed & valid documents

CHAPTER SUMMARY

- The W3C XML 1.0 Recommendation defines XML documents as a class of data objects (textual data documents and many other data formats). Since XML is a restricted form of SGML, then XML documents must also be conforming SGML documents. To think of XML documents simply as text documents is too limiting and detracts from XML's major features: its extensibility with respect to data, its straightforward structure, and its human legibility.
- An XML processor, or parser, is a piece of software that reads XML documents and provides access to their content and structure. In this way, the XML processor does front-end screening for the application. A fatal error is an error in the document that the XML processor must detect and then report to the application. Once a fatal error is detected, the XML processor does not continue normal processing.
- The W3C Recommendation states that documents have a physical structure made up of storage units called entities and a logical structure containing a prolog section and one or more elements.
- The XML declaration statement should appear on the first line of the XML document's prolog, and should include the mandatory XML version attribute, the optional language encoding attribute, and the optional language encoding attribute.
- The document type declaration (also called the DOCTYPE definition) should also appear in the prolog section. It defines the type of document and it also states to which document type definition (DTD) or schema the XML document should conform, if applicable.
- The Processing instructions (PIs) are instructions passed by the XML processor to the application. PI names may begin with the characters XML, xml, or something similar.
- Comments are added to provide information to any person working on the XML document, or to temporarily disable sections of markup and content. Comments can be placed anywhere in a document, but it is bad form to place a comment before the first XML declaration statement.
- Elements are the basic building blocks of XML. Each extends from the first angle bracket in its start tag to the last angle bracket of its end tag. They can be nested but they cannot overlap. Empty elements include those that are declared to be empty, as well as those that may, depending on the circumstances, simply have no content.
- Elements can have element content, data content, or mixed content (i.e., element and data content).
- Element names (also called tag names) should identify or hint at the element type within the element. Elements may or may not include one or more name/value pairs called attribute specifications.
- The root element is the parent of all other elements. The root element usually, but not always, is a parent, but is not considered to have a parent. Any parent can have more than one child element, but each child element document has only one parent

element. Child elements are wholly contained within the content of their parent element, and must not overlap with their sibling element(s).

- Entities can be considered to be physical storage units that can hold parseable text entities or non-XML (non-parseable) binary entities. There are generally three uses for entities: to insert "reserved-for-markup" characters into an XML document as content; to refer to often repeated or varying text; and to include the content of external sources. Most entities must first be defined with an entity declaration in the XML document, or in the DTD or schema.
- Character references are a special kind of entity reference, and are used to insert Unicode characters—ones that cannot be typed on the keyboard—into an XML document.
- CDATA sections tell the parser to ignore the markup characters and to pass them on to the application. Care must be taken, however, because any intentional markups in the CDATA are rendered useless.
- Well-formed XML documents meet the W3C's specific grammatical, logical, and structural rules outlined in the W3C's XML 1.0 Recommendation. The W3C has judged that a fatal error has occurred if and when a conforming XML processor detects that an XML document violates the Recommendation's well-formedness constraints.
- An XML document must be well formed, but need not be valid (that depends, though, on the needs of the application for which the XML document is created).
- A valid XML document is a well-formed XML document that also conforms to the rules defined in a document type definition (DTD) or an XML schema.

Review Questions

1. The term "XML document" refers not only to textual data documents, but also to many other structured ______________ (e.g., vector graphics, mathematical equations, etc.).
2. During the processing of an XML document, what is it that performs the front-end screening?
3. When an XML parser encounters a fatal error situation, it must detect and report the fatal error to the application, and then it can resume normal processing. True or False?
4. According to the W3C, what kinds of structures must an XML document have?
   a. sequential
   b. physical
   c. elemental
   d. parsed or unparsed
   e. logical
5. A generic identifier is another name for ______________.

6. Which of the following is NOT part of the XML declaration statement?
   a. the XML version
   b. language encoding
   c. root element
   d. standalone attribute
7. If you don't specify the language encoding, what is the default?
   a. UTF-8
   b. Unicode
   c. UCS-2
   d. UCS-4
   e. other
8. According to the W3C, how many types of markup declarations are there? What are they?
9. Another name for the document type declaration is the DOCTYPE definition. True or False?
10. Although ________________ are not textually part of the XML document, they are instructions that are passed by the XML processor to the application.
11. Which of the following strings causes a parser to interpret—incorrectly and prematurely—that a comment has ended?
    a. ?
    b. < or >
    c. !*
    d. —
    e. none of the above
12. Which of the following statements is true?
    a. Comments are not part of the textual content of an XML document. The XML processor is not required to pass them along to an application.
    b. Comments are part of the textual content of an XML document. The XML processor is required to pass them along to an application.
    c. Comments are part of the textual content of an XML document, but the XML processor is not required to pass them along to an application.
    d. Comments are not part of the textual content of an XML document, but the XML processor is still required to pass them along to an application.
    e. none of the above
13. How far does an element extend?
14. There are two types of empty elements: those elements that are declared empty and those that have not been declared empty but are simply called ________________.

15. Which of the following statements is true?
    a. It is acceptable to have more than one element on one line, but it is not acceptable to overlap elements.
    b. It is acceptable to have more than one element on one line, and it is acceptable to overlap elements.
    c. It is not acceptable to have more than one element on one line, and it is not acceptable to overlap elements.
    d. It is not acceptable to have more than one element on one line, but it is acceptable to overlap elements.
    e. none of the above.
16. What does it mean for an element to have element content?
17. An element cannot have both element content and data content. True or False?
18. In an !ELEMENT declaration, what does #PCDATA mean?
19. On what factors does a developer decide whether to have more attributes instead of more elements, or vice versa?
20. Which of the following is NOT a good attribute name?
    a. type
    b. _1st_time
    c. 2ndtype
    d. my:type
    e. :_._._
21. Take a look at the following and then fill in the blank at the end:

```
<message>
      <to>NNice@TLSales.com</to>
      <from>Ric@ACME.com</from>
      <subject>Orders</subject>
      <text>
        Your order can be picked up anytime.
      </text>
</message>
```

    There are ______________ elements in this file.
22. Based on the following file:

```
<message to="NNice@TLSales.com" from="Ric@ACME.com"
                  subject="Orders">
      <text>
        Your order can be picked up anytime.
      </text>
</message>
```

    How many attributes are there?

23. Based on the following XML document:

```
<message to="NNice@TLSales.com" from="Ric@ACME.com"
      subject="Orders">
      <flag/>
            <text>
                  Your order can be picked up anytime.
            </text>
</message>
```

From the syntax, the empty element is of the ______________ type.

24. All attribute values must be quoted. Both single and double quotation marks can be used. True or False?

25. An item can be included in an XML document by referencing it. Which of the following cannot be legitimately referenced?

   a. a left-angle bracket

   b. an entire document

   c. a collection of DTD definitions

   d. all of the above

   e. none of the above

HANDS-ON PROJECTS

Project 2-1

In this project, you use the simple text editor MS Notepad to modify a basic XML document. The XML document eventually is integrated into the *www.TLSales.com* Web site that you are going to create. At this point, however, your task is to add a customer service (custsrv) contact, in its own sibling element (also referred to as sister element) within the <contacts> element of this document. Meanwhile, for this first project, we are going to use elements only. The next project introduces attributes.

As you progress through this project, you will find that simple XML files can be made quite easily with an editor such as Notepad. Currently, Internet Explorer V5.X and Netscape V6.X handle XML files differently. An editor such as XML Spy can also offer an easy way to view XML files, because it contains a lot of MS Internet Explorer functionality.

1. Create a personal folder to hold your working files. The folder should be called **C:\home*username***, where *username* is your name.

2. Copy the file called **contacts.xml** out of the **CH02** folder on your data disk into your **C:\home\username** folder.

3. Using **Notepad**, open your new file called **contacts.xml**, found inside the **C:\home\username** folder. Note that one sales contact is already listed in the document.

4. **Update** the comment **(<!-- ... -->)** line so that it reflects your personal information—for example, your name and the chapter number.
5. Construct a new sibling element to <SALES>. Name it <CUSTSRV> and add **Nancy Nice** as data for the <NAME> child element within <CUSTSRV>. Use **NNice@TLSales.com** and **1 515 123-4567** as data for the <EMAIL> and <PHONE> child elements, respectively.
6. When you're finished, the XML document should look like the following:

```
<?xml version="1.0" encoding="UTF-8"?>
<-- edited by Student Name-->
<CONTACTS>
  <SALES>
       <NAME>Jim Sleek</NAME>
       <EMAIL>JSleek@TLSales.com</EMAIL>
       <PHONE>1 800 123-4567</PHONE>
  </SALES>
  <CUSTSRV>
       <NAME>Nancy Nice</NAME>
       <EMAIL>NNice@TLSales.com</EMAIL>
       <PHONE>1 515 123-4567</PHONE>
  </CUSTSRV>
</CONTACTS>
```

7. Save the file, and Close Notepad.
8. Using Internet Explorer, open your **C:\home\username\contacts.xml** file again. Because the file has a file type associated with it, to prevent a different editor from coming up you may have to use Windows NT Explorer to navigate to the file. **Highlight** the file, then **right-click** to bring up a context menu, and then use the **Open With** Internet Explorer option.
9. Try to edit the file. Notice that Internet Explorer lets you open and close the elements by manipulating the + and – focus points, but it does not allow you to edit the file. This is the expected default behavior. Close Internet Explorer.
10. Download and install Netscape V6. Accept all of the recommended defaults, changing nothing, during the installation. When the activation screen appears, click the **Cancel** button, and then click **Cancel** again. You receive a **Windows Integration** message box. Choose **No**. Do not make this your default browser.
11. When the Netscape browser opens, click **File**, **Open File**, navigate to your **C:\home\username\contacts.xml file**, and open it. Notice that this time you only see the unformatted data without the XML tags. This is normal behavior for Netscape V6, which is different from that of Internet Explorer. Close Netscape V6.
12. Using Notepad again, add another employee relations contact to the list using the following specifications. To do this, construct a new sibling element called <EMPLREL> using **Frank Hire** as data for the **<NAME>** child element. Use **Hire@TLSales.com** and **1 515 123-4568** as data for the **<EMAIL>** address and **<PHONE>** child elements, respectively. You should now have three contacts in the file.

13. Save the file, and Close Notepad.
14. Install XML Spy. To do so, double-click the executable file found on the CD included with this book. Accept the terms of the license agreement and all of the defaults as the installation proceeds. When you are finished, you have an XML Spy IDE icon on the desktop.
15. Double-click the **XML Spy IDE** icon to open XML Spy. The XML Spy Licensing Manager appears. Click **ENTER a new key-code**. Please refer to the instructions within XMLSpy for registering your XMLSpy product. The information must be entered exactly as it appears. This information is case and space sensitive, and all three pieces of information are part of the signature of the key-code algorithm.
16. Open the **contacts.xml** file using the XML Spy editor. You should see a screen that looks like the one shown in Figure 2-19. Expand all of the menus if you have to, until you can see the image. If the editor returns errors, you have to fix those before proceeding.

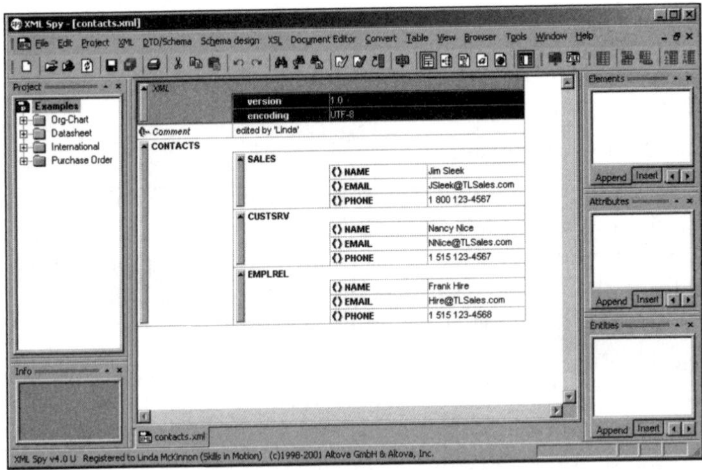

Figure 2-19 XML Spy-enhanced grid view

17. To get acquainted with this editor, construct one last element. This time, use the XML Spy editor, using the Enhanced Grid view. Call the new element **PRESIDENT**, and use your own data. To do this, place your cursor inside the **CONTACTS** white space, right-click, and use the context menu to **Add Child Element**, and enter **PRESIDENT** in the resulting input field. Right-click the blue field next to PRESIDENT to create the <NAME>**,** <EMAIL>, and <PHONE> elements. At any time, you can change the view back to text mode by clicking the menu and choosing the View Text View option. You can use your information or create a new person on your own.

18. You can click the **yellow check mark** in the task bar of XML Spy to check your file for well-formedness. Click **OK**.
19. Save the file.
20. Before closing the XML Spy editor, add two more sales contacts using the following information. Use whatever view you are most comfortable with.

    Click on **SALES** for Jim Sleek. Click **XML**, **Insert**, **Element**. Type **SALES**, then click on the **dark blue bar** to the right of SALES. Right-click. Scroll to **Add Child**, click **Element**, then type in **NAME**, and follow the same procedure to insert the name. Repeat this procedure to add telephone and email information.

NAME	EMAIL	PHONE
Anna Gold	Agold@TLSales.com	1 800 123-4567
Terry White	Twhite@TLSales.com	1 800 123-4567

21. We now have three sales people in the contacts list. Use an empty element tag called **<HEAD/>** to indicate that Anna Gold is the head of the sales department. Do this without affecting the other elements within the <SALES> element. To do so, click Anna's **SALES white space**. Right-click. Scroll to **Add Child**, and click on **Element**. Type **HEAD**, and press **Enter**. This creates the <HEAD/> tag. This procedure is called declaring an empty element.
22. Check your file for well-formedness. Save the file, and Close the XML Spy editor.

Project 2-2

This project is going to use the same data as the previous project. However, now you are asked to rethink the file, and then re-create it by moving the information in the child elements <NAME>, <EMAIL>, and <PHONE> into attributes in the <SALES>, <CUSTSRV> and <EMPLREL> elements. You may have to refer to your notes. But, as you recreate the file, you find that there is, unfortunately, no way to accommodate the requirement for flagging Anna Gold as the head of the Sales Department. So, that is not a requirement this time.

You see that an XML file does not need to have an .xml extension to be an XML file and that XML data can be contained within elements or coded as attributes. Although they appear equivalent, coding data as attributes has its limitations.

1. Make a copy of your **contacts.xml** file, and save it as **attribs**. Open the new **attribs** file in XML Spy, and change the comment line to include the ***name of this new assignment*** and ***your name***.
2. Recode the file converting the child elements into attributes. To do so, click **NAME** in EMPLREL. Then right-click, and scroll to **Insert or Append**, and click **Attribute**. Type **NAME** and press **Enter**. On the right side, type **Frank Hire** and press **Enter**. Repeat the process for Frank's email and phone information. Remove the **<NAME>**, **<EMAIL>**, and **<PHONE>** elements by highlighting and then

pressing **Delete**. Repeat the process for all the contacts. Occasionally check the file for well-formedness by using the **XML**, **Check well-formedness** feature on the menu bar. You can switch between the Enhanced Grid view and the Text view depending upon which you find easier.

3. Save the file and Close the XML Spy editor.

Project 2-3

In this project, you install and configure a personal Web server. Some basic content has been supplied for it. Once the Web server is up and running, you deploy your file **C:\home\username\contacts.xml**, and view the results using both the Internet Explorer and Netscape browsers. You are asked to make notes of the differences in behavior.

You find that there are numerous incompatibilities between different applications when it comes to deploying XML. Although the XML code works correctly inside an IDE such as XML Spy, there is no guarantee that it is going to function correctly with all browsers or Web services. Thus, it is a very good idea to check and deploy your work as you progress through a project.

1. If you have not done so, create a home folder for your files. Double-click **My Computer**. Double-click **Local Disk C:**. If a home folder is not there, create a **home** folder. Create a folder under the **home** folder with ***your name***. This will now be referred to as your C:\home*username* folder.
2. Copy content from **CH02\WWWContent** to your folder. You should now have a folder structure that looks like this: **C:\home\username\WWWContent\tlsales.** If there is an index.html file inside the tlsales folder, then you have done this correctly.
3. Create a personal user Web service for yourself in IIS. To do this, click **Start**, scroll to **Settings**, and then click **Control Panel**. Click **Start**, **Control Panel** if using Windows XP.
4. Double-click **Administrative Tools**, then double-click **Computer Management**. (Click the Classic View link in the Control Panel when using Windows XP.)
5. Expand the **Services and Applications** folder, then expand the **Internet Information Services** folder.
6. Expand the **Web Sites** folder, and then **Default Web Site** folder, and right-click.
7. Select **New**, then click **Virtual Directory**.
8. Once the Virtual Directory Creation Wizard appears, click **Next**.
9. Under **Alias**, type ***your user name*** with no spaces, and click **Next**.
10. Under **Directory**, click **Browse**. Open folders until the path reads: **Local Disk C:\home\username\WWWContent\tlsales**.
11. Click **OK**, then click **Next**.

12. Click **Execute** (**Such as ISAPI applications or CGI**).
13. Click **Next**, then click **Finish**.
14. Right-click **Default Web Site**, and click **Stop**.
15. Right-click **Default Web Site**, and click **Start**. Exit from the Services and Applications Folder.
16. To test the server, double-click on **Internet Explorer**. In the address box, type **http://localhost/*username*/index.html**, and press Enter. Remember that your user name was used as the Alias for the personal Web server in Step 9 above. The Web page for TLSales should appear. The **"We Are Hiring"** link should work, but the **Our Product Catalog** link should not.

CASE PROJECTS

The following two case projects show you how to integrate your newly created XML file into the TLSales Web site, and then how to apply a chosen style regime to that file.

By the end of this exercise, you see that although it is possible to code XML files directly for display by a browser, it is probably not a good idea to rely on the most common browser applications until their display capability improves. Until then, there is still a need for XML-to-HTML transformation. We discuss transformation in Chapter 6.

Case Project 2-1

You are going to change the link on the index page of the *http://localhost/username/* Web server to point to your contacts.xml file rather than to the existing hire.html file. Before proceeding, make a backup copy of the index.html page that was supplied to you. Replace the text for the link called "We are hiring ..." to read "Our new staff". Then recode the link itself so that it links to the contacts.xml file instead of the hire.html file. Place a copy of your contacts.xml file in the pages folder, and test the link, using both the Internet Explorer and Netscape browsers. Both should display the unformatted XML data. The data is unformatted at this time.

Case Project 2-2

Add a directive to your contacts.xml file to point to a cascading style sheet that can format the unformatted XML data. We have created a very basic, cascading style sheet for you to use. All you have to do is to code a directive statement into your contacts.xml file to utilize it. Now code a processing instruction (PI) statement into your contacts.xml file to link the contacts.css style sheet to your contacts.xml file. Test the new link using both the Internet Explorer and Netscape browsers. Improve on the HTML coding in the file as you wish, if time permits.

CHAPTER

3

XML CREATION AND EDITING SOFTWARE

In this chapter, you will learn:

- About the three basic categories of XML authoring tools: simple text editors, graphical text editors, and integrated development environments
- About several prominent authoring tools
- To integrate XML with your existing document and knowledge management system
- How to review, install, configure, and use applications from all the authoring tool categories

This chapter introduces an important piece of XML software: the XML authoring tool, also called the XML editor. Choosing your authoring tool dictates the look, structure, and interoperability of your XML documents during the creation, modification, conversion, updating, and viewing processes, and is therefore a very important decision.

There are three basic categories of XML authoring tools: **simple text editors**, **graphical text editors**, and **integrated development environments (IDEs)**. Several authoring applications are available within each category. Many authoring tools are stretching their classification boundaries as they become further developed and upgraded. Graphical text editors, for example, have taken on characteristics of IDEs in recent years, and might even be classified in an intermediate category between graphical editors and IDEs. Since XML is an open standard, you are not tied to any particular classification or tool. If you tire of one editor or are in a location where you can't use your customary editor (for example, if you are creating mathematical expressions), you will likely be able to switch editors and your documents will work as well as before. Exceptions can occur, though, when licensing is involved or when another component must be created or installed before the program can be used. Later, you see how some editors require that the separate document type definition (DTDs), schemas, or style sheets referenced by an XML document must be available to the editor before the editor will allow you to access or manipulate the document.

SIMPLE TEXT EDITORS

These types of simple applications have few features. For example, you can't change the look and feel of your text with these programs; they only allow you to write ASCII (although not UNICODE) text. Nevertheless, these simple applications are all capable of producing XML documents, since all XML tags and symbols use characters found on the standard keyboard. In fact, you can easily write XML in any text editor or word processor that can save to plain text format.

Although simple text editors are XML's most basic and economical creation and editing tools, they are limited in their display capabilities. Some use only one font, while others only let you use a few different colors. Many authors consider them to be boring. However, they are still among the most widely used text manipulation tools, especially when the creation or modification of a document is not extensive. They are simple and powerful enough, portable because of their small size, and found on virtually every platform as part of a basic operating system installation. Using XML's logical structure, whitespace, and comments, some developers are capable of creating whole documents using nothing but text editors. Despite all the predictions you've heard, simple text editors are still widely used. In a pinch, they can help you get the job done. Plus, if you've ever used one of these low-powered applications, you really appreciate using the more sophisticated tools discussed later.

Some examples of text editors include:

- Microsoft Notepad
- Microsoft WordPad
- vi (found on virtually every UNIX-based platform)
- Emacs (originated on UNIX-based platforms—where it has become more and more popular—but also occasionally installed on Windows systems)
- Apple/Macintosh's SimpleText or SimpleText Pro

Figure 3-1 illustrates what an XML file would look like if it had been created with Microsoft Notepad, and Figure 3-2 shows the same file created in a UNIX/Linux environment with vi.

GNU Emacs—usually just called Emacs—is a more extensible and customizable text editor than vi, Notepad, or WordPad, and can also be used to create or modify XML documents. Emacs was originally developed in 1975 by Richard Stallman; formerly of the Massachusetts Institute of Technology, he left to establish the GNU project and, later, the Free Software Foundation. Development of Emacs has continued through today. Emacs has long been the preferred UNIX-variant (it functions on virtually all UNIX variants) text editor by many. Emacs capabilities include:

- Online documentation, including a tutorial
- Extensibility through its Emacs Lisp language

- Support for many languages and their scripts
- Many extensions that add functionality, including a Web browser
- Variable width and variable height fonts
- Functionality on MS Windows NT, Windows 9X, Windows 2000, and Windows XP
- And many more features

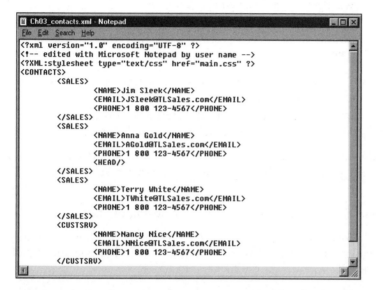

```
Ch03_contacts.xml - Notepad
File Edit Search Help
<?xml version="1.0" encoding="UTF-8" ?>
<!-- edited with Microsoft Notepad by user name -->
<?XML:stylesheet type="text/css" href="main.css" ?>
<CONTACTS>
        <SALES>
                <NAME>Jim Sleek</NAME>
                <EMAIL>JSleek@TLSales.com</EMAIL>
                <PHONE>1 800 123-4567</PHONE>
        </SALES>
        <SALES>
                <NAME>Anna Gold</NAME>
                <EMAIL>AGold@TLSales.com</EMAIL>
                <PHONE>1 800 123-4567</PHONE>
                <HEAD/>
        </SALES>
        <SALES>
                <NAME>Terry White</NAME>
                <EMAIL>TWhite@TLSales.com</EMAIL>
                <PHONE>1 800 123-4567</PHONE>
        </SALES>
        <CUSTSRV>
                <NAME>Nancy Nice</NAME>
                <EMAIL>NNice@TLSales.com</EMAIL>
                <PHONE>1 800 123-4567</PHONE>
        </CUSTSRV>
```

Figure 3-1 contacts.xml created with Microsoft Notepad

```
xterm
<?xml version="1.0" encoding="UTF-8"?>
<!-- edited with vi by user name -->
<?XML:stylesheet type="text/css" href="main.css"?>
<CONTACTS>
        <SALES>
                <NAME>Jim Sleek</NAME>
                <EMAIL>JSleek@TLSales.com</EMAIL>
                <PHONE>1 800 123-4567</PHONE>
        </SALES>
        <SALES>
                <NAME>Anna Gold</NAME>
                <EMAIL>AGold@TLSales.com</EMAIL>
                <PHONE>1 800 123-4567</PHONE>
                <HEAD/>
        </SALES>
        <SALES>
                <NAME>Terry White</NAME>
                <EMAIL>TWhite@TLSales.com</EMAIL>
                <PHONE>1 800 123-4567</PHONE>
        </SALES>
        <CUSTSRV>
                <NAME>Nancy Nice</NAME>
                <EMAIL>Nice@TLSales.com</EMAIL>
"Ch03_contacts.xml" 36L 1111C
```

Figure 3-2 contacts.xml created with UNIX/Linux vi

The name Emacs was originally an abbreviation of Editor MACroS. When it was first developed, the custom was to give macro packages names ending in "mac" or "macs." Also, the prefix "e" was not yet used as an abbreviation on its original operating system (using such an abbreviation makes it is easier to invoke Emacs at a command line interface).

To obtain Emacs, visit the GNU Project Web site at *http://www.gnu.org/software/software.html#HowToGetSoftware*. For further information on GNU, Emacs or the Free Software Foundation, visit Mr. Stallman's Web site at http:*//www.gnu.org/gnu/the-gnu-project.html*.

GRAPHICAL TEXT EDITORS

Using simple text editors can be a slow process. Some developers have difficulty getting a feel for their XML documents when they are confined to using (only) markup elements—with no colors, highlights, and other features—even if they are going to be eventually publishing their documents complete with stylesheets, DTDs, schemas, etc.

To overcome this difficulty, many dedicated XML editors are designed to look and act like modern word processor applications. Unlike simple text editors, graphical XML editors can:

- Represent the markup more clearly by coloring the tags
- Hide the markup completely and apply a stylesheet immediately to give the various document parts their own emphasis or style (style and stylesheets are discussed in more detail in Chapters 6 and 11)
- Provide menus of options
- Allow drag-and-drop editing
- Allow click-and-drag highlighting
- Provide special user-interface mechanisms for manipulating XML markup, such as attribute editors or drag-and-drop relocation of elements
- Provide a menu of legal elements, which is a good tool for rigidly structured XML applications (e.g., filling out forms, entering data into a database)

Using a dedicated editor, developers can simply type the content or content references, choose fonts and colors, and save the document, essentially, as a Web page. This approach is called "what you see is what you get" or WYSIWYG (pronounced "whizzeewig").

A popular feature in higher-end XML authoring tools is automatic structure checking. By resisting any attempt to add an element that doesn't belong in a given context, the tool tries to prevent the author from making syntactic or structural mistakes while writing and editing.

While promoting good document structure and simultaneously preventing inadvertent mistakes, structure checking can also slow your progress when you experiment with the order of the document elements, most commonly during the initial drafting phase of a document. For example, imagine you are setting up a human resource system and you are trying to decide what to use for a parent element: should you use an employee's name, with child elements containing other relevant information (address, phone number, Social Security number, department name, employment start date, classification, work location, etc.)? Perhaps you would prefer, for legibility or computer resource utilization purposes, that the department name should be the parent element, with child elements being the employee names and their child elements? Or your preference might be classifications "on top," with employees listed beneath them? Or would you group your employees according to their work locations (the New York office, the Calcutta office, the Singapore office, etc.)? Now, imagine that you are experimenting with your human resource data structure, or even with your inventory. For example, are motorcycle spark plugs "engine/mechanical system parts" or "electrical system parts"? Do you categorize them first by system, part number, or name? You can see that if your XML text editor begins to resist changes and insertions, then time can be lost accommodating the text editor's tendencies, no matter how noble the original intention of the developers were.

Most developers believe that a high-quality XML authoring environment should be configurable. In addition to the features listed above, the ideal authoring tool should allow you to:

- Customize the editor to enforce the structure (for reasons listed above)
- Check the validity of your XML documents (see the definition of validity in Chapter 2)
- Present a selection of valid elements from which to choose
- Create macros to automate frequently used editing steps
- Map keys on the keyboard to macros
- Define your display properties (e.g., preferences for large type with color, small type with tags displayed, etc.)

The first graphical editors for structured markup languages were based on SGML, of which XML is a restricted form. However, because SGML was much bigger and more complex, those editors were often prohibitively expensive and difficult to maintain. XML's relative simplicity has allowed for the development of simpler and more affordable editors. Still, because XML developers have been requesting more and more features, even the XML editors are growing in number, size, complexity, and price. Following are brief descriptions of some graphical text editors.

Microsoft XML Notepad

XML Notepad is Microsoft's dedicated XML graphical text editor. Its interface consists of a two-pane display. On the left is the document's element structure, on the right are the corresponding element values. A typical presentation is shown in Figure 3-3.

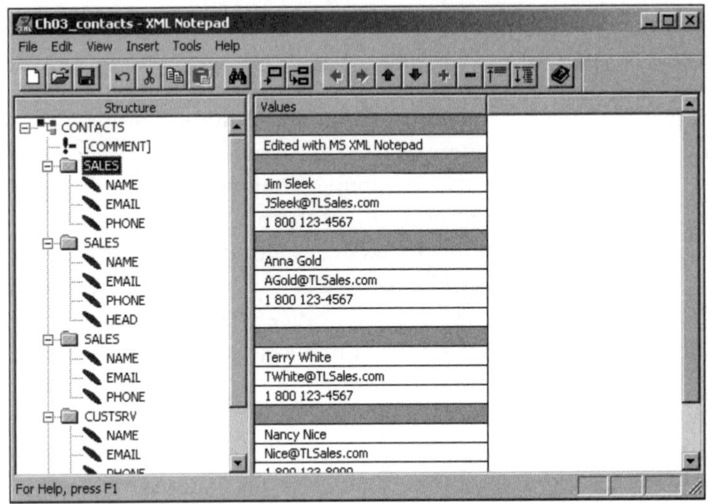

Figure 3-3 contacts.xml created with Microsoft XML Notepad

To download a copy of XML Notepad, see the following Microsoft Developer Network (MSDN) Web site: *http://msdn.microsoft.com/library/default.asp?url=/library/en-us/dnxml/html/xmlpaddownload.asp*. To create a well-formed XML document with XML Notepad, follow the steps found in the document titled, "HOWTO: Use XML Notepad to Create an XML Document" found at *http://support.microsoft.com/support/kb/articles/Q296/5/60.asp*

XAE

Developed by Paul Kinnucan, the **XML Authoring Environment for Emacs (XAE)** is add-on software that enables you to use Emacs (and XEmacs, the version of Emacs that functions within the UNIX/Linux Graphical User Interface system called the X Window System) and your system's HTML browser to create, transform, and display XML documents.

You have to install Emacs and Java on your system prior to installing XAE. XAE can be obtained through the host Web site at *http://xae.sunsite.dk/*.

XML Pro

XML Pro is a product of Vervet Logic, a software development company located in the Indiana University Research Park in Bloomington, Indiana, USA. XML Pro is a Sun Java-based XML modeling application that runs on any Java 2 virtual machine that has version 1.2 of the Java Runtime Environment (JRE 1.2, also called Java 2 or JDK 1.2) installed. XML Pro is integrated with the IBM XML 4J Parser and can be installed on Windows 95 or 98, Windows NT 4.0, Solaris UNIX, and Linux. XML Pro can function as a standalone editing application or it can be integrated with enterprise XML suites. For example, Vervet promotes the purchase of XML Pro in a bundle with Open Text's Near & Far Designer, a DTD creation and editing tool.

A typical XML Pro display is shown in Figure 3-4.

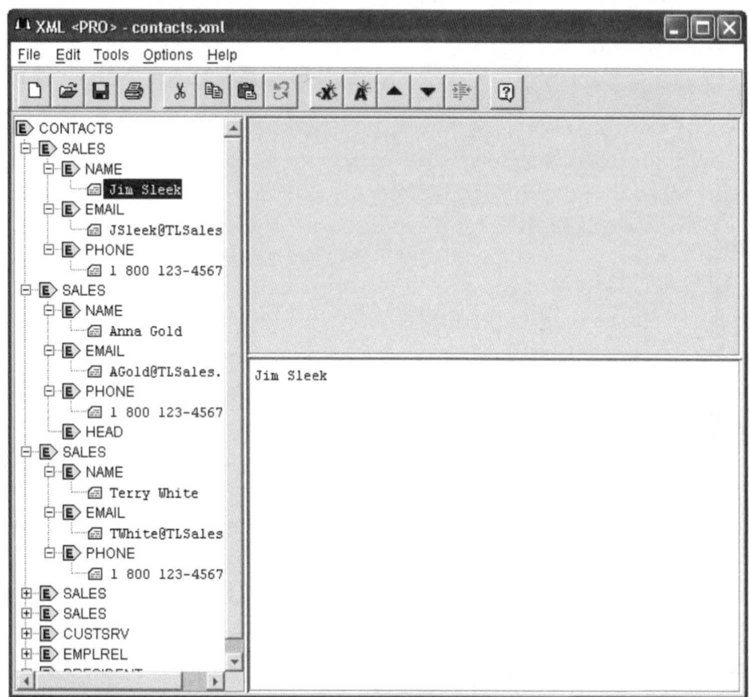

Figure 3-4 contacts.xml created with XML Pro by Vervet Logic

You can download the latest trial version of XML Pro at *www.vervet.com/demo.html*.

Peter's XML Editor

Peter Reynolds built this XML editor while studying for an MBA with the Open University and working as manager of the software development team with Berlitz GlobalNET in Dublin, Ireland. Although he admits to having dedicated limited time to developing this editor, it has become an effective, if somewhat modest, development tool. A typical Peter's XML Editor display is shown in Figure 3-5.

A download version and further information can be found at Mr. Reynolds' Web site at *http://www.iol.ie/~pxe/index.html*.

Adobe FrameMaker + SGML

Adobe FrameMaker is considered to be a high-end editing and compositing tool for publishers. It originally came with its own markup language (MIF), but focused on SGML and XML as they became more prominent. Its extended package (Adobe FrameMaker +SGML) reads and writes SGML and XML documents. However, when modifying an existing XML document, the extended package must be able to find and interpret a DTD.

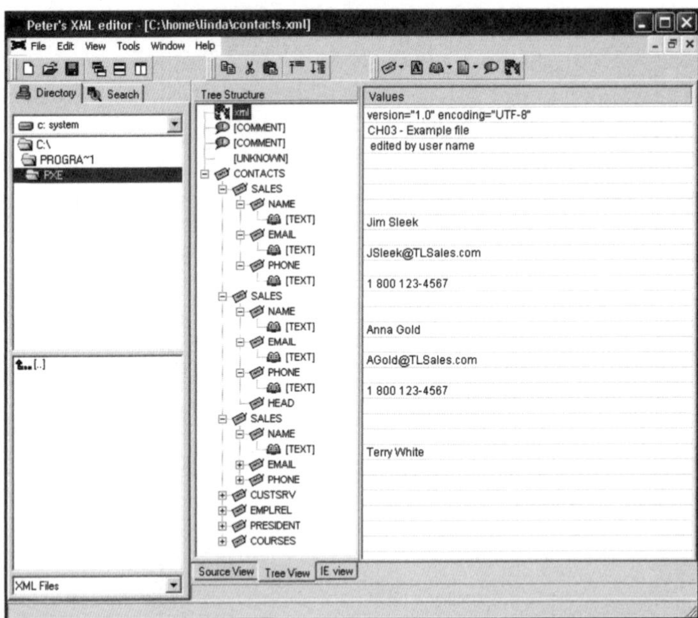

Figure 3-5 contacts.xml created with Peter's XML Editor

When integrated with Quadralay WebWorks Publisher Standard Edition, Adobe FrameMaker and Adobe FrameMaker+SGML let you publish to XML. While doing so, you can generate a cascading style sheet automatically. With FrameMaker, XML tags can then be mapped from the paragraph style names. With FrameMaker+SGML, XML tags can be generated directly from the document's element tags. Either way, high-quality XML that matches the original structure of the document can be produced.

When integrated with HTML editors, FrameMaker can be used to customize and fine-tune publishing of HTML and XML to the Web. This enables the publishing of FrameMaker content so that it fits seamlessly into a Web site's design.

For further information regarding Adobe FrameMaker, go to the Adobe Web site at *http://www.adobe.com/products/framemaker/main.html*.

SoftQuad XMetaL

XMetaL's interface resembles a word processor and makes it easy for anyone to create XML content or convert documents from other formats, including Microsoft Word and Microsoft Excel. Some versions provide templates with replaceable text, custom dialog boxes, and drop-down menus. Currently available for Windows-based PCs only, XMetaL can also be integrated with existing publishing and document management systems and provides document checkout—for document revision and/or approval—and check-in capability. Thus, it is in transition from a strict WYSIWYG word processing application to a more integrated environment.

SoftQuad Software, owned by the Corel Corporation, is XMetaL's developer, and is a founding member of the W3C, XML.org and the Organization for the Advancement of Structured Information Standards (OASIS). SoftQuad and its team of XML experts—among them Peter Sharpe, James Clark, Tim Bray, and Lauren Wood—are also helping to develop XML standards through their affiliation with the W3C.

You can download a trial version of XMetaL from the SoftQuad Web site at *http://www.softquad.com/top_frame.sq*.

Conglomerate

Conglomerate is also in transition from a hybrid word processing environment to an integrated development environment. Its developers claim it is a complete and open system for working with documents and is intended to replace WYSIWYG word processing applications. It lets the user create, revise, archive, search, convert, and publish information in several media (such as print and online), using a single source document. It also provides XML developers with the ability to revise and merge documents while easily keeping track of the changes. The system consists of a graphical front end for all user operations, and a server/database combination that performs storage, searching, revision control, transformation, and publishing. Conglomerate is designed to scale extremely well. Conglomerate is copyrighted by Hans Petter Jansson et al, and is free software, licensed under the GNU GPL, so it is based on open, well-known, and well-supported standards.

The Conglomerate code base is apparently still unfinished but reasonably stable, and is going to be rewritten, based on GnomeCanvas. Source code for UNIX and Windows is available from the developers' FTP server. If you download it, you also need to install Fluxlib 0.2.8—also developed by Mr. Jansson et al—which is also available through their Web site at *http://www.conglomerate.org/*.

Microsoft Word and XML Creation

The text you're reading now was initially created using Microsoft Word. MS Word is one of the most basic word processing tools used in modern mass publishing. In fact, MS Word is even used as the source tool to generate books about other, more sophisticated text generation tools! However, MS Word, especially earlier versions, is not well-suited for generating XML. It loads extraneous tags into the documents it creates, so that the documents become "heavy" and the extraneous tags risk confusion with the tags intended for XML/SGML use. To illustrate, try the following procedure.

Note: The following steps assume you have Microsoft Word installed on your computer. If you do not, read through the steps without performing them so you become familiar with the concepts.

1. Start Microsoft Word. Click **File**, and then click **Open**. The Open dialog window opens.
2. Locate and double-click **contacts.xml**. When contacts.xml opens, type a simple word or phrase at the end of the document. See Figure 3-6.

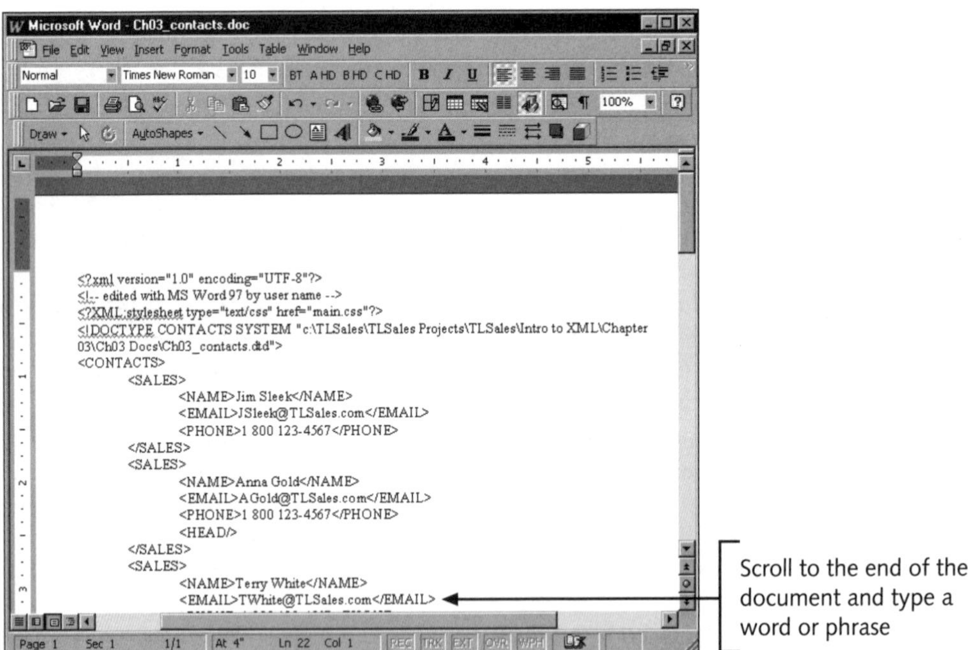

Figure 3-6 contacts.xml created with MS Word

3. Click **File** on the menu bar, and then click **Save As**.
4. In the Save As dialog box, type a new name for the file, such as **Ch03_ contacts**. Click the **Save as type** list arrow, and then click **Rich Text Format (*.rtf)**. Click the **Save** button to save the Word document as an .rtf file.

5. Click **File** again, and then click **Save As Web Page**. In the Save As dialog box, accept Ch03_contacts.htm as the file name, make sure the file type is Web Page, and then click **Save**.

6. Open the Notepad application by clicking Start, Programs, Accessories, Notepad. (Note that **Programs** is **All Programs** when using Windows XP.)

3

7. When Notepad starts, click **File** on the menu bar, and then click **Open**. Use the Open dialog box to locate the .rtf file you created in Step 4, such as Ch03_contacts.rtf. You might have to click the **Files of type** list arrow and then click **All Files** to view all file types. Then double-click the .rtf file you created to open it.

8. When your file is displayed, you see your contact information near the bottom. Notice all the tags MS Word has inserted on your behalf! Take a look at Figure 3-7 to see what happened with the Ch03_contacts.rtf example.

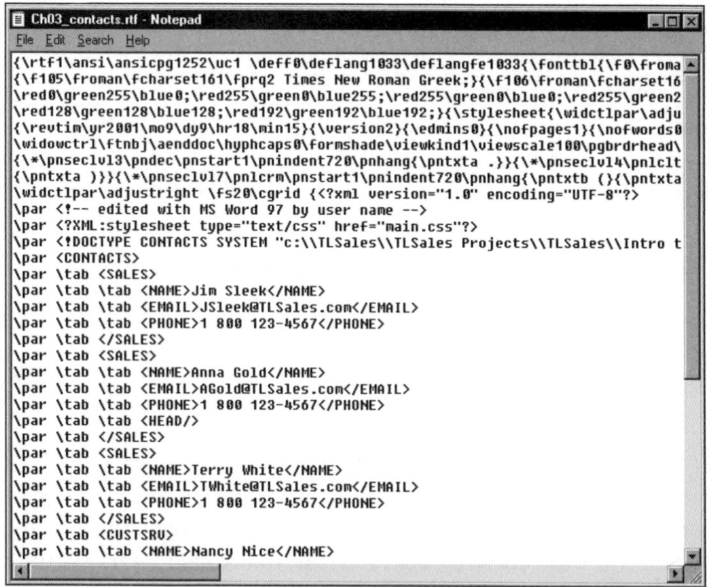

```
Ch03_contacts.rtf - Notepad
File Edit Search Help
{\rtf1\ansi\ansicpg1252\uc1 \deff0\deflang1033\deflangfe1033{\fonttbl{\f0\froma
{\f105\froman\fcharset161\fprq2 Times New Roman Greek;}{\f106\froman\fcharset16
\red0\green255\blue0;\red255\green0\blue255;\red255\green0\blue0;\red255\green2
\red128\green128\blue128;\red192\green192\blue192;}{\stylesheet{\widctlpar\adju
{\revtim\yr2001\mo9\dy9\hr18\min15}{\version2}{\edmins0}{\nofpages1}{\nofwords0
\widowctrl\ftnbj\aenddoc\hyphcaps0\formshade\viewkind1\viewscale100\pgbrdrhead\
{\*\pnseclvl3\pndec\pnstart1\pnindent720\pnhang{\pntxta .}}{\*\pnseclvl4\pnlclt
{\pntxta )}}{\*\pnseclvl7\pnlcrm\pnstart1\pnindent720\pnhang{\pntxtb (}{\pntxta
\widctlpar\adjustright \fs20\cgrid {<?xml version="1.0" encoding="UTF-8"?>
\par <!-- edited with MS Word 97 by user name -->
\par <?XML:stylesheet type="text/css" href="main.css"?>
\par <!DOCTYPE CONTACTS SYSTEM "c:\\TLSales\\TLSales Projects\\TLSales\\Intro t
\par <CONTACTS>
\par \tab <SALES>
\par \tab \tab <NAME>Jim Sleek</NAME>
\par \tab \tab <EMAIL>JSleek@TLSales.com</EMAIL>
\par \tab \tab <PHONE>1 800 123-4567</PHONE>
\par \tab </SALES>
\par \tab <SALES>
\par \tab \tab <NAME>Anna Gold</NAME>
\par \tab \tab <EMAIL>AGold@TLSales.com</EMAIL>
\par \tab \tab <PHONE>1 800 123-4567</PHONE>
\par \tab \tab <HEAD/>
\par \tab </SALES>
\par \tab <SALES>
\par \tab \tab <NAME>Terry White</NAME>
\par \tab \tab <EMAIL>TWhite@TLSales.com</EMAIL>
\par \tab \tab <PHONE>1 800 123-4567</PHONE>
\par \tab </SALES>
\par \tab <CUSTSRV>
\par \tab \tab <NAME>Nancy Nice</NAME>
```

Figure 3-7 Extra information inserted by MS Word

9. Now open another Notepad window by clicking **Start**, **Programs**, **Accessories**, **Notepad**. (Note that **Programs** is **All Programs** when using Windows XP.)

10. When Notepad starts, click **File** on the menu bar, and then click **Open**. Use the Open dialog box to locate the .htm file you created in Step 5, such as Ch03_contacts.htm. You might have to click the **Files of type** list arrow and then click **All Files** to view all file types. Then double-click the .htm file you created to open it.

11. When the .htm file is displayed, you see your contacts listed, but the XML tags have been altered, and many extra tags have been inserted by MS Word again. Look at Figure 3-8 to see what happened with the Ch03_contacts.htm example.

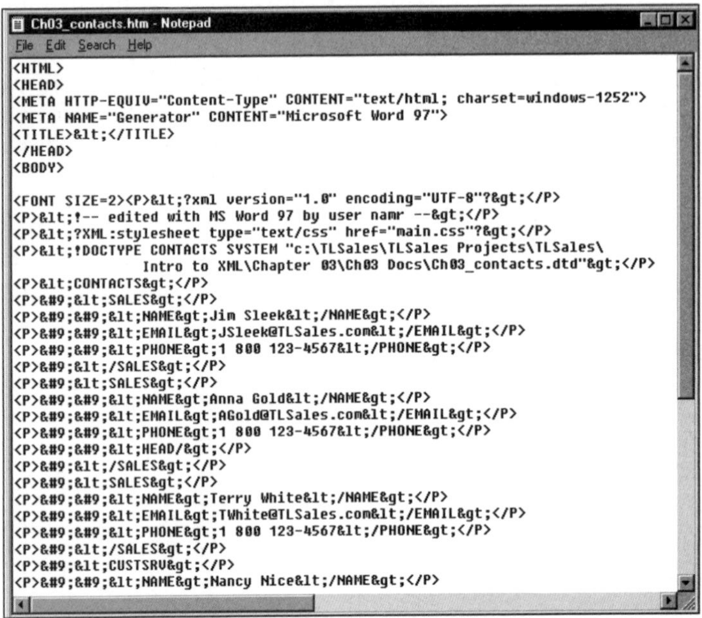


```
<HTML>
<HEAD>
<META HTTP-EQUIV="Content-Type" CONTENT="text/html; charset=windows-1252">
<META NAME="Generator" CONTENT="Microsoft Word 97">
<TITLE>&lt;</TITLE>
</HEAD>
<BODY>

<FONT SIZE=2><P>&lt;?xml version="1.0" encoding="UTF-8"?&gt;</P>
<P>&lt;!-- edited with MS Word 97 by user namr --&gt;</P>
<P>&lt;?XML:stylesheet type="text/css" href="main.css"?&gt;</P>
<P>&lt;!DOCTYPE CONTACTS SYSTEM "c:\TLSales\TLSales Projects\TLSales\
            Intro to XML\Chapter 03\Ch03 Docs\Ch03_contacts.dtd"&gt;</P>
<P>&lt;CONTACTS&gt;</P>
<P>&#9;&lt;SALES&gt;</P>
<P>&#9;&#9;&lt;NAME&gt;Jim Sleek&lt;/NAME&gt;</P>
<P>&#9;&#9;&lt;EMAIL&gt;JSleek@TLSales.com&lt;/EMAIL&gt;</P>
<P>&#9;&#9;&lt;PHONE&gt;1 800 123-4567&lt;/PHONE&gt;</P>
<P>&#9;&lt;/SALES&gt;</P>
<P>&#9;&lt;SALES&gt;</P>
<P>&#9;&#9;&lt;NAME&gt;Anna Gold&lt;/NAME&gt;</P>
<P>&#9;&#9;&lt;EMAIL&gt;AGold@TLSales.com&lt;/EMAIL&gt;</P>
<P>&#9;&#9;&lt;PHONE&gt;1 800 123-4567&lt;/PHONE&gt;</P>
<P>&#9;&#9;&lt;HEAD/&gt;</P>
<P>&#9;&lt;/SALES&gt;</P>
<P>&#9;&lt;SALES&gt;</P>
<P>&#9;&#9;&lt;NAME&gt;Terry White&lt;/NAME&gt;</P>
<P>&#9;&#9;&lt;EMAIL&gt;TWhite@TLSales.com&lt;/EMAIL&gt;</P>
<P>&#9;&#9;&lt;PHONE&gt;1 800 123-4567&lt;/PHONE&gt;</P>
<P>&#9;&lt;/SALES&gt;</P>
<P>&#9;&lt;CUSTSRV&gt;</P>
<P>&#9;&#9;&lt;NAME&gt;Nancy Nice&lt;/NAME&gt;</P>
```

Figure 3-8 HTML code inserted by MS Word

12. Close all the open windows, and then delete the .rtf and .htm sample files you created.

It should be clear now why MS Word, despite all its document production benefits in other contexts, is not as good a tool for XML creation. Meanwhile, if you had viewed the file with Notepad in .doc or .txt format, you would have seen that additional information had been added to the contacts file, but the extra characters would have been unreadable. In the .rtf and .htm formats, you can see what the additional information is conveying, or is trying to convey. No wonder then that the size of the .htm-formatted file is 2 kilobytes, while the .rtf-formatted file is 4 kilobytes. That same file in .doc format is 20 kilobytes long! These examples were created with MS Word 97. MS Word 2000 and Word 2002 (as part of the Microsoft Office 2000 suite and Office XP suite, respectively) now have options to allow you to save documents in Web page formats. The options have some positive impact with respect to XML.

Converting MS Word and Other Formats to XML Documents

If you have created documents in non-XML formats (e.g., earlier versions of MS Word or other word processing formats, HTML, or database queries), then you can use non-XML converters (also called "N-converters) to convert those non-XML documents to XML.

There are several Web sites where you can find lists of such conversion tools, either non-XML to XML or vice versa. Here are some examples:

- The Web site of Lars Garshol; especially his page titled "XML tools by category—A part of Free XML Tools" at *http://www.garshol.priv.no/download/xmltools/cat_ix.html*
- The "General and specific tools for converting to and/or from XML" page at the XMLSOFTWARE Web site at *http://www.xmlsoftware.com/convert/*

Specific conversion applications can be researched through any World Wide Web search engine. For example, Arbortext's Epic E-Content Engine (E3) can capture and revise content from many sources, including MS Word, and can convert XML to many other formats. XML Spy (discussed in the next section) is also compatible with MS Word documents.

Integrated Development Environments

An integrated development environment looks like a single application program, but is much more than that. IDEs are a combination of text and code editors, compilers, debuggers, and GUI developers. They may be stand-alone applications, or may come bundled with other compatible applications. IDEs provide a user-friendly framework for many modern programming languages (e.g., Microsoft's Visual Basic, or IBM's Visual Age for Java). HTML IDEs, especially those used for Web site development (such as Macromedia's DreamWeaver or Microsoft's FrontPage) may already be familiar to you.

XML IDEs not only let you create and edit XML documents, they usually include the functions listed above, plus all the major aspects of XML design, creation, and modification, such as:

- XML editing and validation
- XML DTD editing and validation (some IDEs include schema)
- Extensible Stylesheet Language (XSL) editing and transformation (XSL is an XML-related language that is discussed in detail in Chapter 6)

Larger, sophisticated IDEs facilitate the building of large projects by teams of developers. One method provided by the sophisticated tools is the provision of shared file repositories that use check-in and checkout systems, ensuring that no two developers can modify the same file simultaneously. If a file is already open, the IDE applies a lock to it so that anyone else who tries to open the file is advised that it is already being used. That status message also includes the identity of the developer who is currently working on the file.

Some IDE tools may also provide **versioning**, which means that at certain points in the development cycle, the developer may decide to save the whole project in its state at that time. Thus, the developer creates a particular version of the project. Versioning such as this allows developers to return to that version of the project at some point in the future to either start upgrading from that point again, or simply to compare code with whatever version they are presently working on. The versioning process also provides specific information, such as when a project was last updated (i.e., saved) and by whom. A versioning tool like this is important for effective file management.

At certain strategic points in the project cycle, all of the project files are moved into a development or staging environment, where they are tested before they are deployed in a production environment. Figure 3-9 depicts developers working independently on their respective files. During this time, those files are created and/or edited, and a small amount of testing is performed on each individual's desktop. The files they are working on are likely housed inside a common repository. This is achieved by setting up folder or file system shares over the network. At a certain time, the developers close and version their code, and a Web master moves their files into a development or staging environment for testing. The development or testing environment is modeled after the final production environment, but is usually smaller in scale. Once the files are tested and all bugs are worked out of the code, the files are then promoted by the Web master into the production environment, where they are made available to the end user. Rarely are files moved directly from a developer's desktop into production. That is not considered a best practice.

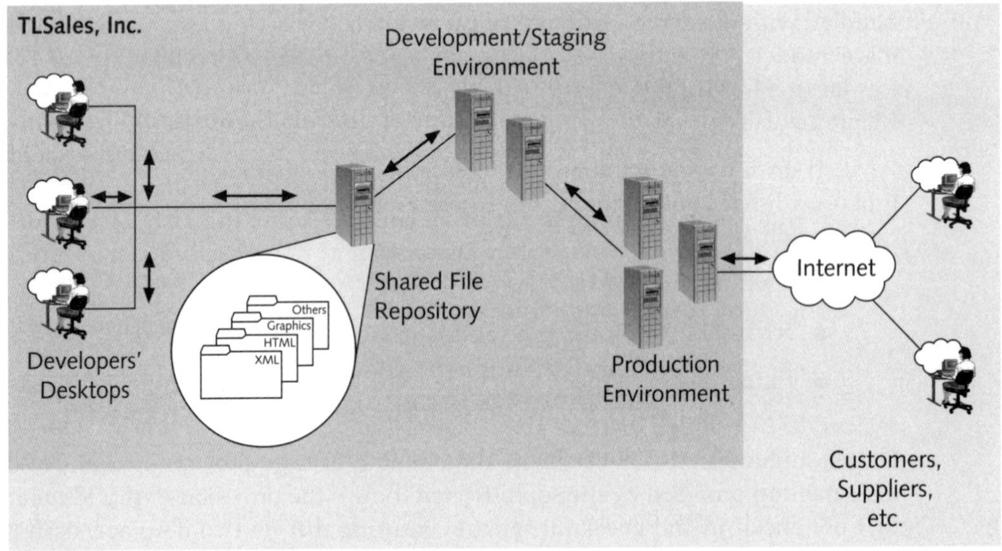

Figure 3-9 An Integrated Development Environment

Although you will be using XML Spy in the Hands-on projects in this and subsequent chapters, it is worthwhile to present a few details about the other integrated development environment applications.

Xeena

Xeena is slightly different from the applications presented so far. It is a visual XML editor from the IBM Haifa Research Laboratory that runs on Win32 and UNIX platforms. Xeena is a Java application built on top of the Java Swing component set and XML parser (an application) for Java. Not quite a full IDE, Xeena is "IDE-capable." It is different from the authoring tools that are in transition from text editor to IDE, which could be termed "editor-plus." Xeena is more like an "IDE-minus."

Xeena provides the ability to edit valid XML documents derived from any valid DTD. The Xeena editor takes a given DTD as input and then automatically builds a palette containing the elements defined in the DTD. Authors can create, edit, or expand any document derived from that DTD by using a visual tree-directed strategy. This requires a minimum learning curve, since only valid constructs or elements are presented to authors, depending on the context they are working in (i.e., Xeena has a context-sensitive palette). Since Xeena is aware of the DTD grammar, it makes only the authorized element icons sensitive, which automatically insures that all generated documents are valid according to the given DTD. There is a recent version of Xeena that also supports XML schema, as well. Xeena also:

- Offers intuitive viewing and editing of XML documents in a tree view
- Includes an XML source viewer
- Provides easy customization of the display
- Offers an editor that is a multiple-document interface (MDI) application with full support to edit multiple XML documents and copy, cut, and paste from one document into another

What makes Xeena IDE-capable is that it is capable of being integrated with other document management applications, document versioning systems, and repositories. It can be also configured as a team authoring tool, with checkout and check-in functionality. Figure 3-10 illustrates how Xeena displays an XML file.

Notice, in the figure, that there seems to be a DOS-like command line window behind the Xeena window. It was intentionally left in to illustrate that, although Xeena is generally started from your desktop by clicking Start, Programs, Xeena, it can also be started from a DOS command line. Xeena opens the command line window on its own and sends progress and error messages to it. However, during routine operations, you need not consult that command line environment, although you might find it informative.

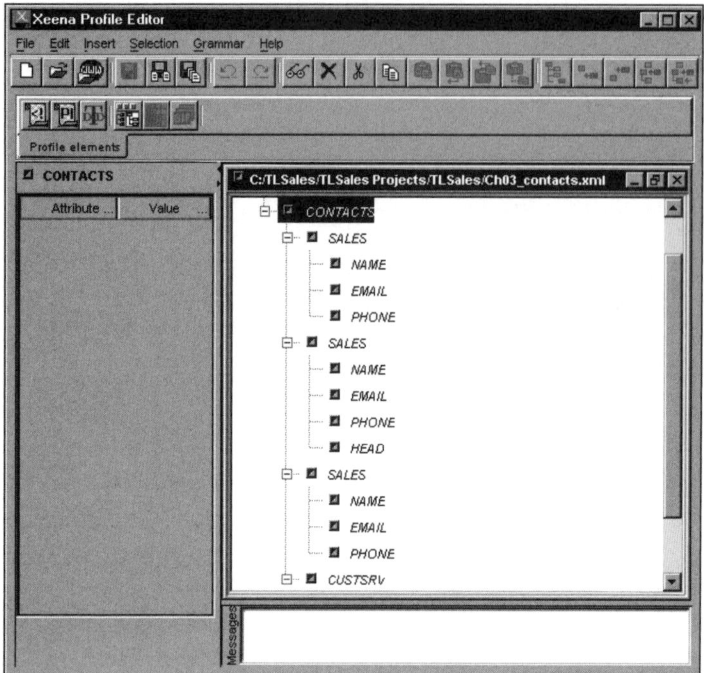

Figure 3-10 contacts.xml created with IBM's Xeena

For further information on Xeena, or to download a trial version, go to its Web site at *http://www.alphaworks.ibm.com/tech/xeena*.

You are introduced to Xeena in Hands-on project 3-2 at the end of this chapter.

XML Spy

Altova GmbH (Austria)/Altova, Inc. (US) originally established under the name Icon Information-Systems in Austria in the early 1990s, focuses entirely on XML software products. They released their first version of XML Spy in February 1999. XML Spy is a 32-bit, Windows application that supports all the major character-set encoding schemes, including Unicode. It can also import text files, Word documents, and data from Access, Oracle, and SQL server databases.

XML Spy now also supports both DTDs and XML schema. Its editor provides five different document views: a grid view for structured editing, a database/table view that shows repeated elements, a text view of lower-level work, a graphical XML schema design view, and an integrated browser view. Figure 3-11 shows an XML file as it would appear in XML Spy.

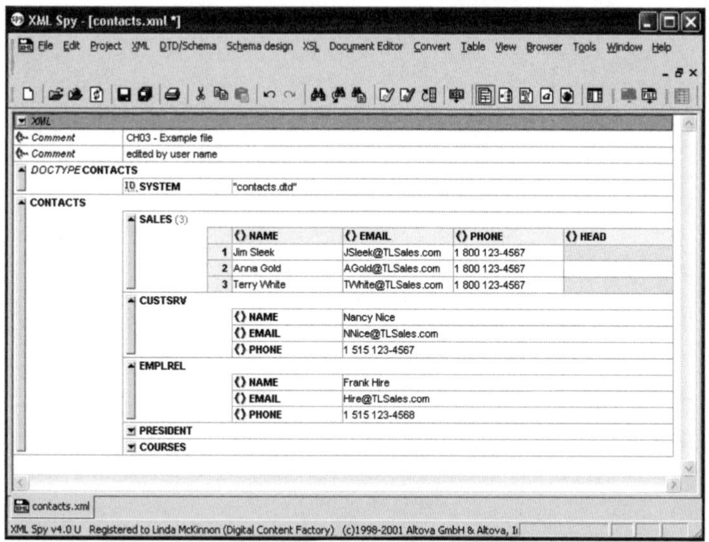

Figure 3-11 contacts.xml created with Altova's XML spy

At Altova's website *(http://www.xmlspy.com)*, you can download XML Spy's free, 30-day evaluation version. You will be using XML Spy in this chapter's Hands-on projects.

Turbo XML

TIBCO Software's Turbo XML is an IDE that combines three additional XML applications: XML Authority, XML Instance and XML Console. It is the first XML IDE to offer comprehensive support for the XML Schema Recommendation. You can investigate Turbo XML and other TIBCO XML software, as well as download a trial version of Turbo XML, at the TIBCO Web site, *http://www.tibco.com/products/extensibility/solutions/turbo_xml.html*. Figure 3-12 shows an XML file as it would appear in Turbo XML.

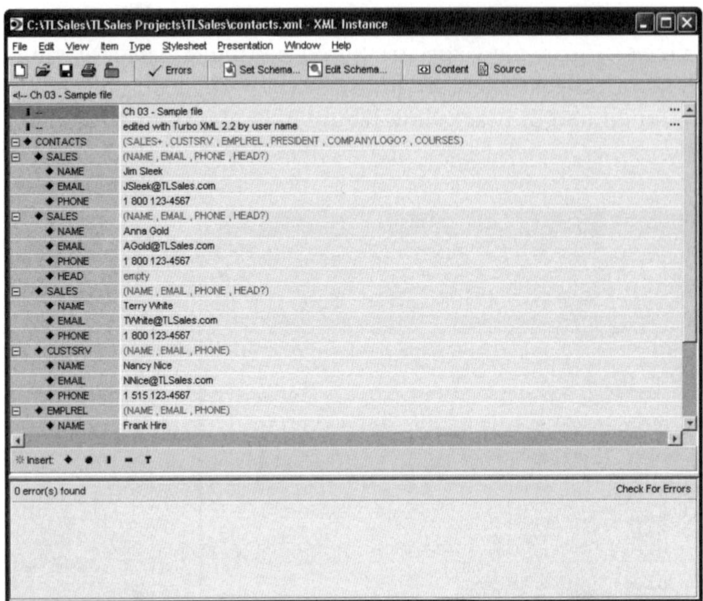

Figure 3-12 contacts.xml created with TIBCO's Turbo XML

Komodo

A cross-platform, multilanguage IDE developed on Mozilla, Komodo supports all of the features that you expect in an IDE, including: an editor with several syntax features (including background syntax checking); an integrated debugger; a "file watcher" for monitoring log files; a project manager for organizing multiple files into projects; a sample project to demonstrate functionality; customizable preferences; online help, and more. It can be found at *http://aspn.activestate.com*.

Arbortext Epic Editor

Arbortext has been around a long time in the world of electronic publishing. Its product, Epic Editor (preceded by a product called Adept), designed for creating XML and SGML content, can be used by teams of authors in several locations; it can be used with large amounts of material, and can be used to create multiple output formats (e.g., the World WideWeb, CD-ROM, print, and wireless).

Epic Editor allows the creation of text and tables, the placement of graphics, and the configuration of links. Epic Editor is used to author Web content and many types of business and technical documents. It has over two dozen key features, some of which are:

- The creation, editing and comparison of compound documents (i.e., documents made up of independent file entities)
- Content Management System (repository) support; repository support for Oracle and Documentum

- Standard DTDs and stylesheets for DocBook, CALS, HTML, XHTML, and others; DOM Support for Level 1 and core Level 2; Turbo Styler to quickly create stylesheets
- A document map that provides a fully editable, structured view of the document
- A math equation editor
- External file entity handling that allows you to view the *content* of file entities directly in the windows of the parent document (other XML editors, by contrast, only display *icons* for file entities)
- Seven kinds of graphic attributes (e.g., resolution, cropping, scale-to-fit, etc.); 12 types of graphic formats (.bmp, .cgm, .gif, .jpg, .tif, etc.)
- Multilingual menus, messages, and online help
- Programming Language support in C, C++, Java, Visual Basic, Perl, TCL, and others
- Real-time validity checking
- XML file saving as SGML or HTML; SGML files can be saved as XML or HTML
- 17 Spelling Dictionaries; 13 Thesauruses
- Table Support: Epic Editor supports both CALS and HTML tables; Excel spreadsheets can be imported
- UNIX and Windows platform support
- XML import/export compatibility with Word and FrameMaker

For further information regarding Arbortext Epic Editor, refer to Arbortext's Web site at *http://www.arbortext.com/*.

Integrating XML with Your Existing Document or Knowledge Management System

If you were to believe all the publicity surrounding XML as the future of World Wide Web-related communications, commerce, and research, then you might be convinced to hurry and convert your Web site, database, and other systems and files so that they are all compliant with, or at least support, the XML specifications. Several of the applications discussed in this chapter can be beneficial for such a conversion. You see and use several others in the chapters to come.

At this stage of XML development, however, it is not necessarily recommended that you rush into a wholesale conversion. Granted, you may be ready for XML and its related languages, applications, and documents, and XML may be capable enough to help you right now. Or, maybe your existing system is doing an adequate job, by and large, or that there really isn't much need for XML just yet. But chances are that you could start integrating XML capability into your system on a limited basis. If so, sooner or later you may be involved in some sort of conversion or integration project. If that is the case, the information in this last section may be useful to you. Not all staff members involved in these projects, as well-trained and experienced as they may be in other IT fields, are totally aware of the many considerations and justifications that come into play before and during such a project. This section does not pretend to provide you with a true cost-benefit analysis method, but it is intended to assist you if you are planning to implement a document or knowledge management system upgrade or conversion.

Initial Considerations

Before designing and implementing a new document or workflow solution, you should examine your current systems and processes, your needs, your business partners (suppliers, customers, transportation firms, etc.) and their capabilities, and your other audiences. Also consider what level of document and work flow management you currently have. Are you still at the most basic level of document management, i.e., converting paper documents into digital format and then sorting them on a computer system (Level 1)? Or does your organization provide means for authors or users to load electronic documents onto a Web server after converting their documents into Web pages (Level 2)? Perhaps you are advanced to the point where you have more elaborate systems that automate work flow, the development of personalized Web content, and publication to multiple channels, plus provide the means for workgroups—whether local or remote—to collaborate on documents (Level 3)?

Other factors to consider when deciding to upgrade your system are whether:

- Document creation or modification is frequent or infrequent
- Documents are of one format only or of multiple formats (the spectrum might range from a single or a few hardcopy mailings to numerous hits on a Web site, with orders for hardcopy or softcopy documentation)
- Documents are provided in one language or more than one language
- Document access, or provision, is considered low-volume or high-volume
- Documents being accessed or provided are dissimilar, or similar
- The documents are accessed externally or only internally
- Certain customers require specific, customized information
- Document flow is always from internal to external, versus the provision of information or content by "outsiders" (from remote physical locations or from those outside the organization)

Business and Technology Considerations

The costs involved in upgrading, though perhaps obvious, may include:

- New or better systems such as development systems, data storage systems, network equipment, air conditioning, backup and recovery equipment, etc.
- Required software
- New staffing requirements
- Training for existing staff
- Consultants, contract staff, or other services
- Incresed power or other operating costs (storage, security, etc.)

The basic benefits of upgrading may include:

- Increased sales revenue
- A reduction in operating costs (especially for creating or updating Web site content)
- Intangible benefits, such as customer satisfaction
- A more efficient operation because more or better information can be obtained or provided more quickly (including payment of accounts, obtaining inventory, and other peripheral services)

The benefits and costs associated with upgrading the document creation and management system in your organization can be further defined:

- How many staff members are presently authors (i.e., responsible for creating or modifying documents)?
- For how many document pages is each author responsible?
- What does it cost, in salary and overhead, to maintain an average document.page?
- How many net document pages are added per year (where "net" means the total number of added documents minus those removed)?
- What would it cost, in salary and overhead, to create an average new document page?
- How many document pages are modified per year?
- What would it cost, in salary and overhead, to modify an average document page?
- Into how many languages must each new or modified page be translated? What would it cost to translate an average document page?
- What is the cost estimate for a new system (hardware, software, new storage facilities, and other related costs)?

- Would a new system require obtaining more staff? Reducing staff members? Training existing staff members? What costs would be associated with it?
- What would the average estimate for "efficiency rating" be for new staff, or for newly trained staff? How would that translate into average cost per new or modified page?
- Would efficiencies be realized by reusing existing content and format information? How would that be calculated with respect to savings (per page, per staff member, or per year)?
- Would efficiencies be realized from automating the document creation and management system (i.e., from control of versions, from checkout/check-in systems, from the use of document repositories, etc.)? How would those savings be reflected?
- Would efficiencies be realized from automating the publication to alternate forms of output (print, online, hardcopy, CD-ROM, or others)? How would those savings be reflected?
- Would the new system result in lower or higher document maintenance costs per page? When would the change take effect?

It would be beneficial to tabulate the impact of the costs and benefits and others that you might be able to add to the list. At some point, it would be wise to consult with your organization's accounting, tax, and other business advisors, especially if investment payout periods exceed a length specified in organizational policies, or if estimated returns on investment fall below organizational policy thresholds. Remember, though, that automated IDE-style installations should be reserved for high-end document environments, where there are many documents and authors, and where information is gathered, translated, and transferred quickly and in high volumes.

There are relevant cost-benefit spreadsheets available on the Internet, too. One source is Arbortext, at *http://www.arbortext.com/*. Once there, follow the "think tank," "Presentations/Articles" link, and then click "Cost Savings Toolkit."

Bear in mind that these upgrades and integration projects are a fact of life in many organizations—in many they are a recurring periodic exercise, in fact—and yet they still seem to arise with little warning to many of their eventual project team members. And then, once the project starts, they often progress quickly. So this section is also intended to awaken you to the present state of your systems, to help get you up to speed a little more quickly if you work on or lead such a team, and to introduce you to some terms with which you might not already be familiar.

Chapter Summary

- There are three basic categories of XML authoring tools: simple text editors, graphical text editors, and integrated development environments (IDEs). There are also applications that fall between graphical text editors and IDEs; they started years ago as text editors, but have undergone continuous development that has pushed them ever closer to IDE status.
- Simple text editors are XML's most basic and economical authoring tools. Although limited in their capabilities, they are still widely used because of their simplicity and portability, and the fact that one or another forms part of every basic operating system installation.
- In contrast to simple text editors, dedicated graphical XML editors have more features, such as: colored markup tags, real-ime stylesheet application, menus of options, drag-and-drop editing, click-and-drag highlighting, etc.
- Using a dedicated editor allows a developer to use a WYSIWYG strategy. These editors also provide automatic structure checking (which can be a benefit, but also hindrance, occasionally), and validity checking.
- Despite its almost universal use, MS Word, especially the earlier versions, is not suitable for generating XML because it adds extraneous tags and other information to the documents it creates. Later versions, such as Word 2000 or Word 2002, though not completely XML-compatible, are an improvement over earlier versions.
- There are conversion applications available that can convert non-XML documents (such as MS Word documents, HTML documents, and others) into XML documents and vice versa. In fact, some of the IDE tools discussed in this chapter also perform such conversions.
- Integrated development environments (IDEs) often look like a single application program, but are much more. They are a combination of editors, compilers, debuggers, and GUI developers. They may stand alone or come bundled with other compatible applications. XML IDEs usually include all the major aspects of XML design, creation, and modification: editing and validation, DTD or schema editing and validation, XSL editing and transformation, versioning, file repositories, and the ability to build and use staging environments for testing.
- If you are considering installing or upgrading a document management system, especially a sophisticated IDE type of installation, you should review your current systems and processes, your needs, your business partners and their capabilities, and your other audiences. Also consider what state your document management is already in, whether it's the basic conversion of paper documents to digital format, the loading of electronic documents on to a Web server, or a more elaborate and automated system.

- There are several document-related factors to consider before implementing a document management solution. Also, all the benefits (including both the tangible revenue-related ones and the intangible customer satisfaction and efficiency-related ones) and the costs must be weighed. Consultations with accounting, tax, and other business advisors are recommended.

Review Questions

1. How many basic authoring tool classifications are there? What are they?
2. Which of the following are not advantages to simple text editors?
   a. They provide automatic validity checking.
   b. They are simple to use, yet powerful enough.
   c. They add extraneous tags.
   d. They are portable because of their small size.
   e. They are found on virtually every platform as part of a basic operating system installation.
3. Simple text editors support ASCII and UNICODE. True or false?
4. Match the following editors to their respective operating systems:

a. Notepad	1. Macintosh
b. WordPad	2. UNIX
c. vi	3. Windows
d. Emacs	4. UNIX
e. SimpleText Pro	5. Windows

5. Which of the following is a feature of a graphical text editor? (Choose all that apply.)
   a. provides colored tags for markup
   b. provides menus of options
   c. provides the ability to hide markup
   d. provides drag-and-drop editing
   e. provides automatic structure checking
   f. all of the above
6. Automatic structure checking is the ability of a text editor to resist an attempt to add an element that doesn't belong in a given context, so as to prevent the author from making syntactic or structural mistakes. True or false?

7. Which of the following constitutes the configurability desired by developers of graphical text editors? (Choose all that apply.)
   a. customize the editor to enforce the structure
   b. provide versioning
   c. allow the use of staging environments
   d. present a selection of valid elements from which to choose
   e. create macros to automate frequently used editing steps
   f. map keys on the keyboard to macros
8. The first graphical editors for structured markup languages were based on:
   a. GML
   b. XML
   c. HTML
   d. SGML
   e. MathML
9. What do earlier versions of MS Word do that make them undesirable for creating XML documents?
10. Applications that convert non-XML documents to XML are called ________________.
11. A text editor that combines text and code editors, compilers, debuggers, and GUI developers is called a graphical text (or "WYSIWYG") editor. True or false?
12. Macromedia's DreamWeaver and Microsoft's FrontPage are two IDEs for ________________.
   a. GML
   b. XML
   c. HTML
   d. SGML
   e. all of the above
13. Checkout and check-in systems provide many features, but cannot prevent two or more developers from trying to modify the same file simultaneously. True or false?
14. Which of the following is *not* provided by versioning?
   a. At some point in the future, you can return to a version of the project to start upgrading from that point again.
   b. At some point in the future, you can simply compare code with whatever version you are currently working on.
   c. A testing environment is provided prior to publishing a document on a Web server.
   d. Specific information is provided, such as when a project was last updated (i.e., saved) and by whom.

15. A(n) ________________ allows XML documents to be tested before they are published to a Web server. (Choose all that apply.)
    a. XML parser
    b. XML application
    c. staging environment
    d. integrated development environment
    e. WYSIWYG editor
    f. none of the above
16. Files are rarely moved directly from a developer's desktop into production. That is not considered a ________________.
17. Which of the basic levels of document management is characterized by an organization letting its authors and users load electronic documents on to a Web server after converting their documents to Web pages?
    a. first level
    b. second level
    c. third level
    d. fourth level
    e. none of the above
18. The ability to publish to several different kinds of media (for example, to the World Wide Web, to CD-ROM, or to hardcopy documents) is termed ________________ publishing.
19. Which of the following is a basic benefit of upgrading a document management system? (Choose all that apply.)
    a. increased sales and revenues
    b. reduced operating costs (especially with respect to creating or updating Web site content)
    c. intangible benefits, such as customer satisfaction
    d. a more efficient operation because more or better information can be obtained or provided more quickly
    e. all of the above
20. A(n) ________________ of documents commonly means more documents are added than removed.

21. Benefits from automated document management and publication include: (Choose all that apply.)
    a. reusing existing content and format information.
    b. automating the document creation and management system.
    c. automating publication to alternate forms of output.
    d. all of the above
    e. none of the above
22. Automated IDE-style installations should be reserved for ______________ environments.
23. Prior to installing Java-based XML editors, you must first install a ______________.
    a. Java Software Development Kit (SDK)
    b. Java development environment
    c. Java class
    d. all of the above
    e. none of the above
24. A Java-based XML editor is a programming package that enables a programmer to develop applications for a specific platform. True or false?
25. Generally, when editors are shown with two-pane displays, ______________ appear on the left while the document's element values appear on the right.

Hands-on Projects

Project 3-1

In this project, you install and test two different Win32 (i.e., Windows 32-bit application) XML editors: Microsoft XML Notepad and Peter's XML Editor. There is a two-fold purpose for doing this: to give you an understanding of how easy it is to install an XML editor, and to show you that XML editors can coexist on the same system. You also have an opportunity to view your existing files using these different editors. Simple Win32 XML editors are easy to obtain and install, whereas JAVA-based editors are challenging. Each XML editor has its own personality. Some have more or fewer features and functions than others. Also, a Win32 XML application does not have any prerequisites other than the MS Windows operating system itself.

These exercises assume that your hard drive is represented by C:. If your hard drive is represented by another letter, substitute that letter for C:.

To install MS XML Notepad:

1. Using your Web browser, navigate to the Microsoft Developer Network Web site at *http://msdn.microsoft.com/library/default.asp?url=/library/en-us/dnxml/html/xmlpaddownload.asp*, and download a trial version of XML Notepad. Double-click the **xpsetup.exe** file. This installation does not require any more configuration than that.
2. Once XML Notepad is installed, start it by clicking **Start**, **Programs**, **Microsoft XML Notepad**, **Microsoft XML Notepad**. (Note that **Programs** is **All Programs** when using Windows XP.)
3. On the menu bar, click the **File** button and then **Open**. Open the *home/username/contacts.xml* file on your hard drive. Click each **plus box** to expand every folder. What you see then should resemble Figure 3-13.

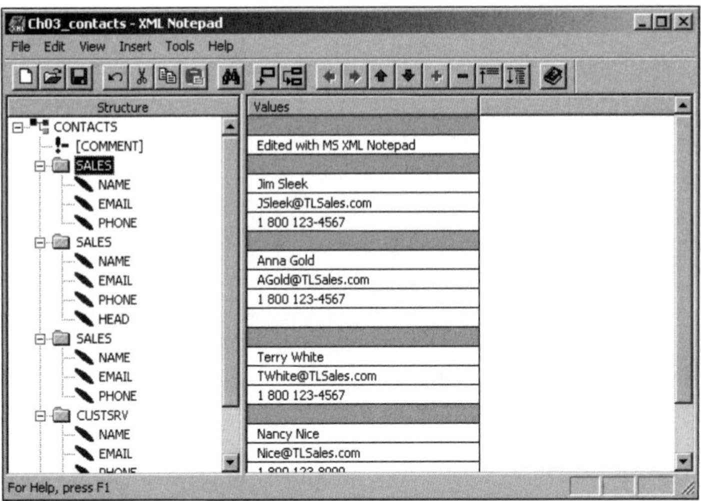

Figure 3-13 XML Notepad display

4. To add a new sales contact, click a **SALES** folder, click **Insert** on the menu bar, and then click **Duplicate Subtree**. In the Values pane, enter your name, e-mail address, and phone number for the element you just created.
5. If the new SALES element for that new contact now appears at the bottom of the list, highlight the SALES object at the bottom of the list, and use the **Up Arrow** button to place the new element with all the other elements.
6. Take a minute to view all the drop-down menus and review the features available with XML Notepad. View the Help files as well.
7. Save the modified file and exit.

To install Peter's XML Editor:

1. Using your Web browser, navigate to Peter Reynolds' Web site at *http://www.iol.ie/~pxe/index.html* and download a trial version of Peter's XML Editor. Double-click the **pxe.exe** file. Like XML Notepad, this installation does not require any more configuration than this.

If you have trouble installing Peter's XML Editor and you are using j2sdk1.4.0, try installing pxe.exe on a Windows XP computer with no JDK installed. If you still cannot install Peter's XML Editor, read but do not perform the following steps.

2. Open Peter's XML Editor by clicking **Start, Programs, Peter's XML Editor** (Note that **Programs** is **All Programs** when using Windows XP.)
3. On the menu bar, click the **File** button, and then **Open**. Reopen the **contacts.xml** file. Click each **plus box** to expand every folder. What you see should resemble Figure 3-14.

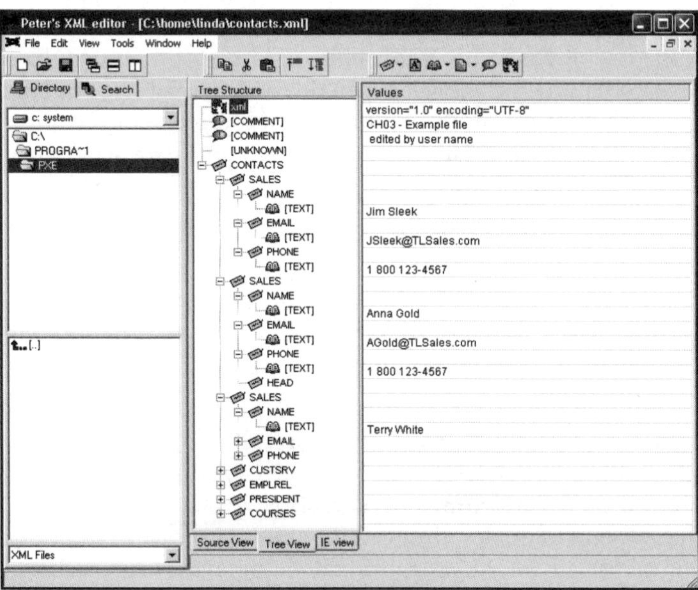

Figure 3-14 Peter's XML editor display

4. To add a new sales contact, you can copy and paste. Click a **SALES** element and then press **Ctrl+C** to copy it. Click the **CONTACTS** element and then press **Ctrl+V** to paste the SALES element at the bottom of the Tree Structure pane. Expand all the elements of the SALES element you pasted, if necessary. In the Values pane, replace the current text with your name, e-mail address, and phone number.

5. Take a minute to view all the drop-down menus and review all the available features of Peter's XML Editor. View the Help files as well.
6. Save the file, and exit.

Project 3-2

In this project, you install and test two different Java-based XML editors: XML Pro and Xeena. As in Project 3-1, you have an opportunity to view your existing files using these two different editors, as well as investigate their available features.

Prior to installing the two editors, you must install the J2 SDK Java Development Environment, which is a prerequisite for Java-based editors. The Java Development Environment requires updating your system's PATH environment variable to indicate where the Java software development kit binaries are stored. Software development kits (SDK) are programming packages that enable a programmer to develop applications for a specific platform. To modify the PATH environment variable, you follow a procedure similar to the one outlined below under "Installing Sun Microsystems J2 SDK Version 1.4.0." Once the PATH environment variable is updated, the Java environment is able to locate its own classes, but only as long as you maintain the SDK's default folder structure. This is also how the XML editors locate the Java SDK. Some Java-based XML editors need a specific SDK. Some editors are capable of being configured to use more than one SDK. It is not uncommon for some of the more advanced XML editors to make DTDs mandatory. That is, some XML editors do not open an XML document unless a DTD already exists for that file.

To install Java Development Environment: Sun Microsystems J2 SDK Version 1.4.0:

1. Using your Web browser, navigate to the Java Web site at *http://java.sun.com* and download the latest version of the Java SDK (version 1.4.0). Then double-click the EXE file you downloaded, and accept all of the defaults to install the Java SDK.
2. As mentioned above, now modify the system's PATH environment variable. To do this, on your desktop, right-click **My Computer**, then on the shortcut menu click **Properties**. When the System Properties dialog window appears, click the **Advanced** tab, and then **Environment Variables** to view the **System Variables** section. On the Systems Variables, find the PATH environment variable by scrolling down the listing. Highlight the **Path** variable and click **Edit**. On the Variable field, add **;C:/jdk1.4.0/bin** to the end of the PATH. Click **OK** to close the tabs and dialog windows.
3. Test to insure that the Java SDK is installed. Open a DOS command window, and at the prompt enter **java-fullversion**, and press **Enter**. The system should respond with "java full version 1.4.0."
4. At this point, it is best practice to restart the system before installing the Java XML editors. This ensures that the operating system internalizes the modified PATH environment upon startup.

Before installing XML Pro, make sure that you have installed the JDK.

To install XML Pro:

1. Using your Web browser, navigate to the Vervet Logic site at *http://www.vervet.com/product-index.html*, and locate the XML Pro trial download link. Make sure that you download the version of XML Pro that does *not* include the JDK—you have already installed a JDK.
2. On the registration screen, complete all the entries.
3. Using Windows Explorer, navigate to the file you downloaded, and then double-click the **xmlpro2.0.1-demo-NOJRE.exe** file to start installing XML Pro.
4. Install XML Pro accepting all of the defaults in the Setup wizard.
5. To open XML Pro, click the **Start** button, point to **All Programs**, point to **XML Pro 2.0**, and then click **XML Pro.**
6. To open the contacts.xml file, click **File** on the menu bar, and then click **Open**. Locate and double-click **contacts.xml**.
7. The contacts.xml file opens in XML Pro, as shown in Figure 3-15. Take a minute to click all the menus and review the features available with XML Pro. View the help files as well.

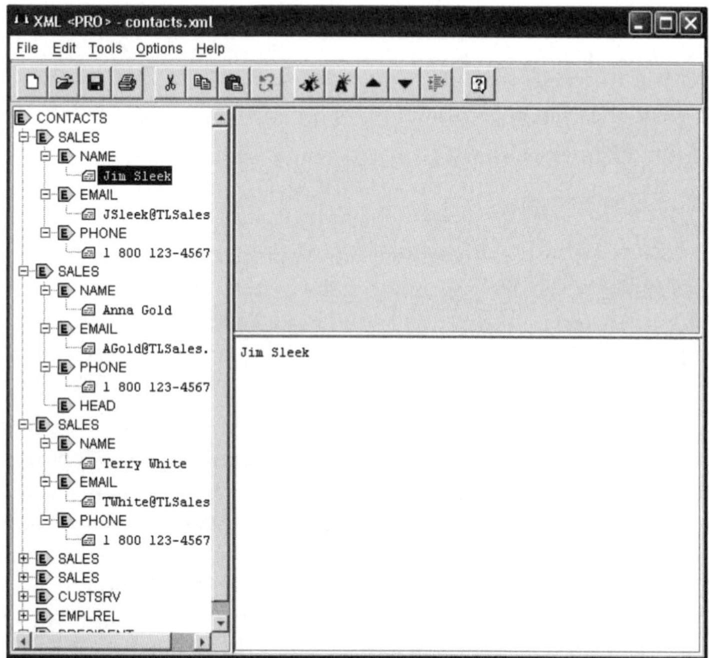

Figure 3-15

8. Close the file without saving it.

To install Xeena:

1. Using your Web browser, navigate to the Xeena Web site at *http://www.alphaworks.ibm.com/tech/xeena*, and download a trial version of Xeena. Double-click the **Xeena-1.1.exe** file.
2. Click **Yes** to accept the Software License Agreement. Click **Yes** for the Swing license. Accept the default destination folders. For Select components, be sure to choose Java 2 (Runtime Environment or SDK). The next screen asks you to browse to where the SDK is installed; go to the appropriate folder or type the appropriate path, and click **OK**. Ignore the Proxy host screen, click **Next**, click **Next** again, click **Next** again, and click **Finish**.
3. Open the Xeena editor by clicking **Start, Programs, Xeena, Addressbook Example**. (Note that **Programs** is **All Programs** when using Windows XP.)
4. View all the drop-down menus, and review the features available with Xeena. View the Help files as well.
5. Close the file. Close the editor as well.

Project 3-3

In this project, you collect all of your files and organize them within the XML Spy IDE environment for future projects.

From this point on in this book, XML Spy will be your authoring, editing, and document management tool.

You also test your files to make sure that they work before deploying them to your Web site. Otherwise, publishing a file to a Web site just to test its basic functionality is very time consuming. In rapid test environments—where numerous changes are made and then tested before publishing to the Web server—developers create and use an environment where they can pretest their code prior to publishing it to the Web server.

Organization of project files is a mandatory step during the development of any project. Because all of these files are related, the relationships between the files need to be carefully documented. If changes are made to the file names or locations, it affects the management of the project, forcing the project to be properly updated. The IDE environment also has an integrated browser utility that you can use to preview files prior to deploying them to a Web site. You see in later chapters that this IDE environment has a built-in parser that allows you to easily work with the data without having to interrupt your work flow by having to work through a separate step to view the results of transformations.

To organize files and test the new environment inside XML Spy:

1. Open the XML Spy editor.
2. Start a new project by clicking **Project** on the menu bar, and then clicking **Project, New Project**. Highlight the New Project item and, using the

drop-down menu, click **Project, Save Project**. Save the project to your home folder on the hard disk. Enter ***your name*** (username) in the File name field.

3. Highlight the **XML Files** folder, right-click to access the shortcut menu, and click **Add Files**. Using the open dialog box, add your finished XML files to the XML Spy environment. Make sure that the source of the files is your own home folder, which represents your work on the last project.
4. Highlight the **HTML Files** folder, right-click to access the shortcut menu, then click **Add Files**. Using the open dialog box, add the *index.html file* that is found in the C:/home/username/WWWContent/tlsales folder.
5. Double-click the **index.html** file. It should resemble Figure 3-16. Notice that XML Spy gives you a browser view of the file, by default. Also notice that the graphic and the cascading style sheet are missing. Follow the steps below to open both the missing graphic and the style sheet.

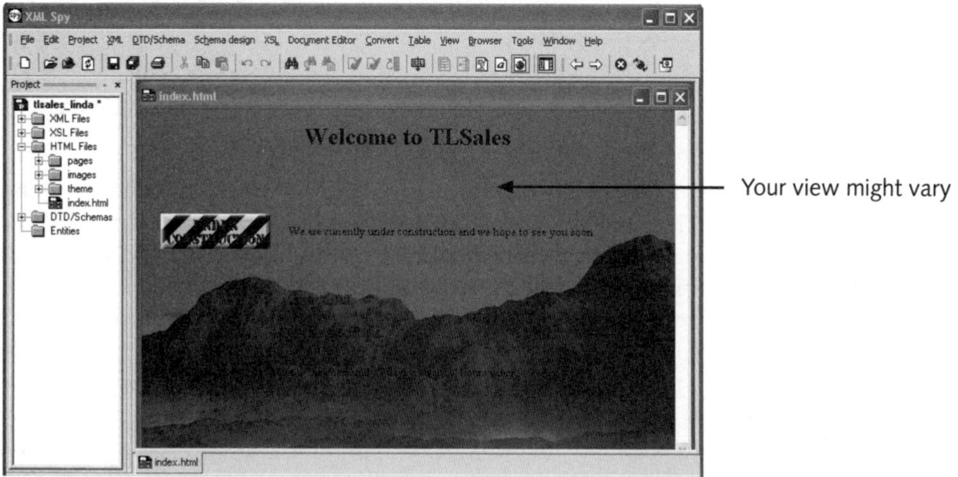

Figure 3-16 index.html displayed by the XML Spy browser function

6. Highlight the **HTML Files** folder, right-click to access the shortcut menu, and click **Add Project Folder**. Add a folder called **theme**. Click **OK**. Right-click the theme folder, and click **Add Files**. Using the open dialog box, add the **contacts.css** file that is found in the C:/home/username/WWWContent/tlsales/theme folder. You may have to change the Files of type to ***.*** (all files).
7. Highlight the **HTML Files** folder, right-click to access the shortcut menu, and choose **Add Project Folder**. Add a folder called **images**. Click **OK**. Right-click the images folder, and click **Add Files**. Using the open dialog box, add all of the files you see in the folder to the project. Press **Ctrl + A** to select all the files.
8. Navigate to the C:/home/username/WWWContent/tlsales/images folder, highlight the **HTML Files** folder, right-click to access the shortcut menu, and click **Add Project Folder**. Add a folder called **pages**. Click **OK**. Right-click the pages folder,

and select **Add Files**. Using the open dialog box, add the **hire.html** file. You may have to navigate to the C:/home/username/WWWContent/tlsales/pages folder.

9. Double-click **hire.html** and make sure it opens.
10. Double-click the **index.html** page to display its graphic and link.
11. Save the project by highlighting the file in the project pane and then clicking **File, Save**. Save the project as ***your username*** inside the C:/home/username folder.
12. Click **Project, Project Properties** and note the name of the new project file. It should be called C:/home/*username*/*username*.spp. (Your drive letter might vary.)
13. Go to the *username*.spp file, and open it with MS Notepad (not with MS XML Notepad). Notice that the file is only a list of references to the original files stored with your Project Files. If you move or rename those files, the project has to be updated. It is best practice to use the XML Spy editor to keep track of all your project files and not to move them using a file utility such as Windows Explorer.
14. Save and close the project.

CASE PROJECTS

A test environment can save developers valuable time, particularly when they want to quickly test to see if something works before the files are published to a Web server. The choice of authoring tool ultimately depends upon what you are trying to achieve. These tools differ from project to project, and in a large development environment (particularly one where Java is involved) very specific versions of prerequisite software (e.g., an SDK) may be required to accommodate other development teams working on the same project. The XML tools that are finally chosen are the result of many hours of planning. Developing DTDs and XML files is a difficult task. It is expected that every developer document the features and functions of their their DTDs so that other developers can utilize and extend their functionality.

Case Project 3-1

After testing several pieces of software, it has been decided that XML Spy will be the team tool used to develop the TLSales Web site. To save time and make the environment more efficient, you now update the existing XML Spy environment to reflect what is currently running inside the Personal Web server. The process for development is to create and pretest all of the XML and related files using XML Spy. Part of the development cycle is to occasionally publish the files into the Personal Web server to verify the functionality of the entire site. The easiest way to facilitate this requirement is to configure both XML Spy and the Personal Web server to share the same folders and files. Proceed to set up the environment inside XML Spy so that the files that it uses are the same files that the Personal Web server is serving from the document root.

Case Project 3-2

As a developer you are often asked to extend or work with files that have been developed by another developer. You have been assigned the task of figuring out what the DTD coded requirements of another developer's project are. Fortunately, in this case the other developer has created specific documentation on this DTD file. It can be accessed via the Help Contents within the editor itself. The specific file that you are to evaluate is the address book example inside the Xeena XML tool. Handle this assignment as if you have to communicate some improvements back to the original developer before it is released to the customer.

CHAPTER

4

CREATING DOCUMENT TYPE DEFINITIONS

In this chapter, you will learn:

- About document modeling and DTDs
- The difference between internal and external DTDs
- About element declarations
- The purpose for attribute list declarations
- About entity and notation declarations
- The importance of DTDs and namespace declarations

Prior to XML, Web site developers and other Web-related document developers in many fields had to do their best to fit their data and information to the HTML document model. Often the fit was far from perfect. XML provides a standard set of tools for developers to create a new kind of markup document, or even whole new markup languages (other languages are also called XML vocabularies or applications; in this book, the word "application" refers to those major processing software module(s) that use XML documents). Each XML-related language is a unique markup solution that meets the specific needs of an organization or industry, or speaks to some other sort of specialized audience.

If you or your organization is in such a position, then you may be glad to know that a wide variety of XML vocabularies have already been developed and are available. However, if you can't find an XML vocabulary to meet your needs, then you might consider writing your own, though it may be challenging. Although each XML vocabulary is unique and may vary significantly from the others in scope and intent, all vocabularies have two important aspects in common:

- They represent a markup language that is designed to describe a specific type of content.
- They are written using XML, which makes all of them members of the same extended markup family, built according to the same standard, and readable by any XML-compliant browser.

However, each unique vocabulary must be built to a consistent set of standards and functions, within an exacting set of content rules and structures. XML allows you to create these rules and structures using a concept called **document modeling**. Documents called document type definitions (DTDs) and XML schemas are the vehicles by which that modeling is conducted. Those documents define or **declare**, all of the components that an XML language or document is allowed to contain, as well as the structural relationships among those components. Thus, each unique XML vocabulary along with its related XML documents is created according to the content and structure rules declared within its respective DTD or schema (each language can only have one of those documents, and that one document must be either a DTD or a schema). Whether the choice is DTD or schema, their functionality is similar: they should contain a complete set of markup properties tailored to the needs of the XML language and documents being used or developed.

The XML languages that are already available also come with their own DTDs or schemas. If you choose to develop your own XML language, and you also choose to develop DTDs for that new language, then be advised that, because DTDs are often used by more than one document and because DTDs are not written in XML, DTD development can be a long process, from planning through coding, testing, and commissioning—even to the documentation stage. This chapter introduces you to basic DTD concepts and development techniques. Schemas (which differ significantly from DTDs in a number of areas and are becoming increasingly popular) are discussed in the next chapter.

If you are working with DTDs or schemas in greater depth than what is introduced in this book, then you are advised to obtain one or more of the several informative books already available that discuss these concepts in more detail. Such manuals may be better suited to guide you further as you learn to design and draft these documents and their related XML documents.

Document Modeling and DTDs

Historically, the most prevalent type of document model has been the DTD. Refer to the diagram in Figure 4-1.

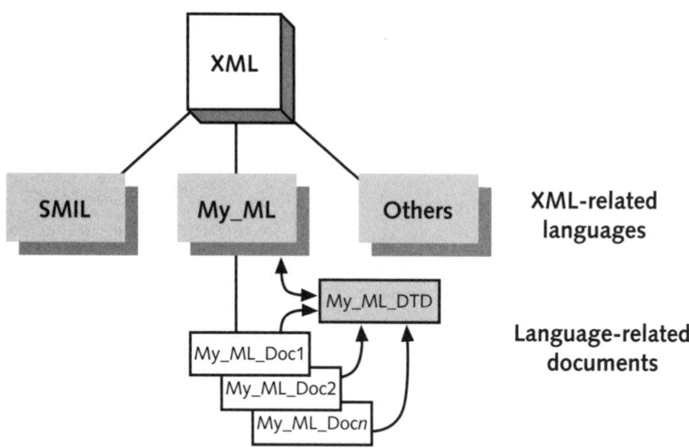

Figure 4-1 XML document relationships

SGML introduced the concept of a document type declaration (the statement within the prolog of an XML document that states what type of document it is and sometimes refers to a document type definition) and had provided for the development of document type definitions (as an internal subset of an XML document or as an actual separate, external document). XML, as a restricted form of SGML, inherited the DTD concept, complete with its syntax. Meanwhile, the reference to "My_ML" in Figure 4-1 simply reflects the fact that anyone can develop their own specific XML-related language, documents, and DTDs. Each XML vocabulary or document, functioning according to its respective DTDs or schemas, can be processed using standard XML tools; for example, Web browsers, such as Internet Explorer and Netscape Navigator, have built-in XML processors.

A DTD defines a document type in the following ways:

- The DTD declares a set of allowed elements. You can't use any element names in your related documents other than those that are declared in the DTD. In this way, the DTD forms the **vocabulary** of the language.
- The DTD also defines the content model for each element. The **content model** is a pattern that indicates what elements or data can be nested within other elements, the order in which the elements or data appear, how many are allowed, and whether they are required or optional. The content model is the method by which the DTD forms the **grammar** of the language.
- The DTD declares a set of allowed attributes for each of its elements. Each **attribute declaration** defines the name, datatype, default values (if any), and behavior (required or optional) of the attribute.

- The DTD includes other mechanisms, such as entity declarations (the specifying of a name for an entity plus the definition of what the entity represents) and notation declarations (labels generally applied to specific types of nonparsed binary data and occasionally to text data), to facilitate content management (for example, to facilitate the importing of data from an external file). Entity and notation declarations are discussed in more detail later in this chapter.

As illustrated in Figure 4-2, the DTD consists of at least four kinds of declarations: element declarations, attribute list declarations, entity declarations, and notation declarations. The "Other content" consists of comments, prologs, and other statements, if applicable. The various sets of declarations help to define and clarify the components and structures of an XML-related language and its related XML documents. They are so important that a large portion of the W3C XML Recommendation is dedicated to defining the various declarations that are allowed in XML.

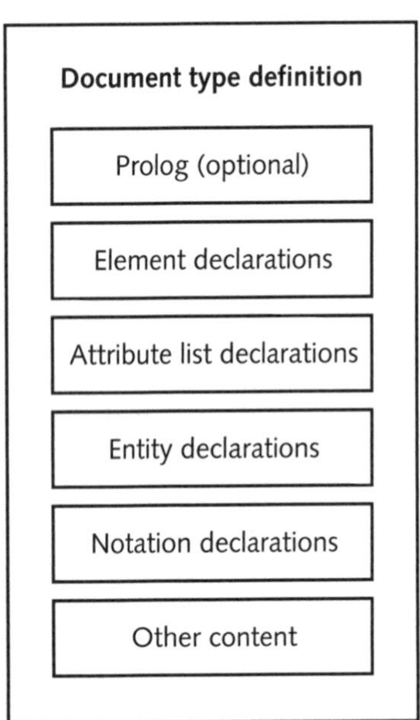

Figure 4-2 Basic DTD schematic

From a more general perspective, the declarations allow a DTD and its documents to communicate metainformation about their content to the XML processor. Metainformation includes the type, frequency, sequencing and nesting of elements, attribute information, the various entities employed, the names and types of external files that may be referenced, and the formats of some external (non-XML) data that also may be referenced.

A typical declaration (in this case, an element declaration) is shown in Figure 4-3. Note that the combination of the start indicator (<!) and the uppercase keyword is called the **declaration identifier**. Note that there is no white space allowed in the declaration

identifier between the start indicator and the keyword; the start indicator cannot be separated from the keyword.

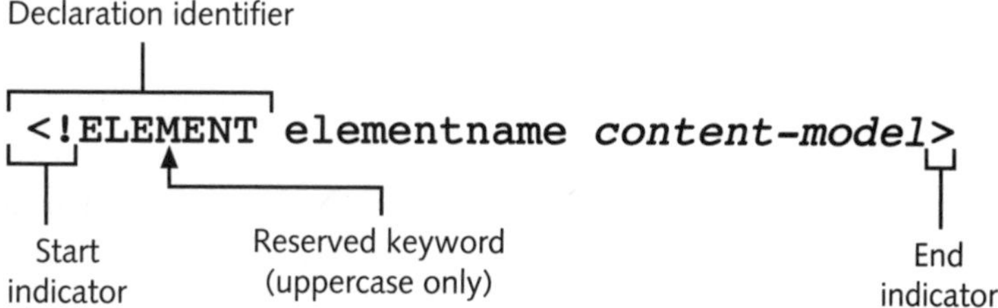

Figure 4-3 Typical DTD declaration syntax

When composing DTDs, pay attention to the ordering of the declarations. If you happen to include the same declaration more than once, the first one takes precedence over any others.

When Document Type Declarations and DTDs Are Necessary

XML is powerful because it enables you to create your own elements and then to give those elements unique and meaningful tag names. For some applications, it may matter whether elements occur in an arbitrary order or whether their tag names overlap. To ensure that an XML document has meaning for all applications, and to enable stylesheets (see Chapter 11) to work with it, there must be some constraint on the document's structure—on the sequence and nesting of tags. Declarations in a DTD are where these constraints can be expressed.

That said, XML content can be processed without a document type declaration and, therefore, without a DTD. Further, it is possible to write XML in a free-form style, where elements can occur in a fairly arbitrary order and where elements can be not only nested, but they can also overlap. From a strictly syntactic perspective, that is acceptable.

On the other hand, here are some instances where DTDs are recommended, if not absolutely required:

- *Default attribute values*—If an XML document or language relies on any kind of default attribute values, at least part of the declaration (that is, the DTD or schema portion) must be processed in order to obtain the correct default values.
- *Handling of white space*—The semantics associated with white space in element content (where it is of little consequence) differs from the semantics associated with white space in mixed content (the interspersing of text with elements) where it may be significant. Without a DTD, there is no way for the processor to distinguish between these cases, and all elements are effectively mixed content.
- *Authoring environments*—Most authoring environments need to read and process document type declarations in order for authors to comply with the content models of the document, especially their publishers' models.

- *Authoring methods*—In situations where people compose or edit data regularly (as opposed to automated environments where data is entered into or generated directly from databases), a DTD is probably going to be required if any structure is to be created, understood, and maintained.

INTERNAL VERSUS EXTERNAL DTDS

As discussed in Chapter 2, the structure of a conforming XML document consists of two major components: the prolog and the root element (which contains the other elements). A document type declaration statement (also called a DOCTYPE definition) should always be included in the prolog. That declaration states what class or type the document is and may also refer to a DTD to which the document should adhere. For the sake of this chapter, assume that it does, indeed, provide a reference to a DTD.

Within its document type declaration statement, the document may actually contain an **internal DTD** (also called an **internal subset**), or it may provide the name and location of an **external DTD** (also called an **external subset**), or it may have both. In other words, there may be a stand-alone internal DTD, an external DTD, or a combination of an internal DTD plus a reference to another, external DTD.

Internal DTDs

Refer to Figure 4-4, which is an example of an XML document that contains an internal DTD. The standalone document declaration, (i.e., standalone="yes") occurs in the XML declaration. The value "yes" indicates that only internal declarations need to be processed, that no external DTD or schema needs to be processed. A value of "no" indicates that both the internal and any external declarations must be processed.

If the standalone specification is "yes", then look for an internal DTD in the document type declaration statement. In that statement, the internal DTD reference is introduced after the opening square bracket ([ ) following the keyword DOCTYPE and the class specification CONTACTS (since the document is a contact list for TLSales). The internal DTD consists of the next several ELEMENT declarations, and concludes at the closing square bracket ( ]) just above the comment statement.

Private External DTDs

The DTD portion of the document doesn't always have to be stored inside the related XML document. Instead, it can be saved in a file for reference by one document or by several different documents. As shown in Figure 4-5, "standalone" has been set to "no" in the XML version statement, which indicates that an external DTD or schema must be processed as well as all internal declarations. In this case, the external DTD is a file named "contacts.dtd", as designated in the document type declaration statement. Further, there is an indication that contacts.dtd can be found locally on the server—in the same directory as the XML document itself, in this case—since the keyword SYSTEM has been inserted after the class specification CONTACTS and there are no additional directories, or paths, specified with contacts.dtd.

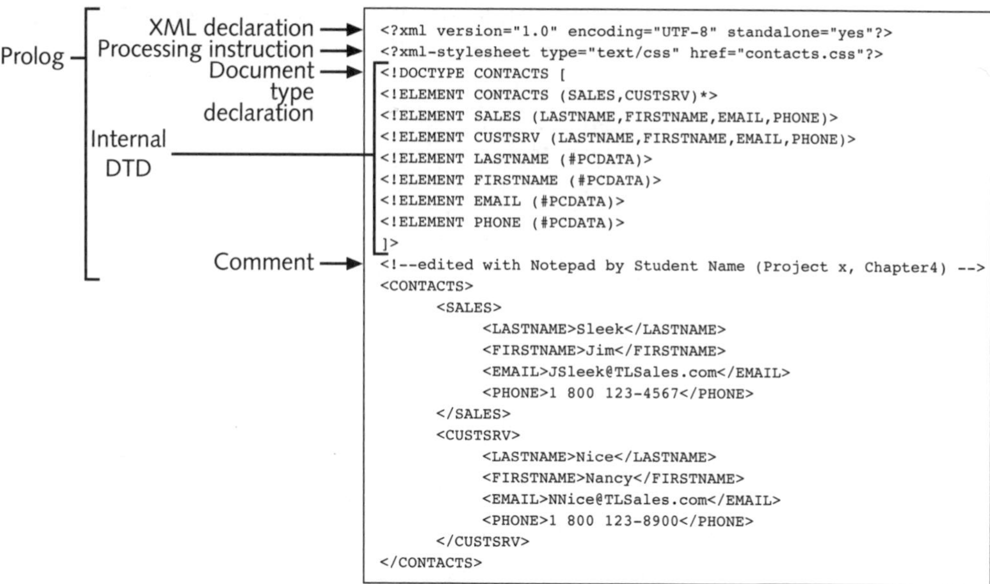

Figure 4-4 XML document with internal DTD

Prolog: XML declaration, Processing instruction, Document type declaration, Comment

```
<?xml version="1.0" encoding="UTF-8" standalone="no"?>
<?xml-stylesheet type="text/css" href="contacts.css"?>
<!DOCTYPE CONTACTS SYSTEM "contacts.dtd">
<!--edited with Notepad by Student Name (Project x, Chapter4) -->
<CONTACTS type="external">
      <SALES>
            <LASTNAME>Sleek</LASTNAME>
            <FIRSTNAME>Jim</FIRSTNAME>
            <EMAIL>JSleek@TLSales.com</EMAIL>
            <PHONE>1 800 123-4567</PHONE>
      </SALES>
      <CUSTSRV>
            <LASTNAME>Nice</LASTNAME>
            <FIRSTNAME>Nancy</FIRSTNAME>
            <EMAIL>NNice@TLSales.com</EMAIL>
            <PHONE>1 800 123-8900</PHONE>
      </CUSTSRV>
</CONTACTS>
```

Reference to external DTD

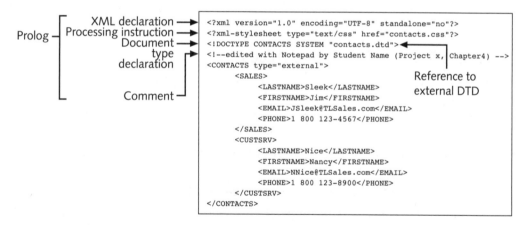

Figure 4-5 XML document with external DTD reference

This XML document should follow the syntax and structure rules found in contacts.dtd. The contacts.dtd DTD is termed private, since it is available only to the user of the system or to those who are able to access the system over a local network.

External DTDs with Different URLs

Figure 4-6 shows another example of an XML document with an external DTD. However, this time the document refers to an external DTD that is located on the same World Wide Web site, but in a different file directory from where the XML document is apparently located. In this case, the Web site is identified by its specific **Universal Resource Locator (URL)**, and a path to the specific directory has been appended to the URL.

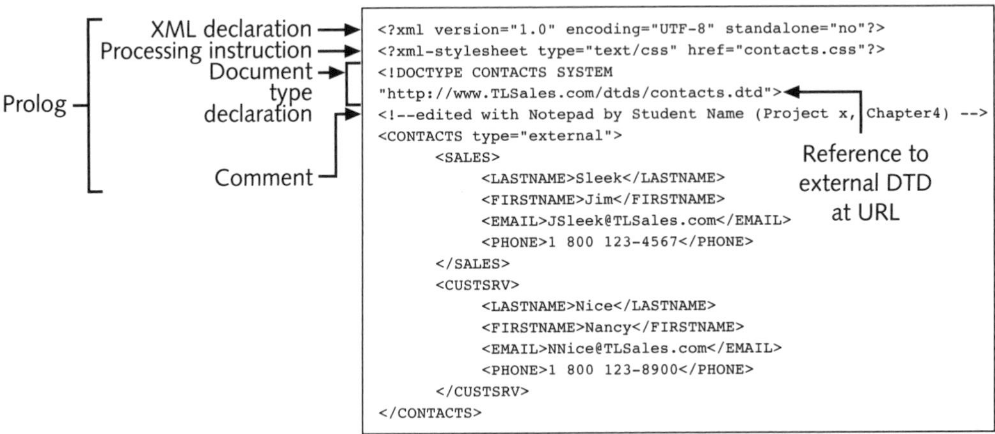

Figure 4-6 XML document with external DTD URL reference

In this case, when the XML processor reads the document type declaration statement, it accesses the DTD through the Web site and directory, and then continues processing the XML document according to the specifications in the DTD.

External DTDs for Public Access

Previously, you saw how to access an external DTD located at a Web site that is different from the Web site where the XML document is located. If a DTD is intended for public use, however, then there is a different method for referring to it. Figure 4-7 shows an example of this type of reference.

In the document type declaration statement, the reference has been changed to resemble the following basic syntax:

```
<!DOCTYPE root_elementname PUBLIC FPI URL>
```

Notice how the keyword PUBLIC has replaced the previous keyword SYSTEM. The coding immediately following the PUBLIC keyword ("-//TLSales//Contacts.dtd Version 2.0//EN") is called the **formal public identifier (FPI)**. The "-" in the first field of the FPI indicates that the DTD is defined by a private individual or organization, not one approved by a nonstandards body (in which case, you would use a "+") or by an official standard (in which case, you would reference the relevant standard itself, such as ISO/IEC 10646). The text "TLSales" in the second field is a unique name that indicates the owner and maintainer of the DTD. The text "Contacts.dtd Version 2.0" in the third field indicates the type of document, along with a unique identifier (the version number, presuming versions are updated periodically). The two-letter specification "EN" in the fourth field indicates that the document is written in English. In this case, the XML processor accesses the PUBLIC DTD at that Web site as it processes the XML document.

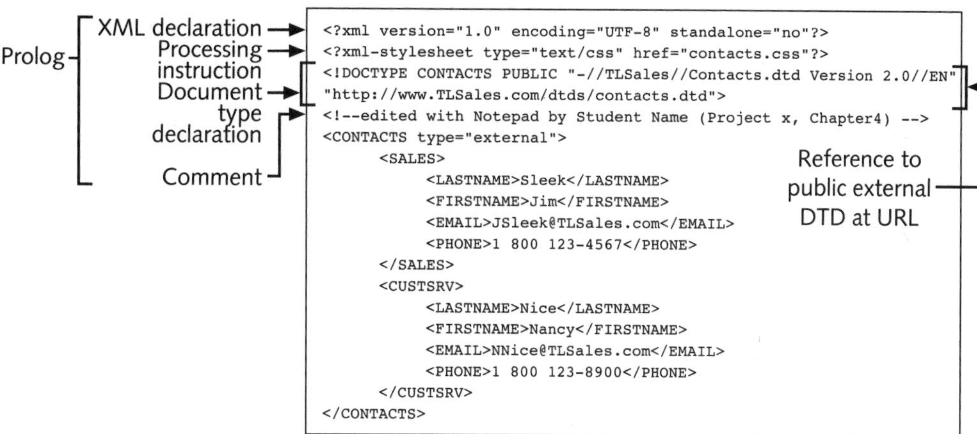

```
<?xml version="1.0" encoding="UTF-8" standalone="no"?>
<?xml-stylesheet type="text/css" href="contacts.css"?>
<!DOCTYPE CONTACTS PUBLIC "-//TLSales//Contacts.dtd Version 2.0//EN"
"http://www.TLSales.com/dtds/contacts.dtd">
<!--edited with Notepad by Student Name (Project x, Chapter4) -->
<CONTACTS type="external">
      <SALES>
            <LASTNAME>Sleek</LASTNAME>
            <FIRSTNAME>Jim</FIRSTNAME>
            <EMAIL>JSleek@TLSales.com</EMAIL>
            <PHONE>1 800 123-4567</PHONE>
      </SALES>
      <CUSTSRV>
            <LASTNAME>Nice</LASTNAME>
            <FIRSTNAME>Nancy</FIRSTNAME>
            <EMAIL>NNice@TLSales.com</EMAIL>
            <PHONE>1 800 123-8900</PHONE>
      </CUSTSRV>
</CONTACTS>
```


Figure 4-7 XML document with public external DTD reference

Internal DTDs and External DTDs

Figure 4-8 shows an example of an XML document that provides an internal DTD and also refers to an external DTD.

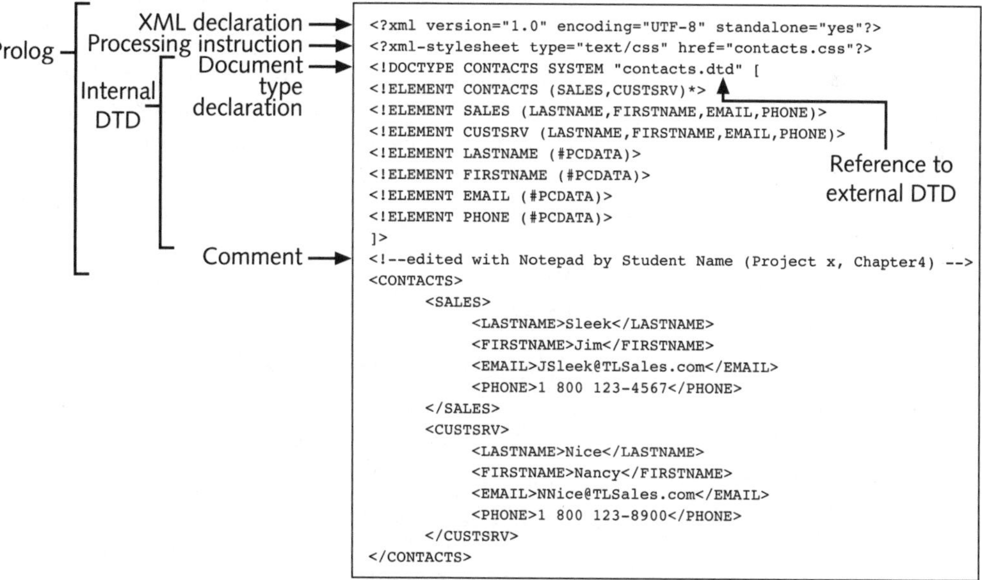

```
<?xml version="1.0" encoding="UTF-8" standalone="yes"?>
<?xml-stylesheet type="text/css" href="contacts.css"?>
<!DOCTYPE CONTACTS SYSTEM "contacts.dtd" [
<!ELEMENT CONTACTS (SALES,CUSTSRV)*>
<!ELEMENT SALES (LASTNAME,FIRSTNAME,EMAIL,PHONE)>
<!ELEMENT CUSTSRV (LASTNAME,FIRSTNAME,EMAIL,PHONE)>
<!ELEMENT LASTNAME (#PCDATA)>
<!ELEMENT FIRSTNAME (#PCDATA)>
<!ELEMENT EMAIL (#PCDATA)>
<!ELEMENT PHONE (#PCDATA)>
]>
<!--edited with Notepad by Student Name (Project x, Chapter4) -->
<CONTACTS>
      <SALES>
            <LASTNAME>Sleek</LASTNAME>
            <FIRSTNAME>Jim</FIRSTNAME>
            <EMAIL>JSleek@TLSales.com</EMAIL>
            <PHONE>1 800 123-4567</PHONE>
      </SALES>
      <CUSTSRV>
            <LASTNAME>Nice</LASTNAME>
            <FIRSTNAME>Nancy</FIRSTNAME>
            <EMAIL>NNice@TLSales.com</EMAIL>
            <PHONE>1 800 123-8900</PHONE>
      </CUSTSRV>
</CONTACTS>
```


Figure 4-8 XML document with internal and external DTDs

If there is an internal DTD *and* an external DTD, then the declarations in the internal DTD are added to the declarations in the external DTD. If there are declarations in the internal DTD that directly contradict those in the external DTD, then processing stops with an error. Some manuals state that the internal declarations prevail over the external declarations due to precedence, but that is not necessarily the case.

DTDs and Valid XML Languages and Documents

Valid XML languages and their documents are those well-formed XML documents that contain both a document type declaration (that refers to a proper DTD or XML schema) and that conform to the constraints of that DTD or schema. The respective W3C Recommendations for XML and XML schemas identify all of the criteria in detail.

In order to determine if a document is valid, the XML processor must read the entire document type declaration (including both internal and external subsets). For some applications, however, validity may not be required, and it may be sufficient for the processor to read only the internal subset.

ELEMENT DECLARATIONS

Element declarations, also called **element type declarations**, specify the names of elements and the nature of their content. Each declaration statement can define only one element. Since it is likely that there is more than one element in an XML language or document, the DTD must contain as many element declarations as there are elements. For example, if there are six elements, then there must be six element declarations in the DTD.

Figure 4-9 expands the element declaration shown previously in Figure 4-3, to show that element declarations are made up of element declaration identifiers, element names, and the content model. As in other declarations, the keyword is the reserved uppercase word ELEMENT. The keyword combines with the start indicator to form the element declaration identifier.

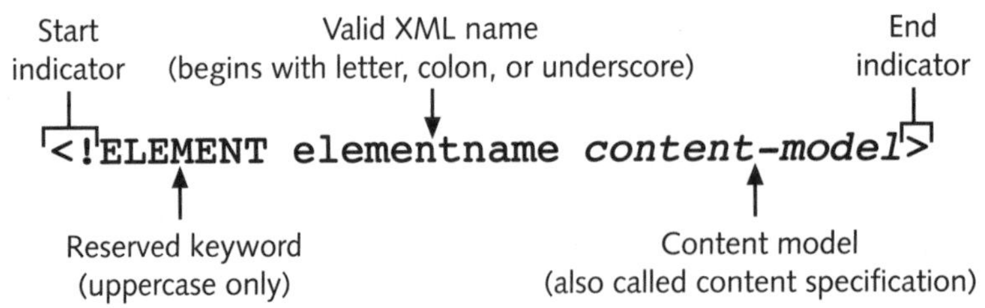

Figure 4-9 Element declaration syntax

Element Names

The element name follows XML naming conventions:

- It can begin with a letter, a colon, or an underscore (no numbers).
- Subsequent characters may be alphanumerics, underscores, hyphens, colons, and periods.

- It cannot contain certain XML-specific symbols, such as the ampersand (&), the at symbol (@), or the less than symbol (<).
- It cannot contain white space.
- It cannot contain parenthetic statements (i.e., words enclosed in parentheses or brackets).

All names specified under the other declarations—that is, the attribute list declarations, entity declarations, and notation declarations—also follow these XML name conventions.

When developing an XML language or XML documents, it is a best practice to develop a style convention for your names and to conform to it throughout the document. Some developers and authors suggest that element names appear in lowercase, which is mandatory for XHTML. Although this is acceptable, it can occasionally create confusion when attributes are involved. (Attributes are discussed later in this chapter.) Some developers use title case, where the first letter is uppercase but the subsequent letters are lowercase; some adopt the Java-related convention of capitalizing the second word of an element name consisting of two or more words. In this book, element names usually appear in uppercase, surrounded by angle brackets (e.g., <ITEM>, which is an element you encounter later in this chapter), except when basic syntax is presented and discussed. Then no angle brackets are included. However, in those cases, the generic element name specified is "elementname", "child_elementname" or similar, to prevent confusion.

It is important to remember that element names are case sensitive. For example, if an element name is specified in the DTD as being in title case, then in subsequent related XML documents, it must also be specified in title case. Otherwise, the document does not pass a validity test against its DTD. Whatever you adopt as your style convention, you must consistently maintain it to avoid parsing errors and application errors.

The Content Model

The content model (or content specification) defines what an element may contain. There are several types of content that you can specify, outlined as follows.

Elements Containing Parsed Character Data Only

An element that contains parsed character data only has the following syntax:

```
<!ELEMENT elementname (#PCDATA)>
```

The reserved uppercase keyword/symbol combination "#PCDATA" indicates that the element contains parsed (or parseable) **character data**, which means that the characters comprising the content of the element are to be checked by the XML parser. The parser checks for entity references and then replaces the reference with the actual entity values. For this process to be completed successfully, however, the entities must not contain elements of their own.

Character data refers to plain text with no markup symbols (such as <, &, ;, or "). However, the term "character data" is very general. There is no reference to whether the content is alphabetic or numeric. By contrast, XML schemas, which are discussed in more detail in the next chapter, provide for additional, more precise specifications such as integers, date format, floating point decimals, and others.

Elements Containing Other Elements Only (Element Content)

Elements that contain only other elements are said to have **element content**. On the other hand, elements that contain both other elements and #PCDATA are said to have mixed content. Mixed content elements are discussed in the next section. Meanwhile, an element that only contains one or more child elements has the following syntax:

```
<!ELEMENT elementname (child_elementname)>
```

or

```
<!ELEMENT elementname (child_elementname1, …
   child_elementnamen)>
```

In this basic syntax, which can be modified with specific expressions, the name of the child element(s) follows the parent element name and is placed in parentheses. If there is more than one child element, all the names are **sequenced** within the one set of parentheses and each name is separated from the others by a comma. An element declaration is also required in the DTD for each child element listed in the parent element declaration.

It is considered a best practice in XML to declare the child elements in the DTD in the same order as they appear in the parent element declaration, but it is not mandatory to XML. If the child elements are declared out of order in the DTD and a related XML document is eventually tested for validity against that DTD, the related XML document is still found to be valid.

If you want to specify the exact order of the appearance of child elements, there is a method to do so, which is discussed later in this chapter. A content model that contains more than one element name uses specific operator symbols to indicate appearance order, frequency, etc.

Elements Containing Mixed Content

As mentioned previously, elements that contain both character data and child elements are said to contain mixed content. A mixed content element declaration has the following syntax:

```
<!ELEMENT elementname (#PCDATA | child_elementname1 |
child_elementname2 | etc. …. )*>
```

If you intend for an element to contain mixed content, then in the DTD, you specify within the parentheses #PCDATA (to declare that the element may contain parseable data), and then add the names of all the relevant child elements that are allowed to appear as an alternative to data. Separate the child element names with vertical lines (the vertical lines are also referred to as "pipes").

When using a mixed content declaration, you can't use the operator symbols, which are available with "element content only" declarations and are inside the parentheses. You also cannot specify the number of occurrences or the order of appearance of the child elements. For these reasons, mixed content declarations should be avoided when possible. They are of limited use to most developers, and are commonly used only to translate simple documents into XML.

4

Later in the "Operators Used with Element Content" section, you see an example of a mixed content element declaration, along with a literal translation.

Elements That Are Not Intended to Hold Content (Empty Elements)

For these elements, the declaration states "This element is not intended to hold any content." The syntax is straightforward; all you need to do is insert the reserved uppercase keyword EMPTY after the name of the element, as follows:

```
<!ELEMENT elementname EMPTY>
```

These types of empty elements were discussed in Chapter 2, where they were called "declared empty elements" to differentiate them from elements that are capable of containing data, but that simply may not contain content at one time or another. Declared empty elements function as markers to indicate that some action may take place during execution by the application: a search may be executed on the data and, based on the presence of an empty element or based on the empty element's attributes, its parent element(s) may be selected for display or other manipulation. Figure 4-10 illustrates declared empty elements.

Notice in Figure 4-10 how Mr. Sleek and Ms. Nice have been designated as the heads of their departments by the insertion of the empty <HEAD/> tag. Later, the application might search for and list the company's department heads. That tag could not be inserted properly—that is, the document would not be valid—unless the DTD (in this case, the referenced contacts.dtd document) contained an empty element declaration like the following:

```
<!ELEMENT HEAD EMPTY>
```

Although these elements may not hold any content, they can still be assigned attributes.

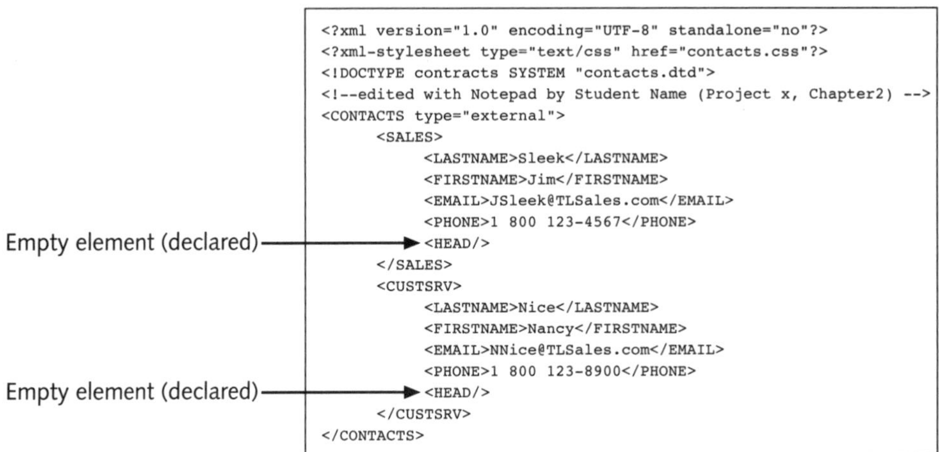

```
<?xml version="1.0" encoding="UTF-8" standalone="no"?>
<?xml-stylesheet type="text/css" href="contacts.css"?>
<!DOCTYPE contracts SYSTEM "contacts.dtd">
<!--edited with Notepad by Student Name (Project x, Chapter2) -->
<CONTACTS type="external">
      <SALES>
            <LASTNAME>Sleek</LASTNAME>
            <FIRSTNAME>Jim</FIRSTNAME>
            <EMAIL>JSleek@TLSales.com</EMAIL>
            <PHONE>1 800 123-4567</PHONE>
            <HEAD/>
      </SALES>
      <CUSTSRV>
            <LASTNAME>Nice</LASTNAME>
            <FIRSTNAME>Nancy</FIRSTNAME>
            <EMAIL>NNice@TLSales.com</EMAIL>
            <PHONE>1 800 123-8900</PHONE>
            <HEAD/>
      </CUSTSRV>
</CONTACTS>
```


Figure 4-10 Declared empty elements

Elements with No Content Restrictions (Elements with Any Content)

This declaration indicates to an XML validator that it doesn't have to perform a check on the specified element's content. Therefore, there are no content restrictions on the elements. Appropriately, the syntax is as follows:

```
<!ELEMENT elementname ANY>
```

In this type of element declaration, all you need to do is insert the reserved uppercase keyword ANY after the name of the element. This specification can be useful when a developer is building and testing an XML vocabulary or document. Time and processor resources can be saved when content doesn't need to be validated all the time. This specification might also be used during document conversion. However, for those elements to which ANY has been specified, the ANY specification should eventually be changed to something more precise and descriptive to provide better control over structure and content.

The ANY element declaration should be avoided in a production environment because it disables all content checking for its element.

Operators Used with Element Content

A content model that contains more than one element name uses specific operator symbols to indicate appearance, order, frequency, etc. These operators include the comma (,), the vertical line (|), the question mark (?), the plus sign (+), and the asterisk (*), which are described here. Remember that these symbols can be used singly or in combination with one another. When using elements in combination, use parentheses (the "(" and ")" symbols) to nest them; they can be nested this way to any depth you require.

The comma allows you to specify a required sequence of child elements. It also serves as an "and" operator. The use of a comma in an element content declaration is shown in the following example:

```
<!ELEMENT FAMILY (MOM, DAD, ELDER_CHILD, YOUNGER_CHILD)>
```

The literal translation of this syntax is: "There is an element named <FAMILY> that consists of one element named <MOM>, one element named <DAD>, one element named <ELDER_CHILD>, and one element named <YOUNGER_CHILD>, in that order."

The vertical line, or the pipe, allows you to specify a list of candidate child elements; however, when the element appears in the respective XML document(s), only one of those child elements can appear within the parent element. Thus, the pipe also serves as an "or" operator, as shown in the following example:

```
<!ELEMENT TROUBLE (ELDER_CHILD | YOUNGER_CHILD)>
```

The literal translation is: "There is an element named <TROUBLE> that consists of either an element named <ELDER_CHILD> or an element named <YOUNGER_CHILD>".

The question mark allows you to specify that the child element is optional; whether it is included or not is decided by the XML document author. A question mark is used in the following example:

```
<!ELEMENT MORE_TROUBLE (DOG?)>
```

The literal translation is: "There is an element named <MORE_TROUBLE > that may or may not contain an element named <DOG>".

The plus sign is used to specify that at least one (i.e., not zero) of the child element(s) is required. However, there is no restriction on the number of times that any of the specified child elements can appear within the parent element in the XML document. There is also no restriction on the order of their appearance. The plus sign is used in the following example:

```
<!ELEMENT ON_SALE (CHEVY | FORD | NISSAN | VW)+>
```

The literal translation is: "There is an element named <ON_SALE > that contains at least one <CHEVY>, <FORD>, <NISSAN>, and/or <VW>". The child elements within the <ON_SALE> element, could be just one <VW>, or a collection like <CHEVY> <VW> <CHEVY> <FORD> <NISSAN> <VW> <FORD> <NISSAN> <NISSAN>, or more.

The asterisk (some call it the "star") is used to specify that zero or more of the child element(s) may appear. There is no maximum or minimum. The asterisk is used in the following example:

```
<!ELEMENT ON_SALE (#PCDATA | CHEVY | FORD | NISSAN | VW)*>
```

You may recognize this as an example of the mixed content element declaration discussed earlier. Its literal translation is: "There is an element named <ON_SALE> that may or may not contain a child element. If it does, then the child element is parsed character data interspersed with one or more <CHEVY>, <FORD>, <NISSAN>, or <VW> child element(s)." Thus, there may not be any child elements in the <ON_SALE> parent, or there may be just one <VW>, or there could be a collection like <CHEVY> <VW> <CHEVY> <FORD> <NISSAN> <VW> <FORD> <NISSAN> <NISSAN>, or more. There may be some character data by itself, or there may be character data combined with one or more of the <CHEVY>, <FORD>, <NISSAN>, or <VW> child elements.

Example of a Complex Declaration: an Order Form Element (ORDER)

So far, the empty declarations and examples have been simple. However, element declarations can be complex. In this section, you see how a more complex declaration is required to describe all the child elements that appear in a simple order form.

For this example, imagine that you are designing an order form for TLSales, and that it looks like Figure 4-11.

No. xxxxxx-xxxxx-xxx

TLSales, Inc.

Order

Customer Name
Street Address
City State Country Zip
Phone Contact Name email

Order taken by Date

Part No. or Description	Each	Qty	Disc	Total-BTax	Tax	Total-ATax
			Totals			

Order filled by Date
Carrier Shipping Date
Comments

Figure 4-11 Complex declaration – an order form

This example focuses on the middle section of the order form; the one that describes the item(s) being ordered. Notice that several pieces of information are needed per item (consider an item to be equivalent to the completion of one row of the tabulation in the middle of the order form) for the order to be processed. Look at Figure 4-12 to see the corresponding section of the related XML document. It is referred to as a draft simply because its DTD has not yet been developed; this example is intended to give some insight into one aspect of its design.


```
<ORDER>
     <ODR_NO>123456-78901-234</ODR_NO>
     <CUSTOMER>
          <NAME>Acme, Inc.</NAME>
          <ST_ADDR>123 Any Dr.</ST_ADDR>
          <CITY>Mytown</CITY>
          <STATE>MO</STATE>
          <COUNTRY>USA</COUNTRY>
          <ZIP_CODE>644444-444</ZIP_CODE>
          <PHONE>613-555-1213</PHONE>
          <CT_NAME>B. Jones</CT_NAME>
          <EMAIL>bjones@acme477.com</EMAIL>
     </CUSTOMER>
     <ITEM>
          <DATE>03-21-03</DATE>
          <ODR_TKR>D. Wilson</ODR_TKR>
          <DESC>
               <PT_NO>7746-56-34-23</PT_NO>
          </DESC>
          <EACH>12.99</EACH>
          <QTY>2</QTY>
          <DISCOUNT>10</DISCOUNT>
          <TTL-BTAX>23.38</TTL-BTAX>
          <TX_ST>08</TX_ST>
          <TTL-ATAX>25.26</TTL-ATAX>
          <RUSH/>
          <NOTE>Stainless steel. Net 30 days</NOTE>
     </ITEM>
.
.
.
</ORDER>
```

Figure 4-12 Sample data in order form's XML document

The middle portion of Figure 4-12 illustrates how the <ITEM> element and its child elements might appear once an item has been properly ordered. In fact, all the item information from the form is intended to be inserted into the <ITEM> element and its child elements. Notice that there seems to be extra information, information that does not appear on the order form itself, but that has been obtained by the TLSales staff member who took the order. This information helps TLSales to better fill the order. Look at Table 4-1, which describes the <ITEM> element and all its child elements, even ones with information that does not appear on the physical order form. This tabulation also helps the author of the DTD to create the appropriate declarations for the various elements.

Drawing upon the information in Table 4-1, as well as the order form itself plus the draft <ITEM> element and child elements, the DTD author might create a declaration for the <ITEM> element that resembles Figure 4-13.

Table 4-1 TLSales order form: a description of the <ITEM> element and its child elements

Element Name	Description	Other Specifications
<ITEM>	One or more items ordered by entry on order form	The parent element, consisting of several child elements; at least one of these elements must appear
<DATE>	Date of order	Mandatory; must appear
<ODR-TKR>	Name of staff member who took order (i.e., filled in order form)	Mandatory
<DESC>	Description of item being ordered	Mandatory; mixed content: contains character data or PT_NO element.
<EACH>	Price of each item	Mandatory
<PT_NO>	Part number corresponding to item	One of the optional inputs for the <DESC> element
<QTY>	Number of items being ordered	Mandatory
<DISCOUNT>	Amount of discount from regular price	Optional; percentage of regular price
<TTL-BTAX>	Total cost before taxes are applied	Mandatory
<TX-ST>	State tax applied against item	May or may not be applied; percentage of regular price
<TX-OTHER>	Other taxes applied against item	May or may not be applied; percentage of regular price
<TTL-ATAX>	Total cost after taxes are applied	Mandatory
<RUSH>	Indicates whether delivery of item should be expedited (i.e., ASAP)	Empty element; optional
<NOTE>	Any special notes or instruction (e.g., specifications, billing, features, etc.)	Zero or more may be inserted

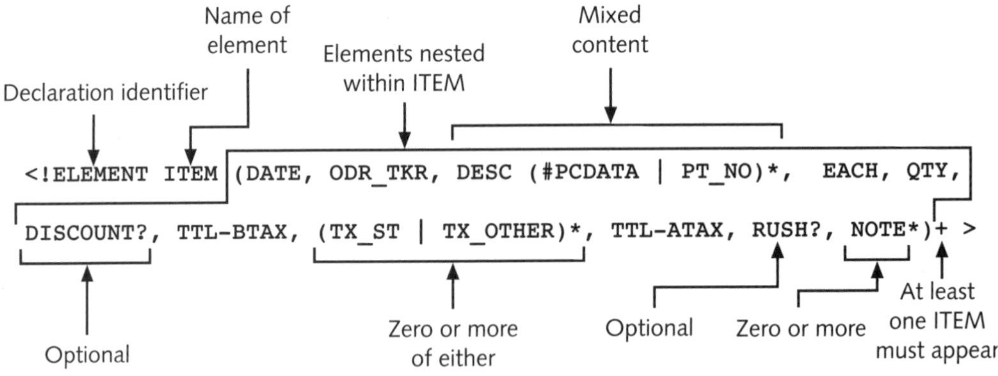

Figure 4-13 Order form—DTD declaration

The notations in Figure 4-13 indicate how the declaration addresses the descriptions and specifications listed in Table 4-1. The <ITEM> element is an example of a complex element declaration. As a content model, it contains several of the content types (e.g., mixed, element) and element content operators (the asterisk, the plus sign, the question mark, etc.).

Attribute List Declarations

Attributes, also known as attribute specifications, allow you to specify additional information for your elements. Attributes take the form of name-value pairs, and appear inside an element's start tag, immediately after the element's name. The basic syntax for an attribute in an XML document (not in a DTD) is shown in the following example using the root element <CONTACTS>:

```
<CONTACTS type="external">
```

The attribute name is type and the attribute's value is specified to be "external". Type is a commonly used attribute name; however, don't confuse the attribute's name with the attribute's actual type. HTML developers might recognize that XML attributes work similarly to HTML attributes. Both languages have SGML as their predecessor. In addition, as illustrated here, specific attributes and their respective values are generally defined for individual elements on a case-by-case basis.

Syntax for Attribute List Declarations in a DTD

Although you can freely add attributes to your XML vocabularies and documents, those vocabularies and documents are not valid unless their attributes also have been defined in the respective DTDs. Attributes are defined in DTDs by attribute list declarations. Figure 4-14 illustrates the basic syntax of an attribute list declaration (ATTLIST).

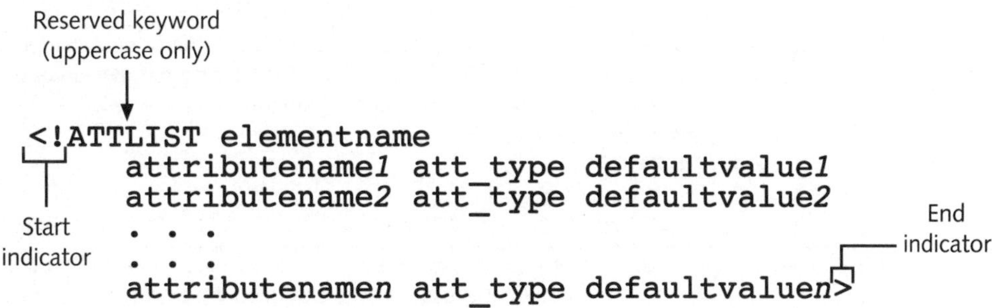

Reserved keyword (uppercase only)
<!ATTLIST elementname
attributename1 att_type defaultvalue1
attributename2 att_type defaultvalue2
. . .
. . .
attributenamen att_type defaultvaluen>
Start indicator
End indicator

Figure 4-14 ATTLIST declaration syntax

Following is a simple one-attribute example of an attribute list declaration, based on the XML document example specification used previously:

```
<!ATTLIST CONTACTS
type CDATA #REQUIRED>
```

Each attribute list declaration identifies an element that has attributes, and then describes the nature of the attributes for that element. In this example, the element is named <CONTACTS>, the name of its attribute is type, the type of values the attributes may hold is CDATA, and the default value for the attribute is #REQUIRED. (Actually, by definition, #REQUIRED indicates that no default value exists.) During initial processing, the XML parser reads this attribute specification and passes the specification data along to the application.

Attribute Types and Default Values

In the example given, the type of attribute was specified to be CDATA, which is one of XML's ten possible attribute types, all of which are described in Table 4-2.

Table 4-2 Attribute types

Attribute type specification	Description of attribute type
CDATA	The attribute's value is a simple character string. Any text is allowed except that which is used for markup, such as <, ", or &, for example. (For them, use the <, ", and & entity references, respectively.) This use of CDATA is not to be confused with the entity-related concept called CDATA sections.
ENTITY	The attribute's value must be the name of a single entity. The entity must be declared in the DTD. Example: <!ATTLIST warning symbol ENTITY #IMPLIED> <!ENTITY skullxbones SYSTEM "images/poison.jpg"> <warning symbol="skullxbones">
ENTITIES	The attribute's value may be multiple entity names, separated by white space.
ID	The attribute's value is a proper, unique XML name (a unique identifier). All of the ID values used in a document must be different. IDs uniquely identify individual elements in a document. Elements can have only a single ID attribute. Example: <!ATTLIST CUST cust_no ID #REQUIRED> <CUST cust_no="20021031-37">
IDREF	The attribute's value must be the value of a single ID attribute on some element in the document, usually an element to which the current element is related. Example: <!ATTLIST EMPLOYEE empl_no ID #REQUIRED dept_no IDREF #IMPLIED> allows <EMPLOYEE empl_no = "20021345"> and <EMPLOYEE empl_no = "20021447" dept_no = "200114">

Table 4-2 Attribute types (continued)

Attribute type specification	Description of attribute type
IDREFS	The attribute's value may contain multiple IDREF values, separated by white space.
List of names (also called "enumerated")	The attribute's value must be taken from a specific list of names. This is also called "enumerated" because the possible values are all explicitly enumerated in the declaration. Example: contractor=(YES I NO) Alternatively, you can specify that the names must match a notation name. (Notation declarations are discussed later in this chapter.)
NMTOKEN	Name token attributes are a restricted form of string attribute (they begin with a letter). In general, an NMTOKEN attribute must consist of a single word or string with no white spaces within it, but there are no additional constraints on the word. It doesn't have to match another attribute or declaration. Example: company="Thomson"
NMTOKENS	The attribute's value may contain multiple NMTOKEN values, separated by white space. Example: company="Thomson Learning"
NOTATION	Consists of a sequence of name tokens, but matches one or more notation types (instructions for processing formatted or non-XML data).

In the example, the default value specified for the type of <CONTACTS> is #REQUIRED. However, in the XML document example at the beginning of this section, in the <CONTACTS> element the value for the attribute named type was "external". How are these related? Table 4-3 describes the four possible default value specifications for attributes.

Table 4-3 Attribute default values

Default Value	Explanation
#REQUIRED	The attribute must have an explicitly specified value for every occurrence of the element in the document
#IMPLIED	The attribute value is not required, and no default value is provided. The user may supply one if they choose to do so. If a value is not specified, the XML processor must proceed without one.
"value"	Any legal value can be specified as the attribute's default. The attribute value is not required to be specified for each occurrence of the element in the document. If a value is not specified explicitly, then the attribute for this element is given the specified default value.
#FIXED "value"	An attribute declaration may specify that an attribute has a fixed value. In this case, the attribute is not required, but if it occurs, it must have that specified value. If it is not present, the element is treated as though it has specified default value for that particular attribute.

The description of the #REQUIRED default value from Table 4-3 indicates that whenever the element <CONTACTS> appears, a value for the attribute named type must be specified. In the example at the beginning of this section, the type attribute in <CONTACTS> was given the value "external". Therefore, it is presumed that, at some point in the application, there is a need for a list of TLSales.com staff members whose contact information can be made available to the public (that is, externally). The <CONTACTS> element and its attribute specification "type="external" " is useful at that point.

Handling White Space

During the development of XML documents and DTDs, white space is added so that the developer can visualize the document's structure and function(s), and also to track development progress. Maintenance of the white space during subsequent processing isn't usually of significance. At times, depending on the task facing the developer, the creation or maintenance of white space may be significant. The most commonly used example is the reproduction of poetry, where stanzas must be isolated from one another, and other structural features must be maintained. In those cases, the developer must be aware of the content model of the elements in question. Generally, white space is considered significant in mixed content (the interspersing of text with elements) and is insignificant in element content.

XML processors generally must pass all characters that are not markup through to the application. White space maintenance is not a consideration unless the processor is advised. If it is so advised and if the processor is a validating processor, then it must also inform the application about which white space characters are significant. There is a special attribute "XML:space" that may be used to indicate explicitly that white space is significant. On any element that includes the attribute specification XML:space="preserve", all white space within that element (and within child elements that do not explicitly reset XML:space) is considered significant and is maintained.

The only legal values for XML:space are "preserve" and "default". The value default indicates that the default processing is desired. In a DTD, the XML:space attribute must be declared as an "enumerated" type with only those two values as choices.

Finally, with respect to white space in parsed text, XML processors are required to normalize all end-of-line markers to a single-line feed character (&#A;). Although document authors are rarely concerned with this, it can eliminate some cross-platform portability issues.

Language Identification

Many document processing applications (for example, Web browsers) can benefit from information about the natural language in which the content and attributes of a document are written. XML provides the attribute XML:lang to enable you to specify the language, using the following as values:

- The two-letter language codes found in ISO 639, titled "Code for the representation of the names of languages"

- Language identifiers registered with the Internet Assigned Numbers Authority (IANA), listed in Request for Comments 1766, and found at *http://www.ietf.org/rfc/rfc1766.txt*
- Language identifiers of your own design, as long as the identifiers begin with "x-" or "X-"

Here are a couple of simple examples:

```
<MERCH_US xml:lang="EN-US">Green shirts</MERCH_US>
```

or

```
<PRODUITS_FRANCE xml:lang="fr">Chemises verts</PRODUITS_
FRANCE>
```

You may have noticed the inclusion of the two-letter language subcode "US" with the language code "EN" in the first example. For some languages, there are dialect or regional dialect subcodes available.

Attribute Value Normalization

When required, the XML processor performs all attribute value normalization on attribute values. That is, the referenced character(s) replace their respective references, entity references are resolved, and white space is also resolved.

ENTITY DECLARATIONS

Entities are defined as storage units that hold strings or blocks of parsed data such as text entities, and unparsed data such as graphics, audio files, or video files, among others. Entities are powerful DTD and content management tools. All entities used in an XML language or document must first be defined with an entity declaration in an internal or external DTD. The **entity declaration** specifies a name for the entity and defines what the entity represents (a string of text or an external file, etc.).

In Chapter Two, the discussion of entities centered on general entities. Discussion of the other type of entity, parameter entities, was intentionally delayed until this chapter, since they are relevant to DTDs.

General entities are references that are expended by the parser and then passed along to the application. The following example is a general internal entity representing a specific date:

```
<!ENTITY DATE "January 1, 2003">
```

The next example is a general external entity representing a file that contains a diagram, photograph, or some other type of graphic:

```
<!ENTITY PIX  SYSTEM "picture04.tif">
```

Subsequently, at appropriate places in their respective XML languages or documents, the entity references—in their distinctive form "&entity name;"—can be used as content between the tags in an element. The following example shows how each of the above entities might be referred to in their respective XML documents:

```
<NEW_FISC_YR>&DATE;</NEW_FISC_YR>
<FIGURE04>&PIX;</FIGURE04>
```

Parameter entities are different from general entities and are not used within the XML documents or languages. They are used only in the DTDs for those documents or languages. Their declaration syntax is similar to that for general entity declarations, but their syntax is also reminiscent of the syntax for attribute type specifications, which was previously discussed. Figure 4-15 illustrates typical declaration syntax.

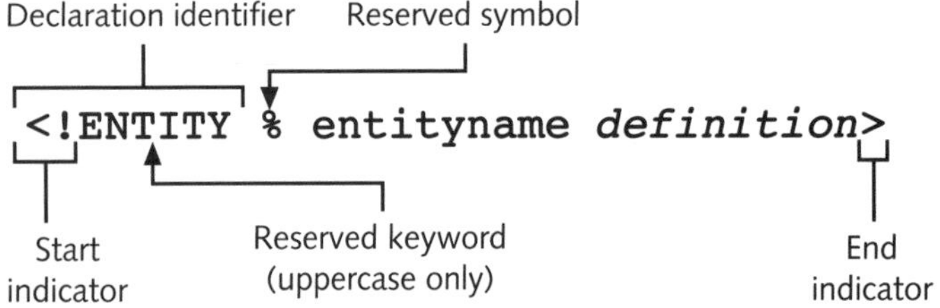

Figure 4-15 Parameter entity declaration syntax

To use the parameter entity reference, insert " % entityname; " into an element declaration, as in the following:

```
<!ELEMENT % ENTITYNAME;>
```

The parameter entity references are expanded as the XML processor reviews the DTD. In this way, the data contained in the entity itself is brought into the process as the XML document or language is being validated and not later, when the XML processor passes the document to the application (as is the case with general entities).

Internal Parameter Entity

An application of an internal parameter entity is shown in Figures 4-16 and 4-17. Note how, in the example's "Before" scenario, shown in Figure 4-16, the <SALES> and <CUSTSRV> elements are composed of the same child elements: <LASTNAME>, <FIRSTNAME>, <EMAIL>, and <PHONE>. The element declarations are also identical: only one of each of these elements occurs, and they occur in the same order in both <SALES> and <CUSTSRV>. This is an ideal situation in which to use a parameter entity reference.

In the "After" scenario, shown in Figure 4-17, a parameter entity called CONT_INFO is declared to be composed of references to the <LASTNAME>, <FIRSTNAME>, <EMAIL>, and <PHONE> elements. Later, the declarations of <SALES> and <CUSTSRV> include the parameter entity CUST_INFO.

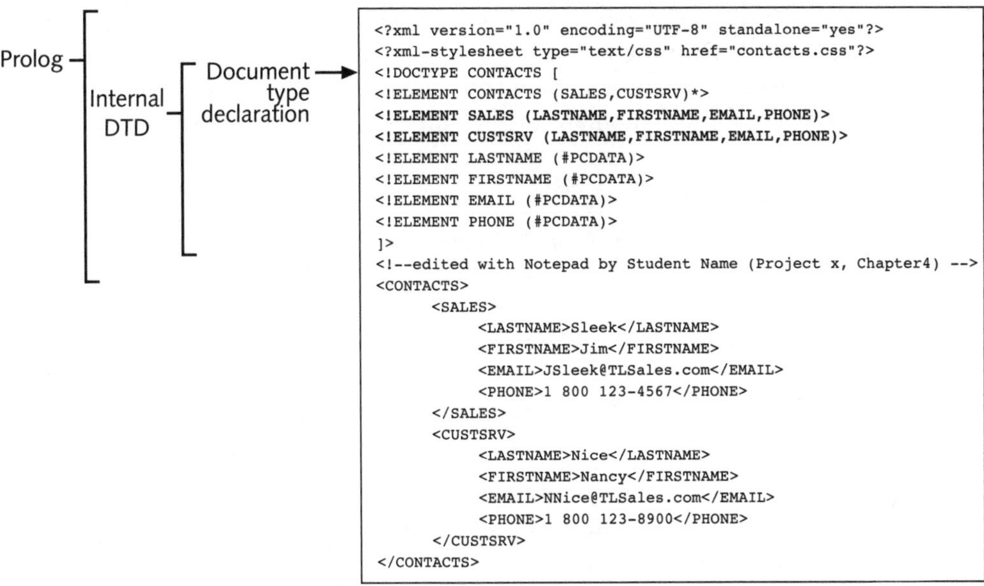


```
<?xml version="1.0" encoding="UTF-8" standalone="yes"?>
<?xml-stylesheet type="text/css" href="contacts.css"?>
<!DOCTYPE CONTACTS [
<!ELEMENT CONTACTS (SALES,CUSTSRV)*>
<!ELEMENT SALES (LASTNAME,FIRSTNAME,EMAIL,PHONE)>
<!ELEMENT CUSTSRV (LASTNAME,FIRSTNAME,EMAIL,PHONE)>
<!ELEMENT LASTNAME (#PCDATA)>
<!ELEMENT FIRSTNAME (#PCDATA)>
<!ELEMENT EMAIL (#PCDATA)>
<!ELEMENT PHONE (#PCDATA)>
]>
<!--edited with Notepad by Student Name (Project x, Chapter4) -->
<CONTACTS>
      <SALES>
           <LASTNAME>Sleek</LASTNAME>
           <FIRSTNAME>Jim</FIRSTNAME>
           <EMAIL>JSleek@TLSales.com</EMAIL>
           <PHONE>1 800 123-4567</PHONE>
      </SALES>
      <CUSTSRV>
           <LASTNAME>Nice</LASTNAME>
           <FIRSTNAME>Nancy</FIRSTNAME>
           <EMAIL>NNice@TLSales.com</EMAIL>
           <PHONE>1 800 123-8900</PHONE>
      </CUSTSRV>
</CONTACTS>
```

Figure 4-16 Before use of internal parameter entity

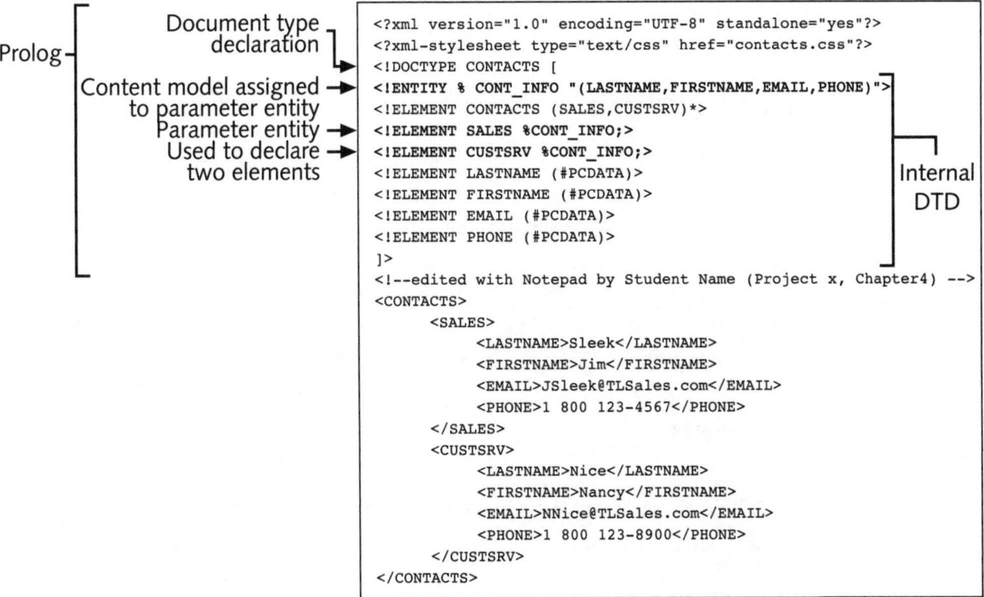


```
<?xml version="1.0" encoding="UTF-8" standalone="yes"?>
<?xml-stylesheet type="text/css" href="contacts.css"?>
<!DOCTYPE CONTACTS [
<!ENTITY % CONT_INFO "(LASTNAME,FIRSTNAME,EMAIL,PHONE)">
<!ELEMENT CONTACTS (SALES,CUSTSRV)*>
<!ELEMENT SALES %CONT_INFO;>
<!ELEMENT CUSTSRV %CONT_INFO;>
<!ELEMENT LASTNAME (#PCDATA)>
<!ELEMENT FIRSTNAME (#PCDATA)>
<!ELEMENT EMAIL (#PCDATA)>
<!ELEMENT PHONE (#PCDATA)>
]>
<!--edited with Notepad by Student Name (Project x, Chapter4) -->
<CONTACTS>
      <SALES>
           <LASTNAME>Sleek</LASTNAME>
           <FIRSTNAME>Jim</FIRSTNAME>
           <EMAIL>JSleek@TLSales.com</EMAIL>
           <PHONE>1 800 123-4567</PHONE>
      </SALES>
      <CUSTSRV>
           <LASTNAME>Nice</LASTNAME>
           <FIRSTNAME>Nancy</FIRSTNAME>
           <EMAIL>NNice@TLSales.com</EMAIL>
           <PHONE>1 800 123-8900</PHONE>
      </CUSTSRV>
</CONTACTS>
```

Figure 4-17 After insertion of internal parameter entity

One of the distinct advantages of using parameter entity references is readily apparent: a great number of keystrokes can be saved—while maintaining accuracy—when you need to repeat a number of similar element declarations. Further, if a number of parameter entities have been created for your elements and those entities are not satisfactory or you want to experiment, then you only need to modify the parameter entities or create new ones. You don't have to alter the original elements themselves.

External Parameter Entity

In a manner similar to the internal parameter entity just discussed, parameter entities can be added to external DTDs wherever they are: in the same directory as the XML document, in a private DTD at another Web site, or in a public DTD at another Web site. The advantages listed for internal parameter entities are multiplied if you are using external DTDs, especially if several XML documents access each DTD. Finally, another use of the external parameter entity is to use it to reference public standards, like the W3C's XHTML 1.0 transitional DTD, and then to combine it with the some of your own elements.

In the respective DTD, add the following entity declaration:

```
<!ENTITY % XHTML1-trans-DTD PUBLIC "-//W3C//DTD
   XHTML 1.0 Transitional//EN" SYSTEM
   "http://www.w3.org/TR/xhtml1/DTD/xhtml1-transitional.dtd">
```

After this reference is inserted, you need only refer to it by its parameter entity name "%XHTML1-trans-DTD;" in the DTD.

NOTATION DECLARATIONS

XML was designed primarily for dealing with text data; however, it also handles unparsed data, or non-XML data, such as audio, video, other graphics, etc., by using notation declarations. **Notation declarations** usually apply labels to specific types of nonparsed binary data, but they can also play a role with text data, too. You can use notation declarations to label text data that has specific formats (for example, date formats). Once labeled, the data can be passed directly to the application, which processes it according to its coded instructions. A typical notation declaration appears in Figure 4-18.

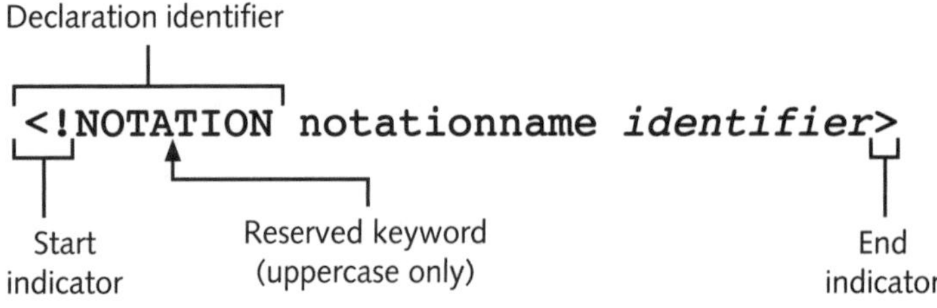

Figure 4-18 Notation declaration syntax

Whatever takes the place of the generic term "identifier" in Figure 4-18 is presumed to mean something to the application to which the XML document is passed. If these notation declarations are to be used, then it is up to the application developers to communicate what the application interprets and uses. Table 4-4 lists some examples of identifiers. Since no one can anticipate the needs of any given application, and since no one has developed a universally accepted standard identifier scheme, the list in Table 4-4 may not be very useful. However, it does illustrate that the format used for identifying and locating the various resources resembles what XML developers have seen before, which was part of the previous discussion of entities.

4

Table 4-4 Examples of external identifiers used with notation declaration

External Identifiers	Description
SYSTEM "ISO 4217:1995"	ISO standard for world currencies
SYSTEM "ISO 8601:1998"	ISO Standard for date formats
SYSTEM "..\winnt\system32\notepad.exe"	MS Notepad, located on the local system, might be used to display data contents, for example
PUBLIC "-//TLSales//NotDecl GfxFmt//EN" "http://tlsales.com/fmts/gfx.htm"	An FPI for a (fictitious) online resource

The effect of the declaration syntax is to create a label that is to be used in conjunction with attribute or unparsed external entity declarations. Attribute declarations have already been discussed. Unparsed entities import nonparsed data. The declaration syntax for such unparsed entities is shown in Figure 4-19.

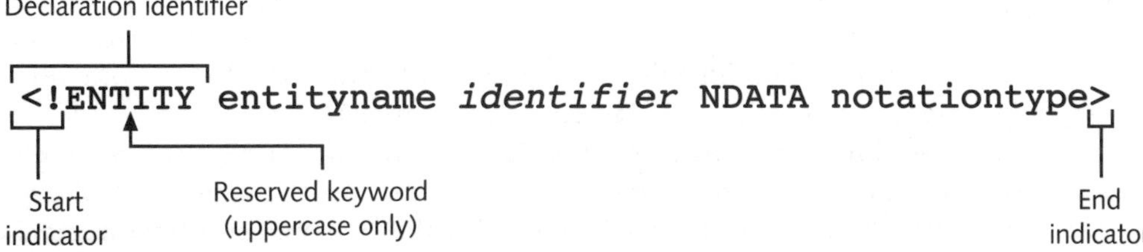

Figure 4-19 Unparsed entity declaration syntax

The following example concerns some video MPEG footage obtained at an association awards dinner. In the example, a notation type named MPEG is declared, using its MIME type (video/MPEG) as its identifier. There is a declared empty element named <VIDEO> that has an attribute called "location". Location's value, "ASSOCIATION", is the name of an entity. The unparsed entity ASSOCIATION references the video file, which, in turn is passed to the VIDEO element within the parent element AWARDS in the XML document proper.

```
<!DOCUMENT AWARDS [
<!ELEMENT AWARDS ANY>
<!ELEMENT VIDEO EMPTY>
```

```
<!ATTLIST VIDEO
location ENTITY #REQUIRED
>
<!NOTATION MPEG SYSTEM "video/mpeg">
<!ENTITY ASSOCIATION "videos/assoc_award.mpg" NDATA MPEG>
]>
<AWARDS>
<VIDEO location="ASSOCIATION"/>
</AWARDS>
```

During XML processing, the processor interprets the empty VIDEO element and finds the entity named ASSOCIATION as the value of the "location" attribute. The processor then recognizes that the ASSOCIATION entity is to remain unparsed because of the NDATA keyword. So the processor passes the file "assoc_award.mpeg" to the application for processing. At that point, it is hoped that the application developer built the processing capability into the application. If there is no such capability, then:

- An error may result
- The user may be prompted by the application (presumably asking the user what they want done with the file)
- The application may ignore the file and continue
- The application may "hang" (worst case)

DTDs and Namespace Declarations

Figure 4-20 depicts two versions of the contacts.xml document. Notice in the top document, that the <CONTACTS ... > start tag contains an xmlns="http://www.TLSales.com/dtds/" attribute. In the bottom document, the equivalent start tag is named <ns:CONTACTS ... > and contains an xmlns:ns="http://www.TLSales.com/dtds/" attribute. These attributes are called *namespace declarations*. The xmlns portion states this is an *XML* namespace declaration. Such declarations indicate to the XML parser that the elements in their respective documents conform to the specifications in the W3C's Namespaces in XML Recommendation of January 1999. The difference between the two Figure 4-20 documents, as indicated in the figure, is the namespace declaration in the version of contacts.xml on the top is called a default namespace declaration, while that in the document on the bottom is called a prefix namespace declaration (notice also in that document, each of the other elements in the document has a "ns:" prefix).

```
<?xml version="1.0" encoding="UTF-8" standalone="no"?>
<?xml-stylesheet type="text/css" href="contacts.css"?>
<!DOCTYPE contacts SYSTEM "contacts.dtd">
<!--edited with Notepad by Student Name (Project x, Chapter4) -->
<CONTACTS xmlns="http://www.TLSales.com/dtds/">
      <SALES>
           <NAME>Jim Sleek</NAME>
           <EMAIL>JSleek@TLSales.com</EMAIL>
           <PHONE>1 800 123-4567</PHONE>
           <HEAD/>
      </SALES>
      <CUSTSRV>
           <NAME>Nancy Nice</NAME>
           <EMAIL>NNice@TLSales.com</EMAIL>
           <PHONE>1 800 123-8900</PHONE>
           <HEAD/>
      </CUSTSRV>
</CONTACTS>
```

Default namespace

```
<?xml version="1.0" encoding="UTF-8" standalone="no"?>
<?xml-stylesheet type="text/css" href="contacts.css"?>
<!DOCTYPE contacts SYSTEM "contacts.dtd">
<!--edited with Notepad by Student Name (Project x, Chapter4) -->
<ns:CONTACTS xmlns:ns="http://www.TLSales.com/dtds/">
      <ns:SALES>
           <ns:NAME>Jim Sleek</ns:NAME>
           <ns:EMAIL>JSleek@TLSales.com</ns:EMAIL>
           <ns:PHONE>1 800 123-4567</ns:PHONE>
           <ns:HEAD/>
      </ns:SALES>
      <ns:CUSTSRV>
           <ns:NAME>Nancy Nice</ns:NAME>
           <ns:EMAIL>NNice@TLSales.com</ns:EMAIL>
           <ns:PHONE>1 800 123-8900</ns:PHONE>
           <ns:HEAD/>
      </ns:CUSTSRV>
</ns:CONTACTS>
```

Prefix namespace

Figure 4-20 Namespaces in DTDs

Namespace declarations were developed to overcome the necessity for always having to create unique names for datatypes with similar functions. They become necessary when you have to differentiate between similar names in the DTDs and the related documents (i.e., when you want to avoid "name collisions"). For example, in Figure 4-20, there is a <NAME> element nested within each of the <SALES> and <CUSTSRV> elements. However, what if contacts.xml were a lot larger and there was a need to use an element name like <NAME> elsewhere, say, to differentiate a department, division, or location? Normally, you would have to use another unique name, like <DEPT_NAME>, for example. But the use of namespace declarations allows you to use <NAME> again, provided it had a unique prefix attached to it (e.g., <dpt:NAME>).

Do not be confused by the references to URLs in the creation of namespace declarations. Despite the appearance, a namespace is not really a physical device or location, but a logical device that only represents a collection of declarations for elements and components (incidentally, elements and other components are also called datatypes). Thus, that collection is represented by a unique name, which takes the form of a Uniform Resource Identifier (URI). The term URI is a generic term for all types of names and addresses for objects on the World Wide Web. In fact, the namespace name is actually a uniform resource locator (URL), which you may recognize as the global address of a document or resource on the Web. URLs are one form of URI; they are already well-known, and thus programmer-friendly. But, during the processing of a document that contains a namespace with a URL, no browsers or other applications actually access the URLs. The URL names are all that is being used, simply to add uniqueness to the datatype names. The W3C Recommendation titled "Namespaces in XML," dated January 1999, recommends the use of URLs as namespace names because URLs indicate domain names that are recognized as being functional across the Internet. Thus, although they add to uniqueness, they are not rejected syntactically by validators or other processors.

Please remember that you cannot use prefixes that begin with `xml`, `XML`, xMl, or any such combination. They are reserved for use by XML and XML-related specifications.

The scope of every namespace declaration is restricted to the element for which it is declared. In the Figure 4-20 examples, the namespace has been declared in the root <CONTACTS ...> element, so it is effective throughout the document. However, namespace can be declared for child elements (also called subelements) but, then, the namespace is valid only for the scope of that subelement—that is, for the subelement in question and its own subelements—but not within its sibling elements or any other elements outside its scope.

Default Namespace Declarations

In Figure 4-20, the declaration within the <CONTACTS ...> start tag in the top document, as mentioned earlier, is called a default namespace declaration. It indicates to the XML parser that, if the parser encounters an element with no prefix, then the declarations for those elements would, by default, be found in the DTD document at the *http://www.TLSales.com* Web site, in the Web site's dtds directory. Remember what was stated earlier, though: there is no accessing the URL for definitions. The namespace declaration is used as a logical device only, to establish uniqueness for the element name. The uniqueness is not that evident, here, though. What is really happening is this: when the parser encounters an element name that has no apparent prefix, it recognizes the element as though it has "http://www.TLSales.com/dtds/" appended to the name (e.g., <NAME> is actually <http://www.TLSales.com/dtds/:NAME>. So there is uniqueness; it's just not as obvious.

For the document author, however, the effect is simply that certain element names—those of the author's choice—within the element do not need prefixes. That reduction in element name complexity adds to the legibility of the document and the cleanliness of its structure.

Default namespace declarations can be used in conjunction with prefix namespace declarations, and often *are* used that way.

Prefix Namespace Declarations

In Figure 4-20, the <ns:CONTACTS ...> element, in the bottom document, contains the declaration xmlns:ns=http://www.TLSales.com/dtds/ in its start tag. That declaration is called a prefix namespace declaration and it indicates to the XML parser that the parser will enounter at least one element with the "ns:" prefix attached to the element's name. It also tells the parser that the respective element, attribute, entity, and other declarations for those elements could be found at *http://www.TLSales.com* in the Web site's dtds directory.

The parser will never actually access the TLSales Web site, so there is no need to install a DTD document there. In fact, there is no compulsion even to create a *www.TLSales.com* Web site. The namespace declaration is simply used as a logical device, to establish uniqueness for those elements whose names begin with the prefix "ns:". When the parser encounters an element with the prefix "ns:", it will recognize that element as though it had the whole Web site URL appended to its name as a prefix – that is, <ns:NAME> would be treated as though it was named <http://www.TLSales.com/dtds/:NAME>. In effect, the declaration has told the parser that all the elements whose names begin with "ns:" belong to the same "ns:" club. Those elements are uniquely different from any other elements, even if those elements have the same base name. The fact they have different prefixes makes them different from one another.

As you can see, with prefix namespace declarations, the uniqueness of element names is more obvious than it was with default namespace declarations.

Declaring Namespaces in the DTD

Namespace declarations are powerful, special applications of attributes. But, like all attributes, they must be declared in the respective DTDs. Because default namespace declarations and prefix namespace declarations differ somewhat, their declarations in DTDs also differ. The following sections discuss each.

If you are going to use more than one namespace declaration in a document, then you have to declare *all* the xmlns attributes in your DTD.

Declaring Default Namespaces

Creating the appropriate declarations to set up for the default namespace attribute is fairly straightforward. From Figure 4-20, you can see that the <CONTACTS ...> element contains two subelements: <SALES> and <CUSTSRV>. So, within the contacts.dtd file, ensure that the declaration for the <CONTACTS> element is:

```
<!ELEMENT CONTACTS (SALES, CUSTSRV)* >
```

A literal translation of that declaration is fairly easy: "There is an element named <CONTACTS> that contains zero or more occurrences of elements named <SALES> and/or <CUSTSRV>."

Once the element declaration is in place, you have to create a declaration for the attribute to be found within the start tag for <CONTACTS>. That declaration looks like:

```
<!ATTLIST CONTACTS xmlns CDATA #FIXED
   "http://www.TLSales.com/dtds/" >
```

Here is a literal translation: "Within the scope of the element named <CONTACTS>, a default namespace attribute named "xmlns" is in effect. The value for that attribute contains parseable character data. The value is fixed (i.e., it does not vary), and the value is http://www.TLSales.com/dtds/. For <CONTACTS> and its subelements, treat their names as if the value for the default namespace was appended as a prefix to their names."

Remember, the XML parser understands that xmlns is specifically a namespace attribute. So when it recognizes the xmlns attribute, it knows what it is, and starts the proper subroutines to deal with it.

If you are going to use more than one namespace declaration, then you have to insert all of the appropriate declarations into your DTD. That means you have to keep track of which prefixes go with which element names, and ensure that they don't cause name collisions within the DTD.

Declaring Prefix Namespace Attributes

Creating the appropriate declarations to set up for the prefix namespace attribute is just a little more complex than that for the default namespace declaration. This time, from the bottom document in Figure 4-20, you can see that the <ns:CONTACTS ...> element contains two subelements: <ns:SALES> and <ns:CUSTSRV>. But, now, within the contacts.dtd file, you may find it surprising that the declaration for the <ns:CONTACTS> element is still:

```
<!ELEMENT CONTACTS (SALES, CUSTSRV)* >
```

The literal translation is the same as before: "There is an element named <CONTACTS> that contains zero or more occurrences of elements named <SALES> and/or <CUSTSRV>." Now that this element declaration is in place, you have to create a slightly different declaration for the attribute to be found within the start tag for <ns:CONTACTS>. That declaration looks like:

```
<!ATTLIST ns:CONTACTS xmlns:ns CDATA #FIXED
   "http://www.TLSales.com/dtds/" >
```

Here is the literal translation: "Within the scope of the element named <ns:CONTACTS>, a prefix namespace attribute named "xmlns:ns" is in effect. The value for that attribute contains parseable character data. The value is fixed (i.e., it does not vary), and the value is http://www.TLSales.com/dtds/. The value for the namespace is represented by the prefix ns:. For <CONTACTS> and its subelements, if you encounter an element name with the prefix ns:, treat the names as if the value for the default namespace was appended as a prefix to the names."

If you are inserting more than one prefix namespace into a document, then you must also insert a separate attribute declaration to that effect into your DTD. So, if in Figure 4-20, you wanted to add a separate namespace attribute to the <SALES> element—for example, <SALES xmlns:sales="http://www.TLSales.com/sales/" >—then you would add the following to your DTD:

```
<!ATTLIST sales:SALES xmlns:sales CDATA #FIXED
   "http://www.TLSales.com/sales/" >
```

Then the new namespace declaration is in effect for the full extent of the <SALES> element. That is, the xmlns:sales namespace declaration eclipses the xmlns:ns namespace declaration. Once the processor reached the end of the <SALES> element, though (that is, once it encountered the <CUSTSRV> element), then the xmlns:ns namespace declaration is in effect again.

Limitations of DTDs with Respect to Namespace Declarations

Because the concept of DTDs predates the development of the W3C Namespaces in XML Recommendation, among other reasons, DTDs do not provide the same level of support for namespaces that XML schemas do. Schema specifications were developed at approximately the same time as the W3C namespace specifications, so they are more flexible and comprehensive. A more comprehensive discussion of namespaces is provided when schemas are covered in the next chapter.

Document Analysis and Testing

During XML document development, especially during DTD or schema development, it is beneficial to go through the process of document analysis, and record the results.

Document analysis is the process of determining the effectiveness of XML document development. The people best qualified to perform this type of analysis are the users and creators of the documents. Several document analysis sources are readily available on the Internet, in libraries, and from other sources. Analysis includes, but is not necessarily limited to:

- XML document and DTD testing for well-formedness and validity
- Document layout analysis with respect to access, knowledge integration, and content extraction (for learning and for data/information extraction for subsequent processing)
- Structure (recognition, visualization, and representation) of all components (e.g., documents, hypertext, and nonparsed components)

- Access to textual information embedded in Internet images
- Document image processing for Internet/intranet transmission: data compression, sound/color analysis, etc.
- Authoring, editing, and presentation systems for complex multimedia documents
- Workflow management; possible reformatting for multimodal mobile access

To begin with, a good practice would be to test your XML DTDs and documents using at least two validating XML parsers on at least two different operating system platforms. Test and check the documents and DTDs for conformance to the W3C XML Recommendation, appropriateness to their intended task(s), and compliance with guidelines or requirements obtained in consultation with your users or other clients. All results from document analysis and testing should then be kept in a hard-copy report for handy reference. Parts of the results may also be kept in some sort of XML-related syntax, such as DTD modules, to be incorporated into subsequent XML authoring and processing.

Here are some reminders regarding DTDs:

- DTDs should be designed to be flexible, reusable, and practical.
- XML DTDs must be designed to comply with the XML well-formedness and validity constraints.
- Base subsequent DTD development on your document analyses.
- XML DTDs themselves must be valid XML and must not use any of the additional features of SGML that are not allowed in XML.
- Documents conforming to the DTDs must also be valid XML documents.

DOCUMENTATION

An XML application is not considered complete or stable until it is documented. Developers should provide complete and detailed documentation with every DTD suite (the XML documents, the relevant DTDs, and other referenced entities). The documentation should be designed to be used by both XML novices and experts, and it should detail the syntax, proper use, and client-specific definition for each element in a DTD. Additional relevant information about each element, such as probable audio/visual presentation, should also be included as comments. You should also produce documentation for all XML documents (including all their relevant DTDs, etc.) that interoperate with the subject XML document/DTD suite.

Chapter Summary

- Each XML-related language is a unique markup solution that meets a specific need or speaks to a specialized audience. For each XML language, other related XML documents are created. Document type definitions (DTDs) or schemas are developed to specify structures and content models for the languages and documents.
- If you're moving toward an XML-based operation, you might consider selecting one of many available existing vocabularies, or you might consider developing your own XML-related language and documents.
- DTDs and schemas facilitate XML document modeling by: declaring a set of allowed elements, defining the content model for each element, declaring the allowed attributes, etc.
- A document may contain: a stand-alone internal DTD; a reference to an external DTD; or a combination of an internal DTD plus a reference to another, external DTD. There are several types of external DTDs: private external DTDs on the same system; private external DTDs, but at a different URL; and public external DTDs at a different (possibly remote) URL.
- A content model defines what an element may contain. There are several types of element content: parsed character data only; other elements only; mixed content (character data plus elements); empty elements; and elements with no content restrictions.
- There are five operator symbols that you can use singly or in combination in a DTD to indicate the order and frequency, etc., of the appearance of its elements.
- Attributes are name-value pairs that provide additional information about elements. There are ten attribute types and four generic specifications for attribute default values. Plus, there are special attributes for maintaining white space and for specifying in which language a document is written.
- During processing and validation, the XML parser performs all attribute value normalization on attribute values: character references are replaced by the referenced character(s); entity references are resolved; and white space is also resolved.
- Parameter entities are only used in DTDs and not within the XML documents or languages. Parameter entities are normalized when the DTD is accessed. By contrast, general entities are normalized when the XML document is presented to the application.
- Use notation declarations to label text data that has specific formats. However, notation declarations rely heavily on the application's ability to handle the data once the data has been passed to it.
- Namespace declarations, which are special attributes, prevent name collisions. However, they require the insertion of appropriate declarations into the respective DTDs.

- It is recommended that document analysis be undertaken during the development of XML documents, and DTDs and schemas, and periodically thereafter, and that the results be recorded and kept. XML documents are not considered complete or stable until they are documented.

Review Questions

1. What two things do all XML-related vocabularies have in common?
2. If you are investigating existing XML vocabularies, which of the following steps should you take?
   a. Read all the documentation available for all your candidate vocabularies.
   b. Look at their sample documents.
   c. Test their markup on your own data.
   d. Find out what parsers and tools have been developed to help display all documents written to that vocabulary.
   e. all of the above
3. DTDs predate SGML. True or false?
4. How many kinds of declarations are there in a typical DTD? What are they?
5. The ______________ within a DTD allow it and its documents to communicate metainformation to the XML processor.
6. In a typical declaration statement, what do you call the combination of the start indicator (<) and the uppercase keyword?
7. In which of the following situations is the use of a DTD recommended?
   a. when an XML document or language relies on default attribute values
   b. when you need to handle white space
   c. when dealing with complex mathematical equations
   d. when people compose or edit data regularly
8. According to location, what kinds of DTDs are there? (Choose all that apply.)
   a. public internal
   b. internal
   c. private external
   d. public external
   e. all of the above

9. From the following document type declaration statement, what kind of DTD is being referred to?

```
<!DOCTYPE CONTACTS SYSTEM "http://www.TLSales.com/dtds/
contacts.dtd">
```

   a. public access external DTD
   b. private external DTD
   c. private internal DTD
   d. public internal DTD
   e. internal DTD, plus external DTD

10. Regarding formal public identifiers, match the following fields to the description of the information in the field:

a. first field	1. "maintainer"
b. second field	2. language
c. third field	3. "definer"
d. fourth field	4. document type

11. An element declaration statement can define more than one element. True or false?

12. What are the five types of element content?

13. Regarding element declaration operator symbols, match the following symbols with their respective interpretations:

a. asterisk (*)	1. optional
b. comma (,)	2. zero or more
c. question mark (?)	3. sequence
d. plus sign (+)	4. choice of one
e. vertical bar (|)	5. one or more

14. Regarding attribute type specifications, what is the difference between NMTOKEN and NMTOKENS?

15. What does the default attribute value #IMPLIED mean?

16. On any element which includes the attribute specification ______________, all white space within that element (and within child elements that do not explicitly reset ______________) is considered significant and is maintained.

17. XML provides the attribute XML:lang to enable you to specify the language, using as values:
   a. codes found in ISO 639
   b. codes found in RFC 1766
   c. codes found in ISO/IEC 10646
   d. codes of your own design, with certain stipulations

18. When the time comes, the XML processor performs all attribute value normalization on attribute values: character references are replaced by the referenced character(s), entity references are resolved, and white space is also resolved. True or false?
19. How would you refer to the following code?

    ```
    <!ENTITY PIX SYSTEM "picture04.tif">
    ```

    a. notation declaration, external graphic entity
    b. private internal DTD, external graphic entity
    c. general entity, internal graphic entity
    d. general entity, external graphic entity
    e. parameter entity, external graphic entity
20. When does the XML processor expand parameter entity references?
21. When you see code such as the following, what type of reference is being used?

    ```
    <! ELEMENT SALES %CONT_INFO;>
    ```

22. Notation declarations apply ________________ to specific types of ________________ data.
23. Regarding notation declarations, if the application developer has not built processing capability into an application, what might be expected to happen?
    a. An error may result.
    b. The user may be prompted by the application.
    c. The application may ignore the file and continue.
    d. The application may "hang."
    e. all of the above
    f. answers a, b, and c, but not d or e
24. Which of the following indicates that a default namespace may be in use? (Choose all that apply.)
    a. <ns:NAME>
    b. xmlns="http://www.TLSales.com/dtds"
    c. <NAME>
    d. <!ATTLIST ns:SALES xmlns:ns CDATA #FIXED "http://www.TLSales.com/sales/" >
25. An XML application is not considered complete or stable until ________________.

HANDS-ON PROJECTS

Project 4-1

In the next three projects, you define your own XML vocabulary that describes information about a company. You could use an XML Schema to define the vocabulary, but for these projects, you use a Document Type Definition (DTD).

4

In the following steps, you use the XML Spy Integrated Development Environment (IDE) to create a DTD in a new XML Spy project. The project that you create is called company, and the new DTD is called company.dtd. You will store both in a new Chapter4 folder.

To create a new project:

1. Click **Start**, point to **Programs** (point to **All Programs** in Windows XP), point to **XML Spy Suite**, and then click **XML Spy IDE**. The XML Spy window opens.
2. Click **Project** on the menu bar, and then click **New Project**. A new project appears in the project window.
3. To save the project, click **Project** on the menu bar, and then click **Save Project**. The Save As dialog box opens. Click the **Save in** list arrow and navigate to the C:/home/<*yourname*> folder.
4. In the Save As dialog box, click the **Create New Folder** button. Type **Ch04** as the name of the new folder, and then press **Enter**. Double-click the **Ch04** folder to open it.
5. In the File name text box, type **company** as a project file name, and then click **Save**.

Now that you have created a new project named company, you can create a new DTD named company.dtd. Then you must add the DTD file to the appropriate XML project. To do so, you add the DTD file to the DTD/Schemas item.

To create a new DTD and add it to the company project:

1. Click **File** on the XML Spy menu bar, and then click **New**. The Create new document dialog box opens containing a list of document types. Locate and click **dtd Document Type Definition**, and then click **OK**.
2. To save the new DTD, click **File** on the menu bar, and then click **Save As**. The Save As dialog box opens.
3. Click the **Save in** list arrow and navigate to the C:/home/<*yourname*>/Ch04 folder, if necessary. In the File name text box, type **company** as the DTD file name, and then click **Save**.
4. To add the DTD to the DTD/Schemas folder in the Project window, right-click the **DTD/Schemas** folder, and then click **Add Files**. The Open dialog box opens, listing company.dtd in the project directory. Double-click **company.dtd** to add this file to the company project.

The XML Spy IDE allows you to work with DTDs using different views. The default view is Enhanced Grid view. To examine the syntax of a DTD, you use the Text View, which allows you to directly view and edit the source code of the DTD.

To view the DTD source code:

1. To switch to Text View, click in the company.dtd window, click **View** on the menu bar, and then click **Text View**. The source code of the company.dtd file appears in the Project window.
2. Examine the code in the window. When you created the DTD, XML Spy created a default DTD document similar to the one shown in Figure 4-21. The first line contains the XML declaration with two attributes: the version and the document's language encoding. The second line is a comment containing the name and version of the XML application that created the file and the author's name. The third line is the default root element and is declared as empty.

Notice that each tag is a different color. This feature is called **syntax coloring** and it helps you to quickly identify the structure of the DTD.

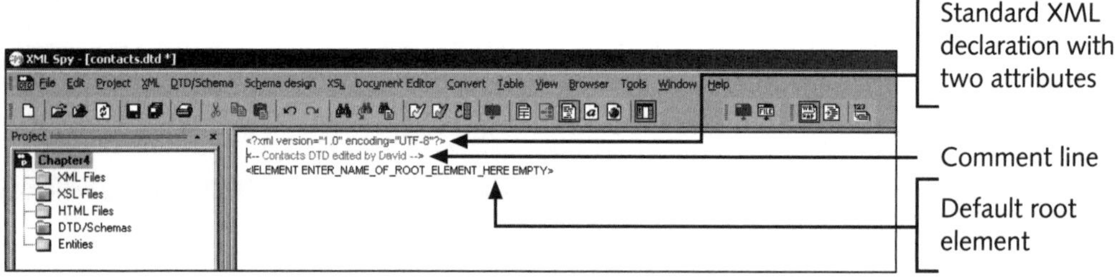

Figure 4-21

3. Click **File** on the menu bar, and then click **Save** to save the DTD file. Leave this file and project open in XML Spy for the next project.

Project 4-2

Now that you have created a DTD in an XML Spy project, the next two projects show you how to build a content model that represents a simplified structure of a small company.

At the root of the model is the company element. A company has a name and several departments. Each department itself has a name, a manager, and zero or more employees. (The manager may be the only employee in a department.) Each employee has a name and an employee ID.

To create a content model:

1. Make sure that company is the current project, that you are viewing company.dtd in Text View, and that you have completed Project 4-1. If you have not, perform

the steps in Project 4-1 to open the company project and the company.dtd file, switch to Text View, and then continue with this project.

2. Replace the default root element text *ENTER_NAME_OF_ROOT_ELEMENT_HERE* with the name **Company**. Replace the empty declaration with the list of child elements (**Name, Department+**).

   In this example, a company will have only one name, but it can have one or more departments. The + (plus sign) following the *Department* child element denotes a cardinality of one-or-more. The cardinality refers to the number of times a child element can appear within a parent element, meaning that a company can have one-or-more departments. By default, the cardinality of a child element is one-and-only-one.

   The root element should now look like the following code:

```
<!ELEMENT Company (Name, Department+)>
```

3. On the line below the Company element, add the Name element by typing the following:

   <!ELEMENT Name (#PCDATA)>

   This element is declared as containing parseable character data and will be used to represent simple names. Notice the relationship between the Company and Name elements—the Company element has a Name element as a child element.

Notice that after you type **<!**, a list of tags appears. This is a feature of the XML Spy Text View called **Intelligent Editing** and allows you to select context-sensitive identifiers.

4. On the line below the Name element declaration, declare a department element by typing the following:

   <!ELEMENT Department (Name, Employee*)>

   Notice that Department also has a Name child element. The Name child elements of both Company and Department refer to the same declaration. In this example, a department can have zero or more staff. The * (asterisk) indicates a cardinality of zero-or-more.

5. Since you already have declared the Name element, the next declaration is the Employee element. On the line below the Department element declaration, type:

   <!ELEMENT Employee (FirstName, LastName, EmpID)>

6. Continue to add the child elements of Employee by typing:

   <!ELEMENT FirstName (#PCDATA)>
   <!ELEMENT LastName (#PCDATA)>
   <!ELEMENT EmpID (#PCDATA)>

Your DTD should appear as follows:

```
<?xml version="1.0" encoding="UTF-8"?>
<!-- edited with XML Spy v4.3 U (http://www.xmlspy.com)
by [your name] -->
<!ELEMENT Company (Name, Department)>
<!ELEMENT Name (#PCDATA)>
<!ELEMENT Department (Name, Employee*)>
<!ELEMENT Employee (FirstName, LastName, EmpID)>
<!ELEMENT FirstName (#PCDATA)>
<!ELEMENT LastName (#PCDATA)>
<!ELEMENT EmpID (#PCDATA)>
```

7. Click **File** on the menu bar, and then click **Save** to save the DTD file. Leave this file and project open in XML Spy for the next project.

Project 4-3

In this project, you continue to build on the DTD from Project 4-2. You convert the Employee ID from a child element into an attribute of the Employee element, add choice elements to identify employee work status, and add an example of an empty element. You also create attribute lists with default values, enumerated lists, and multiple attributes.

You will also use this DTD in Project 4-4 to create a well-formed valid XML file.

To add an attribute to the DTD:

1. Make sure that company is the current project, that you are viewing company.dtd in Text View, and that you have completed Projects 4-1 and 4-2. If not, perform the steps in Projects 4-1 and 4-2, and then continue with this project.
2. You now convert the EmpID element into an attribute of Employee. Begin by deleting **<!ELEMENT EmpID (#PCDATA)>** from the DTD.
3. Delete the **EmpID** child element from the Employee declaration's element list.
4. Insert a line below the Employee element and add an attribute specification to the Employee element by typing:

   <!ATTLIST Employee EmpID ID #REQUIRED>

   The employee ID attribute, EmpID, is now defined as a required and unique attribute of Employee. Every Employee must have a unique EmpID value within an XML document using this DTD. The Employee element and attribute should appear as follows:

   ```
   <!ELEMENT Employee (FirstName, LastName)>
   <!ATTLIST Employee EmpID ID #REQUIRED>
   ```

Since employees can either be full time or part time, you need to add choice elements to the DTD that allow the appropriate information to be stored based upon an employee's work status. Then you can add the default attribute for this element and other elements, including attributes for numbered lists.

To add a choice element:

1. At the end of the child element list for the Employee element, type **(PartTime | FullTime)**. An Employee element must now have either a PartTime or FullTime child element, but not both. The element declaration should now look like this:

```
<!ELEMENT Employee (FirstName, LastName, (PartTime |
FullTime))>
```

2. At the end of the DTD file, add the PartTime element and attribute by typing:

```
<!ELEMENT PartTime EMPTY>
<!ATTLIST PartTime HourlyRate CDATA “$9.75”>
```

   Notice that the PartTime element is an empty element; it has neither child elements nor parsed character data (#PCDATA). It has one attribute, HourlyRate, which has a default value equal to a hypothetical minimum wage. If the HourlyRate attribute has been omitted in an XML document, when the validating parser reads the PartTime element, it automatically adds the attribute with the default value of “$9.75”.

3. Following the PartTime attribute list, add the FullTime element by typing:

```
<!ELEMENT FullTime (StockOptionGrant*)>
<!ATTLIST FullTime Salary CDATA #REQUIRED
                  BenefitPkg (Tier1 | Tier2 | Tier3) “Tier1”>
<!ELEMENT StockOptionGrant EMPTY>
<!ATTLIST StockOptionGrant TotalOptions CDATA #REQUIRED
                  StrikePrice CDATA #REQUIRED>
```

   The FullTime element has a single child element and list of two attributes. The asterisk in the declaration of FullTime indicates that the element may contain zero or more StockOptionGrants child elements. Notice that the second attribute, BenefitPkg, restricts the possible values to a selection within the enumerated list, and declares a default value of “Tier1”. The DTD should now appear as follows:

```
<?xml version="1.0" encoding="UTF-8"?>
<!-- edited with XML Spy v4.3 U (http://www.xmlspy.com)
by [your name] -->
<!ELEMENT Company (Name, Department+)>
<!ELEMENT Name (#PCDATA)>
<!ELEMENT Department (Name, Employee*)>
<!ELEMENT Employee (FirstName, LastName, (PartTime |
FullTime))>
<!ATTLIST Employee EmpID ID #REQUIRED>
<!ELEMENT FirstName (#PCDATA)>
<!ELEMENT LastName (#PCDATA)>
<!ELEMENT PartTime EMPTY>
<!ATTLIST PartTime HourlyRate CDATA "$9.75">
<!ELEMENT FullTime (StockOptionGrants*)>
<!ATTLIST FullTime Salary CDATA #REQUIRED
                BenefitPkg (Tier1 | Tier2 | Tier3) "Tier1">
<!ELEMENT StockOptionGrants EMPTY>
```

```
<!ATTLIST StockOptionGrants TotalOptions CDATA #REQUIRED
                    StrikePrice CDATA #REQUIRED>
```

4. Click **File** on the menu bar, and then click **Save** to save the DTD file. Leave this file and project open in XML Spy for the next project.

Project 4-4

In this project, you use the DTD that you created in the first three projects to create a valid XML document that conforms to the DTD.

To create an XML document:

1. Make sure that company is the current project, that you are viewing company.dtd in Text View, and that you have completed Projects 4-1, 4-2, and 4-3. If not, perform the steps in Projects 4-1, 4-2, and 4-3, and then continue with this project.
2. To create a new XML file click **File** on the menu bar, and then click **New**. The Create new document dialog opens.
3. In the list box, click **xml Extensible Markup Language**, and then click **OK**. The New file dialog box opens.

   You can now associate either a DTD or XML Schema with your document. You also can choose not to associate a vocabulary if you do not want to validate your document. In this project, you want to base your document on the DTD that you have created.
4. Click **DTD**, and then click **OK**. The XML Spy dialog box opens.
5. Click the **Window** button, expand the **DTD/Schemas** branch in the Project files window, if necessary, click **company.dtd**, and then click **OK**.
6. The fully resolved filename for company.dtd appears in the Choose a file text box. Click **OK** to accept it. An Enhanced Grid view of an XML Document appears in the main window.
7. To save the new XML document, click **File** on the menu bar, and then click **Save As**. The Save As dialog box opens.
8. Click the **Save in** list arrow, and then navigate to the C:/home/<*yourname*>/Ch04 folder, if necessary. In the File name text box, type **acme** as the file name, and then click **Save**.

As you did with the company.dtd file, you now add the new XML document to the company project and then view the source code of acme.xml. In the same way that the XML Spy IDE allows you to work with the source code for DTDs, it also allows you to work directly with the source code for XML documents in Text View.

To add an XML document to the project and then examine the source code:

1. To add the XML document to the XML Files item in the Project window, right-click the **XML Files** folder, and then click **Add Files**. The Open dialog box opens.
2. Click the **Look in** list arrow, and then navigate to the C:/home/<*yourname*>/Ch04 folder, if necessary. Click **acme.xml**, and then click **Open**. The acme.xml document is added to the XML Files Item in the Project window.

3. To switch to Text View, click in the XML Files window, click **View** on the menu bar, and then click **Text View**. The default XML document for acme.xml appears.
4. When you created the XML document, XML Spy created a default document similar to the one shown in Figure 4-22. Notice that XML Spy has already added a number of elements to the default XML document.

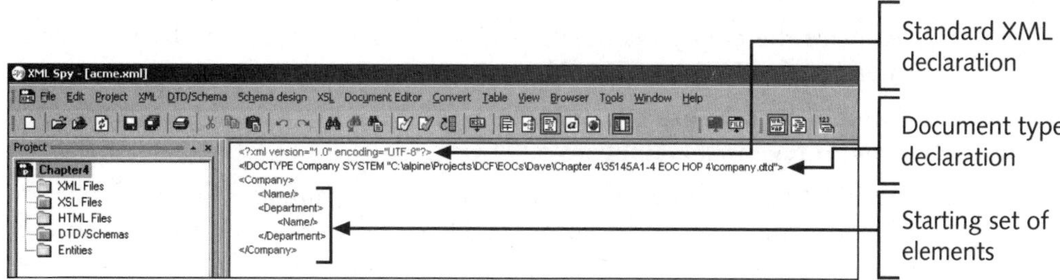

Figure 4-22

The first line of the document contains the standard XML declaration with two attributes: the version and the document's language encoding.

The third line is the Document Type Declaration, which provides information to the XML parser about the DTD. The first identifier following the word DOCTYPE is the root element Company. The next identifier is SYSTEM, which denotes that the following URI references a DTD on the local system.

Do not confuse Document Type Declaration (DOCTYPE) with the Document Type Definition (DTD). The DTD provides information about an XML vocabulary, while the DOCTYPE provides information to the XML parser about the DTD.

The remaining lines form a minimal set of elements provided by XML Spy to help get you started.

5. Click **File** on the menu bar, and then click **Save** to save the DTD file. Leave this file and project open in XML Spy for the next project.

Project 4-5

In this project, you add information to the XML document about your company, department, and employees. You also learn how to validate the XML document.

The first step to building any successful company is to have a creative name. Your company is named AcmeCo, so you begin by replacing the Company NAME element with

AcmeCo. Then you can replace the Department NAME element with the department name, IT. After naming elements and completing the document, you should make sure the content is valid.

To begin building your company:

1. Replace the empty *Name*, *<Name/>*, element directly under the Company element with **<Name>AcmeCo</Name>**.
2. Replace the empty Name, *<Name/>*, element directly under the Department element with **<Name>IT</Name>.**
3. Double-click **company.dtd** under the DTD/Schema folder in the Project window to review the company DTD.

   Your XML document now has a named company, and the company has a named department. Look at the company DTD. Make sure you have typed everything correctly. Do you need anything else to complete a valid XML document? Since a department can have zero (or more) employees, you should have a valid XML document.
4. Return to the acme.xml document by double-clicking **acme.xml** under XML Files in the Project window.
5. Validate the document to verify that you correctly typed the employee ID attribute value. Click **XML** on the menu bar, and then click **Validate**. If the document is valid according to the company.dtd, a green check mark appears at the bottom of your main window, as shown in Figure 4-23.
6. If a red X appears instead, verify that your code is correct as follows:

```
<?xml version="1.0" encoding="UTF-8"?>
<!DOCTYPE Company SYSTEM "C:\Home\[yourname]\Ch04\
Company.dtd">
<Company>
  <Name>AcmeCo</Name>
  <Department>
         <Name>IT</Name>
  </Department>
</Company>
```

A company is only as good as the people it employs, so now you must staff the IT department. Part of the process to add an employee is to give her a unique employee ID. Recall that you declared EmpID as an ID attribute. Values for EmpID must conform to the XML naming rules and cannot begin with a number. For this project, you use an underscore and number to create a unique value for each employee ID attribute.

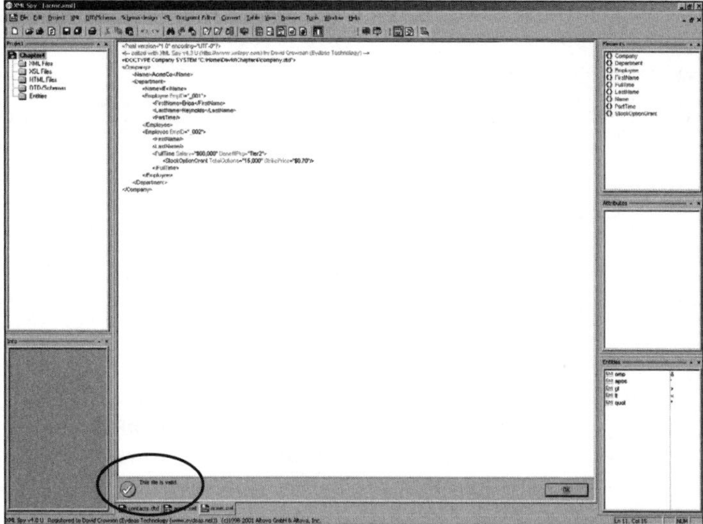

Figure 4-23

To add employees:

1. Insert a line directly under the Name element of Department. On the new line, type:

```
<Employee EmpID="_001>
   <FirstName>Erica</FirstName>
   <LastName>Reynolds</LastName>
   <PartTime/>
</Employee>
```

   This Employee has FirstName and LastName elements, and also has a PartTime element. Recall that an Employee had to have either a PartTime or FullTime child element. The PartTime element is empty, but it has an attribute HourlyRate with a default value of "*$9.75*". A validating parser automatically includes this attribute in the element, but a non-validating parser, which does not use DTDs, is going to miss the default attribute value.

2. Click **XML** on the menu bar, and then click **Validate**. If you typed everything correctly, your document should still be valid.

3. A Department can have multiple employees, so add another. Directly below the previous Employee element, type:

```
<Employee EmpID="_002">
   <FirstName>David</FirstName>
   <LastName>Campbell</LastName>
   <FullTime Salary="$60,000" BenefitPkg="Tier2">
          <StockOptionGrant TotalOptions="15,000"
                                 StrikePrice="$0.70">
```

```
            </StockOptionGrant>
        </FullTime>
    </Employee>
```

4. Click **XML** on the menu bar, and then click **Validate**. Your XML document should still be valid and look like the following:

```
<?xml version="1.0" encoding="UTF-8"?>
<!DOCTYPE Company SYSTEM "C:\Home\[yourname]\Ch04\
company.dtd">
<Company>
  <Name>AcmeCo</Name>
  <Department>
         <Name>IT</Name>
         <Employee EmpID="_001">
                <FirstName>Erica</FirstName>
                <LastName>Reynolds</LastName>
                <PartTime/>
         </Employee>
         <Employee EmpID="_002">
                <FirstName>David</FirstName>
                <LastName>Campbell</LastName>
                <FullTime Salary="$60,000" BenefitPkg=
                   "Tier2">
                        <StockOptionGrant TotalOptions=
                           "15,000" StrikePrice="$0.70">
                        </StockOptionGrant>
                </FullTime>
         </Employee>
  </Department>
</Company>
```

5. Save the files, and leave them open for the next project.

Project 4-6

In this final project of the chapter, you create an XML document with an internal DTD. You create a new XML document called *contact.xml* that contains a person's name, phone number, fax number, and e-mail.

To create an internal DTD:

1. To create a new XML file, click **File** on the menu bar, and then click **New**. The Create new document dialog opens.
2. In the list box, click **xml Extensible Markup Language**, and then click **OK**. The New file dialog box opens.

   You can now associate either a DTD or XML Schema with your document. You also can choose not to associate a vocabulary if you do not want to validate your document. In this project, you create an internal DTD, so you do not need to choose either option.

3. Click **Cancel**. An Enhanced Grid view of an XML Document appears in the main window.
4. Switch to Text View by clicking **View** on the menu bar, and then clicking **Text View**. The default XML document for contact.xml appears.
5. Following the XML declaration, type:

```
<!DOCTYPE Contact [
        <!ELEMENT Contact (Name, PhoneNumber, FaxNumber,
            Email)>
        <!ELEMENT Name (FirstName, LastName)>
        <!ELEMENT FirstName (#PCDATA)>
        <!ELEMENT LastName (#PCDATA)>
        <!ELEMENT PhoneNumber (#PCDATA)>
        <!ELEMENT FaxNumber (#PCDATA)>
        <!ELEMENT Email (#PCDATA)>
]>
```

   The Document Type Declaration in this example specifies an internal subset of element declarations. Note that the root name appears following the DOCTYPE identifier. For this example, the complete local vocabulary is declared within the square brackets of the DOCTYPE declaration.

Now you are ready to add the content to the file, validate the document, and save it. Then you can add the XML document to the project.

To create the XML content:

1. Following the DOCTYPE declaration, type:

```
<Contact>
        <Name>
                <FirstName>Jack</FirstName>
                <LastName>Cunningham</LastName>
        </Name>
        <PhoneNumber>204-555-1234</PhoneNumber>
        <FaxNumber>204-555-4321</FaxNumber>
        <Email>JackC@acmeCo.com</Email>
</Contact>
```

2. Validate the document to verify that you correctly typed the employee ID attribute value. Click **XML** on the menu bar, and then click **Validate**. If the document is valid according to the employee.dtd, a green check mark appears at the bottom of your main window.

3. If a red X appears instead, verify that your code is correct, as follows:

```
<?xml version="1.0" encoding="UTF-8"?>
<!DOCTYPE Contact [
        <!ELEMENT Contact (Name, PhoneNumber, FaxNumber, Email)>
        <!ELEMENT Name (FirstName, LastName)>
        <!ELEMENT FirstName (#PCDATA)>
        <!ELEMENT LastName (#PCDATA)>
        <!ELEMENT PhoneNumber (#PCDATA)>
        <!ELEMENT FaxNumber (#PCDATA)>
        <!ELEMENT Email (#PCDATA)>
]>

<Contact>
        <Name>
                <FirstName>Jack</FirstName>
                <LastName>Cunningham</LastName>
        </Name>
        <PhoneNumber>204-555-1234</PhoneNumber>
        <FaxNumber>204-555-4321</FaxNumber>
        <Email>JackC@acmeCo.com</Email>
</Contact>
```

4. To save the new XML document, click **File** on the menu bar, and then click **Save As**. The Save As dialog box opens. Click the **Save in** list arrow, and then navigate to the C:/home/<*yourname*>/Ch04 folder, if necessary. In the File name text box, type **contact** as the file name, and then click **Save**.
5. To add the XML document to the XML Files folder in the Project window, right-click the **XML Files** folder, and then click **Add Files**. The Open dialog box opens.
6. Click the **Look in** list arrow, and then navigate to the **C:/home/<*yourname*>/Ch04** folder, if necessary. Click **contact.xml**, and then click **Open**. The contact.xml document is added to the XML Files Item in the project window.
7. Click **File** on the menu bar, and then click **Exit** to exit XML Spy.

Case Projects

Project 4-1

Although DTDs are being rapidly replaced by schemas, in some cases there are still many existing requirements for DTDs. In the future, you may be creating schemas or converting DTDs to schemas. You should realize that although these tools are easy to use, they do not necessarily give you the best code. However, knowing that it can create the code allows you to use them as working examples for syntax which can be used for copy and paste operations.

Using your notes and previous files in this chapter, create a DTD called product.dtd and an XML document called product.xml file, based on the following specifications:

- Create an external DTD file called product.dtd.
- Create a root element called <CATALOG>.
- Create an element called <ITEM> that has the sibling elements <PRODUCT_DESC,> <IMAGE> and <PRICE>.
- Implement the ability to create many <ITEM>s in the document.
- <PRODUCT_DESC> is a mandatory element containing text that should be able to contain any character data.
- <IMAGE> is an element containing text that contains the name of a graphics file.
- <PRICE> is an element containing text and should be able to contain a dollar sign ('$').
- <PRICE_CURR> is an attribute that implements a choice of either CDN or US dollars, with US as the default, if nothing is selected.

Save your work in the yourname folder. Save all your files and exit.

After you have created the product.dtd file, to save time and typing, use the DTD/Schema menu to generate a sample XML document with sample data.

CHAPTER

5

CREATING XML SCHEMAS

In this chapter, you will learn:

- About the disadvantages of using DTDs
- About the W3C XML Schema Recommendations
- About schemas
- How to identify schema components
- How to use mixed content elements
- How to use empty element content
- How to use facets to define data precisely

In Chapter Four, you saw how document type definitions (DTDs) provide a mechanism for modeling XML languages and documents—that is, for describing the structure of information within those languages and documents. However, DTDs have some shortcomings, which were already known when the first edition of the Extensible Markup Language (XML) 1.0 (First Edition) specification was accepted as a Recommendation by the World Wide Web Consortium (W3C) on Feb 10, 1998. Several XML-related modeling languages, most notably XML Schema, were developed to overcome the limitations of DTDs.

This chapter discusses the W3C Schema Recommendation, the standard by which XML schemas will be composed in the future. Following this discussion is an in-depth review of a simple schema that has been derived from a simple XML DTD. During the review, the basic components of a schema are introduced, as well as their options and even some alternate methods. The Hands-on Projects at the end of the chapter provide instructions for performing the conversion from the same DTD to the schema, and then for creating XML schemas from scratch.

Understanding Some Disadvantages of Using DTDs

Although DTDs are currently the most widely used tool in defining document types, the DTD has several drawbacks, including the following disadvantages:

- DTDs have their own syntax, which differs from true XML, which means that a DTD can't be processed with a standard XML parser. It would be better, and it would make learning easier, if the tools used to process XML documents could also be used to process their document models.
- DTDs have limited ability to describe the data in elements and attributes. For example, you can't indicate when character data should be numbers, date format, or currency, for example.
- DTDs have limited support for namespaces, so they can't define or restrict the content of elements based on context sensitivity.

To expand on the last point, it is possible to specify with a DTD that a company element must have a name element, an address element, and a phone element associated with it. However, a contact element for the company element also needs a name and a phone number, but unfortunately must have different elements defined for these items, like cont_name or cont_ph. Thus, in a DTD, you only get to specify the structure of the name or phone element once. DTDs are not hierarchical and therefore require you to specify new names for similar elements in different contexts of the same document.

There are other limitations to DTDs, but they go beyond the grasp of this introductory book. Of course, XML's DTD modeling language could be revised or extended to eliminate its shortcomings, but not without also revising or extending SGML's DTD language. Although that's not an impossible task, it would create difficulties when you consider what would be involved across all the SGML-related languages and their descendants. SGML tools, after all, are designed to be able to process all SGML-related documents. Modeling languages that have hierarchical **schemas** that specify validation criteria were developed to overcome these shortcomings. Here are some of the better-known offerings:

- XML Schema
- Document Content Description (DCD)
- Regular Language description for XML (RELAX)
- RDF (Resource Description Framework) Schema
- BizTalk
- Schema for Object-oriented XML (SOX)
- Tree Regular Expressions for XML (TREX)
- Schema for Object-oriented XML (Schematron)
- Document Definition Markup Language (DDML)

The W3C XML Schema Recommendations

The shortcomings of DTDs were already known when the first edition of the Extensible Markup Language (XML) 1.0 Recommendation was endorsed in February 1998. Soon thereafter, the W3C formed their XML Schema Working Group, which published an XML Schema Requirements document that listed and discussed the goals of the XML Schema language. The group subsequently continued to work on the new **XML Schema Definition Language (XSD)**, as part of the W3C's XML Activity.

XSD development was facilitated by the experience that had been gained using DTDs and previous schema languages. The Working Group intended for XSD to become the most flexible and powerful type of schema available. A working draft was released in April 2000, and a two-part Candidate Recommendation was produced in October 2000. (The first part was dedicated to schema structures; the second, to datatypes.) That document was reviewed by W3C members and other interested parties, and a pair of two-part Proposed Recommendations were produced in March 2001. On May 2, 2001, the W3C's XML Schema Part 1: Structures, and XML Schema Part 2: Datatypes, were endorsed by the Director as W3C Recommendations.

Part 1 of the Schema Recommendation can be found at *www.w3.org/TR/xmlschema-1/* and Part 2 can be found at *www.w3.org/TR/xmlschema-2/*. A good companion primer is also available at *www.w3.org/TR/2001/REC-xmlschema-0-20010502/primer.html*.

It is predicted that schemas will one day replace DTDs. But, for now, DTDs still enjoy some advantages over schemas:

- *Tool support*—All SGML-related tools and many XML-related tools can already process DTDs.
- *Deployment*—A large number of document types are already defined using DTDs (for example, HTML, XHTML, DocBook, etc.).
- *Expertise and practical application*—Development in these two areas has grown since DTDs were introduced with the SGML standard ISO 8879 in 1986.

The two-part XML Schema Recommendation is an application of XML and, as such, is a large, complex standard. On the one hand, it lets you specify almost any kind of XML relationship, but, on the other hand it requires a lot of learning and a significant amount of work to implement it properly. In this book, as in other reference documents, it is referred to as **XML Schema**. (It is also called **XSchema** by some.) Individual schemas, developed according to XML Schema, are simply called schemas or XML schemas.

XML Schema, by facilitating the development of better data descriptions and the definition of shared markup vocabularies, helps to overcome one of the main problems for XML in the world of e-commerce and, especially, business-to-business (B2B) communication: the fact that systems using XML created for one company or industry cannot understand XML documents created for another company or industry. Many companies have been using different DTDs or schemas from one another, and their systems have had difficulty deciphering the differences among those models. With XML Schema, different organizations can still create specific schema information for their own use, but, because they are starting from a common standard, they can also generate compatible information that is easier for other systems to understand and use.

SCHEMA DESCRIPTION

Figure 5-1 depicts the relationships among SGML, XML, languages related to XML, and some fictitious documents, schemas, and DTDs related to XML. Notice that the DTD concept was developed for content modeling in SGML-related languages. Thus, DTDs are the schema mechanism for SGML. XML inherited DTDs from SGML. One of the fictitious XML-related languages, called My_ML1, has several documents the contents of which are based on a content model document that, in turn, is based on SGML's DTD specifications. Thus, the content model document is called My_ML1.dtd, and is called a DTD.

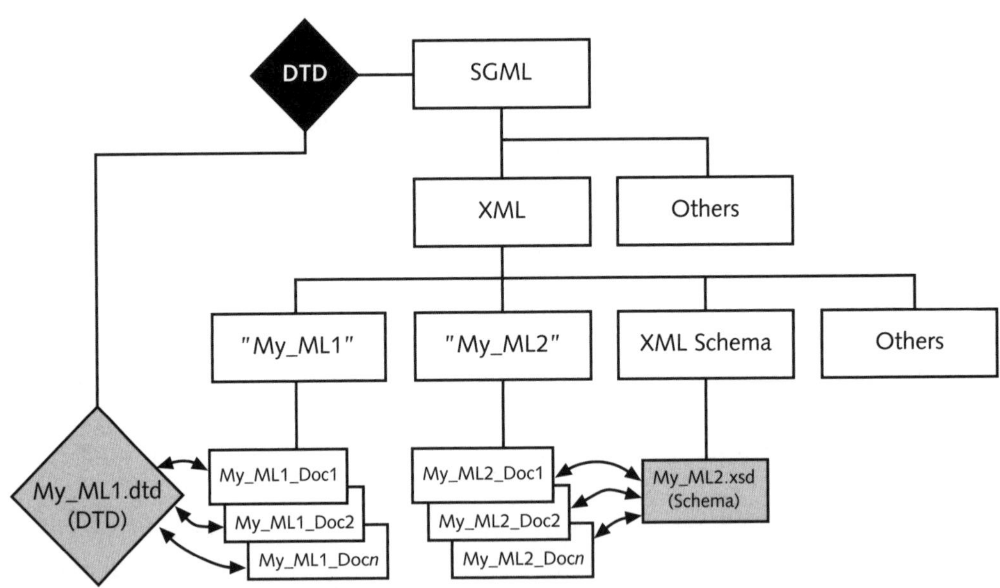

Figure 5-1 SGML, DTD, XML, schema, and document relationships

XML schemas were developed to overcome the shortcomings of DTDs and, eventually, to replace DTDs. Like a DTD, a schema is a model for describing the structure and content of data. But XML Schema was developed as a content modeling language, an application of XML, and not as an application of SGML. So XML Schema pertains only to XML and XML-related languages and, thus, schemas pertain to XML-related languages and documents. The second fictitious XML-related language, My_ML2, has been included in the figure for this reason. My_ML2, has a content model descended from XML Schema; its content model document is, thus, called a schema.

"Schema" is a term borrowed from database technology, where it is used to describe the structure of data in relational tables. In the context of XML, a schema describes a model for a whole class of documents. The model describes the possible arrangement of elements, attributes, and text in a schema-valid document. In schemas, models are described in terms of constraints. A **constraint** defines what can appear in a given language or document. There are basically two kinds of constraints: content model constraints and datatype constraints. **Content model constraints** define the elements that can appear and, in this way, the schema establishes the **vocabulary**. They also describe the pattern of appearance—the number and type of components, the order they appear in, and whether they are required or optional, and, in this way, they also determine the **grammar**. **Datatype constraints** describe the units of data that the schema considers valid.

Remember that the purpose of any document model, including schemas, is to provide a means to validate a document at machine speed. Any well-formed document that conforms to a schema's constraints is considered valid. In a large-scale environment, where vast amounts of information are being received from many and varied sources and sent to many and varied destinations, the ability to check document validity at high speed is an important business consideration. No one wants to process content if it is not in the proper schema. The earlier, faster, and more easily you catch errors and transact business, the more efficient and profitable your business will be.

Although schemas and DTDs perform similar document modeling functions, the lexicons surrounding them can be quite different. If you are familiar with object-oriented languages such as C++ and Java, then you recognize the terminology used by XML schema enthusiasts when they state, for example, that individual schemas define a **class** of XML documents, and that XML documents that conform to a particular schema are called **instance documents**. That terminology is used in this chapter and in others where schemas are referenced. Note that instances and schemas may not exist as documents, although they may exist as byte streams, fields in database records, or as collections of XML "Information Items." However, to simplify and clarify the discussions in this chapter, they are displayed as documents and files.

Schema Components

Figure 5-2 shows a simple external XML DTD ready to be converted to an XML schema.

From the DTD, you can see that its respective conforming, or valid, XML documents each have a root element named <CONTACTS> and that the root element, as a parent element, contains four child elements named <DEPT>, <NAME>, <EMAIL>, and <PHONE>. There is at least one such listing, because there is a plus sign following the word <DEPT>. Every time a <DEPT> element occurs, it is followed by one <NAME>, <EMAIL>, and <PHONE> element. The content of all of the <DEPT>, <EMAIL>, <NAME>, and <PHONE> elements is specified to be parsed character data. Each <DEPT> element has an attribute called dept_name and the value of the attribute is chosen from the enumerated list Sales, Custsrv, Emplrel, and President.

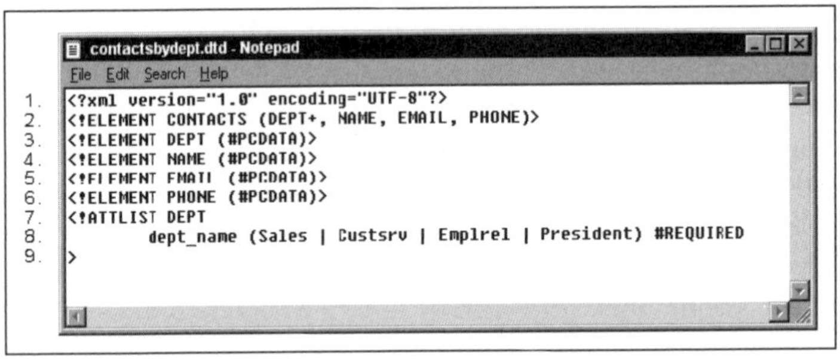

```
<?xml version="1.0" encoding="UTF-8"?>
<!ELEMENT CONTACTS (DEPT+, NAME, EMAIL, PHONE)>
<!ELEMENT DEPT (#PCDATA)>
<!ELEMENT NAME (#PCDATA)>
<!ELEMENT EMAIL (#PCDATA)>
<!ELEMENT PHONE (#PCDATA)>
<!ATTLIST DEPT
        dept_name (Sales | Custsrv | Emplrel | President) #REQUIRED
>
```

Figure 5-2 A simple DTD: contactsbydept.dtd

Figure 5-3 illustrates the result of using XML Spy to convert this DTD to a simple XML schema. Note the file extension .xsd, which indicates that the file is a schema. The file extension seems to be a holdover—perhaps a tribute—from the first days of XML Schema development, when the project was called XML Schema Definition Language (XSD).

The Prolog

The first three lines of the schema are its prolog. The first line is the familiar **XML declaration** (also called the **header**). Like every XML document, the schema begins with this declaration, which states that the document is written in XML. Nothing should precede this header. The tag is essentially <?xml … ?>, the XML version number is 1.0, and the document's language encoding specification is UTF-8. (If there were no language encoding specified, it would default to this value anyway.) For a detailed discussion of the attributes found in the header, please refer to Chapter Two. The next two lines are comment lines. In this example, the comments indicate who has worked on this schema (the generic "Student Name"), and what application was originally used to create it ("XML Spy v4.0"), even though it is being displayed using Microsoft Notepad.

contactsbydept.xsd - Notepad

File Edit Search Help

```
1. <?xml version="1.0" encoding="UTF-8"?>
2. <!-- edited with XML Spy v4.0 U (http://www.xmlspy.com) by Student Name -->
3. <!--W3C Schema generated by XML Spy v4.0 U (http://www.xmlspy.com)-->
4. <xs:schema xmlns:xs="http://www.w3.org/2001/XMLSchema" elementFormDefault="qualified">
5.     <xs:element name="CONTACTS">
6.         <xs:complexType>
7.             <xs:sequence>
8.                 <xs:element name="DEPT" type="DEPTType" maxOccurs="unbounded"/>
9.                 <xs:element ref="NAME"/>
10.                <xs:element ref="EMAIL"/>
11.                <xs:element ref="PHONE"/>
12.            </xs:sequence>
13.        </xs:complexType>
14.    </xs:element>
15.    <xs:complexType name="DEPTType">
16.        <xs:simpleContent>
17.            <xs:restriction base="xs:string">
18.                <xs:attribute name="dept_name" use="required">
19.                    <xs:simpleType>
20.                        <xs:restriction base="xs:NMTOKEN">
21.                            <xs:enumeration value="Sales"/>
22.                            <xs:enumeration value="Custsrv"/>
23.                            <xs:enumeration value="Emplrel"/>
24.                            <xs:enumeration value="President"/>
25.                        </xs:restriction>
26.                    </xs:simpleType>
27.                </xs:attribute>
28.            </xs:restriction>
29.        </xs:simpleContent>
30.    </xs:complexType>
31.    <xs:element name="EMAIL" type="xs:string"/>
32.    <xs:element name="NAME" type="xs:string"/>
33.    <xs:element name="PHONE" type="xs:string"/>
34. </xs:schema>
```

Figure 5-3 Corresponding XML schema: contactsbydept.xsd

The Schema Element: Namespaces and Qualified/Unqualified Locals

Several lines in the schema in Figure 5-3 illustrate how schemas handle element declarations. The fourth line of the example schema, beginning with "<xs:schema ... ", is the start tag for the **schema element**, which is the first element of the schema and is equivalent to the root element of an XML document. The <schema> element, therefore, is the parent element of all the other elements in the schema. The other elements, which were referred to as child elements in the discussions of XML documents and DTDs in the previous chapters, are referred to as **subelements** in discussions of schemas. In this case, the <xs:schema ... > start tag also includes two attribute specifications, the namespaces and the qualified or unqualified local elements.

Namespaces in Schemas

In the <xs:schema ... > start tag, it appears that there is an attribute being defined (xmlns:xs), which is given a value *http://www.w3.org/2001/XMLSchema*. As you have learned, this is called a **namespace declaration**. Because schemas provide more support for namespaces, this chapter briefly reviews the namespace concept and provides additional information about them.

Remember that each namespace indicates to the XML processor that the definitions and treatments of elements and other datatypes in the schema are adopted from the W3C's Namespace Recommendation, as indicated by the specification of the URL *http://www.w3.org/2001/XMLSchema* as the value of the xmlns:xs attribute. In other words, the processor is told that, when it encounters datatypes preceded by the prefix "xs:" (which represents the URL), the meaning of those datatypes are identical to the definition found for them in the W3C Schema recommendation. Thus, they have standard definitions and so require no further definition before they are processed.

Each namespace represents a collection of element types and other datatype names and is identified by a unique name. That unique name takes the form of a **Uniform Resource Identifier (URI)**, the most common of which are **Uniform Resource Locator (URLs)**. Do not be misled or confused by the reference to URLs when it comes to creating and referring to namespaces. Although URLs are readily identified as Web addresses, here they are not actually used as addresses for anything. There is no invocation of browsers or other applications to check or retrieve data from the URLs; they are simply used to specify the names used in the schema. In the W3C Recommendation titled "Namespaces in XML," the W3C recommended the use of URLs as namespace names because URLs indicate domain names that are known to work throughout the Internet. Thus, they make names unique and are not rejected by the processor or the application. At least, they won't be rejected on the basis of syntax.

The namespace declaration informs the processor about the URI, and also provides an abbreviation for the URI. The abbreviation is used thereafter instead of the full URI or URL. For example, in the declaration *xmlns:xs=http://www.w3.org/2001/XMLSchema*:

- The "xmlns" portion states "this is a namespace declaration".
- The "xs" portion is the abbreviation that is used to relate the respective elements and other datatypes to the namespace.
- The *http://www.w3.org/2001/XMLSchema* portion is the unique URI or URL.

After the namespace is defined, the element or other datatype name becomes a unique hybrid name, consisting of a prefix (which is the abbreviation for the URI portion of the namespace), then a colon, and then the local portion (the characters to the right of the colon). The local portion is generally the most meaningful to the context of the element or datatype.

Here is an example of such a hybrid name:

```
<xs:sequence>
```

In this example, the local part of the unique name is "sequence," and the URI part is the prefix "xs," which according to the declaration in the schema element tag, actually stands for http://www.w3.org/2001/XMLSchema. Although the examples and projects presented in this book are simple, a typical schema in an e-commerce environment actually uses elements and types from multiple schemas, each with its own different namespace.

In other schema-related textbooks, Web sites, and documents, the prefix used for this type of lesson is "xsd." The reason that the authors use "xs" is that XML Spy v4 uses that prefix by default and XML Spy v4 is the selected XML editor for this text.

All namespaces shown in Figure 5-3 have employed prefixes in their declarations, like the following:

```
<xs:schema xmlns:xs="http://www.w3.org/2001/XMLSchema"  ... />
```

But namespaces do not have to be declared explicitly with prefixes. Look at the following example:

```
<schema xmlns="http://www.w3.org/2001/XMLSchema" ... />
```

5

Subsequently, when the parser encounters an element or attribute name with no prefix in the schema, then the URL mentioned in the above declaration/attribute is presumed to be the namespace to which the element or attribute is associated. A variation of the default namespace is the following: a default namespace can be undeclared if an empty string is used for its value in the declaration. Consider the following example, in which no namespace is associated with the element or attribute name:

```
<schema xmlns="" ... />
```

In the schema validation process, the processor checks an instance document to see if it conforms to one or more schemas. Thus, there has to be a method to allow that checking. The target namespace provides that method. In the schema(s), the element and attribute declarations and type definitions are checked against corresponding elements and attributes in the instance documents.

First, in the schema, one should declare a target namespace by specifying a URL as a value for the targetNamespace attribute, and specify that both locally defined elements and locally defined attributes must be unqualified. (The qualification of local elements and attributes can be globally specified by a pair of attributes—elementFormDefault and attributeFormDefault—on the schema element, or can be specified separately for each local declaration using the form attribute.) The targetNamespace attribute is normally placed within the schema element, although this is not a universal rule or practice. It can be placed within any element declaration. Its syntax follows:

```
targetNamespace="http://www.tlsales.com/Sch01"
```

Then, the instance document(s) should also declare a namespace, using the same URL as the target namespace in the schema declaration. The declaration should be placed in the root element tag (generally) and use a syntax similar to the following:

```
xmlns:xxx="http://www.tlsales.com/Sch01
```

Any prefix could be used in the declaration. The prefix used should be appropriate to the document. The letters "xxx" in the above syntax are simply one example of a prefix. Later, the XML processor examines the instance document, reads the URI/URL in the namespace declaration, and looks for a schema with the identical URI/URL specified for the targetNamespace attribute of the schema element. Figure 5-4 illustrates the validation process.

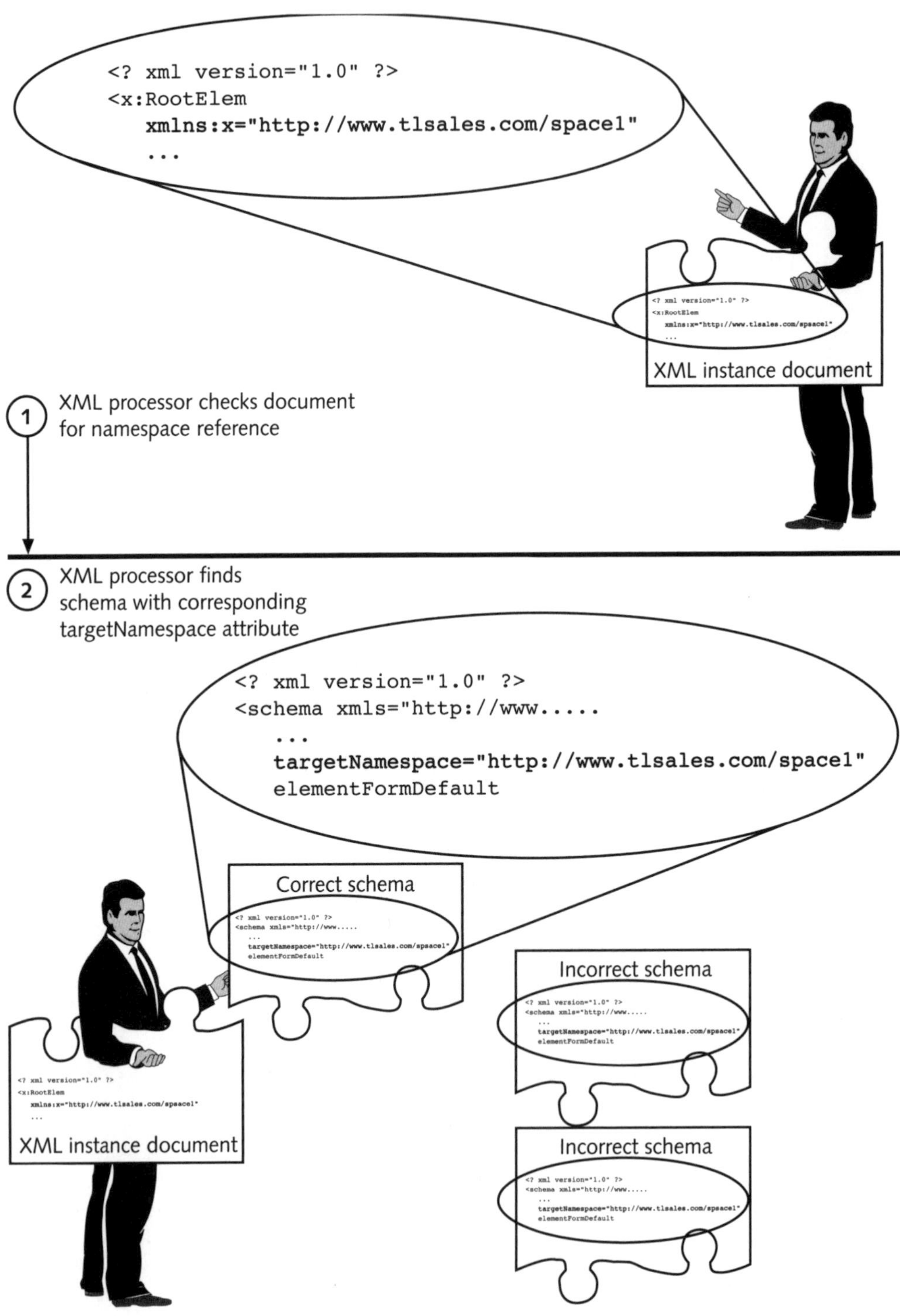

Figure 5-4 XML schema document validation

That is why target namespaces are so named. A namespace has been declared in the schema that sets the basis for validating elements and attributes in a document. In other words, target namespaces in the schema facilitate validation of conforming instance documents.

In the Figure 5-3 schema, there is neither a target namespace specification, nor a default namespace specification. This may indicate that this schema document is a support namespace, also called a chameleon namespace. The author has probably decided to use a homogeneous namespace design, wherein several schema documents have been created, but all the schemas share one common umbrella namespace. The namespace attribute/declaration appears in the main schema document, but the support schema documents do not have their own namespace declarations. In the main schema, there is probably a statement like:

5

```
<xs:include schemaLocation="contactsbydept.xsd"/>
```

or

```
<xs:import namespace="http://www.tlsales.com"
  schemaLocation="contactsbydept.xsd"/>
```

When the parser encounters either of these elements, with their respective attribute/value pairs, it accesses the document (in this case, contactsbydept.xsd) and treats it like a support schema. Once accessed by the parser, the supporting schema adopts the namespace declared in the main schema document, in a manner similar to a chameleon taking on the colors of its surroundings. A "no target, no default" schema document like this is also said to be observing a **chameleon namespace** design. Homogeneous/chameleon namespaces can provide great flexibility in design, but they can also get you into trouble inadvertently if you are not diligent with element types. However, these concepts are beyond this introductory course. Chameleons are only mentioned here to bring your attention to their existence in case you run into a schema with no default or target namespace declared.

Qualified and Unqualified Locals

The schema element tag in the example presented in Figure 5-3 also includes an attribute named elementFormDefault, the value of which is specified to be qualified. To explain the function of that attribute, first note that **local elements** are those in a schema that are declared in subelements of the schema element, but not in the scope of the schema element itself. Elements that are declared in the <schema> element are called **globally declared elements**.

During the schema design phase, for various reasons, the designer has to decide whether or not the name of the origin namespace of each local element should be displayed (or **exposed**) in the element's tag in the instance documents. The exposing of the origin namespace of those locally declared elements is called **qualifying** them. The designer incorporates the attribute elementFormDefault as a sort of binary on/off switch to illustrate their choice. If the value of the elementFormDefault attribute is specified as qualified, the identity of the namespaces is shown in the tags of the local elements in the instance documents. Figure 5-5, wherein several terms have been bolded (they normally do not appear that way), illustrates this.

```
<? xml version="1.0" ?>
<schema xmls="http://www .....
   ...
   targetNamespace="http://www.tlsales.com/space1"
   elementFormDefault="qualified">
      <element name="A" type="string" />
      <element name="First" type="FirstType" />
      <complexType name="FirstType" />
            <element name="Second" type="SecondType" />
            <element name="Third" type="ThirdType" />
            <element ref="A" minOccurs="0" />
            <element name="B" type="string" />
      </complexType>
      <complexType name="SecondType" />
            <element name="C" type="string" />
            <element name="D" type="boolean" />
      </complexType>
      <complexType name="ThirdType" />
            <element name="E" type="string" />
            <element name="F" type="boolean" />
      </complexType>
      .
      .
```

Schema (qualified)

```
<? xml version="1.0" ?>
<spl:First xmlns:spl="http://www.tlsales.com/space1" />
      <spl:Second>
            <spl:C> True or False: Are you OK? </spl:C>
            <spl:D> True </spl:D>
      </spl:Second>
      <spl:Third>
            <spl:E> True or False: Is this easy to understand? </spl:E>
            <spl:F> True </spl:F>
      </spl:Third>
      <spl:A> This is a global comment </spl:A>
      <spl:B> This is a local comment </spl:B>
      .
      .
```

Instance document

Figure 5-5 Qualified locals

In this case, because the elements named <A> and <First> have been declared within the schema element, but not within subelements of the schema, they are termed global elements. The elements named <Second>, <Third>, <C>, <D>, <E>, and <F> are local elements. In the schema, the first bolded term, qualified, indicates that this schema requires its conforming instance documents to expose the identity of the namespaces pertaining to all local elements declared in the schema (that is the <Second>, <Third>, <C>, <D>, <E>, and <F> elements). The identity of the namespaces pertaining to the global elements <First> and <A> also have to be exposed. In the conforming instance document, the prefix sp1: precedes all the element tags, since sp1: represents the target namespace referred to in both the schema and the instance document.

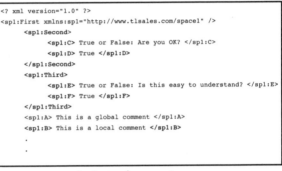

On the other hand, if the value of the attribute elementFormDefault is specified as unqualified, the identity of the namespaces pertaining to the schema's global elements is exposed, but not the namespaces pertaining to the schema's local elements. Figure 5-6 illustrates this. Comparing the instance documents of Figures 5-5 and 5-6, reveals how, in Figure 5-6, the tags for the <Second> and <Third> elements, as well as the tags for the elements named <C>, <D>, <E>, and <F>, do not contain the prefix sp1: this time. Only the <First> element and the <A> element still retain that prefix. In other words, when unqualified is specified as the value for elementFormDefault in the schema document, the tags for those elements that have been locally declared in the schema contain their respective element names when they appear in the respective instance documents, but do not show any namespace reference.

5

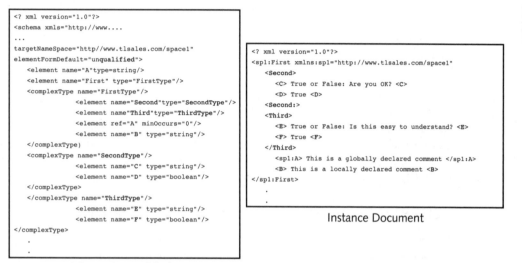

```
<? xml version="1.0"?>
<schema xmls="http://www....
...
targetNameSpace="http//www.tlsales.com/space1"
elementFormDefault="unqualified">
    <element name="A"type=string/>
    <element name="First" type="FirstType"/>
    <complexType name="FirstType"/>
                <element name="Second"type="SecondType"/>
                <element name"Third"type="ThirdType"/>
                <element ref="A" minOccurs="0"/>
                <element name="B" type="string"/>
    </complexType)
    <complexType name="SecondType"/>
                <element name="C" type="string"/>
                <element name="D" type="boolean"/>
    </complexType>
    </complexType name="ThirdType"/>
                <element name="E" type="string"/>
                <element name="F" type="boolean"/>
</complexType>
    .
    .
```

Schema (unqualified)

```
<? xml version="1.0"?>
<spl:First xmlns:spl="http://www.tlsales.com/space1"
   <Second>
     <C> True or False: Are you OK? <C>
     <D> True <D>
   <Second:>
   <Third>
     <E> True or False: Is this easy to understand? <E>
     <F> True <F>
   </Third>
     <spl:A> This is a globally declared comment </spl:A>
     <B> This is a locally declared comment <B>
</spl:First>
   .
   .
```

Instance Document

Figure 5-6 Unqualified locals

The <CONTACTS> Element: Element Types and Compositors

Figure 5-7 highlights the next element declaration following the schema element start tag in our contactsbydept.xsd example, the element <CONTACTS>. The <CONTACTS> declaration actually spans more than one line—lines 5 to 7, in fact—because of the type of element that <CONTACTS> is. In the schema, the xs:complexType element tag on line 6 declares that <CONTACTS> is a **complex type** element: an element that contains attributes and/or subelements.

The complex type is one variety of **element** type—also referred to as **data type** or **content type**. These types determine the appearance of elements and their content in the related XML instance documents. Besides complex types, the other element type is the simple type. **Simple type** elements contain no attributes or subelements, just character data. Simple types are discussed in more detail later in this section.

```
5.     <xs:element name="CONTACTS">
6.         <xs:complexType>
7.             <xs:sequence>
```

Figure 5-7 Lines 5 through 7 of contactsbydept.xsd

Because the subelements within <CONTACTS> follow a specified sequence, the xs:sequence element is specified on line 7. The sequence element indicates that the elements contained within it must appear in an XML document in the same order as they appear in the sequence element. The sequence element is one type of compositor, called the **sequence compositor**. Compositors are specialized XML Schema components that allow you to define groups of elements and attributes within the schema and, thus, within the related XML documents.

There are three types of compositors: sequence compositors, which are illustrated in contactsbydept.xsd; **choice compositors**, which indicate that only one element can appear in the XML document at that point and that the element must be chosen from among the several choices which appear in the choice element; and **all compositors**, which indicate that one or more of the elements within the all element can appear in the XML document in any order, as an unordered set of elements.

The <DEPT> Element: Attributes and Cardinality

As stated above, the sequence element in the schema defines an ordered sequence of subelements. The four subelements are then declared in order, from line 8 to line 11, as shown in Figure 5-8.

```
            <xs:sequence>
8.              <xs:element name="DEPT" type="DEPTType" maxOccurs="unbounded"/>
9.              <xs:element ref="NAME"/>
10.             <xs:element ref="EMAIL"/>
11.             <xs:element ref="PHONE"/>
            </xs:sequence>
```

Figure 5-8 Lines 8 through 11 of contactsbydept.xsd

The first subelement within <CONTACTS> is called <DEPT>. It is different from the other subelements, because it contains character data and an attribute named dept_name, the value of which is eventually selected from among several choices by the instance document author. The subelements <NAME>, <EMAIL>, and <PHONE>, which follow <DEPT>, do not have attributes; they only contain character data.

Within the declaration of the subelement <DEPT>, there is an attribute named "type" which has been given a value DEPTType by the schema designer. This attribute indicates that another complexType has been created, has been named DEPTType, and can be found later in the schema. The complexType was created automatically by XML Spy when it processed the ATTLIST declaration in lines 7 and 8 of the DTD and saw that every

<DEPT> element would have a required attribute called dept_name. The name DEPTType was chosen by the schema's designer and follows a common (but not mandatory) XML convention: combining the element name DEPT with the word type. Otherwise, the name could be anything that a schema author chooses. The complexType element DEPTType is also examined later in this section.

In the DTD corresponding to the schema, the plus sign (+) next to DEPT indicates its **cardinality**, that is, the number of times the <DEPT> element may occur in instance documents. The plus sign indicates that a <DEPT> element must occur at least once, but that there is no limit to the number of times it may occur. As the DTD was converted to a schema, XML Spy substituted equivalent schema-related attributes to indicate that cardinality: minOccurs (the minimum number of occurrences) and maxOccurs (the maximum number of occurrences). The program also provides the specifications for these properties. However, while there appears to be a specification for maxOccurs, minOccurs has not been specified, because it doesn't need to be. The plus sign in the DTD indicated "at least once" and minOccurs' default value is one.

5

The default value for maxOccurs' is also one, but, since the <DEPT> element may occur more than once, that default cannot be allowed to prevail. So the maxOccurs attribute is used to specify a maximum occurrence value; therefore specifications for maxOccurs can be any positive integer or the word "unbounded," which would indicate that there is no limit to the number of times <DEPT> may occur. Unbounded is selected because it is intent of the schema that <DEPT> can occur once or as many times as the document author may want.

Notice that the other elements (<NAME>, <EMAIL>, and <PHONE>) only occur once for each time a <DEPT> element appears. Thus, their default minOccurs and maxOccurs values suffice. So, although you could specify values for minOccurs and maxOccurs, it is not necessary to do so for <NAME>, <EMAIL>, and <PHONE>.

Line 3 of the DTD indicates that the content of the <DEPT> element is made up of parsed character data. At first glance, the <DEPT> element declaration in the schema doesn't seem to address that requirement. However, the declaration of the complexType element named DEPTType, to be discussed later, does. At this point, the declaration of the <DEPT> element is complete. Since there are no subelements within <DEPT>, its declaration takes only one line, and its element declaration tag finishes with a />.

The <NAME>, <EMAIL>, and <PHONE> Subelements: Simple Types and Schema Structures

Declarations for the three remaining subelements under <CONTACTS>, that is, <NAME>, <EMAIL>, and <PHONE>, follow the <DEPT> element declaration. Lines 4, 5, and 6 of the DTD indicate that these elements contain parsed character data only, with no subelements and no attributes. Thus, according to definitions stated previously, they are simple types of elements and their declarations are expected to be single lines. Simple types are typically of two kinds: those that are defined in the W3C Schema Recommendation (XML Schema), and those that are defined by the schema designer according to specific needs. Table 5-1 lists several simple element types that are already defined in XML Schema. You may refer to XML Schema for a comprehensive listing. Remember that, when you reference the simple types found in XML Schema, they are usually preceded by a prefix such as xs:, as used in this text, or xsd:, which is often found elsewhere.

Table 5-1 Simple types defined in W3C XML schema recommendation

Name of Simple Type	Definition
Binary	Contains binary values (e.g., 1001, 11101)
Boolean	Contains values such as True or False, 1 or 0
Date	Contains a date in YYYY-MM-DD format
Decimal	Contains a decimal value, positive or negative
ENTITY, ENTITIES	Contains an ENTITY or ENTITIES attribute type, as described in the W3C XML Recommendation
ID	Contains an ID attribute type, as described in the W3C XML Recommendation
int, integer	Contains an integer
Language	Contains a language identifier (e.g., en-US, de, fr)
Qname	Contains an XML qualified name (i.e., contains a namespace reference plus a local name, separated by a colon)
String	Contains a string of text characters
Time	Contains a time reference (e.g., 08:13:47.639)
AnyURI	Contains a Uniform Resource Identifier reference; the value can be absolute or relative

Authors of schemas can approach simple element type declarations in one of two ways: the "nesting doll" (also called the Russian doll) approach, where a full element declaration is inserted every time the element is needed, as shown in Figure 5-9, or a flat catalog approach, using global element references.

In the generic schema in Figure 5-9, the element named <First> appears within three subelements (<Second>, <Fourth>, and <Sixth>) and is fully declared within each one. In each case, the declarations are identical, which is to be expected, since the element name is the same. The tree diagram at the bottom of the figure illustrates the hierarchical structure of this simple schema.

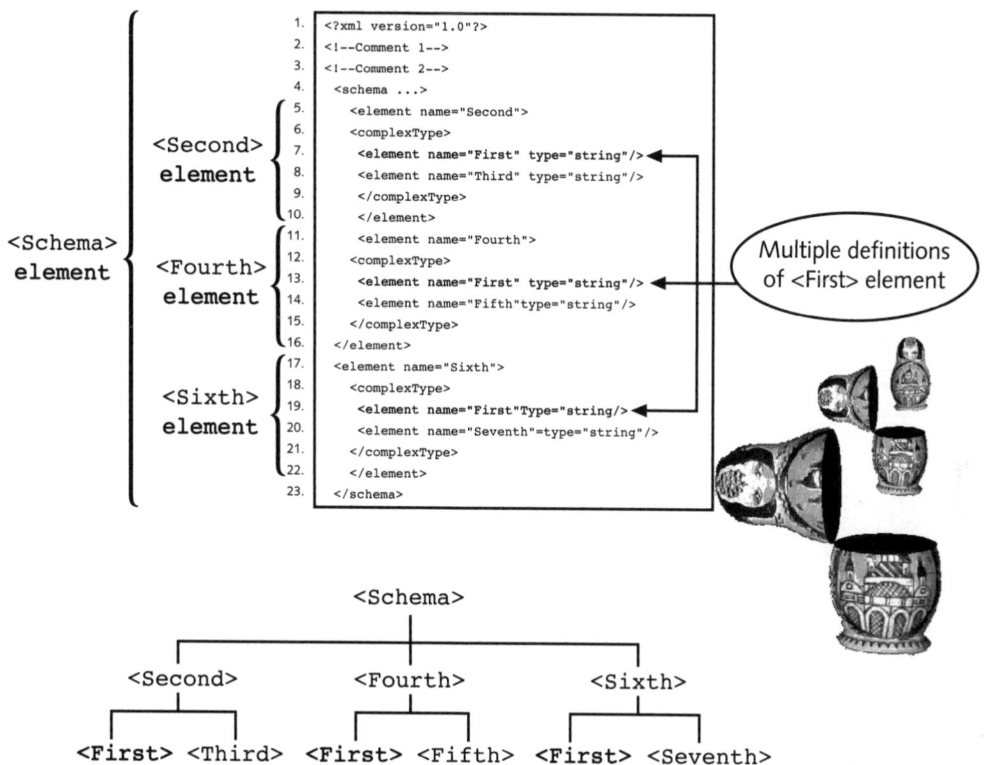

Figure 5-9 Simple nesting doll/Russian doll schema structure

Many programmers call this a **Russian doll approach**, since the elements are cloaked one within another. (You may recall seeing Russian dolls where several hollow dolls of different sizes are enclosed within one another.) There is nothing wrong with this approach; however, compared to the global reference approach to be discussed next, the XML processor uses more resources when processing this schema. Further, if changes are to be made to the First element, then the changes must be made in three locations, within each of the subelements that contain the First element. This uses up more of the programmer's time and may introduce a risk that the changes may not be made uniformly across the three locations (depending on the technique used to make the changes). That is not a big issue for a small schema like this, but could be a significant issue with a larger schema that has several conforming instance documents.

Figure 5-10 illustrates a different approach, commonly called a **flat catalog approach**, that employs global references and is intended to create a flatter schema structure. Notice how the ref=First declaration, within the declarations of the <Second>, <Fourth>, and <Sixth> elements, points to the <First> element, which now is declared within the schema element. The ref=First reference means that, at the time of processing, the processor should look for the declaration of the <First> element within the schema element, then consider looking for a <First> element to be included within the <Second>, <Fourth>, and <Sixth> elements in a conforming XML document.

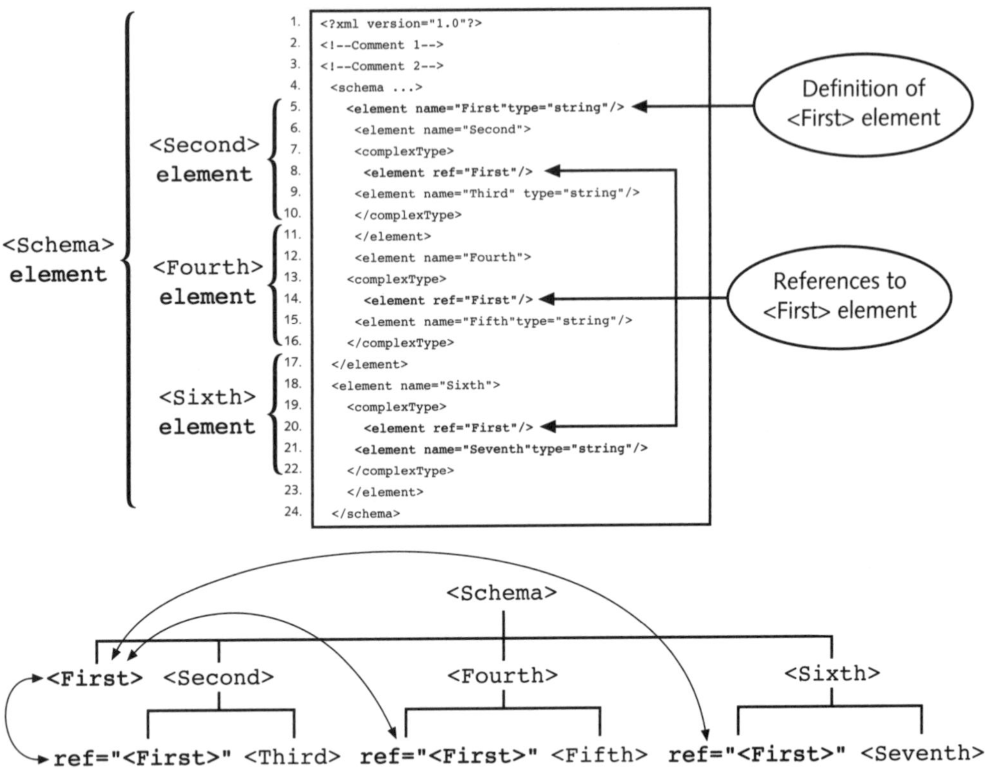

Figure 5-10 Simple flat catalog schema structure

With this approach, the <First> element is fully declared only once and in a very specific location, within the schema element itself and not within any of the subelements beneath the schema element. Then, in any subelements that would contain the <First> element, the slightly different—and generally more simple and compact—syntax is used to refer to the <First> element. During processing, the XML parser can refer back to the <First> element declaration in the schema element.

This reference is termed a **global reference** (some designers also call it an **archetype**) because the element being referred to is declared within the schema element and not within any subelements below the schema element. This way, all the subelements below the schema element can refer to <First> without error. If <First> were declared within one of the subelements beneath the schema element (for example within <Sixth>), then <First> could not be referenced from elements stemming from <Second> or <Fourth>, which are <Sixth>'s siblings. It could only be seen from those elements stemming from <Sixth>. Because of this principle (each element declaration being visible only within the element where it is defined and all its descendants), the schema document language is called a **scoped** language.

The advantages to the flat catalog approach include the following:

- A programmer can group all the common simpleType elements together in one location, immediately within the <schema> element.
- The schema's hierarchy is inherently flatter.
- Programmer and processor resources are saved.
- If a change has to be made to one of the common elements, then it needs only to be made in one location. (This reduces the risk of nonuniform changes to elements.) The references inherit the changes automatically.

The lines in the Figure 5-9 and Figure 5-10 schemas have been numbered, and indicate that the catalog approach may not be an advantage in a very simple schema. However, the savings would be readily apparent in any schema larger than the example used in those figures.

Referring back to the schema example we have been using in this chapter, it appears that XML Spy's default approach is to use the flat catalog approach, not the nesting doll. The simple types named <EMAIL>, <NAME>, and <PHONE> are fully declared within the schema element (at the bottom near the end tag, which is another XML convention). Then, in the <CONTACTS> complex element, there are "refs" to the respective simple types. The "ref" elements could also contain other context-specific attributes pertinent to the simple types (for example, indications of cardinality) that would not be specified in the global declarations. However, in this simple example, the authors have chosen not to do so.

Global references found in the various subelements of a flat catalog approach can only point to simple types, not complex types. If <First> had been a complex type, then the flat catalog approach could not have been used. After the line 8 to 11 single-line element reference declarations have been completed, then the sequence (line 12), complexType (line 13), and element (line 14) end tags are inserted to terminate the <CONTACTS> element declaration. For your convenience, those lines have been reproduced in Figure 5-11.

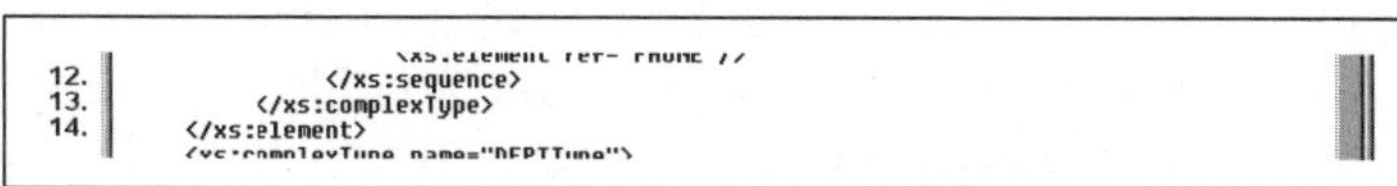

```
12.         </xs:sequence>
13.      </xs:complexType>
14.   </xs:element>
```

Figure 5-11 Lines 12 through 14 of contactsbydept.xsd

The DEPTType Complex Type Declaration: Simple Content Types and Inheritance

At line 8, in the <DEPT> element declaration, the designer inserted type=DEPTType to indicate to the XML processor that <DEPT> was a complex type of element and that another complex type declaration, named DEPTType, would follow. That declaration covers from line 15 to line 30, as shown in Figure 5-12.

```
15. <xs:complexType name="DEPTType">
16.     <xs:simpleContent>
17.         <xs:restriction base="xs:string">
18.             <xs:attribute name="dept_name" use="required">
19.                 <xs:simpleType>
20.                     <xs:restriction base="xs:NMTOKEN">
21.                         <xs:enumeration value="Sales"/>
22.                         <xs:enumeration value="Custsrv"/>
23.                         <xs:enumeration value="Emplrel"/>
24.                         <xs:enumeration value="President"/>
25.                     </xs:restriction>
26.                 </xs:simpleType>
27.             </xs:attribute>
28.         </xs:restriction>
29.     </xs:simpleContent>
30. </xs:complexType>
```

Figure 5-12 Lines 15 through 30 of contactsbydept.xsd

Line 15 is a typical complex type element declaration and provides DEPTType as the value for the name attribute. So far, the declaration looks identical to the one for <CONTACTS>. But line 16 is where the DEPTType declaration deviates from the <CONTACTS> declaration. The xs:simpleContent element name indicates to the XML processor that the complex type named DEPTType is a **simple content element**, which contains character data *only* and *no* subelements. Simple content elements may also contain attributes but, at line 16, the processor cannot yet determine whether DEPTType has attributes. This declaration is different from the complex type element <CONTACTS>, which contained subelements.

At this point, it may be helpful to consider the complexType declaration, from line 15 to line 30, as a container of elements, attributes, and other parameters that are useful for defining the complex type <DEPT> element. The container nature of the DEPTType complexType becomes more apparent as you become more familiar with it and especially when you are doing the Hands-on Projects at the end of this chapter. Line 17 gives further direction to the XML processor. It sets the stage for adding attributes by telling the processor that a restriction is applied to the element. Adding base=xs:string indicates that the kind of character dataq allows is string data, and that the string data is restricted. In subsequent lines, the text strings are restricted to Sales, Custsrv, Emplrel, or President.

You have already encountered the principle of XML **inheritance**, which comes in two forms: restriction and extension. **Restriction** allows you to restrict the content model of the base type. A very simple restriction might be the consideration of only positive integers after the base model has been defined as integers. Restriction allows you to create subsets from a set. The line 17 example is a little more complicated. **Extension**, on the other hand, allows you to expand on to (that is, to append additional elements to) the content model of the base type.

The dept_name Attribute: Use and Facets

Line 18 is an attribute declaration element, and it informs the processor that an attribute is used to express the restriction to the complex type named DEPTType, that is, the restriction that was alluded to in line 17. The attribute's name is dept_name. Because the name does not have an xs: prefix, it is not defined in the XML Schema Recommendation. So a definition must be provided. Further, according to the *required* value that was specified for the use attribute in the <xs:attribute> element start tag, a value for the dept_name attribute must be provided in any conforming XML document. Otherwise, the document is not valid. Besides *required*, the other commonly specified values for the use attribute are:

- *optional*—The attribute is optional.
- *fixed*—The value of the attribute is fixed. Another attribute named value must also appear. The value specified for the value attribute determines the value of the use=fixed attribute.

Line 19 indicates that the attribute is a simple type. In fact, all attributes must be simple types.

Line 20 tells the processor that there is a restriction placed on the value of the attribute. The base attribute type will be NMTOKEN (name token). As discussed in Chapter Four, name token attributes are a restricted form of string attribute, since they must begin with a letter and not an underscore. As you may recall, an NMTOKEN attribute must consist of a single word or string with no white spaces interspersed in it, but there are no other constraints on the word. NMTOKEN attributes meet the base="xs:string" parameter in line 17, too.

Lines 21 through 24 present the choices for the value of the dept_name attribute. Here, one type of **facet**—the enumeration—is used to define the values from which one can choose a department name. (Facets are discussed later in more detail.) Each line provides one choice. Meanwhile, from the xs:enumeration element tag, you can see that this term is defined in the XML Schema Recommendation. Thus, the attribute's value must be taken from the names explicitly listed here, the simple types listed within the dept_name attribute declaration element. Only one can be chosen. To clarify, it is indicated in line 8 that only one department name can be chosen at a time. After the department name (or abbreviation) is selected, then its <NAME>, <EMAIL>, and <PHONE> elements, and their respective information, must be inserted. However, after the <PHONE> information is inserted for the first department, another <DEPT> element can be created to begin the cycle anew. And there is no limit on the department contacts that can be entered, since maxOccurs equals "unbounded" in line 8. Note how each department name or abbreviation also meets the restrictions listed on lines 17 and 20.

Now that the DEPTType complex type, the dept_name attribute, and its respective department name abbreviations have been declared in the schema, the attribute restriction (line 25), simpleType (line 26), DEPTType attribute (line 27), DEPTType restriction (line 28), simple element content (line 29), and DEPTType complexType (line 30) end tags can be inserted to terminate the DEPTType complexType element declaration.

Globally Referenced Simple Types (Archetypes)

Lines 31 to 33, as shown below in Figure 5-13, list the full declarations of the simple type elements referenced in lines 9 through 11.

```
31.     <xs:element name="EMAIL" type="xs:string"/>
32.     <xs:element name="NAME" type="xs:string"/>
33.     <xs:element name="PHONE" type="xs:string"/>
```

Figure 5-13 Lines 31 through 33 of contactsbydept.xsd

To paraphrase previous statements, these are simple types because they do not have attributes or subelements. (They can easily be described on one line.) The prefix xs: in type="xs:string" indicates that string is a simple type already defined in the XML Schema Recommendation. Further, references to these types are called global references or archetypes because the elements are declared within the schema element and not within any subelements below the schema element. Thus, they can be seen and referred to from every subelement in the schema.

Mixed Content Elements

Like DTDs, schemas also support the creation of mixed content elements: those elements that contain subelements as well as character data at the same level. However, where DTDs cannot exert control over the order of the child elements or over the number of times they appear, schemas can do so, because they have more complete syntax.

Here is an example of a portion of a schema that contains a mixed content element. It is a model for a request to the executive assistant of each department to provide contact information. Naturally, because the element contains other elements as well as text, the element is a complex type. Note the use of the attribute named "content" with its value mixed, which is included in the complexType element start tag.

```
<xs:element name="contact_req" >
      <xs:complexType content="mixed" >
            <xs:element name="dept_exec_asst"
               type= "xs:string" />
            <xs:element name="time_lmt_days" >
                  <xs:simpleType base="xs:integer" >
                        <xs:maxInclusive value="5" />
                  </xs:simpleType>
             </xs:element>
      </xs:complexType>
</xs:element>
```

A conforming XML document (such as the actual request letter) might contain the following:

```
<contact_req>
Dear <dept_exec_asst>Pat Green</dept_exec_asst>:
Please provide the name, e-mail address, and phone number
of the designated department contact by <time_lmt_days>
5</time_lmt_days>working days from the date of this memo.
Thanks in advance for your cooperation.
Dale Burgess, President
</contact_req>
```


EMPTY ELEMENT CONTENT

Schemas also provide the ability to declare empty content elements. They are declared by using the xsd:complexType element type, but they deliberately omit the definition of a subelement within the complex type element. Here is an example of the declaration of the empty element <HEAD> that might ultimately be contained within the definition of the <CONTACTS> element:

```
<xs:element name="HEAD">
      <xs:complexType>
      </xsd:complexType>
</xsd:element>
```

USING FACETS TO DEFINE DATA MORE PRECISELY

The schema used as an example in this chapter used inheritance (restrictions or extensions) to more precisely define the values of attributes. It also illustrated how enumeration, one type of facet, could be used to more precisely define the values from which one can choose a department name to begin the description of a departmental contact. As indicated there, facets are a means for providing a more precise definition for data contained within a simple type element or attribute. Their syntax is usually simple:

```
<facetname value="facetvalue"/>
```

In Hands-on Project 5-4, you create a simple type subelement called DiscountCode under a Customer element and you are required to define the value of the DiscountCode as an integer with a value less than 999. Here's what that simple type element might look like:

```
<xs:element name="DiscountCode">
       <xs:simpleType>
              <xs:restriction base="xs:integer">
                     <xs:minInclusive value="1"/>
                     <xs:maxInclusive value="999"/>
              </xs:restriction>
       </xs:simpleType>
</xs:element>
```

By now, you are familiar with most of the terms listed above. Notice that the minInclusive and maxInclusive facets provide the lower and upper boundaries, respectively, of the range of integers for the DiscountCode value. These facets—minInclusive, maxInclusive, and enumeration—are very popular and very valuable. Another popular facet named "pattern" is used in many ways. Most commonly, pattern is used for the designation of UPCs, ISBNs, and other inventory-control numbers. UPC stands for Universal Product Code and is a number associated with an individual product (for example, a bottle of your favorite soda) or an individual item (the 28-ounce bottle of your favorite soda) for inventory purposes, pricing, or shipping purposes. Many organizations use UPCs or other bar code numbers (often identified by the more generic term "stock keeping unit" or SKU); there are approximately a dozen commonly used formats. If a company's products do not normally have UPCs (or ISBNs in the publishing world), the company can invent its own arbitrary numbering system. Whatever system they use, the number usually appears on orders, order confirmations, shipping documents, etc.

Whatever numbering system is adopted by an organization, the pattern of the number can be specified in XML document models. Here is the schema coding for the older style, fixed-length UPC code commonly used by food merchandisers:

```
<!--UPC Bar Code for identifying products -->
<xsd:simpleType name="UPCcode">
      <xsd:restriction base="xsd:string">
              <xsd:pattern value="\d{1}-\d{5}-\d{5}-\{1}"/>
       </xsd:restriction>
</xsd:simpleType>
```

Another example of the use of the pattern facet is the specification of an International Standard Book Number (ISBN), the international code for identifying published material such as books, pamphlets, audio books on cassettes or CDs, machine-readable tapes, floppy disks, and CD-ROMs, to name a few. Schema coding for an ISBN might look like this:

```
<!-- International Standard Book Number (ISBN) -->
 <xsd:simpleType name="ISBN">
       <xsd:restriction base="xsd:string">
             <xsd:pattern value="\d{1}-\d{5}-\d{3}-\d{1}"/>
       </xsd:restriction>
</xsd:simpleType>
```


These are just a few of the most commonly used facets available with XML schemas. Other facets are described briefly in Table 5-2.

Table 5-2 Other schema facets

Facet Name	Description
Length	Specifies the length of a value. Limited to the value 2147483647. Items larger than this limit are not validated correctly.
minLength	Specifies the minimum length of a value, e.g., length of abbreviation for language, state, province, or country. Limited to the value 2147483647. Items larger than this limit are not validated correctly.
maxLength	Specifies the maximum length of a value, e.g., length of a delivery address. Limited to the value 2147483647. Items larger than this limit are not validated correctly.
maxExclusive	Defines a maximum exclusive upper bound of a datatype value. For example, "less than 10" would require a maxExclusive value of 10 or a maxInclusive of 9.
minExclusive	Defines the exclusive lower bound of a datatype value. For example, "at least two" would require a minExclusive value of two.
duration	Specifies a time period. The value designates a Gregorian year, month, day, hour, minute, and second. The number of seconds can include decimal digits. An optional preceding minus sign (-) can indicate a negative duration. If the sign is omitted, a positive duration is presumed. Example: to indicate a duration of two years, three months, six days, five hours, and 16 minutes, state P2Y3M6DT5H16M. Minus six hours looks like: -P6H.
totalDigits	Defines the maximum number of digits in the value of a given datatype. Derived from "decimal." The value of totalDigits must be a positive integer.
fractionDigits	Specifies the maximum number of digits in the fractional part of a value of a given datatype. Also derived from "decimal." The value of fractionDigits must be a nonnegative integer.
whiteSpace	Specifies what to do with white space in a datatype. Value must be preserve, replace, or collapse. If the datatype is specified as a string, the value of whiteSpace is usually specified as preserve.

Be careful when specifying facets with simple datatypes. Not all facets apply to all datatypes. You can consult the W3C XML Schema Recommendation to check which facets go with which simple datatypes.

Chapter Summary

- The shortcomings of DTDs were already known by the time the first edition of the Extensible Markup Language (XML) 1.0 Recommendation was endorsed by the W3C Director in early 1998. The W3C's XML Schema Working Group developed the "XML Schema Part 1: Structures" and "XML Schema Part 2: Datatypes" Recommendations from 1998 to 2001. Together, they are called "XML Schema," or "Xschema." Schemas are expected to replace DTDs one day, although, at present, DTDs still have some advantages.
- With schemas, document models are described in terms of constraints, which define what can and cannot appear in a given XML language or document. There are two kinds of constraints: content model constraints and datatype constraints.
- The first line of the schema—the XML declaration, also called its header—is mandatory. The rest of the prolog, if any, is not. The schema element, the first element of the schema, is equivalent to the root element of an XML document, and is the parent element of all the other elements in the schema.
- Schemas provide more XML namespace support than DTDs. Target namespace provides the method for the processor to check an instance document to see if it validates against a schema. If a namespace is neither a target namespace nor a default namespace, then it is probably a supporting schema to another main schema (i.e., it is "chameleon namespace").
- Element types determine the appearance of elements and their content in instance documents. There are two kinds of element types: complex types, which are elements that contain attributes and/or subelements; and simple types, which contain no attributes or subelements, only character data.
- Compositors are specialized XML Schema components that allow you to define groups of elements and attributes within the schema and, thus, within the schema's related XML documents. There are three types of compositors: sequence, choice, and all.
- The authors of schemas have two choices with respect to schema structure: the nesting doll (also called Russian doll) structure, or a flat catalog approach.
- It is useful to consider a complexType declaration as a container of elements, attributes, and other parameters that help to define the respective complex type element.
- XML inheritance comes in two forms: restriction and extension.

- Globally referenced simple element types are also called archetypes. They are global because they are situated in the schema element, so they can be referenced from all the subelements in the schema.
- Like DTDs, schemas also provide the ability to declare empty content elements and mixed content elements. However, unlike DTDs, schemas are more flexible and powerful; they allow you to better specify the order of appearance and the number of appearances of mixed content elements.
- The most popular and valuable facets used with schemas tend to be minInclusive, maxInclusive, enumeration, and pattern. The values for minOccurs and maxOccurs indicate an element's cardinality (i.e., the number of times the DEPT element may occur in instance documents).

Review Questions

1. The DTD document modeling language cannot be revised or extended to overcome its shortcomings. True or False?
2. Which of the following is not an advantage that DTDs still have over schemas:
    a. All SGML-related tools and many XML-related tools can already process DTDs.
    b. All the existing browsers already support DTDs.
    c. Expertise and practical application has progressed since the introduction of DTDs with the SGML standard ISO 8879 in 1986.
    d. A large number of document types are already defined using DTDs.
3. Schema is a term borrowed from ______________ technology, where it is used to describe the ______________. In the context of XML, a schema describes a model for a whole class of ______________.
4. In schemas, models are described in terms of ______________.
    a. datatypes
    b. attributes
    c. elements
    d. constraints
5. If you are familiar with programming languages such as ______________, then you recognize the terminology used by XML practitioners.
    a. SGML
    b. Visual Basic
    c. C++ and Java
    d. Fortran and Cobol
6. The schema element in the schema is equivalent to what in an XML document?

7. When the XML processor encounters xmlns:xs="http://www.w3.org/2001/XMLSchema in the schema element tag, what is it being told?
8. Which of the following indicates a default namespace?
   a. "xmlns:xs=http://www.w3.org/2001/XMLSchema"
   b. "xmlns="http://www.w3.org/2001/XMLSchema"
   c. "defaultNamespace="http://www.tlsales.com/Sch01"
   d. all of the above
   e. none of the above
9. What is a default namespace?
10. What has to happen in order for an XML instance document to be validated against a schema?
    a. A targetNamespace attribute is normally declared within the schema's schema element, and the instance document(s) also declares a namespace, using the URL "ww.w3.org/2001/XMLSchema" in its root element tag.
    b. All namespace declarations must mention "www.w3.org/2001/XMLSchema."
    c. A defaultNamespace is normally declared within the schema element, and the instance document(s) also declares a namespace, using the same URL as the schema's default namespace, in its root element tag.
    d. A targetNamespace is declared within the schema's schema element, and the instance document(s) also declares a namespace, using the same URL as the schema's target namespace, in its root element tag.
    e. Both the schema and the instance document must have target and default namespaces and neither should mention "www.w3.org/2001/XMLSchema."
11. What kind of design does a schema have when it has no target namespace declaration and no default namespace declaration?
12. Fill in the blanks: When a schema designer has to decide whether or not to expose the name of the origin namespaces for each local element in instance documents, he or she incorporates the ______________ as a sort of binary ______________.
13. Whenever you see element tags that look like <sp1:name> and </sp1:name> in an instance document, then you know that "the locals are qualified." True or false?
14. Complex type is one variety of:
    a. element type
    b. data type
    c. content type
    d. all of the above
    e. a and b, but not c

15. Which of the following are types of compositors? (Choose all that apply.)
    a. choice
    b. cardinal
    c. simple
    d. qualified/non-qualified
    e. all
    f. sequence

16. Why did XML Spy automatically create the complexType, which was eventually named DEPTType by the designer/author?
17. The plus sign (+) next to the DEPT element in the DTD was equivalent to what in the schema?
    a. minOccurs default; maxOccurs default
    b. minOccurs unbounded; maxOccurs unbounded
    c. minOccurs default; maxOccurs unbounded
    d. minOccurs unbounded; maxOccurs default
    e. minOccurs 1; maxOccurs default
    f. none of the above
18. If you are looking over a schema document, and you see an element such as "ref=address," what should you realize?
19. What do the nesting doll, Russian doll, and the flat catalog refer to? How do they differ from one another?
20. What are the two forms of XML inheritance? Which would you use to create a subset from a content model of your base type?
21. If you have a schema and it contains a mixed content element named "notice," which of the following is false?
    a. The "notice" element is a complex type.
    b. The "notice" element tag contains an attribute named "mixed" with a value equal to "content."
    c. The complexType element tag contains an attribute named "complex" with a value equal to "mixed."
    d. The "notice" element tag contains an attribute named "content" with a value equal to "mixed."
    e. The complexType element tag contains the "content" attribute with the "mixed" value.
22. Schemas are the preferred method over DTDs for code extensibility and reusability. True or false?

23. Fill in the blanks. With schemas, declare empty content elements by using the ______________ element type but by deliberately ______________ the definition of a subelement within the ______________.
24. What popular facet is used for the designation of UPCs, ISBNs, and other inventory-control numbers?
25. If you are using a base of integers and you want to designate a value of "less than 10" you could use a maxExclusive value of 10 or a maxInclusive of ______________.

HANDS-ON PROJECTS

Project 5-1

In this project you design a schema.xsd file for the contacts list, instead of a DTD file. To do so, you use a quick method to create a small schema from existing DTD and XML files. This project also illustrates that DTDs and schemas can be similar in how they work, even if they are coded differently. Generally speaking, the schema does most of the tasks that a DTD does, but offers more control.

To convert a DTD file to a schema:

1. Use Windows Explorer to create a folder named **Ch05** in the C:\home\<*yourname*> folder. Then copy the files in the Ch05\Project_5-1 folder on your Data Disk to the C:\home\<*yourname*>\Ch05 folder.
2. Click **Start**, point to **Programs** (point to **All Programs** in Windows XP), point to **XML Spy Suite**, and then click **XML Spy IDE**. The XML Spy window opens.
3. Click **Project** on the menu bar, and then click **Open Project**. Click the **Look in** list arrow, and then navigate to C:\home\<*yourname*>\Ch05, if necessary. Click the **contacts** project, and then click **Open**.
4. Double-click the **DTD/Schemas** folder in the Project pane. Double-click the **contactsbydept.dtd** file. Click **View** on the menu bar, and then click **Text View** to see the code shown in Figure 5-14.

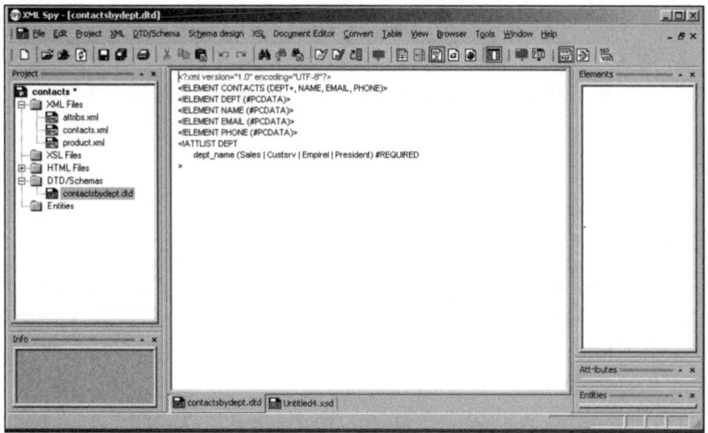

Figure 5-14

5. Click **DTD/Schema** on the menu bar, and then click **Convert DTD/Schema**. The Convert DTD/Schema dialog box opens.
6. Click the **W3C Schema**, **Complex types**, and **Make global definition** option buttons. Then click **OK** to convert the DTD to a schema.
7. Save the new file as **contactsbydept.xsd** in the C:/home/<*yourname*>/Ch05 folder, as shown in Figure 5-15.

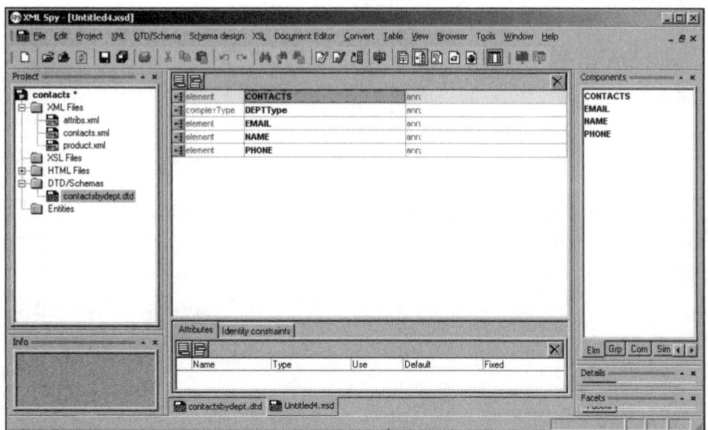

Figure 5-15

Now you are ready to examine the schema and then compare the schema elements to the DTD elements.

To examine and compare the schema:

1. Double-click the **CONTACTS** element icon to expand the Schema Design view of the element.

2. Click the **CONTACTS** element in the middle pane. You can see that it has been converted to a complex element because it contains other elements.
3. Click the **NAME** element in the middle pane. This has been converted to a simple element because it is a leaf and does not contain any other elements or attributes.
4. Save the file.
5. To view the coded contactsbydept.xsd file, click **View** on the menu bar, and then click **Text view**.
6. Click the **DEPT** element and examine the Details area in the right pane. Notice in the original DTD shown earlier in Figure 5-14, the DEPT element was coded as DEPT+. Select the equivalent code in the XML schema: **maxOccurs="unbounded"**. Switch to Schema Design view.
7. Click the **DEPT** element in the upper-middle pane.
8. Click the **Attributes** tab in the lower-middle pane.
9. Click the **NMTOKEN Type** in the lower-middle pane, and then click the **Enumerations** tab in the lower-right pane.
10. In the original DTD shown earlier in Figure 5-14, the DEPT element has !ATTLIST defined as dept_name with a finite list of values: Sales | Custsrv | Emplrel | President. Switch to Text view, and then select the equivalent code in the XML schema:

    ```
    <xs:enumeration value="Sales"/>
    <xs:enumeration value="Custsrv"/>
    <xs:enumeration value="Emplrel"/>
    <xs:enumeration value="President"/>
    ```

11. Leave contactsbydept.xsd open in XML Spy for the next project

Project 5-2

In this project you create an XML schema from scratch as a document model for a customer list, and use it to validate the elements and the data within the elements in an XML document. Then you create a valid XML file that conforms to the new schema. Although you have conversion tools to convert DTDs to schemas, the results might not be what you want or need. Plan carefully to make sure that a schema file will be extensible and reusable.

To create a new customer schema:

1. In the XML Spy Project pane, click the **DTD/Schemas** folder.
2. To create a new schema, click **File** on the menu bar, and then click **New**. Click **xsd W3C Schema**, and then click **OK**. An empty schema opens.
3. Double-click in the highlighted field and replace the default root element text *ENTER_NAME_OF_ROOT_ELEMENT* with the name **TLSales**. This view is the Schema Design view and now displays TLSales as a global component in the top pane and shows attributes in the lower pane. The upper-right pane, called the helper pane or Component Navigator, displays TLSales in the Elm tab.

4. To save the new schema, click **File** on the menu bar, and then click **Save As**. The Save As dialog box opens. Click the **Save in** list arrow, and then navigate to the **C:/home/<*yourname*>Ch05** folder, if necessary. In the File name text box, type **customer.xsd** as the file name, and then click **Save**.

Now you are ready to create a document model you can use for customer lists.

To create a generic document model:

1. Define a specific namespace by clicking **Schema design** on the menu bar, and then clicking **Schema settings**. In the Schema settings dialog box, click the **Target namespace** option button and type **http://tlsales.com/namespace** in the Target namespace text box. Click **OK**.
2. Now you add elements to the schema. To do this, click the **TLSales** element component icon. A single blue box with the TLSales element appears.
3. Double-click the text under the box to edit it. Type **TLSales customer schema**.
4. Right-click the **TLSales** element and point to **Add Child,** and then click **Sequence** on the shortcut menu. A hexagon with a line and three dots appears. This is called the Sequence compositor.
5. Right-click the **Sequence compositor**, point to **Add Child,** and then click **Element** on the shortcut menu. Type **Address** as the name of the element. See Figure 5-16.

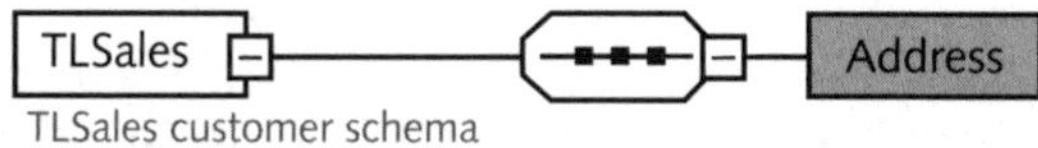

Figure 5-16

6. Right-click the **Sequence compositor** again, point to **Add Child,** and then click **Element** on the shortcut menu. Type **Customer** as the name of the element, and press **Enter**. This current configuration will allow for one Customer with an Address only. You will change this configuration to have as many customers as necessary.
7. Right-click the **Customer** element, and then click **Unbounded** on the shortcut menu. A small infinity symbol appears under the Customer element, as shown in Figure 5-17, indicating a one-to-many relationship. You could also modify the minOcc and maxOcc fields in the Details area of the right pane.

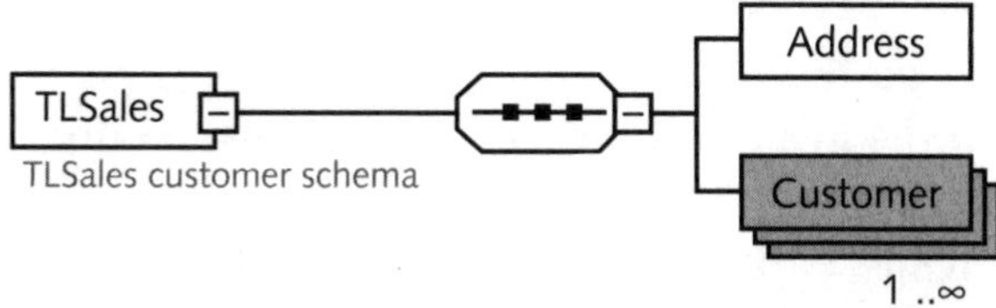

Figure 5-17

Project 5-3

In this project you add subelements to the Address element to store the XML data.

To add subelements to the Address element:

1. Right-click the **Address** element, point to **Add Child**, and then click **Sequence**. Right-click the new **Sequence compositor**, point to **Add Child**, and then click **Element**. Type **Name** as the name, as shown in Figure 5-18.

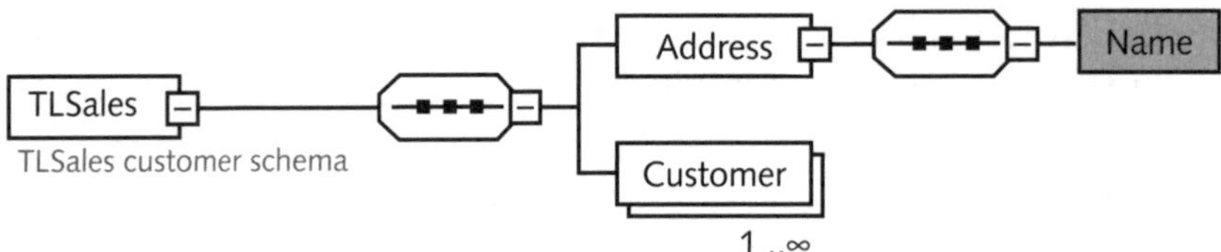

Figure 5-18

2. You need to restrict the Name element to occur only once and to contain only text data. To do this, make sure the **Name** element is selected. In the XML Spy details pane, click **type** and then click **xs:string**. The minOcc and maxOcc fields both default to a value of 1, which is what you want. The Name element icon should now have three small lines in the top-left corner, denoting string text. Press **Enter**.
3. You now need to create two more elements using drag and drop. Click the **NAME** element. Hold down the **Ctrl** key and drag until you see the small + (plus sign) appear, and then release. Be sure to release the mouse before you release the Ctrl key. See Figure 5-19. If necessary, drag the copied element into place.

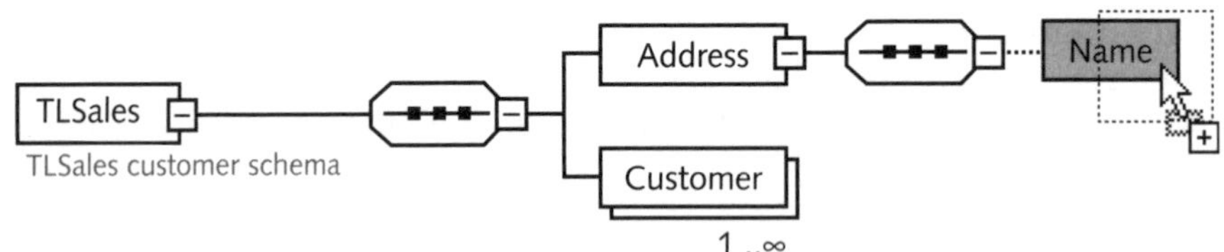

Figure 5-19

4. Double-click the second **Name** element and change the element name to **Street**.
5. Add one last element called **City**. Now you can configure the schema view to edit specific settings.
6. Click **Schema design** on the menu bar, and then click **View config**. A Schema display configuration pane appears.
7. Click the **Append** icon, which is the upper-left icon in the Element tab, click the list arrow, and then click **type**.
8. Click **OK**. The content model displays the type under each element. You can display as much or as little of these details as necessary.

Project 5-4

In this project you add subelements to the Customer element. These will be simple types, meaning simple content models.

To add subelements to the Customer element:

1. Create the following sub-elements: First, Last, Phone, Fax, Email, and DiscountCode.
2. Change the requirements for Fax so that it is optional. Right-click the **Fax** element, and then click **Optional** on the shortcut menu. The element now appears with a dotted outline. See Figure 5-20.

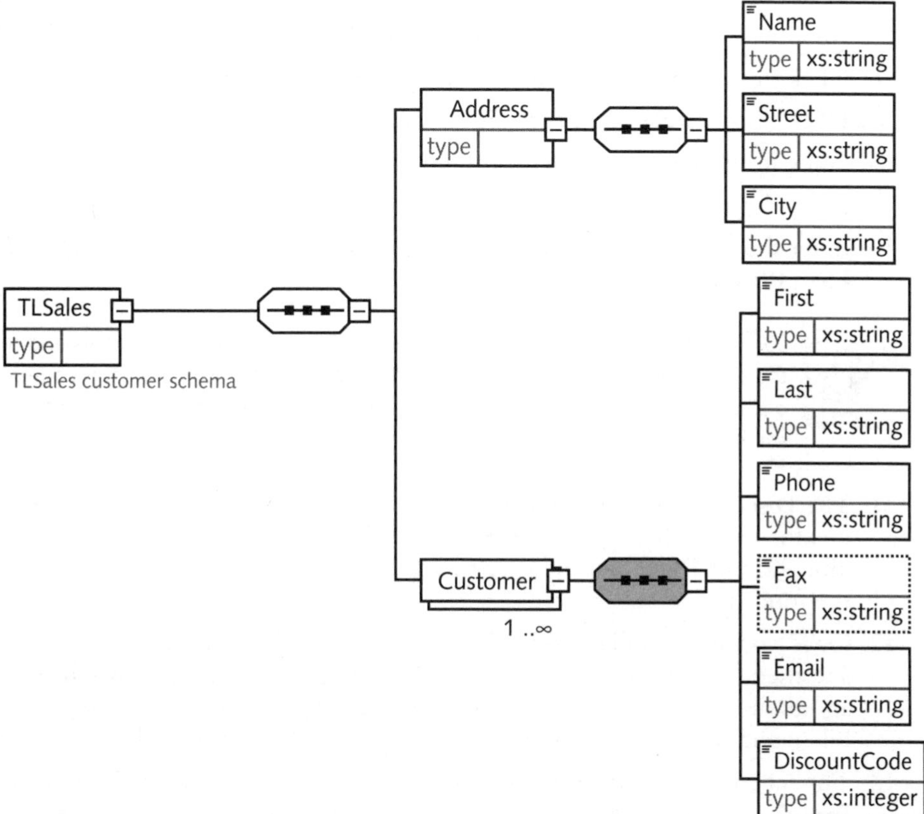

Figure 5-20

3. Change the requirements for the DiscountCode element so that it is an integer and limited to a value less than 999. Click the **DiscountCode** element, and then click the **xs:integer** entry form in the details pane. Click the **maxIncl** field of the Facets tab and enter **999** as the maximum value allowed.
4. Save the file and save the project, and then close the customer.xsd schema file, but leave the XML Spy open for the next project.

Project 5-5

In this project, you create an XML file from scratch based on the customer.xsd schema. This helps you to see how XML files relate to the schema that validates them.

To create an XML file based on a schema:

1. Create a new XML file by clicking **File** on the menu bar, and then clicking **New**.
2. In the Create new document dialog box, click **XML Extensible Markup Language**, and then click **OK**.
3. In the New file dialog, click the **Schema** option button, and then click **OK**.
4. In the XML Spy dialog box, click **Browse**, find and click **c:\home\<*yourname*>\Ch05\customer.xsd**, and then click **Open**.
5. An empty XML file appears. Click the **Address** list arrow, and then click **Address**.
6. Click in the **Name** text box, and then type your name.
7. Click in the **Street** text box, and then type your street address.
8. Click in the **City** text box, and then type your city name.
9. Expand the Customer tag by clicking the **Customer** list arrow.
10. Enter the following elements the same as you did in Steps 6 through 8: **First**, **Last**, **Phone**, and **Email**.

So far all the elements you have entered have been required elements and of the data type string. No other restrictions have been placed on the content of these elements. You could type in "abc" as the value of each element and still have a valid XML file.

11. The DiscountCode element has a data type restriction of integer. It also has a maxInclusive value of 999. Enter several different values for this element, such as **abc**, **99**, and **1001**, and then try to save the file by clicking the **Save** button on the toolbar.
12. Once you successfully enter valid data, save the file. Click **File** on the menu bar, and then click **Save As**. In the Save As dialog box, click the **Save in** list arrow, and then navigate to the C:/home/<*yourname*>/Ch05 folder, if necessary. In the File name text box, type **customer.xml** as the file name, and then click **Save**.
13. The schema allows for one optional field: Fax. To insert this field, right-click the **Email** element, point to **Insert**, and then click **Element**.
14. In the list below the new Element, click **Fax**, and then enter your fax number or another valid fax number.

    You should now be able to save without any validation errors. To explore the file, you can try to rearrange your data, enter new fields, add additional customers to the file, etc., to see how the XSD will react to your changes.
15. Save the file and save the project.

Project 5-6

In this project you create a global AddressType component that is used to create a template to handle the difference between United States (US) and Canadian address formats.

To create a global component:

1. In XML Spy, click **File** on the menu bar, and then click **Open**. Navigate to the C:/home/<*yourname*>/Ch05 folder, if necessary, and double-click the **customer.xsd** file.
2. In the working pane, right-click the **Address** element, point to **Make Global,** and then click **Complex type**. Address now appears in a yellow box, indicating that the Address element is now a global component.
3. Click the **Display all Globals** icon. (This icon is located in the upper-left corner of the middle pane, not on the toolbar.) The schema now displays two global components, the TLSales and AddressType elements.
4. Click the **Com(plex)** tab of the Component Navigator to verify that AddressType is also visible.
5. Click the **AddressType** component icon to view the new content model.
6. Click the **Display all Globals** icon again. This is the view that will be used to create the different Address formats.
7. Click the **Append** icon at the top of the component pane, and then click **ComplexType** on the shortcut menu.
8. Type **Cdn-Address** in the text box, and then press **Enter**.
9. Click the **Cdn-Address** component icon to see the new content model.
10. Click the **base** item in the details pane, and then click **AddressType**. A copy of the AddressType content model appears in a yellow box. This is the generic part of the Address to which you can now add the requirements for a Canadian postal code.
11. Right-click the **Cdn-Address** element, point to **Add Child,** and then click **Sequence** to add another Sequence compositor. The new compositor is displayed outside of the generic global AddressType content model box.
12. Right-click the new Sequence compositor, point to **Add Child,** and then click **Element**. Type **PostalCode** as the new element name, and then press **Tab**. Click **xs:string** in the type list box. Create a second element called **Province** with the same requirements as PostalCode, as shown in Figure 5-21.

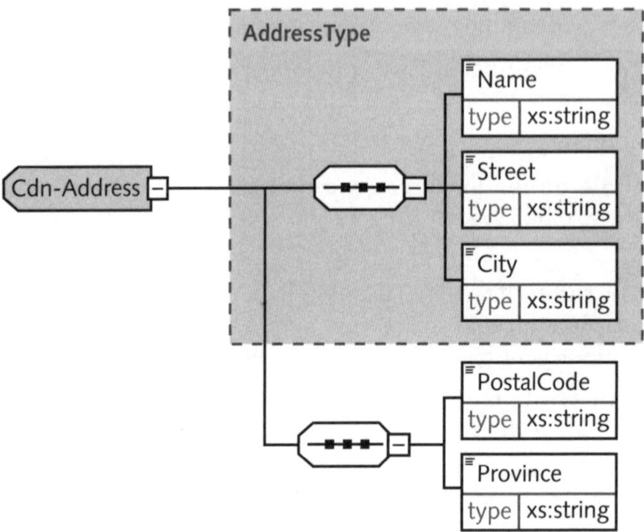

Figure 5-21

13. Create the second Address model for the US requirement. Type **US-Address** as the name for the new global complex type. The Zip code should be a xs:positiveinteger and the Province should be changed to State. The final model should resemble Figure 5-22.

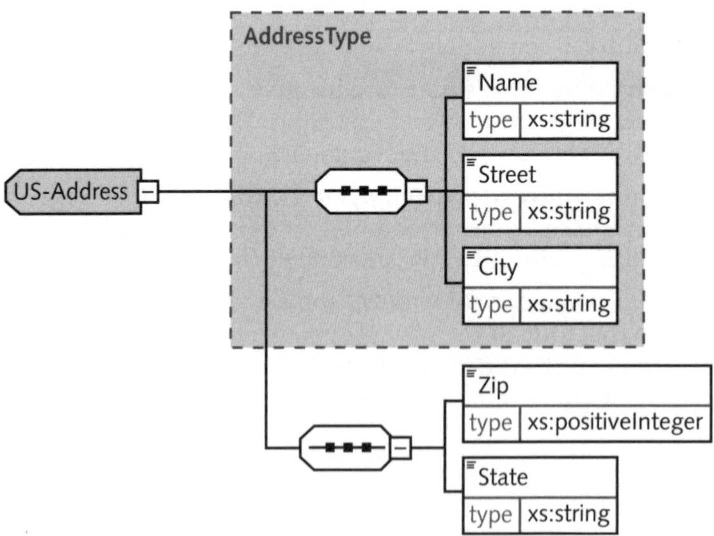

Figure 5-22

14. Save the file and save the project. Leave customer.xsd open in XML Spy.

Project 5-7

To complete the Customer schema definition, you need to make the Customer element global and add some element attributes that will be used to restrict the data selection to specific data sets. In the AddressType content model, you want to explore how an element or content model can be designed for reuse. In the Customer content model, you focus on restricting and further controlling the type of data that an element can contain. A good schema should encompass both.

To restrict data selection:

1. Switch to schema view for the TLSales element. Right-click the **Customer** element, point to **Make Global,** and then click **Element**. A small arrow appears on the Customer element. The isRef field in the details pane is also checked.
2. Click the **Display all Globals** icon to return to the schema overview. The Customer element is now available in the component list in the Elm tab.
3. Define the Customer element attributes. Click the **Customer** element to make it active. Click the **Append** icon, and then click **Attribute**.
4. Enter **OneTime** as the attribute name. Select **xs.boolean** as the type and make it required. Use the same method to create two more attributes for the Customer element called Regular and Senior with the same properties as onetime.
5. Create an attribute called Discount and limit it to contents using the Enumeration feature. Click the **Append** icon in the Attribute pane. Enter **Discount** as the attribute name and select **xs:positiveInteger** as the Type. Click the **Enumerations** tab of the Facets pane.
6. Click the **Append** icon in the Facets pane and enter **5**. Use the same method to add 10, 15, 20, and 25 as discount values.
7. Save the file and save the project.
8. As a final step you may want to look at the text view of this model and study the structure and syntax for the code. Then close XML Spy.

CASE PROJECTS

Case Project 5-1

You have been asked to validate a newly created customer schema file called customer.xsd to see if it creates a valid XML file called customer.xml before it is deployed for use in the accounting department. As part of this process, you must document this process for the users in accounting.

Create the customer.xsd and customer.xml files, and then validate the XML file. Record the steps so that another user can successfully perform the same task.

Case Project 5-2

Using the customer.xsd file that you have, create another schema file called Cdn-customer.xsd, like the one shown in Figure 5-23, to facilitate a corporate expansion. Your specifications are to make the sequence compositor unbounded. Change the TLSales child element sequence to Customer, then Address. Change the Address element type to Cdn-Address. Finally, ask someone else to test the Cdn-customer.xsd file by creating a valid Cdn-customer.xml file prior to deployment.

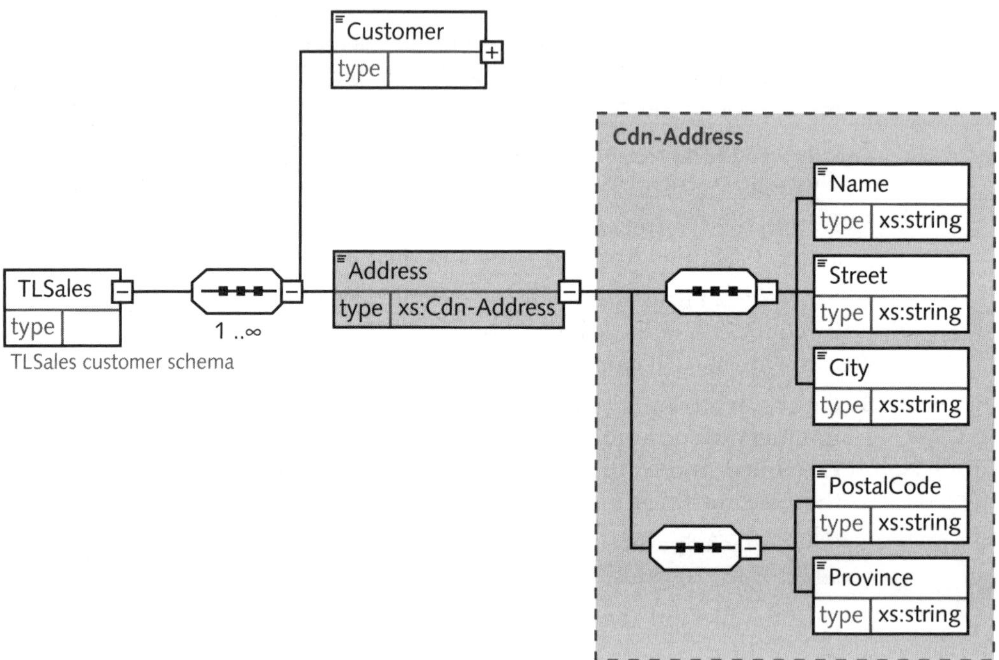

Figure 5-23

CHAPTER

6

Creating XML Transformations

In this chapter, you will learn:

- Why you should transform XML data
- About the nature of transformation
- About XSL, XPath, and XSLT
- About the steps involved in a simple XSLT transformation
- How to perform two XSLT transformations

In previous chapters, the emphasis has been on the structure of XML documents for data storage. In this chapter, you learn about transforming XML documents, so the emphasis shifts from structuring XML documents to transferring and outputting the information found in them. Transforming the data contained in XML documents prepares that data for further processing. In this chapter, you learn why transformations are necessary, and how to perform one. Further, you review a simple transformation to understand the considerations, concepts, and syntaxes involved. Later, in the Hands-on Projects, you perform a transformation, using XML Spy and your browser.

WHY TRANSFORM XML DATA?

Recall that XML is a simple, standard way to interchange structured data. Even in its raw form, XML is reasonably easy to read and write. However, whether the XML data is viewed or printed by people, or whether it is provided directly to another software application, it is very rarely used in its raw or original form. First, it has to be transformed into another format. To communicate effectively with a human reader, XML data might have to take the form of a document that can be displayed or printed, or of an audio, graphics, or video file. To transfer XML data between applications on the same or different systems—for example, to load data into an application where the required format might be a comma-separated-values file, a SQL script, an HTTP message, or a sequence of calls on a particular programming interface—that data likely has to be transformed from the data model used by one application to the model used in another. For example, an invoice can be presented on a screen or printed page, but it can also be used as a form in accounting or tax preparation application. Sports statistics, displayed on TV sets and browsers everywhere, are also summarized, indexed, and aggregated in databases. You transform XML data so the same data can serve different purposes.

Converting XML to HTML for display is probably the most common application of transformation today. Consequently, it is the one that is used in the examples and Hands-on Projects in this chapter. Once you transform the XML data into HTML format, you can display it on any browser.

TRANSFORMING XML DOCUMENTS

There are two phases to the transformation process. The first phase is a structural transformation, in which the data is converted from the structure of the incoming XML document to the structure of the desired output. The second phase is a formatting transformation, in which the new structure is changed to the required format (e.g., HTML, PDF, DB2, Oracle, etc.). Figure 6-1 illustrates the basic transformation process. The terms found in the figure are explained as the chapter progresses.

This chapter focuses primarily on the transformation of XML documents using the Extensible Stylesheet Language Transformation (XSLT) language, which is one aspect of the Extensible Stylesheet Language (XSL) trio—XSL, XSLT, and XPath. Each is discussed in the following paragraphs.

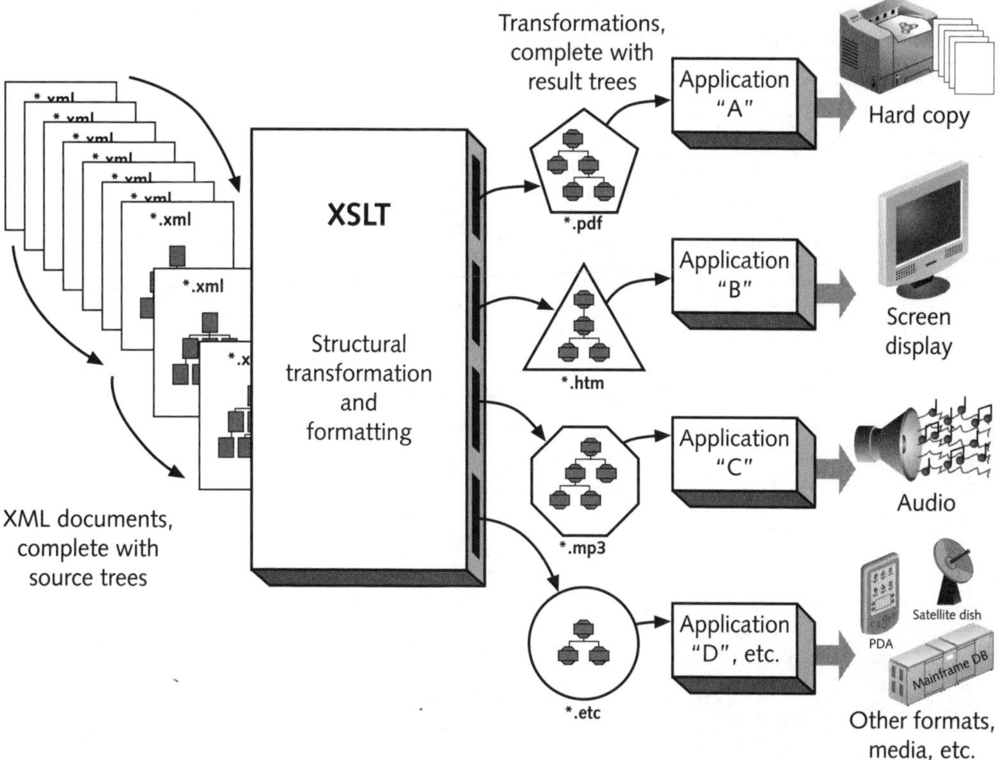

Figure 6-1 Basic XSLT transformation process

XSL

The XSL proposal was drafted and submitted to W3C in August of 1997, and a W3C XSL Working Group was formed in January of 1998. (Remember, the first edition of the W3C XML Recommendation itself was in the final endorsement stages at that time; it was endorsed in February 1998.) Originally, XSL's developers envisioned that XSL would be developed into a platform- and media-independent formatting language composed of two parts, a formatting language and a transformation language. The formatting language was to be a set of XML elements that would describe the various parts of page media, such as tables, headers, and footnotes. These descriptive elements would be the "formatting objects." The transformation language was intended to convert an XML document into a **result tree**, consisting of the XSL formatting objects. Thus, if the concept envisioned by the original developers had come to pass, XSL transformations would have consisted of a two-stage process: a structural transformation followed by formatting. However, as illustrated in Figure 6-2, during its development, the original XSL concept actually evolved into the following three XML-related languages:

- ***XSL***—the XML vocabulary for specifying formatting objectives and other semantics
- ***XSL Transformation (XSLT)***—the language for transforming XML documents
- ***XML Path Language (XPath)***—an expression language used to access or refer to parts of an XML document. Aspects of XPath are also enlisted by other XML-related languages (for example, as you will see later in this chapter, XSLT uses XPath for its transformations.)

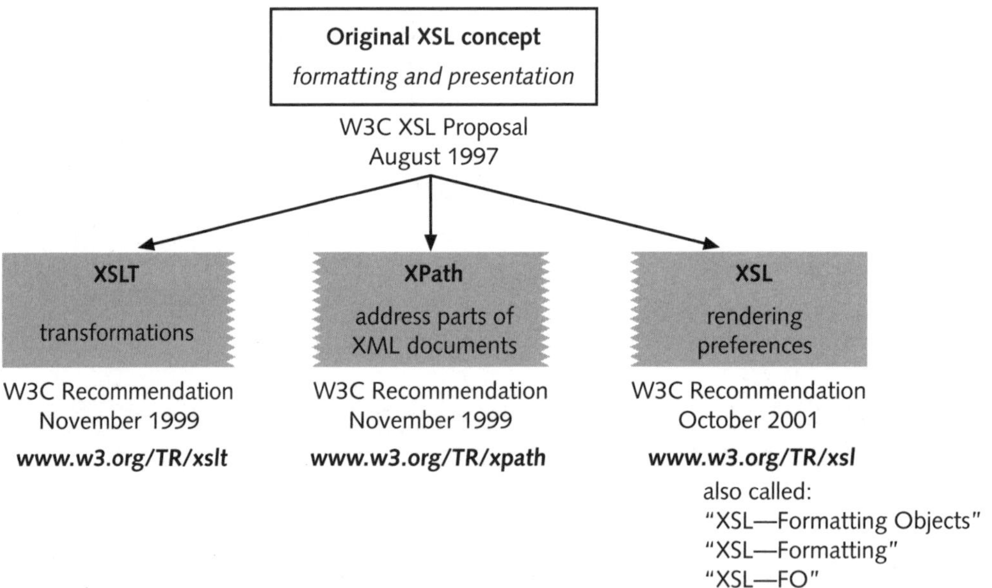

Figure 6-2 The XSL-related languages

The XSL Version 1.0 Recommendation was endorsed in October of 2001. Focusing on paged media, XSL 1.0 makes it possible to transform XML documents into professional quality products through the use of complex document formatting based on formatting objects and other properties.

XSL is a language for expressing style sheets. Just as **Cascading Stylesheets (CSS)** are used with HTML documents (and XML documents, too, as you see in Chapter 11), an XSL stylesheet is a file that describes how to display an XML document of a given type. XSL shares the functionality and is compatible with CSS2, the latest version of CSS, although it uses a different syntax. But XSL also adds advanced styling features, expressed by an XML document type, that define two sets of elements: **formatting objects** and attributes (in part, borrowed from CSS2 properties and adding more complex ones).

An XSL engine takes an XML document and an XSL stylesheet, and produces a rendering of the document. XSLT 1.0 and XPath still play a major role to significantly change the original structure of an XML document, plus locate and extract data. Now, XML documents and data can be formatted and rendered for both the World Wide Web and for print media.

XPath

As mentioned earlier, the XML Path Language 1.0 is a language for addressing parts of an XML document. (XPath has been a W3C Recommendation since November of 1999.) Its use is essential for those occasions when you want to prescribe exactly which parts of a document are to be transformed. XPath allows you to say, for example, "select all paragraphs belonging to the chapter element," "select the third list item," and so on.

XPath is a language for finding the information in an XML document. Using XPath, you can specify the locations of document structures or data in an XML document, and then process the information using XSLT. In practice, it can be difficult to determine where XSLT stops and where XPath starts, but they were developed as two different standards in the W3C. XPath considers documents to be composed of nodes in a tree-like structure. Most XML practitioners have heard of XPath, but mainly in the context of XSLT or the XPointer linking language. Thus, their experience with XPath may be limited. However, XSLT uses XPath extensively as a standard method to match nodes in an XML source tree, a process you learn about later in this chapter.

XSLT

XSLT is designed for transforming one XML document into another and uses its own kind of stylesheet to do so. Do not confuse XSLT stylesheets with Cascading Style Sheets (CSS). Cascading Style Sheets concentrate on how data is displayed (you learn more about CSS in Chapter 11). XSLT stylesheets actually change the structure and type of an XML document (for example, to automatically generate tables of contents, cross-references, indexes, etc.). XSLT stylesheets, therefore, have different components and are built differently than CSS documents. XSLT stylesheets can also transform an XML document into another XML document, one using a different XML vocabulary from the original.

The increasing popularity of XML does not mean that other ways of converting data will disappear. There will always be multiple data standards. For example, newspapers will likely use different formats for exchanging news articles, or use formats different from those used in the broadcast media. There will always be a need to do things like extract information from documents, for example, to extract identities, addresses, or dollar amounts from purchase records and add that information to revenue databases. As a result, conducting commerce (e-commerce or regular commerce) and linking organizations will demand innovations for extracting and combining data from one set of XML documents to generate another set of XML documents.

Though it was not originally intended as a general-purpose XML transformation language, XSLT was also designed to be used independently of XSL. It has become widely accepted for purposes outside of XSL, such as generating HTML Web pages, other text formats, audio and video presentations, and database input from XML data. Thus, XSLT is now often used as a general-purpose XML processing language.

However, XSLT is different from conventional programming languages because it is based on template rules that specify how XML documents should be processed. Although conventional programming languages are often sequential, template rules can be followed in any order because XSLT is a declarative language. XSLT, like XPath, considers documents to be composed of nodes in a tree-like structure. The XSLT stylesheet declares what output should be produced when a pattern in the XML document is matched.

At this writing, the XSL Working Group is working on XSLT 2.0 and XPath 2.0. The Requirement documents for those two second editions were released in February, 2001.

Sample Transformation—the TLSales Contacts List

For the remainder of the chapter, you examine a sample transformation to illustrate XSLT transformation concepts, syntax, and structure. This transformation involves extracting a portion of the TLSales, Inc. contact list, currently stored as an XML document called contacts.xml, and displaying the extracted portion in a browser, in HTML format. You will perform this transformation in Hands-on Project 6-1.

The transformation process is illustrated in Figure 6-3.

Briefly summarized, the process is:

1. An XML parser, or processor, is started and given an XML data document.
2. From references within the XML document, the XML parser locates a DTD (or a schema, if the author has specified one) and an XSLT stylesheet.
3. The parser then validates the XML document and XSLT stylesheet (since both should be well-formed XML documents).
4. The parser relinquishes control to the XSL parser. That processor, using the XSLT stylesheet as its guide, performs the specified transformation and generates the appropriate result tree document. The result tree document is, in turn, used as the source document for subsequent processing by the respective application.

data.dtd
data.xml
data.xslt
data.dtd
data.xml
These are valid.
OK, thanks.
data.xslt
data.xml
data.dtd
2. The XML parser finds the dtd.
3. The XML parser then finds the XSLT stylesheet and validates the XML document and the stylesheet.
4. The XML parser hands the valid documents to an XSL parser.
data.xml
data.htm
1. The XML parser is started and is given the XML document that contains the source tree.
6. The XSL parser creates the result tree document which is processed by the application.
5. The XSL parser then processes the documents.

6

Figure 6-3 Basic XML/XSL parsing

Acquiring XSL Parsers

XSL processors (parsers) are readily available. You can find several by checking the W3C Web site at *www.w3.org/Style/XSL/* or by reading "The XML Cover Pages—Extensible Stylesheet Language (XSL)" by Robin Cover at *xml.coverpages.org/xsl.html.* Some are stand-alone processors and some can be integrated with IDEs. For the Chapter 6 Hands-on Projects, the XML Spy IDE already contains an XSL parser. However, XML Spy does not come with one already installed, but supports several. Before you start Project 6-1, you should download and install an XSL parser and integrate it with XML Spy. However, if one hasn't been integrated, you are prompted to take appropriate action.

Examining the XML Source Document

Examine the source XML document in Figure 6-4. Notice that the root element is named <CONTACTS> and that it contains nine child elements, eight identifying contacts in several TLSales, Inc. departments. These include five contacts in Sales, one each in Customer Service and Employee Relations, and the President.

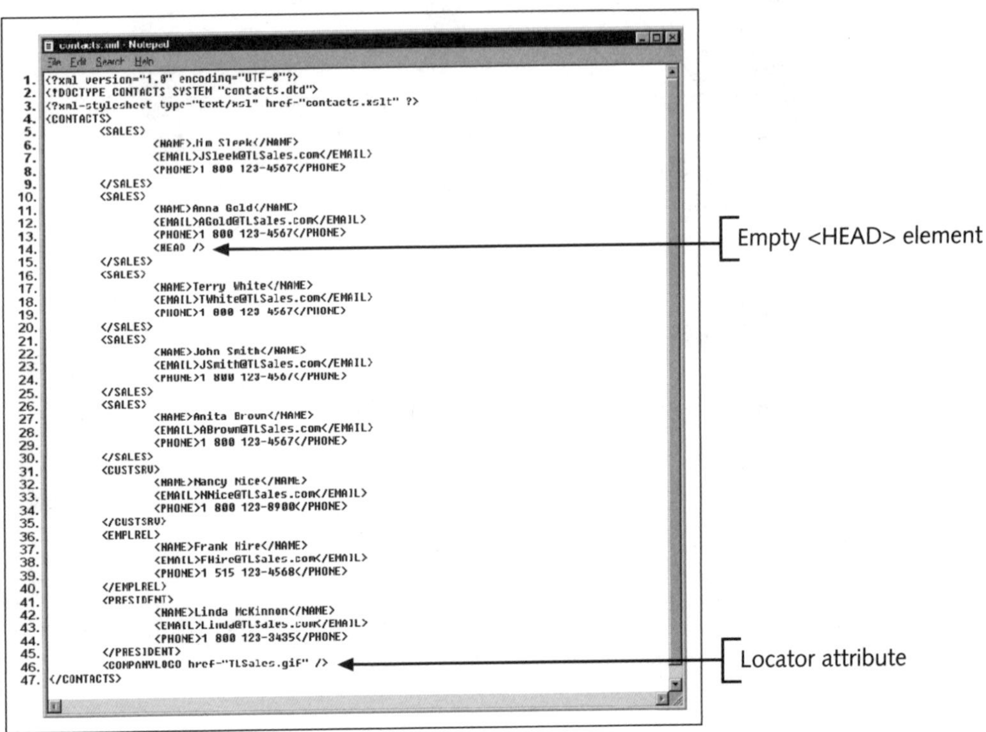

```
1. <?xml version="1.0" encoding="UTF-8"?>
2. <!DOCTYPE CONTACTS SYSTEM "contacts.dtd">
3. <?xml-stylesheet type="text/xsl" href="contacts.xslt" ?>
4. <CONTACTS>
5.         <SALES>
6.                 <NAME>Jim Sleek</NAME>
7.                 <EMAIL>JSleek@TLSales.com</EMAIL>
8.                 <PHONE>1 800 123-4567</PHONE>
9.         </SALES>
10.        <SALES>
11.                <NAME>Anna Gold</NAME>
12.                <EMAIL>AGold@TLSales.com</EMAIL>
13.                <PHONE>1 800 123-4567</PHONE>
14.                <HEAD />
15.        </SALES>
16.        <SALES>
17.                <NAME>Terry White</NAME>
18.                <EMAIL>TWhite@TLSales.com</EMAIL>
19.                <PHONE>1 800 123 4567</PHONE>
20.        </SALES>
21.        <SALES>
22.                <NAME>John Smith</NAME>
23.                <EMAIL>JSmith@TLSales.com</EMAIL>
24.                <PHONE>1 800 123-4567</PHONE>
25.        </SALES>
26.        <SALES>
27.                <NAME>Anita Brown</NAME>
28.                <EMAIL>ABrown@TLSales.com</EMAIL>
29.                <PHONE>1 800 123-4567</PHONE>
30.        </SALES>
31.        <CUSTSRV>
32.                <NAME>Nancy Nice</NAME>
33.                <EMAIL>NNice@TLSales.com</EMAIL>
34.                <PHONE>1 800 123-8900</PHONE>
35.        </CUSTSRV>
36.        <EMPLREL>
37.                <NAME>Frank Hire</NAME>
38.                <EMAIL>FHire@TLSales.com</EMAIL>
39.                <PHONE>1 515 123-4568</PHONE>
40.        </EMPLREL>
41.        <PRESIDENT>
42.                <NAME>Linda McKinnon</NAME>
43.                <EMAIL>Linda@TLSales.com</EMAIL>
44.                <PHONE>1 800 123-3435</PHONE>
45.        </PRESIDENT>
46.        <COMPANYLOGO href="TLSales.gif" />
47. </CONTACTS>
```


Figure 6-4 The contacts XML document

A **locator attribute** provides information to the processor regarding remote resources. In line 46, href is an ordinary locator attribute, since it refers to the location of the company logo image file—a property of the <COMPANYLOGO> element.

One of the child elements, the <SALES> element identifying Anna Gold, also contains an empty element <HEAD> that indicates that Anna is the head of the Sales Department. <HEAD> can be used for other types of processing, like a search script developed to look for and display department managers.

In the prolog portion of the contacts.xml document, at line 3 is the document type declaration statement. The declaration tells the processor that the XML document is a CONTACTS type of document, and then points the processor to the external document type definition (DTD), which the processor should use to validate the XML document.

Line 4 of the XML document is its processing instruction statement. With type="text/xsl", the processor is told to apply an XSL type of stylesheet. (If the value of type were "text/css", then the processor would apply a cascading style sheet.) href="contacts.xslt" tells the processor where to look for the stylesheet file. The interpretation, here, is "look in the same directory in which you found this XML document." If the stylesheet is found in a different location, a directory path is included with the filename. "type" and "href", the way they are applied in line 4, are pseudo-attributes. **Pseudo-attributes** are not really attributes in the strictest sense. They look like attributes, but they appear in the <?xml-stylesheet ...?> processing instruction, not in the start tag of an element. They use attribute/value-like syntax, but they do not describe any properties of any element. What they do is describe certain properties of the stylesheet mentioned in the declaration. Table 6-1 lists six pseudo-attributes that may appear in such a declaration. href is a locator pseudo-attribute, since it refers to the location of the XSLT stylesheet.

Table 6-1 Pseudo-attributes used in <?xml-stylesheet...?> declarations

Pseudo-attribute	Explanation
alternate	"yes" or "no"; default is "no"
charset	optional; the character set pertaining to the stylesheet
href	required; indicates the location of the stylesheet; format is URI
media	optional; indicates the type of target media
title	optional; names the stylesheet
type	required; indicates the kind of stylesheet, e.g., "text/xsl" indicates XSL stylesheet

Interpreting the DTD

Figure 6-5 illustrates the DTD that is used to build contacts.xml. Notice that, in line 3, a plus sign appears next to the element name <SALES> within the element <CONTACTS>. The plus sign indicates that at least one <SALES> child element must appear within the <CONTACTS> element. On the same line, the question mark (?) next to <COMPANYLOGO> indicates that the appearance of a <COMPANYLOGO> element, which is declared empty in line 8, is optional within <CONTACTS>. From the examination of the <CONTACTS> root element in contacts.xml, it is clear that the author chose to include <COMPANYLOGO>.

```
contacts.dtd - Notepad
File Edit Search Help
1. <?xml version="1.0" encoding="UTF-8"?>
2. <!-- edited with XML Spy v4.0 U (http://www.xmlspy.com) by Student Name -->
3. <!ELEMENT CONTACTS (SALES+, CUSTSRV, EMPLREL, PRESIDENT, COMPANYLOGO?)>
4. <!ELEMENT SALES (NAME, EMAIL, PHONE, HEAD?)>
5. <!ELEMENT CUSTSRV (NAME, EMAIL, PHONE)>
6. <!ELEMENT EMPLREL (NAME, EMAIL, PHONE)>
7. <!ELEMENT PRESIDENT (NAME, EMAIL, PHONE)>
8. <!ELEMENT COMPANYLOGO EMPTY>
9. <!ELEMENT NAME (#PCDATA)>
10. <!ELEMENT EMAIL (#PCDATA)>
11. <!ELEMENT PHONE (#PCDATA)>
12. <!ELEMENT HEAD EMPTY>
```

Figure 6-5 The contacts DTD

On line 4, another question mark appears next to the element name <HEAD> within the <SALES> element. Again, it indicates that the element <HEAD>, which is declared empty in line 12, may or may not appear within a <SALES> element. The contacts.xml file indicated that an empty <HEAD> element appears in the <SALES> element specific to Anna Gold.

Examining the Source Tree

Figure 6-6 illustrates the source tree structure defined within the contacts.xml file that was developed according to the contacts.dtd file and eventually validated against it. Note that the source tree is not just an element tree. Thus, it does not simply show the various elements in contacts.xml. The source tree also illustrates all the types of nodes, including elements, attributes, and declarations. If contacts.xml contained any namespaces—which it does not—then they would also appear in Figure 6-6. The source tree is presented here so that, once the complete transformation has eventually taken place, you can compare the source tree with the result tree. Otherwise, source trees are valuable design tools for planning transformations.

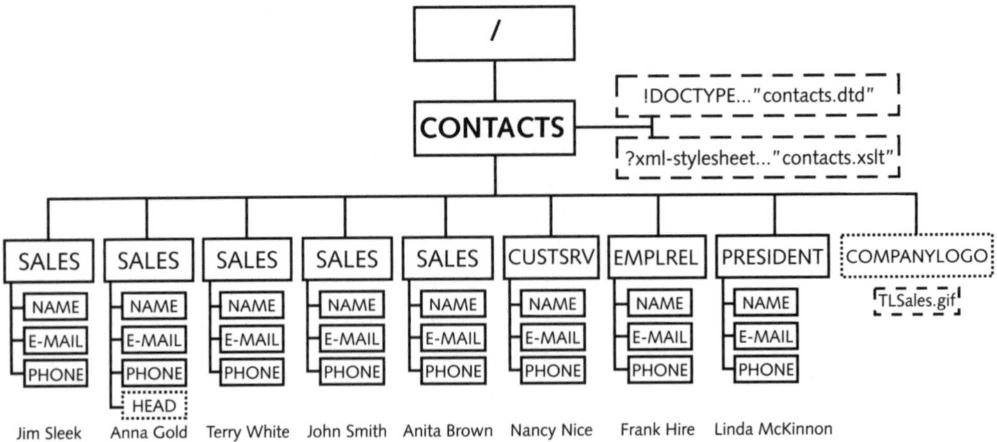

Figure 6-6 The contacts source tree

Note that the root node—represented by the box with the " / " in it and signifying the whole document, including the prolog—is at the top of the source tree structure. Beneath it is the document node CONTACTS with its DOCTYPE definition and XML-stylesheet declaration. Beneath them, from left to right, are the child elements from contacts.xml. The order matches the order presented in contacts.xml. COMPANYLOGO, at the right side, is in a dotted-line box, which is a way of indicating that it is an empty element. Beneath COMPANYLOGO is the name of the Graphics Interchange Format (.gif) file containing the company logo's graphic image, which is the value of the "href" pseudo-attribute in the <COMPANYLOGO> element. The staff names were included at the bottom of the diagram to indicate that the order of the elements here corresponds to the order in the source contacts.xml document. Note the declared empty <HEAD> child element within Anna Gold's <SALES> element.

Examining the XSLT Stylesheet

Figure 6-7 illustrates the XSLT stylesheet contacts_sort.xslt. The first line of the document is the XML declaration (also called the header). The XSLT stylesheet is a well-formed XML document and so must conform to XML document conventions. However, this is the only prolog-style statement required. The first element tags follow immediately. Line 2 is the stylesheet element. This tag indicates to the processor that this XML document is a stylesheet. The tag xsl:transform could also be used instead of xsl:stylesheet, since it is considered a synonym for that term. The xsl:transform tag would also use the same attributes as xsl:stylesheet. This XSLT stylesheet, like all XSLT stylesheets, uses the namespace xmlns:xsl=http://www.w3.org/ 1999/XSL/Transform. Every conventional XSLT element tag in this stylesheet usually begins with the prefix "xsl:" to indicate to the processor which version of XSLT to refer to and to show that the tag conforms to the W3C XSLT Recommendation. (If authoring stylesheets yourself, you could specify a different prefix.) Further, if a tag does not have an "xsl:" prefix, then the XSL parser passes the statement to the next processing phase. In this case, the next processing phase is the browser, which is an HTML-rendering application. The xsl:stylesheet tag is followed by a version attribute, indicating the version of XSLT to which the stylesheet conforms. In this case, for the version of XSLT, the value is 1.0.

An XSLT stylesheet is a complete and well-formed XML document. The <xsl:stylesheet> element usually forms the document element of the document (i.e., the equivalent of the root element, but not to be confused with the concept of root nodes, discussed previously). However, an XSLT stylesheet may also be embedded in a non-XML resource or it may occur in an XML document other than as the document element. For more information about embedded stylesheets, refer to *www.w3.org/TR/xslt* under "Embedded Stylesheets" for further details.

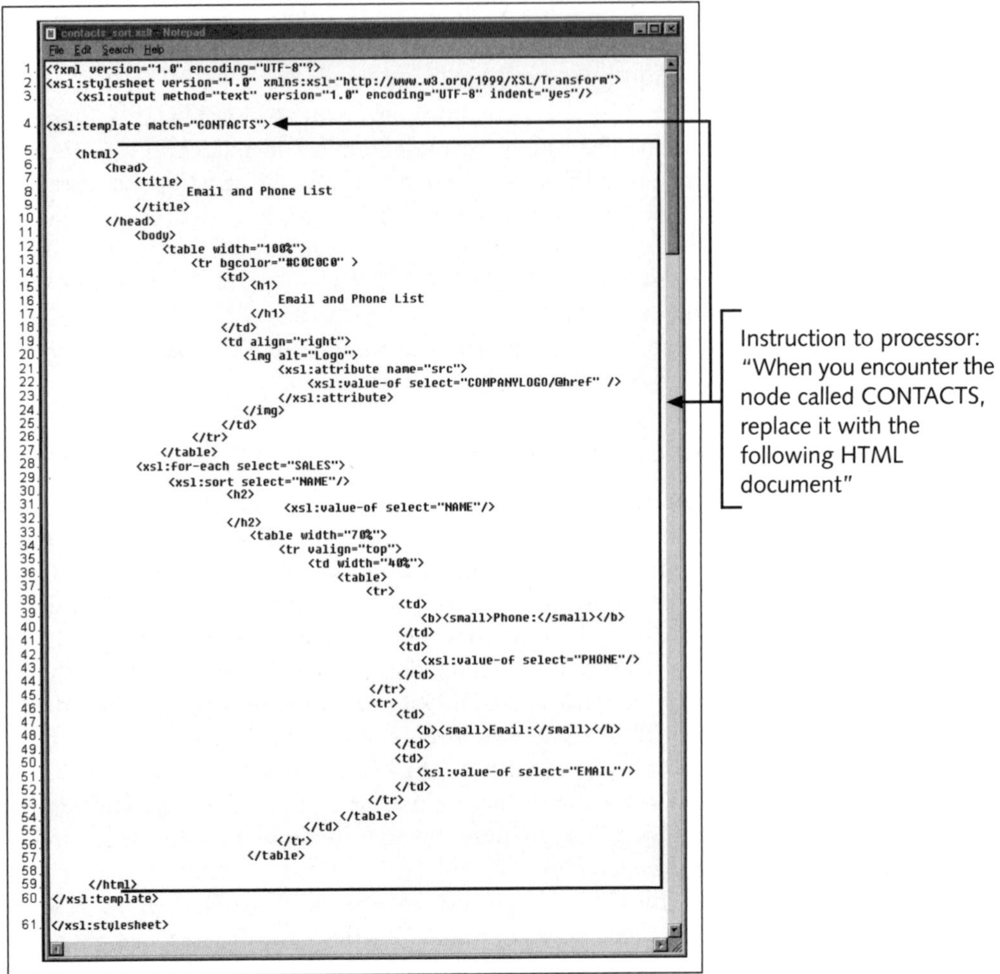

```
<?xml version="1.0" encoding="UTF-8"?>
<xsl:stylesheet version="1.0" xmlns:xsl="http://www.w3.org/1999/XSL/Transform">
    <xsl:output method="text" version="1.0" encoding="UTF-8" indent="yes"/>

<xsl:template match="CONTACTS">

    <html>
        <head>
            <title>
                Email and Phone List
            </title>
        </head>
            <body>
                <table width="100%">
                    <tr bgcolor="#C0C0C0" >
                        <td>
                            <h1>
                                Email and Phone List
                            </h1>
                        </td>
                        <td align="right">
                            <img alt="Logo">
                                <xsl:attribute name="src">
                                    <xsl:value-of select="COMPANYLOGO/@href" />
                                </xsl:attribute>
                            </img>
                        </td>
                    </tr>
                </table>
            <xsl:for-each select="SALES">
                <xsl:sort select="NAME"/>
                    <h2>
                        <xsl:value-of select="NAME"/>
                    </h2>
                    <table width="70%">
                        <tr valign="top">
                            <td width="40%">
                                <table>
                                    <tr>
                                        <td>
                                            <b><small>Phone:</small></b>
                                        </td>
                                        <td>
                                            <xsl:value-of select="PHONE"/>
                                        </td>
                                    </tr>
                                    <tr>
                                        <td>
                                            <b><small>Email:</small></b>
                                        </td>
                                        <td>
                                            <xsl:value-of select="EMAIL"/>
                                        </td>
                                    </tr>
                                </table>
                            </td>
                        </tr>
                    </table>

    </html>
</xsl:template>

</xsl:stylesheet>
```

contacts_sort.xslt - Notepad
File Edit Search Help
Instruction to processor: "When you encounter the node called CONTACTS, replace it with the following HTML document"

Figure 6-7 The Sales contacts stylesheet

The <xsl:stylesheet> element may contain, as direct children, any of the several elements listed in Table 6-2. Any element occurring as a child element of the document element <xsl:stylesheet> is referred to as a **top-level element**. Top-level elements are elements that provide additional specifications to the stylesheet. Some of the top-level elements listed in Table 6-2 are discussed in further detail later in this section. For details regarding the other elements, check the W3C XSLT Recommendation at *www.w3.org/TR/xslt*.

Table 6-2 Top-level elements

Element Name	Explanation
xsl:include	Lets you include an additional XSLT stylesheet; has an `href` attribute whose value—a URI reference—identifies and provides the location of the stylesheet to be included
xsl:import	Lets you import a stylesheet; importing is the same as including except that the definitions and template rules in the importing stylesheet take precedence over those in the imported stylesheet
xsl:strip-space	If an element name matches a name test in an xsl:strip-space element, then the element name is removed from the set of whitespace-preserving element names
xsl:preserve-space	If an element name matches a specific name test in an xsl:preserve-space element, then the element name is added to the set of whitespace-preserving element names
xsl:output	Allows stylesheet authors to specify how they wish the result tree to be produced; discussed in more detail later in this section
xsl:key	A stylesheet declares a set of keys for each document using this element; a key is a kind of generalized identifier
xsl:decimal-format	Declares a decimal-format, which controls the interpretation of a format pattern used by the format-number function. A name attribute specifies a particular format. If there is no name attribute, then the element declares the default decimal-format.
xsl:namespace-alias	Declares that one namespace URI is an alias for another namespace URI.
xsl:attribute-set	Defines a named set of attributes; a following name attribute specifies the name of the attribute set
xsl:variable	With this element, you add an attribute called "name," and specify a parsed character data-related name as a value. That specified value becomes a variable name that can, thereafter, be combined with other specifications (for example, element names) to search for data or to create display specifications. For more details and examples, refer to *www.w3.org/TR/xslt*. One of two elements that can be used to bind variables (the other is xsl:param). For the difference, see xsl:param, below.
xsl:param	An element that can be used to bind variables (the other one is xsl:variable). Also uses an attribute called "name." The difference between xsl:param and xsl:variable is that the value specified on the sl:param variable is only a default value for the binding. When its stylesheet is implemented, parameters can be specified for the variable name that can be used in place of the default value. For more details and examples, refer to *www.w3.org/TR/xslt*.
xsl:template	An instruction to the processor regarding how to transform a node for output, more details are provided in the discussion below

6

Except for the <xsl:import> element or its alternate, the <xsl:include> element, which must come first when they are used, the top-level elements may occur in any order. Furthermore, the <xsl:stylesheet> element may contain elements that do not originate in the XSLT namespace, as long as the expanded names of such elements have non-null URIs (i.e., you cannot specify a namespace like "xmlns:abc=" "" and then attempt to use abc: as a prefix for an element name). They are otherwise acceptable, as long as they do not attempt to alter the behavior of XSLT elements and functions from that found in the W3C XSLT Recommendation. An XSLT processor is free to ignore such top-level elements, and *must* ignore the top-level element without giving an error if it does not recognize the element's namespace URI. In line 3, the stylesheet instructs the processor regarding what output should be produced when a pattern in the XML document is matched. An XSLT processor may produce the result tree as a sequence of bytes, although it is not required to be able to do so. The <xsl:output> element allows stylesheet authors to specify how they wish the result tree to be displayed. If an XSLT processor outputs the result tree, it should do so as specified by the <xsl:output element>; however, it is not required to do so. Meanwhile, the <xsl:output> element is only allowed as a top-level element.

The method attribute in the <xsl:output> element identifies the method that should be used for displaying the result tree. The value must be a qualified name (that is, it must contain a prefix, a colon, and a local name portion). If there is no prefix, then there are only three options for the values specified for the method attribute: xml, html, or text. Occasionally, under certain circumstances, the default value may be html (for details, check *www.w3.org/TR/xslt*). Usually, though, the default is xml. If the value is a qualified name with a prefix, then the value is expanded into its expanded name, which should then specify the output method. In this instance, however, the result tree is specified to be a well-formed XML document. In this case, although XML is specified as the output method, lines 5 through 59 actually seem to override XML by providing HTML tags. The XML information is provided, but the HTML tags prevail. This is explained later, when <xsl:template ... > tags are discussed in more detail. However, in a separate trial for comparison purposes, the authors removed all the HTML-related lines, leaving only the XML/XSLT lines. The output of that trial is shown in Figure 6-8.

Notice how the XML output, when displayed in Notepad, appears as one continuous line. For the sake of readability, Figure 6-8 shows the line broken into three segments. Despite the ugliness of this display, the proper information has been extracted.

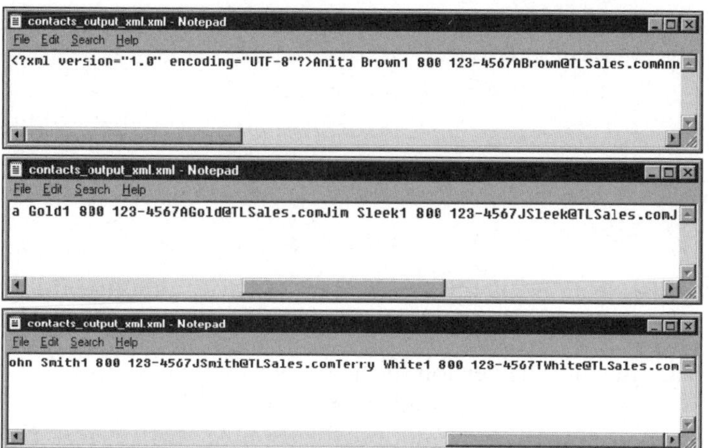

Figure 6-8 Sales contacts output in XML format

There are ten possible attributes allowed within the <xsl:output> element. They are listed in Table 6.3.

Table 6-3 List of available xsl:output attributes

Attribute Name	Explanation
method	The format of the output; optional; values = xml, html, text, name
version	The version of the output format version specified; optional; value = version number (decimal)
encoding	The character set used for encoding; optional; value = text specification (e.g., UTF=8, UTF=16, etc.); not case sensitive
omit-xml-declaration	Optional; values = "yes," "no;" "yes" indicates that the XML declaration (i.e., <?xml...?>) should be omitted in the output; "no" indicates otherwise
standalone	Optional; values = "yes," "no;" "yes" indicates that the result should be a stand-alone document; "no" indicates otherwise
doctype-public	Optional; value = text; indicates the public identifier to be used in the <!doctype> declaration in the output
doctype-system	Optional; value = text; the system identifier to be used in the <!doctype> declaration in the output
cdata-section-elements	Optional; value = list of names; a list (separated by white space) of elements the content of which is to be output in CDATA sections
indent	Optional; values = "yes," "no". "Yes" indicates that the output should be indented to indicate the hierarchic structure (for readability). "No" indicates that the output should not be indented.
media-type	Optional; value = mimetype; the media type of the output

Of these ten attributes, four are specified in the top-level <xsl:output> element in line 3 of the *contacts_xml.xslt* example:

- method
- version
- encoding
- indent

The output method has been explicitly specified to be XML, although the specificaton could have been omitted and XML would still have been the default.

The version attribute specifies the version of the output method. In this case, XML version 1.0 is to be used for creating the result tree. If the XSLT processor does not support a specified version of XML, it should use a version of XML that it does support. The XML version specified in the stylesheet's XML declaration should correspond to the version of XML that the XSLT processor uses for outputting the result tree. The default value is version 1.0.

Encoding specifies the preferred character encoding that the XSLT processor should use to output the result tree. The value should either be a character set registered with the Internet Assigned Numbers Authority (IANA) or should start with "x-". XSLT processors are required to respect values of UTF-8 and UTF-16. In fact, if no encoding attribute is specified, then the XSLT processor should use either of those two values. If another value is specified and the XSLT processor does not support it, then the processor may signal an error. Occasionally, you may see a result tree containing a character that cannot be represented in the output encoding used by the XSLT processor. If that character occurs in a context where XML recognizes character references, then the character should be displayed as a character reference (character references were discussed previously in Chapter 2). Otherwise—for example, if the character occurs in the name of an element—the XSLT processor should signal an error.

Indent specifies whether the XSLT processor may add additional white space when displaying the result tree; the value must be either yes or no. If the value is yes, then the XML output method may add white space to the result tree output in order to make the output more presentable. If the value is no, then there should be no additional white space. The default value is no.

If you are using XML documents that contain mixed content (i.e., there are elements that contain both elements and text), then it is not advisable to specify the indent value as yes.

Query Contexts and Template Rules

As mentioned previously, both XSLT and XPath consider documents to be composed of nodes in a tree-like structure. Before processing can begin, the relevant **query context** portion of the source tree—the portion of the contacts.xml document that contains the information that is manipulated and copied to the output—must be selected with a combined XSLT/XPath expression. Another valuable thing to remember is that XSLT is different from conventional programming languages because XSLT is based on **template rules** that specify how XML documents should be processed. A template rule is specified with the <xsl:template ... > element. Further, unless you specify a name attribute and its respective value, then you must specify a match attribute. The value specified for the match attribute identifies the source node or nodes to which the new template rule applies. That value is an XPath expression. Meanwhile, the content listed between the <xsl:template ... > start tag and the </xsl:template> end tag is the template that appears in the output.

Line 4 of the contacts_xml.xslt file, which is reproduced below in Figure 6-9, uses the top-level element <xsl:template> to begin the first—and only, in fact—template rule in the stylesheet, and to specify that the <CONTACTS> node is query context.

```
4.  <xsl:template match="CONTACTS">
```

Figure 6-9 Line 4 of contacts_xml.xslt

Note that the XPath expression used to select the relevant portion of the XML document is CONTACTS. What it specifies, in other words, is that the relevant query context of the contacts.xml document is the node called <CONTACTS>. Stated yet another way, <xsl:template match="CONTACTS"> has **set the context** (also called **matched the context**) for subsequent queries. It is like saying to the processor, "When you encounter the node called <CONTACTS>, substitute the HTML document template defined between this <xsl: template ... > start tag on line 4 and the </xsl:template> end tag on line 60, near the end of this stylesheet." In this case, it is sufficient to select the document node (i.e., document element) <CONTACTS> because no changes are to be made above it, in the prolog. In addition, it simplifies the selection of child nodes later in the stylesheet.

This concept of the **query context**—that is, the context being processed by an XSL template at any given moment—is important both during the planning and design phases and, later, during troubleshooting. If your XSL file isn't creating the output file you're expecting, understanding the processor's progress through its contexts could help you determine why it is malfunctioning and how you might debug the problem. A reminder regarding context appears later, in the discussion of the processing of contacts.xml according to contacts.xslt.

The discussion so far has centered around matching a specific node: the document element node named <CONTACTS>. If, for other purposes, you need to match to another type of node, consult Table 6-4 to find the syntax for doing so. The examples listed in Table 6-4 pertain to the contacts.xml document depicted in Figure 6-4. Later in this discussion, you see a match to an attribute.

Table 6-4 Syntax for matching to nodes

Node Name	Syntax	Explanation
Document root	<xsl:template match="/">	Match the document's root node
Element	<xsl:template match= "docnodename">	Match the document node
	<xsl:template match= "docnodename/nodename">	Match a child to the document node
	<xsl:template match= "docnodename//nodename">	Match the nodename grand-child(ren) of the document node
	<xsl:template match= "docnodename/*/nodename">	Match all the nodename descendants of the document node
Attribute	<xsl:value-of select= "@attributename">	Match on the value of the specified attribute
	<xsl:value-of select= "nodename/@*">	Match on the value of all the attributes of the specified node.
Namespace	<xsl:template match= "documentnodename"> <xsl:value-of select= "@xs:xmlns"/>	Match on the document node and select the namespace value.
Comment	<xsl:template match="comment()">	Convert a comment from XML's <!—comment --> form to a form that another markup language can use
Processing Instruction	<xsl:template match= "/processing instruction()">	Match on all the processing instructions in the document root
	<xsl:template match= "/processing instruction(piname)">	Match on a specific processing instruction piname in the document root
Text	xsl:template match="text()">	Match on all text

An alternative to including the template in the stylesheet is to store the template in a file elsewhere and call it from the <xsl:template> tag. For example, a stylesheet could declare that the "templatename" template be inserted by the following syntax:

```
<xsl:template name="templatename">
...
</xsl:template>
```

The HTML Document Template

Lines 5 through 59 of contacts_xml.xslt (those lines are reproduced below in Figure 6-10) define the HTML format document to be inserted as a template for the <CONTACTS> node during processing.

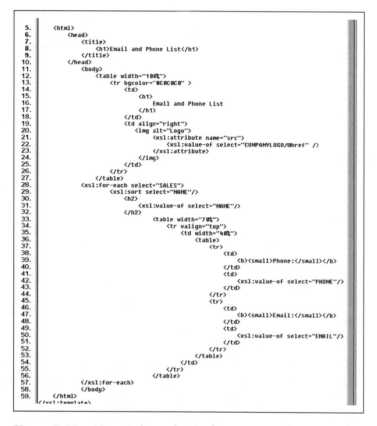

```
5.  <html>
6.      <head>
7.          <title>
8.              <h1>Email and Phone List</h1>
9.          </title>
10.     </head>
11.         <body>
12.             <table width="100%">
13.                 <tr bgcolor="#C0C0C0" >
14.                     <td>
15.                         <h1>
16.                             Email and Phone List
17.                         </h1>
18.                     </td>
19.                     <td align="right">
20.                        <img alt="Logo">
21.                             <xsl:attribute name="src">
22.                                 <xsl:value-of select="COMPANYLOGO/@href" />
23.                             </xsl:attribute>
24.                         </img>
25.                     </td>
26.                 </tr>
27.             </table>
28.         <xsl:for-each select="SALES">
29.                 <xsl:sort select="NAME"/>
30.                     <h2>
31.                         <xsl:value-of select="NAME"/>
32.                     </h2>
33.                             <table width="70%">
34.                                 <tr valign="top">
35.                                     <td width="40%">
36.                                         <table>
37.                                             <tr>
38.                                                 <td>
39.                                                     <b><small>Phone:</small></b>
40.                                                 </td>
41.                                                 <td>
42.                                                     <xsl:value-of select="PHONE"/>
43.                                                 </td>
44.                                             </tr>
45.                                             <tr>
46.                                                 <td>
47.                                                     <b><small>Email:</small></b>
48.                                                 </td>
49.                                                 <td>
50.                                                     <xsl:value-of select="EMAIL"/>
51.                                                 </td>
52.                                             </tr>
53.                                         </table>
54.                                     </td>
55.                                 </tr>
56.                             </table>
57.         </xsl:for-each>
58.         </body>
59. </html>
</xsl:template>
```

Figure 6-10 Lines 5 through 59 of contacts_xml.xslt

The HTML codes in lines 6 through 10 specify that the final browser page produced has the phrase "E-mail and Phone List" in the head section of the frame of the browser window. That phrase may come in handy if other users want to find the frame in a "Favorites" or "Bookmarks" listing, for example. Lines 11 through 58 define the body of the template HTML document. If you are familiar with HTML coding, you can see that lines 12 through 27 define a single-row, two-column (i.e., a two-cell) table which is to appear at the top of the browser page. The table is to be full width, and its first row is to have a silver background—judging from the bgcolor=#C0C0C0 (that is the RGB hexadecimal-style color code for silver) attribute/value pair specified for the first table row element <tr> in line 13. The title of the page, which is contained in the first cell in the table, is "E-mail and Phone List" (line 16), identical to the browser window's head specification (line 8).

Finding the Logo Image; the Current Template Rule

Lines 21 through 23, reproduced in Figure 6-11, list some XSLT elements that specify where to find a logo image.

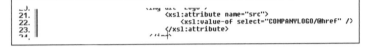

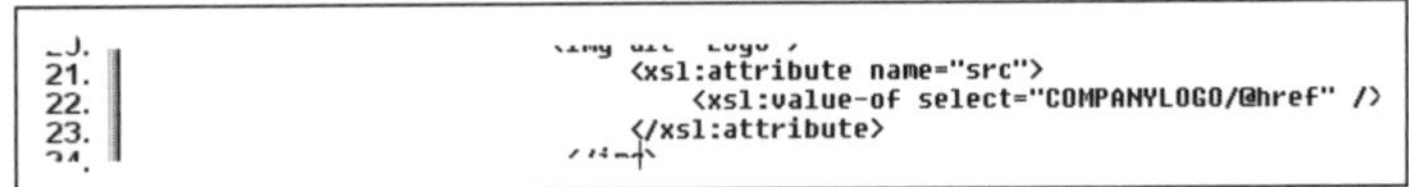

```
21.     <xsl:attribute name="src">
22.         <xsl:value-of select="COMPANYLOGO/@href" />
23.     </xsl:attribute>
```

Figure 6-11 Lines 21 through 23 of contacts_xml.xslt

That logo image is to be added to the table in the second cell. Here is the translation of those three lines:

- An attribute is added to the HTML image tag <img alt="Logo">. The attribute's name is src (line 21).
- The value of the new src attribute is the value extracted from the href locator pseudo-attribute found in the node <COMPANYLOGO> within the <CONTACTS> node (we know, from looking at the contacts.xml document in Figure 6-4, that the value is "TLSales.gif") (line 22).
- This is the end of the attribute definition (line 23).

The attribute expression implements the **current template rule**. At any point in the processing of an XSLT stylesheet, if another template rule is chosen by matching a pattern like "attribute", the template rule corresponding to "attribute" suspends the current "<xsl:template>" template rule for the extent of the instantiation of "attribute". When the "attribute" template rule is finished, control passes back to the "<xsl:template>" template rule.

The term **instantiation** refers to the creation of a data structure with its own set of subroutines, which operate on specific data.

Examining Repetitive Loops and Sorting

Lines 28 through 57, reproduced in Figure 6-12, define the most important information to be harvested from contacts.xml: the names, e-mail addresses, and phone numbers of the Sales Department contacts.

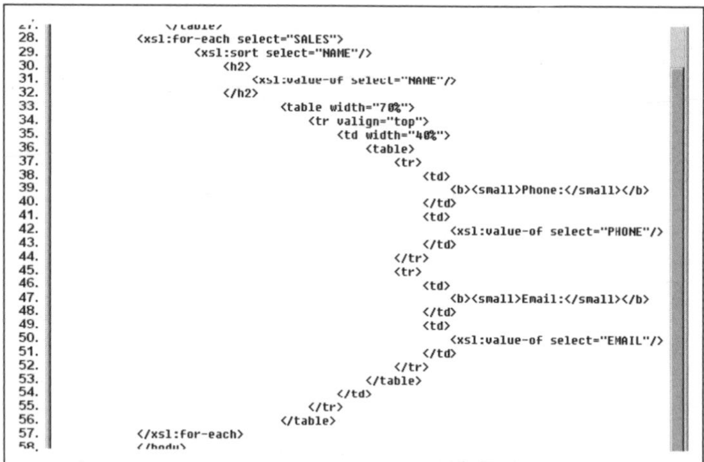

```
28.     <xsl:for-each select="SALES">
29.         <xsl:sort select="NAME"/>
30.           <h2>
31.             <xsl:value-of select="NAME"/>
32.           </h2>
33.               <table width="70%">
34.                 <tr valign="top">
35.                   <td width="40%">
36.                     <table>
37.                       <tr>
38.                         <td>
39.                           <b><small>Phone:</small></b>
40.                         </td>
41.                         <td>
42.                           <xsl:value-of select="PHONE"/>
43.                         </td>
44.                       </tr>
45.                       <tr>
46.                         <td>
47.                           <b><small>Email:</small></b>
48.                         </td>
49.                         <td>
50.                           <xsl:value-of select="EMAIL"/>
51.                         </td>
52.                       </tr>
53.                     </table>
54.                   </td>
55.                 </tr>
56.               </table>
57.     </xsl:for-each>
```

Figure 6-12 Lines 28 through 57 of contacts_xml.xslt

The expression on line 28 ("<xsl:for-each select="SALES">") combines the XSLT element <xsl:for-each> with the XPath expression SALES. It tells the processor to "find all the SALES nodes in this, the CONTACTS node (as defined on line 4)". The "for-each" is a repetitive loop that processes all the subsequent instructions (until the </for-each> end tag is encountered) for each SALES node encountered. So each SALES node is searched. In addition, the nodes are searched in document order (i.e., as they appear in the document) unless a sort specification is provided. The for-each loop expression activates the current template rule again, for the extent of the instantiation of the for-each template rule. In any for-each loop, the context in which the processor is working changes to whatever SALES node it finds itself reading. On one pass, the context may be "CONTACTS/SALES/NAME=Jim Sleek"; on the next, it may be "CONTACTS/SALES/NAME=John Smith".

Line 29 provides the sort specification referred to in the previous paragraph. <xsl:sort select= "NAME"/> tells the processor to search the SALES nodes in alphabetical order according to the values found in the NAME node beneath each SALES node. <xsl:sort> can only appear as a child of <for-each> or <apply-templates>. The attribute select is not the only one available to <xsl:sort>. Other attributes include lang, data-type, order, and case-order. For further details, check *www.w3.org/TR/xslt#sorting*.

Displaying the Output

Lines 30 to 32 instruct the processor to take the value found in the respective node NAME (as they are read in alphabetical order according to line 29) and output that value in Heading2 format (lines 30 through 56 are reproduced in Figure 6-13, below). Lines 33 through 56 define another table; this time, it will be two rows by two columns.

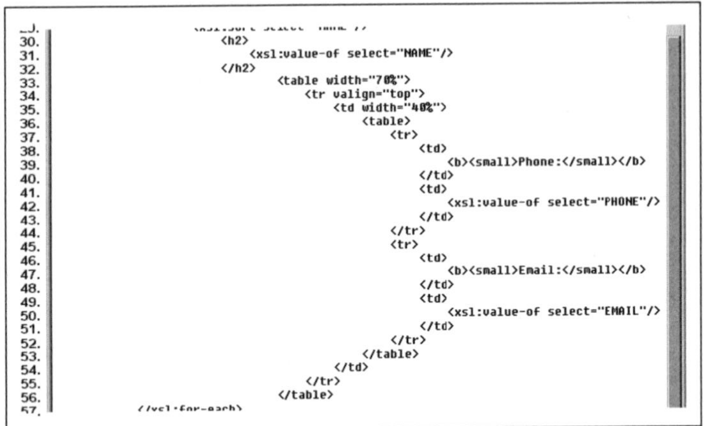

```
30.         <h2>
31.             <xsl:value-of select="NAME"/>
32.         </h2>
33.             <table width="70%">
34.                 <tr valign="top">
35.                     <td width="40%">
36.                         <table>
37.                             <tr>
38.                                 <td>
39.                                     <b><small>Phone:</small></b>
40.                                 </td>
41.                                 <td>
42.                                     <xsl:value-of select="PHONE"/>
43.                                 </td>
44.                             </tr>
45.                             <tr>
46.                                 <td>
47.                                     <b><small>Email:</small></b>
48.                                 </td>
49.                                 <td>
50.                                     <xsl:value-of select="EMAIL"/>
51.                                 </td>
52.                             </tr>
53.                         </table>
54.                     </td>
55.                 </tr>
56.             </table>
```

Figure 6-13 Lines 30 through 56 of contacts_xml.xslt

Notice that one of these tables is created each time another SALES node is read. In Line 39, the processor is told to print Phone: in small bold print in the top-left cell in the table. At line 42, the processor is told to print the value of the node PHONE found within the respective SALES node in the top-right cell of the table. Later, at line 48, the processor is instructed to print E-mail: in small bold print in the bottom-left cell of the table. Finally, at line 51, the processor is told to print the value of the node E-MAIL, found within the respective SALES node, in the bottom-right cell of the table.

The End of the For-each Loop

Please refer to Figure 6-14. At line 57, the processor reaches the end of the <for-each> loop. It returns to line 28 and repeats the SALES node investigation and subsequent table building until it encounters no new SALES nodes. Then, at last, the processor passes line 57 and is finished processing the contacts.xml document according to this stylesheet.

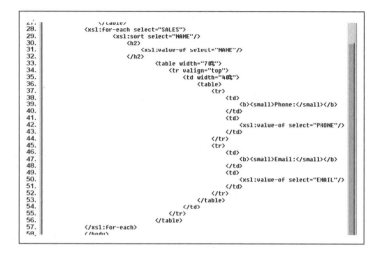

```
28.         <xsl:for-each select="SALES">
29.             <xsl:sort select="NAME"/>
30.               <h2>
31.                   <xsl:value-of select="NAME"/>
32.               </h2>
33.                       <table width="70%">
34.                         <tr valign="top">
35.                           <td width="40%">
36.                             <table>
37.                               <tr>
38.                                 <td>
39.                                   <b><small>Phone:</small></b>
40.                                 </td>
41.                                 <td>
42.                                   <xsl:value-of select="PHONE"/>
43.                                 </td>
44.                               </tr>
45.                               <tr>
46.                                 <td>
47.                                   <b><small>Email:</small></b>
48.                                 </td>
49.                                 <td>
50.                                   <xsl:value-of select="EMAIL"/>
51.                                 </td>
52.                               </tr>
53.                             </table>
54.                           </td>
55.                         </tr>
56.                       </table>
57.         </xsl:for-each>
```

Figure 6-14 Lines 28 through 57 of contacts_xml.xslt

Figure 6-15 displays the output of the XSL parser after that output file has been passed to a browser (in this case, Microsoft Internet Explorer). Notice that the Sales Department contacts are in alphabetical order, as prescribed in the XSLT stylesheet, and *not* as they appear in the original contacts.xml document.

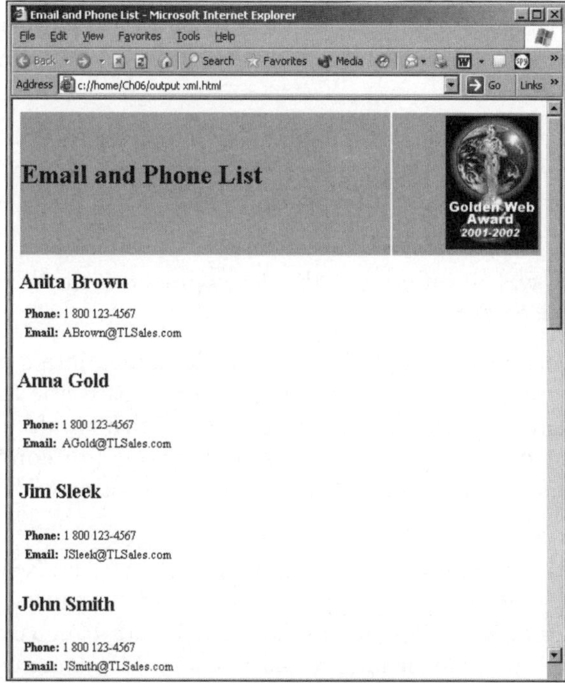

Figure 6-15 Sales contacts—HTML format

6

Notice that not all the information from all the nodes in the contacts.xml document is displayed in Figure 6-15. It follows, then, that the output information—that is, the results tree in Figure 6-16—is not identical to the source tree of Figure 6-6.

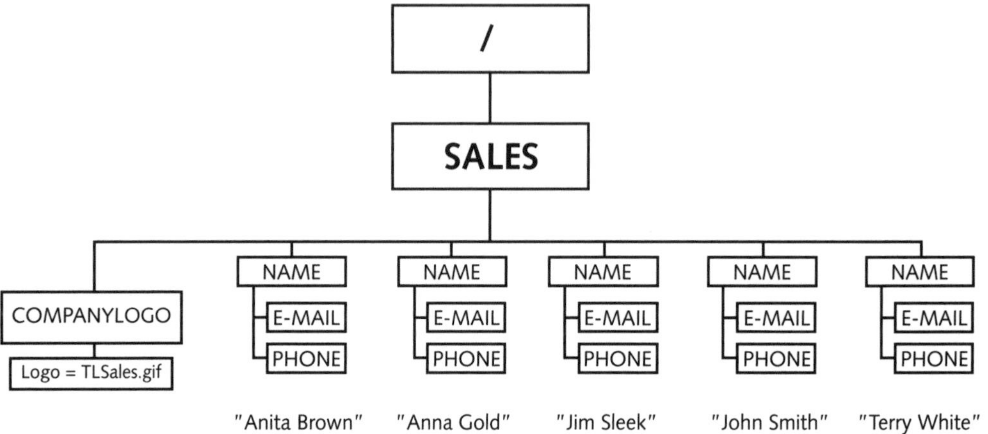

Figure 6-16 Sales contacts result tree

Chapter Summary

- Whether XML data is to be viewed immediately, or is to be fed to another software application, it is rarely used in its raw or original form. First, it has to be transformed into another format.
- There are two phases to the transformation process: a structural transformation (where the data is converted from the structure of the incoming XML document to the structure of the desired output) and formatting (in which the new structure is displayed in the required format).
- The development of XSLT was an offshoot of the development of the W3C Extensible Stylesheet Language (XSL).
- The original XSL developers envisioned XSL would be developed into a platform- and media-independent formatting language composed of two parts: the formatting language (a set of XML elements, called "formatting objects," that would describe the various parts of page media) and the transformation language (for converting the structure of a source XML document into a result tree consisting of XSL formatting objects).
- The original XSL concept evolved into three programming languages: XSL (the XML vocabulary for specifying formatting objectives and other semantics), XSLT (the language for transforming XML documents), and XML Path Language (XPath, an expression language used to access or refer to parts of an XML document).

XPath and XSLT both consider documents to be composed of nodes in a tree-like structure.

- During a basic transformation, the XML parser validates the XML document and its referenced XSLT stylesheet against a referenced DTD or schema. Then the XSL parser starts using the XSLT stylesheet as its guide, performs the specified transformation.
- Source and result (node) trees are a valuable design and planning tool. But, they should not simply illustrate the elements in the source XML document. They should also illustrate all the types of nodes (e.g., elements, attributes, declarations, etc.) in source documents and in transformations.
- XSLT stylesheets instruct the XSL processor regarding what output should be produced when a pattern in the XML document is matched. All XSLT stylesheets use namespaces. An XSLT stylesheet is a complete and well-formed XML document. Its <xsl:stylesheet> element usually forms the document element. Top-level elements, which add stylesheet specifications, occur as child elements of the <xsl:stylesheet> element. Except for the <xsl:import> and <xsl:include> elements, top-level elements may occur in any order.
- Unless a template is called in from another location, the content listed on the stylesheet between the "<xsl:template ... >" start tag and the "</xsl:template>" end tag is the template for the information that appears in the output.
- XSLT processing is subject to the current template rule. That is, at any point in the processing of an XSLT stylesheet, when processing is adhering to one template rule, if a new template rule is invoked, then that new template rule suspends the current template rule for the extent of the instantiation of the new template rule. When processing of the new template rule is finished, control passes back to the original template rule.

6

Review Questions

1. What is the primary reason for performing XML transformations?
2. What are the two phases of transformation?
3. When was XSLT developed as a W3C Recommendation?
   a. during XSL development
   b. during XML development
   c. during XPath development
   d. during HTML development
   e. all of the above
4. What is considered to be the most common application of transformation today?

5. Match the following:

a. defines a set of elements called formatting objects	1. XPath
b. language for transforming XML documents	2. XSL
c. language for finding the information in an XML document	3. XML
d. allows the separation of the data from the data presentation	4. XSLT

6. Transformations are affiliated with source node trees, while XSLT stylesheets are affiliated with result node trees. True or false?
7. XSLT and XPath both consider documents to be composed of ________________ in a tree-like structure.
8. Briefly describe a basic transformation process.
9. Pseudo-attributes are a kind of attribute, but they appear in the <?xml-stylesheet ...?> declaration. True or false?
10. A(n) ________________ provides information to the ________________ regarding remote resources.
11. Which of the following should not be included in a source tree?
    a. namespaces
    b. declarations
    c. template rules
    d. elements
    e. attributes
    f. all of the above
12. On an XSLT stylesheet, which element could be used instead of the <xsl:stylesheet> element?
13. When authoring XSLT stylesheets and referring to the namespace "xmlns:xsl=http://www.w3.org/1999/XSL/Transform", you must use the prefix "xsl:". True or false?
14. In which of the following locations can you place the <xsl:stylesheet> element?
    a. in an element other than the document element
    b. in a non-XML resource
    c. in a document element
    d. all of the above
    e. a and c, but not b or d
15. An element occurring as a child element of an xsl:stylesheet element is called a(n) ________________.
16. The XML version mentioned in the XSLT stylesheet's XML declaration should correspond to the version of XML that the processor uses for outputting the result tree (i.e., the version mentioned in the <xsl:output> element). True or false?

17. When specifying a value for the encoding attribute of <xsl:output>, which of the following can you use?
    a. UTF-8
    b. ANSI 9964
    c. UTF-16
    d. any character set registered with IANA
    e. any character set starting with "x-"
    f. all of the above
18. If your source XML documents contain mixed content elements (i.e., elements which contain both elements and text), then what should you specify for the indent attribute of <xsl:output>?

19. What is a query context?
20. In the following expression, which components are mostly XSLT and which are mostly XPath?

```
"<xsl:template match="CONTACTS">
```

21. Match the start tags in a-c with the processing instructions in 1-2.
    a. <xsl:template match="docnodename//nodename">
    b. <xsl:template match="docnodename/nodename">
    c. <xsl:template match="docnodename/*/nodename">
       1. Match all the nodename descendants of the document node.
       2. Match the nodename grandchild(ren) of the document node.
       3. Match a child to the document node.
22. Here is a rule that was introduced in this chapter. From among the choices follwing it, choose its name.

    "At any point in the processing of an XSLT stylesheet, when processing is adhering to one template rule, if a new template rule is invoked, then that new template rule suspends the current template rule for the extent of the instantiation of the new template rule. When processing of the new template rule is finished, control passes back to the original template rule."
    a. the template suspension rule
    b. the current template rule
    c. the template transformation rule
    d. the basic transformation rule
    e. none of the above
23. The for-each is a repetitive loop that processes all the subsequent instructions (until the </for-each> tag is encountered) for its designated node. Each node is searched in ________________ order unless a ________________ specification is provided.

24. <xsl:sort> can only appear as a child of:
    a. <template>
    b. <for-each>
    c. <value-of>
    d. <apply-templates>
    e. <attribute>
25. What does the following coded instruction mean?

    ```
    <xsl:value-of select="PHONE">
    ```

    a. The processor is being told that following instructions will affect the value of the <PHONE> node.
    b. The processor is being told to change the value of all nodes except <PHONE>.
    c. The processor is being told to change, and then print, the value of the node <PHONE>.
    d. The processor is being told to print the value of the node <PHONE>.
    e. none of the above

Hands-on Projects

Project 6-1

One common XML transformation is to convert an XML document to HTML and display the results in a browser. Doing so involves using an XSLT stylesheet and XML file. In this project, you use XSLT elements to display the content of the SALES element from the contacts.xml file. In the following projects, you add to one XSL transformation and build another from scratch.

The following Hands-on Projects require that MSXML Parser 3.0 is installed on your system. Please refer to the "Read This Before You Begin" page at the beginning of this book for instructions on how to find this application.

You start Project 6-1 by copying the project files you need to the home/*yourname*/ Ch06 folder on your hard disk. These projects assume that this folder is on drive C; if you are using a different drive, substitute its letter for drive C in the instructions.

To copy the project files and open the contacts project:

1. Open Windows Explorer. Create a new folder called **Ch06** in the C:/home/*yourname* folder.
2. Copy the **contacts.spp**, **contacts.xml**, **contacts.dtd** and **contacts.xslt** files located in the Ch06\project_6-1 folder on your Data Disk to your **C:/home/*yourname*/Ch06** folder. If you are asked to replace the current files, click **Yes to all**.

Now you are ready to start XML Spy and open the contacts project.

3. Click **Start**, point to **Programs** (point to **All Programs** in Windows XP), point to **XML Spy Suite**, and then click **XML Spy IDE**.
4. Click **Project** on the menu bar, and then click **Open Project**. The Open dialog box appears.
5. Click the **Look in** list arrow, navigate to C:\home*yourname*\Ch06, if necessary, click **contacts.spp**, and then click **Open**.

   If you click the expand boxes in the Project window, you will notice that the project has three files: an XML document, contacts.xml; an XSL transformation, contacts.xslt; and a DTD, contacts.dtd.

Now you can open and review the XML document to prepare for the transformation.

To review the XML document:

1. Expand the **XML Files** branch in the Project pane, and then double-click **contacts.xml** to open the XML document.
2. Click **View** on the menu bar, and then click **Text view** to view the source code.

   Notice that the XML document contains a list of individuals and contact information. Each person's name and contact information is contained within a SALES, CUSTSRV, or PRESIDENT element.
3. Examine Line 4. The xml-stylesheet declaration identifies the stylesheet that will be used with this document. You will review this stylesheet next.
4. Click **XML** on the menu bar, and then click **Validate** to validate the XML document. A green circle with a check appears in the lower-left corner of the XML Spy window.

After you validate the XML document, you can open and review the XSL transformation, which you'll perform in Project 6-2.

To open and review the XSL transformation:

1. Expand the **XSL Files** branch in the Project pane, and then double-click **contacts.xslt** to open the XSL transformation. The XSL transformation opens in Text view in the XML Spy window.
2. Examine the transformation file. Following the XML declaration, the transformation begins with the xsl:stylesheet root element, which specifies the XSL version and namespace prefix. The xsl namespace prefix is used as a convention, but you can use any other prefix. The next line is the xsl:output element, which specifies that this transformation will produce an HTML result tree.

   Note that the first template matches the root of the source tree, and begins the definition of the result tree with the document, head, and body HTML elements.
3. In the HTML code, find the xsl:apply-templates element that matches the CONTACTS element. When the transformation engine is processing the source tree, this element will cause the xsl:template matching CONTACTS to process the element and then return to the line following the xsl:apply-templates.

Find the xsl:for-each element in the template that matches CONTACTS. This element will apply the transformation information for each instance of the SALES element within CONTACTS.

4. Leave XML Spy open. In the next project, you will perform a transformation on the XML document.

Project 6-2

In this project, you transform the XML document that you reviewed in Project 6-2. The transformation will result in an HTML document, and display the child element data for the SALES elements using the XML Spy HTML browser. After examining the generated HTML code, you will add to the XSL transformation to capture the PRESIDENT and CUSTSRV contact information.

To apply the transformation and then review the HTML:

1. If necessary, return to the contacts.spp XML Spy project you opened in Hands-on Project 6-1.
2. Click the **contacts.xml** tab pane to display the XML document. Click **XSL** on the menu bar, and then click **XSL Transformation** to transform the file. An HTML encoding of the document appears. See Figure 6-17.

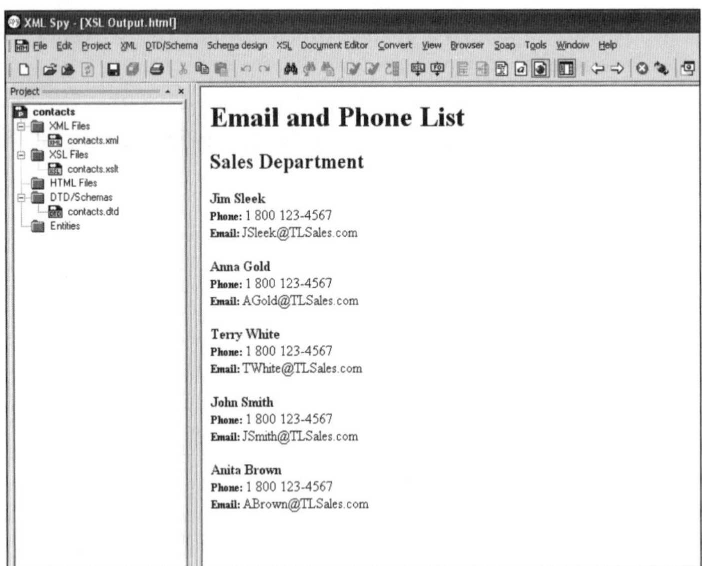

Figure 6-17

3. To review the HTML document generated by the transformation, click **View** on the menu bar, and then click **Text view** to display the source code.

4. Examine the HTML code, noting how it compares with the XSL transformation and XML document information. In particular, notice that for each SALES element, there is a block of similar HTML code that was generated by the xsl:for-each element.
5. Once you have finished examining the code, click **File** on the menu bar, and then click **Save As**. Type **example1.html** as the filename, and then click **Save** to save the file in the Ch06 folder.

Now you are ready to complete the transformation. You will add XSL code to the transformation so that the PRESIDENT and CUSTSRV element information is also displayed in the HTML document.

To complete the transformation:

1. Double-click the **contacts.xslt** file to open the transformation file.
2. Immediately before the line *<h2>Sales Department</h2>*, type the following:

```
<h2>President</h2>
<xsl:for-each select="PRESIDENT">
        <b><xsl:value-of select="NAME"/></b>
        <br/>
        <b><small>Phone: </small></b>
        <xsl:value-of select="PHONE"/>
        <br/>
        <b><small>Email: </small></b>
        <xsl:value-of select="EMAIL"/>
        <br/>
</xsl:for-each>
<h2>Customer Service</h2>
<xsl:for-each select="CUSTSRV">
        <b><xsl:value-of select="NAME"/></b>
        <br/>
        <b><small>Phone: </small></b>
        <xsl:value-of select="PHONE"/>
        <br/>
        <b><small>Email: </small></b>
        <xsl:value-of select="EMAIL"/>
        <br/>
</xsl:for-each>
```

Note that XML Spy enters some closing tags for you.

3. Click **File** on the menu bar, and then click **Save** to save the change. If you receive a message about a missing schema, click **OK**.
4. Under the XML Files branch in the project pane, double-click the **contacts.xml** file to display the XML document. Click **XSL** on the menu bar, and then click **XSL Transformation** to transform the file. The new HTML document appears. Notice that the President and Customer Service Representative are now listed. The new HTML document should resemble Figure 6-18.

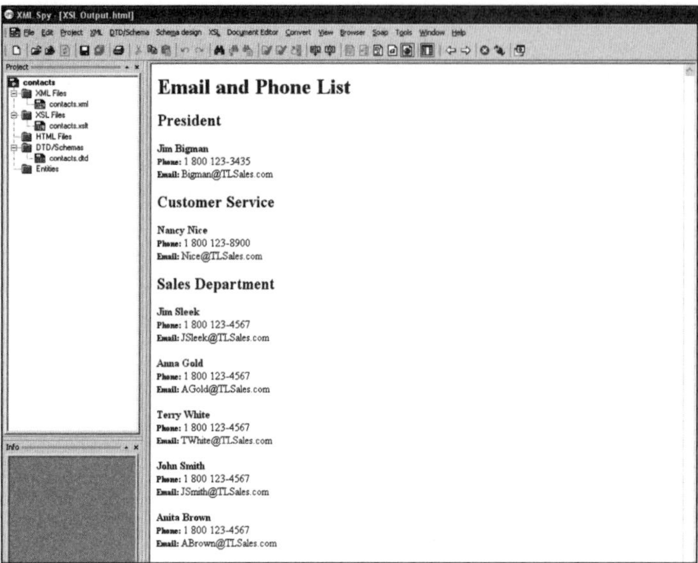

Figure 6-18

5. Switch to Text view to examine the HTML source code. Note the differences between this transformation and the first, especially how your changes to the transformation affected the output.
6. Click **File** on the menu bar, and then click **Save As**. Save the file as **example2.html** in the Ch06 folder.

Project 6-3

In the contacts.dtd file that you have been using in the previous projects, there can only be one PRESIDENT and one CUSTSRV child element in the CONTACTS element, but there can be several SALES child elements. In this project, you will continue to build on the contacts XSL transformation by sorting the SALES contacts information using a xsl:sort statement.

To generate sorted output:

1. With the contacts project you worked with in Project 6-2 open in XML Spy, double-click the **contacts.xslt** file in the Project pane. The XSL transformation document appears.

   Recall that xsl:sort elements can only be a child element of xsl:apply-templates or xsl:for-each elements, and that the xsl:sort element must immediately follow the parent element.

2. Insert **<xsl:sort select="NAME">** directly beneath the <xsl:for-each select="SALES"> element. The transformation code for the SALES element should look as follows:

```
<h2>Sales Department</h2>
<xsl:for-each select="SALES">
         <xsl:sort select="NAME"/> </xsl:sort>
         <b><xsl:value-of select="NAME"/></b>
         <br/>
         <b><small>Phone: </small></b>
         <xsl:value-of select="PHONE"/>
         <br/>
         <b><small>Email: </small></b>
         <xsl:value-of select="EMAIL"/>
         <br/><br/>
</xsl:for-each>
```


3. Click **File** on the menu bar, and then click **Save** to save the change.
4. Under the XML Files branch in the Project pane, double-click the **contacts.xml** file to display the XML document. Click **XSL** on the menu bar, and then click **XSL Transformation** to transform the file. The new HTML document appears. Notice that the names under the Sales Department are now sorted, and should begin with Anita Brown.
5. Click **File** on the menu bar, and then click **Save As**. Save the file as **example3.html** in the Ch06 folder.

Project 6-4

In this project, you add a list of employees to the beginning of the XML document. This means that two separate templates must process the same elements. You will achieve this by using modes. A mode is an attribute of both the xsl:template or xsl:apply-template elements, and allows you to process the same section of the XML document more than once.

To modify the XSL transformation and apply the transformation:

1. With the contacts project you worked with in Project 6-3 open in XML Spy, double-click the **contacts.xslt** file in the Project pane. The XSL transformation document appears.
2. In the xsl:apply-templates element matching CONTACTS, add the **mode="main"** attribute immediately after the select="CONTACTS" attribute. The element should now appear as follows:

```
<xsl:apply-templates select="CONTACTS" mode="main"/>
```

3. In the xsl:template matching CONTACTS, add the **mode="main"** attribute immediately after the match="CONTACTS" attribute. The element should now appear as follows:

```
<xsl:template match="CONTACTS" mode="main">
```

4. Immediately following the <body> tag in the xsl:template matching the root, type the following:

```
<h1>Employee Summary</h1>
<xsl:apply-templates select="CONTACTS" mode="emplist"/>
```

5. Immediately before the xsl:template matching CONTACTS, type the following:

```
<xsl:template match="CONTACTS" mode="emplist">
    <xsl:for-each select="*">
            <xsl:sort select="NAME"/>
            <b><xsl:value-of select="NAME"/></b>
            <br/>
            </xls:sort>
    </xsl:for-each>
</xsl:template>
```

6. Double-click the **contacts.xml** file in the Project pane to display the XML document. Click **XSL** on the menu bar, and then click **XSL Transformation** to transform the file. The new HTML document appears.

   Notice the new header and sorted list of employees. The new HTML document should resemble Figure 6-19.

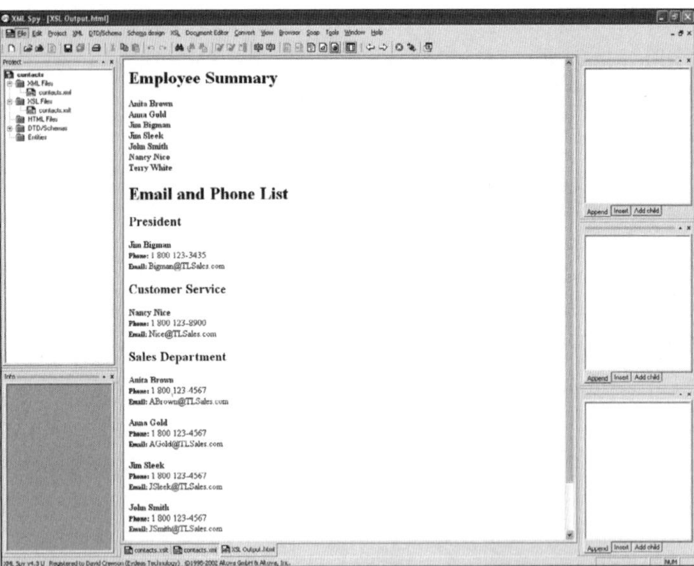

Figure 6-19

Project 6-5

XSL provides two conditional processing statements: xsl:if and xsl:choose. In this project, you use both condition elements to enhance the HTML output by adding a job title to each employee in the Employee Summary section, and by identifying the department head in the Sales Department. You also create and initialize a variable that you will use within the conditional statement.

To add a xml:choose element:

1. With the contacts project you worked with in Project 6-4 open in XML Spy, double-click the **contacts.xslt** file in the project pane. The XSL transformation document appears.
2. In the xsl:template matching CONTACTS in the EMPLIST mode, add the following code immediately before the line break (<br/>) element:

```
<xsl:variable name="NodeName"><xsl:value-of select="local-
name()"/></xsl:variable>


<xsl:choose>
<xsl:when test=" $NodeName='PRESIDENT'">, President</xsl:when>
<xsl:when test="$NodeName ='CUSTSRV'">, Customer Service</xsl:
when>
<xsl:when test="$NodeName ='SALES'">, Sales</xsl:when>
<xsl:otherwise>, Unknown</xsl:otherwise>
</xsl:choose>
```

6

This block of code begins with the creation of a variable, NodeName, which is initialized to the name of the context element by using the XPath function call local-name(). The condition compares the value within the NodeName variable with a set of possible element values. The xsl:choose element is similar to a switch statement used in C++ or Java because it tests for a number of specific conditions, and provides a sink or default element if none of the conditions have been matched. Notice that, unlike a switch statement, each xsl:when element can contain unrelated expressions.

The second XSL conditional processing statement is the xsl:if element. You will use this statement to identify the head of the sales department. You may have noticed in the contacts DTD that the SALES element has an optional HEAD child element. If HEAD exists within a SALES element, then an appropriate identifier will be displayed in the resulting HTML document.

To add an xml:if element and then apply the transformation:

1. Immediately following the xsl:value-of element in the SALES xsl:for-each loop in the template matching CONTACTS, type the following:

   ```
   <xsl:if test="HEAD">, <em>Head of Department</em></xsl:if>
   ```

   The block of code should appear as follows:

   ```
   <h2>Sales Department</h2>
   <xsl:for-each select="SALES">
       <xsl:sort select="NAME"/>
       <b><xsl:value-of select="NAME"/></b>
   ```

```
        <xsl:if test="HEAD">, <em>Head of Department</em>
</xsl:if>
        <br/>
        <b><small>Phone: </small></b>
        <xsl:value-of select="PHONE"/><br/>
        <b><small>Email: </small></b>
        <xsl:value-of select="EMAIL"/><br/><br/>
</xsl:for-each>
```

2. Click **File** on the menu bar, and then click **Save** to save your work.
3. Double-click the **contacts.xml** file in the project pane to display the XML document.
4. Click **XSL** on the menu bar, and then click **XSL Transformation** to transform the file. A new HTML document appears in the main window with job titles for every employee in the Employee Summary and a department head identifier for Anna Gold in the Sales Department.
5. Click **File** on the menu bar, and then click **Save As** to save the file as **example4.html** in the Ch06 folder.

Project 6-6

Another application of XSL transformation is to convert XML documents from one grammar to another. As you have noticed, all of the child contact elements in the contacts.xml document use the element type to identify the job type. In this project, you will transform contacts.xml into a second XML file where every employee is an EMPLOYEE element, and the job type is stored as an attribute.

To create a new XSL transformation:

1. Click **File** on the menu bar, and then click **New**. A Create new document dialog opens.
2. Click **xslt Extensible Stylesheet Language**, and then click **OK**. A new XSL transformation document appears in the main window. Notice that the default transformation that XML Spy produces creates a shell stylesheet with a xsl:stylesheet element and a xsl:output element. Observe that the method attribute of the xsl:output element is set to "xml". Since your transformation will create another XML document, the method and all other default attribute values are sufficient for this project.
3. To save the XSL transformation, click **File** on the menu bar, and then click **Save As**. The Save As dialog opens. Save the file as **contacts2.xslt** in the Ch06 folder.
4. In the project pane, right-click the **XSL Files** branch, and then click **Add Files**. The Open dialog appears.
5. Navigate to C:/home/yourname/Ch06, if necessary, click **contacts2.xslt**, and then click **Open**. The contacts2.xslt file appears under the XSL Files branch in the project pane.

6. Immediately below the xsl:output element, type the following code:

```
<xsl:template match="/">
    <CONTACTLIST>
         <xsl:apply-templates select="CONTACTS"/>
    </CONTACTLIST>
</xsl:template>
```

This is the xsl:template that matches the source tree's root element. It creates the result tree's root and then refers to the xsl:template matching CONTACTS.

7. Following the XSL code you just entered, type the following code:

```
<xsl:for-each select="*">
          <xsl:sort select="NAME"/>
          <EMPLOYEE>
              <xsl:attribute name="branch">
                main</xsl:attribute>
              <NAME>
                   <xsl:value-of select="NAME"/>
              </NAME>
              <POSITION>
                   <xsl:value-of select="local-name()"/>
              </POSITION>
              <PHONENUM>
                   <xsl:value-of select="PHONE"/>
              </PHONENUM>
              <EMAIL>
                   <xsl:value-of select="EMAIL"/>
              </EMAIL>
         </EMPLOYEE>
</xsl:for-each>
```

Some of the XSL code will look familiar to you, but note a few differences. The template iterates through the child elements of CONTACTS, sorting them by name and organizing them as EMPLOYEE elements. The xsl:attribute on the line immediately below the EMPLOYEE element declares a branch attribute within EMPLOYEE and initializes the value to "main". The XPath function local-name() that returns the local part of an element's name, without the namespace prefix.

8. Click **File** on the menu bar, and then click **Save** to save your work.

Now you are ready to apply the transformation.

To apply the transformation:

1. Double-click the **contacts.xml** file in the project pane to display the XML document.
2. Modify the xml-stylesheet declaration to reference contacts2.xslt, if necessary. The fourth line should appear as follows:

```
<?xml-stylesheet type="text/xsl" href="contacts2.xslt"?>
```

6

3. Click **XSL** on the menu bar, and then click **XSL Transformation** to transform the file. A new XML document appears in the main window.
4. Click **View** on the menu bar, and then click **Text view** to view the source code. Notice the EMPLOYEE attribute and the value of the POSITION elements.
5. Click **File** on the menu bar, and then click **Save As** to save the file as **examples.html**. Then close XML Spy.

CASE PROJECT

Create an XSLT stylesheet named basic.xslt that produces an HTML page for the TLSales product list. Start by copying the product.xml, product.dtd, and all the image files from the Ch06\Case_Project folder on your Data Disk to your home\yourname\Ch06 folder. After copying these files, change the paths for some elements in the file to reference your home\yourname\Ch06 folder.

CHAPTER

7

LINKING IN XML

In this chapter, you will learn:

- About XML Linking Language (XLink)
- How to apply XLink to create links in XML
- How to validate XLinks
- How to use the XML pointer language (XPointer)
- About XPointer points and ranges
- About XLink and XPointer implementations

One of the major attractions and successes of the World Wide Web is its ability to link resources at one local location to remote resources at another location. However, simple HTML hyperlinking structures sometimes aren't adequate for XML documents and languages. For XML developers, the solution was to develop a specific language for linking XML documents: the XML Linking Language (also called XLink). XLink, used generally for linking to a particular document, also calls upon the XML Pointer Language (XPointer), which extends XPath concepts and utilities to point to specific locations within a document. XLink also uses XML Base (or XBase), a base utility that defines Uniform Resource Identifiers (URI) similar to HTML BASE. This chapter explains these languages, shows how XLink links and XPointer links are created, and provides hands-on opportunities to create and integrate them with your existing projects.

XLink and XPointer technologies are still under development, and the related W3C Recommendations are generally ahead of the XLink and XPointer application developers. As a result, the common browsers—or common versions of those browsers—are not likely to implement them to your satisfaction. That is why the Hands-on Projects at the end of the chapter look more like demonstrations than actual projects. The browser developers are catching up, though their progress has been slow. If you are interested in using links in your XML documents, it would serve you well to monitor the progress of these languages, their respective applications and implementations, and their W3C Recommendations and other standards. An excellent place to start is at the W3C Web site, at *www.w3.org*.

UNDERSTANDING THE XML LINKING LANGUAGE (XLINK)

The **XML Linking Language** (commonly called **XLink**, but also called **XML Linking** and, occasionally, **XLL**) allows you to create links in XML documents using XML syntax. You can use it to create simple HTML-like unidirectional links (i.e., one source/one destination) or sophisticated links with several sources and destinations.

Initial development of XLink began in late 1996 and early 1997. The XML Linking Language 1.0 was published as a W3C Recommendation on June 27, 2001, so it has become the sanctioned W3C solution for linking in XML. XLink was created to overcome the limitations of HTML links, which include the following:

- Reconciling XML's functionally relevant element names such as <PRODUCT> or <contact> with HTML's predefined and specific elements such as <A> (for "anchor") or <IMG> (for "image")
- Linking your document with multiple sources and destinations, when HTML identifies only one source and destination per link
- HTML has only one link actuation technique (the user must move the mouse pointer to the hyperlink and click it)
- Locating link definitions in separate locations (for example, link databases), so that the write permission for their corresponding documents does not have to be given to as many individuals
- Using standard XML constructs (e.g., concepts, syntax, formats, etc.)
- Complying with XML's rules for well-formedness and validity
- Being readable and writable by humans
- Indicating to the reader or developer something about the nature and behavior of the link (title, destination, traversal rules, etc.)
- Remaining compatible and complementary with HTML
- Providing other XML-related functionality

XLink also draws upon the concepts and techniques found in the following Recommendations:

- Extensible Markup Language (XML) 1.0 (Second Edition), W3C, 2000
- Namespaces in XML (XML Names), W3C, 1999
- XML Base (XBase), W3C, 1999
- XML Pointer Language (XPointer) 1.0, W3C, 1998
- XML Path Language (XPath) 1.0, W3C, 1999
- RFC 2396: Uniform Resource Identifiers, IETF (Internet Engineering Task Force), 1995
- RFC 2732: Format for Literal IPv6 Addresses in URLs, IETF, 1999

Types of XLinks

For XML and XLink, **links** are defined by the W3C as explicit relationships between addressable units of information or services in XML documents (i.e., between resources or even portions of resources). The links may be of two types according to activation: **hyperlinks** (that is, links that are intended primarily to be viewed and used at the discretion of human users), or they may be links that are intended only for computer functioning, with certain automatic instructions for the system. While HTML can provide links that require human activation, XLink links are capable of providing both types of functionality.

XLink links are also divided into two types according to structure: simple and extended. Each can be configured to require human activation or to automatically provide instructions to the system.

Using Simple Links

A **simple link** (which is also referred to as a simple-type link) is a link that associates exactly two participating resources, one local and one remote, with an arc traversing from the local one to the remote one (resources, arcs, and traversal are discussed later in this chapter). Thus, a simple link is always an outbound link. The simple link is the category into which HTML <A> and <IMG> links fall.

Figure 7-1 illustrates a simple link. There is one local and one remote resource, with a single traversal arc from the local resource to the remote resource. For example, Figure 7-1 could represent the name of a TLSales course appearing in text that, when clicked, leads to information about the course content and costs.

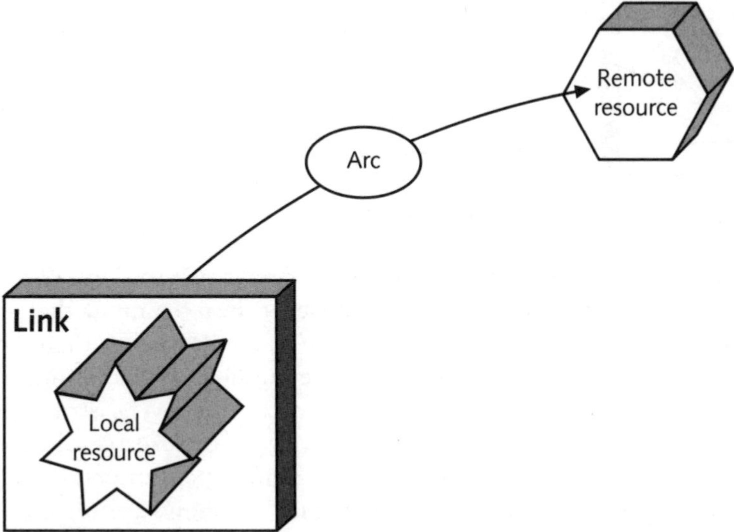

Figure 7-1 A generic simple-type link

Additional comments about simple links are found in the next section, which discusses extended links. An example of a simple link is provided in the section titled "Applying XLink to Create Links."

Using Extended Links

Extended links offer full XLink functionality, including inbound and third-party arcs (arcs between remote resources), as well as arcs that can simultaneously connect a local resource to several remote resources. As a result, the structure of an extended link can be fairly complex, and may include elements for pointing to remote resources, elements for containing local resources, elements for specifying arc traversal rules, and elements for specifying human-readable resource and arc titles (resources, arcs, and traversal are discussed in the next two sections). Figure 7-2 illustrates a fairly typical extended link situation.

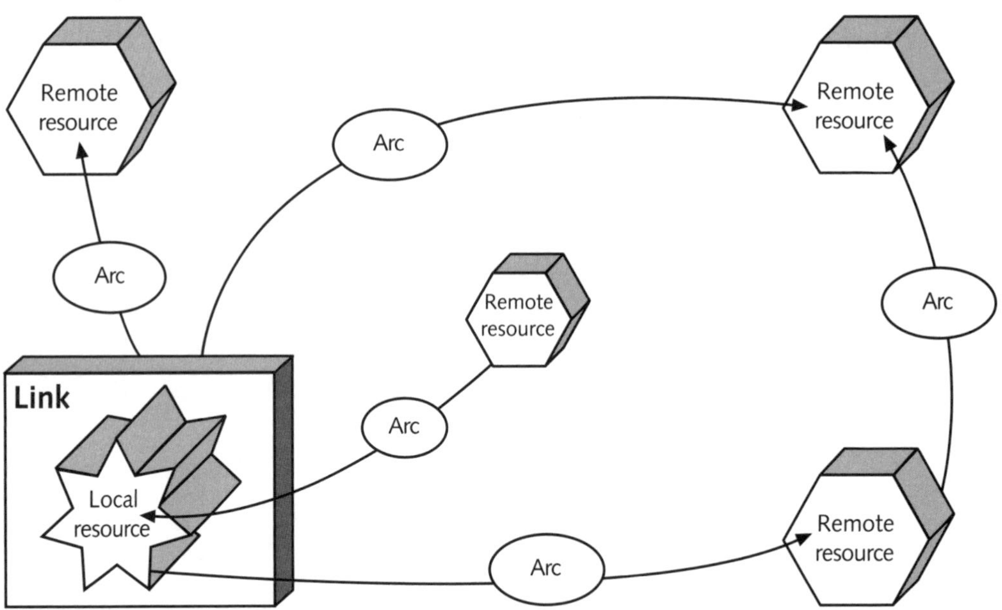

Figure 7-2 Generic extended-type link situation

If you are a newcomer to XLinks, it may be convenient at first to think of simple links, conceptually, as a subset of extended links. However, bear in mind that simple and extended links differ syntactically. The purpose of a simple link is to provide, when applicable, a convenient shorthand version of an equivalent extended link. You could convert a simple link back into extended link format, but several structural changes would be needed, since a properly constructed simple link is capable of combining all the basic functions of a combined extended-type element, a locator-type element, an arc-type element, and a resource-type element. Figure 7-3 shows a comparison between the XML code of a simple link and an equivalent extended link. Please note that the coding of the simple link could be made even shorter if, for example, default behavior for XLink attributes like xlink:type and xlink:show were to be declared within the affiliated DTD or schemas.

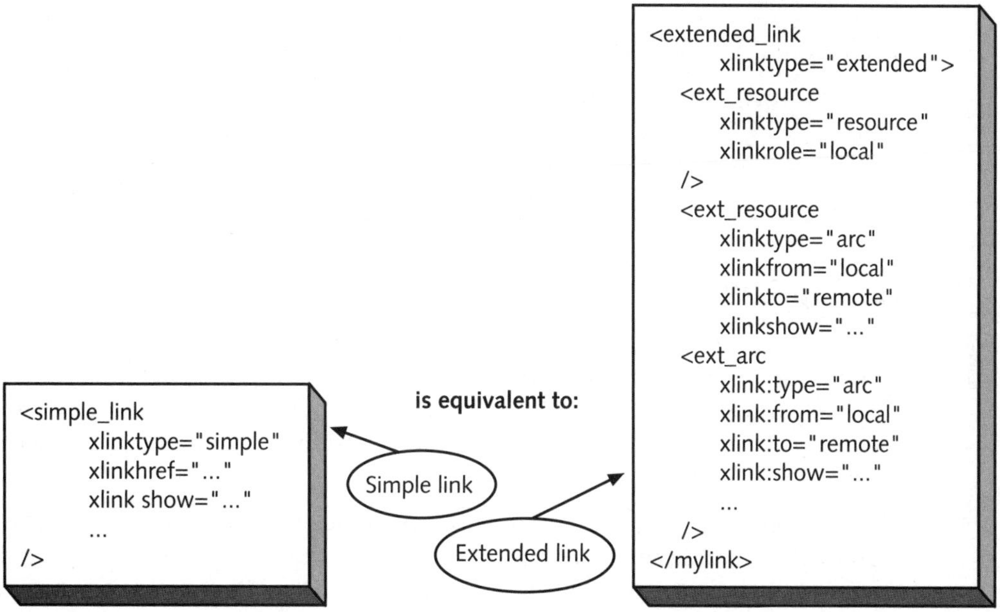

```
<simple_link
        xlinktype="simple"
        xlinkhref="..."
        xlink show="..."
        ...
/>
```

is equivalent to:

Simple link

Extended link

```
<extended_link
        xlinktype="extended">
    <ext_resource
        xlinktype="resource"
        xlinkrole="local"
    />
    <ext_resource
        xlinktype="arc"
        xlinkfrom="local"
        xlinkto="remote"
        xlinkshow="..."
    <ext_arc
        xlink:type="arc"
        xlink:from="local"
        xlink:to="remote"
        xlink:show="..."
        ...
    />
</mylink>
```

Figure 7-3 Comparison of XLink code: simple link vs. extended link

Despite the impression given by Figure 7-3, simple-type links are not always superior to extended-type links. As stated above, simple-type links are just used as a shorthand form for otherwise extended links, and are only appropriate for certain simple situations, like the one illustrated in Figure 7-3. Otherwise, extended links—although they may be complex—are still far more flexible and powerful.

Using Resources

Resources include files, images, documents, programs, etc. There are several types of XLinks resources. Table 7-1 describes the most common ones. Please note that the definitions overlap and that the resources may also be portions of resources.

Table 7-1 Common resource types

Type of Resource	Explanation/Definition
Starting resource	A resource from which a traversal is begun
Ending resource	A destination resource for a traversal
Local resource	An XML element that participates in a link by being a linking element or a child to a linking element
Remote resource	A resource, or portion of a resource, that participates in a link, addressed with a URI reference; it may even be in the same XML document or inside the same linking element

Traversing Links

In Table 7-1, you probably noticed the term **traversal**. Traversal simply means to follow a link from where it starts to where it ends. The process of traversal, then, always involves a pair of participating resources. All information about how to traverse a pair of resources, including the direction of traversal and any subsequent application behavior resulting from the link, is called an **arc**.

If two resources participate in a link, but there is only one source and one destination, then the link is **unidirectional**. However, if there are two arcs connecting the same pair of resources, but they switch places as starting and ending resources, then the link is **multidirectional**. Keep in mind that a multidirectional link, as the W3C mentions in the XLink Recommendation, should not be confused with "going back" (i.e., pressing the back button) after traversing a link.

The W3C defines an **outbound** arc as one that has a local starting resource and a remote ending resource (i.e., the link direction is away from the linking element). Conversely, if the ending resource is local but the starting resource is remote, then the arc is **inbound**. A variation of these concepts is the arc where neither the starting resource nor the ending resource is local. That is termed a **third-party** arc, a concept that may seem foreign to those familiar to the world of HTML.

APPLYING XLINK TO CREATE LINKS IN XML

In XML, similar to HTML, resource links are represented by elements. According to XLink, the linking elements are found in the appropriate XML documents. Unlike HTML, however, which only provides the <A> and <IMG> (for anchor and image, respectively) elements for linking, you may give the XLink elements any name you choose. What eventually makes them behave as links are the attributes you later assign to them. The W3C uses the term "assert" in those cases. Paraphrasing the XLink Recommendation, "links are asserted by elements that have start tags containing the appropriate linking attributes."

Declaring An XLink Namespace Is Required

In order to create linking elements, a declaration of the XLink namespace is required. However, for XLinks, the declaration must be within the linking element's start tag. Here is an example of such an XLink namespace declaration:

```
<elementname xmlns:xlink="http://www.w3.org/1999/xlink" ... >
```

Using the XLink's Global Attributes in XLink

It was stated earlier that XLink linking elements (which are also called XLink links or XLinks) are denoted by the linking attributes placed in their start tags. These attributes are called global attributes. Not only do they indicate which elements are linking elements, but global attributes also allow the developers to specify other properties about the links and their resources, such as when to load the linked resources, how they should appear once they are loaded, etc. First and foremost, though, XLink links always have an attribute named "type," which is one of the ten global XLink attributes.

The global attributes provided by XLink are grouped according to their functions in Table 7-2.

Table 7-2 The XLink global attributes

Attribute Name	Definition/Explanation
XLink definition/assertion attribute	
type	Indicates the XLink element type (simple, extended, locator, arc, resource, or title); a value for this attribute *must* be supplied, and must be one of: simple, extended, locator, arc, resource, title, or none. See Table 7-3.
Locator attribute: allows an XLink application to find a remote resource (or resource fragment)	
href	May be used on simple-type elements; must be used on locator-type elements; value must be a URI reference or must result in a URI reference after a specific escaping procedure described in XLink 1.0
Semantic attributes: describe the meaning of resources within the context of a link	
role	May be used on extended-type, simple-type, locator-type, and resource-type elements; value must be a URI reference, with some constraints as found in XLink 1.0.; the URI reference identifies some resource that describes the intended property
arcrole	May be used on arc-type and simple-type elements; value must be a URI reference, with constraints as described in XLink 1.0; the URI reference identifies some resource that describes the intended property; if no value is supplied, no particular role value is to be inferred
title	May be used on extended-type, locator-type, resource-type, arc-type, and simple-type elements; used to describe the meaning of a link or resource in a fashion readable by humans; a value is optional (if one is supplied, it should contain a string that describes the resource); this information is highly dependent on the type of processing being done

Table 7-2 The XLink global attributes (continued)

Attribute Name	Definition/Explanation
Behavior attributes: signal behavior intentions for traversal to a link's remote ending resource(s)	
show	May be used on the simple-type and arc-type elements; used to communicate the desired presentation of the ending resource on traversal from the starting resource; when used on arc-type elements, they signal behavior intentions for traversal to whatever ending resources are specified
actuate	May be used on the simple-type and arc-type elements; similar comments to "show", above; used to communicate the desired timing of traversal from the starting resource to the ending resource
Traversal attributes	
label	May be used on resource-type and locator-type elements; value must be an NCName (i.e., any name that begins with a letter or underscore and has no space or colon in it, because its author may add a namespace prefix to it)
from	May be used on the arc-type element; value must also be an NCName; if a value is supplied, it must correspond to the same value for some label attribute on a locator-type or resource-type element that appears as a direct child inside the same extended-type element as does the arc-type element
to	May be used on the arc-type element; the value must also be an NCName; as with "from", if a value is supplied, it must correspond to the same value for some label attribute on a locator-type or resource-type element that appears as a direct child inside the same extended-type element as does the arc-type element

With respect to the show attribute, although that attribute is not absolutely required, when it is used, conforming XLink applications should give it the treatment specified in XLink 1.0. That is, the values specified for it must be one of:

- "new" for open a new window
- "replace" for replace the existing window
- "embed" for embed the new resource inside the existing one
- "other" means behavior of the application is unconstrained and the application should look for direction from other markup present in the link
- "none" means behavior is also unconstrained, but no other markup is present to help the application determine the appropriate behavior

Further, regarding the actuate attribute, the value specified must be one of:

- "onLoad" is used when the application should traverse to the ending resource immediately on loading the starting resource; however, if a single resource contains multiple arcs that have behavior set to show="replace" and actuate="onLoad", then application behavior is unconstrained

- "onRequest" is used when the application should traverse from the starting resource to the ending resource only on a post-loading event (e.g., when a user clicks on the starting resource, or software finishes a countdown)
- "other" is used when behavior is unconstrained and the application should look to other markup to determine the appropriate behavior
- "none" is used when behavior is unconstrained by this specification, but no other markup is present to help the application determine the appropriate behavior

Meanwhile, as stated in Table 7-2, a value for the type attribute *must* be supplied, and must be one of: simple, extended, locator, arc, resource, title, or none. Table 7-3 explains these values.

Table 7-3 Values for the type attribute

type Attribute Value	Explanation/Definition
simple	Provides syntax for a common outbound link (two participating resources; e.g., HTML-style `<A>` and `<IMG>` links); less functionality; no special internal structure; conceptually a subset of extended links, but with different syntax
extended	Provides full functionality (e.g., inbound arcs, third-party arcs, links with multiple participating resources); can be fairly complex; can be used to find linkbases (thus, can help an XLink application process other links)
locator	Addresses the remote resources participating in an extended link
arc	Provides traversal rules among an extended link's participating resources
resource	Supplies local resources that participate in an extended link
title	Describes the meaning of an extended link or resource in human-readable terms; provides human-readable labels for the link
none	Provides its element no XLink-specified meaning; any XLink-related content or attributes have no XLink-specified relationship to its element, for example, "none" is useful occasionally in helping XLink applications to avoid checking for the presence of an href

Once a type attribute has been specified, then that specification designates the XLink **element type** as simple, extended, locator, arc, resource, title or none. That designation complies with XLink convention, where a linking element containing a type attribute whose value is "V" is called a "V-type element". For example, the following linking element, called <payments> is referred to as a "locator-type element":

```
<payments xlink:type="locator" ....>
```

Accordingly, the element type dictates the XLink-imposed constraints that such a linking element must follow. The element type also influences the behavior of XLink applications when they encounter the linking element.

Restrictions on XLink Types and Attributes

As linking elements are developed and defined, two restrictions apply.

The first restriction is, given an element of a particular type, only certain attributes can be combined with them. Table 7-4 summarizes the hierarchy of declared attributes in a linking element. Customarily, the simple-type element only requires an href locator attribute, so Table 7-4 really applies only to extended-type elements.

Table 7-4 Corresponding parent/child attributes in linking elements

Parent element type	Allowed child attributes
simple	No child attributes applicable
extended	locator, arc, resource, title
locator	title
arc	title
resource	No child attributes applicable
title	No child attributes applicable

The second restriction is, given a particular declared element type, only some combinations of XLink attributes apply. Table 7-5 indicates the restrictions to the combinations of global attributes and type attribute values that cooperate in the definition of a linking element. Each R indicates that one or more of the type attribute values must be supplied (that is, they are required) before the linking element can function. Each O indicates which type attribute values can be used (that is, they are optional). If a table entry is left blank, that indicates that the type attribute value must not be used.

Table 7-5 Combinations of global attributes and type attribute values

Global Attribute Name	type attribute values					
	simple	extended	locator	arc	resource	title
type	R	R	R	R	R	R
href	O		R			
role	O	O	O		O	
arcrole	O			O		
title	O	O	O	O	O	
show	O			O		
actuate	O			O		
label			O		O	
from				O		
to				O		

A Simple-Type XLink Example

Following is a brief example of the application of the previous two tables in a simple-type linking element named <contacts>.

```
<!-- contacts is a simple-type element that needs an href
attribute to point to a resource. -->
<contacts xmlns:xlink="http://www.w3.org/1999/xlink"
                xlink:type="simple"
                xlink:href="administration.xml"
                xlink:show= "new" />
```

Figure 7-4 illustrates this simple-type link.

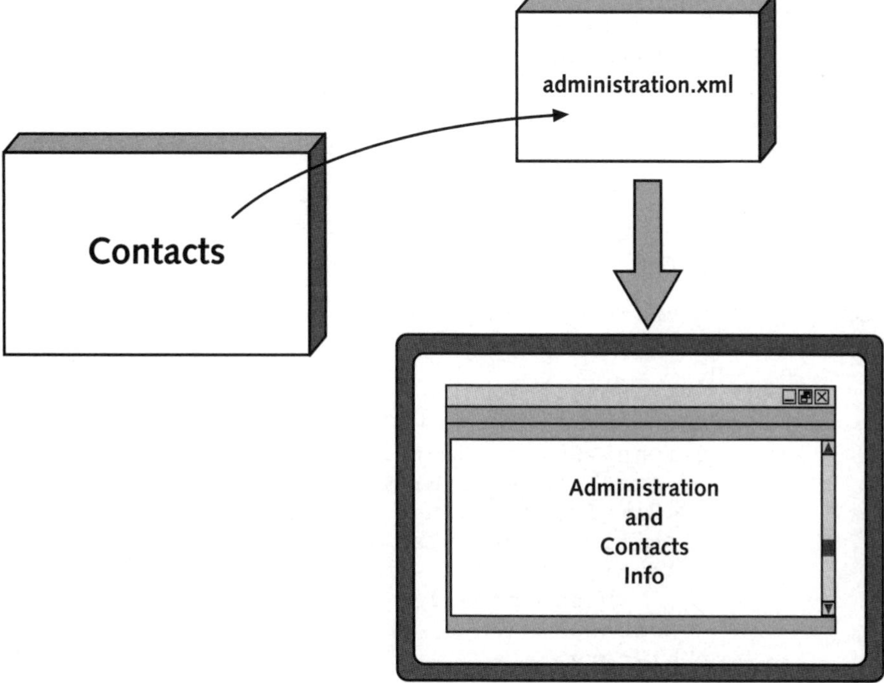

Figure 7-4 The simple-type contacts link

Notice how the link element <contacts> declared the XLink namespace first, then its simple type. The element then specified the resource to be accessed, and used the optional attribute show to instruct the application to open a new window to display the results of the link.

An Extended-Type XLink Example

A common situation for Human Resource professionals in every organization is the tracking of the professional development of their fellow employees. Suppose you are one of TLSales' HR professionals and you want to express in XML the relationship between TLSales' employees and their respective environments (that is, their work history prior to employment and their training at TLSales after they were hired). This includes making links from an employee to a description of their experience, and also making links to descriptions of where they had previously worked. The data for each employee might be written similarly to the way it has been written for Mr. Sleek in the TLSales Sales Department:

```
<?xml version="1.0"?>
   <HRInfo>
      <surname>Sleek</surname>
      <name>Jim</name>
         <hired>Dec 1, 1895</hired>
         <terminated></terminated>
            <background>
               <education>Columbia University,
               1994</education>
               <SSN>101010101010</SSN>
            </background>
   </HRInfo>
```

Also, brief descriptions of Mr. Sleek's work history may be included in separate files such as the following:

```
<?xml version="1.0"?>
   <workhistory>
      <company>Smith, Smith, Smith & Smith</company>
         <state_city>NY NYC</state_city>
         <timeframe begin="1994" end="1995"/>
         <title>Floor Sales/Pitchman</title>
         <duties>
            <DutyList>Sales, demos, inventory, </DutyList>
         </duties>
   </workhistory>
```

As you can see, fulfilling the requirement to create a file that relates employees like Mr. Sleek to their respective experience and work history is a task beyond a simple strategy like adding <A> or <IMG> element links to HTML documents. There are several extra factors to consider, including:

- One employee has probably had several kinds of experience (here, one link may connect one resource to many other resources).
- One employee has likely worked with several organizations.

- All links must be meaningful. Having one kind of work experience is likely not equivalent to having worked for a specific company, and this should be conveyed in the documents.

Now that there is a sufficient amount of information with which to build an extended-type link, the resources must now be specified. But, the employee and environment documents are stored in separate documents outside of this XML document, so those documents are beyond HR's control. In that case, use XLink's locator-type element type(s) to refer to them. Remember, the strategy is not to impose an element name (you won't be allowed to, anyway), but to mark remote resources as locators using XLink attributes.

```
<environment xmlns:xlink="http://www.w3.org/1999/xlink"
    xlink:type="extended">
    <!-- The resources involved in our link are the
    employee -->
    <!-- their experience and their work history -->
    <employee    xlink:type="locator" xlink:label="employee"
          xlink:href="sleek.xml"/>
    <experience xlink:type="locator" xlink:label="training"
          xlink:href="inventory.xml"/>
    <experience xlink:type="locator" xlink:label="training"
          xlink:href="checkout.xml"/>
    <experience xlink:type="locator" xlink:label="training"
          xlink:href="orderdesk.xml"/>
    <history   xlink:type="locator" xlink:label="workhistory"
          xlink:href="smithx5.xml"/>
    <history   xlink:type="locator" xlink:label="workhistory"
          xlink:href="petersdriveinn.xml"/>
</environment>
```

This is acceptable so far, but one thing is missing: how do you specify the relationships among the resources? Do this by specifying arcs between them (see the bold print, below):

```
<environment xmlns:xlink="http://www.w3.org/1999/xlink"
    xlink:type="extended">
    <!-- The resources involved in our link are the
    employee -->
    <!-- their experience and their work history -->
    <employee    xlink:type="locator" xlink:label="employee"
          xlink:href="sleek.xml"/>
    <experience xlink:type="locator" xlink:label="training"
          xlink:href="inventory.xml"/>
    <experience xlink:type="locator" xlink:label="training"
          xlink:href="checkout.xml"/>
    <experience xlink:type="locator" xlink:label="training"
          xlink:href="orderdesk.xml"/>
    <history   xlink:type="locator" xlink:label="workhistory"
          xlink:href="smithx5.xml"/>
```

```
  <history   xlink:type="locator" xlink:label="workhistory"
        xlink:href="petersdriveinn.xml"/>
   <bind xlink:type="arc" xlink:from="employee"
         xlink:to="training"/>
   <bind xlink:type="arc" xlink:from="employee"
         xlink:to="workhistory"/>
</environment>
```

As you can see from this case, when using XLink, all that is needed is an XML document containing elements and attributes like those above. Further, in the same document, all the resources and relationships are clearly specified. Figure 7-5 illustrates this extended-type link.

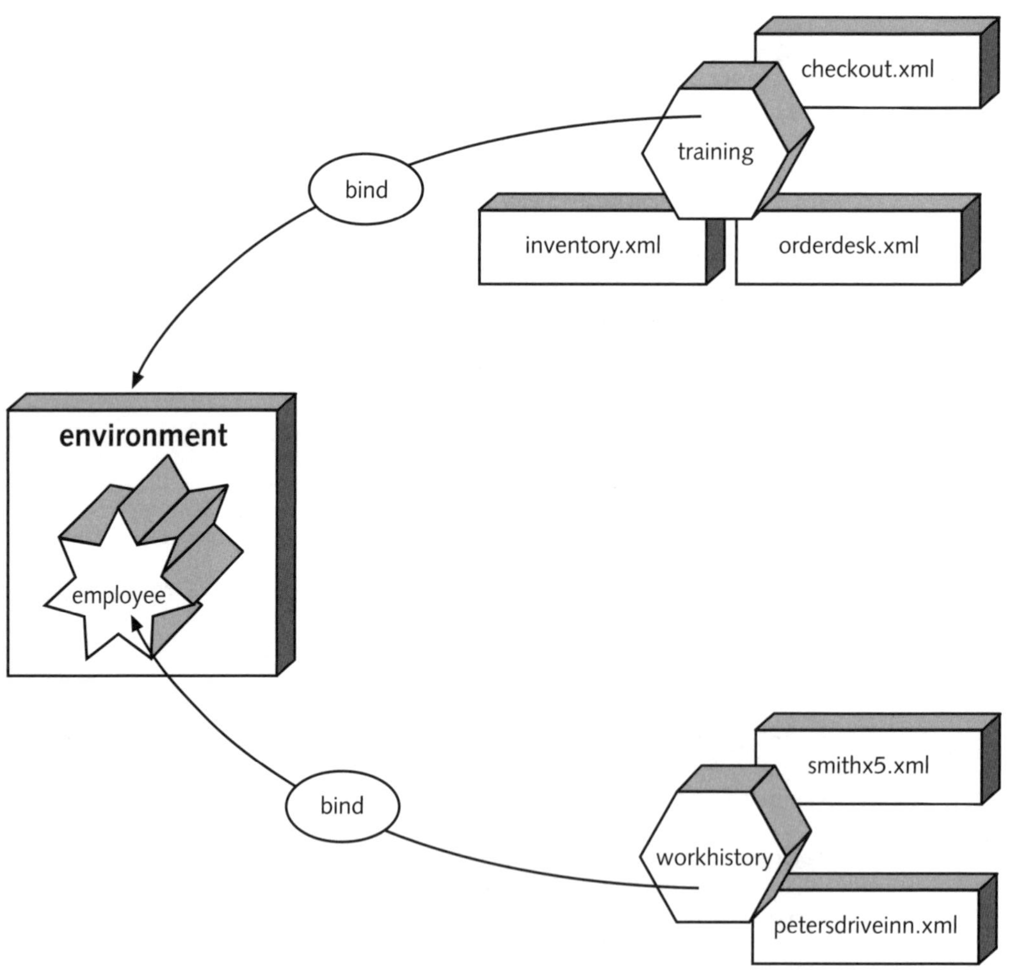

Figure 7-5 A simple extended-type link: an employee's environment

VALIDATING XLINKS

In order for the XLink linking elements to function correctly and reliably, their respective elements and documents must be well-formed and valid. That means that the XLink linking elements and attributes must be declared in the referenced DTDs and schemas. To best illustrate how this should be done with various elements and attributes, a number of examples are presented.

Example 1: Employee Information with a Resource-type Linking Element

The first example focuses on some simple employee information, using a local resource-type linking element. Again, the employee is Mr. Sleek of the Sales Department.

7

The <employee> element appears as follows:

```
<employee xlink:label="jsleek">
   <name>Jim</name>
   <surname>Sleek</surname>
</employee>
```

An entry in a DTD for the linking element <employee> might look like:

```
<!ELEMENT  employee    (name,surname)>
<!ATTLIST  employee
           xlink:type       (resource)    #FIXED "resource"
           xlink:title      CDATA         #IMPLIED
           xlink:label      NMTOKEN       #IMPLIED
           xlink:role       CDATA         #IMPLIED>
```

Note that the linking element has another two XLink-based attributes besides xlink:type. As mentioned before, xlink:title is a semantic attribute used to give a short description of the resource. The second attribute, xlink:label, is a traversal attribute used to identify the element later when arcs are built. The third attribute, xlink:role, is used for describing a property of the resource.

It is important to note also that the subelements <name> and <surname> of the <employee> resource-type element have no significance for XLink. Thus, for this example, you can presume that they are declared elsewhere in the DTD.

Example 2: Remote Employee Information with a Locator-type Linking Element

As mentioned previously in this chapter, locator-type linking elements are used to point to remote resources. For example, presume that you are building a link to a remote resource pertaining to the Sales Department. The locator-type <department> linking element might appear as follows:

```
<department xlink:label="sales" xlink:href="sales.xml"/>
```

Here is the DTD coding for the <department> locator-type element:

```
<!ELEMENT  department     EMPTY>
<!ATTLIST  department
           xlink:type     (locator)       #FIXED "locator"
           xlink:title    CDATA           #IMPLIED
           xlink:role     CDATA           #IMPLIED
           xlink:label    NMTOKEN         #IMPLIED
           xlink:href     CDATA           #REQUIRED>
```

Remember that locator-type elements can have the same title, role, and label attributes as resource-type elements. However, they also require an href semantic attribute, which ultimately does the pointing to the remote resource.

Example 3: Remote Employee Information Using Inbound Link Arcs

Remember that an inbound link consists of an arc from an external resource (which is located with a locator-type element), toward an internal resource (specified with a resource-type element). Arc-type elements use additional child to and from attributes to designate the start and end points of the specified arc. Again, using Mr. Sleek, look at the arc-type element <empl_record> (i.e., the employee record):

```
<empl_record xlink:type="arc" xlink:from="jsleek"
  xlink:to="sales"/>
```

In addition to the traversal attributes "to" and "from," arcs may include the show, title, actuate, and arcrole attributes. The DTD, then, would include the following coding:

```
<!ELEMENT  acted       EMPTY>
<!ATTLIST  acted
    xlink:type    (arc)       #FIXED "arc"
    xlink:title   CDATA       #IMPLIED
    xlink:show    (new|replace|embed|other|none)  #IMPLIED
    xlink:from    NMTOKEN     #IMPLIED
    xlink:to      NMTOKEN     #IMPLIED>
```

Example 4: Extended-type Linking Element

Combining the examples from the previous section results in the following arc from a local to a remote resource:

```
<!-- A local resource -->
<employee xlink:label="jsleek">
<name>Jim</name>
<surname>Sleek</surname>
</employee>
```

```
<!-- A remote resource -->
<department xlink:label="sales" xlink:href="sales.xml"/>
<!-- An arc that binds them -->
<empl_record xlink:type="arc" xlink:from="jsleek"
   xlink:to="sales"/>
```

In order to encapsulate relationships, an overall container element is needed—that is, an extended-type linking element. Recall that extended-type links may point to remote resources and local resources, and may also contain arcs and a title.

Figures 7-6 through 7-9 depart somewhat from the existing discussion, to illustrate the evolution of a simple, generic extended-type linking element named <extLink>. The first coding for the extended-type link (shown in Figure 7-6) consists, naturally, of its start tag and end tag. The start tag contains the xlink:type attribute which specifies that the element is an extended-type link. The little rectangle above the code box indicates the creation of the link.

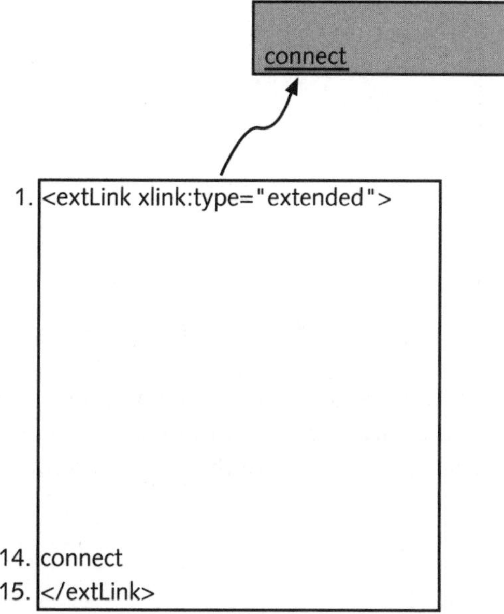

Figure 7-6 Evolution of an extended link element; Phase 1: creating the XLink element

Figure 7-7 illustrates the references to the remote resources: cross-hatched balls of different sizes that represent two different HTML documents. Each document is specified to be of a locator type, meaning they are the remote resources of an extended link. Both get the label "hatchball", though, to indicate that only one arc is necessary to initiate contact with both remote sources.

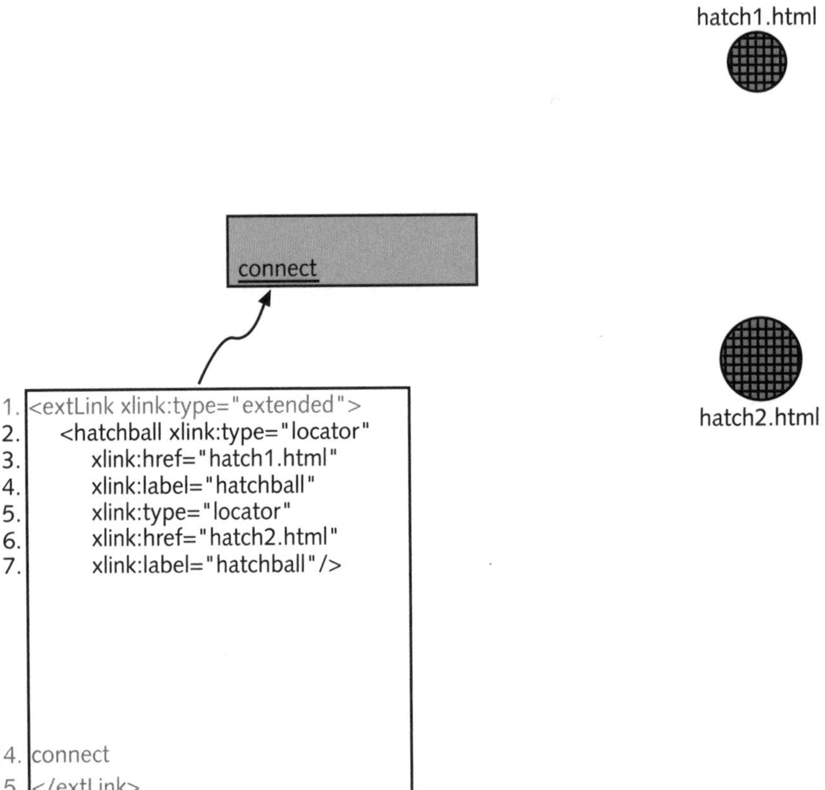

Figure 7-7 Evolution of an extended link element; Phase 2: refer to remote resources

Figure 7-8 illustrates the creation of the local resource. Its element name is <stripeball>. The type is specified to be "resource", indicating that it is the local resource participating in the link. Its label, though, is "not-hatch", to ensure there is no confusion with the remote hatchball resources.

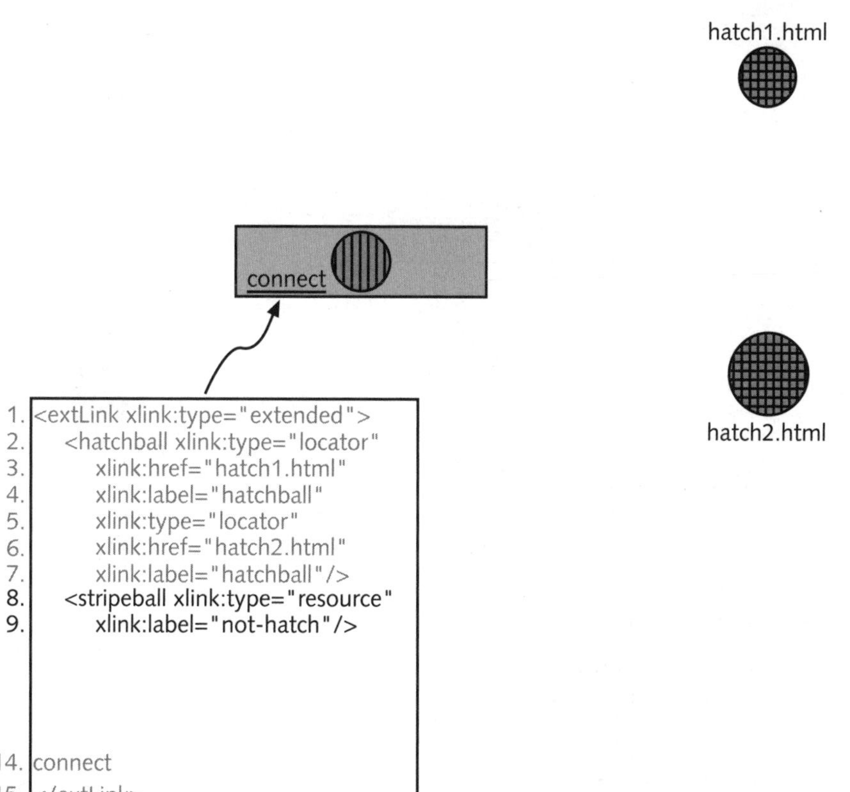

Figure 7-8 Evolution of an extended link element; Phase 3: refer to local resource

Figure 7-9 illustrates the creation of an element named <go>, the type of which is specified to be arc. It is given an arbitrary title of X and is told that it arcs from the local resource, labeled "not-hatch," to all the remote resources that have been given the label "hatchball" (in this case, you have already seen that there are two such remote resources). The word "connect" acts as the visible presence for the <extLink> element; that is, as the hyperlink.

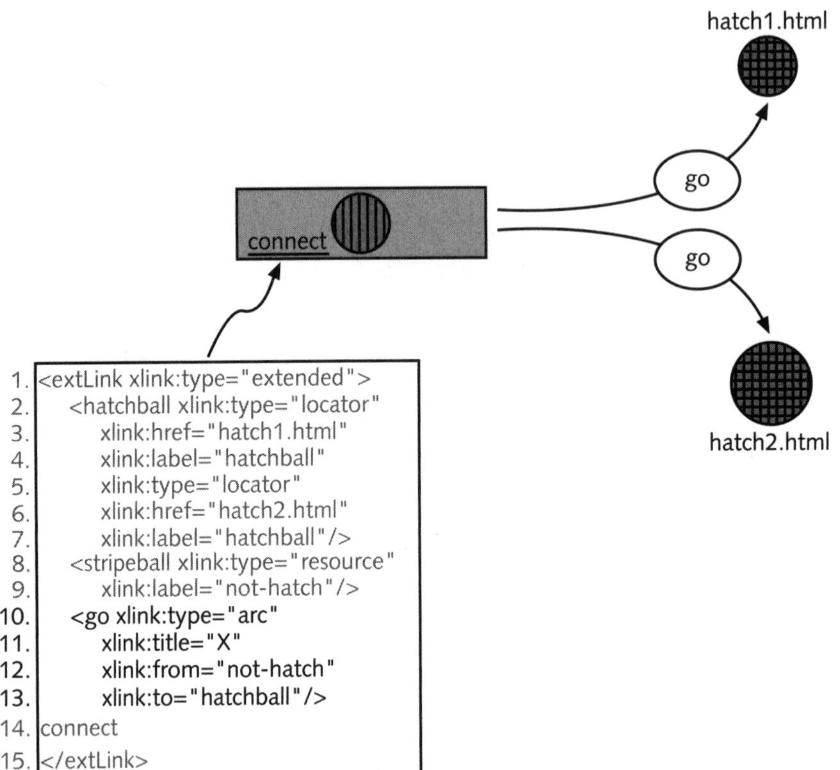

Figure 7-9 Evolution of an extended link element; Phase 4: creating arcs

Remember, if it facilitates comprehension, consider extended-link elements to be meaningful containers for resources and arcs. Returning to the TLSales example and Mr. Sleek, note in the following DTD code how the extended-type element called <staff> contains the now-familiar <employee>, <department>, and <empl_record> elements:

```
<!ELEMENT  staff  (employee,department,empl_record)*>
<!ATTLIST  staff
   xmlns:xlink    CDATA        #FIXED
                                  http://www.w3.org/1999/xlink"
   xlink:type     (extended)   #FIXED "extended"
   xlink:titlev   CDATA        #IMPLIED>
```

Combining all the previous TLSales elements results in a complete and valid extended-type link, which should validate against the DTD code above. From the quick illustration in Figures 7-6 through 7-9, you should now recognize the components of the following extended link. Again, the one-to-many link is something that is not possible in HTML.

```
<staff xlink:title="TLSales Staff Information">
     <employee xlink:label="jsleek">
          <name>Jim</name>
          <surname>Sleek</surname>
     </employee>
     <department xlink:label="HRInfo" xlink:title="Sales"
               xlink:href="sales.xml"/>
     <department xlink:label="HRInfo"
       xlink:title="Partners"
               xlink:href="partners.xml"/>
     <empl_record xlink:type="arc"
               xlink:from="jsleek"
               xlink:to="HRInfo"/>
...
</staff>
```


Validating Simple Links

Recall again that, conceptually, simple-type linking elements can be considered a subset of extended links. They can exist as a notation for linking elements where you don't require the power and flexibility—and resource overhead—of an entire extended-type link. All the XLink-related aspects of a simple link are encapsulated in one element. Further, XLink doesn't care about the subelements of a simple-type link, only about the linking element itself and its attributes.

To review, the valid XLink attributes for a simple-type link are href, title, role, arcrole, show, and actuate. The following is an example of DTD code for a typical simple-type link element:

```
<!ELEMENT director (#PCDATA)>
<!ATTLIST director
     xmlns:xlink      CDATA    #FIXED
       "http://www.w3.org/1999/xlink"
     xlink:type     (simple)  #FIXED "simple"
     xlink:href     CDATA     #IMPLIED
     xlink:show     (new)     #FIXED "new"
     xlink:actuate  (onRequest)     #FIXED "onRequest">
```

Here is the simple-type element link that corresponds to the above DTD code:

```
<president xlink:href="gwbushjr.xml">George W. Bush Jr.
</president>
```

Using the XML Pointer Language (XPointer)

So far in this chapter, all links have been to whole resources, although there have been several mentions of linking to subresources, portions of resources and similar terms. However, if you need to provide a more precise link to a paragraph, citation, or other portion of a larger resource, XPointer is recommended.

In the words of the W3C, "[XML Pointer Language], which is based on the XML Path Language (XPath), supports addressing into the internal structures of XML documents and external parsed entities. It allows for examination of a hierarchical document structure and choice of its internal parts based on various properties, such as element types, attribute values, character content, and relative position."

XML Pointer Language (XPointer) Version 1.0 became a Candidate Recommendation of the World Wide Web Consortium on September 11, 2001. At that point, the document was considered stable by the XML Linking Working Group and was available for public review. To view it, go to *www.w3.org/TR/2001/CR-xptr-20010911/*.

XPointer was developed to extend the ability of XPath to find subresources. You were already introduced to some XPath concepts in Chapter 6. XPath is a declarative language used for addressing and pattern matching. Being an extension of XPath means XPointer can reach more precise locations in a document without having to download more data than necessary or without needing to provide additional elements, attributes, or other components to the document. However, you can still add markup to documents (like the id attribute to element start tags) and take advantage of the flexibility that it gives you. Thus, since XPointer can extend the XPath capability, then it follows that XPointer is also being used in conjunction with XLink to access resources more precisely, just by the nature of the configuration of a linking element.

To see how XPointer works with XLink, look at the example of the simple-type linking element named <MEETING> in Figure 7-10. Note that the XPointer features are placed in the linking element <MEETING> through the use of the locator attribute "xlink:href".

From " ... etc.", you can see that terms have been left out at this point for the sake of simplicity. The XPointer-related terms are explained later in this chapter.

```
<MEETING xmlns:xlink="http://www.w3.org/1999/xlink"
                              xlink:type="simple"
                              xlink:show="new"
                              xlink:href="http://www.TLSales.com/mtg_agenda.xml#
                                   xpointer(/child::*[position()=2])...etc./>
agenda
</MEETING>
```

Figure 7-10 An XPointer working with XLink

The extension to XPath works like this: you may have noticed already that XPointer expressions resemble XPath expressions in syntax and effect, but XPointer adds some new features to meet its own needs. Those additional features, variously called extensions, XPointer references, fragment identifiers, and other names, enable XPointer to:

- Use URI references to address into the internal structure of XML documents
- Address points and ranges, in addition to the whole (XPath) nodes (Users can now select parts of documents using their mouse.)
- Use string matching in its searches

These additional features are discussed in more detail in upcoming sections. To summarize, the major advantage provided by the new XPointer extensions is the ability to refer more precisely to XML document subresources. This provides a level of precision that HTML and XLink and XPath could not reach previously. Plus, as you see later in this chapter, with XPointer, the user is even given the ability to click on more precise pieces of information, which can also save time and bandwidth, and provide documents with more precise and clearer information.

Addressing a Document's Internal Structure with a Universal Resource Identifier (URI)

In the example shown in Figure 7-10, the value specified for the locator attribute xlink:href was a URI that allows the application to drill down to a subresource within the specified URL. The example shown in Figure 7-11 illustrates just the URI value portion, minus the "...etc.", of the locator attribute, so that you can see the URI's basic parts a little more clearly.

All of the parts of the Figure 7-11 URI are discussed in detail as the chapter progresses. Note that the URI reference begins with a Web site address (*http://www.TLSales.com*), followed by the name of the specific XML document to be searched (mtg_agenda.xml) at that site. The XPointer-specific information follows that, and is connected to the Web site URI and XML document portions by a **hash symbol** (#), also called a pound sign, or a number sign connector.

There are two types of such **connectors**; each instructs the parser to initiate link behavior in a specific manner. The hash connector initiates link behavior similar to HTML; the entire linked resource is downloaded, and the focus is then shifted to the identified fragment.

The other connector is the vertical bar character (|), also called the **pipe**. When the pipe is used, subsequent behavior is left to whatever is written in the application, which may or may not download the entire resource, depending on its author's needs and intents. At any rate, downloading of the entire resource can be prevented, and only discrete subresources can be retrieved and served back to the requestor in the application. This way, bandwidth can be conserved and other connection costs can also be optimized. For the remainder of this chapter, the more basic hash symbol connector is used.

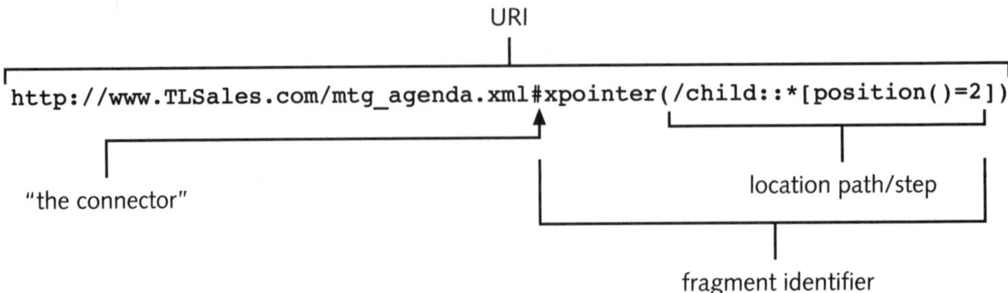

Figure 7-11 A generic XPointer URI

The **fragment identifier** begins immediately after the connector and is composed of the keyword xPointer combined with the location (also called the locationpath) or even the location steps (in the Figure 7-11 example, the location path is equal to just one location step). The location is discussed in the next section.

At various points in the following sections, the XPointer reference may be called one of several names: fragment identifier, XPointer reference, XPointer, reference, location, link target, and others. No matter which term is used, they all refer to the same concept. They are listed here because this concept especially seems to have many name variations, depending on the organization, industry, region, and backgrounds of those who use it. If you continue a career of XML XLink development, be prepared to hear several variations.

Figure 7-12 represents a typical Web page that includes the link named "agenda." Note that, as the mouse pointer is placed over "agenda", that the whole URI—the URL plus the hash connector and the fragment identifier—is displayed in the status bar at the bottom of the window (in Figure 7-12, "etc." again substitutes for the fragment identifier in the identifier). When clicked, this link initiates the display of whatever content is to be found at the referenced location.

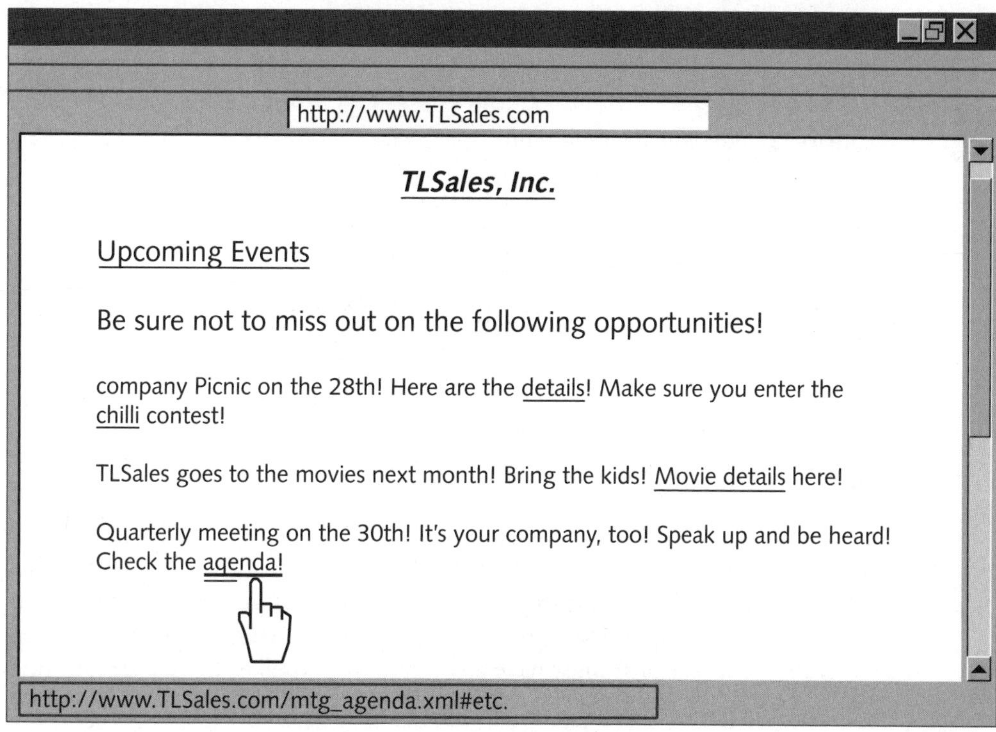

Figure 7-12 XPointer construct on a generic web page

Fragment Identifier Components: Location Steps and Location Paths

As stated previously, XPointer fragment identifiers are composed of the xPointer keyword followed by the basic addressing component, the **location** (i.e., a description of a subresource location). XPointer location descriptions can represent very precise locations in XML documents, especially on those occasions when they are used in tandem combinations.

The location, then, is composed of a **location path** which, in turn is made up of one or more **location steps.** If there is more than one location step in the location path, then the location steps are separated by a forward slash (/) character. Please refer to the generic example in Figure 7-13.

The location steps contain components like (XPath) nodes, axes, node tests, and zero or more predicates, as well as the (XPointer) points and ranges (all of these concepts are explained later in this chapter). Figure 7-14 illustrates individual location step.

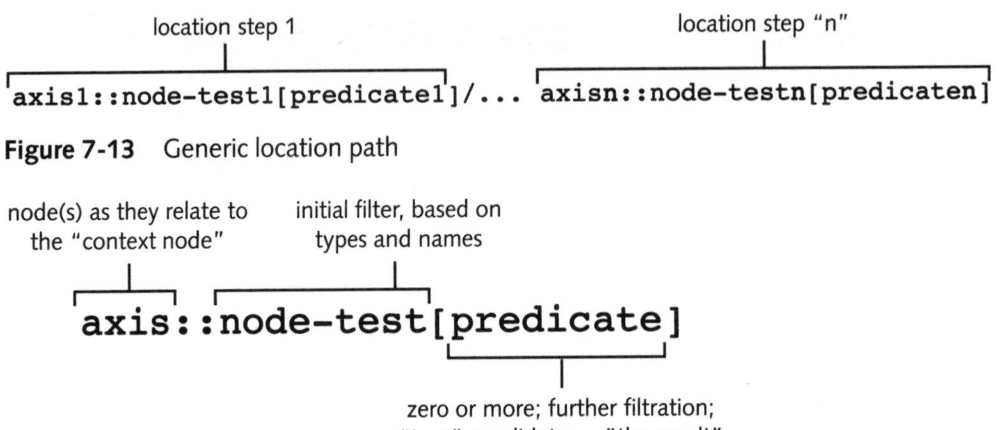

Figure 7-13 Generic location path

Figure 7-14 Generic location step

The steps are evaluated left to right, starting with the context defined in the location step at the far left. Thus, whatever result is finally distilled from the step at the far right must have also survived the far-left step. In other words, whatever results there are to the location step (that is, whatever locations survive the final predicate screen, a concept discussed later in the next sections) must have answered "yes/true" to the conditions imposed by it.

If a location path is prefixed with a forward slash (/), then the screening must have begun with the document's root node as the initial context. (Recall that each XPath context consists of the context node(s), integer-value positions and sizes, and variable bindings, function libraries, and namespace declarations.)

Before these concepts can be explained, please note that the formal grammar for XPointer and other XML-related languages is **Extended Backus-Naur Form (EBNF)** notation, an example of which is illustrated in Figure 7-14, and which is described in W3C XML Recommendation 1.0 and other references. EBNF has been around since 1960 and is commonly used to describe programming grammar and syntax. However, rarely does a variation of EBNF actually play a role as it does in the description of location steps in XPointer extensions. In EBNF parlance, the "::" means "the expression on the left is defined by the expression on the right."

Referring to the TLSales, Inc. management team XML document (mgt_team.xml) shown in Figure 7-15, in the expression `child::MGT[position()=3],` child is an axis name, MGT is a node test, and `[position ()=3]` is the predicate. Here, the parser is basically being told to check the child elements of the context node, and select the data from the third element named <MGT>. You aren't expected to be able to read this example expression or the next one, yet.

```
<?xml version="1.0" encoding="UTF-8" standalone="yes"?>
<?xml-stylesheet type="text/css" href="contacts.css"?>
<!—edited with Notepad by Student Name (Project x, Chapter 7) -->
<MGT_TEAM>
    <MGT id="sales.mgr">
        <LASTNAME>Gold</LASTNAME>
        <FIRSTNAME>Anna</FIRSTNAME>
    </MGT>
    <MGT id="custsrv.mgr">
        <LASTNAME>Smith</LASTNAME>
        <FIRSTNAME>Dale</FIRSTNAME>
    </MGT>
    <MGT id="mktg.mgr">
        <LASTNAME>Jones</LASTNAME>
        <FIRSTNAME>Chris</FIRSTNAME>
    </MGT>
    <MGT id="admin.mgr">
        <LASTNAME>Wong</LASTNAME>
        <FIRSTNAME>Kelly</FIRSTNAME>
    </MGT>
    <MGT id="prod.mgr">
        <LASTNAME>Manocha</LASTNAME>
        <FIRSTNAME>Pat</FIRSTNAME>
    </MGT>
    <MGT id="exec.mgr">
        <LASTNAME>McKinnon</LASTNAME>
        <FIRSTNAME>Linda</FIRSTNAME>
    </MGT>
</MGT_TEAM>
```

Figure 7-15 TLSales management team (mgt_team.xml)

Here is another example based on mgt_team.xml and creating a location path with one or more location steps, such as:

```
/descendant::MGT/child::LASTNAME
```

In this example, the parser is instructed to examine all the descendant elements of the context node, and select data from all the <LASTNAME> elements that have an <MGT> element as a parent. You can see that, from the nature of this example, the parser will be looking with more precision for the specified data.

XPointer Axes

The **axis**, shown in Figure 7-14, may represent one or more XPath-style nodes, within which the subresource is found. These axes become more familiar with practice and by examining the options available to you. Axes provide "look at" instructions to the parser. The parser is told what its position is when it commences its search and in which direction to search. XPointers use the same axes as XPaths. Table 7-6's list of available axes should clarify this concept.

Table 7-6 Axes available to XPointer

Axis Name	Instruction to Parser
child	Look at the children of the context node
descendant	Look at all descendants (i.e., the children, children's children, etc.) of the context node
parent	Look at the parent node of the context node (if you are at the root, this is "empty")
ancestor	Look at all ancestor nodes from the parent back to the root (that includes the parent of the context node, the parent's parent, and so forth, back to and including the root node)
following-sibling	Look at the sibling nodes to the right; that is, look at the following siblings of the context node (remember, a sibling is a node on the same level as the context node)
preceding-sibling	Look at the sibling nodes to the left; that is, look at all the preceding siblings of the context node
following	Look at all the nodes in the document that follow the context node, excluding descendants and excluding attribute nodes and namespace nodes
preceding	Look at all preceding nodes in the document, excluding any ancestors and excluding attribute nodes and namespace nodes
attribute	Look at the attributes of the context node
namespace	Look at the namespace declarations in the context node
self	Look at the context node itself
descendant-or-self	Look at the union of the context node and its descendants
ancestor-or-self	Look at the union of the context node and its ancestors

XPointer Node Tests

The **node test** is a preliminary filtering test (based on element names or a type of processing instruction or something similar). Although XPointers use the same axes as XPaths, XPointers use some node tests that XPaths do not. Table 7-7 lists the node tests you can use with XPointers, and what they match. The concept of node tests, similar to axes, will be clearer after you examine Table 7-7 and practice a little.

Table 7-7 Node tests you can use with XPointers

Node Tests	Matches
*	Any element
node()	Any node
text()	A text node
comment()	A comment node
processing-instruction()	A processing instruction node
point()	A point in a resource
range()	A range in a resource

Note in particular the last two node tests: point () and range(). These correspond to the two new constructs added in XPointers—points and ranges. They are addressed in more detail later in this chapter.

Recall that to extend XPath to include points and ranges, the XPointer specification created the concept of a "location," which can be an XPath node, a point, or a range. However, node tests are still called node tests, not location tests, even though they function correctly with the new points and ranges.

XPointer Predicates

The **predicate** is the final filter, the one that focuses most on context size and position, the results of which are considered to have indicated a boolean-like "yes/true" response to its conditions. XPointers support the same types of predicate expressions as XPaths. Predicate expressions become clear to you as you practice and as you examine the examples in this chapter. Meanwhile, there are numerous references you can read to become familiar with predicate expressions, most notably the W3C's XPath Recommendation 1.0. The following are the types of expressions you can use in XPointer predicates:

- *Node sets*: a location path can be used as an expression.
- *Booleans*: true/false determinations; "or" and "and" expressions can be used
- *Numbers*: represent floating-point numbers; include a special "Not-a-Number" (NaN) value, positive and negative infinity, and positive and negative zero; the +, – (must be preceded by white space), div and mod operators are allowed
- *Strings*: a sequence of zero or more Unicode characters (later, several related functions are demonstrated)
- *Result tree fragments*: parts of XML documents that are not complete nodes or sets of nodes; created by document () functions, etc.

XPointer Location Set Functions

Table 7-8 lists several kinds of XPointer functions that return specific location sets.

Table 7-8 XPointer location sets returned by certain functions

Functions	Explanation / Description
id()	Returns all the elements whose ID attribute values match the one specified
here()	Returns a location set with one location: the current location
origin()	Same as here(), except that this function is used with out-of-line links
root()	Returns a location set with one location: the root node

The id() function is well-known; you can use it to return locations with ID attribute values that are a match to that specified in the location part of the extension. The id() function is discussed in a little more detail at the end of this section. The here() function refers to the current element, not just the current node; it is useful because XPointers are usually stored in text nodes or attribute values. The origin() function is much like the here() function, but you use it with out-of-line links, which are not covered in this text due to time and space constraints. And the root() function works like the / character—it refers to the root node, corresponding to the beginning of the prolog.

Pointing to IDs: The id() Function

The simplest example of an XPointer refers to an ID attribute in the element(s) to which you want to point. For example, a TLSales management team list may use the element <MGT> in the manner depicted previously in Figure 7-15, which lists TLSales' management team.

Referring again to Figure 7-15, if you intend to point specifically to Kelly Wong, for example, the fragment identifier of your XPointer might be expressed as #id(admin.mgr). The full URI would, therefore, be *http://www.TLSales.com/mgt_team.xml#id(admin.mgr)*.

Counting Elements: The position() Function

You have also seen the XPath-related position() function in action several times in this chapter. It simply acts as a counter for the various elements that the parser might encounter in the early processing stages. Earlier you were shown the expression `child::MGT[position()=3]`. This instructed the parser to look among the child elements to the context node, and to fetch the data from the third <MGT> element found there.

XPointer Examples

Table 7-9 lists several XPointer reference examples. They all refer to the agenda for TLSales' regular meeting, the mtg_agenda.xml document depicted in Figure 7-16.

Table 7-9 XPointer reference examples

Reference/Search Example	Explanation / Description
*	All the element children of the context node
.	The context node itself
* *	The parent of the context node
@*	All the attributes of the context node
@ID	The ID attributes of the context node
text()	All text node children of the context node
ITEM	The <ITEM> element children of the context node
//ITEM	All the <ITEM> descendants of the document root
ITEM[4]	The fourth <ITEM> child of the context node
ITEM [first()]	The first <ITEM> child of the context node
*/TIME_REQ	All the <TIME_REQ> grandchildren of the context node
ITEM[TIME_REQ]	The <ITEM> children of the context node that have <TIME_REQ> children
/AGENDA/ITEM[4]/SUMMARY	The <SUMMARY> element of the fourth <ITEM> element of the <AGENDA> element

Figure 7-16 contains the agenda referred to by the examples in Table 7-9.

```
<?xml version="1.0" encoding="UTF-8" standalone="yes"?>
<?xml-stylesheet type="text/css" href="contacts.css"?>
<!--edited with Notepad by Student Name (Project x, Chapter 7) -->
<AGENDA>
      <ITEM id="1Q_REVS">
            <SPONSOR>Gold</SPONSOR>
            <TIME_REQ units="hours">1.0</TIME_REQ>
            <SUMMARY>
                  <COMMENT>Improved over 4Q</COMMENT>
            </SUMMARY>
      </ITEM>
      <ITEM id="COMPLAINTS">
            <SPONSOR>Smith</SPONSOR>
            <TIME_REQ units="hours">0.5</TIME_REQ>
            <SUMMARY>
                  <$REQD amount="$Cdn">0</$REQD>
            </SUMMARY>
      </ITEM>
      <ITEM id="ADV_PLAN">
            <SPONSOR>Jones</SPONSOR>
            <TIME_REQ units="hours">1.0</TIME_REQ>
            <SUMMARY>
                  <COMMENT>Reduce radio; more WWW</COMMENT>
                  <$REQD amount="$Cdn">2.5 million</$REQD>
            </SUMMARY>
      </ITEM>
      <ITEM id="Q_A">
            <SPONSOR>Manocha</SPONSOR>
            <TIME_REQ units="hours">0.5</TIME_REQ>
            <SUMMARY>
                  <COMMENT>Improved</COMMENT>
                  <$REQD amount="$Cdn">0</$REQD>
            </SUMMARY>
      </ITEM>
      <ITEM id="REORG">
            <SPONSOR>McKinnon</SPONSOR>
            <SUMMARY>
                  <COMMENT>On schedule/under budget</COMMENT>
            </SUMMARY>
      </ITEM>
</AGENDA>
```

Figure 7-16 Meeting agenda (XML document)

UNDERSTANDING XPOINTER POINTS AND RANGES

With XPath, you can locate data only at the node level. In Chapter 6, when you studied XSL transformations, XPath was adequate because you were working with XML data in terms of nodes. However, such an approach is not adequate for all purposes, especially for referencing subresources with XLink. For example, a user working with a displayed XML document might find it useful to click the mouse at a particular point, or even select a range, to access additional or alternate XML content. Meanwhile, such information might not start and end on node boundaries, and thus might contain parts of various trees and subtrees. To obtain finer control over XML data, you can work with points and ranges in XPointer. A **point** is a specific location in a document. A **range** is made up of all the XML content between two points, which can include parts of elements and text strings.

To support points and ranges, XPointer extended XPath's nodes into locations. Every location is an XPath node, point, or range. Therefore, XPath's node sets have become location sets in the XPointer specification.

XPointer Points

To define an XPointer point, you use two items—a node and an index that can hold a zero or a positive integer. The node identifies the point's origin; the index indicates how far away the referenced point is from that origin.

There are two different types of points—node-points and character-points, so their index values should be expressed differently. The first type to be discussed is node-points, because the concept of child nodes is important to both, but is better illustrated with node points. After the two types of points are discussed, then you are shown how to create points. Once the syntax is understood with respect to the concepts, examples are presented.

Node-points

Any origin node (also called the container node) may or may not have child nodes. If it does, then the point found in the node is called a **node-point**. The index of a node-point is measured in child nodes. Here, the index of a node-point must be equal to or less than the number of child nodes in the origin node. If you use an index of zero, the point is immediately before any child nodes. An index of zero indicates the point before any child nodes, and a nonzero index *n* indicates the point immediately after the nth child node. For example, an index of 2 means a point is located immediately after the second child node.

Character-points

If the origin node can only contain text but no child nodes, then the index is measured in characters. As a result, these are called **character-points**.

The index of a character-point must be a positive integer or zero, and less than or equal to the length of the text string in the node. An index of zero indicates that the point is immediately before the first character. If the index is 4, then the point is immediately after the fourth character. Character-points cannot be preceded or followed by siblings or children. Note that XPointer collapses all consecutive white spaces into a single white space. Also, there is no placement of points inside start and end tags, processing instructions, comment, or any markup. The characters referred to are strictly within the data.

Creating Character-points and Node-points

To create a point, use the start-point() function. Here is the syntax:

```
xpointer(location path/node test/start-point()
   [position()=position-number])
```

Examples: Character-point and Node-point

Please refer to mtg_agenda.xml in Figure 7-16. If you want to place a reference character-point just before the "t" in Smith, in the second ITEM element (the one that addresses COMPLAINTS), then do the following:

```
xpointer(/AGENDA/ITEM[2]/SPONSOR/text()/start-point()
   [position()=3])
```

Referring to the same meeting agenda figure, if you want to place a reference node-point just before the TIME_REQ node in the third item (ADV_PLAN), then code it this way:

```
xpointer(/AGENDA/ITEM[3]/node()/start-point()
   [position()=1])
```

The long form references to these examples are, respectively:

```
http://www.TLSales.com/mtg_agenda.xml#xpointer(/AGENDA/
  ITEM[2]/SPONSOR/text()/start-point()[position()=3])
```

and

```
http://www.TLSales.com/mtg_agenda.xml#xpointer(/AGENDA/
  ITEM[3]/node()/start-point()[position()=1])
```

XPointer Ranges

A range consists of all the XML structure between two points: a start point and an end point. However, both have to be in the same document and the start point cannot occur after the end point. If the start point and the end point coincide at the same location, then the range is said to be collapsed.

Furthermore, a range does not have to be completely contained within one subtree of a document, either. It can extend from one subtree to another. All you need are a valid start point and a valid end point, and they both must be situated in the same document.

To create a range, use the following syntax:

```
xpointer(location path/node test/start-point()
      [position()=position-number] to
      (location path/node test/start-point()
      [position()=position-number])
```

Referring to the agenda in Figure 7-16 again, if it is your intent to find out the quick summary statement regarding Quality Assurance (Q_A) at TLSales, Inc., then use the following reference:

```
xpointer(/AGENDA/ITEM[4]/SUMMARY/COMMENT/text()/
      start-point()[position()=0] to
      /AGENDA/ITEM[4]/SUMMARY/COMMENT/text()/
      start-point()[position()=8])
```

XPointer Abbreviations

XPointer has added some abbreviated forms of reference, mostly to facilitate the common practices of referring to elements by location or ID. Table 7-10 contains several examples of such abbreviations.

Table 7-10 XPointer abbreviations

Intent	Original Code	Abbreviated Code

You want to locate Ms. Gold's Comment regarding First Quarter Revenues in mtg_agenda.xml. The comment looks like this:
 	
<COMMENT>Improved over 4Q</COMMENT>
	`http://www.TLSales.com/mtg_agenda.xml#`
	
	`xpointer(/child::*[position()=1]/`
	
	`child::*[position()=3]/child::*[position()=1])`
		According to XPath, the child:: part is optional, and the predicate [position()=x] can be abbreviated as [x]. In XPointer, you can also omit the square brackets. Here's the result:
		
		`http://www.TLSales.com/mtg_agenda.xml#1/3/1`

You can use words as location steps, not just numbers. But the words must correspond to ID values of elements. In the mtg_agenda.xml document, the fifth ITEM element has an id=REORG. You may want to read its (child) SPONSOR element (which shows "McKinnon").	`http://www.TLSales.com/mtg_agenda.xml#`
	
	`xpointer(/child::*[id("REORG")]/`
	
	`child::*[position()=1]`
		Use the element's ID value as a location step, and you get this: `http://www.TLSales.com/mtg_agenda.xml#REORG/`

The last example uses an id() function. To do this, you must ensure that the ID attributes are declared in a DTD or schema. However, not all XML documents have DTDs or schemas, so XPointer provides the capability to specify alternative patterns with multiple XPointers. Here is how one of these "crossfires" might look:

```
http://www.TLSales.com/mtg_agenda.xml#xpointer(id("REORG"))
  xpointer(//*[id="REORG])/1
```

If the first XPointer fails, the second XPointer should take over. It locates any element that has an attribute named "id" with the specified value.

Selecting an Implementation

Many XML developers, programmers, or authors express concerns about the fact that the IT industry has fallen behind the W3C on XLinking and XPointing, and that implementations, especially browsers, are slow to adopt the concepts and practices mentioned in the respective Recommendations. The following lists were gleaned from several sources (including the W3C). The list may not be comprehensive and there is no guarantee or warranty regarding the performance of any of these applications.

The following is a list of XPointer implementations:

- Fujitsu XLink Processor, developed by Fujitsu Laboratories Ltd., is an implementation of XLink and XPointer.
- libxml is the Gnome XML library's beta implementation of XPointer. The full syntax is supported, but the test suite does not cover all aspects yet.
- 4Xpointer is an XPointer Processor written in Python by Fourthought, Inc.

The following is a list of XLink implementations:

- Mozilla M17 Browser (Mozilla) is an open source browser with restricted XLink support.
- Link (Justin Ludwig) is a small, XLink-aware XML browser.
- psgml-xpointer.el (David Megginson) is a very useful extension to psgml for emacs that generates XPointer expressions.
- Reusable XLink XSLT transformations (Fabio Arciniegas A.) are XSLT templates that allow the transformation of extended links to HTML and JavaScript representations.
- XMLhack and XLink news are the latest XLink news and software releases.
- X2X (empolis UK Ltd.) is an XML XLink engine that allows linking between documents and information resources without needing to change the resources that are being linked.
- Fujitsu XLink Processor (Fujitsu Laboratories Ltd.) is an implementation of XLink and XPointer.
- xlinkit.com is a lightweight application service which provides rule-based XLink generation and checks the consistency of distributed documents and Web content.

- Amaya, the W3C editor/browser, now supports XLinks simple links, too.
- XLink2HTML is a set of XSLT stylesheets for the creation of HTML representations of XLink elements.
- XTooX is a free XLink processor that turns extended-type, out-of-line links into inline links. Available under the GNU Lesser General Public License.

Chapter Summary

- Simple HTML hyperlinking structures are inadequate for XML documents and languages. As a result, specific languages have been developed for linking XML documents: the XML Linking Language (XLink) for linking between documents and the XML Pointer Language (XPointer).
- The W3C defines a link as an explicit relationship between addressable units of information or services. XLink and XPointer links can be categorized in two ways: hyperlinks, intended for viewing and responding to by humans, and links that are intended only for automatic response by computer systems.
- XLink links are not restricted to specific names like HTML's predefined <A> or <IMG> (for anchor and image). You can give an XLink link whatever name you wish. It is not the name, but the attributes specified for an element, that make it a linking element.
- A simple link associates exactly two participating resources, one local and one remote, with an arc traversing from the local to the remote. A simple link is always an outbound link. Extended links offer full XLink functionality (outbound, inbound, and third-party arcs; links that have arbitrary numbers of participating resources, etc.). The structure of an extended link can be fairly complex.
- Local-to-remote links are outbound, while remote-to-local links are inbound. Links among remote resources are third-party.
- XLinks require the use of namespaces but, in the case of XLinks, the declaration must be placed within the linking element's start tag.
- XLink's global attributes also allow developers to specify the basic attribute types of XLinks, which dictate certain aspects of the links' other properties and resources. XLink links always have an attribute named "type", the value of which is fundamental to a link's purpose and behavior.

- For the XLink linking elements to function correctly and reliably, their respective elements and documents must be well-formed and valid. That means that the XLink linking elements and attributes must be declared in the referenced DTDs and schemas, if applicable.
- XLinks link to whole resources. If you need to provide a more precise link to a paragraph, citation, or other portion of a larger resource, use XPointer constructs.
- XPointer links use URI references, which begin with Web site addresses, followed by the name of the specific XML document, a specific XPointer connector (usually a # symbol), and then the fragment identifier (composed of the xpointer keyword followed by a location path that is made up of one or more location steps).
- In the location steps, the axis may represent one or more XPath-style nodes, within which the subresource is found. The node test is a preliminary filtering test, and the predicate is the final filter (it focuses most on context size and position).
- The simplest example of an XPointer is a reference to an ID attribute in the element to which you want to point. That is why it is recommended that ID attributes be added to significant elements in XML documents to facilitate XLinking and XPointing.
- A point is a specific location in a document. A range is made up of all the XML content between two points, which can include part of elements and text strings. There are two different types of points—node-points and character-points. Their index values are expressed differently.

Review Questions

1. What are three shortcomings of HTML linking?
2. How does the W3C define "link"?
3. Match the XML standards in a, b, and c to their descriptions in 1, 2, and 3.

a. XBase	1.	contains specifications to create links to specific locations within a document
b. XLink	2.	contains specifications to create links to a document
c. XPointer	3.	URI-defining facility

4. Which of the following are true regarding simple links (also called simple-type links)?
   a. the category into which HTML-style <A> and <IMG> links would fall
   b. may be either an inbound or an outbound link
   c. associates exactly two participating resources, one local and one remote
   d. named because its href attribute has the value "simple"
   e. Its arc goes to the local resource from the remote resource.

5. The purpose of a ______________ link is to provide a convenient shorthand version of an equivalent ______________ link.
6. In the text, several properties of extended-type links were described. Which of the following elements might appear in an extended link?
   a. elements for specifying human-readable resource and arc titles
   b. elements specifying arc traversal rules
   c. elements pointing to remote resources
   d. elements containing local resources
   e. all of the above
7. Match the following:

a. resource	1. resource from which traversal is begun
b. remote resource	2. participates in a link by being a linking element or being a child to a linking element
c. starting resource	3. includes files, images, documents, programs, etc.
d. ending resource	4. addressed with a URI reference
e. local resource	5. destination resource for a traversal

8. To use your linking elements, the declaration of the XLink namespace is required. But where is it located?
9. What is an arc?
10. Match the following:

a. multidirectional	1. two resources: one source and one destination
b. outbound	2. neither the starting resource nor the ending resource is local
c. unidirectional	3. two arcs connecting the same pair of resources, but the resources switch places as starting and ending
d. inbound	4. direction is away from the linking element
e. third party	5. ending resource is local; starting resource is remote

11. XLink links always have an attribute named ______________, which is one of XLink's ten ______________ attributes.
12. What is the name of the locator attribute that allows an XLink application to find a remote resource?
13. Which of the following is *not* a value for the behavior attribute "show"?
    a. replace
    b. here
    c. embed
    d. other
    e. none

7

14. As linking elements are developed and defined, what two restrictions apply?
15. XLink linking elements and attributes need not be declared in the referenced DTDs and schemas; XLink is only concerned with subelements. True or false?
16. What three features make XPointer an "extension" to XPath?
17. The major advantage provided by the new XPointer extensions is the ability to refer more precisely to XML document subresources, introducing a level of precision that HTML, XLink, and XPath couldn't reach previously. True or false?
18. What is the difference between a fragment identifier and a location path? What is the difference between a location path and a location step?
19. What are the components of a location step that is made up of an axis, a nodetest, and zero or more predicates?
    a. nodetest
    b. URL
    c. axis
    d. URI
    e. predicate
20. Match the following:

a. preceding	1. Look at the sibling nodes to the right.
b. following	2. Look at the sibling nodes to the left.
c. preceding-sibling	3. Look at the nodes that follow the context node.
d. following-sibling	4. Look at all preceding nodes in the document.

21. Which of the following does *not* refer to an XPointer reference?
    a. fragment identifier
    b. link target
    c. location
    d. XPointer
    e. all of the above
    f. none of the above
22. Which of the following is included in the XPointer concept of a location?
    a. range
    b. URI
    c. XPath node
    d. point
    e. all of the above

23. Which of the XPointer functions (that is, the ones that return location sets) is most widely known at present?
24. Which of the following means "all the element children of the context node"?
    a. *@
    b. .
    c. **
    d. @id
    e. *
25. The index of a node-point is measured in ______________.
    a. character points
    b. child characters
    c. characters
    d. child nodes

7

HANDS-ON PROJECTS

In the following Hands-on Projects, you create and examine XML linking and referencing methods using XLink and XPointer. These technologies have only recently been recommended by the World Wide Web Consortium (*www.w3c.org*), and at this time, there is a very limited amount of software available that implements these standards.

You begin by examining some of the files that you will build upon and inspect. In Hands-on Project 7-2, you will implement a simple link, similar in behavior to an HTML link. In the subsequent projects, you are presented files that implement the functionality of extended links and pointer references, but you are not able to run them because no browsers currently support the new specifications.

Note: The following projects assume that your hard disk is the C drive. If you are using another drive, such as D, substitute its letter as appropriate.

Project 7-1

In this project, you set up and review an XML document that includes an XLink.

To set up the project files:

1. In Windows Explorer, create a new folder called **Ch07** in C:/home/yourname.
2. Copy all of the files located in the Ch07/Project_7-1 folder on your Data Disk to your C:/home/yourname/Ch07 folder. If asked to replace the current files, click **Yes to all**.
3. Click **Start**, point to **Programs** (point to **All Programs** in Windows XP), point to **XML Spy Suite**, and then click **XML Spy IDE**. The XML Spy window opens.

4. Click **Project** on the menu bar, and then click **Open Project**. The Open dialog box appears.
5. Click the **Look in** list arrow, and then navigate to C:\home\<yourname>\Ch07. Click **contacts.spp** and then click **Open**.

   If you expand the folder in the Projects pane, you will notice that the project has three files: an XML document, coxntacts.xml, a cascading style sheet, contacts.css, and a DTD, contacts.dtd.

Now you are ready to examine the XML document that contains the XLink codes and the style sheet for the document.

Examine the XML document and its style sheet:

1. Expand the **XML Files** branch in the Project pane, and then double-click the **contacts.xml** file. The XML document opens in the main window. Click **View** on the menu bar, and then click **Text view** to view the XML source code.

   Notice that the xml-style sheet declaration references the contacts.css cascading style sheet. Cascading Style Sheets provide a simple method to define the presentation of XML documents.
2. You can view the formatted XML document in the XML Spy HTML browser by clicking **View** on the menu bar, and then clicking **Browser view**. The formatted document appears in the main window.
3. Return to the XML document's source code by clicking **File** on the menu bar, and then clicking **Text view**.

   The CONTACTS element has an XLink namespace declaration referencing http://www.w3c.org/1999/xlink. This namespace is used for the global attributes set of XLink. Although the elements that require links are in a separate namespace, they become XLink elements by incorporating the xlink:type attribute.
4. To examine the style sheet, expand the **XSL Files** branch in the Project pane, and then double-click the **contacts.css** file. The cascading style sheet opens in the main window.

   A style sheet consists of style rules that tell a browser how to display a document. Each rule is made up of a selector, and a set of style property and value pairs contained within curly braces, {}. The values of the style properties define how an element should be presented. Each element defined in the DTD has a corresponding style sheet selector in contacts.css. See Chapter 11 for complete information about cascading style sheets.
5. Expand the **DTD/Schemas** branch in the Project pane, and then double-click the **contacts.dtd** file. The document type definition opens in the main window.

   The DTD looks similar to the DTD used in the Hands-on Projects in Chapter 6 with the addition of two new element declarations. The WHATSNEW element contains a child element called SITE that you use to create a link in the XML document. The important thing to note is that the SITE element is a straightforward element; there is nothing exceptional about it. You add linking capabilities by adding XLink attributes to the element.

Project 7-2

In this project, you add a link to the XML document that you reviewed in Project 7-1. You construct a simple XLink that is the XML equivalent to an HTML hyperlink because it provides access to an external Web page identified by a Uniform Resource Identifier (URI).

To format the link, you create a style rule in the contacts.css style sheet. The resulting link appears similar to the familiar blue underlined format and the hand pointer that appears when a user points to the link. Because not all browsers currently support XLink functionality, you must use Netscape Navigator 6.2 to view the link.

To add a link to the XML document and modify the style sheet:

1. With the contacts project from Project 7-1 still open in XML Spy, double-click the **contacts.xml** file in the Project pane to return to the XML document. The XML document appears in the main window.
2. Recall that a simple link is a one-way link between a source and destination resource, and provides the same type of functionality as an HTML hyperlink. You add the following link to the XML document immediately before the CONTACT end tag, </CONTACT>:

```
<WHATSNEW>
    Check out what's new at
    <SITE xlink:type="simple" xlink:href="http://www.course.com">
            www.course.com
    </SITE>
</WHATSNEW>
```

   Your document should now resemble Figure 7-17.
3. Click **File** on the menu bar, and then click **Save** to save your work.
4. So that the link looks like a default HTML link with a hand pointer, you can create a new style sheet rule in contacts.css. Double-click the **contacts.css** file in the XSL Files branch of the project pane. The cascading style sheet appears in the main window.
5. After the last style sheet selector, type the following style rule:

```
SITE     {
    color: #0000FF;
    text-decoration: underline;
    cursor: hand
    }
```

   Every time a SITE element is referenced in the browser, the data is presented as a blue underlined text with a hovering hand cursor. The contacts.css file should now resemble Figure 7-18.

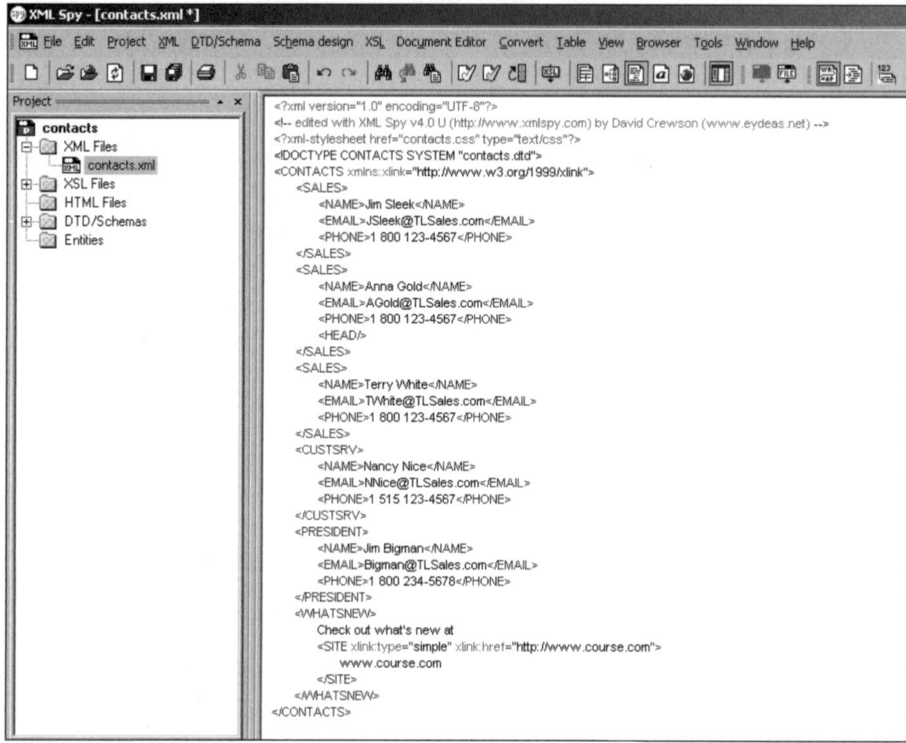

Figure 7-17

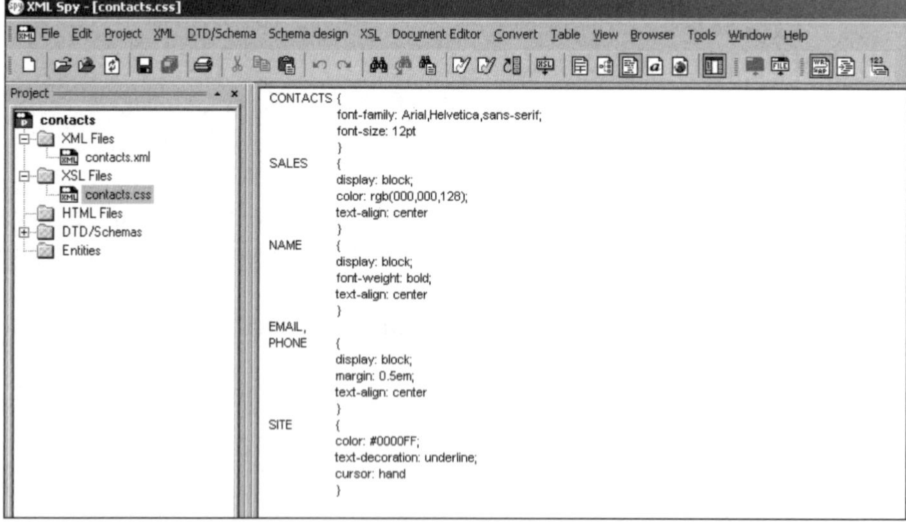

Figure 7-18

6. Click **File** on the menu bar, and then click **Save** to save your work.

To view the link in Netscape Navigator 6.2:

1. Click **Start**, point to **Programs** (point to **All Programs** in Windows XP), point to **Netscape 6.2**, and then click **Netscape 6.2**. The Netscape browser window opens.
2. In the Address bar text box, type **C:\home\<yourname>\Ch07\contacts.xml**, and then press **Enter**. The formatted XML document opens.

   Your document with the new link at the bottom of the page will resemble Figure 7-19.

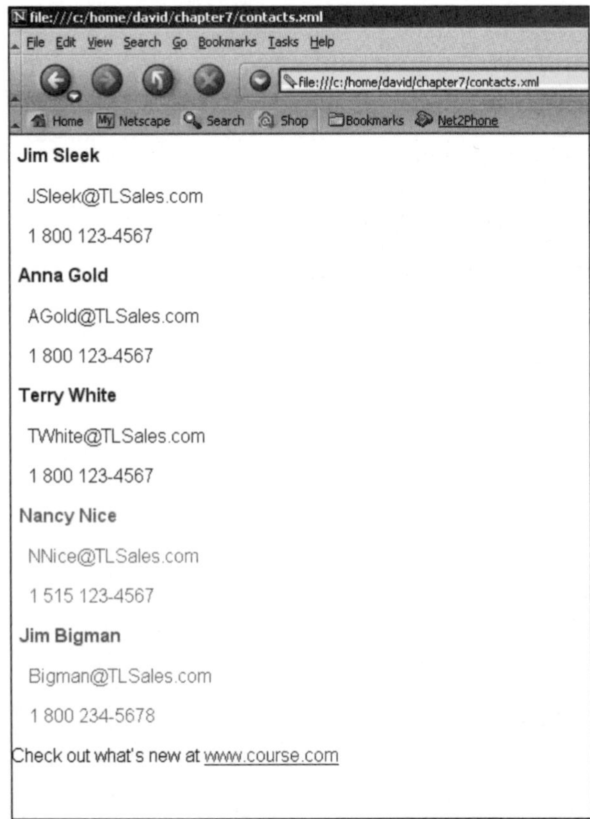

Figure 7-19

3. Click the **www.course.com** link to navigate to the external Web site.
4. Click **Go** on the menu bar, and then click **Back** to return to the XML document. Click **File** on the menu bar, and then click **Exit** to quit Netscape Navigator.

7

Project 7-3

In this project you examine an XML document with extended links. At the time of writing, XLink was a recent W3C Recommendation, but little or no software provides the complete functionality. In particular, none of the key Web browsers currently implements extended links, so for the next Hands-on Project, you examine the code required to implement an extended link, but cannot display it in a browser.

To examine the sales.xml document:

1. Right-click the **XML Files** branch in the Project pane, and then click **Add Files** on the shortcut menu. The Open dialog box appears.
2. Click the **Look in** list arrow and then navigate to C:\home\<yourname>\Ch07, if necessary. Click **sales.xml**, and then click **Open**. Sales.xml is added to the project.
3. Double-click the **sales.xml** file under the XML Files branch in the Project pane. The XML document opens in the main window. Click **View** on the menu bar, and then click **Text view** to view the source code. The coded XML document appears in the main window, as shown in Figure 7-20.

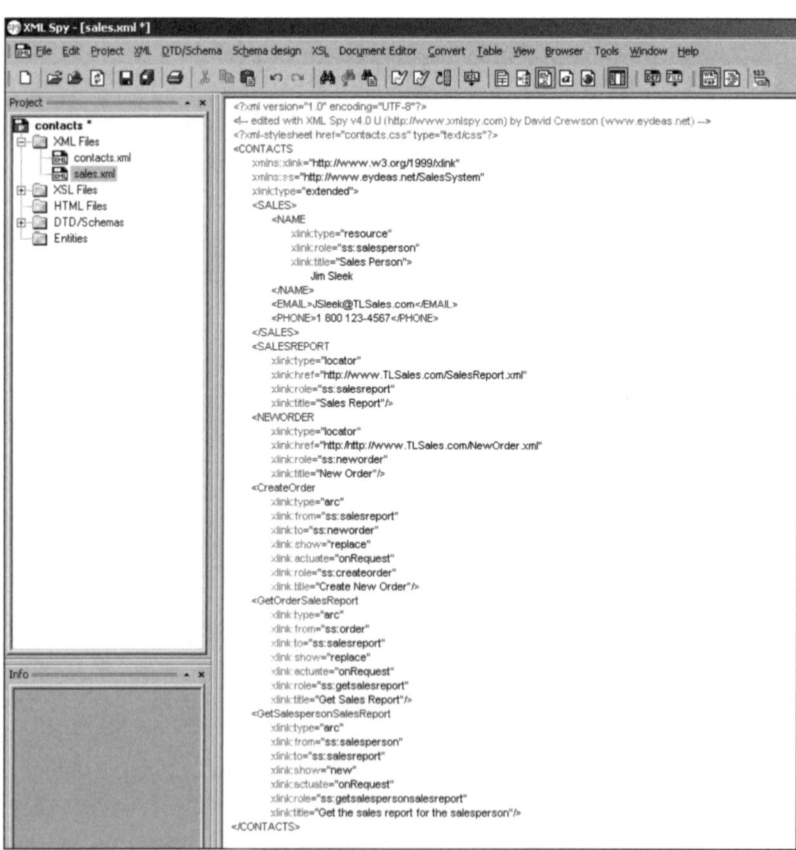

Figure 7-20

Notice that the file is still using the CONTACTS and SALES elements, and has introduced some additional elements. Because this file is provided as an example, there is no corresponding DTD to validate it.

In the CONTACTS element, the xlink:type attribute is set to extended. This indicates that the element contains child elements that participate in extended linking. Also notice that the ss namespace has been defined. This namespace is used to create unique labels to identify child elements of CONTACTS that participate in the extended links.

Next, you examine the resources and the links. Recall that a resource is a component that can be identified.

To examine the resources and the links:

1. In the sales.xml document, find the three resources that participate in the document's extended links, one internal and two external. The NAME element contains the internal resource declaration xlink:type="resource" that identifies the element as participating as an internal or inline resource. The xlink:role attribute defines a unique identifier to the resource that is used in the link definition. The xlink:title is used by browsers to provide human-readable descriptions about the link, such as in the case of a ScreenTip.
2. Find the SALESREPORT and NEWORDER elements. These elements represent external resources and are identified by the xlink:type="locator". They participate in the link by referencing or locating the external resource defined by the xlink:href attribute. The value identifies a URI specifying the location of the reference.
3. The method of connecting resources is by an arc. Find the three arcs in the document, each one specifying the rules for each link. The CreateOrder and GetOrderSalesReport link the external resources in both directions. In HTML, you would have to modify both resources to create a duplex, or two-way, link, but with XLink, even though both resources exist in separate locations, they were linked without need to modify the resources themselves.
4. Find the xlink:from and xlink:to attributes of the arc-type element. These attributes identify the source and destination resources. The xlink:show determines how the destination resource is displayed. In this case, the resource replaces the current resource in the browser window. The xlink:actuate attribute tells the browser to wait for the request before loading the resource. The role and title serve the same purpose as in the resources.
5. Find the GetSalespersonSalesReport, which links the local NAME element with the SALESREPORT element located externally. Notice that the xlink:show attribute is set to new. When the link is activated, the destination resource appears in a new browser window.

   If you were able to view the document in a browser, you would observe the information in the NAME element displayed in the window. If you were to click "Jim Sleek," a new window with the sales report would open. From the new window, you would be able to toggle between the sales report and new order documents.

Project 7-4

In the last project, you examined how XLink arcs connect various XML document resources. In this project, you examine how you can point to specific portions of the document using XPointer expressions. These expressions can be appended to a URI to enable a link to point to an element, a group of elements or even a portion of an element.

The file order.xml represents information about a single sales order. The salesreport.xml refers to information within the order. You begin by reviewing the order document, and then observe how XPointer expressions in the salesreport document refer to single points with the order. Note that at the time of writing, XPointer is not an available feature in most browsers for the same reason as XLink.

To examine the external resource:

1. Right-click the **XML Files** branch in the Project pane, and then click **Add Files** on the shortcut menu. The Open dialog box appears.
2. Click the **Look in** list arrow, and then navigate to C:\home\<yourname>\Ch07, if necessary. Press and hold the **Ctrl** key, and then click **order.xml** and **salesreport.xml** to select these documents. Click **Open**. Order.xml and Salesreport.xml are added to the project.
3. Double-click the **order.xml** file under the XML Files branch in the Project pane. The XML document opens in the main window. Click **View** on the menu bar, and then click **Text view** to view the source code.
4. The order document is shown in Figure 7-21. Examine the document, noting structure of the document, and the relationship of the NAME element to the root element (/ORDER/SALES/NAME).

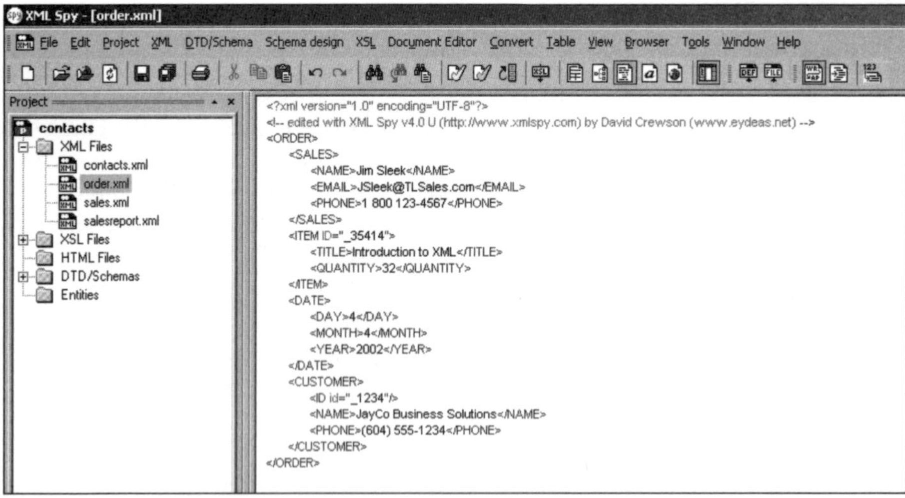

Figure 7-21

Now you can examine an XPointer expression.

Examine an XPointer expression and the linking document.

1. Double-click the **salesreport.xml** file under the XML Files branch in the Project pane. The XML document opens in the main window. Click **View** on the menu bar, and then click **Text view** to view the source code. The XML document opens, as shown in Figure 7-22.

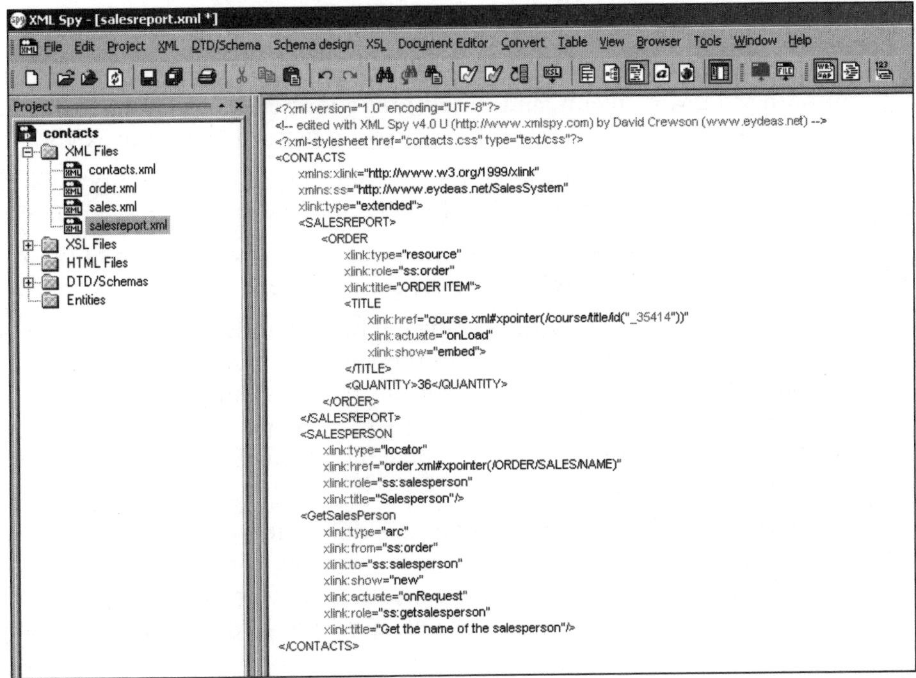

Figure 7-22

2. In the SALESREPORT element, notice how the value for TITLE is obtained. TITLE contains an xlink:href attribute that identifies a URI called order.xml. The reference location is further refined using the XPointer expression

   xpointer(//ORDER/ITEM/ID("_35414")/TITLE.

   This expression finds the value of the TITLE element where its parent element, ITEM, has an ID type attribute with a value of "_35414".

3. Review the structure from the order.xml document:

```
<ORDER>
        -- elements removed --
        <ITEM REF="_35414">
                <TITLE>Introduction to XML</TITLE>
                <QUANTITY>32</QUANTITY>
        </ITEM>
        -- elements removed --
  <ORDER>
```

   Looking closer at the expression, recall that the "//" instructs the parser to search all of the ITEM elements, and the id() function selects the ITEM with the appropriate value. The evaluation of the expression is Introduction to XML.

   Note that ID is not the name of the attribute, but the attribute type. In this case, assume that the REF attribute has been defined in the DTD as an ID type.

   The xlink:show attribute instructs the parser to insert the value of the referenced TITLE element value into the salesreport document.

4. Find the SALESPERSON locator-type. This XPointer expression is part of an external resource that participates in the GetSalesPerson link. The xlink:href attribute refers to the NAME element in the order.xml file. Note that the path of the expression, /ORDER/SALES/NAME, is the path from the root to the NAME element in the external resource. The NAME element is the reference point for this resource.

   The GetSalesPerson arc-type handles this link as it would any other resource. When the link is selected, a new browser window appears with the NAME fragment of the external resource as the active document. Because the XPointer is contained in a locator-type resource element, the actual reference is completely transparent to the arc-element.

Project 7-5

XPointer gives you flexibility when retrieving information. Now that you know how to reference a specific element in an XML document, you can examine how XPointer can reference a point or a range within an XML document. The XPointer scheme introduces the concept of points and ranges, which you examine in this project. You continue to work with the salesreport.xml file from Project 7-4.

A point is a spot in an XML document defined by an XPointer expression. It can be an element, an attribute, a processing instruction, or any position within these objects. In order to define a point, both a container node and an index must be identified. Depending on the type of element determines what the point references.

A range is the entire XML structure between two points: a start-point and an end-point. The start-point begins immediately before the first node in the range, and the end-point references the point immediately following the last node in the range.

To examine an XPointer point and range:

1. With salesreport.xml open in the XML Spy IDE, find the BUYER element. The xlink:href attribute indexes the second element within order.xml URI. Assume that the referenced code appears as follows:

```
<CUSTOMER>
    <ID id="_1234"/>
    <NAME>JayCo Business Solutions</Name>
    <PHONE>(604) 555-1234</PHONE>
</CUSTOMER>
```

   The point defined in CUSTOMER refers to the value in the NAME element. If CUSTOMER contained CDATA instead of elements, then the point would refer to the location immediately following the second character.

2. Find the DATE element in the salesreport document. This element is similar in functionality to the CUSTOMER element except that the xlink:href identifies a range.

```
order.xml#xpointer(/ORDER/DATE/DAY/range-
  to(/ORDER/DATE/YEAR))
```

   The date portion of the order.xml file looks as follows:

```
<ORDER>
    -- omitted elements --
    <DATE>
            <DAY>4</DAY>
            <MONTH>4</MONTH>
            <YEAR>2002</YEAR>
    </DATE>
    -- omitted elements --
</ORDER>
```

   The /ORDER/DATE/DAY portion of the expression references the DAY element and is defined as the start point of the range. The range-to() function follows and defines the end point. The range of elements that is inserted into the salesreport document consists of the DAY, MONTH, and YEAR elements from the order document.

3. Close XML Spy.

CASE PROJECT

The technologies of XLink and XPointer are currently under development, and its future is yet to be determined. Use a Web search engine to find information about XLink and XPointer, or visit at least three of the following Web sites. Then determine whether you think the XLink and XPointer technologies are important developments. Do you think they will determine the future of the Web? If so, in what way? What opportunities could they provide and to whom? Write two to three pages defending your position.

- www.w3.org/TR/2001/CR-xptr-20010911/
- www.w3.org/TR/xlink/
- www.w3.org/XML/Linking
- www.xml.com/pub/a/2000/09/xlink/
- www.oasis-open.org/cover/xll.html

CHAPTER

8

INTRODUCTION TO XHTML

In this chapter, you will learn:

- About XHTML
- About the advantages of XHTML
- About XHTML and DTDs
- About the differences between XHTML and HTML syntax
- How to extend an XHTML document
- How to convert Web sites to XHTML
- About XHTML utilities and services provided by W3C

HTML has contributed significantly to the phenomenal success and growth of the World Wide Web, currently the fastest growing communications medium. As it developed and proliferated, HTML provided the capability for developers everywhere to display billions of documents on millions of terminal screens. However, the documents displayed have been fairly generic, because HTML contains a predefined and standardized set of elements that serve basic roles of structuring information without many formatting frills.

On many fronts, document and application developers and user agent designers continue to develop new kinds of data, new ways to describe data, and new products and services. Since the mid-1990s, non-standard HTML coding has also proliferated across the Web, affecting millions (if not billions) of document pages, applications, and scripts. Consequently, browser developers have had to add more so-called "flexible coding" to their products to accommodate those poorly coded Web sites, documents, and scripts. That flexibility—the algorithms required to guess what the Web sites were trying to express—has actually caused the manufacturers to create larger browser applications, which require more hard disk space, RAM, and CPU resources.

You have probably noticed that more alternate computing, browsing, and marketing platforms are available today, such as personal digital assistants (PDAs) and handheld computers, portable telephones (e.g., cellular, satellite), global positioning systems, "smart" home appliances, and others. Several of these alternate technologies already use the Web for communication and control. It is reasonable to expect that more types of these devices will be introduced and, eventually, the sheer numbers of these Web-dependent devices will be astonishing. Each platform has different requirements and capabilities with respect to system resources and power consumption, as well as the operating systems, applications, and Web-related languages available to them. How will the innovations communicate with new and existing Web-related platforms and facilities? Will their communication applications (e.g., browsers) also be required to include algorithms to guess the meaning of poor coding? How much computer resources and electrical power will be wasted? Will their data and datatypes be accommodated?

One solution to these issues has been the promotion, adoption, and growth of XML. However, will the existing HTML-based Web sites and documents have to change to other XML-related languages? How long will it take? How much will it cost?

This chapter introduces and discusses the Extensible Hypertext Markup Language (XHTML), a markup language that is actually a reformulation of HTML (that is, it contains all the existing HTML components), but adopts XML standards, including a strict adherence to XML syntax. Along with an introduction to XHTML's major features and advantages, the chapter also discusses the process of converting existing HTML documents to XHTML, introduces free utilities that can facilitate that conversion, and provides insight into how XHTML 1.0 can be extended to accommodate new data types.

UNDERSTANDING XHTML

The **Extensible Hypertext Markup Language** is HTML that has been refined into an XML application. That is, XHTML consists of all the predefined components (i.e., elements, attributes, entities, etc.) in HTML version 4.01 combined with XML standards and syntax, including the provision for introducing unique components, as you would find in other XML-related languages. Thus, XHTML closely resembles HTML 4.01, but is a stricter and cleaner version of it. Unlike XML, which was not designed to replace HTML, but to complement it, XHTML is designed to eventually replace HTML as the primary tool for designing Web sites.

Earlier in this book, XML was defined as a markup language and a metalanguage, designed to *describe* data. HTML, by contrast, was originally designed to *display* data. Recall that, in XML-related documents, the content has to be marked up and structured correctly with appropriate elements, for example. Proper markup and structure results in well-formed documents. Well-formed documents that conform to their respective DTDs or schemas are considered valid documents. It follows, then, that if every XHTML document is a complete XML document that also conforms to the XML Recommendation, then it must be compatible with all general-purpose XML tools and processors.

Because XHTML is a reformulation of HTML 4 as an application of XML, it is the first step toward a modular and extensible XML-based Web. Therefore, XHTML is a bridge for Web page designers: it can prepare them for the Web of the future, while it maintains compatibility with today's HTML 4-based browsers.

XHTML is not the answer to every markup problem. Its basic set of HTML-related elements may not be detailed enough for your purposes, and its present extensibility provisions may be limited. However, it is a good general-purpose, compact language for developing Web sites, so as a jumping-off point for development, it is very capable. And development of the W3C's XHTML family of standards is progressing rapidly, so extensibility and modularization will only improve.

A Brief History of HTML and XHTML

Tim Berners-Lee began work on HTML as an application of SGML in late 1990. A specification for HTML was released on the Internet in 1991 and a draft definition was released in 1993. The W3C's HTML Working Group was formed in 1995 and, in November 1995, HTML 2.0 (RFC 1866) became an IETF Proposed Standard.

Even while early HTML standardization attempts were underway, a discussion document called HTML+ (containing proposals intended to form a superset of HTML) was circulated in November 1993. Although HTML+ was not to be, it led the way to HTML 3.0, which provided many additional capabilities over HTML 2.0, and which was to be HTML 2.0's successor. But, the differences were too vast, and standardization and deployment of HTML 3.0 never took place either. Published in March 1995, it died the following September. However, some of its more stable components eventually appeared in HTML 3.2 and HTML 4.0. HTML 3.2 was approved as a W3C Recommendation in January 1997. It was an amalgamation of HTML 2.0, with some features that had survived from HTML 3.0, plus other extensions already implemented by browser manufacturers. It was readily embraced as the successor of HTML 2.0.

July 1997 saw the first draft of HTML 4.0, which included a mature form of the Cougar HTML DTD model that had been introduced in July 1996 and had undergone considerable modification. HTML 4.0 also included several new and powerful features, including more ideas that had survived from HTML 3.0. Finally, HTML 4.0 became a W3C Recommendation in December 1997, and was revised in April 1998. HTML 4.0's DTDs (called Strict, Transitional, and Frameset) would later be adopted and adapted by XHTML 1.0. The W3Cs HTML 4.01 Recommendation, which added some upgrades and bug fixes to HTML 4.0, was released in December 1999.

XHTML 1.0, the W3C's first XHTML Recommendation, was released on January 26, 2000. It was referred to as "HTML 5" by some. XHTML 1.0 was the first major change to HTML since HTML 4.0 was released in 1997. As stated previously, with XHTML 1.0, HTML became an XML application. XHTML 1.0 uses HTML 4 tags extensively, so it can be interpreted by existing browsers. XHTML documents, being XML-related, are also easier to process and maintain. Additionally, through the use of already available utilities, some of which are discussed later in this chapter, you can easily convert existing HTML documents to XHTML. Figure 8-1 illustrates the evolution of XHTML.

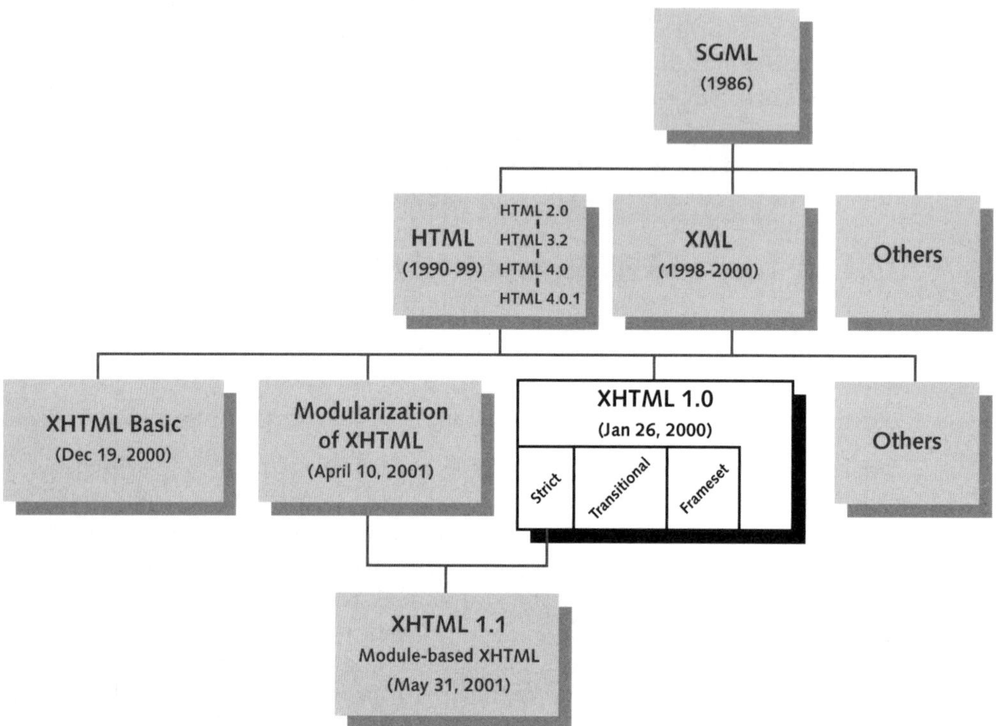

Figure 8-1 Evolution of the XHTML family

Since the approval of XHTML 1.0, there have been several new additions to the XHTML family, all of which address the future of XHTML: modularization. XHTML modularization involves specifying of well-defined sets (also called collections) of XHTML components that can be quickly and economically combined and extended by document authors and application and product designers who create and cater to all the alternate computing platforms. The application and product designers can specify the elements and modules that are supported by their respective devices. Other developers can then more comfortably and easily provide content for those modules and, thus, for the devices.

The adoption of modularization standards also means that developers can tailor their content to various devices. The devices can load the software needed to read and manipulate the modules and other content.

After XHTML 1.0, the next W3C XHTML specification was a modularization-related Recommendation titled "XHTML Basic," approved in December 2000. XHTML Basic specifies the minimal set of modules required to create XHTML-related languages for those computing platforms, such as PDAs, pagers, and mobile telephones that cannot support all of XHTML's features. Thus, XHTML Basic is intended to be a common base or a common language that can be extended or otherwise supported by the software developed for those platforms.

The W3C Recommendation titled "Modularization of XHTML" was approved in April 2001. It provides a means to extend XHTML 1.0 so that it also can be used on the alternate computing platforms by specifying the appropriate abstract module framework and abstract modules.

Modularization of XHTML was used, in fact, to create the W3C Recommendation titled "XHTML 1.1 - Module-based XHTML" that, with the W3C Recommendation titled "Ruby Annotation," was released as a sort of hybrid Recommendation on May 31, 2001. Usually referred to as "XHTML Modularization," **XHTML 1.1** is a reformulation of XHTML 1.0 - Strict, one of the three variants of XHTML 1.0 that is discussed later in this chapter. **Ruby Annotation** is text typically inserted in documents to indicate pronunciation or annotation (particularly in East Asian documents).

If you examine the XHTML 1.1 specifications, you see that the modularized XHTML has a number of predefined core modules—governing text extension, forms, objects, tables, images, etc.—that have their own sets of predefined elements, attributes, and document models. For example, a table always has <table>, <col>, or <tr> elements, among several others. Ruby also has predefined elements. Further, with each predefined core module or element, there are also predefined underlying functionalities and relationships among them (in a table, for example, columns always display from left to right; rows, from top to bottom).

So, to create new specific XHTML-related document types (i.e., a new language and documents), developers only need to create any necessary unique modules for their industry or organization and the platform(s) they use, and then combine them with predefined and reusable XHTML core modules. This speeds language and document development as well as eventual parsing and validation, and helps to facilitate the development of functional compatibility.

Any further detailed discussion of the XHTML family of modularization Recommendations is beyond the scope of this introductory discussion. The XHTML modularization family of specifications represents a new generation of XHTML.

For more information regarding the XHTML family of W3C Recommendations, see the W3C's HTML home page at *www.w3.org/MarkUp/#standard*.

ADVANTAGES OF XHTML

There are several advantages to using XHTML instead of HTML or to converting HTML documents to XHTML:

- XHTML resembles HTML
- XHTML coding must meet tougher XML-compliant standards
- XHTML is extensible
- XHTML is portable
- XHTML is modular
- XHTML is backward and future compatible

XHTML Resembles HTML

Millions of developers are already familiar with HTML. As you see later in this chapter, HTML and XHTML coding are similar. If you are familiar with HTML 4 design, XHTML should be easy to learn and use. The HTML-XHTML resemblance, combined with other XHTML advantages, can allow you to quickly create robust XHTML-related markup languages and documents that are immediately useful and will remain useful for the foreseeable future.

XHTML Must Meet XML-compliant Coding Standards

Recall that XHTML is an application of XML. XHTML-related languages and documents, because they have to meet stricter XML rules, are cleaner, more predictable, and better behaved when manipulated by any editors, validators, browsers, and other XML-compliant software.

As XHTML becomes more widely known and used, more Web sites, Web languages, and Web-related documents will meet XHTML/XML standards, and they will become more compatible with XML-compliant browsers and other applications. Eventually, those applications—especially the browsers—may be pared down, sped up, and given new features, because they will no longer have to accommodate non-standard Web programming and markup.

Another benefit from XML-compliance is the moving of style specifications from the actual markup in the documents themselves to separate external stylesheets. That reliance on stylesheets means faster and more flexible development of style support.

XHTML is Extensible

Although HTML was an SGML application, it was not an XML application. Thus, adding any new group of elements would have required changing the entire HTML language specification. XHTML, on the other hand, is XML-related so it is easier to extend—that is, to introduce unique organization- or industry-related elements or additional attributes. Adding new logical components in such a manner increases functionality. To introduce them and put them to use, then, becomes as simple as declaring a namespace, defining the components in another—that is, additional—DTD or schema, and adding or modifying a stylesheet. An example XHTML 1.0 extension can be found near the end of this chapter.

XHTML is Modular

XHTML is already fairly modular. XML has approved several module-related W3C Recommendations, and appropriate DTDs and schemas are being developed. As the development of XHTML modularity continues, XHTML languages and documents—and their descendants—integrate existing XHTML core modules with unique industry or organizational modules. Ultimately, this modular approach facilitates the development of documents and languages to serve almost any Internet or intranet purpose, and contributes to future portability to meet the needs of alternate computing devices.

XHTML is Portable

The W3C's XHTML family is, and continues to be, designed so that applications on alternate platforms can communicate and exchange XHTML-based data. Eventually, it should be possible to develop XHTML-conforming languages and content that any XHTML-conforming user agent uses, and vice versa. When new devices are developed, they are more quickly and comfortably adopted into the family of Web-related communications.

XHTML is Backward and Future Compatible

Properly constructed XHTML documents are compatible with most HTML browsers in use today. XHTML documents are also compatible with existing and future XML-related browsers and applications. So, XHTML documents are both backward and future compatible.

XHTML Variants and DTDs

The W3C Recommendation released on January 26, 2000, describes XHTML 1.0 as its own family of document types (also called **variants**), which are successors to those defined earlier by HTML 4. As in HTML 4, the variants are called Strict, Transitional, and Frameset. Each variant has its own DTD that declares a logical structure for using XHTML in a particular manner. The XHTML 1.0 Recommendation also defines the respective Strict, Transitional, and Frameset DTDs.

As discussed in Chapter 4, DTDs are used by SGML applications, such as HTML and XHTML, and each DTD consists of at least four kinds of declarations: element declarations, attribute list declarations, entity declarations, and notation declarations. Remember that, as the DTD declares a set of allowed elements, it specifies the vocabulary of the document or language. The DTD also defines the grammar of the language by specifying the content model for each element. The content model is the pattern that indicates what elements or data can go inside another element, in what order they appear, how many of each can appear, and whether they are required or optional. The DTD declares a set of allowed attributes for each element and each attribute declaration defines the name, datatype, default values (if any), and behavior (e.g., if it is required or optional) of the attribute(s). Finally, the DTD provides other mechanisms (entity declarations and notation declarations) to make managing the model easier. Thus, an XHTML DTD describes in precise, computer-readable language the allowed grammar, vocabulary, attribute values, and other mechanisms for the valid markup of an XHTML document.

Each XHTML developer must determine which variant to use. Suppose that you have already chosen and now must specify the name of an XHTML variant. You do so by inserting the appropriate specification in the DOCTYPE declaration at the beginning of the XHTML document. (The DOCTYPE declaration is discussed in more detail as the chapter progresses.) Once the parser reads that declaration statement, it knows which variant is being used and validates the document against the specified DTD. Here is an example of such a statement:

```
<!DOCTYPE html PUBLIC "-//W3C//DTD XHTML 1.0 Strict//EN"
    "http://www.w3.org/TR/xhtml1/DTD/xhtml1-strict.dtd">
```

This statement tells the parser that the DTD is to use the strict variant, and that the DTD is found within the directory structure at the public W3C Web site. The W3C maintains and updates all the DTDs and other informational resources at this Web site.

The XHTML 1.0 Strict Variant

Recall that there are three variants of XHTML 1.0. The Strict variant is used when you want really clean structural markup, free of tags associated with layout. Strict variant and its associated DTD are used with W3C's Cascading Style Sheet language (CSS) to generate the desired fonts, colors, and layout effects. Again the DOCTYPE declaration statement for the Strict variant should be:

```
<!DOCTYPE html PUBLIC "-//W3C//DTD XHTML 1.0 Strict//EN"
    "http://www.w3.org/TR/xhtml1/DTD/xhtml1-strict.dtd">
```

The Strict DTD contains elements, attributes, and other components that have not been deprecated or that do not appear in framesets. Figure 8-2 shows how the DOCTYPE definition statement appears in a simplified, generic, Strict variant-related XHTML document. In this figure, the DOCTYPE definition has been placed in bold text for emphasis.

```
<?xml version="1.0"?>
<--The following document declaration defines the document
                                type and specifies the DTD-->
<!DOCTYPE html PUBLIC "-//W3C//DTD XHTML 1.0 Strict//EN"
   "http://www.w3.org.TR.xhtml1-strict.dtd">
<--The rest of this example document resembles HTML-->
<html xmins="http://www.w3.org/1999/xhtml">
   <head>
      <title> Welcome to TLSales, Inc.!</title>
   </head>
   <body>
      <p> We Hope You Like Our Merchandise!</p>
   </body>
</html>
```

Figure 8-2 XHTML document declaring a Strict DTD variant

The XHTML 1.0 Transitional Variant

The Transitional variant is commonly used by those who are writing Web pages for the general public to access. Although the developers can take advantage of XHTML features such as style sheets, they may also want to make small adjustments to their markup so that those who visit their Web sites with older browsers—ones that can't understand style sheets—can still see the text and formatting. Thus, the DTD and documents use the body element with attributes such as bgcolor, text, and link.

The DOCTYPE declaration statement for the Transitional variant is similar to that for the Strict variant. Here is an example of what it looks like:

```
<!DOCTYPE html PUBLIC "-//W3C//DTD XHTML 1.0 Transitional
//EN"
     "http://www.w3.org/TR/xhtml1/DTD/
     xhtml1-transitional.dtd">
```

The Transitional DTD includes everything in the Strict DTD, plus deprecated elements and attributes. Figure 8-3 shows how the proper DOCTYPE definition statement appears in a typical, generic Transitional variant-related XHTML document.

```
<?xml version="1.0"?>
<--The following document declaration defines the document
                                type and specifies the DTD-->
<!DOCTYPE html PUBLIC "-//W3C//DTD XHTML 1.0 Transitional//EN"
   "http://www.w3.org.TR.xhtml1-transitional.dtd">
<--The rest of this example document resembles HTML-->
<html xmins="http://www.w3.org/1999/xhtml">
   <head>
      <title> Welcome to TLSales, Inc.!</title>
   </head>
   <body>
      <p> We Hope You Like Our Merchandise!</p>
   </body>
</html>
```

Figure 8-3 XHTML document declaring a Transitional DTD variant

If you are developing XHTML documents that call upon the Transitional DTD, remember to include both the <lang> and <xml:lang> elements. Some browsers do not recognize <xml:lang>, so they use <lang>. However, those that recognize <xml:lang> give it precedence over the <lang> element.

The XHTML 1.0 Frameset Variant

Use the Frameset variant when you want to partition the browser window using frames. The Frameset DTD includes everything in the Transitional DTD, plus frames. Here is the Frameset DOCTYPE declaration statement:

```
<!DOCTYPE html PUBLIC "-//W3C//DTD XHTML 1.0 Frameset//EN"
"http://www.w3.org/TR/xhtml1/DTD/xhtml1-frameset.dtd">
```

This DTD is almost identical to the Transitional DTD. The only difference is that, in Frameset XHTML documents, the content portion of the html element is not called the body element; it is instead called the frameset element. The proper DOCTYPE definition statement appears in Figure 8-4.

```
<?xml version="1.0"?>
<--The following document declaration defines the document
                                     type and specifies the DTD-->
<!DOCTYPE html PUBLIC "-//W3C//DTD XHTML 1.0 Frameset//EN"
   "http://www.w3.org.TR.xhtml1-frameset.dtd">
<--The rest of this example document resembles HTML-->
<html xmins="http://www.w3.org/1999/xhtml">
   <head>
      <title> Welcome to TLSales, Inc.!</title>
   </head>
   <body>
      <p> We Hope You Like Our Merchandise!</p>
   </body>
</html>
```

Figure 8-4 XHTML document declaring a Frameset DTD variant

If it is appropriate, convenient, and secure, consider installing copies of the most frequently accessed DTDs on your local system or network. However, if you do so, you also have to change the system identifier (SYSTEM, plus a URI has to be included) in the DOCTYPE definition statement. Using a local copy of the DTD can considerably speed the loading of your documents. Of course, it is up to you to keep track of any changes to the respective DTDs and standards.

Understanding the Difference Between XHTML Syntax and HTML Syntax

In this section, you explore the differences between XHTML and HTML. Recall that because XHTML is an application of XML, it must use clean and structured syntax. XHTML is therefore different from HTML in terms of document structure and logical structure. XHTML documents have a different structure from HTML documents because they must include a prolog that includes an XML declaration and document type declaration. XHTML documents must also be well formed, with all elements nested in the root html element.

The logical structure of XHTML documents is also different from HTML documents because element names must be lowercase, and all elements must be closed properly.

Figure 8-5 presents two documents: a simple HTML document on the right, and an equivalent XHTML document on the left. This figure forms the basis for comparison of document structure and components.

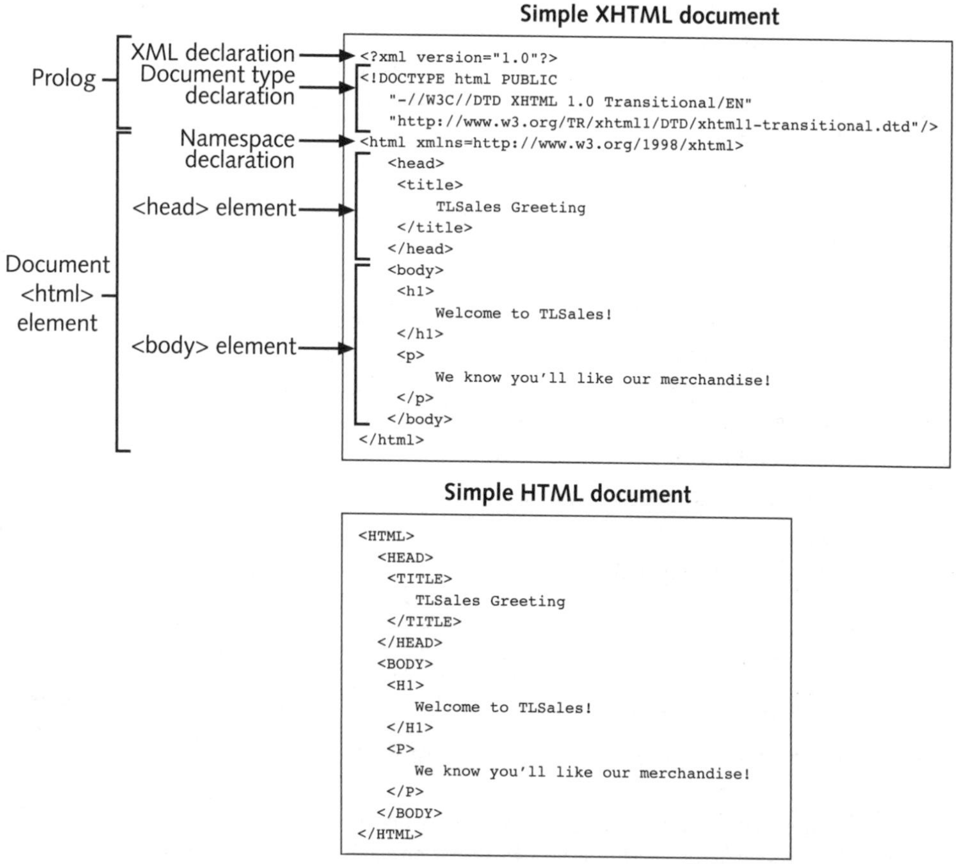

Simple XHTML document

Prolog: XML declaration; Document type declaration

Document <html> element: Namespace declaration; <head> element; <body> element

```
<?xml version="1.0"?>
<!DOCTYPE html PUBLIC
   "-//W3C//DTD XHTML 1.0 Transitional/EN"
   "http://www.w3.org/TR/xhtml1/DTD/xhtml1-transitional.dtd"/>
<html xmlns=http://www.w3.org/1998/xhtml>
   <head>
    <title>
        TLSales Greeting
    </title>
   </head>
   <body>
    <h1>
        Welcome to TLSales!
    </h1>
    <p>
        We know you'll like our merchandise!
    </p>
   </body>
</html>
```

Simple HTML document

```
<HTML>
  <HEAD>
   <TITLE>
      TLSales Greeting
   </TITLE>
  </HEAD>
  <BODY>
   <H1>
      Welcome to TLSales!
   </H1>
   <P>
      We know you'll like our merchandise!
   </P>
  </BODY>
</HTML>
```

Figure 8-5 Structural differences between HTML and XHTML documents

The Prolog and Basic Elements

Like other XML-related documents, an XHTML document consists of two major parts, a prolog and a document element. With XHTML, the document element is named <html> and consists of the sibling <head> and <body> elements. Figure 8-5 shows that the prolog consists of an XML declaration and a document type declaration (also called a DOCTYPE definition). The DOCTYPE definition is mandatory, because it indicates the type of XHTML document it is and which DTD the document is to be validated against. The document in Figure 8-5 is an html type and is validated against xhtml1-transitional.dtd.

Well-formedness

In XHTML documents, all elements must be nested within the root html element. Declaring the default namespace is also required. For all versions of XHTML, the default namespace is *www.w3.org/1999/xhtml*. The other elements may have subelements (i.e., child elements) of their own, or may simply contain text or attributes. Unless they are declared empty, the subelement tags must be in pairs, and the elements must be correctly nested within their respective parent element. The proper basic document structure resembles the following:

```
<html>
<head> <title>... </title></head>
<body> ... </body>
</html>
```

Within <html>, the <head> element contains the <title> element. The <title> element must also be properly nested within the <head> element. The <body> element of the document consists of all elements and other content down to the </body> end tag, just before the </html> end tag. Again, the <body> and <head> elements are siblings; both are child elements of the html element.

In HTML, some elements have been forgiven for being improperly nested. For example, look at the left side of Figure 8-6, where the end tag of the first (parent) element </b> is encountered before the end tag of the second (child) element </i>.

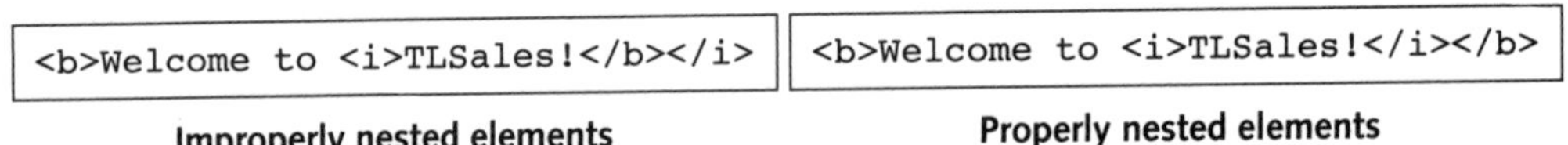

Figure 8-6 Improper versus proper element nesting

While this may be allowed in HTML, it is *never* allowed in XHTML. In XHTML, as in all XML-related documents, all elements must be properly nested within one another, as illustrated on the right side of Figure 8-6.

Now that you have learned how the document structure of XHTML documents is different from HTML documents, examine the differences in logical structure, which involve elements, attributes, and other components. Figure 8-7 shows some differences in logical structure between XHTML and HTML.

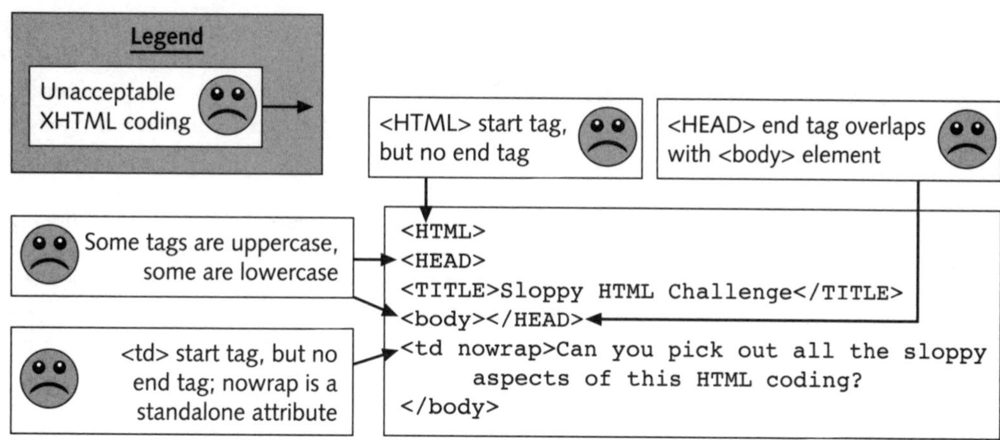

Figure 8-7 Acceptable HTML, unacceptable XHTML

8

Element Names Must Be Lowercase

As stated in Chapter 1, there are similarities between XML-related documents, such as XHTML and HTML. For example, for both specifications, the root—or document—element is called <html> or <HTML>, respectively. The difference, as shown in Figure 8-5, is that XHTML element syntax follows the XML convention. In HTML, it doesn't matter whether <HTML> is lowercase, uppercase, or a combination of the two. By contrast, XHTML, like all XML-related languages, is case sensitive. So, with XML-related languages, it does matter: even if elements have similar tag names like <Name>, <NAME>, or <name>, they all signify different elements. With XHTML, the case sensitivity is even more constricting: the <html> element name, like all component names, must be in lowercase only. That departs from other XML vocabularies. Other XML-related languages do not have a lowercase-only restriction on component names.

The document in Figure 8-7, with its mixed element name cases (lowercase and uppercase) or the document containing the components on the right side of Figure 8-6 would not be considered XHTML. However, the document containing the components on the left of Figure 8-6 would be interpreted as XHTML.

XHTML Elements Must Be Properly Closed

In Chapter 2, you saw how elements are declared in XML in their respective DTDs and schemas to be nonempty (those that are able to contain data, and so should have both start and end tags) and those that are declared empty (which only have a start tag, but the start tag contains an ending forward slash). Further, when an element—empty or nonempty—is included in a document, it must be properly opened and closed. XHTML follows that XML convention, too.

In Figure 8-7, you see that by XHTML standards, the <HTML> and <td> elements are not acceptable because although they have start tags, they have no end tags. The <HTML> element is also not acceptable because it is not lowercase, as discussed previously. The document on the left of Figure 8-8 is also not acceptable because it contains two improperly closed elements. The document on the right shows those elements with proper end tags.

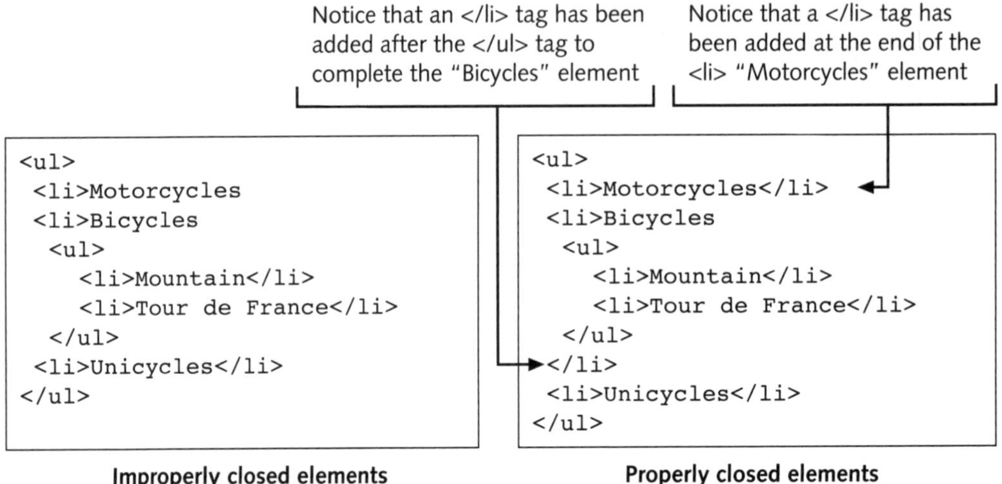
Notice that an </li> tag has been added after the </ul> tag to complete the "Bicycles" element
Notice that a </li> tag has been added at the end of the <li> "Motorcycles" element
<ul>
<li>Motorcycles
<li>Bicycles
<ul>
<li>Mountain</li>
<li>Tour de France</li>
</ul>
<li>Unicycles</li>
</ul>
<ul>
<li>Motorcycles</li>
<li>Bicycles
<ul>
<li>Mountain</li>
<li>Tour de France</li>
</ul>
</li>
<li>Unicycles</li>
</ul>
Improperly closed elements
Properly closed elements

Figure 8-8 Improperly versus properly closed elements

The improperly closed Motorcycles <li> element is fairly obvious and can be easily remedied, but the improperly closed Bicycles <li> element is not so obvious. In fact, it is a very common oversight in such nested lists to forget that an inside child list must also be enclosed within proper <li> and </li> tags. This is another significant departure from the older-style HTML because, in HTML it is occasionally acceptable to leave the end tags out. But, in XHTML all elements capable of holding data must have an end tag. (Whether they ultimately contain data depends on the intentions of the developers and the behavior of the applications.)

As you know, in XML any element can be treated as an empty element, as long as it is declared empty in the DTD or schema. In HTML, however, several HTML elements are commonly *expected* to be empty. Among these are line break <br>, horizontal rule <hr>, image <img>, and metainformation <meta>. In XHTML, however, these elements would have to be declared empty, and their start tags would have to end with />. Table 8-1 lists two common examples where this technique has been used for elements that have been declared empty in their DTD or schema.

Table 8-1 XHTML syntax for common declared empty elements

Definition/Intent	Incorrect Syntax	Correct syntax
Introduce a line break at the end of a line of poetry	Two roads diverged in a wood, and I-- 	Two roads diverged in a wood, and I--
Introduce a horizontal rule (i.e., horizontal line) after some text	Our office location is indicated on the following map. <hr>	Our office location is indicated on the following map. <hr/>

For each of the Table 8-1 examples, a second method could also be used. That is, instead of using /> at the end of the start tags (i.e., <br /> or <hr />), you could use a pair of tags, such as
</br> and <hr></hr>, where an end tag immediately follows the start tag, with no data between them. However, this second method is not recommended because, occasionally unpredictable results occur. It is best to use the method indicated in the table.

To ensure that the declared empty element's start tag is recognized by most browsers, consider adding an extra white space before the / symbol.

Recall that HTML does not differentiate between uppercase or lowercase characters. However, XHTML element names must be lowercase only; XHTML attribute names are to be lowercase, too. As in other XML-related documents, the specified values of XHTML attributes also must be placed between double quotation marks. Figure 8-9 presents several expressions that all seem to specify the width of a table. Notice that, of the five combinations of element names, attribute names, and attribute values, only one is correct.

Example Attribute=Value	Decision	Rationale
<table WIDTH="80%">	Incorrect	Attribute name is uppercase
<table WIDTH=80%>	Incorrect	Attribute name is uppercase; no quotes around value
<table width=80%>	Incorrect	No quotes around attribute value
<TABLE width="80%">	Incorrect	Attribute name is lowercase; quotes around value; but element name is uppercase!
<table width="80%">	**Correct**	Element name and attribute name are lowercase; quotes around value

Figure 8-9 Proper and improper attribute syntax

In HTML, several attributes—the boolean attributes, which play the role of boolean variables—can be minimized. That is, if their name appears in the start tag of an element, that means that the value of the attribute is "true". If their name didn't appear, then that implied that their value was "false". This created a breed of stand-alone attributes, such as the nowrap attribute in the <td> element in Figure 8-7, whose name was accepted as the value of the attribute. To HTML developers, stand-alone attributes are convenient to insert and interpret, and save coding time.

With the adoption of XML syntax, these stand-alone attributes are not allowed in XHTML. Table 8-2 illustrates the new, expanded treatment of these specific XHTML attributes.

Table 8-2 XHTML treatment of HTML minimized attributes

Definition	HTML Minimized Attributes	XHTML Equivalents
Display the definition in compact form	<DL compact>	<dl compact="compact">
Define this input element as checked	<INPUT checked>	<input checked="checked">
Declare this object, but don't do anything with it	<OBJECT declare>	<object declare="declare">
This input text cannot be altered	<INPUT readonly>	<input readonly="readonly">
This input item is unavailable	<INPUT disabled>	<input disabled="disabled">
This option is predefined as selected	<OPTION selected>	<option selected="selected">
Defer the execution of this script	<SCRIPT defer>	<script defer="defer">
Use a server side image map	<IMG ismap>	<img ismap="ismap">
No action in this area	<AREA nohref>	<area nohref="nohref">
Alter the appearance of the horizontal rule	<HR noshade>	<hr noshade="noshade">
Suppress word wrapping here	<TD nowrap>	<td nowrap="nowrap">
Multiple selections are possible from this listing	<SELECT multiple>	<select multiple="multiple">
This frame cannot be resized by a user	<FRAME noresize>	<frame noresize="noresize">

In HTML 4.01, for the elements <a>, <applet>, <frame>, <iframe>, <img>, and <map>, you could specify a name attribute, and give it a value. Now, with XHTML, the name attribute has been deprecated. The attribute id should be used instead. All the former name attribute values can be used for id. Instead of:

```
<img src="TLSales.gif" name="picture3" />
```

use this:

```
<img src="TLSales.gif" id="picture3" />
```

However, to continue working with older browsers for a while, use both the name and id attributes, with identical values, like this:

```
<img src="TLSales.gif" id="picture3" name="picture3" />
```

In this case, to ensure that your XHTML document remains compatible with today's browsers, you should add an extra space before the / symbol in the empty img element.

Extending an XHTML 1.0 Document

This section shows you how to create a simple extension in an XHTML 1.0 document. Figure 8-10 shows that three documents will play an active role: the HTML file named extend.html, an additional DTD file created for this extension, named extend.dtd, and a cascading stylesheet file named extend.css. This example also enlists support from the XHTML 1.0 Transitional DTD at the W3C Web site.

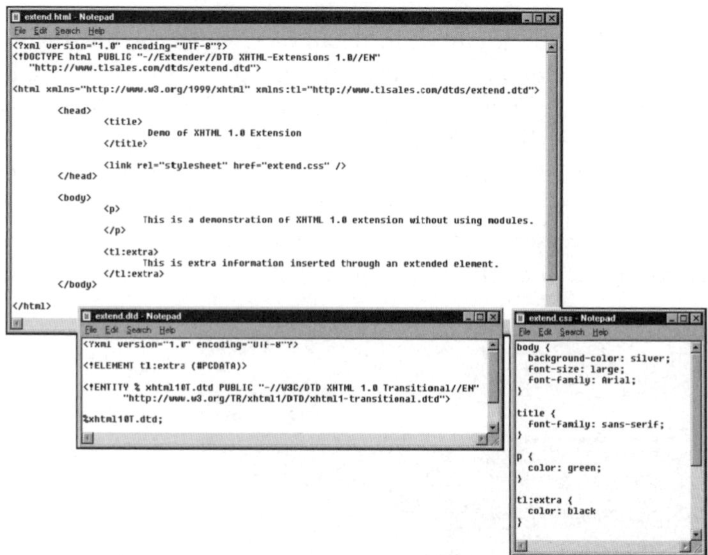

Figure 8-10 Changes required to extend an XHTML 1.0 document

The HTML file contains the components necessary for an XHTML file: a prolog with a DOCTYPE definition, an <html> element with a start tag that contains a default namespace declaration, and <head> and <body> elements. The HTML file also has content within the <body> element: a typical <p> element that demonstrates XHTML's extensibility, and another extending element named <tl:extra>. Notice that, for this example, the extending element uses a namespace declaration format, consisting of the namespace prefix tl, a colon, and the element name. This ensures that the new extending element is unique, and its definition/declaration does not clash with any declarations in the Transitional DTD at the W3C Web site. Although the corresponding namespace declaration could be placed in the <body> element start tag, it has been placed within the start tag of the root <html> element so that it can be applied throughout the whole document, and not just within one or another element.

In some texts, extending elements such as the <tl:extra> element are placed as siblings to <head> and <body>. Avoid doing this if you can. It creates clashes between the XHTML document and the XHTML DTDs.

Now, look at the new extend.dtd file. Because declarations already exist in the Transitional DTD for the <html>, <head>, <body>, <title>, and <p> elements, they do not need to be declared here. In fact, if declarations were included for them, then a validating editor or IDE might create error messages to that effect. It's better to avoid trouble. But you do need a declaration for the new tl:extra element. Because you also need to enlist the support of the Transitional DTD, you must declare it as a parameter entity in the DTD, too. Immediately after the declaration, you add a command %entityname (in this example, it is %xhtml10T.dtd), so that this DTD indeed causes the parser to consult with the Transitional DTD.

Cascading stylesheets (CSSs) are discussed in detail in Chapter 11 but for now, notice how a specification has been added to extend.css for the new element: it will be in black and use other default properties inherited from its parent elements. If the extend.html were a larger, production Web page document, you would have to find a stylesheet (XSLT or CSS), and then insert the specification in the appropriate location. Once these three documents have been created or modified, they need to be published to the Web server, and accessed by a browser. Figure 8-11 illustrates the result of adding the new <tl:extra> element to the extend. html document.

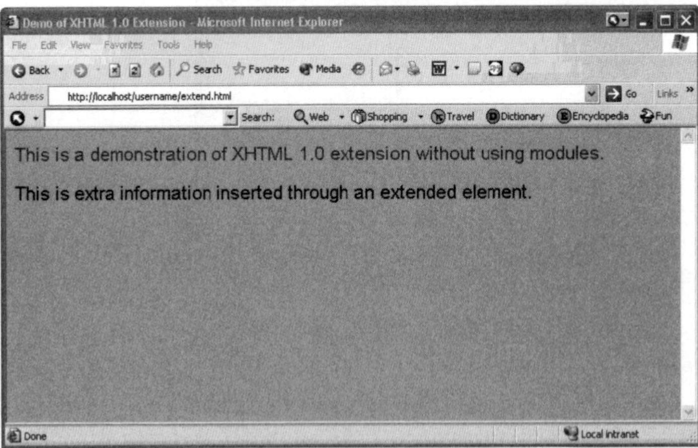

Figure 8-11 Results from extending an XHTML 1.0 document

You can use the technique presented in Figure 8-11 to insert any element to the HTML document. Again, the data in the <tl:extra> element inherits its characteristics (except for its color, which you specified in the stylesheet file) from its parent elements.

Converting Web Sites to XHTML

It is not recommended that you convert a Web site from HTML to XHTML manually, especially when several utilities are available to help you. However, if you decide to convert manually, prior to converting your Web site you should become familiar with XHTML's XML-related syntax rules. Then use a procedure similar to the following, which has been drafted from the several smaller-scale conversions:

1. Create a prolog for every applicable document: the most important addition is the DOCTYPE declaration. If this is to be a Web site conversion—likely requiring some backward compatibility with older browser versions—the transitional DOCTYPE declaration is recommended. Although the browsers themselves won't process the statement, it is used when your XHTML files are validated.
2. Change tag and attribute names to lowercase: XHTML is case sensitive and only accepts lowercase HTML tags and attribute names. You can use a fix-up utility to insert lowercase tags and attribute names. See Chapter 3 for a list of utilities that can help you. If you or your organization has generated the HTML code, conversion may go smoothly. However, if outsiders have been hired in the past, or if you have copied code from the Internet, then this could be a complex task.
3. Insert quotation marks around all attribute values: this is a time-consuming job, so use a specialized utility.
4. Repair empty element tags: in case there may be a problem with some browsers, consider inserting a space to the right of the forward slashes (/). A global search and replace tool can aid you.
5. Validate the Web site documents: validate the new XHTML document against the document type definition specified in Step 1. Use the W3C DTD validator at the following location: *http://validator.w3.org/*. This Web site is discussed in detail in the next section.

For a description of an actual HTML to XHTML Web site conversion, see the following Web site: *www.w3schools.com/xhtml/xhtml_howto.asp*. The step-by-step description of their manual operation, as well as their additional comments regarding the reasons for some of their actions, are instructive.

XHTML Utilities and Services Provided by W3C

To facilitate the transition from older HTML versions to XHTML, and to convert sites automatically, the W3C provides compatibility guidelines (located in Appendix C of the XHTML 1.0 Recommendation), and access to three utilities.

W3C's HTML Validation Service

W3C provides a free service that checks HTML and XHTML documents for conformance to W3C Recommendations and other standards. Using their form at *http://validator.w3.org/*, you can validate a document by providing a URI for the document and then choosing validation parameters from the following:

- A selection of 33 character encoding schemes, from UTF-8 to EUC-JP (Japanese UNIX) to KOI8-R (Russian) and more
- A selection of eight document type specifications: HTML 2.0, HTML 3.2, HTML 4.01 Strict, HTML 4.01 Transitional, HTML 4.01 Frameset, XHTML 1.0 Strict, XHTML 1.0 Transitional, and XHTML 1.0 Frameset.

As illustrated in Figure 8-12, the validation service then examines the document at the URI you provide, in accordance with the options you have chosen.

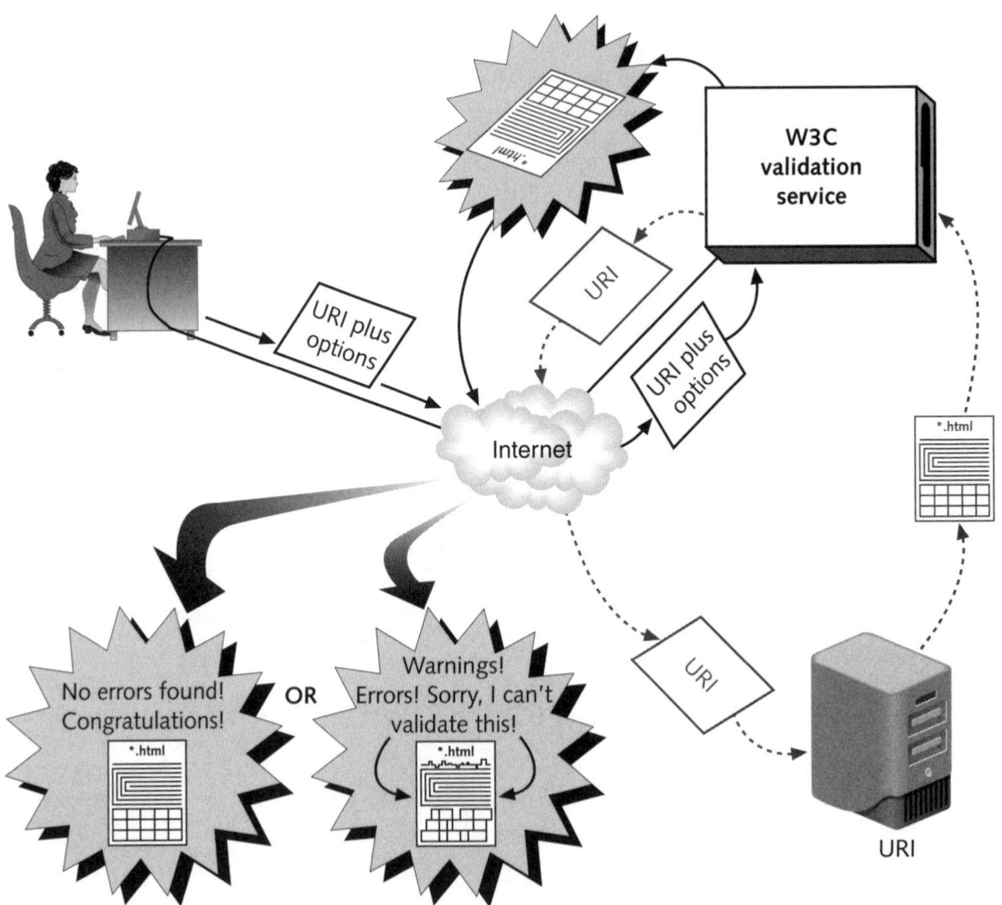

Figure 8-12 W3C validation service: URL document check

Alternatively, by using the W3C's related form at *http://validator.w3.org/file-upload.html,* you can validate documents on your computer by uploading them, as illustrated in Figure 8-13.

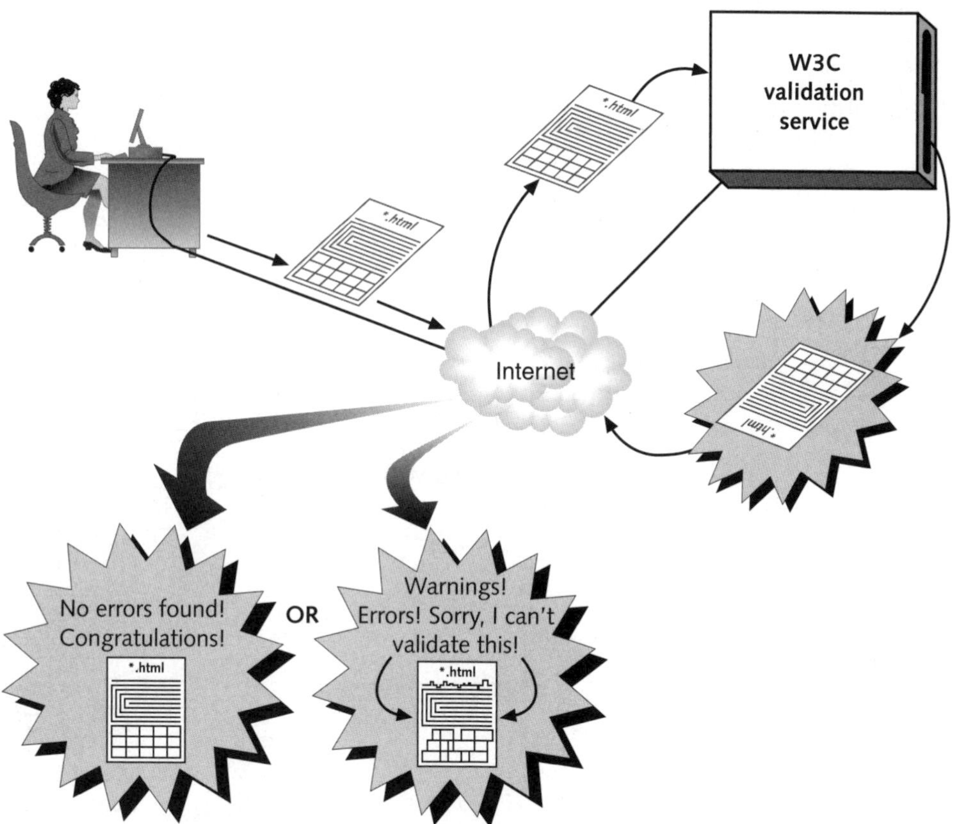

Figure 8-13 W3C validation service: file upload

Either way, you have the same validation parameters available to choose from. New features are being added to the W3C validation site constantly. You can find a summary of the most recent changes to the service by going to *http://validator.w3.org/*, and clicking "What's New."

HTML TIDY

HTML TIDY (also spelled Tidy, which is the way it is referred to here) is a free downloadable utility for editing HTML. Mistakes are fixed automatically and sloppy HTML editing is "Tidy'd" up into more easily understood markup. Tidy is available as open source software, and also converts existing HTML content into well-formed XML for delivery as XHTML. As illustrated in Figure 8-14, Tidy can fix many problems automatically, but it won't generate a clean version of a document when it finds problems it cannot handle confidently and unambiguously. In those cases, Tidy brings those issues to your attention by logging them as errors.

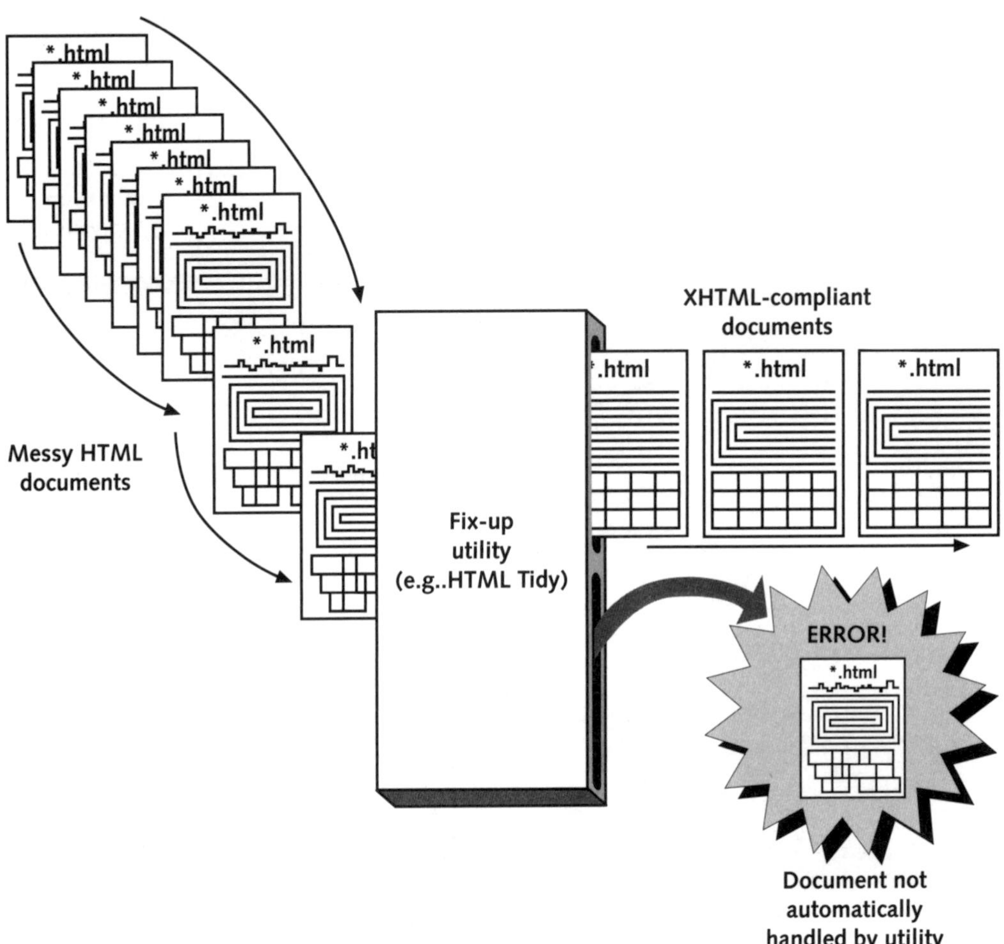

Figure 8-14 HTML fix-up utility

Tidy can also help you determine how and where to make your pages more accessible to people with disabilities. Tidy is available for most platforms, and has been integrated into many authoring environments. You can investigate it further at *www.w3.org/People/Raggett/tidy/*.

You have a chance to work with Tidy in Hands-on Project 8-1 at the end of this chapter.

Amaya: W3C's Editor/Browser

Amaya is an open source software project hosted by W3C. Amaya is a multipurpose active client that performs the following tasks:

- Retrieves documents from the Web and presents them to the user
- Provides an authoring tool that allows you to edit existing documents and to create new ones

- Allows you to publish these documents on remote Web servers.
- As both a browser and an authoring tool, has been specifically developed to be a test bed client with which to experiment, test, and demonstrate a wide range of new developments in World Wide Web protocols and data formats, as well as new extensions to existing ones.

Since the Web is based on client-server architecture, both a client and a server are needed to test and demonstrate new Web specifications. Within the realm of the W3C, Amaya plays this role on the client side; a product called Jigsaw plays the same role on the server side.

Amaya has a what you see is what you get (WYSIWYG) style of interface, similar to that of the most popular commercial browsers. (There are several reproductions of Amaya's interface in Hands-on Project 8-3.) With that interface, users can generate HTML and XHTML pages and CSS style sheets (without needing to know HTML or CSS), as well as MathML expressions and SVG drawings. At this writing, the current Amaya release supports HTML 4.01, XHTML 1.0, XHTML Basic, XHTML 1.1, HTTP 1.1, MathML 2.0, many CSS 2 features, and SVG support.

As an editor and authoring tool, Amaya correctly considers HTML to be an SGML application. It recognizes DTDs when manipulating the document structure, and it performs only valid operations. The advantage to this approach is that Amaya leads to well-structured documents, which facilitates safe processing by subsequent applications. Amaya is also available on both UNIX and Windows 95/NT platforms.

For more information on Amaya, check the following sources:

- The Amaya home page, at *www.w3.org/Amaya/*, where you can download a copy of the Amaya software
- "An Introduction to Amaya"—the February 20, 1997, W3C Note document found at *www.w3.org/TR/NOTE-amaya-970220.html*

You have a chance to work with Amaya in Hands-on Project 8-3 at the end of this chapter.

Chapter Summary

- HTML has contributed significantly to the phenomenal success and growth of the Internet and the World Wide Web. But, its shortcomings are now starting to threaten the pace of future Web expansion.
- XML technologies, including XHTML, are considered a possible remedy to current Web expansion challenges.
- The W3C approved XHTML 1.0 in January 2000. An XML-related language, XHTML was the first major change to HTML since HTML 4.0 in 1997. Since XHTML 1.0, three more XHTML Recommendations, all modularity related, have also been approved.

- XHTML adheres to XML conventions, including a strict and robust syntax, as well as well-formedness and validation requirements.
- The major advantages to XHTML are its relationship to XML, its familiarity to the many existing HTML developers, its extensibility, its modularity, its portability, and that fact that it is backward and future compatible.
- XHTML 1.0 comes in three variants (Strict, Transitional, and Frameset), corresponding to three respective DTDs. In other words, each variant has a specific DTD that declares a logical structure for using XHTML in a particular and specific manner. The XHTML variants are successors to those defined earlier by HTML 4.
- Typical XHTML documents consist of two major parts: the prolog, which contains the important DOCTYPE declaration, and the root element named <html>, which, in turn, consists of the sibling <head> and <body> elements. The <html> start tag must contain a default namespace declaration.
- XHTML is even more case sensitive than other XML-related languages. All tag names and attribute names must be lowercase.
- The <html> root element must be called <html>. All other elements must be properly nested, and all XHTML elements must be closed. Attribute values must be enclosed in quotes, and attribute minimization, condoned in HTML, is forbidden in XHTML.
- To facilitate the transition from older HTML versions to XHTML, W3C provides compatibility guidelines as an appendix to HTML 1.0. W3C also provides access to three utilities that aid in performing document conversions.

Review Questions

1. Which of the following is not an XHTML variant?
   a. Frameset
   b. Strict
   c. Transitional
   d. Conditional
2. Which of the following is in the proper chronological order of their development?
   a. SGML, HTML, XML, XHTML 1.0
   b. SGML, HTML 4, XML, XHTML 1.0
   c. SGML, XML, HTML 3.2, XHTML 1.1
   d. SGML, XML, HTML 4, XHTML 1.0
   e. none of the above

3. From which of the following did XHTML originally inherit its DTD concept?
   a. SGML
   b. XML
   c. HTML 4
   d. Cougar
   e. HTML 3.2
4. The modern browsers' flexibility manifests itself in larger browser applications, because they have to include algorithms to guess what the non-standard Web sites are trying to express. True or false?
5. Like XML, which was developed to complement HTML, XHTML is intended to replace HTML. True or false?
6. XHTML 1.1, together with Ruby Annotation, is referred to as:
   a. XHTML Extension
   b. XHTML Modularization
   c. XHTML Portable
   d. all of the above

7. Which of the following is an appropriate DOCTYPE declaration statement for the Transitional variant, where the DTD is kept at the W3C Web site?
   a. <!DOCTYPE html PUBLIC "-//W3C//DTD XHTML 1.0 Strict//EN" "http://www.w3.org/TR/xhtml1/DTD/xhtml1-transitional.dtd">
   b. <!DOCTYPE html SYSTEM "-//W3C//DTD XHTML 1.0 Transitional//EN" "http://www.w3.org/TR/xhtml1/DTD/xhtml1-transitional.dtd">
   c. <!DOCTYPE html PUBLIC "-//W3C//DTD XHTML 1.0 Transitional//EN" "http://www.w3.org/TR/xhtml1/DTD/xhtml1-transitional.dtd">
   d. <!DOCTYPE html PUBLIC "-//W3C//DTD XHTML 1.0 Transitional//EN" "http://www.w3.org/TR/xhtml1/DTD/xhtml1-frameset.dtd">
8. Which of the following is the most common XHTML variant?
   a. Conditional
   b. Frameset
   c. Strict
   d. none of the above
9. The Frameset DTD is almost identical to the Transitional DTD. The only difference is that, in frameset XHTML documents, the content portion of the <html> element is called the <frameset> element, not the <body> element. True or false?

10. Which of the following is not an advantage of XHTML over HTML?
    a. It is an XML application.
    b. It is extensible.
    c. It is modular.
    d. It is portable.
    e. It is backward and future compatible.
    f. none of the above
11. When introducing a line break at the end of a line of poetry, which is the preferred syntax?
    a. Nobody loses all the time
    b. Nobody loses all the time
    c. Nobody loses all the time
</br>
    d. Nobody loses all the time
    e. Nobody loses all the time
</br>
    f. all of the above
12. Which of the following is proper syntax?
    a. <INPUT "checked"=checked>
    b. <input checked=checked>
    c. <INPUT input="checked">
    d. <input checked="checked">
    e. <input input="checked">
    f. none of the above
13. Since the release of XHTML 1.1 - Module based XHTML, DTDs are already being developed that are composed of interchangeable parts. True or false?
14. To prevent confusion in browsers, do not use "<img src="TLSales.gif" id="picture3" name="picture3" />. True or false?
15. Which of the following is not likely to be aided by a global search and replace?
    a. installing a prolog
    b. changing tag and attribute names
    c. inserting quotation marks around attribute values
    d. repairing empty element tags
16. Which of the following won't generate cleaned-up coding if there are problems that it cannot handle confidently and unambiguously?
    a. Tidy
    b. Validator

c. Amaya

d. Netscape

e. Internet Explorer

f. none of the above

17. W3C's HTML validation service is a free service that checks HTML and XHTML documents for conformance to W3C Recommendations and other standards, and replaces incorrect coding. True or false?

18. Amaya is so powerful and versatile that it can serve as both a client and a server with which to experiment and demonstrate new Web specifications. True or false?

19. What does Tidy do?

 a. checks code for conformance to W3C standards

 b. edits HTML

 c. checks Web applications

 d. all of the above

 e. none of the above

20. Which of the following do not apply to Amaya?

 a. retrieves documents from the Web

 b. allows you to edit existing documents and to create new ones

 c. allows you to publish documents on remote Web servers

 d. has been specifically developed to be a testbed client

 e. all of the above

 f. none of the above

21. Some components from the defunct HTML 3.0 eventually appeared in HTML 3.2 and HTML 4.0. True or false?

22. What are the root elements supposed to be named in XHTML?

 a. <root>

 b. <document>

 c. <html>

 d. <frameset>

 e. <body>

 f. any of the above

23. Both XHTML and HTML allow you to leave out </li> tags when you have several nested lists. True or false?

24. Because the Strict variant is used when you want extremely clean structural markup, free of any tags associated with layout, the Strict variant and its associated DTD ignore any Cascading Style Sheet language documents. True or false?

25. If you install copies of the most frequently accessed DTDs on your local system or network, you don't have to change the system identifier as long as you keep track of any changes to the respective DTDs and standards. True or false?

HANDS-ON PROJECTS

Project 8-1

In this project, you explore the differences between HTML and XHTML by modifying an index.html file and refining it to meet XHTML specifications. To do so, you install and use a tool called HTML Tidy. Tidy is a utility that parses an HTML file and converts it into a well-formed document. You will use Tidy's output-xhtml option to convert the source file into an XHTML file. Tidy will convert as much of the file as possible for you, and flag the areas that need to be manually updated.

Tidy does not completely convert HTML code to XHTML, but it does correct errors such as fixing end tags that are missing, mismatched, or out of order; adding slashes (/) to end tags; including quotation marks around attribute values; and inserting the appropriate DOCTYPE element.

Start by downloading HTML Tidy and copying the project files for Chapter 8 to the appropriate folder. Then you examine the index.html file and run HTML Tidy to find and correct coding errors.

To download HTML Tidy and copy the project files:

1. In Windows Explorer, create a new folder called **Ch08** in C:/home/<*yourname*>.
2. Using your browser, navigate to http://sourceforge.net/projects/tidy to open the HTML Tidy Home page. Follow its instructions to download a copy of Tidy to your C:/home/<*yourname*>/Ch08 folder.
3. Copy the **index.html** file located in the Ch08/Project_8-1 folder on your Data Disk into your **C:/home/<*yourname*>/Ch08** folder.

Now you can view index.html and run HTML Tidy to fix errors in the file.

To view the HTML file and run HTML Tidy:

1. Click **Start**, point to **Programs** (in Windows XP, point to **All Programs**), point to **Accessories**, and then click **Notepad**. The Notepad window opens.
2. Click **File** on the menu bar, and then click **Open**. The Open dialog box appears.
3. Click the **Look in** list arrow, and navigate to C:/home/<*yourname*>/Ch08, if necessary. Click the **files of type** list arrow, and then click **All Files**. Click **index.html** and click **Open**. See Figure 8-15.
4. To open a command console, click **Start**, and then click **Run**. In the Open text box, type **cmd** to open a Command Prompt window, and then click **OK**.

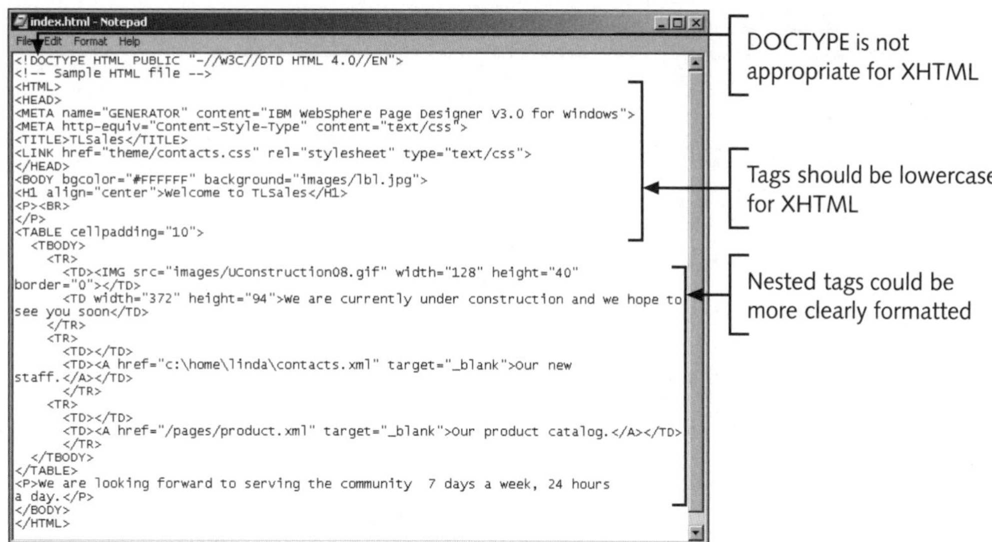

Figure 8-15

5. Type **cd home/<*yourname*>/Ch08** at the command prompt to navigate to this chapter's home folder.
6. You are now ready to use HTML Tidy to check the index.html file for XHTML errors. At the command prompt, type:

   tidy --output-xhtml true -f errs.txt -im index.html

   The --output-xhtml option instructs Tidy to generate XHTML output. Make sure that a double dash precedes the instruction for this option only. The *–im* option instructs the utility to modify the index.html file using tabbed layout, and the *-f* option directs all error messages to the *errs.txt* file. Press **Enter**.

To view the updated file:

1. Start another session of Notepad. (Click **Start**, point to **Programs** or **All Programs**, point to **Accessories**, and then click **Notepad**.) Open the newly modified **index.html** file and compare the changes with the original file. See Figure 8-16.

   Note: If you do not find any differences between the modified and original version of index.html, make sure that index.html is not marked read-only. In Windows Explorer, right-click **index.html** and then click **Properties**. In the index.html Properties dialog box, click the **Read-only** option button or check box, if necessary, so that it is not selected.

   Notice that a DOCTYPE declaration has been added with a XHTML specification. Tidy also changed the case of the tags to lowercase and has rearranged the nested tags.

8

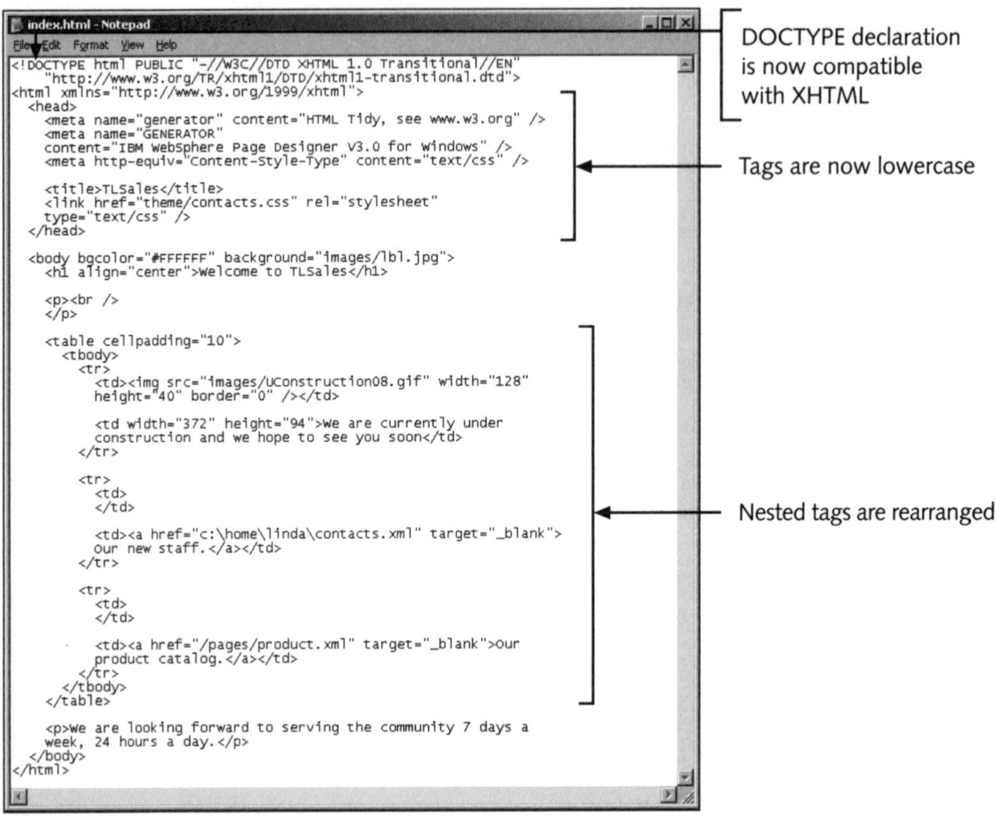

```
<!DOCTYPE html PUBLIC "-//W3C//DTD XHTML 1.0 Transitional//EN"
    "http://www.w3.org/TR/xhtml1/DTD/xhtml1-transitional.dtd">
<html xmlns="http://www.w3.org/1999/xhtml">
  <head>
    <meta name="generator" content="HTML Tidy, see www.w3.org" />
    <meta name="GENERATOR"
    content="IBM WebSphere Page Designer V3.0 for Windows" />
    <meta http-equiv="Content-Style-Type" content="text/css" />

    <title>TLSales</title>
    <link href="theme/contacts.css" rel="stylesheet"
    type="text/css" />
  </head>

  <body bgcolor="#FFFFFF" background="images/lbl.jpg">
    <h1 align="center">Welcome to TLSales</h1>

    <p><br />
    </p>

    <table cellpadding="10">
      <tbody>
        <tr>
          <td><img src="images/UConstruction08.gif" width="128"
          height="40" border="0" /></td>

          <td width="372" height="94">We are currently under
          construction and we hope to see you soon</td>
        </tr>

        <tr>
          <td>
          </td>

          <td><a href="c:\home\linda\contacts.xml" target="_blank">
          Our new staff.</a></td>
        </tr>

        <tr>
          <td>
          </td>

          <td><a href="/pages/product.xml" target="_blank">Our
          product catalog.</a></td>
        </tr>
      </tbody>
    </table>

    <p>We are looking forward to serving the community 7 days a
    week, 24 hours a day.</p>
  </body>
</html>
```

index.html - Notepad
File Edit Format View Help
DOCTYPE declaration is now compatible with XHTML
Tags are now lowercase
Nested tags are rearranged

Figure 8-16

2. Tidy automatically generated a file named errs.txt that summarizes modifications and lists the errors found in the document. Start another session of Notepad and open **errs.txt**. See Figure 8-17. Review the log of changes that Tidy made. Your list might contain additional errors.
3. Close the copy of Notepad containing the original copy of index.html, but leave the revised index.html and errs.txt open for the next project. To make index.html compliant with XHTML standards, you must correct the errors in errs.txt.

Project 8-2

In this Hands-on Project, you resolve XHTML errors in the index.html file you worked with in Project 8-1. To correct the summary and alt attribute errors reported in errs.txt, you must open index.html and edit the source code to make it a well-formed XHTML document.

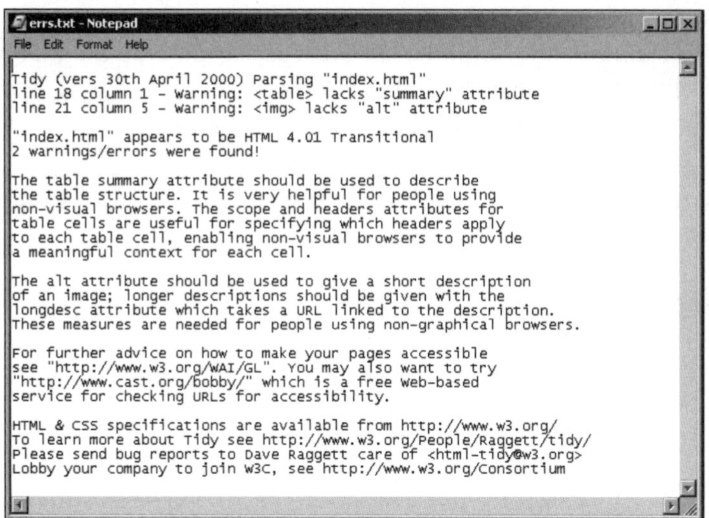

errs.txt - Notepad

File Edit Format Help

```
Tidy (vers 30th April 2000) Parsing "index.html"
line 18 column 1 - Warning: <table> lacks "summary" attribute
line 21 column 5 - Warning: <img> lacks "alt" attribute

"index.html" appears to be HTML 4.01 Transitional
2 warnings/errors were found!

The table summary attribute should be used to describe
the table structure. It is very helpful for people using
non-visual browsers. The scope and headers attributes for
table cells are useful for specifying which headers apply
to each table cell, enabling non-visual browsers to provide
a meaningful context for each cell.

The alt attribute should be used to give a short description
of an image; longer descriptions should be given with the
longdesc attribute which takes a URL linked to the description.
These measures are needed for people using non-graphical browsers.

For further advice on how to make your pages accessible
see "http://www.w3.org/WAI/GL". You may also want to try
"http://www.cast.org/bobby/" which is a free Web-based
service for checking URLs for accessibility.

HTML & CSS specifications are available from http://www.w3.org/
To learn more about Tidy see http://www.w3.org/People/Raggett/tidy/
Please send bug reports to Dave Raggett care of <html-tidy@w3.org>
Lobby your company to join W3C, see http://www.w3.org/Consortium
```

Figure 8-17

To revise index.html:

1. Make sure that both the revised copy of index.html and errs.txt are open in separate Notepad windows.
2. The first error reported in errs.txt states:

   line 18 column 5 - Warning: <table> lacks "summary" attribute

   You can read about the significance of this error further down in the error file. To fix the error, find the following element:

   <table cellpadding="10">

   Add the summary attribute as follows:

   <table cellpadding="10" summary="This table is to format the links.">
3. The second error states:

   line 21 column 15 - Warning: <img> lacks "alt" attribute

   The description of the error follows the description of the previous error. To fix the error, find the following img tag:

   <img src="images/UConstruction08.gif" width="128" height="40" border="0"/>

   Add an alt attribute:

   **<img alt="Site Under Construction"
src="images/UConstruction08.gif" width="128"
height="40" border="0">**

4. To save your changes, click **File** on the menu bar, and then click **Save**. Confirm the changes by running index.html in HTML Tidy again. Type the following at the command prompt in the command console:

   tidy --output-xhtml true –f errs.txt –im index.html.

5. Open the **errs.txt** file using Notepad. You corrected the errors involving the summary and alt attributes. See Figure 8-18. If you did not correct these errors, check the syntax you used and try again.

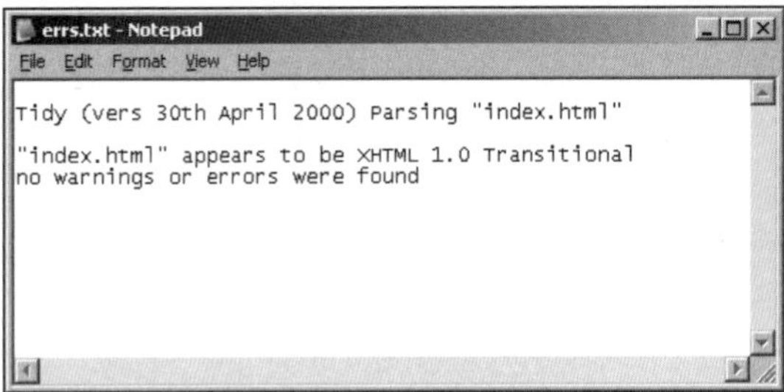

errs.txt - Notepad
File Edit Format View Help
Tidy (vers 30th April 2000) Parsing "index.html"
"index.html" appears to be XHTML 1.0 Transitional
no warnings or errors were found

Figure 8-18

Project 8-3

In this project, you create an XHTML file using the Amaya XHTML editor. Amaya is an open source software project hosted by W3C. In this project you download and install Amaya and then create an XHTML document.

To copy the project files and install Amaya:

1. In Windows Explorer, copy **hire.html**, **product.html**, **bikes.xml**, **bike.jpg** and **lbl.jpg** from the Ch08/Project_8-3 folder on your Data Disk into your C:/home/<*yourname*>/Ch08 folder.
2. Using your browser, navigate to *www.w3.org/Amaya/user/BinDist.html* to open the Amaya Home page. Follow its instructions to download a copy of amaya-WindowsNT-6.1.exe or the latest version for the Windows NT/2000/XP platform to your C:/home/<*yourname*>/Ch08 folder.
3. The file that you have just downloaded is a self-extracting installation file and will configure Amaya on your system. In Windows Explorer, double-click **amaya-WindowsNT-6.1.exe** or the latest edition of this program. The InstallShield Self-extracting EXE dialog box opens. Click **Yes** to begin the installation.
4. Select all of the default choices on the dialog boxes as they appear. When the Setup Complete dialog opens, click **Finish** to complete the installation.

To create an XHTML document:

1. To start Amaya, click **Start**, point to **Programs** (in Windows XP, point to **All Programs**), point to **Amaya**, and then click **amaya**. The Amaya window opens.
2. Click **File** on the menu bar, point to **New**, and then click **New XHTML 1.1 document**. The New XHTML 1.1 document dialog box opens using the default Formatted View.
3. In the text box, type **C:\home\<*yourname*>\Ch08\main.html** to name and save the file. Click **Confirm**. A new file window opens. See Figure 8-19.

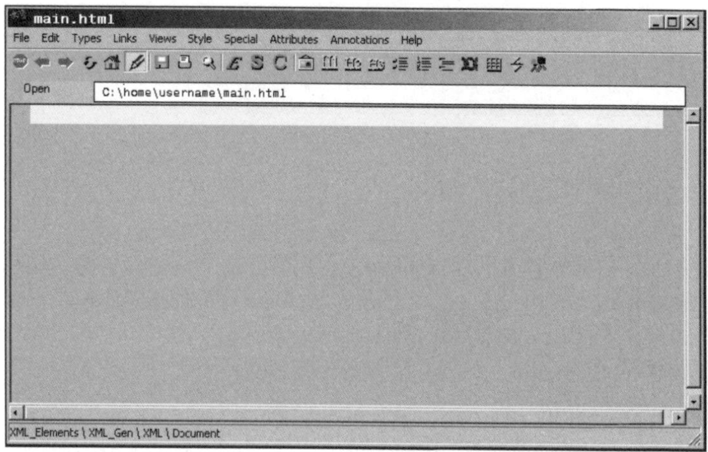

Figure 8-19

4. To change the page title, click **Types** on the menu bar, and then click **Change Title**. The Change Title dialog box opens. Type **TLSales** in the text box and then click **Confirm**.

   Recall that Amaya is a WYSIWYG XHTML editor; if you make a change in the Formatted View document pane, changes are made to the underlying document.
5. To view the code that the editor automatically created, click **Views** on the menu bar, and then click **Show source**. The underlying source code appears in a separate window, shown in Figure 8-20. You can edit the file in either window, and then synchronize the changes by clicking **File** on the menu bar, and then clicking **Synchronize**.
6. In the formatted view window, click **File** on the menu bar, and then click **Save** to save your work. Keep the source code window open so you can use it in the next project.

8

TLSales

File Edit Types Links Views Style Special Attributes Annotations Help

```
<?xml version="1.0" encoding="iso-8859-1"?>
<!DOCTYPE html PUBLIC "-//W3C//DTD XHTML 1.0 Transitional//EN"
    "http://www.w3.org/TR/xhtml1/DTD/xhtml1-transitional.dtd">
<html xmlns="http://www.w3.org/1999/xhtml">
<head>
  <meta http-equiv="Content-Type" content="text/html; charset=iso-8859-1" />
  <title>TLSales</title>
  <meta name="GENERATOR" content="amaya 5.2" />
</head>

<body>
</body>
</html>
```

Figure 8-20

Project 8-4

Now that you have installed Amaya and created a document, you are ready to add content. In this project, you begin to create a home page for the TLSales Web site. The Web page will include a title, a table with links, an image, and a background. Start by adding a title and table to the Web page.

To create a heading and a table:

1. With main.html open in Amaya from Project 8-3, click in the Formatted View window, if necessary.
2. Click the **H1** button on the toolbar to create a heading. Type **Welcome to TLSales** in the editing window.
3. To format the heading, click **Style** on the menu bar, and then click **Format**. The Format dialog box opens.
4. In the Align area, click option button next to the centered image, as shown in Figure 8-21, and then click **Done** to center the heading.
5. Click **File** on the menu bar, and then click **Synchronize** to synchronize the source code view. Switch to the Source View window, and notice it now includes code for the heading you just added:

   <h1 style="text-align: center">Welcome to TLSales</h1>

   Switch back to the Formatted View window.
6. To create a table, start by pressing the **Enter** key twice to insert a blank line.
7. Click the **Table** button on the toolbar. A table dialog opens.
8. Type **2** in the Number of Columns text box, type **4** in the Number of Rows text box, and type **1** in the Border text box. Click **Confirm**. A table appears in the document window. See Figure 8-22.

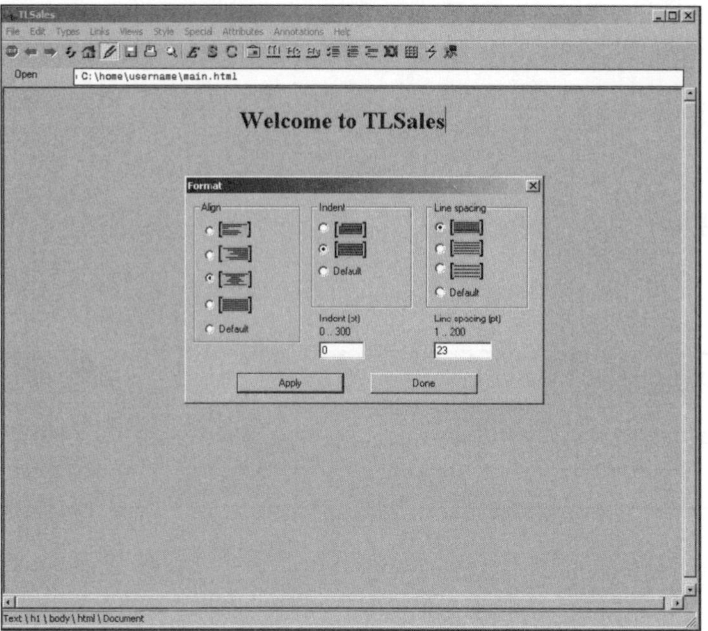

Figure 8-21

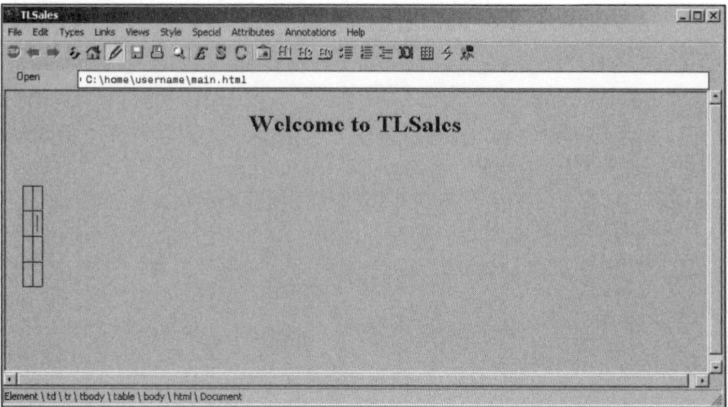

Figure 8-22

Project 8-5

In this project, you add three links to the main.html document—two links to HTML files and one link to an XML file. The links are all contained within cells of the table that you created. After you add the links, you adjust the cell spacing to make the text easier to read.

To create links:

1. Click in row 2, column 2 of the table. Type **Our staff**, and then select that phrase.
2. To create the link, click **Links** on the menu bar, and then click **Create or change link**. The pointer changes to a hand pointer.
3. Click the selected text with the hand pointer. The Attribute dialog box opens.
4. Type **hire.html** in the Attribute text box, and then click **Confirm**. The text in the document editor now appears blue.
5. Repeat Steps 1–4 for the two additional links in the table below:

Text	Row	Col	Link
Our Staff	2	2	hire.html
Catalog	3	2	product.html
Newest Bikes	4	2	Bikes.xml

6. To modify the table's cellspacing attribute, you must select the entire table element. Drag from the area directly above the table, to the area directly below the table to select the entire table. If only part of the table is selected, or if one of the cells is not completely selected, try again.
7. Click **Attributes** on the menu bar, and then click **cellspacing**. The Attributes dialog opens. Type **4** in the text box as shown in Figure 8-23. Click **Apply**, and then click **Done**.

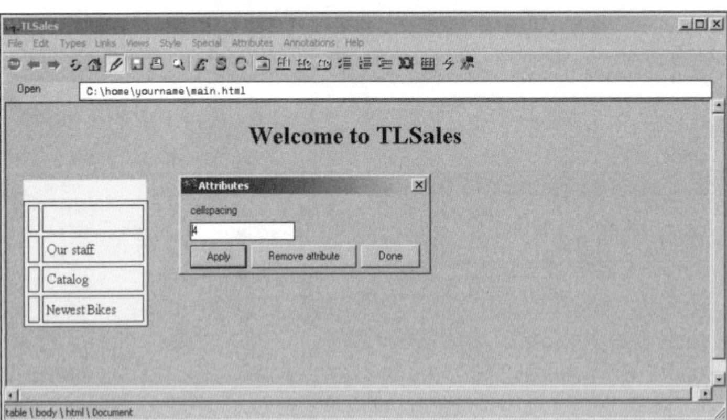

Figure 8-23

8. Click **File** on the menu bar, and then click **Save** to save your work.

Project 8-6

The final step in developing the XHTML Web page is to add the graphics and then view it in a browser. If you can, view the Web page in both Internet Explorer and Netscape Navigator to check the differences.

To add graphics and test the Web page:

1. To add a graphic to the table, click in row 1, column 1. Click **Types** on the menu bar, and then click **Image(img)**. The Images directory dialog box opens.
2. In the Insert image text box, type **bike.jpg**, and in the Alternate Text text box, type **Built for Speed!**. Click **Confirm**. The graphic will not appear until you open the file in a browser.
3. To add a background image, click the background of the window, click **Style** on the menu bar, and then click **Background image**. The Background image dialog box opens. Type **lbl.jpg** in the Images directory text box, and then click the **no-repeat** option button in the Repeat Mode section. Click **Confirm**. The background image appears.
4. To save the file, click **File** on the menu bar, and then click **Save.**
5. Click **Views** on the menu bar, and then click **Show source**. A source view window appears. Review the XHTML code that Amaya created. Notice how the tags are all well formed and properly nested.
6. Test your new page in both Internet Explorer and Netscape Navigator by typing **C:\home\<yourname>\Ch08\main.html** in the Address boxes. The Web page should resemble Figure 8-24 in Internet Explorer.

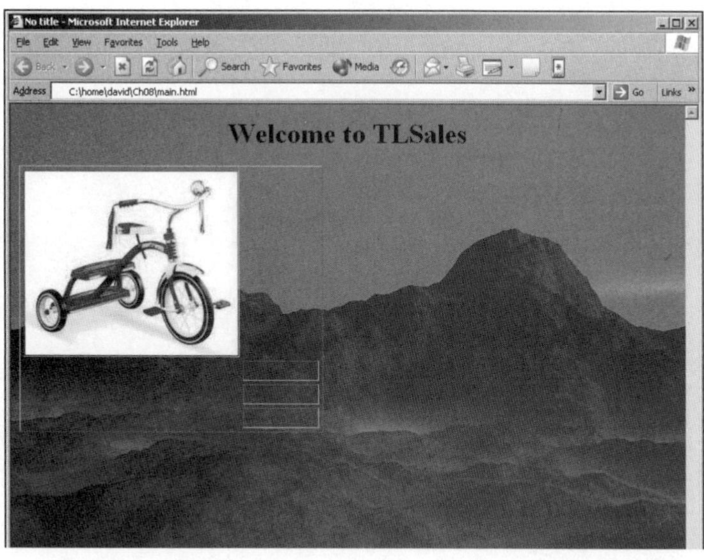

CASE PROJECT

Knowing that the correct syntax and nesting used for elements and their attributes, including nesting behavior, is defined in the companion DTD files for XHTML; you should make sure that you have the most current and accurate files available. These files are known as xhtml1-strict.dtd, xhtml1-transitional.dtd, and xhtml1-frameset.dtd. Sometimes errors are made or the tools that you are using are at various levels of development and support.

1. Validate the XHTML code that you just created in Amaya with Tidy. It should pass inspection.
2. Validate the XHTML code that you edited in XML Spy. To do this, create an empty XHTML file, and cut and paste all the code from main.html into it. Be careful not to overwrite the XML Spy prolog and declarations statements (comment out the Amaya prolog and declarations). Your goal here is to use the XML Spy reference to the xhtml1-strict.dtd within XML Spy. You find that the tables may not validate. Move on to step three.
3. Compare the definition of the table element in the xhmtl1-strict.dtd file that Amaya uses to that of XML Spy. You may have to use the Windows search and find utility to locate the DTD files on the local drive. Or you may have to look at the DTD files as published at *www.w3.org*. You find that XML Spy handles this differently, and that is why the table element does not validate as is.

What to do when this happens? Remain aware that there are standard DTDs available. We would recommend that you use the DTD files as specified on the *www.w3.org* site. That way your code will always be industry compliant.

CHAPTER

9

INTRODUCTION TO VECTOR MARKUP LANGUAGE (VML)

In this chapter, you will learn:

- About the basic digital imaging technologies
- About the Vector Markup Language (VML)
- How to create and view VML documents
- About VML templates
- How to use predefined shapes
- How to alter VML images
- How to use the <group> element

Individuals and organizations are generating more visual content on the Web every day, driven by the needs of information and research exchange and the rapid growth in e-commerce. With millions of Web sites and billions of pages of content, data must be presented quickly when requested, while optimizing the use of system and network resources.

During the past decade, several technical developments have taken place. For example, conversion software has been developed that is readily available and relatively easy to use, compression algorithms have been used to help reduce bandwidth loading, and faster network hardware is being built. Data can be easily converted to graphic images and these images can be published and communicated easier, faster, and more cost-effectively. Recent developments have also involved XML-related applications and documents.

In this chapter, you are introduced to the Vector Markup Language (VML), the most commonly used XML-related graphic language. Some basic concepts are discussed first to lay a foundation for understanding ofVML, its principles, evolution, and features.

VML may not remain the most popular XML-related graphic language. Scalable Vector Graphics (SVG) or descendant of SVG or VML may supercede VML. For now, however, VML is the most widespread and best known of the vector graphic languages.

UNDERSTANDING DIGITAL IMAGING TECHNOLOGIES

It was not long ago that the generation of visual graphic material consisted of many steps:

- Information was collected and transported to an artist, who then created an image (often after more than one try, as the artist and the client fine-tuned the message and the images).
- A printer was hired to transform the artwork into a robust presentable format (possibly involving several copies of the same or different sizes).
- The final copy was then transformed (likely scanned) into a digital representation, at the client's, the artist's, or the printer's shop
- The graphic image, now in one or more digital formats, was stored on the network, separate from the rest of the relevant applications.
- The graphic image was summoned when needed, and then manipulated to fit a screen.
- The same image might was manipulated differently—maybe even converted to a different digital format—to be printed.

Admittedly, a process such as the one described above might be considered "worst case," but certainly not beyond the realm of possibility. Often, processes such as these were aggravated by imprecise instructions, missed deadlines, copyright infringement, or payments gone awry. Over the years and throughout many organizations, more efficient procedures and methods have been developed, such as hiring full-time specialists, relying on dedicated, talented, and ambitious staff members, combining functions in contractors' shops, or purchasing specialized hardware and software.

There are two basic digital imaging technologies: those involving bitmap graphics and those involving vector graphics. Although VML involves vector graphics, each technology is discussed here.

Bitmap Graphics

A **bitmap** graphic file (also known as a **raster** graphic file) is a file with data structured so that it corresponds bit for bit with an image displayed on a screen or printed on a page. In other words, the image data is mapped to precise locations in the raster, which is the area of the computer screen that displays the viewable image. Bitmapped graphics are images made up of dot patterns, similar to the patterns of black and white or colored dots that once made up newspaper and magazine photographs.

A bitmap is characterized by the width and height of the respective image in picture elements **(pixels)** and the number of data bits per displayed pixel. Those bits govern the number of shades of gray or the combination of red, green, and blue colors per pixel, plus the intensity of those colors. Bitmap files representing colored images contain between one and eight bits for each of the red, green, and blue pixels. Bitmap files also occur in various formats, depending on the algorithms used to compress the data within them. The formats are usually referred to by the extensions given to their files, such as .gif, .tif, .jpg, .png, and .bmp. Without being compressed, the bitmap files would take up more storage space. The format also determines whether a file can be exchanged between platforms and applications. Some formats have more advanced features than others. For example, .tif files provide more detail than .jpg files.

Figure 9-1 illustrates a black and white 10 pixel by 10 pixel example of a bitmap rendering of a smiley face image. The header of the bitmap file specifies that the file format is BM (for bitmap), that both the width and height of the pixel display is 10 pixels, and that the colors are black and white. Following the header is the first defining byte with no black (1) bits in it, just white (0) bits. So no pixels in the first part of the display are black. However, the second byte has black bits in the fifth and sixth pixel positions, defining the eyebrow of the smiley face shown in the lower portion of the figure. The rest of the face is defined in the information contained in the subsequent bytes. For color renderings, more information is needed per pixel to render the appropriate combination of red, green, and blue.

Thus, bitmap graphics are rendered by controlling the composition of each display pixel or each printed dot. Bitmapped images, then, do not need any running-time calculation, but they may require a lot of random access memory on motherboards, on video adapter cards, or within printers.

Bitmap images require fast processors, since video monitors may require an image change (also called a refresh) between 50 and 200 times per second, depending on monitor characteristics. Some output devices, such as dot matrix printers, laser printers, and display monitors, are called bitmap or raster devices. They contain rasterizers, which are combinations of hardware and software that translate objects into bitmaps. This means that all objects must be translated into bitmaps before being produced through the raster device. Applications that manipulate bitmapped images are called paint programs.

Besides the fact that they are found everywhere, the advantage to bitmap graphics and paint programs is the ability they give you to enhance the details of an image; you can literally modify each pixel. However, bitmap graphics do not provide much flexibility: once the image has been created, significant changes cannot easily be made. To change a bitmap graphic, you must use the appropriate software (which would likely include the software to uncompress and then recompress the files) on a system with certain minimum requirements. You cannot access bitmaps, make quick or significant changes, and re-draw the bitmap images quickly. Other disadvantages to bitmaps on the Web are that their generally large file sizes cause them to download slowly, and they are usually stored external to their HTML document. This causes the processor to work harder, makes the images more difficult to distribute, and causes extra system administration problems.

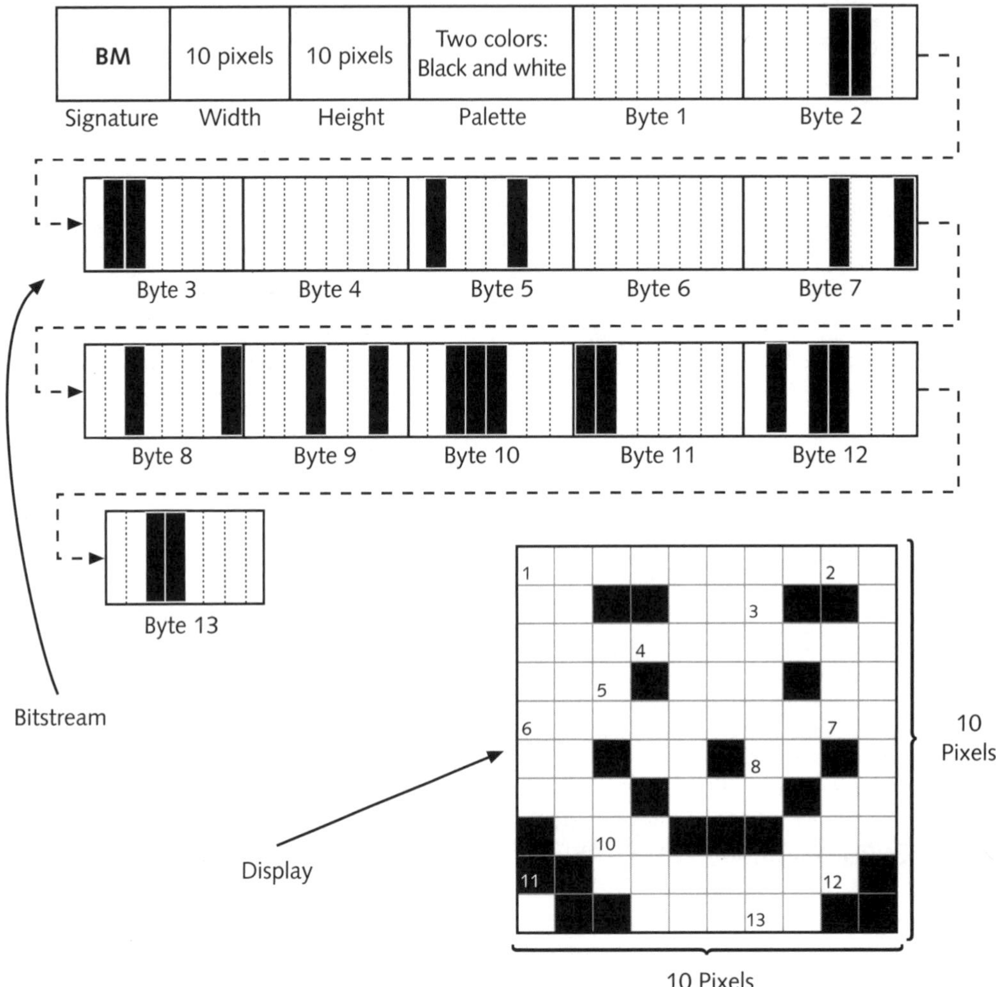

Figure 9-1 Simplified bitmap example

Vector Graphic Images

Vector graphic images are those objects created by drawing a series of lines, polygons, and text, while providing only the starting position and direction for each line. Vector graphic images are also called **object-oriented graphics**, though they are not related to object-oriented programming.

A computer draws a vector graphic by referring to mathematical descriptions (i.e., specific geometrical formulas) and attributes in the vector images file. In other words, vector graphics always use a certain algorithm to create a line or rectangle, for example, to draw an image on the screen or send it to a printer. That means that the computer performs real-time calculations as it draws the image. Figure 9-2 illustrates a simplified version of a vector graphic rendering, as well as its bitstream. Notice how the bitstream describes the image as a display list, which contains a mathematical description of every object in the image, including their locations and dimensions, as well as other attributes such as fill colors, line stroke widths, and layer. Please note, however, that not all the necessary information can be represented in such a simplified diagram.

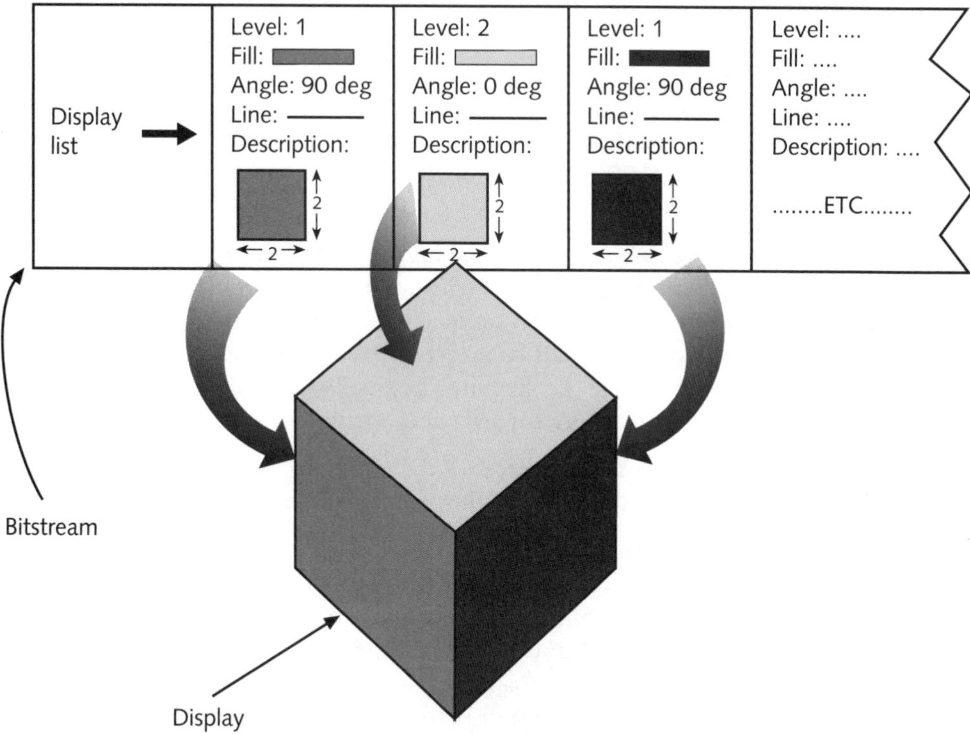

Figure 9-2 Simplified vector graphic example

Vector graphics are widely used in word processing, graphics editing, and publishing and presentation software. In fact, almost all sophisticated graphics systems, including computer aided design (CAD) and drafting systems, and animation software, use vector graphics. Fonts created with vectors are called vector fonts, scalable fonts, object-oriented fonts, or outline fonts. (You might have heard one or more of these terms before.) Applications that create and manipulate vector graphics are called drawing programs.

This may seem contradictory at first, but .gif, .png, and other bitmapped formats can store vector graphics. In these cases, vector graphics are translated into bitmaps only after all sizes and resolutions have been specified. That's also why many printers (particularly

PostScript printers, for example) can use vector graphics: those printers have raster image processors (RIPs) that perform the translation within the printer at the last possible moment before printing.

Advantages of Vector Graphics

The advantages of using vector graphics include their flexibility, their smaller file size, and their faster download speed.

Flexibility is multifaceted. The first aspect of flexibility is scalability: vector graphic representations can be written to any device, with any resolution, and at any size, with no loss of clarity and no distortion. Such images look just as good displayed at higher resolutions and magnifications as at lower resolutions. By contrast, bitmapped images can become jagged with higher magnification. With vector graphics, you can easily render an object at different sizes and transform it in other ways without worrying about image resolution and pixels.

The flexibility of vector graphics (drawing) programs means that overlapping elements can be manipulated independently without using different layers for each one. This becomes evident in the Hands-on projects at the end of this chapter. Further, once vector objects are created, they can be selected, resized, moved, and reordered at any time; these are significant changes far beyond the pixel detailing of bitmap manipulation. You also can search vector graphics for data and attributes.

Vector graphics are also flexible because they interact easily with other image files using almost any computer system. Vector files are just simple text files.

Vector graphic files use smaller amounts of memory to represent their objects no matter the actual size of the objects. If the graphics files are altered to create bigger or smaller images, there is almost no difference in the size of their already smaller definition files. This means savings in RAM and in hard disk storage space. Finally, since vector graphic files are more compact than bitmapped graphic files, their download times (at least for simpler images) are shorter, leading to faster download times for Web users.

Disadvantages of Vector Graphics

The disadvantages of vector graphics are that more powerful processors may be needed to handle them, and that altering fine image details may be beyond vectors.

If you are inserting many complex or small objects using vector techniques, you might need a more powerful and faster system, because each individual character may be created by hundreds of line objects. Similarly, if you intend to create hundreds or thousands of objects in a single display, then it may take significant time to recalculate vector information, pass the information to a rasterizer, store the data in RAM, and quickly transfer and refresh it to a screen while redrawing the objects not only at one time, but at perhaps hundreds of times a second. As a way to work around these bottlenecks, some programmers develop specialized software to save processing time, while still allowing the use of vector fonts and images to produce fine results in hard copy.

The second drawback to vector graphics is that some vector objects cannot be modified pixel by pixel because of their data structure. If you want to fine-tune or control certain pixels, you must use a bitmapped technique.

UNDERSTANDING THE VECTOR MARKUP LANGUAGE (VML)

Currently, the most common graphics-based XML application is the **Vector Markup Language (VML)**. VML is widespread because Microsoft Internet Explorer 5 and later versions have incorporated VML as a method to interpret vector-based graphics. Further, Internet Explorer (IE) does not require you to download plug-ins to display or interpret VML's file format.

The W3C (*see www.w3.org/TR/NOTE-VML*) describes VML as "an application of the Extensible Markup Language (XML) 1.0, which defines a format for the encoding of vector information together with additional markup to describe how that information may be displayed and edited." VML is designed to help developers address the problems and disadvantages of using bitmap technology.

Also, because it is an application of XML, VML is both open and standards based. For example, as shown in Figure 9-3, it is fully compliant with other W3C standards such as Cascading Style Sheets, HTML, XML and others.

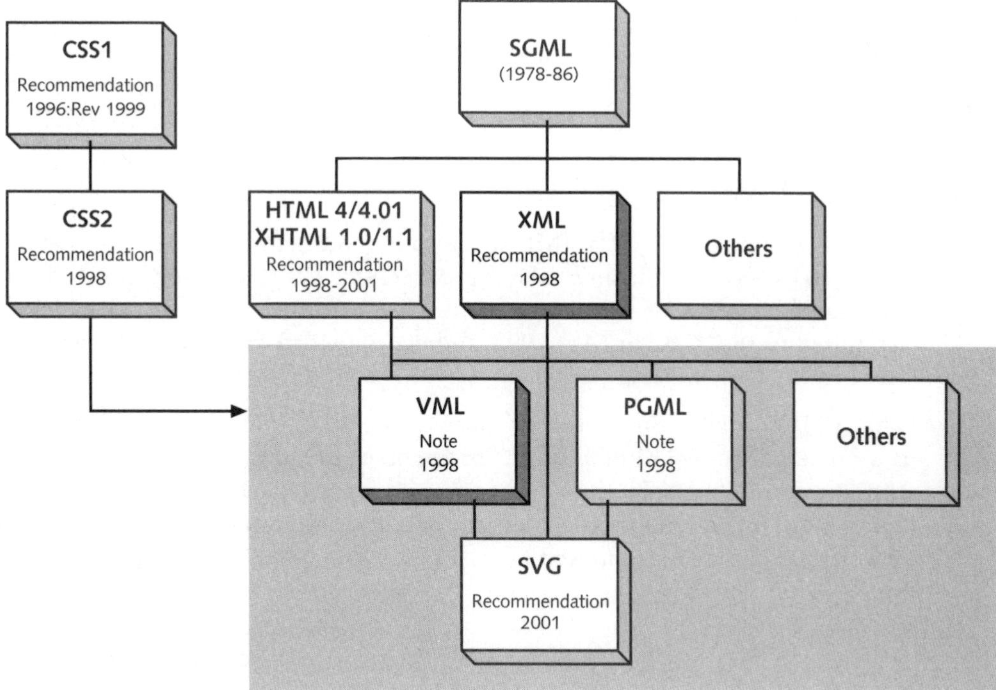

Figure 9-3 VML in relation to other standards

True to its vector graphics heritage,VML uses mathematical descriptions to create graphics. VML delivers its vector graphics definitions within the lines of HTML 4.0-compliant pages, so the graphic definitions are integrated with the HTML coding, rather than relying on external files as bitmapped graphics do. The HTML code and VML code must be well-formed to ensure the intended functionality.

Because VML uses existing HTML and **Cascading Style Sheets (CSS)** mechanisms, VML supports the markup of vector graphic information in the same way that HTML supports the markup of textual information. For example, all top-level VML elements support the <style> element and its related attributes, in the same manner that all HTML elements support it. Because VML also supports CSS, you can style and position shapes as you like.

That VML was designed to provide a textual way to describe vector graphics also means that its elements, attributes, and other prescriptive text are easily cut and pasted for use in other authoring tools. Because VML is a text-based encoding system, the source code can also be viewed in your browser.

VML also contains some Microsoft Office-related features, which allows it to cooperate with VML generation by current Microsoft Windows 2000 and XP technologies. When you use VML elements, they must be properly "triggered" with namespace and behavior declarations.

If you use pure VML, there are no external bitmap files or other binary files to accommodate; an image can be generated using nothing but VML. However, you can combine bitmaps with vector data by including the bitmap reference in a vector path. Further, there are limited transformation attributes (such as chromakey, gamma, picture, and black level adjustments) that are applied to the bitmap data from within the HTML/VML document.

History of VML

In 1998 an initial draft of a VML specification was authored jointly by Autodesk Inc., Hewlett-Packard Company, Macromedia Inc., Visio Corporation, and Microsoft Corporation. (Most of the representatives were from Microsoft.) That document was submitted to the W3C in May 1998, and was intended for review, discussion, and comment by W3C members.

That VML specification document survives as a W3C "Note." As the W3C states, a Note is a dated, public record of an idea, comment, or document. As such, it does not represent any commitment by the W3C to pursue work related to it. Neither does its Note status indicate any endorsement of its content, nor any present or future allocation of resources to the issues addressed by it.

Here is a quick summary of those VML design requirements that are articulated in the VML Note of 1998:

- VML documents must retain the information required for further editing (thus, VML must be extensible; every relevant application must be able to add any necessary editing data).
- VML must support the interchange of data between applications (i.e., one application must be able to read and edit the data of another application.
- VML documents must use the existing mechanisms of HTML and CSS (this facilitates implementation, and ensures that implementations can reuse existing code and techniques).
- VML must be backward compatible with existing user agents (i.e., with existing Web browsers), VML must also contain provisions to allow alternate bitmap representations of graphics.
- VML must provide efficient representations of vector graphics, by using such methods as defining a compact representation of path elements, and using concise names for frequently used attributes and more verbose and descriptive names for less frequently used attributes.
- VML must allow the implementation of subsets where an application does not require full VML functionality. For example, normally a viewer implements the full specification, but an editor should be able to implement only the subset required for its own data.
- VML must support editing by hand (the structure of the graphic should be obvious, and the syntax should be familiar to HTML programmers).
- VML should support scripting, including the requirements of animation.

Recall that VML was originally designed to provide a textual way to describe vector graphics that can be easily cut and pasted for use in a wide variety of authoring tools. Further, VML was written so that it could be integrated into existing HTML 4.0 markup.

The VML specification never attained W3C Recommendation status, despite the support from Microsoft and others, including the incorporation of VML graphic-rendering functionality into Microsoft's Internet Explorer 5 browser and later versions. It looks like no further development will take place. In fact, both the VML Note and the (rival) Precision Graphics Markup Language Note (also submitted in 1998) were overtaken and passed by the development of the Scalable Vector Graphics specification, which became a W3C Recommendation in mid-2001. These other documents are discussed in the next section.

Other Vector Graphics Specifications

VML was not the first or only vector graphics specification to be submitted to the W3C. However, because Microsoft incorporated VML into Internet Explorer, VML gained a distinct advantage.

The following sections examine two additional specifications. One, the Precision Graphics Markup Language (PGML), is still a W3C Note. The other, Scalable Vector Graphics (SVG), was developed as a result of four vector graphic specification proposals (VML among them) that W3C received in 1998. SVG, from a Recommendation standpoint, has surpassed the others.

PGML

In 1998, another XML-related graphics standard was submitted to the W3C: the **Precision Graphics Markup Language (PGML)**. As with VML, PGML is a vector graphics-related application of XML that also uses CSS style attributes. PGML was also granted Note status by the W3C in 1998.

PGML was developed by technical representatives of Adobe Systems, Inc., IBM Corporation, Sun Microsystems, Inc., and Netscape Communications Corporation for professional design and publishing. PGML is based on Adobe's PostScript language and its portable document format (PDF) file format.

There are several similarities between PGML and VML. For example, both are text-based markup languages. Both strive to be HTML and CSS2 compliant. Despite claims to the contrary, both PGML and VML were driven primarily by their respective companies' desire to establish their own technologies as the premier standard for vector graphics. Both PGML and VML have enabled their editing applications (i.e., Word for VML, Illustrator for PGML) to create, save, and export XML versions of their Web-oriented document files. This means that many developers can start creating Web content more freely and easily by using applications that are already familiar to them. Still, both languages are considered verbose and cumbersome, although programmers are heartened by the fact that, ultimately, most of the code is generated by the editing applications and not written by hand.

PGML and VML may use different syntax for graphic objects, but their feature sets are similar. They both allow for paths, and including images, text, and predefined shapes, for instance. In addition, both depend on a namespace mechanism to identify unknown XML tags and to reliably and safely add new XML tags.

Significant differences between PGML and VML include:

- The VML specification includes only a partial DTD, while the PGML specification includes a complete and verified DTD.
- PGML uses a more confusing matrix coordinate system for creating and editing shapes; VML uses text and descriptive terms, and refers to shape types that can be combined to form other shapes that, in turn, are scalable.
- PGML provides a transparency setting for <group> objects. VML doesn't provide this for grouped objects as a whole, but provides opacity and chromakey attribute settings wit hin the <shape> and <shapetype> subelements within a group.

- PGML includes animation features for motion paths and changing color and opacity over time. VML has no animation support.
- VML has slightly better font mapping support than PGML.
- PGML has better color specification support than VML.
- When it comes to creating graphics from scratch, the two specifications do that differently, too: PGML uses <path>, <img>, and <text>; VML uses <shape> and <shapetype>.

PGML and the other vector graphic-related submissions received by the W3C at approximately the same time were proposals that their companies contributed to spur discussion and consultation. Whether any survive remains to be seen. But, both contributed to the development of a true W3C Recommendation: Scalable Vector Graphics 1.0, which is discussed next.

Scalable Vector Graphics (SVG)

In early 1999, the W3C created their **Scalable Vector Graphics (SVG)** Working Group after having received four standards proposals for vector graphics.

- PGML (March 1998)
- VML (May 1998)
- Web Schematics on the World Wide Web, a proposal submitted by representatives of the Council for the Central Laboratory of the Research Councils in March 1998 (also given Note status by the W3C)
- The DrawML Specification, submitted by Håkan Lothigius of Excosoft AB, a Swedish IT consulting company, in December 1998; DrawML resembles Web Schematics, but relies on Java functionality

After almost three years of drafting, discussion, consultation, and development, the SVG group's proposal was endorsed by the W3C as Recommendation SVG 1.0 in 2001. SVG is an open-standard, vector graphics language created under the auspices of the W3C by representatives from Adobe, Apple, Autodesk, BitFlash, Canon, CSIRO, Corel, Excosoft, HP, IBM, ILOG, Intranet Solutions, Inc., Kodak, Lexica, Macromedia, Microsoft, Netscape, Opera Software, Oxford Brookes University, OASIS, Quark, RAL (CCLRC), Sun, Visio, Xerox, and the W3C itself. Many other industry, academic, e-mail, and chat group members, as well as members of the general public, helped to develop SVG. See Figure 9-4.

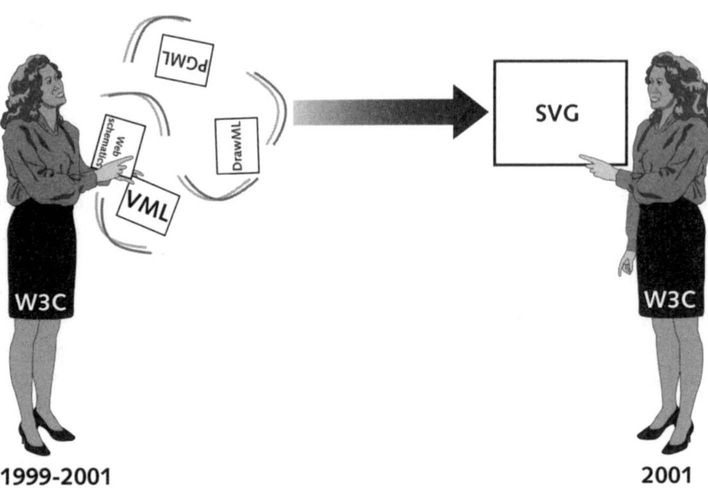

Figure 9-4 Evolution of SVG

The SVG Recommendation is published under the W3C Document Copyright Notice and License. The bindings within the Recommendation are published under the W3C Software Copyright Notice and License, and the Recommendation comes with Patent Statements. If you intend to use or modify SVG, all these documents are worth examining first, if only to clarify your rights and duties.

SVG is stable and comes with its own mature DTD. Although some SVG development has taken place since 1999, SVG is not yet widely implemented. Nevertheless, there are SVG graphics on the Web. To view them, you need to install a plug-in from Adobe's Web site first. The plug-in adds SVG functionality to current Netscape 4 or higher or Internet Explorer 5 or higher browsers. One of the benefits of the plug-in is better zooming performance: the plug-in facilitates scaling such as that found at the client end. You don't have to wait for a server on the Web to download different resolution bitmaps every time you zoom in or out.

All Web browsers might eventually come with built-in SVG capability, so there will be no further need for plug-ins. Until then, VML remains more ubiquitous and popular. However, SVG is considered the major graphic format for the future. There will be a period during which SVG has to break in, to gain acceptance and momentum. In the meantime, Web designers must learn to use SVG and to make it more accessible to everyone.

VML Advantages

This section summarizes the advantages VML offers Web site graphic development and deployment. Some of the advantages stem from its vector graphics heritage. Other advantages stem from VML's Internet Explorer affiliation.

First, VML is incorporated within the current version of Microsoft's Internet Explorer browser, so it is accessible to a wide audience and requires no additional downloads or plug-ins to be functional.

The second advantage is faster download capability. As discussed previously, the standard bitmap-based graphics, using .gif, .jpg, and other formats, are referenced externally at Web site servers and then are described pixel by pixel, resulting in relatively slow downloads. Compared to most of those bitmap image files, text-based VML files are smaller. This means faster downloads in general, especially to remote dial-up users.

VML documents are easily and quickly created, updated, and published to their servers. You can create and update the VML code directly with common applications, such as Microsoft Office 2000 or Office XP applications, but if you are familiar with VML coding, you can even use an application as simple as Notepad.

By using VML, developers can cut and paste vector graphics from one location to another, and later edit the images with no loss of quality. This promotes ordinary user interaction, while it lets all developers scale VML graphics to interact with page elements and objects.

By contrast, bitmap image files need to be edited and regenerated using an application similar to the application that created the graphic originally. To store the image, the data must be compressed, and not all compression applications are alike. Then, when called up by a browser, the image files must be uncompressed, which affects speed of delivery and appearance.

VML does not require using a rasterizer. Existing operating system facilities, such as those found in the Win32 Graphical Device Interface (GDI), the Windows standard for representing graphical objects and transmitting them to output devices, or Macintosh QuickDraw, the underlying graphics display system for Apple Macintosh computers, can be used. This has a particular benefit to printing.

These advantages all contribute to faster, newer approaches to Web site design, and have also allowed VML to thrive when it comes to creating timely business charts and graphs, provide menu or advertising graphics, or even to break into the world of geographic information systems (where VML's map making and drawing strengths can be quickly and easily employed alongside XML-related spatial databases).

Creating and Viewing VML Documents

There are numerous ways to produce a VML-based graphic. If you are proficient with the VML language, then you can use a text editor. Microsoft Office 2000 and XP applications also allow you to generate VML data. So you can use Microsoft Excel, Word, and PowerPoint to create pictures in a document (even incorporate bitmap images such as a .gif or .jpg), then save the document in HTML/VML.

One easy method is to cut a VML sample from a Web site, and then paste a text editor. Then you can change shapes, colors, and other features. For example, using Microsoft IE and a search engine, search for Web sites by entering a query composed of search terms (also called descriptive words or keywords) such as: "vml animations" or "vml examples." The search engine presents a list of candidate Web sites that it considers relevant to your search. Click a URL and explore it. If you find a graphic image in which you are interested, click View on the menu bar, then click Source. A new window opens and the HTML and other related code for that page is presented. If the graphic image is a VML image, the source includes VML coding (VML elements are listed and discussed later in this chapter). When you find what you want, copy and paste the code into a new or existing HTML or XHTML Web document. As always, you must ensure that your DTDs or schemas contain appropriate declarations for the new coding.

In the Hands-on Projects at the end of this chapter, you use the XML Spy IDE. XML Spy incorporates VML display features similar to those found in Internet Explorer, so you can see your results quickly.

You may also download Microsoft's VML Generator, found at the Microsoft Developer News (MSDN) Library at *msdn.microsoft.com/library/default.asp?url=/workshop/author/vml/default.asp*. This editor is almost WYSIWYG in nature. Adding or changing shapes, colors, line weights, or fill patterns, involves modifying the code and clicking the Refresh button.

When trying to view VML pages, which are HTML pages containing VML markup and data, your options are not as plentiful. The only Web browser that currently supports VML is Internet Explorer version 5 (with the VML option installed) and Internet Explorer 5.5. As stated previously, no additional downloads or plug-ins are required.

VML Document Creation: Syntax and Features

Now that you have been introduced to VML, its heritage, its related standards, you are ready to examine its syntax. Remember that VML is an application of XML, and so XML's syntax must be strictly adhered to. Also remember that VML uses the existing mechanisms of HTML 4 and Cascading Style Sheets (as defined in the W3C's CSS1 and CSS2 Recommendations). Therefore, all top-level VML tags support the <style> element in the same manner that all HTML elements support it.

The Prolog and Other Basics

As indicated in Figure 9-5, a VML document, such as other XML/HTML-like documents, consists of two main parts, the prolog, and the <html> element. In turn, the <html> element consists of the <head> element and the <body> element.

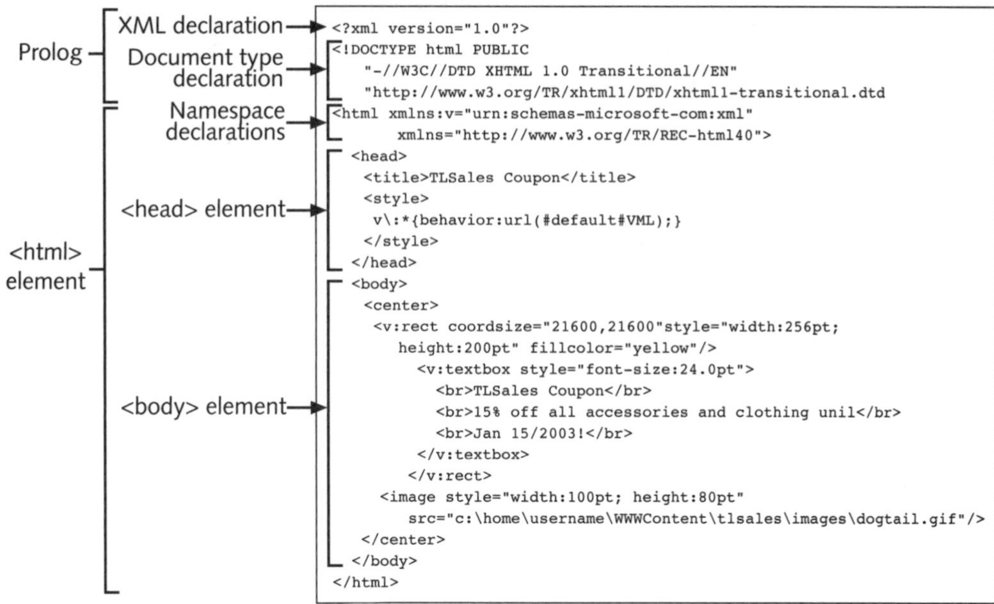


```
<?xml version="1.0"?>
<!DOCTYPE html PUBLIC
    "-//W3C//DTD XHTML 1.0 Transitional//EN"
    "http://www.w3.org/TR/xhtml1/DTD/xhtml1-transitional.dtd
<html xmlns:v="urn:schemas-microsoft-com:xml"
       xmlns="http://www.w3.org/TR/REC-html40">
 <head>
  <title>TLSales Coupon</title>
  <style>
   v\:*{behavior:url(#default#VML);}
  </style>
 </head>
 <body>
  <center>
   <v:rect coordsize="21600,21600"style="width:256pt;
      height:200pt" fillcolor="yellow"/>
        <v:textbox style="font-size:24.0pt">
          <br>TLSales Coupon</br>
          <br>15% off all accessories and clothing unil</br>
          <br>Jan 15/2003!</br>
        </v:textbox>
      </v:rect>
    <image style="width:100pt; height:80pt"
       src="c:\home\username\WWWContent\tlsales\images\dogtail.gif"/>
  </center>
 </body>
</html>
```

Figure 9-5 Sample VML document

VML documents follow both HTML and XHTML syntax. The examples in this chapter reflect the stricter XML-related XHTML syntax (discussed in the previous chapter). Thus, the elements appear in lowercase to comply with the XML/XHTML well-formedness requirements.

The sample VML/XHTML document in Figure 9-5 also has a prolog similar to all other XHTML-related documents, although the prolog is not necessary if VML is used with HTML. The prolog consists of an XML declaration and a DOCTYPE declaration indicating the DTD variant.

The <head> element contains the <title> element and the <style> element. For the document to be well-formed, both those elements must be properly nested within the <head> element. Further, the <style> element contains the behavior declaration, which is discussed later in this chapter.

VML Namespace Declarations

For VML to render properly, you must declare two namespaces: the VML namespace and the default namespace for HTML or XHTML.

Both declarations must appear in the start tag for the document's root <HTML> element if the document is an ordinary HTML document; otherwise, if the document is to be XHTML-compliant, then the element is called by its lowercase equivalent, <html>.

To declare a VML namespace, use V= in the declaration. Later in the document, the v prefix precedes each VML-related element tag. Following is the VML namespace declaration that should appear in the <HTML>/<html> start tag. Note that it is a reference to a schema:

```
<html xmlns:v="urn:schemas-microsoft-com:vml">
```

Once inserted, this code tells Internet Explorer that all tags beginning with v: are part of the VML namespace, as opposed to the default HTML namespace.

If you omit this aspect of the document, the VML is displayed. If you are having trouble producing VML output, start your debugging by looking for this declaration.

The default namespace is inserted next, in the same <HTML>/<html> element start tag. If your document is not XHTML-compliant, use the declaration on the second line, below:

```
<html xmlns:v="urn:schemas-microsoft-com:vml"
      xmlns="http://www.w3.org/TR/REC-html40">
```

If your document is XHTML-compliant, the default declaration must reflect that it is. In that case, use the declaration on the second line, below:

```
<html xmlns:v="urn:schemas-microsoft-com:vml"
      xmlns="http://www.w3.org/1999/xhtml">
```

Once inserted, these codes—whichever one you insert—tell Internet Explorer that all tags that do not have a prefix are part of the HTML or XHTML namespaces, respectively.

Recall that VML is supported in the Microsoft Office 2000 and XP applications: Microsoft Word, PowerPoint, and Excel. That means you can use those applications to draw VML objects. If you do so, then you must add yet another namespace declaration, because those applications add their own prefix. Here is the total declaration, if you are creating an HTML document—one that, for this example, will *not* be XHTML-compliant—with those MS Office applications:

```
<html xmlns:v="urn:schemas-microsoft-com:vml"
      xmlns="http://www.w3.org/TR/REC-html40"
      xmlns:o="urn:schemas-microsoft-com:office:office">
```

Another term for using MS Office applications to create VML objects is "using Office extensions." Remember that if you are not using Office extensions, then you can omit the third namespace reference.

Figure 9-6 illustrates the namespace declarations in use in a VML document created with the XML Spy IDE. In this figure, that the VML prolog has been intentionally omitted.

```
coupon.html - WordPad
File Edit View Insert Format Help

<html xmlns:v="urn:schemas-microsoft-com:vml"
      xmlns="http://www.w3.org/TR/REC-html40">
         <head>
            <title>TLSales Coupon</title>
               <style>
                  v\:* {behavior:url(#default#VML);}
               </style>
         </head>
         <body>
            <center>
               <v:rect coordsize="21600,21600" style="width:256pt;height:200pt"
                       fillcolor="yellow">
                  <v:textbox style="font-size:24.0pt">
                     <br>TLSales Coupon</br>
                     <br>15% off all accessories and clothing until</br>
                     <br>Jan 15/2003!</br>
                  </v:textbox>
               </v:rect>
                  <v:image style="width:100pt;height:80pt"
                           src="c:\home\username\WWWContent\tlsales\images\dogtail.gif" />
            </center>
         </body>
</html>

For Help, press F1                                                    NUM
```

Figure 9-6 VML namespace declarations

VML Behavior Declarations

Generally, VML support is provided with Microsoft Internet Explorer 5 or later as a default behavior. This support is achieved using what Microsoft calls "behaviors" (introduced with IE5). If your initial IE browser installation did not include VML behavior, you may need to add it as an option. To do so, look for the vgx.dll in the Program Files\Common Files\Microsoft Shared\VGX folder of your Windows system.

Behaviors are complete and encapsulated subroutines that, when called, extend Internet Explorer functionality. Because they are complete unto themselves, you declare them at the beginning of an HTML document, and then apply them one or more times to those elements in your document that you specify. They provide you with the ability to reuse blocks of code, and to keep your content separate from the code. There are two types of behaviors: the original eleven IE 5 behaviors, which are now referred to as attached behaviors, and custom-defined, element behaviors, which were introduced with IE 5.5.

To ensure that the Internet Explorer VML behavior is used, insert the following into the <style> element subelement of the <head> element:

```
<style>
     v\:* { behavior: url(#default#VML); }
</style>
```

This instructs the browser to pass all of the tags beginning with v: to its VML rendering subroutine. Figure 9-7 shows what this single behavior declaration looks like in a VML document.

Figure 9-7 VML behavior declaration

Like the VML namespace, if you omit this aspect of the document, your VML images are displayed. If you have trouble producing VML output, check the <style> element after you examine your namespace declarations.

Because VML is supported in several recent Microsoft Office applications, if you create VML objects with those programs, then you must add more behaviors to the style element. In that case, the <style> element expands to:

```
<style>
     v\:* { behavior: url(#default#VML); }
     o\:* {behavior:url(#default#VML);}
</style>
```

Later in this chapter, you learn about creating **primitive graphic objects**, those you create from scratch by setting a path for a digital pen to traverse. If your VML document contains one or more of those objects, then you must also add another declaration to the <style> element. Your style element then looks like:

```
<style>
     v\:* { behavior: url(#default#VML); }
     o\:* {behavior:url(#default#VML);}
     .shape {behavior:url(#default#VML);}
</style>
```

The .shape is an object-oriented programming-like class name. In embedded-style behaviors like this, the class name is used as a selector, and begins with a period (.). This causes every element that has been assigned the class name of "shape" to be rendered according to the specifications in the IE behavior.

VML Templates

There are several categories of VML elements; they are roughly categorized according to function or hierarchy. However, some elements can be considered members of more than one category.

The main categories of VML elements are listed in Table 9-1, along with examples of elements that belong to each category.

Table 9-1 Main VML categories

Category	Membership (Examples)
Top-level	<group>, <shape>, <shapetype>, and <background>
Primary	<group>, <shape>
Subelements	Examples include <fill>, <formulas>, <strokeweight>, <handles>, <image>, <imagedata>, plus several more
Predefined	Examples include <rect>, <roundrect>, <line>, <oval>, <polyline>, <curve>, <arc>, plus several more

Most of the elements listed in Table 9-1 are discussed in this chapter. The others are beyond the scope of this introductory-level presentation.

VML applies to each element a default template consisting of the full set of attributes that may apply to that particular element. But, if you specify a particular element—such as <shape>, which is discussed next—you can override the default values for any of the template attributes by specifying the attribute name and its new value within the start tag for the respective element.

The <shape> Element

The <shape> element is used as a first step toward defining a visible vector graphic element. Note that <shape> only defines the containing box for the actual figure you eventually create. Shape elements define what is called a block level box. Inside the containing box, a local coordinate system is defined for any subelements. The coordinate system uses the coordsize and coordorigin attributes. All subsequent positioning information is expressed in terms of this local coordinate space. As a result, position attributes such as left, top, width, and height are not expressed in length units (inches, or millimeters, etc.) as such; they are simply divisions within the box.

To clarify, the coordsize attribute defines how many divisions there are along the base of the containing box, across its width. The coordorigin attribute defines the coordinate at the upper left corner of the containing box. The reason this strategy was developed is that the vectors defining a figure inside the block level box can be specified with respect to its local coordinate system. Later, if the containing box is changed, the outline of the figure is automatically scaled to the new box dimensions.

Meanwhile, to create a figure inside the block level box, you must still use the <path> element as a subelement within <shape> (the <path> is discussed in the next section). Although it is the most basic of the VML graphic elements, <shape> is not used as often as one would expect. Most developers prefer to use predefined shapes such as <rect>, <oval>, <line>, and others.

Table 9-2 shows the attributes, complete with their default values, that make up the <shape> element's default VML template. If you are using <shape>, and you want to override one of the default attribute values, specify that attribute name and assign it a new value in the <shape> element's start tag.

Table 9-2 VML template for the <shape> element

Attribute=value	Namespace	Attribute=value	Namespace
flip=null	CSS	chromakey=null	VML
height=100	CSS	coordorigin="0, 0"	VML
left=0, margin-left=0, center-x=0, etc.	CSS	strokecolor="black"	VML
position="static"	CSS	opacity="100%"	VML
rotation=0	CSS	fillcolor="white"	VML
top=0, margin-top=0, center-y=0, etc.	CSS	coordsize="1000, 1000"	VML
style='visibility=visible'	CSS	strokeweight= "0.75pt"	VML
width=100	CSS	type=null	VML
z-index=0	CSS	adj=null	VML
stroke=true	VML	path=null	VML
wrapcoords=null	VML	alt=null	VML
href=null	VML	id=null	VML
title=null	VML	class=null	VML
v=null	VML	print=true	VML
fill=true	VML	target=null	VML

The namespace designation in Table 9-2 indicates from which namespace the attribute originates.

As an example, here is the minimum VML code needed to produce a shape:

```
<v:shape fillcolor="green"
      style="position:relative;top:1;left:1
      width:400;height:300"
      path="m 1,111,300,400,300,400,1 x e" >
      </v:shape>
```

At a minimum you must define a <shape>'s fillcolor, position, top, left, width, height, and path attributes. However, <shape> only defines the containing box for the shape you eventually create. To create the shape itself, you must still use a <path> subelement within the <shape> element, or specify a path attribute within the start tag of the <shape> element. Both options are discussed next.

Creating Paths: The path Attribute and <path> Element

If you want to define a figure within the <shape> element, use a <path> subelement within the <shape> element, or specify a path attribute within the start tag of the <shape> element.

The path Attribute

Within the <shape> element, you specify the figure you wish to draw by using the attribute "path" and providing, as values for that attribute, an expression that includes a string of x,y coordinates plus one or more specific shape-drawing commands, called pen commands. The path attribute thus defines the figure's outline by describing a path consisting of a sequence of straight lines and/or bézier curves (technically, these represent a list of vector-based drawing operations). Bézier curves (pronounced bez-ee-ay and named after the French mathematician Pierre Bézier) are curved lines defined by at least three specified points, and then by mathematical formulas. The outline is stroked, filled, or otherwise modified according to the values you specify for other attributes. The <shape> syntax, including the path attribute, is as follows:

```
<v:shape path="expression" ... >
```

The set of pen commands referred to are: m, l (the letter "ell"), c, x, e, t, r, v, nf, ns, ae, al, ar, at, wa, wr, qb, qx, and qy. The most common of those commands are summarized in the following Table 9-3.

Table 9-3 Path attribute pen commands

Command	Name	Description
m	moveto	Start a new subpath at the given (x,y) coordinate
l	lineto	Draw a line from the current point to the given (x,y) coordinate which becomes the new current point; to form a polyline, specify a number of coordinate pairs
c	curveto	Draw a bézier curve from the current point to the coordinate given by the final two parameters (the control points are given by the first four parameters)
x	close	Close the current subpath by drawing a straight line from the current point to the original moveto point
e	end	End the current set of subpaths
t	rmoveto	Start a new subpath at the (relative) coordinates specified
r	rlineto	Draw a line from the current point to the given relative coordinate
v	rcurveto	Draw a bézier curve from the current point, using the given coordinate relative

Following is an example that defines and draws a closed square. The path is defined in the expression following the path attribute. A starting point at coordinates 1,1 is defined with the moveto command (m). Next, a line is to be drawn with the lineto command (l) from the starting point to the other three points, in the order they are listed (i.e., 1,200; 200,200; and 200,1). Then the figure is closed—that is, a line is drawn from the last point specified back to the starting point—by the close (x) command. The path is then ended with the end (e) command. Note that according to the style-position attribute the given coordinates are in relative coordinate space; the true size is determined by the width and height specifications. Here, then, is the coding:

```
<v:shape id="rect01"
     fillcolor="gray" strokecolor="black"
     coordorigin="0 0" coordsize="200 200"
     style="position:relative;top:1;left:1;
     width:20; height:20"
     path="m 1,1 l 1,200, 200,200, 200,1 x e">
</v:shape>
```

You can use spaces as delimiters when specifying point coordinates, not just commas. For example, path="m 1 1 l 1 200 200 200 200 1 x e" is equivalent to path="m 1,1 l 1,200, 200,200, 200,1 x e". If you find that you are using zeroes in your path description, and also using commas as delimiters, consider omitting the zeroes. Thus, "path="m 10,10 l 20,10,20,,10, x e"" is equivalent to "path="m 10,10 l 20,10, 20,10, x e""

The <path> Element

Within a <shape> element, or even a <shapetype> element, a wholly contained <path> element can be inserted to serve as an alternative to the previously described path attribute in order to prescribe the custom-designed outline of a figure. Within the <path> element, you can specify the figure you wish to draw by using the attribute v and providing, as values for that attribute, an expression that includes a string of x,y coordinates plus one or more of the pen commands. At this point, the procedure is similar to the one described for the path attribute within <shape>. The v attribute defines the figure's outline by describing a path consisting of a sequence of straight lines and/or bézier curves. So, while the execution commands differ, the pen commands are the same as those listed previously in the path attribute section: m, l (the letter "ell"), c, x, e, t, r, v, nf, ns, ae, al, ar, at, wa, wr, qb, qx, and qy. The most common of those commands were summarized previously in Table 9-3.

The basic <shape> syntax, including the contained <path> element with the v attribute, is as follows:

```
<v:shape ...... >
     <v:path v="m 1,1 l 1,200, 200,200, 200,1 x e" .... />
</v:shape>
```

If a shape contains both a path attribute and a <path> element with a v attribute, the specifications within the <path> element prevail over any values specified for the path attribute in the <shape> element. The values 1, 200, and others define x and y values. The units are relative to the values specified for the coordsize attribute of the parent shape element.

The complete list of attributes you can use with the <path> element are: id, v, limo, fillok, strokeok, shadowok, arrowok, gradientshapeok, textpathok, and textboxrect. Using these attributes gives you more control and more features than if you had just used the path attribute in the <shape> element to draw your figure. For example, the <limo> attribute and the <formulas> element provide greater control of figure scaling.

If you do not require a complex figure, you can conserve resources by using the path attribute. Following is an example of the <path> element in action. It prescribes the shape of a rectangle similar to that drawn by the path attribute in the previous example.

```
<v:shape strokecolor="black" fillcolor="gray"
     coordorigin="0 0" coordsize="200 200"
     style="top:1;left:1;width:20;height:20">
          <v:path v="m 1,1 l 1,200, 200,200, 200,1 x e"/>
</v:shape>
```

9

Note that the v attribute within the <path> element does the same as the path attribute did in the previous path attribute example.

As with the path attribute, you can also use spaces as delimiters when specifying point coordinates, not just commas. For example, <v:path v="m 1 1 1 1 200 200 200 200 1 x e" /> is equivalent to <v:path v="m 1,1 1 1,200, 200,200, 200,1 x e"/>. If you are using zeroes in your path description while you are using commas as delimiters, consider omitting the zeroes. Thus, <v:path v="m 10,10 1 20,10,20,0,10,0 x e" /> is equivalent to <v:path v="m 10,10 1 20,10,20,,10, x e" />.

Using Predefined Shapes

The discussions of the <shape> and <path> elements indicate that you can spend a lot of effort when creating graphic figures with them. VML also provides a number of predefined shape elements that offer several advantages to the <shape>/<path> combination.

Table 9-4 lists VML's predefined shapes and provides examples. The examples are using a common local coordinate space, such as the one depicted in Figure 9-8.

Table 9-4 VML's predefined shapes

Element	Definition
<rect>	Draws a rectangle Rectangle example: <v:rect style='width:200pt;height:150pt' fillcolor="gray" coordorigin="50 500" strokecolor="black" strokeweight="1pt"/>
<roundrect>	Draws a rectangle with rounded corners; note the addition of the arcsize attribute, which accepts values between 0 (square corners) and 1.0 (semicircular) Rounded rectangle example: <v:roundrect style='width:400pt;height:250pt' arcsize="0.25" fillcolor="gray" strokecolor="black" strokeweight="2pt"/>
<line>	Draws a straight line Horizontal line example: <v:line from="150pt,400pt" to="400pt,400pt" strokecolor="black" strokeweight="3pt"> Vertical line example: <v:line from="350pt,500pt" to="350pt,700pt" strokecolor="black" strokeweight="4pt">
<polyline>	Draws the number of lines you specify, connected to one another in head-to-toe fashion Polyline example: <v:polyline points="100pt,300pt,500pt,350pt,550pt,500pt,650pt,600pt,800pt,500pt" strokecolor="black" strokeweight="4pt"/>
<oval>	Draws an oval (or a circle, depending on the attributes) Oval example: <v:oval style='width:100pt;height:300pt' fillcolor="gray" coordorigin= "500 0" strokecolor="black" strokeweight="1pt"/> Circle example: <v:oval style='width:200pt;height:200pt' fillcolor="white" coordorigin="650 400" strokecolor="black" strokeweight="1pt"/>
<image>	Inserts a specified image into a shape; there is an implied rectangle that is the same size as the image Image example: <v:image style="width:150pt;height:400pt" coordorigin="763 100" src="c:\home\username\WWWContent\TLSales\image\VMLwoman.gif" />
<curve>	Draws a curved line Curved line example: <v:curve style='position:relative' from="500,550" control1="600pt,650pt" control2="800pt,715pt" to="900pt,650pt" strokecolor="black" strokeweight="3pt"/>
<arc>	Draws an arc Arc example: <v:arc style='width:200pt;height:200pt' startangle="0" endangle="-90" coordorigin="775 0" strokecolor="black" strokeweight="2pt"/>

The advantages to using these predefined shapes are that they provide a method for drawing frequently used figures, and let you edit the shapes with more natural sounding syntax. For example, in the previous section, a rectangle was defined using a combination of the <v:shape> and <v:path> elements. With the predefined shape elements, you only need to use the <v:rect> element to define a rectangle.

With VML graphics, positive numbers are to the right of the left margin and run downward from the top margin. Figure 9-8 illustrates, using the examples from Table 9-4.

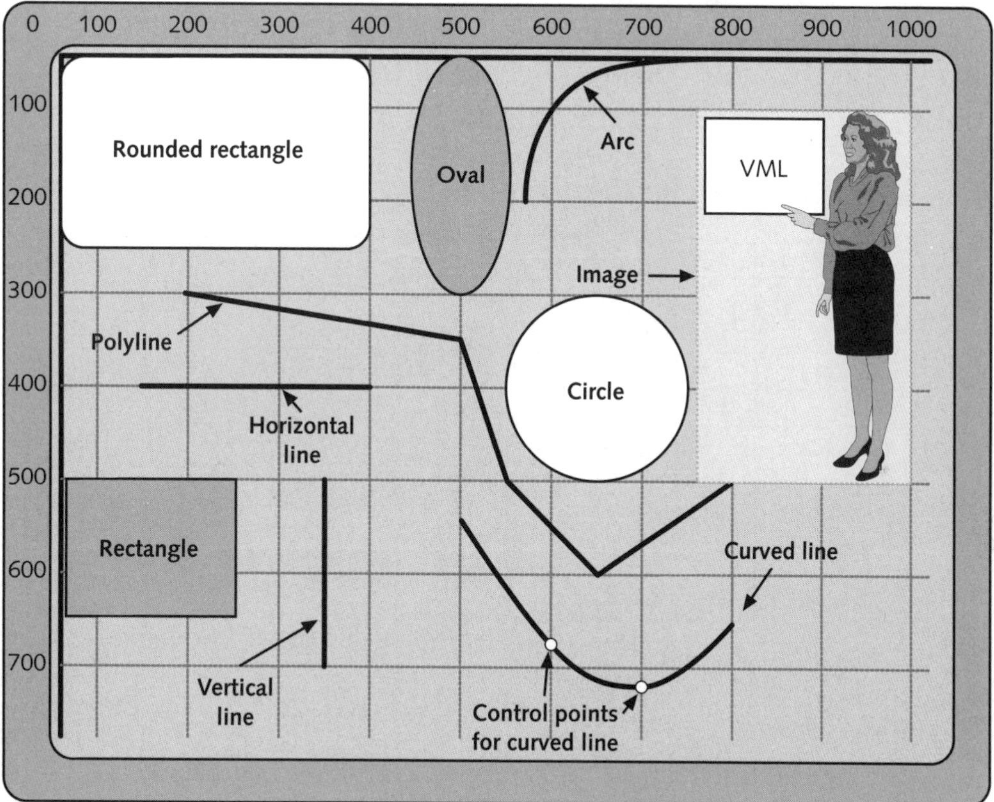

Figure 9-8 Predefined shapes

Table 9-5 lists the default attribute: value pairs (also called the default templates) for VML's predefined shapes. Notice that there are both common and specific attributes listed for each element type.

9

Table 9-5 Default VML templates for the predefined shapes

Attribute	Default Values for VML's Predefined Shapes						
	<rect>	<roundrect>	<line>	<oval>	<polyline>	<curve>	<arc>
id	null	null	null	null	null	null	null
href	null	null	null	null	null	null	null
target	null	null	null	null	null	null	null
class	null	null	null	null	null	null	null
title	null	null	null	null	null	null	null
alt	null	null	null	null	null	null	null
style	'visibility :visible'	'visibility :visible'	'visibility :visible'	'visibility :visible'	'visibility :visible'	'visibility :visible'	'visibility :visible'
opacity	"1.0"	"1.0"	"1.0"	"1.0"	"1.0"	"1.0"	"1.0"
chromakey	"null"	"null"	"null"	"null"	"null"	"null"	"null"
stroke	"true"	"true"	"true"	"true"	"true"	"true"	"true"
strokecolor	"black"	"black"	"black"	"black"	"black"	"black"	"black"
strokeweight	"1"	"0.75pt"	"1"	"0.75pt"	"1"	"1"	"0.75pt"
fill	"true"	"true"	"true"	"true"	"true"	"true"	"true"
fillcolor	"white"	"white"	"white"	"white"	"white"	"white"	"white"
print	"true"	"true"	"true"	"true"	"true"	"true"	"true"
coordsize	"1000, 1000"	"1000, 1000"	"1000, 1000"	"1000, 1000"	"1000, 1000"	"1000, 1000"	"1000, 1000"
coordorigin	"0 0"	"0 0"	"0 0"	"0 0"	"0 0"	"0 0"	"0 0"
arcsize		"0.2"					
from			"0 0"			"0 0"	
to			"10 10"			"10 10"	
position				"0 0"			
size				"100 100"			
points					"0 0 10 10 20 0"		
control1						"10 10"	
control2						"20 0"	
startangle							"0"
endangle							"90"

You use a predefined <rect> element in the first Hands-on project at the end of this chapter.

The <shapetype> Element

The previous section discussed several predefined shapes that may be used as convenient alternatives to explicitly declaring a <shape> element with a path element or attribute. However, on those occasions when a custom-designed figure must be repeatedly used, and when the predefined elements cannot serve the purpose, then the <shapetype> is utilized.

The <shapetype> element defines a figure that is used elsewhere—likely more than once—in your VML document. That is, <shapetype> is used to define the prototype definition of a desired figure. Here is <shapetype>'s syntax:

```
<v:shapetype id="envelope" coordsize="10 10" >
   <v:path v="m 1,1 l 1,5,4,8,7,5,1,5,7,1,7,5,7,1, x e"
      textboxrect="0,2,8,4" fillcolor="red"
      strokecolor="blue"... />
</v:shapetype>
```

Note that you must specify an ID attribute, the attribute name you use later with a <shape> element, to draw a copy of the figure where you want to place one. Remember that the order cannot be changed: the <shapetype> must appear before the figure is drawn.

Where you want to draw the figure, use syntax resembling the following:

```
<v:shape type="envelope" fillcolor="white"
      strokecolor="black"...>
</v:shape>
```

Thus, the <shape> element references a specific <shapetype> element by using a type attribute the value of which—although it is just a name in this example—is actually a relative URL pointing to the specifications within the <shapetype> element.

The <shapetype> element does not cause the figure to be drawn, but only contains the specifications for the figure. When you insert the subsequent and corresponding <shape> element(s), the figure is drawn. Also, in the <shape> syntax, the fillcolor and strokecolor attributes are specified as white and black, respectively. Specifying different values in the <shape> element overrides the values originally specified in the <shapetype> element. You can also alter other aspects of the figure by setting or changing other property attributes within the <shape> element.

Placement of VML Figures

Placing VML figures on a Web page involves answering two questions: what strategy do you use to place them, and once they are in place, how can you fine-tune their positions, especially with respect to one another?

9

There are three VML positioning strategies: static positioning, absolute positioning, and relative positioning. Sometimes placement gives rise to another issue: what if two or more figures overlap? How do you specify which is on top, in the middle, and on the bottom? At that point, z-indexing helps. Finally, what if a figure is to be inserted, but you want to flip it or rotate it? VML provides methods for those maneuvers, too.

All these concepts involve the style attribute in the figure's start tag. That style attribute complies with the syntax described in the W3C's Cascading Style Sheets, Level 2 Recommendation of May 1998.

Static Positioning

VML's default position style is **static positioning**, which instructs browsers to position the shape at the current point in the text flow and ignore any top or left settings there might be in the style attribute.

To illustrate, in the following VML document coding, recognize that the prescribed blue circle is positioned immediately after the text "Place the blue circle here." but before the term "OK?".

```
<body>
Place the blue circle here.
<v:oval style='width:80pt;height:80pt' fillcolor="blue"
   strokecolor="blue" strokeweight="4pt" />
OK?
</body>
```

Using that code, the figure is displayed when and where it is read by the application, just like an inline image. However, on most occasions, you probably want to place figures and images in specific locations. The next sections tell you how to do that.

Absolute Positioning

If you set the value of the style attribute in the figure's start tag to position:absolute, (indicating to the application that you are using **absolute positioning**) the application observes the subsequent attributes you add, as you place the figure's containment box a specified distance from the top left corner (the base point) of its parent element (the positioned element that contains the shape).

For example, in the previous sample of VML code, the blue circle is contained within the <body> element (that is, within the entire Web page). Its base point, then, is at the top left corner of the Web page. Now alter the previous code until it reads like the following sample.

```
<body>
Place the blue circle here.
  <v:oval style='position:absolute;left:20pt;top:10pt;
     width:80pt;height:80pt'
```

```
        fillcolor="blue" strokecolor="blue"
        strokeweight="4pt" />
OK?
</body>
```

Now that the code is altered, the circle's block level box is positioned exactly 20 points to the right and 10 points down with respect to the top left corner of the Web page.

Because you have positioned the figure with the absolute designation, it is not considered part of the text flow. So, it is not likely to be between "Place the blue circle here." and "OK?"

The precise positioning of figures may be absolute or relative. One exception is a figure within a <group> element. Then, precise positioning must be absolute and done with respect to the top left of the parent group.

Relative Positioning

9

With **relative positioning**, you can place (i.e., offset) a figure's block level box in a precise position relative to the current point—the base point—in the text flow. The offset distance is determined by the top and left settings in the style attribute in the figure's start tag. This time, remember that the containing box once again (like it did in VML's default static approach) takes up space in the text flow.

Following the current blue circle example, with the following VML code, the blue circle is positioned 50 points to the left and 15 points lower with respect to the current point in the text flow.

```
<body>
Place the blue circle here.
  <v:oval style='position:relative;left:50pt;top:15pt
     width:80pt;height:80pt' fillcolor="blue"
     strokecolor="blue"
     strokeweight="4pt" />
OK?
</body>
```

Controlling Overlap with the z-index

Occasionally, one figure overlaps another, whether by design or accident. VML's default behavior is to place the figure that is listed last in the code on top of the figure(s) that are listed earlier. However, with VML, you can use the z-index specification in the style attribute of a figure's start tag to specify a layering hierarchy.

The value of the z-index specification can be a negative integer (e.g., -2), zero, or a positive integer (e.g., +3). The figure with the highest positive z-index value is displayed on top of the figures with lower positive z-index values. Or, in the words of the W3C, "positive numbers are in front of the screen. Negative numbers are behind the screen." Meanwhile, if two or more figures have the same z-index value, the layering reverts to default behavior and the figure that is listed last in the code appears on top. Z-indexes can also be applied to <shapetype> and <group> elements.

For example, in the following VML representation, from the respective z-indexes you can see that the blue circle is displayed on top of another figure, a green rectangle.

```
<body>
   <v:oval style='position:relative;left:50pt;top:15pt;
           width:80pt;height:80pt;z-index:3'
           fillcolor="blue" strokecolor="blue"
           strokeweight="4pt" />
   <v:rect style='position:relative;left:50pt;top:15pt;
      width:100pt; height:60pt; z-index:0'
      fillcolor="green" strokecolor="green"
      strokeweight="3pt" />
</body>
```

If you reverse the z-index values, as shown below, the green rectangle is moved to the top.

```
<body>
   <v:oval style='position:relative;left:50pt;top:15pt;
       width:80pt;height:80pt;z-index:0'
       fillcolor="blue" strokecolor="blue"
       strokeweight="4pt" />
   <v:rect style='position:relative;left:50pt;top:15pt;
       width:100pt; height:60pt; z-index:3'
       fillcolor="green" strokecolor="green"
       strokeweight="3pt" />
</body>
```

This technique is also applied to the insertion of a background graphic. For example, if you want the walking stickman to appear in the background on your page, give it a negative z-index value, as follows:

```
<body>
   <v:image style='position:absolute;left:20pt;top:10pt;
      width:400pt;height:400pt; z-index:-3'
      src="c:\home\username\WWWContent\TLSales\
      images\stickman.gif" />
</body>
```

By supplying a negative integer and absolute positioning, you place the graphic in the background and make it independent from the text flow.

Rotating Images

At times you may need to rotate an object or a figure on your page. For example, an airline may want to show a background graphic of an aircraft climbing into the sky. At such times, you specify a value for rotation in the style attribute. The values you specify for a figure rotation are clockwise or counterclockwise degrees about the figure's center, or its axis. The number specified indicates the degrees of rotation. If the number is positive, the rotation is clockwise; if negative, counterclockwise.

Here is a simple airline example:

```
<body>
Everybody likes a summer holiday! Come fly with us!
     <v:image style='position:absolute;left:20pt;top:10pt;
     width:400pt;height:400pt; z-index:-3;
     rotation=-35' src="c:\home\username\WWWContent\
     globeair\images\boeing767.gif"/>
</body>
```

Figure 9-9 illustrates the airline example.

Figure 9-9 Rotation movement

Flipping Images

Sometimes an image fits better or looks better if it is flipped on the page. For example, a figure may fit better with the text, or the posture of someone in a picture may look more dynamic, if they are oriented differently. At these times, use the flip specification within the style attribute. The value you specify for flip dictates whether the figure rotates about its x axis or its y axis, according to Table 9-6.

Table 9-6 Values for the flip specification

Value	Description
x	Invert the figure's x ordinates (i.e., flip the figure about its y axis)
y	Invert the figure's y ordinates (i.e., flip the figure about its x axis)

Figure 9-10 illustrates these movements.

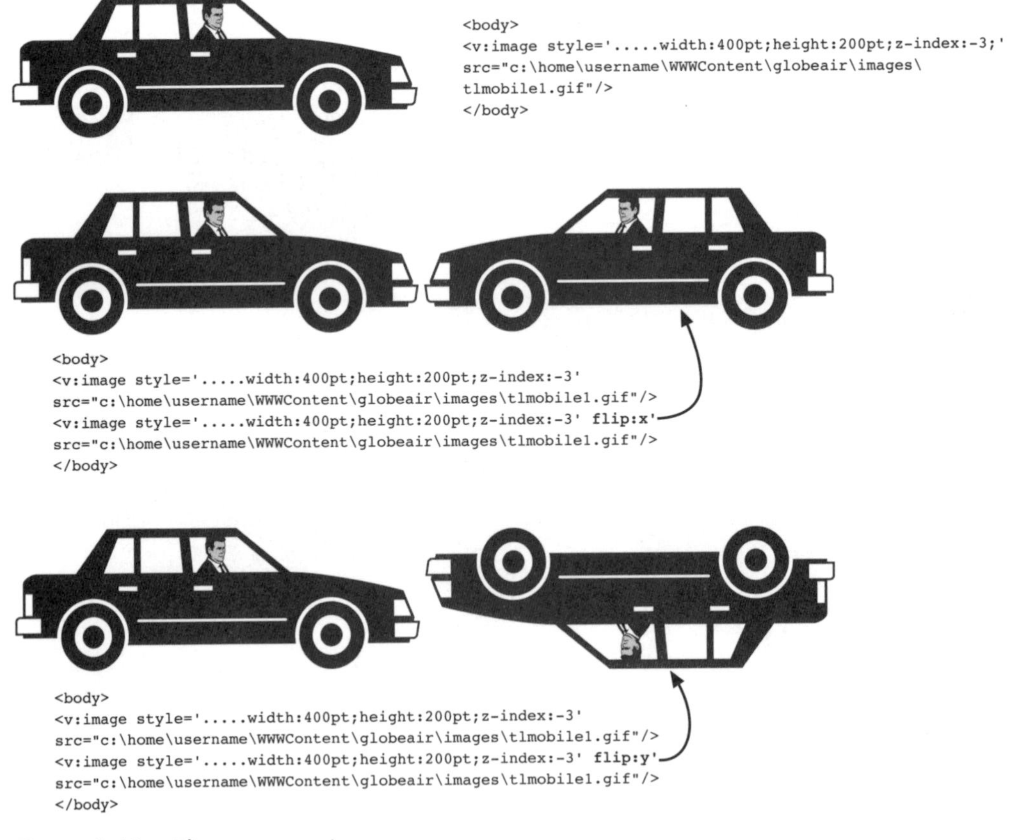

Figure 9-10 Flip movements

Remember that you can also specify both x *and* y for flip.

ALTERING IMAGES

There are several approaches used to alter the appearance of figures drawn with VML:

- Adding color to VML figures with the style attribute
- Changing the fill aspects of VML figures with the <fill> element
- Increasing or decreasing the scale of figures (i.e., scaling them up or down) with the style attribute

In the next few sections, each approach is discussed in turn.

Adding Color to Shapes

There are three ways to specify colors in VML:

- By using the predefined color names; VML observes the HTML 4.0 predefined color names, listed in Table 9-7
- By specifying the RGB function
- By specifying the Hexadecimal value

Table 9-7 HTML 4.0 named colors

No.	Name of Color	Hexadecimal Value	No.	Name of Color	Hexadecimal Value
1	Aqua	#00FFFF	9	Navy	#000080
2	Black	#000000	10	Olive	#808000
3	Blue	#0000FF	11	Purple	#800080
4	Fuchsia	#FF00FF	12	Red	#FF0000
5	Gray	#808080	13	Silver	#C0C0C0
6	Green	#008000	14	Teal	#008080
7	Lime	#00FF00	15	White	#FFFFFF
8	Maroon	#800000	16	Yellow	#FFFF00

Table 9-8 illustrates the three methods at work in the description of a predefined rectangle. In the table, the color terms are bold for emphasis.

Table 9-8 Color specification examples

No.	Method	Example Rectangle Syntax
1	Using predefined color names	<v:rect style='width:200pt;height:150pt' fillcolor="**red**" coordorigin="-600 75" strokecolor="**black**" strokeweight="1pt"/>
2	Specifying the RGB function	<v:rect style='width:200pt;height:150pt' fillcolor="**rgb(255,0,0)**" coordorigin="-600 75" strokecolor="**rgb(0,0,0)**" strokeweight="1pt"/>
3	Specifying the hexadecimal value	<v:rect style='width:200pt;height:150pt' fillcolor="**#FF0000**" coordorigin="-600 75" strokecolor="**#000000**" strokeweight="1pt"/>

Changing the Fill of VML Figures with the <fill> Element

In several examples in this chapter, the fillcolor attribute has been inserted into start tags to generally specify the color of the figure. But, there are times when you may want to alter the way the colors are treated. When that happens, the fillcolor, strokecolor, strokeweight, and other attributes do not provide the options you need. That is when you use a separate element, <fill>. In the next few sections, you learn how the <fill> element improves the appearance of your VML figures.

The fill element has nineteen attributes: alignshapes, angle, aspect, color, color2, colors, focus, focusposition, focussize, id, method, on, opacity, opacity2, origin, position, size, src and type. Table 9-9 lists common <fill> attributes.

Table 9-9 Commonly used <fill> attributes

Attribute Names	Explanation
angle	The angle along which a fill gradient is directed (default = 0)
color, color2, colors	color sets the fill color (default = white); color2 sets a secondary fill color, for patterns (default = white); colors sets intermediate colors in a gradient (default = null)
focusposition, focussize	For radial gradients; focusposition sets the position of the innermost rectangle (default = 0,0); focussize sets the size of the innermost rectangle (default = 0,0)
id	Provides a unique identifier for the figure (default = null)
method	Sets the fill method; options are none, linear, sigma, or any (default = sigma)
origin	Specifies the origin, relative to the upper left of the image (default = auto, the center of the image)
size	Specifies the size of the image (default = auto)
src	Provides the URI of an image to insert for image and pattern fills (default = null)
type	Specifies the fill type; options are solid, gradient, gradientradial, tile, pattern, or frame (default = solid)

Most of the attributes are fairly straightforward. The next few sections show some of them in action.

Creating Gradient Fills

Gradient fills are just a progression from one color to another across the image. For gradient-filled images, you have to specify a value for the type attribute within the <fill> subelement which, in turn, is wholly contained within the image's element. You may also wish to specify additional attributes like "method", "color2", "focus", and "angle". Meanwhile, there are two types of gradient fills available to you: a normal gradient and the gradientradial. Each is mentioned separately.

Following is an example of a normal gradient fill:

```
<body>
     <v:oval style='position:relative;left:50pt;top:15pt;
     width:80pt;height:80pt;z-index:0' fillcolor="black"
     strokecolor="white" strokeweight="1pt" >
          <v:fill method="sigma" angle="30"
             type="gradient" />
     </v:oval>
</body>
```

The example is a circle with a gradient ranging from white to black across it at an angle of 30 degrees.

A gradientradial fill employs an image which, as a fill, contains a small rectangle of one color. The outer regions of the image are another color. The gradient occurs as the fill changes color, beginning at the small rectangle, out to the color of the outer region. The following example is the same circle with a radial gradient ranging from white at the top left down across the image to black at an angle of 30 degrees.

```
<body>
     <v:oval style='position:relative;left:50pt;top:15pt;
     width:80pt;height:80pt;z-index:0' fillcolor="black"
     strokecolor="white" strokeweight="1pt" >
          <v:fill method="sigma" angle="30"
             type="gradientradial" />
     </v:oval>
</body>
```

In the next example, the smaller rectangle is placed offset in the circle, creating a highlight spot.

```
<body>
  <v:oval style='position:relative;left:50pt;top:15pt;
     width:80pt;height:80pt;z-index:0' fillcolor="black"
     strokecolor="white" strokeweight="1pt" >
          <v:fill method="sigma" angle="45" focus="100%"
          focusposition=".25, .75" focussize="0,0
          type="gradientradial" />
  </v:oval>
</body>
```

Creating Pattern Fills

In order to create a pattern fill, you must first have a pattern stored in an image file. Then, in the <fill> element, you set the type attribute value to "pattern", and provide a "src" (source location) attribute with a value that must be set to the URI location of the image file. Further, "pattern" allows you to repeat an image, and specify custom fill colors.

In this next example, the smaller rectangle is placed more toward the center of the circle, creating a highlight spot.

```
<body>
  <v:oval style='position:relative;left:50pt;top:15pt;
     width:80pt;height:80pt;z-index:0'
     fillcolor="white" strokecolor="gray"
     strokeweight="1pt" >
          <v:fill type="pattern"
          src="c:\home\username\WWWContent\
          tlsales\images\plaid.gif"/>
  </v:oval>
</body>
```

Creating Picture Fills

To create a picture fill, you must first have a picture stored in an image file. Then, in the <fill> element, you set the type attribute value to "frame", and provide a "src" (source location) attribute with a value that must be set to the URI location of the image file. However, "frame" does not allow you to repeat an image.

Here's an example:

```
<body>
     <v:oval style='position:relative;left:50pt;top:15pt
     width:80pt;height:80pt;z-index:0' fillcolor="white"
     strokecolor="gray" strokeweight="1pt" >
          <v:fill type="frame"
          src="c:\home\username\WWWContent\tlsales\images\
bikes.gif"/>
     </v:oval>
</body>
```

If you are considering adding a picture image to a VML document, also consider using the <imagedata> element to specify the image to insert instead of calling the image with the <fill> element. During the insertion process, you can then modify the image at the same time. The <imagedata> must be wholly contained within the element pertaining to the respective shape in which you want to insert the picture.

The <imagedata> has 19 attributes; the most commonly used attributes are listed in Table 9-10. The mandatory attribute is src; it must point to an image file for <imagedata> to be effective.

Table 9-10 Commonly used <imagedata> attributes

Attribute Name	Explanation	Attribute Name	Explanation
bilevel	Specifies whether an image is displayed in black and white	gain	Defines the intensity of all colors in an image
blackLevel	Specifies the intensity of black in an image	gamma	Defines the amount of contrast for an image
chromakey	Defines the color in the palette that is treated as transparent	grayScale	Specifies whether a picture is displayed in grayscale mode
cropbottom	Specifies the percentage of the picture to be removed from the bottom	href	Specifies the URL for an image
cropleft	Specifies the percentage of the picture to be removed from the left side	id	Specifies the unique identifier for an image
cropright	Specifies the percentage of the picture to be removed from the right side	src	Defines a source for the image
croptop	Specifies the percentage of the picture to be removed from the top	title	Defines the title of an image
detectmouseclick	Determines whether a mouse click can be detected		

The following example calls for a black and white picture called staff.gif to be included inside a rectangle on the page. 15% of the picture is removed (cropped) from the left side and the remaining picture is stretched to fit the shape.

```
<body>
     <v:rect style='position:relative;left:10pt;top:10pt
                   width:80pt;height:80pt;z-index:0' >
         <v:imagedata type="frame" bilevel="True"
grayscale="True"
          src="c:\home\username\WWWContent\tlsales\images\
staff.gif"
          cropleft=".2" />
     </v:rect>
</body>
```

Increasing or Decreasing Scale

To change the scale of a shape in VML, you respecify the size of the box containing the image. The image is then redrawn within the containing box, meeting your new specifications. To change the containing box size, you alter the values of the width and height in the style attribute, within the element start tag of the image. For example, in the previous section, a red rectangle with a black border was defined in the following manner:

```
<v:rect style='width:200pt;height:150pt' fillcolor="red"
coordorigin="-600 75" strokecolor="black" strokeweight=
"1pt"/>
```

If you want the rectangle to be twice as long and twice as high, you only need to double the width and height specifications, as in the following:

```
<v:rect style='width:400pt;height:300pt' fillcolor="red"
coordorigin="-600 75" strokecolor="black" strokeweight=
"1pt"/>
```

Using the <group> Element

If you have many figures that need to be manipulated, yet they can keep the same relative size and shape compared to one another, you would find it tedious to set their attributes individually. There would also be an increased risk of errors for one or more of the figures. It would be easier and less risky if you could just group them, and *then* specify attributes for the entire group. If you have experience with graphics drawing software, you already know the value of being able to group figures to form one image, so that you can more easily manipulate them. In most programs, the process is called "grouping". In VML, it is no different: the top-level <group> element is used to group several shapes so that they work as one image. This <group> element supports the same attributes as the <shape> element, with some exceptions. But, group only works with four subelements: <group>, <shapetype>, <shape>, and <lock>.

As discussed in previous chapters, placing elements inside other elements is called nesting. You can create a <group> element by nesting any number of other <shape> elements and <group> elements; there is no limit to the levels of nesting, nor to the number of elements or groups you can nest within a group. When a group is inside another group, it is called a nested group.

When elements are grouped, they use the local coordinate space of the group. The new group is then referenced by a single ID. These features allow the figure elements within the group to be scaled and moved together. For example, Figure 9-11 illustrates a two-level nested group in which:

- The helmet, lance, and shield shapes are combined to form the armor group

- The horse, saddle, and bridle shapes are combined to form the steed group
- The armor and steed groups, combined with the rider shape, form the knight group

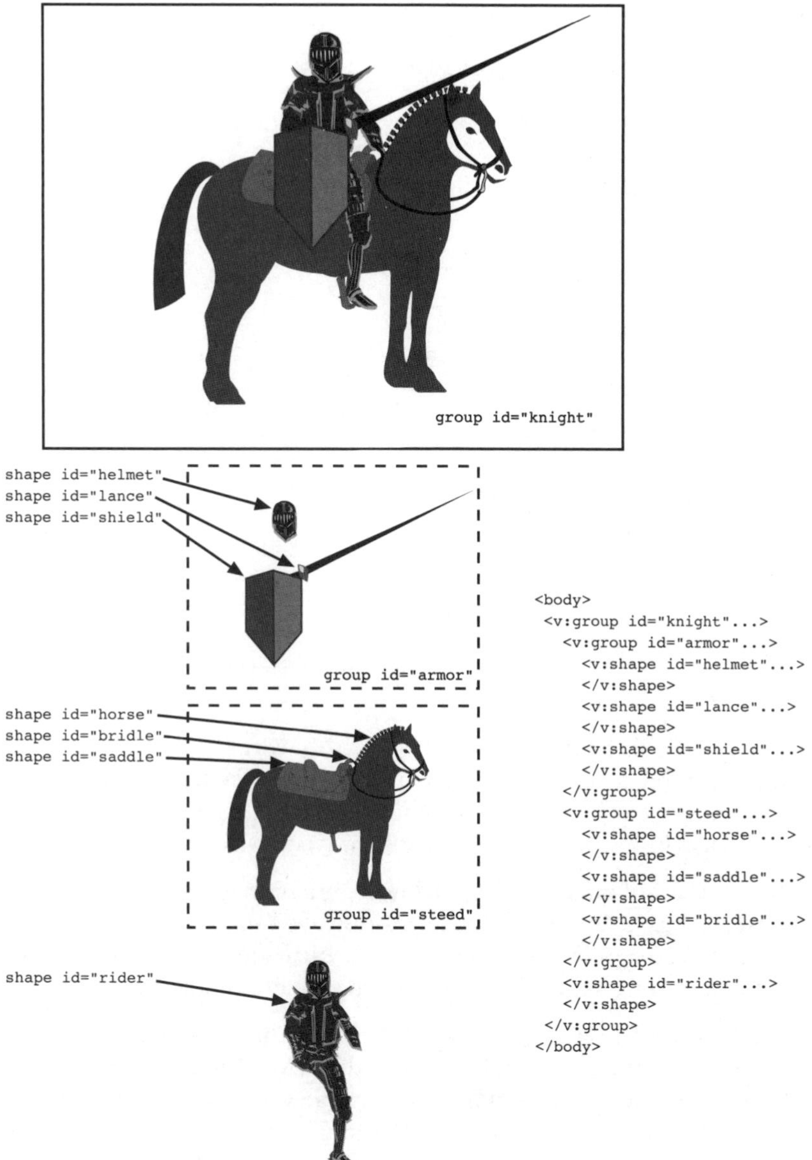
group id="knight"
shape id="helmet"
shape id="lance"
shape id="shield"
group id="armor"
shape id="horse"
shape id="bridle"
shape id="saddle"
group id="steed"
shape id="rider"
<body>
<v:group id="knight"...>
<v:group id="armor"...>
<v:shape id="helmet"...>
</v:shape>
<v:shape id="lance"...>
</v:shape>
<v:shape id="shield"...>
</v:shape>
</v:group>
<v:group id="steed"...>
<v:shape id="horse"...>
</v:shape>
<v:shape id="saddle"...>
</v:shape>
<v:shape id="bridle"...>
</v:shape>
</v:group>
<v:shape id="rider"...>
</v:shape>
</v:group>
</body>

Figure 9-11 Knight group components and code

The following lines of code, also displayed in Figure 9-11, build the basic structure of the knight group (to save time and preserve structural clarity, the shape details have been left out):

```
<body>
   <v:group id="knight"...>
      <v:group id="armor"...>
         <v:shape id="helmet" ...>
         </v:shape>
         <v:shape id="lance" ...>
         </v:shape>
         <v:shape id="shield" ...>
         </v:shape>
      </v:group>
      <v:group id="steed"...>
         <v:shape id="horse" ... >
         </v:shape>
         <v:shape id="saddle" ...>
         </v:shape>
         <v:shape id="bridle" ...>
         </v:shape>
      </v:group>
      <v:shape id="rider" ...>
      </v:shape>
   </v:group>
</body>
```

Chapter Summary

- More visual content is being transferred across the World Wide Web every day. That information must be displayed quickly while the use of system and network resources must be optimized. There has been technical progress: graphic conversion software, compression algorithms, and faster network hardware is always being created.
- There are two basic digital imaging technologies: bitmap graphics, where data corresponds bit for bit with the pixel patterns displayed on a screen or the dots printed on a page, and vector graphics, where mathematical algorithms are used to draw screen and printer images. Each has its advantages and disadvantages.
- The Vector Markup Language (VML), an XML application that is the subject of a 1998 W3C Note, is the most widespread of the XML-related graphic languages, although development and acceptance of Scalable Vector Graphics, already a W3C Recommendation, is accelerating. Since VML is an XML application, it is both open and standards based. It is also fully compliant with other W3C standards such as Cascading Style Sheets, HTML, and XHTML.

- Pure VML has no external bitmap files or other binary files to accommodate; an image can be generated using nothing but the VML language. But, bitmap data is still important, and can be combined with VML's vector data. Plus, there are limited adjustments that VML can provide to that bitmap data.
- You can produce VML documents using text editors, Microsoft Office 2000/XP applications, Microsoft VML Generator application (can be downloaded from the Web), and some non-Microsoft XML IDE's. But, for viewing VML pages, the only Web browser that currently supports VML is Microsoft Internet Explorer 5 and later versions, which have built-in VML support to produce vector-based graphics with no need for supplemental downloads or plug-ins. The proliferation of MS IE has made VML available to millions of users.
- Since VML is an application of XML, its syntax must be adhered to strictly. In a VML document, a minimum of two namespace declarations are necessary: the VML namespace and a default namespace for HTML (or XHTML). If you use Microsoft Office 2000/XP applications to generate VML objects, then you must add yet another Microsoft-related namespace declaration, because those applications add their own prefix. To take advantage of Microsoft IE "behaviors", VML documents require behavior declarations to be inserted in the <style> element. If you omit namespace declarations or behavior declarations, your VML images are displayed.
- VML cooperates with HTML and XHTML. With HTML, VML documents need not have a prolog like they would with XHTML. However, no matter what, a VML document must contain an <html> element which, in turn, consists of the <head> element and the <body> element.
- The <shape> and <path> elements are the most rudimentary of VML's building blocks and can be used to create almost any VML graphic. Most often, though, you use predefined shape elements, such as <line>, <oval>, <rect>, and others, to create your figures. However, if you need to use the same figure repeatedly and the predefined shapes do not help, then consider using the <shapetype> element to create custom shapes.
- There are three methods used to place images on a page: the (default) static positioning, absolute positioning, and relative positioning. If your images overlap, use z-indexing to control the layering. If you want to further alter the positioning of images, try the flip and rotation specifications.
- Three approaches used to alter the appearance of VML figures are: adding color to VML figures with the style attribute, changing their fill aspects with the <fill> element, and scaling them up or down with the style attribute. You can even fill a figure with patterns and pictures.
- Use the top-level element called <group> to combine figures and treat them as though they were one. There is no limit to the levels of this type of element nesting, nor to the total number of figures or other groups of elements that may be included in one <group>.

9

Review Questions

1. Bitmapped graphics and vector graphics consist of images made up of dot patterns. True or false?
2. Which of the following is not an advantage of vector graphics?
   a. better control over fine details
   b. faster downloads
   c. scalability
   d. smaller files mean storage and memory savings
   e. none of the above
3. VML is widespread because it has been incorporated into current versions of ________________.
4. Because VML uses existing HTML and Cascading Style Sheets (CSS) mechanisms, all top-level VML elements support the ________________ element.
   a. <crop>
   b. <prolog>
   c. <group>
   d. <style>
   e. all of the above
5. The VML specification document is a W3C ________________.
   a. specification
   b. note
   c. recommendation
   d. publication
   e. draft
6. VML may not have been the only vector graphics specification to be submitted to the W3C, but it was the first. True or false?
7. If you are considering using the latest W3C vector graphics-related Recommendation, it would be advisable to consult which of the following documents?
   a. the W3C Document Copyright Notice and License
   b. the W3C Software Copyright Notice and License
   c. scalable Vector Graphics 1.0
   d. the SVG Patent Statements
   e. all of the above
8. VML's advantages stem from its ________________ heritage and its ________________ affiliation.

9. VML documents follow both HTML and XHTML syntax. True or false?
10. Which of the following are necessary for all VML documents?
    a. the VML namespace declaration
    b. the Microsoft namespace, for Internet Explorer access
    c. a default namespace declaration
    d. all of the above
11. All declarations must appear in the start tag for the document's root <HTML> (or <html>, if you mean to comply with XHTML) element. True or False?
12. If your document is intended to be XHTML-compliant, which declaration must you use?
    a. `xmlns:v="urn:schemas-microsoft-com:vml"`
    b. `xmlns="http://www.w3.org/TR/REC-html40"`
    c. `xmlns="http://www.w3.org/1999/xhtml"`
    d. all of the above

13. To ensure that IE's VML behavior is used, insert the behavior declaration into the ________________.
14. If your VML graphics do not display, what are the first places in the VML document(s) that it is recommended you look first for errors?
    a. the behavior declaration
    b. the DOCTYPE definition
    c. the prolog
    d. the namespace declaration
    e. none of the above
15. VML applies a default template to every element. To override any particular default value, you must insert the name of the specific attribute, plus its new value, in the start tag of the respective element. True or false?
16. Which of the following are predefined shapes in VML?
    a. <formulas>
    b. <group>
    c. <rect>
    d. <path>
    e. <line>
17. The <shape> element only defines the containment box for the actual figure you eventually want to create. That containment box is also called a(n) ________________.

18. If you do not require a complex figure, then you might conserve resources by defining a figure's outline with a path attribute, as opposed to the <path> element. True or false?
19. On those occasions when a custom-designed figure must be used—and used repeatedly—and when the predefined elements can not serve the purpose, then consider creating a(n) ________________ element.
    a. <shapetype>
    b. <form>
    c. <prototype>
    d. <shape>
    e. <line>
20. Which of the following is VML's default position style?
    a. relative positioning
    b. static positioning
    c. absolute positioning
    d. vector positioning
    e. bitmap positioning
    f. none of the above
21. The figure with the highest positive z-index value is displayed on top of the figures with lower positive z-index values. True or false?
22. If the number you specify for a figure rotation specification is ________________, the rotation is clockwise.
23. If you want to flip a figure about its y axis, you specify "y" as the value for the flip specification. True or false?
24. Which of the following is the hexadecimal color code for black?
    a. #000000
    b. #FFFFFF
    c. #CCCCCC
    d. #BBBBBB
    e. #111111
    f. none of the above
25. You can create a(n) ________________ by nesting any number of <shape> elements and <group> elements.

HANDS-ON PROJECTS

Project 9-1

In this project, you configure a VML document. The only commercial browser that supports VML is Internet Explorer 5 or later, so you are not able to view your work with Netscape Navigator. Microsoft has implemented VML as an extension, called a behavior, that allows Internet Explorer to process VML instructions. All elements of the VML namespace are directed to the behavior for processing.

To configure VML, the document must explicitly declare the VML namespace and associate the namespace with the behavior. In this project, you configure a document to be able to process the vector shapes that you will add in the following projects.

These projects assume that your hard disk is drive C.

To set up the project files and create an HTML document:

1. In Windows Explorer, create a new folder called **Ch09** in C:\home\<yourname>.
2. Copy the **hot.gif** file located in the Ch09/Project_9-1 folder on your Data Disk into your C:/home/<yourname>/Ch09 folder.
3. Click **Start**, point to **Programs**, point to **XML Spy Suite**, and then click **XML Spy IDE**. The XML Spy window opens.
4. Click **File** on the menu bar, and then click **New**. The Create new document dialog box opens. Click **html HTML Document** and then click **OK**. The default source code for a new HTML document appears in the main window.
5. Click **File** on the menu bar, and then click **Save**. In the Save As dialog box, click the **Save in** list arrow to navigate to C:\home\<yourname>\Ch09. Type **coupon.html** in the File name text box, and then click **Save**.

Recall that two namespace declarations are required for a browser to properly render VML. The example that you build does not have to be XHTML compliant, so you declare the html40 namespace with the vml namespace in the HTML start tag.

In the HTML document, modify the root HTML element start tag to include the VML and default namespace declarations.

To configure the HTML document and add style tags:

1. At the beginning of the HTML document, modify the html tag so it appears as follows:

   ```
   <html xmlns:v="urn:schemas-microsoft-com:vml"
         xmlns="http://www.w3c.org/TR/REC-html40">
   ```

   Your document should appear similar to Figure 9-12.

9

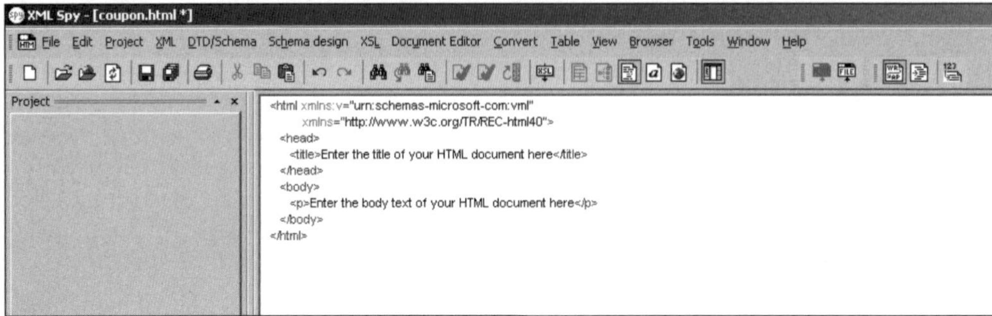

Figure 9-12

2. Replace the default TITLE data with the following:

```
<title>TLSales Coupon</title>
```

VML is defined in Internet Explorer 5+ as a default behavior. Behaviors provide a means for Web developers to extend the functionality of Internet Explorer; default behaviors are simply behaviors included with Internet Explorer. A behavior can be applied to a document using a STYLE element.

3. To ensure that the VML behavior is invoked, insert the following on the line immediately after the TITLE element:

```
<style>
        v\:* {behavior:url(#default#VML);}
</style>
```

This instructs the browser to pass all of the tags beginning with v: to the built-in rendering object. Your document should appear similar to Figure 9-13. If, later in the project, your VML code fails to render the vector images, ensure that the namespace and behavior declarations are correct.

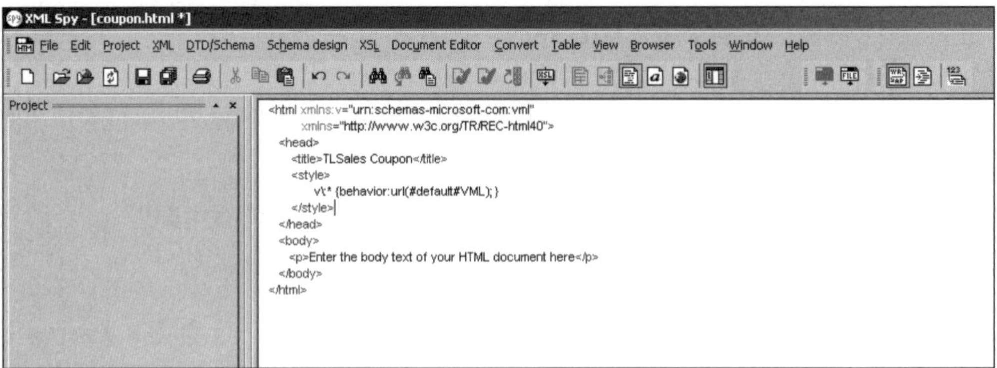

Figure 9-13

4. Click **File** on the menu bar, and then click **Save** to save your work.

Project 9-2

Now that you have an outline for a VML document, you are ready to create an online coupon using a predefined VML object. Customers can print or download this coupon to receive a discount of up to 15% on all products at a hypothetical store. Recall that the only commercial browser that supports VML is Internet Explorer 5 or higher, so you are not be able to view your work with Netscape Navigator.

If you have difficulty viewing shapes in Project 9-2, ensure that the namespace and the behavior declaration syntax is the same as described in Project 9-1.

To draw the coupon:

1. Now that the HTML document has been properly initialized for VML, you are now ready to start adding shapes. With the coupon.html document that you used in Project 9-1 still open in XML Spy, replace the default paragraph element, <p> ... </p>, in the HTML body with the following code to draw a rectangle:

```
<v:rect style= "width:325; height:175" fillcolor="yellow">
</v:rect>
```

   The code block defines a large yellow rectangle using the predefined rect VML shape. VML uses Cascading Style Sheet specifiers to indicate how the objects should appear. You learn more about cascading style sheets in Chapter 11, but for now, observe how the values of each attribute affects the presentation.

2. Within the rectangle element that you just added, type the following code to generate the "TLSales Coupon" text using the predefined VML textbox element.

```
<v:textbox style="font-size:24.0pt; text-align: center;">
        <p>TLSales Coupon</p>
        <p>15% of everything!</p>
        <p>Expires: Jan. 15, 2005</p>
</v:textbox>
```

   Your document should now resemble Figure 9-14.

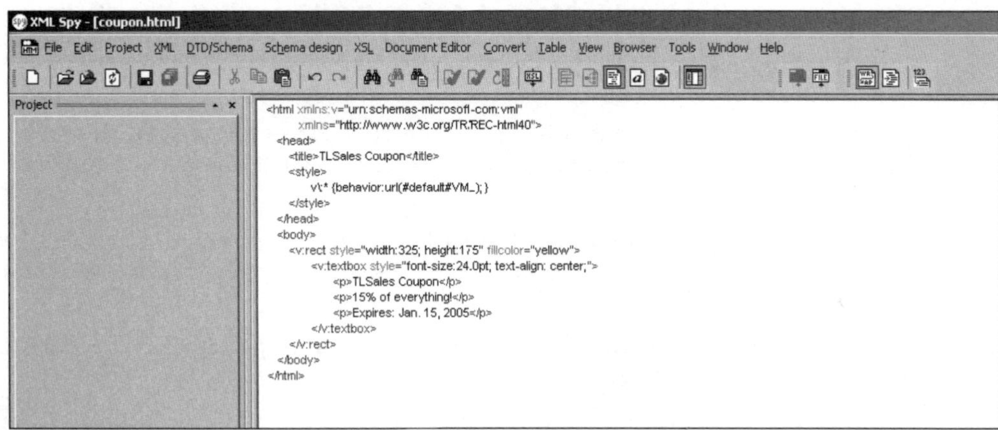

Figure 9-14

3. Click **File** on the menu bar, and then click **Save** to save your work.

   Before viewing the rendered objects in the browser, ensure that you have included the v: namespace prefix before the rect and textbox start and end tags. If you do not include the namespace prefix, Internet Explorer treats the elements as unknown tags and the objects do not render in the browser.

4. Click **View** on the menu bar, and then click **Browser view** to view the coupon. A yellow rectangle with text appears, similar to Figure 9-15.

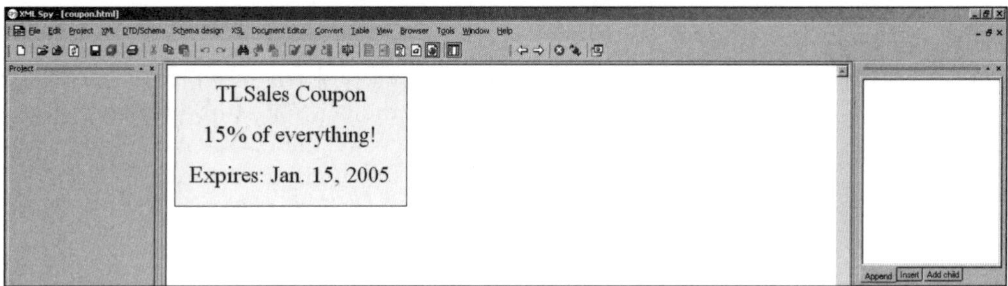
TLSales Coupon
15% of everything!
Expires: Jan. 15, 2005

Figure 9-15

Project 9-3

You can now add a shadow to the coupon and place a VML image in the document. The shadow is a gray rectangle that you should place slightly offset and below the yellow rectangle. You have to adjust the relative positioning and the z-index of the rectangle to properly place the shadow. An image is added above the coupon using a VML image element.

To add a shadow:

1. With the coupon.html document that you used in Project 9-2 still open in XML Spy, switch to Text view, and immediately following the rect element end-tag, </v:rect>, type:

   <v:rect style="width:325; height:175;" fillcolor="#cccccc" />

   The code adds a light gray rectangle to the document the same size as the yellow rectangle.

2. Click **View** on the menu bar, and then click **Browser view** to examine the document using browser view. Notice that the rectangle follows the yellow rectangle in the text flow.

3. To place the rectangle in the proper location, click **View** on the menu bar, and then click **Text view** to return to the source code view. Revise the line from the last step to look like the following:

   <v:rect style="**position:relative; top:2; left:-323;** width:325; height:175;"
   fillcolor="#cccccc" />

   The new rectangle is placed 298 units to the right and 2 units below relative to the default position in the text flow. This is called relative positioning.

4. Click **View** on the menu bar, and then click **Browser view** to examine the document using the browser view. Click the **All on/off** button on the toolbar. Notice that the gray rectangle is on top of the yellow rectangle.

   There are two ways that you can reverse the overlap. The first is to switch the order of the two rectangle elements in the HTML document, or you adjust the z-index. The z-index determines the order that shapes overlap one another. By default, the z-index of a shape is 0.

5. Click **View** on the menu bar, and then click **Text view** to return to the source code view of the document. Update the line from the last step to the following:

   <v:rect style="position:relative; top:2; left:-323; width:325; height:175;
   z-index:-1;" fillcolor="#cccccc" />

   Your HTML document should look similar to Figure 9-16.

6. Click **View** on the menu bar, and then click **Browser view** to return to the browser view to review the change. Click the **All on/off** button on the toolbar. The rendered document should look like Figure 9-17. Notice that the gray rectangle is positioned slightly offset and beneath the yellow rectangle. By setting the z-index of the rectangle to -1, you have set the gray rectangle behind the yellow.

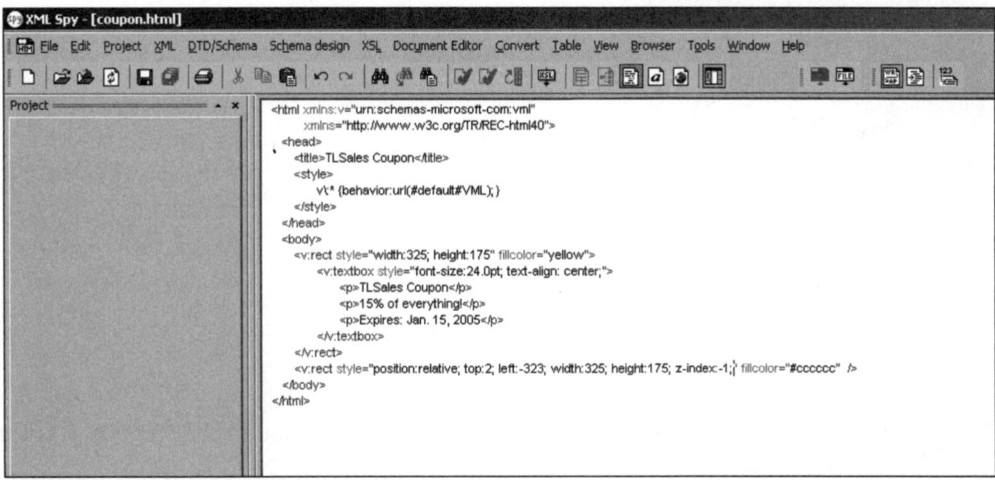

Figure 9-16

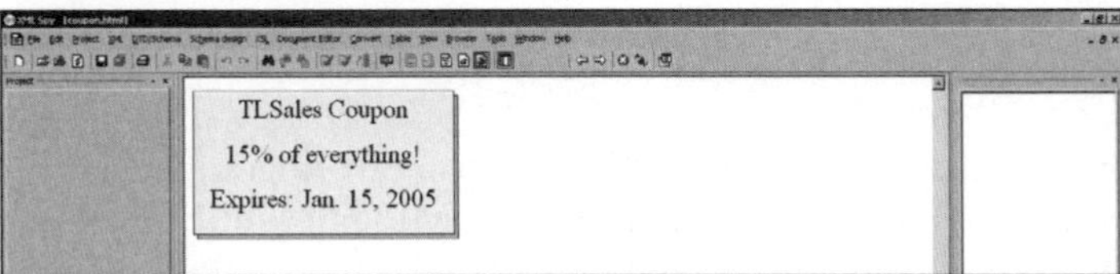

Figure 9-17

7. Click **View** on the menu bar, and then click **Text view** to return to the source code view of the document.

To add an image:

1. You now add an animated gif image above the coupon to add some action to the page. In between the body start tag, <body>, and the rect start tag, <v:rect>, add the following code:

   **<v:image style="width:55pt;height:34pt" src="hot.gif" />
**

   The image is added using a VML predefined image element. The height and width of the image is defined in the style attribute, and the image source is identified by the src attribute.

2. Click **View** on the menu bar, and then click **Browser view** to view the updated coupon. Click the **All on/off** button on the toolbar. You now see the image above the yellow rectangle, similar to Figure 9-18.

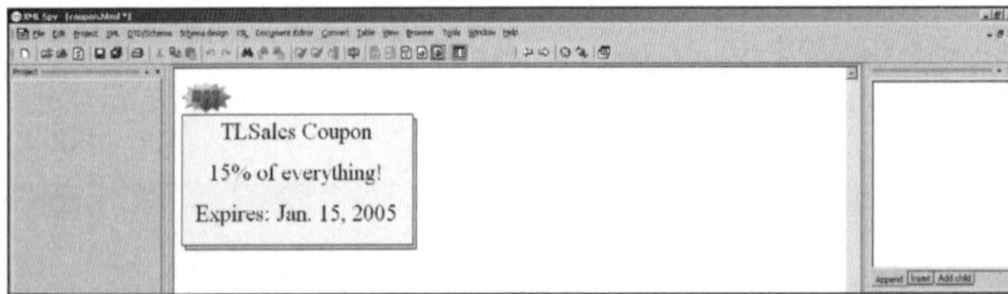
TLSales Coupon
15% of everything!
Expires: Jan. 15, 2005

Figure 9-18

   Notice how the code for the image is added before the code for the yellow rectangle, and it appears above the rectangle in the browser. This is called Static Positioning and is the default positioning method for VML. The images are placed in the current position of the text flow.

3. To return to the source code, click **View** on the menu bar, and then click **Text view**. Save your changes.
4. To view the document using Internet Explorer, click **Start**, and point to **Programs** (point to **All Programs** in Windows XP), and then click **Internet Explorer**.
5. In the Address bar, type **C:\home\<yourname>\Ch09\coupon.html** to view coupon.html in Internet Explorer.
6. Close the Internet Explorer window.

Hands-on Project

Project 9-4

In Project 9-3, you added a VML predefined shape to your document. There are a limited number of predefined shapes available through VML, but you can create any object that you wish using the custom shape element. In this project, you create an octagon using a path element within a shape element and give it a gradient fill. You also add a brief text message to the custom shape.

To add a custom shape and a gradient:

1. With the coupon.html document that you used in Project 9-3 still open in XML Spy, directly below the second rect element, type the following code:

   ```
   <br/>
   <v:shape style="position:relative; top:-30; left:225; width:20mm;
   height:20mm"
           coordsize="17 17" fillcolor="red"
           strokecolor="#999999" strokeweight="3">
   </v:shape>
   ```

   The line break, <br/>, moves the text flow to the line below the yellow rectangle. The shape is confined to a containing box declared in the style attribute to be 20mm x 20mm. Within the containing box, there is an 18 x 18 matrix of equally spaced divisions (0 - 17) defined by the coordsize attribute. The color of the shape is initialized using the strokecolor attribute, and the border color is defined to be a shade of gray with the hexadecimal value of 999999. The width of the border is declared using the strokeweight attribute.

   The custom shape is positioned relative to the text flow position. For now, leave the top and left values set to zero.

   If you were to preview the code that you have added, there would be no additional visual objects in the browser. You need to add a path element to the custom shape to define the object drawing rules.

2. Within the shape element, type the following code:

   ```
   <v:path v="m 5,0 l 12,0 17,5 17,12 12,17 5,17 0,12 0,5 x e " />
   ```

   The path is drawn by a virtual pen that is controlled by a sequence of commands read left to right within the v attribute. The first command in the sequence is m 5,0. (Author's note: The x and y coordinates are separated with a comma, whereas commands and coordinate pairs are separated by spaces. This is by convention; either a comma or a space can separate all items within the v attribute.) The command tells the VML processor to move the pen to the coordinate (5, 0). The next command is the letter l, signifying that a line should be drawn from the current coordinate to (12, 0). The line continues joining coordinate pairs until the x command terminates the line. Finally, the e command ends the line.

3. Click **View** on the menu bar, and then click **Browser view** to view the updated coupon. Click the **All on/off** button on the toolbar. You now see the octagon below the yellow rectangle, similar to Figure 9-19.

9

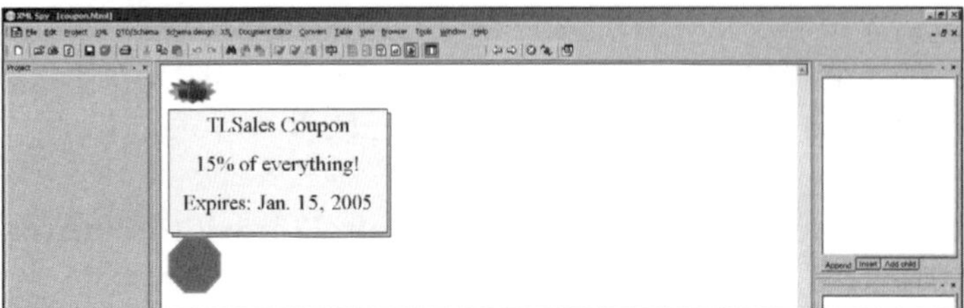
TLSales Coupon
15% of everything!
Expires: Jan. 15, 2005

Figure 9-19

4. Click **View** on the menu bar, and then click **Text view** to return to the source code view.
5. You can add a gradient fill to the octagon that you created. Type the following code directly under the path element within the shape element:

   ```
   <v:fill method="linear" angle="30" type="gradient" />
   ```

   The fill element is used for any type of fill. In this case, you created a linear gradient, set at a 30-degree angle, transitioning from red to white.
6. Click **View** on the menu bar, and then click **Browser view** to view the updated coupon. Click the **All on/off** button on the toolbar. You now see the octagon with a gradient fill.

To add text:

1. Click **View** on the menu bar, and then click **Text view** to return to the source code view.
2. In the same manner that you added text to the yellow rectangle, you add text to the octagon. Immediately following the fill element in the shape element, add the following code:

   ```
   <v:textbox style="text-align:center; font-weight: bold; color:#333333;">
           <h3>Stop and Save!</h3>
   </v:textbox>
   ```

   This code block adds a string to the custom shape. The text is centered in the containing box of the shape, bold and a dark gray color, defined by the hexadecimal color value 333333.
3. Click **View** on the menu bar, and then click **Browser view** to view the updated coupon. Click the **All on/off** button on the toolbar. The rendered document should look like Figure 9-20. Click **View** on the menu bar, and then click **Text view** to return to the source code.

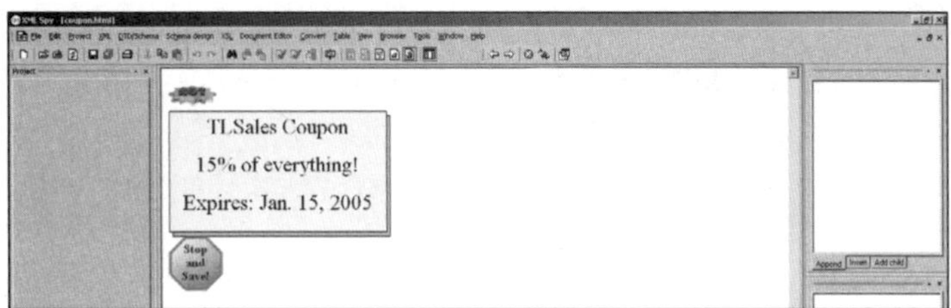
TLSales Coupon
15% of everything!
Expires: Jan. 15, 2005

Figure 9-20

Project

Project 9-5

In Project 9-4, you created a custom shape and added it to your document. You may want to use the shape multiple times, varying the scale, orientation, and position. You can achieve this by using VML shape types to define a template for a shape, and then inserting it into the document using shape elements. In this project, you create a triangle shape and combine two triangles to create a star shape. You manage the triangles together using a group element and then use a combination of relative and absolute positioning to adjust the location of the stars.

To add a custom shape type:

1. With the coupon.html document that you used in Project 9-4 still open in XML Spy, create the shape's prototype by typing the following code immediately after the shape end tag, </v:shape>:

```
<v:shapetype id="triangle" coordsize="12 12"
        fillcolor="red" strokecolor="red">
</v:shapetype>
```

   The shapetype element is identified by an id that will be used as a reference by the shape element. The shape is defined within a 13 x 13 matrix, but as you will see, the scale of the object is determined by the declaration of the size style properties in the style element.

2. Add the path of the shape by adding the following path element within the shapetype element:

```
<v:path v="m 6,0 l 12,10 0,10 x e "/>
```

   The shape prototype is now defined, but do not render in the document until you reference it using a shape element.

3. To add the shape prototype to the document, immediately following the shapetype end tag, </v:shapetype>, add the following code.

```
<v:shape type="#triangle" style="position:relative; left:0; top:0;
        width:12; height:12;" />
```

   Notice that the shape element references the shapetype id in the type attribute. Because an HTML document is parsed sequentially, the shapetype element must precede any referring shape elements.

4. Add a second shape immediately below the previous by typing:

```
<v:shape type="#triangle" style="position:relative; left:0; top:1;
      width:12; height:12; flip:y;" />
```

   The shape is similar to the first shape, with the exception that it is flipped about the y-axis and is lowered by 250 units.

5. So that you can move and scale the shapes together, group the shapes by wrapping the following group element around the two shape elements:

```
<v:group coordsize="12 12" style="position:absolute; top:25; left:275;
      width:60; height:60">
      <--existing triangle shape elements -->
</v:group>
```

   The scale and position for both shape elements are now defined by the single group element. Notice that the grouped shapes are placed using absolute positioning style property. Your code should look similar to Figure 9-21.

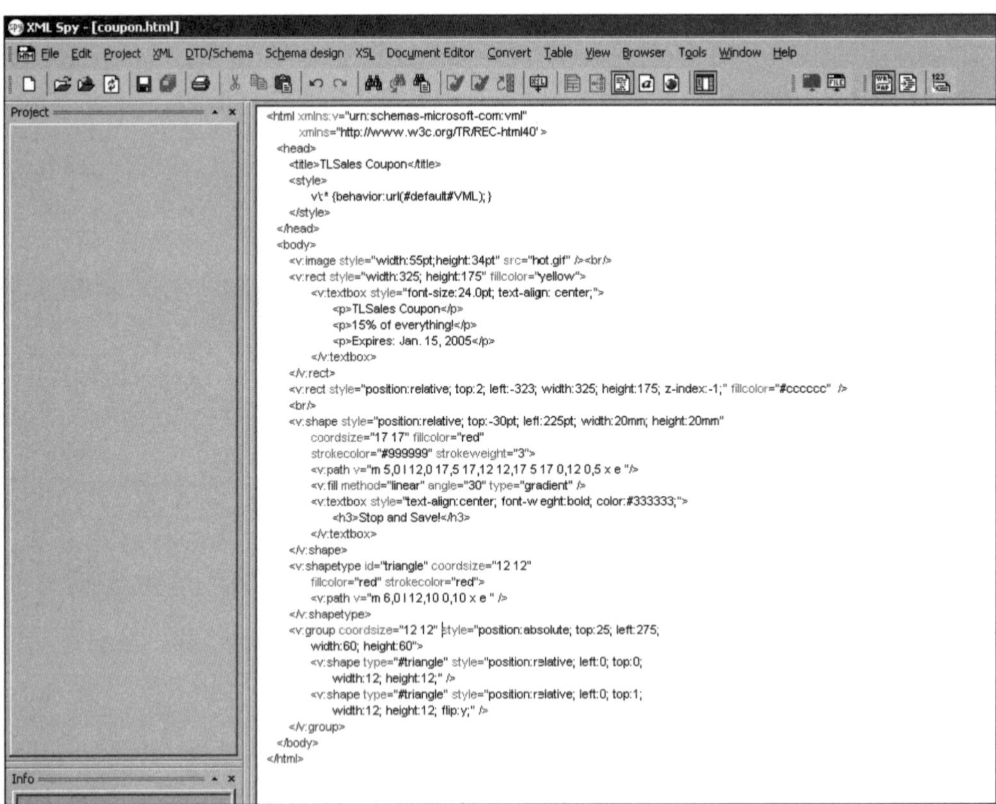

Figure 9-21

6. Click **View** on the menu bar, and then click **Browser view**. The rendered document appears in the main window and should look similar to Figure 9-22.

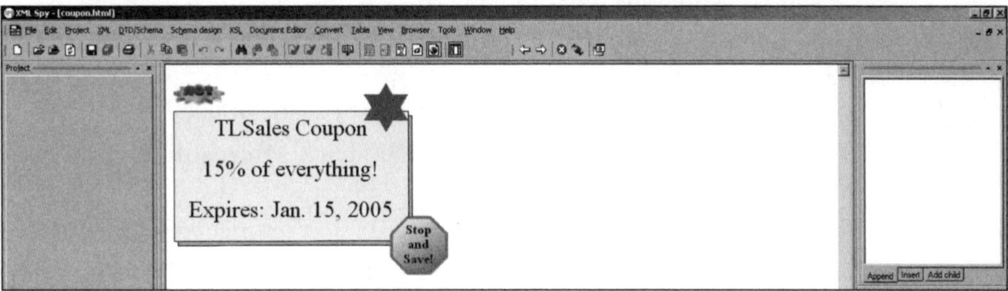

Figure 9-22

Notice that the two triangles are overlapped with one positioned upside-down over the other, creating a star. Also notice that the star is not positioned relative to the text flow, but has been placed relative to the top left corner of the browser window. This is called absolute positioning.

7. Click **View** on the menu bar, and then click **Text view** to return to the source code.

To add another grouped shape:

1. Drag to select the entire group element, including all of the child shape elements. Press **Enter**, click **Edit** on the menu bar, and then click **Copy** to copy the code block.
2. Position the cursor following the group element end tag, </v:group>, click **Edit** on the menu bar, and then click **Paste** to paste the code.
3. Update the attributes of the group element start tag as follows:

   <v:group coordsize="12 12" style="position:absolute; **top:225; left:50; width:30; height:30"**>

   The placement is modified, and the size is reduced.
4. Click **View** on the menu bar, and then click **Browser view**. The rendered document appears in the main window.

   Notice how, without modifying the shape types or the shapes, the second smaller star has been placed below the yellow rectangle. A few changes to the group element attributes modify the aggregated shape as required.
5. Click **File** on the menu bar, and then click **Save** to save your work.
6. Click **File** on the menu bar, and then click **Exit** to exit XML Spy.

Project 9-6

In this project, you observe how other Microsoft applications use VML to model vector images. You use Microsoft Word to draw some shapes, and then examine the HTML that is produced. You must have Microsoft Word installed on your computer to complete this project.

To start Microsoft Word and add vector shapes to a document:

1. Click **Start**, point to **Programs**, and then click **Microsoft Word**. The Microsoft Word window opens.

   You now use the drawing tools to create basic vector shapes in the document.

2. Right-click the menu bar to the right of Help, and click **Drawing** to open the Drawing toolbar.
3. Click the **Oval** button on the Drawing toolbar. In the document window, drag to draw an oval. When you release the mouse button, an oval is placed in the document.
4. Click the **Rectangle** button on the Drawing toolbar. In the document window, drag to draw a rectangle. When you release the mouse button, a rectangle is placed in the document.
5. To group the shapes, start by clicking the rectangle. A selection box surrounds the rectangle. Hold down the **Shift** key and then click the oval. Both shapes are selected framed.
6. Right-click one shape, point to **Grouping** on the shortcut menu, and then click **Group**. A selection box surrounds the area containing the rectangle and oval.
7. Drag the shapes within the document. Notice that both shapes move as one.

To save the document as an HTML document and open it in Internet Explorer:

1. Click **File** on the menu bar, and then click **Save as Web Page**. The Save As dialog box opens.
2. Click the **Save in** list arrow and then navigate to **C:\home\<yourname>\Ch09** folder, if necessary. Type **shapes.html** in the File name text box, and then click **Save**.
3. To open the HTML document in Internet Explorer, click **Start**, point to **Programs** (**All Programs** in Windows XP), and then click **Internet Explorer**. The Internet Explorer browser window opens.
4. In the Address text box, type **C:\home\<yourname>\Ch09\shapes.html**. The shapes document appears with the circle and square combination.
5. To view the HTML code, right-click a blank area of the browser window, and then click **View Source**. A Notepad window opens with the HTML source code.

   Notice the VML namespace declaration in the html element start tag, and the VML behavior declaration in the style element.

6. Scroll down to the bottom of the document. Find the paragraph element containing the VML elements. Organize and indent the elements within the document so that you can read the code. The VML shapes should look as follows:

```
<v:group ...
        <v:oval ... />
        <v:rect ... />
</v:group>
```

7. Close Notepad, Internet Explorer, and Word.

Case Project

Figure 9-23 below is a mix of all the techniques presented in the Hands-on Projects. Create this image using the VML coding techniques shown to you, and the code samples provided in the Chapter 9 Hands-on Projects.

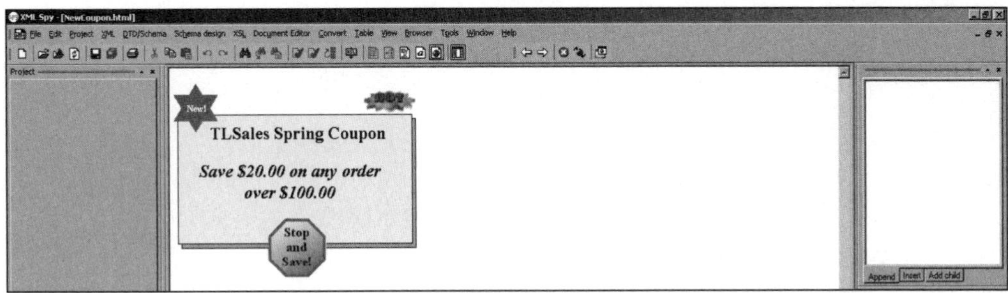

Figure 9-23

CHAPTER

10

INTRODUCTION TO THE SYNCHRONIZED MULTIMEDIA INTEGRATION LANGUAGE (SMIL)

In this chapter, you will learn:

- About the Synchronized Multimedia Integration Language
- How to create a SMIL document
- How to synchronize media objects
- How to hyperlink elements
- How to view and prepare SMIL documents

The **Synchronized Multimedia Integration Language (SMIL)** is an XML-related language that enables authors to create streaming media presentations by combining different types of media. **Streaming media** is a technology for transferring audio, video, and other multimedia data in real time over the Internet or over private networks so that it can be processed as a steady and continuous stream. Streaming results in little or no waiting for downloads. The recipient's browser or plug-in application can start displaying the data before the file or files have been transmitted. Further, streaming is beneficial because most users still do not have fast enough access to quickly download large multimedia files. Prior to streaming, you had to download one or more files to your hard disk, and then play those files. With streaming, just about any user can watch or listen to the content of a requested file almost immediately after selecting it on a Web site.

You can use three methods to deliver streaming media. **True streaming**, which uses a separate streaming server and requires the recipient to obtain a specific media player application for the format of the requested media *prior* to commencement of the streaming process, is the latest technology. **Hypertext Transfer Protocol (HTTP) streaming**, also called progressive download streaming or serverless streaming, uses a standard Web server—not a separate, dedicated streaming server—and also requires the recipient to obtain a specific media player application beforehand. This was the first popular form of streaming. The third method, **clientless streaming**, sends the media player application with the media files during the streaming process.

Streaming media is becoming more common today, and the need for good tools to create streaming presentations is growing. In the past three or four years, a number of competing streaming technologies and standards have been developed.

Chapter 10 discusses SMIL, focusing on the W3C's SMIL 1.0 Recommendation of June 1998. Recently, the W3C has endorsed the more powerful, more sophisticated, and very much larger SMIL 2.0 Recommendation but, as far as the introductory level of this chapter is concerned, a discussion of SMIL 1.0's principles is sufficient.

WHAT IS THE SYNCHRONIZED MULTIMEDIA INTEGRATED LANGUAGE?

The Synchronized Multimedia Integration Language (SMIL; pronounced "smile") is an XML-related language that enables you to create presentations that combine different types of media. It was developed specifically to solve the problems of coordinating the presentation of different types of media while optimizing bandwidth usage.

SMIL allows Web site developers and other authors to:

- Combine text, image, audio, and video media.
- Control multimedia synchronization (i.e., the "temporal behavior" of the various media).
- Control the layout of visual media.
- Provide hyperlinks to include additional media (for jumping to another part of the presentation, for starting a new multimedia presentation, or for opening a Web page).
- Store the media content (i.e., the media objects) on their local systems, or elsewhere ranging from locations on their local area networks to anywhere on the Internet.
- Write SMIL files with complex editors or simple text editors.
- Search SMIL files. SMIL presentation files are text files with metadata components, so they can be searched for names or character strings.
- Divide the multimedia content into separate streams (for example, separate static text or image files from nonstatic audio or video files), and transmit them individually. However, because of single time-line technology, the separate streams are timed and coordinated to look like one longer stream.

- Adapt media streams to the recipient's system characteristics. For example, media objects can be created and stored in multiple versions (e.g., different bandwidth versions to facilitate transmission, different language soundtracks, etc.).
- Reuse any or all media objects in multiple presentations, because each is accessed with a unique Uniform Resource Identifier (URI).

Simply stated, SMIL enables authors to create and transmit everything from the simplest presentations (even using media that might not require streaming) to complex TV-like multimedia presentations, such as movies and training courses. Because SMIL code resembles the XML-related language codes encountered earlier in this text, anyone who can use XHTML or HTML can also use SMIL.

SMIL is different from Java, through which the benefits of multimedia have long been achievable. And the human legibility of SMIL makes it easier for non-Java programmers to use. SMIL documents can also be assembled on the fly by Java servlets or CGI scripts accessing a database.

SMIL 1.0

The full specification of SMIL 1.0, titled Synchronized Multimedia Integration Language (SMIL) 1.0 Specification was endorsed as a W3C Recommendation on June 15, 1998. The Recommendation can be viewed at *www.w3.org/TR/REC-smil/*.

The SMIL 1.0 Recommendation was prepared by the W3C's Synchronized Multimedia Working Group (SYMM-WG), which, at the time of endorsement, included representatives from the following sixteen organizations: Alcatel, Apple, CNET/DSM, CWI, DAISY Consortium, DEC, GMD, Havas, INRIA, Lucent/Bell Labs, Netscape, NIST, Philips, The Productivity Works, RealNetworks, and the W3C. The Working Group was assembled in January 1997. They published their first public draft in November 1997 and, as stated above, the full specification was endorsed as a Recommendation in June 1998.

Microsoft had contributed to SMIL 1.0 development until the last draft, but did not embrace the SMIL 1.0 Recommendation. Microsoft said that SMIL 1.0 overlapped with several existing standards, such as CSS2, HTML, and the DOM, and was, therefore unnecessary. Macromedia did not embrace SMIL because they claimed that SMIL's features were not sophisticated enough, and that those features overlap and potentially conflict with existing standards, such as DOM.

If you wish to view the SMIL 1.0 DTD, go to *www.w3.org/TR/REC-smil/#smil-dtd*.

SMIL 2.0

The W3C's second version of the SMIL specification, titled Synchronized Multimedia Integration Language (SMIL 2.0), was endorsed as a Recommendation on August 7, 2001. It is approximately ten times larger than SMIL 1.0 and can be viewed at *www.w3.org/TR/smil20/*.

Unlike SMIL 1.0, SMIL 2.0 consists of sets of **markup modules**, each of which defines the semantics and syntax for the following nine specific areas of SMIL functionality: animation, content control, layout, linking, media objects, metainformation, structure, timing, and transition effects. Several of these functions are new, and fill the functionality shortcomings observed in SMIL 1.0 by many software developers.

The modules can be used alone or in combination. For example, you could create animation with transition effects. Furthermore, two SMIL 2.0 profiles are defined (for comprehensive SMIL 2.0 presentation, and for handheld and mobile devices). The profiles let you create an XML-based language specific to anticipated device needs.

Through the use of namespaces, SMIL 2.0 also allows the reuse of SMIL 2.0 syntax and semantics in other XML-based languages, specifically, those that need to represent timing and synchronization, such as XHTML and SVG.

SMIL 2.0 was also prepared by the W3C's Synchronized Multimedia Working Group (SYMM-WG). For SMIL 2.0, the Working Group included representatives from the following organizations: Canon, Compaq, CSELT, CWI, Ericsson, France Telecom, Gateway, Glocomm, IBM, INRIA, Intel, Macromedia, Microsoft, Netscape/AOL, NIST, Nokia, Oratrix, Panasonic, Philips, RealNetworks, WGBH, and the W3C.

Figure 10-1 shows that SMIL 2.0 also has nine module types. It also has nine DTDs. By comparison, the older and less sophisticated SMIL 1.0 uses only one. The references to the appropriate DTDs are specified in the DOCTYPE definitions of the respective documents.

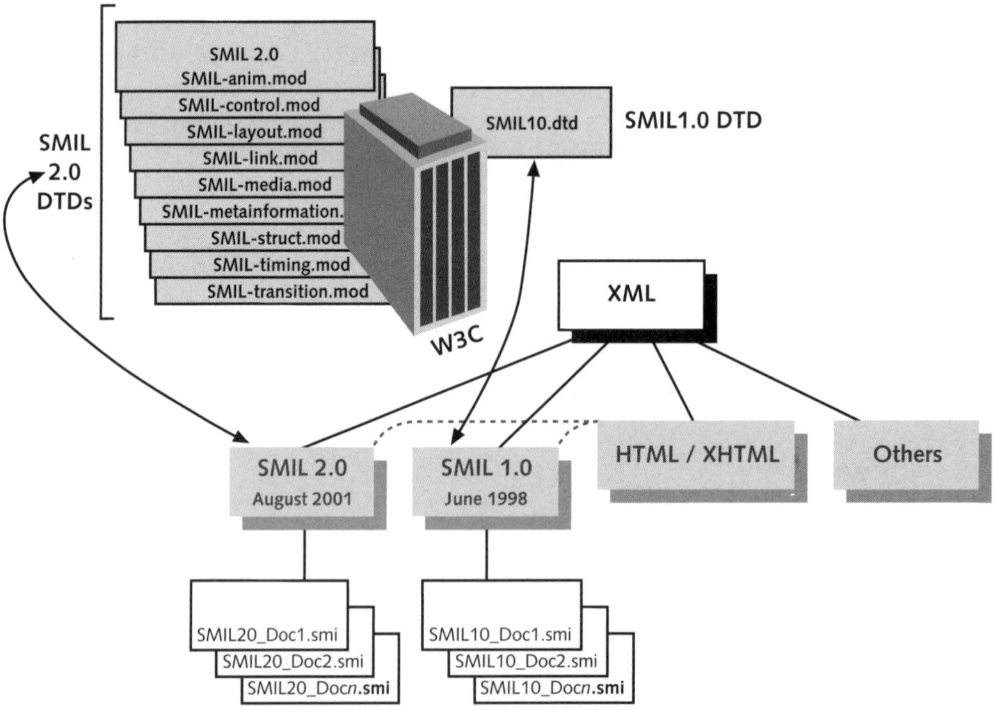

Figure 10-1 SMIL 2.0 vs. SMIL 1.0

Creating a SMIL Document

SMIL documents follow both HTML and XHTML syntax. Like VML, however, SMIL documents follow XHTML more closely, because the element tags must be lowercase. Like all XML-related languages, SMIL is case sensitive.

To create a SMIL presentation, you first have to define regions in your display in which to place the media objects. Then you specify the media objects and assign each to a region. Finally, you determine the order in which to play or display the media objects: in sequence, parallel, or a combination of both.

As indicated in Figure 10-2, an SMIL document, like other XML-related documents, consists of two main parts, the prolog, and the <smil> element, which, in turn, consists of the <head> element and the <body> element.

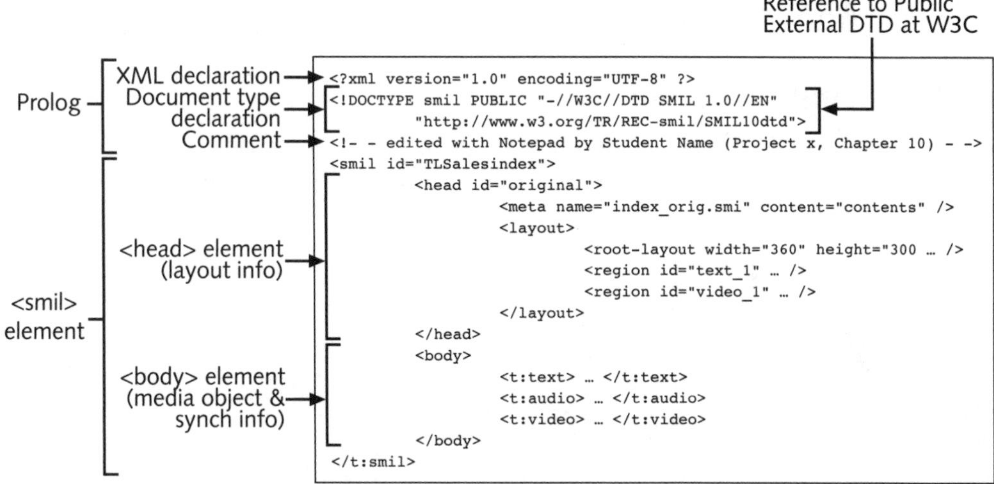

Figure 10-2 A typical SMIL document

SMIL documents are saved as *filename*.smi; that is, they are given whatever name the respective authors feel are appropriate, along with an .smi extension.

The Prolog

The sample SMIL document in Figure 10-2 has a prolog similar to all other XML-related documents. That prolog consists of an XML declaration and a DOCTYPE definition indicating the location of the SMIL DTD. In the case of Figure 10-2, there is also a comment indicating the name of the author and the text editor used.

The document type declaration names the document type definition (DTD) that is used to validate the document. For SMIL, the document type declaration should look like the following:

```
<!DOCTYPE smil PUBLIC "-//W3C//DTD SMIL 1.0//EN"
                "http://www.w3.org/TR/REC-smil/SMIL10.dtd">
```

As you learned in Chapter 4, this form of declaration facilitates accessing an external DTD that is intended for public use. Furthermore, the declaration indicates that the DTD is located at a different Web site from the one at which the XML document is located. Figure 10-1 illustrated the relationship between a SMIL document, the SMIL language, the SMIL DTDs, XML, and other XML-related languages.

In Chapter 4, you also learned how the XML 1.0 Recommendation provides a way to add more declarations to your SMIL document than those found in the external DTD: by including them within the <!DOCTYPE> element. *Do not use this technique with SMIL,* because many SMIL applications do not support it.

The <smil> Element

The most fundamental part of a SMIL document—that is, its "root" element—is the <smil> element. Figure 10-3 illustrates a <smil> element within a simplified SMIL 1.0 document.

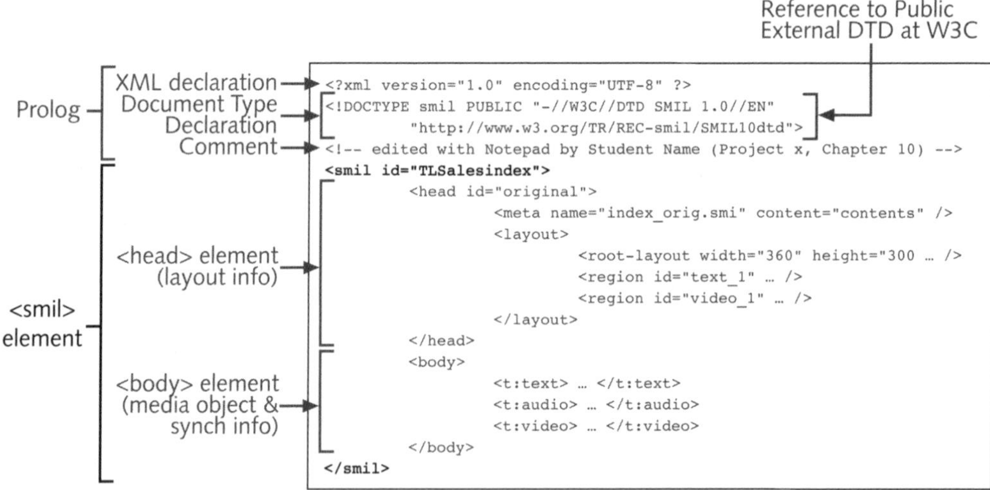

Figure 10-3 The <smil> element

The direct child elements (i.e., the element content) of the <smil> element are <head> and <body>. The <smil> element can contain an id attribute though one is not mandatory, which is an attribute that uniquely identifies the element within a document so that it can be found by an application. Not all applications are written such that they contain the id value, but it is possible to do so. Meanwhile, the value of the id attribute must be a proper XML name. Here is an example:

```
<smil id="TLSalesindex">
```

The SMIL 1.0 Recommendation anticipated that SMIL 1.0 elements and attributes would be used in other XML-based documents. For those cases, the Recommendation states that to allow document developers to include SMIL 1.0 elements and attributes in otherwise non-SMIL 1.0 XML-based documents, the following XML namespace declaration could be added to the root element start tag of those non-SMIL documents:

```
<rootelementname
   xmlns:t="http://www.w3.org/TR/REC-smil" ... >
```

However, as time and practice eventually dictated, SMIL 1.0 components are generally *not* included in other XML-related documents using the classic namespace-related technique. Further, in the SMIL 1.0 documents themselves, namespace declarations are not necessary. As you will see in your Hands-on projects at the end of this chapter, SMIL 1.0 documents are currently linked to other HTML or XHTML documents, and automatically startup SMIL 1.0 player applications, such as RealPlayer. Those applications, in turn, use the SMIL 1.0 documents. So it is not necessary to include the namespace declaration in the XML documents in the classic manner. Microsoft Internet Explorer, for example, uses HTML and TIME behaviors in its HTML or XHTML documents to accommodate linking to SMIL 1.0 documents and calling up the SMIL 1.0 players.

The <head> Element

In SMIL 1.0 documents, the <head> element is contained within the <smil> element. The <head> element has to contain either a <layout> element or a <switch> element, and can also contain any number of <meta> elements. As with other XML-related documents, for the SMIL document to be well-formed, the child elements of the <head> element must be properly nested. The <head> element can also have an id attribute.

The <head> element contains the SMIL document layout information. However, the *layout* information is different from, although related to, the SMIL document's (also called the presentation's) *temporal* behavior. That is, the layout information is not related to the actual media objects in the presentation, nor to their timing or synchronization. That temporal behavior is left to components nested in the <body> element, which are discussed later in this chapter.

The <layout> Element

Everything concerning the layout of media objects in the viewport is stored in the <layout> element, which must be properly nested within the <head> element. If you are going to accept the default layout values for all the media object elements in your document, then you must make the <layout> element an empty element, and then specify a type attribute in the start tag and assign it the value "text/smil-basic-layout". Here is an example:

```
<layout type="text/smil-basic-layout"></layout>
```

Otherwise, you can follow a <layout> element practice similar to that shown in Figure 10-3. There are two child elements that may be found nested within <layout>: <root-layout> and <region>.

The <root-layout> Element

Inside the <layout> element, the <root-layout> element determines the size and other attributes of the SMIL 1.0 player's **viewport**, (i.e., the window within the player that displays the SMIL presentation; occasionally, the viewport is also called the **root-layout region**). A typical SMIL 1.0 player display, with some sample regions is shown in Figure 10-4. Although three regions are shown in the figure, (i.e., region A, region B, and region C) the number, size, and positioning of regions is left to each SMIL document author according to their requirements.

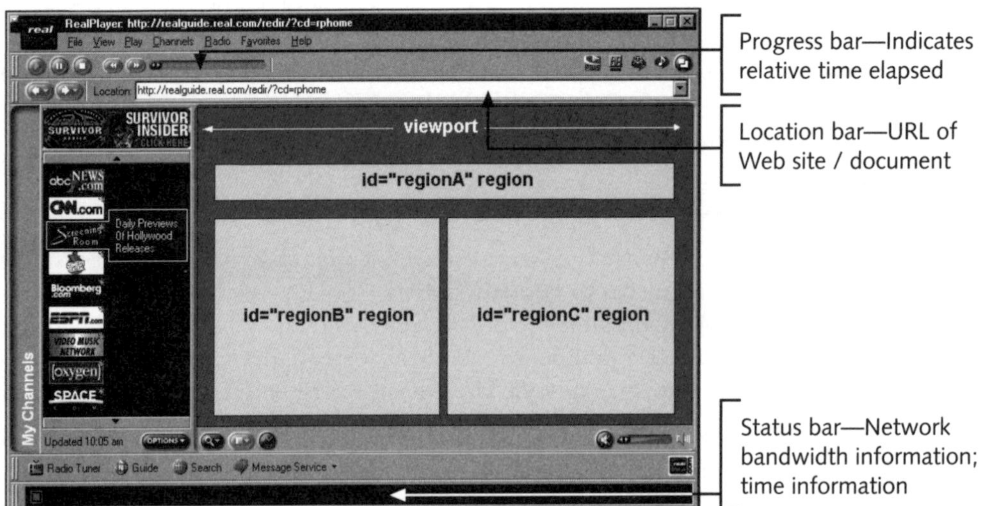

Figure 10-4 Typical SMIL 1.0 player

Because the SMIL player has only one viewport, a SMIL document cannot have more than one <root-layout> element. Meanwhile, the <root-layout> element is a declared empty element and can have the following attributes: background-color, height, width, id, skip-content, and title.

For example, the following source code creates a viewport 300 pixels wide and 200 pixels high with a white background:

```
<root-layout width="300" height="200"
   background-color="white" />
```

Figure 10-3 shows an example of another <root-layout> element. If there is no <root-layout> specification, then the application's default values are used.

The <region> Element

By using one or more <region> elements within the <layout> elements in your SMIL document, you can divide a viewport into regions, and then display one or more visual media objects (i.e., text, image, or streaming video) in each region. In other words, each visual object can be contained within a specific region, and the regions are identified, positioned, and sized by the use of <region> elements.

The regions' identities, positions, and dimensions are controlled by the values specified for the id, left, right, width, height, and z-index attributes in the respective <region> elements. Following is an example of the use of <region> to define two regions in a viewport.

```
<region id="img_reg1" left="10" top="10"
      width="150" height="100" z-index="1" />
<region id="img_reg2" left="25" top="25"
      width="200" height="100" z-index="0" />
```

This code specifies an id attribute for each region. You have to assign unique id attributes to each region like this so that, later, in the <body> element, you can refer to the regions individually by the id values when you define the image, text, or streaming video to insert into each one. At that point, you use an <img> tag with a region attribute—not a <region> element—that has a value identical to the id given to the respective <region> element. For example, if you want a text document to be displayed in the region with the id of "img_reg1", then the value specified for the region attribute of the <text> tag would be "img_reg1". Thus, that <img> element points back to that particular region definition. (This is covered again, when the <body> element is discussed later in this chapter.)

The left, top, width, and height attributes define the position and dimensions of the region. In the previous examples, the values provided are expressed in pixels, which is appropriate for absolute positioning. While width and height are fairly straightforward, left and top are absolute references to the top left corner of the viewport. Using "img_reg1" as an example, "left="10" " and "top="10" " specify that the top left corner of the "img_reg1" is:

- 10 pixels to the right of the viewport's left edge
- 10 pixels below the top of the viewport

Figure 10-5 illustrates the two regions defined in the examples.

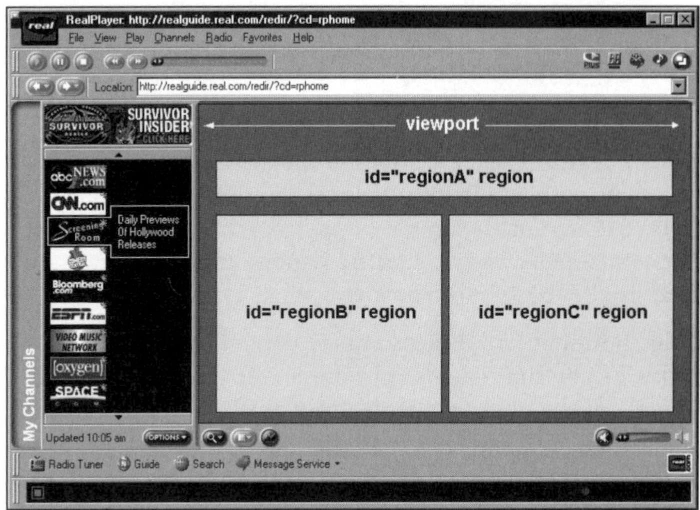

Figure 10-5 Overlapping regions

Not only can you specify region positions *absolutely* by counting the number of pixels, but you can also specify their positions *relatively* to the viewport's dimensions. For example, if you wish to display an image with its right border at 25% of the distance from the viewport's left border to the right, and its top at 33% of the distance down from the top of the viewport, modify the previous example of code to read like the following:

```
<region id="img_reg1" left="25%" top="33%"
   width="150" height="100" z-index="1" />
```

Notice that the dimensions of the region are still specified with pixel measurements.

In Figure 10-5, two regions overlap. If you are concerned about regions overlapping one another and want to prevent it, be careful with the positions and dimensions you specify. However, if you want two or more of your regions to overlap (for example, to create a background motif), then you use the z-index attribute with the <region> element the same way you used it with VML. The same rules apply, too: when two or more regions overlap, the one with the more positive z-index is rendered on top. If neither region has a z-index specified or if their z-index values are identical, then the latest <img> element specified is laid over the earlier one(s).

Most of the time, your media objects are not the same size as the regions you define for them. Here are the typical situations you are generally faced with, and suggestions for remedying them by adding the "fit" attribute and its various values to the <region> start tag. The situations are depicted in Figure 10-6.

1. "Fill; distortion"

   Your object, when displayed, is smaller than its region. You want the object to grow and completely fill the region, even if it distorts the image. Because of the nature of the image, distortion in one direction or another is not an issue with you. Use syntax similar to the following:

```
<region id="img_reg1" left="10" top="10" width="150"
      height="100" background-color="black" fit="fill" />
```

2. "Grow; no distortion"

   Again, your object, when displayed, is smaller than its region. You want the object to grow until one or the other of the object's edges just touches one of the region's edges. This time, because of the nature of the image, you do not want any distortion. Use syntax similar to the following:

```
<region id="img_reg1" left="10" top="10" width="150"
      height="100" background-color="black" fit="meet" />
```

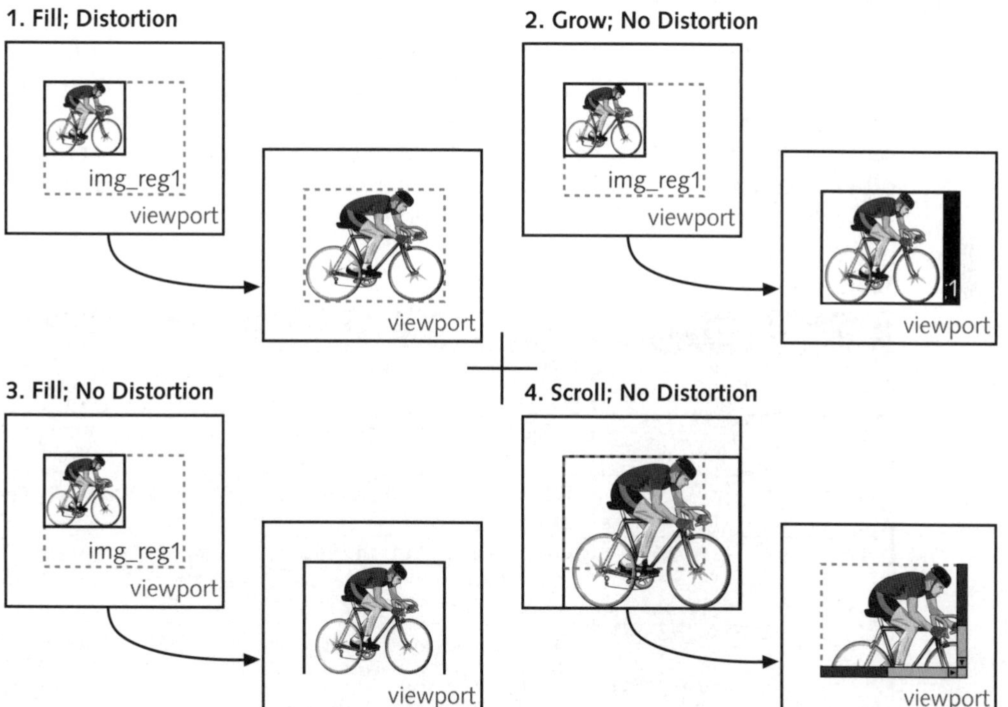

Figure 10-6 Fit attribute remedies

3. "Fill; no distortion"

   Your object, when displayed, is smaller than its region. You want the object to grow and completely fill the region, even if the region seems to crop (or "slice") some of the media object off. Because of the nature of the image, you would rather lose some of the image than have any distortion. Use syntax similar to the following:

```
<region id="img_reg1" left="10" top="10" width="150"
      height="100" background-color="black"
      fit="slice" />
```

4. "Scroll; no distortion"

   Your object, when displayed, is larger than its region. You do not want to reduce the size of the object and you do not want any distortion. Instead, you want the end user to be able to scroll up or down, so that they eventually see all of the image. Use syntax similar to the following:

```
<region id="img_reg1" left="10" top="10" width="150"
      height="100" background-color="black"
      fit="scroll" />
```

The <meta> Element

The declared empty <meta> element is used to provide additional information about a SMIL document, such as the author's name and key words. There is no restriction on the number of <meta> elements you can include. However, the <meta> element can only be included in the <head> element of a SMIL 1.0 document (that is, unlike other elements, such as <switch>, it cannot appear in the <body> element). Table 10-1 lists the attributes you can add to the <meta> element.

Table 10-1 meta> element attributes

Attribute Name	Explanation
content	Required for <meta> elements; specifies the value of the property defined in the meta element
id	Uniquely identifies the element within the document, in case it is being searched for by an application
name	Required for <meta> elements; identifies the property defined in the meta element
skip-content	Introduced in SMIL 1.0 for future extensibility; possible values are "true" (ignore the content of this element) or "false" (process the content of this element)
base	The value of this property determines the base URI for all relative URIs used in the document
title	The title of the presentation

Here is an example to illustrate <meta> element syntax:

```
<meta name="string" content="string"
   skip-content="false" />
```

The <switch> Element

SMIL has the ability to help you adapt your presentation according to the capabilities and other properties of the recipient's system. A special element, called <switch>, makes that possible. Within the <switch> element, you can nest child elements against whose attributes SMIL can conduct Boolean true/false tests on a user's system. The first child element whose attributes all test true prevails over the other child elements and is executed. By default, any child element that contains no test attributes is automatically considered true. In other words, depending on the user's system, a different set of elements and, thus, a different looking or sounding Web presentation (for example, in a different language, at a different resolution, with video instead of static shots or "stills," etc.) might be executed automatically.

However, the <switch> element is more commonly used in the <body> element with the media object elements and the synchronization elements nested there. See "Using the <switch> Element to Specify Media Objects" for more information.

The <body> Element

While the <head> element of the SMIL document contains appearance and layout information, the <body> element contains all the actual content and timing information. Some refer to this as "content and temporal information, plus linking behavior."

The <body> element contains child elements that specify to the SMIL parser and the application what is to be rendered in the defined regions. In other words, the region's visual characteristics are defined in the <head> section, and the audiovisual contents are defined in the <body> section.

The start tag in the <body> element is also allowed to contain the attribute id. The <body> element, on the other hand, can contain the following child elements: <a>, <animation>, <audio>, <img>, <par>, <ref>, <seq>, <switch>, <text>, <textstream>, and <video>. Some of these you may have seen before, some are reasonably self-evident, and some are discussed in more detail as the chapter progresses.

SYNCHRONIZING MEDIA OBJECTS

Any given region of the viewport may have the same content throughout a presentation, or different content at different times. The rendering of different components or media objects, such as <img>, <video>, and <text> can occur either sequentially or in parallel.

Sequential operations are specified with the <seq> element under the <body> element. That is, the <seq> element(s) are child element(s) of the <body> element. The <seq> elements contain one or more child elements, and the contents specified in those elements are played or displayed in sequence, one after another.

Similarly, parallel operations are indicated by the <par> element under the <body> element. Like <seq> elements, then, <par> elements are also child elements of the <body> element. The <par> elements also contain child elements but, in contrast to <seq> element children, the contents of <par> children are played at the same time. Due to the nature of their rendering attributes, however, the children of a <par> element can still appear to overlap in time, or they can appear to be spaced apart in time.

The <body> element itself acts much like a <seq> element—in fact, it is considered to be a special type of <seq> element—because the child elements under <body> are basically played one after the other. However, <body> lacks the time attributes provided with <par> and <seq>.

Because of their time-oriented functions, the <seq> and <par> elements are called **synchronization** elements.

Using the <seq> Element for Synchronization

Recall that the <seq> element indicates that sequential operations are to be undertaken. The child elements of the <seq> element(s), at that point, are played or displayed in sequence, one after another. In other words, the children of a <seq> element form a **temporal sequence**.

Figure 10-7 presents a simplified example of the use of the <seq> element. It's a good idea to use a time line, like that shown in Figure 10-7, during the planning stages, to design the sequences of your media objects.

The <seq> element can contain the follow child elements: other <par> or <seq> synchronization elements; hyperlink elements such as <a>; media object elements such as <animation>, <audio>, <img>, <ref>, <text>, <textstream>, and <video>; and other elements such as <switch>. Table 10-2 lists the attributes that are applicable to the <seq> element.

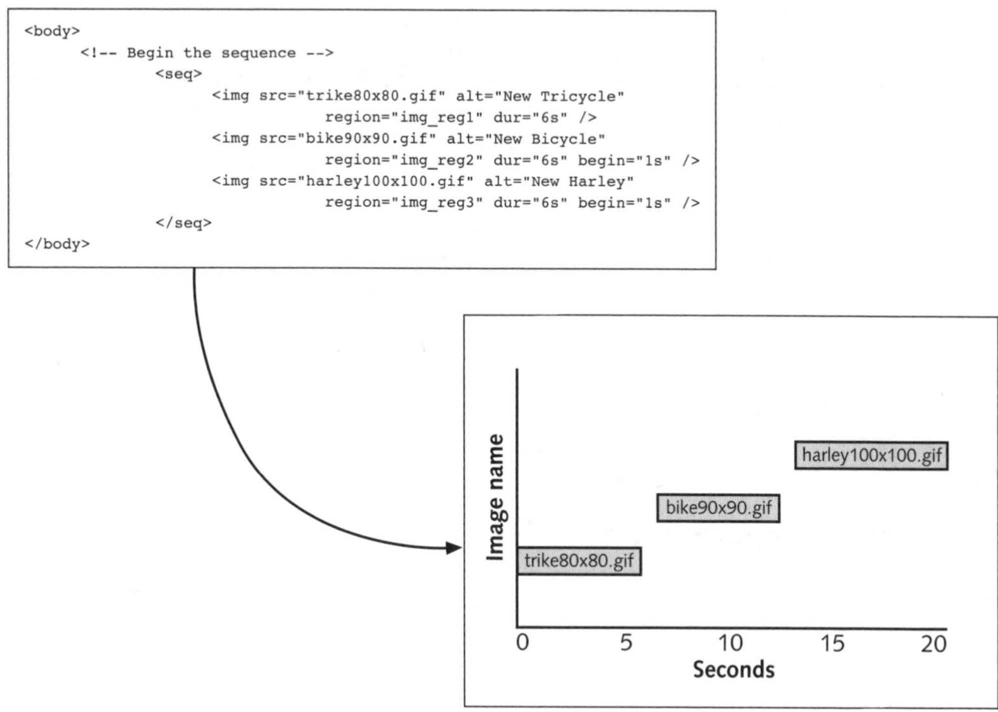

<body>
<!-- Begin the sequence -->
<seq>
<img src="trike80x80.gif" alt="New Tricycle"
region="img_reg1" dur="6s" />
<img src="bike90x90.gif" alt="New Bicycle"
region="img_reg2" dur="6s" begin="1s" />
<img src="harley100x100.gif" alt="New Harley"
region="img_reg3" dur="6s" begin="1s" />
</seq>
</body>
Image name
harley100x100.gif
bike90x90.gif
trike80x80.gif
0
5
10
15
20
Seconds

Figure 10-7 Example of a <seq> element

Table 10-2 Attributes applicable to the <seq> element

Attribute Name	Explanation
abstract	Brief content description
author	Content author's name
begin	The time for the explicit begin of an element (seconds); two types: clock-based delay-value; event-value
copyright	Content's copyright notice
dur	The explicit duration of an element (seconds)
end	The explicit end of an element (seconds)
endsync	Attribute which influences the implicit duration of the <par> element
id	Unique identifier
region	Specifies the abstract rendering surface defined within the <layout> elements
repeat	Number of times object should be repeated; value can be an integer (default value is 1), or the string "indefinite"
system-bitrate	Specifies the approximate bandwidth

Table 10-2 Attributes applicable to the <seq> element (continued)

Attribute Name	Explanation
system-captions	Determines whether closed captioning will be on or off.
system-language	Value is a comma-separated list of language names (RFC1766); determines whether there is a match between end-user system and objects
system-overdub-or-caption	Determines if end users prefer overdubbing or captioning when they are available
system-required	Specifies the name of an extension (e.g., namespaces)
system-screen-size	"True" if the SMIL viewer is capable of displaying a resolution of the given size ("width x height" in pixels)
system-screen-depth	Specifies the depth of the screen color palette in bits per pixel
title	All <seq> elements should have a "title" attribute with a meaningful description

Using the <par> Element for Synchronization

Like <seq>, the <par> element is a media object synchronization element. Unlike <seq>, though, the child elements of a <par> element are played at the same time. Plus, the children of a <par> element can overlap in time.

The children of both the <par> and <seq> elements have attributes used to define a media object **lifecycle**. The begin and end attributes are the most obvious of the life-cycle controls. The begin attribute indicates to a SMIL application/interpreter when to begin displaying the elements contained in the <par> element. The end attribute indicates when the display should end.

You can see these lifecycle controls at work in Figure 10-8, which presents a simplified example of the use of the <par> element. Again, be sure to use a time line, like that shown in Figure 10-8, during the planning stages.

The <par> element can contain the same child elements as the <seq> element, namely: other <par> or <seq> synchronization elements; hyperlink elements such as <a>; media object elements such as <animation>, <audio>, <img>, <ref>, <text>, <textstream>, and <video>; and other elements such as <switch>.

The attributes that are applicable to the <par> element are identical to those listed previously in Table 10-2 for the <seq> element.

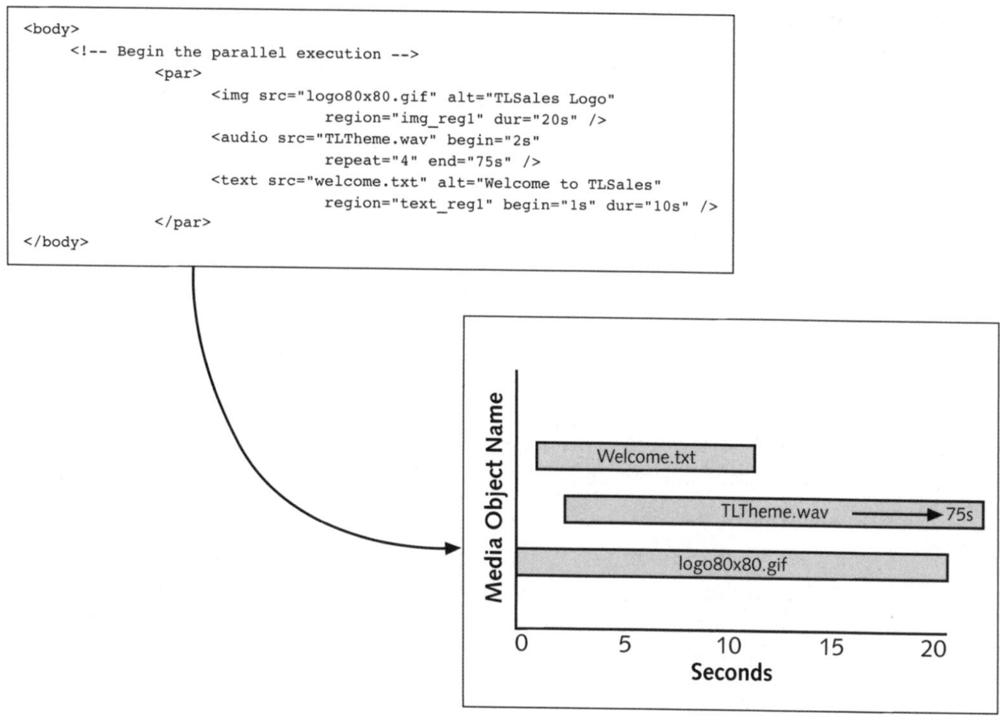

<body>
<!-- Begin the parallel execution -->
<par>
<img src="logo80x80.gif" alt="TLSales Logo"
region="img_reg1" dur="20s" />
<audio src="TLTheme.wav" begin="2s"
repeat="4" end="75s" />
<text src="welcome.txt" alt="Welcome to TLSales"
region="text_reg1" begin="1s" dur="10s" />
</par>
</body>
Media Object Name
Welcome.txt
TLTheme.wav
75s
logo80x80.gif
0
5
10
15
20
Seconds

Figure 10-8 Example of a <par> element

Understanding the SMIL Media Object Elements

This section concerns the SMIL media object elements:

- *<ref>*—Generic media reference (suggested to be used when an author is in doubt about the category to which a media object belongs)
- *<animation>*—Animated vector graphics or other animated images
- *<audio>*—Audio clip
- *<img>*—Still image, such as PNG or JPEG
- *<text>*—Text reference
- *<textstream>*—Streaming text
- *<video>*—Video clip

You can group media objects into the following categories:

- Visual media objects (e.g., images, videos, animations)
- Audio media objects of various formats, such as MP3 and WAV

The W3C, however, groups them as follows:

- Media objects with an **intrinsic** (i.e., built-in, due to their nature) duration; also called **continuous media**. Examples are video and audio files.
- Media objects without intrinsic duration; also called **discrete media**. Examples are text files and still images.

Each visual media object, such as a video image, for example, is displayed by the SMIL interpreter in a region within the viewport. That region is treated as a type of container. The media object is then associated with or included in the region through the use of a URI reference.

Depending on an individual author's treatment of the <region> element, the visual media object may or may not fill the whole container area. Meanwhile, as the end user browses the SMIL document, the same region(s) may host different visual media objects. Or some regions are created, used in a limited fashion, and then not used again as different regions are used.

Remember that to include a visual media object (a text, a video, or another static image) in a SMIL presentation, you must first, under the <layout> element, specify and apply general characteristics to a chosen visual abstract rendering surface (put more simply—to a chosen region of the viewport). Now, under the <body> element, to insert an actual visual image like a JPEG image, you can use the <img> element as shown in the following example code:

```
<img src="smiley32x32.jpg" alt="Smile"
          region="img_reg1" ... />
```

Here, the value of the region attribute in the <img> element start tag is identical to the value given to the id attribute inside the start tag of the <region> element inside the <layout> element. Thus, that value (name) serves as a pointer to the chosen region and links the two components together.

Make sure that the category into which a media object falls is appropriately reflected in the element name. This facilitates the readability of the SMIL document. For example, it would be confusing to create a series of elements with img-related names if some were to eventually contain audio or animation references. However, if there is a doubt about how to group a media object (for example, is an animation the same as a video?), use the generic <ref> element. Thus, the media object elements allow you to include media objects into a SMIL presentation. To do so, the media objects are specified by a URI reference.

Table 10-3 lists the attributes that are applicable to all media object elements. Most have been mentioned and defined in tables for other elements. Consider including the alt attribute in the start tag for all media objects. If the object fails to play or display, you still have opportunity to send a message to the end user; plus, if the alt message appears, that signals that there are malfunctions in the document, the browser, or other SMIL-related applications.

Table 10-3 Attributes that apply to media object elements

Attribute Name	Explanation
abstract	Brief content description
alt	For viewers/players that cannot display a particular object, this specifies alternate message; strongly recommended for all object elements
author	Content author's name
begin	The time for the explicit begin of an element (seconds); two types: clock-based delay-value, and event-value
clip-begin	Specifies the beginning of a subclip of a continuous object as offset from the object's start; various formats, syntax
clip-end	Specifies the end of a subclip of a continuous object that should be played; same syntax as clip-begin
copyright	Content's copyright notice
dur	The explicit duration of an element (seconds)
end	The explicit end of an element (seconds)
fill	Attribute which determines the effective end of the child element and the parent
id	Unique identifier
longdesc	Specifies a URI link to a longer object description; should supplement the description provided by alt
region	Specifies the abstract rendering surface defined within the <layout> elements
src	URI of the media object
system-bitrate	Specifies the approximate bandwidth
system-captions	Determines whether closed captioning is on or off
system-language	Value is a comma-separated list of language names (RFC1766); determines whether there is a match between end-user system and objects
system-overdub-or-caption	Determines if end users prefer overdubbing or captioning when they are available
system-required	Specifies the name of an extension (e.g., namespaces)
system-screen-size	"True" if the SMIL viewer is capable of displaying a resolution of the given size (width x height in pixels)
system-screen-depth	Specifies the depth of the screen color palette in bits per pixel
title	All <seq> elements should have a title attribute with a meaningful description
type	Type of media object referenced by src

Finally, you can attach anchors and links to visual media objects. Media object elements can contain the <anchor> element, which allows you to associate a link with a complete media object.

Using the <switch> Element to Specify Media Objects

As stated earlier, <switch> lets SMIL adapt a presentation according to the capabilities and other properties encountered in the recipient user's system. It does so by providing specific child elements with attributes that allow the execution of one or more Boolean true/false tests against the system settings. The first set of child elements with attribute tests that all prove to be "true" are executed. Any child element which contains no test attributes is, by default, automatically considered to be true.

Basically, <switch> element syntax looks like:

```
<switch>
     <!-- First Test -->
         <elementname testattribute= ... />
     <!-- Second Test -->
         <elementname testattribute= ... />
... etc.
</switch>
```

There are only certain elements that are allowed to be children of <switch>. They are:

- the media object elements <animation>, <audio>, <img>, <ref>, <text>, <textstream>, and <video>
- the synchronization elements <par> and <seq>
- <a>, <anchor>, and <switch>

Table 10-4 lists those test attributes that can appear in the child elements, to be used by <switch>.

Table 10-4 <switch> test attributes

Test Attribute Name	Explanation
<***elementname*** system-language= "*langcode*" />	End-user's system language; values are a list of two character language codes (e.g., en, fr, es, de, etc.; see RFC1766), delimited by commas
<*elementname* system-bitrate= "*integer value*" />	Approximate bandwidth; value is a single integer value (e.g., 9600, 14400, 28800, 56000 etc.)
<*elementname* system-screen-size= "*integerxinteger*" />	Monitor screen resolution; value is comprised of two integers, separated by an "x" (e.g., 800x600)
<*elementname* system-screen-depth= "*integer*" />	Number of bits per pixel color definition; value is an integer value of 4 (16 colors), 8 (256 colors), 16 (65,536 colors), or 24 (16.78 million colors, or true color)
<*elementname* system-captions= "on | off" />	"true" if closed captioning has been turned on; "false" if closed captioning has been turned off
<*elementname* system-overdub-or-caption= "caption | overdub" />	Determines whether end users prefer overdubbing or captioning when the option is available; evaluates "true" if the end-user preference matches this attribute value; "false" if there is no match

Table 10-4 <switch> test attributes (continued)

Test Attribute Name	Explanation
<elementname system-required= *"namespace* | *etc."*	Specifies the name of an extension (e.g., a name-space supporting additional element types); evaluates to "true" if the extension is supported by the implementation, otherwise, this evaluates to "false"

For example, what if you know that some of your end users prefer to communicate in Spanish and that some others have monitors that are capable of 800 × 600 pixel resolution only? How might you code your SMIL document to anticipate communicating your messages to those groups? Figure 10-9 represents one possible simplified solution. There are others; the elements can be mixed and matched in other configurations.


```
<?xml version="1.0" encoding="UTF-8" ?>
<!DOCTYPE smil PUBLIC "-//W3C//DTD SMIL 1.0//EN"
      "http://www.w3.org/TR/REC-smil/SMIL10dtd">
<!-- edited with Notepad by Student Name (Project x, Chapter 10) -->
<smil id="…">
      <head id="…">
            <meta name="…" content="…" />
            <layout>
                  <root-layout width="360" height="300 … />
                  <region id="reg_1" … />
                  <region id="reg_2" … />
            </layout>
      </head>
      <body>
            <switch>
                  <!-- English Language -->
                  <par system-language="en">
                        <text src="us_english.doc" region="reg_1" />
                              <switch>
                                    <!-- English Language Screen Resolution-->
                                    <text src="800x600_us_eng.doc" region="reg_1"
                                                system-screen-size="800x600" />
                                    <text src="1024x768_us_eng.doc" region="reg_1"
                                                system-screen-size="1024x768" />
                                    <text src="other_us_eng.doc" region="reg_1" />
                              </switch>
                  </par>
                  <!-- Spanish Language -->
                  <par system-language="es">
                        <text src="espanol.doc" region="reg_1" />
                              <switch>
                                    <!-- Spanish Language Screen Resolution-->
                                    <text src="800x600_esp.doc" region="reg_1"
                                                system-screen-size="800x600" />
                                    <text src="1024x768_esp.doc" region="reg_1"
                                                system-screen-size="1024x768" />
                                    <text src="other_esp.doc" region="reg_1" />
                              </switch>
                  </par>
            </switch>
      </body>
</smil>
```

Figure 10-9 Simplified <switch> example

HYPERLINKING ELEMENTS

Presentation of a SMIL document may involve accessing other SMIL or non-SMIL applications or plug-ins. For example, a SMIL browser may use an HTML plug-in to display an embedded HTML page. Or, as you encounter in the first Hands-on project at the end of this chapter, an HTML browser may use a SMIL plug-in to display a SMIL document embedded in an HTML page. What lets you create access points like these are the SMIL link elements—namely, <a> and <anchor>—which allow for the in-line description of navigational links between objects. Figure 10-10 presents a simplified schematic of two <a> and two <anchor> hyperlinking elements embedded in a presentation. As the presentation progresses, the <a> and <anchor> links are encountered and activated, and whole (<a> element) or partial (<anchor> element) media objects are retrieved from a local database and from across the Internet.

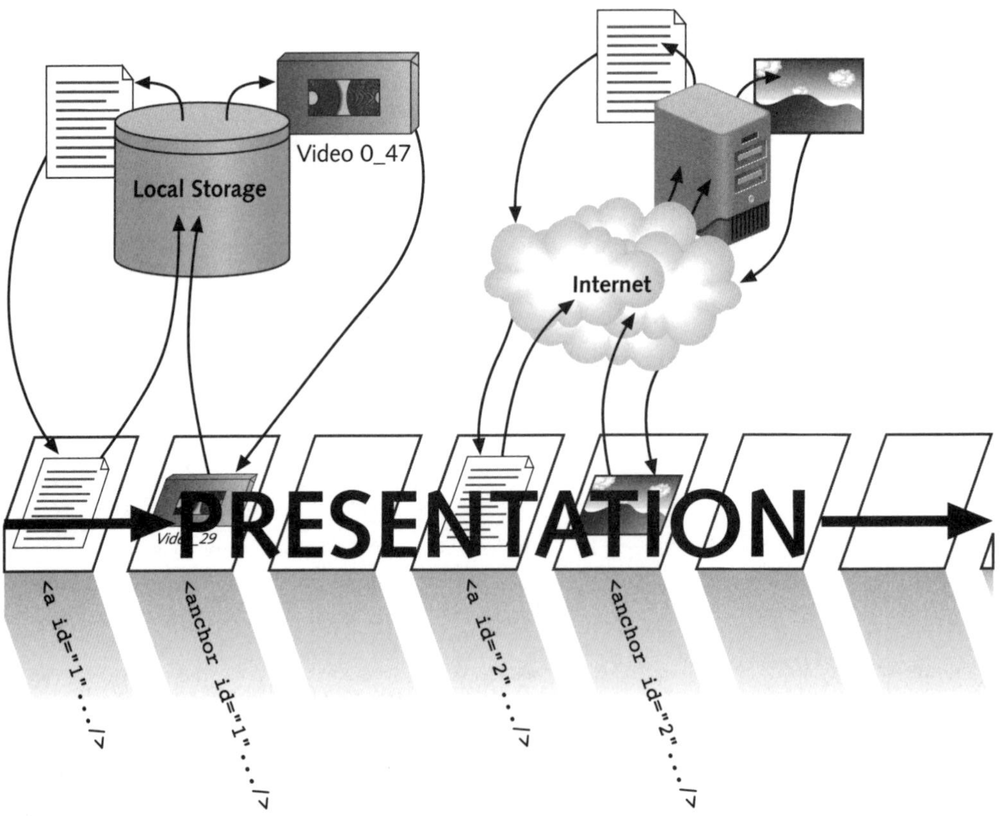

Figure 10-10 Hyperlinking elements in a presentation

The following list includes rules, stipulations, and specifications regarding linking in the SMIL 1.0 Recommendation. If you are contemplating using links, it is recommended that you study the Recommendation in detail.

1. SMIL provides only for unidirectional single-headed (i.e., one source/one destination) in-line links.
2. SMIL supports those locators currently used in HTML, including name fragment identifiers and the # connector. So it understands and uses object locators of the fragmented form "http://TLSales.com/folder/path#image04".

The fragment part is an id value that identifies one of the elements within the referenced SMIL document. If a link containing a fragment part is followed, the presentation should start as if the end user had fast-forwarded through the remote destination presentation to the effective beginning of the element designated by the fragment.

3. If the object addressed by the link has a repeat attribute (e.g., with "N" or "indefinite" values) then all of the specified repetitions of the object are played. Further, if the object addressed by the link is contained within another element that, in turn, contains a "repeat" attribute, then those repetitions are played, too.
4. It is forbidden to link to elements that are the content of <switch> elements.

10

Using the <a> Element to Link Media Objects

The <a> element associates a link with a complete media object, unlike the <anchor> element, which facilitates linking to parts of other media objects. Although the functionality of the <a> element is very similar to the functionality of the <A> element in HTML 4.0, SMIL has added the show attribute, which controls the temporal behavior of the source document once the link on that document has been followed. Table 10-5 lists the attributes that are applicable to the <a> element.

Table 10-5 Attributes used with the <a> element

Attribute Name	Explanation
href	Specifies the URI of the link's destination; this attribute is required for <a> elements
id	Unique identifier
show	Controls the behavior of the source document containing the link when the link is followed; possible values: "replace" (current presentation is paused and replaced by the destination resource; default value); "new" (presentation of the destination resource starts in a new context, not affecting the source resource);"pause" (source presentation is paused, and the destination resource starts in a new context)
title	All <a> elements should have a "title" attribute; the value for "title" should describe the linked media object

The <a> element can contain the following child elements: <animation>, <audio>, <img>, <par>, <ref>, <seq>, <switch>, <text>, <textstream>, and <video>. The <a> element does not influence the synchronization (i.e., ordering or timing) of its child elements. Please note, though, that <a> elements may not be nested.

Here is an example of an <a> element link that starts a new video presentation in a new window:

```
<a href="http://www.TLSales.com/new_merch_2003.smi"
          title= "New Merchandise for 2003" show="new" >
     <video id="import_video01" region= "video_reg01" />
</a>
```

The following example shows a link that starts a replacement presentation instead of the source presentation that displayed the link. It allows a SMIL player to spawn from an HTML browser.

```
<a href="ad_strat_long.smil" show="new"
     region= "pip_window01">
Click here for the tour of our new advertising strategy!
</a>
```

Using the <anchor> Element to Link Parts of Media Objects

Recall that the <a> element is used to associate a link with a *complete* media object. Occasionally, it is useful to associate links with spatial and temporal subparts of a media object. The <anchor> element does that. First, with the id and href attributes, it identifies the linked/destination media object. Then the anchor element allows you to break an object into spatial subparts, using the coords attribute, or temporal subparts, using the begin and end attributes. Table 10-6 lists all the attributes applicable to the <anchor> element.

Table 10-6 <anchor> element attributes

Attribute Name	Explanation
begin	The time for the explicit begin of an element (seconds); two types: clock-based delay-value, and event-value; value is relative to the beginning of the destination media object
coords	Values specify a rectangle within the display area of a visual media object. Coordinates are relative to the top left corner of the visual media object, as shown in Figure 10-11. Values are: "left-x,top-y,right-x,bottom-y" (e.g, coords="50,10,200,110"). If specified as percentages (e.g., coords= "10%,10%,55%,40%"), values are relative to the total width or height of the media object display area.
end	The explicit end of an element (seconds); value is relative to the beginning of the destination media object
href	Contains the URI of the link's destination
id	Unique identifier

Table 10-6 <anchor> element attributes (continued)

Attribute Name	Explanation
show	Controls the behavior of the source document containing the link when the link is followed; possible values: "replace" (current presentation is paused and replaced by the destination resource; default value); "new" (presentation of the destination resource starts in a new context, not affecting the source resource); "pause" (source presentation is paused, and the destination resource starts in a new context).
skip-content	Introduced for future extensibility; possible values are "true" (ignore the content of this element) or "false", (process the content of this element)
title	Like <a>, all <anchor> elements should have a "title" attribute; its value should describe the linked media object

Figure 10-11 illustrates the positioning of the display rectangle, using the <anchor> element with its coords attribute, according to the description of coords in Table 10-6.

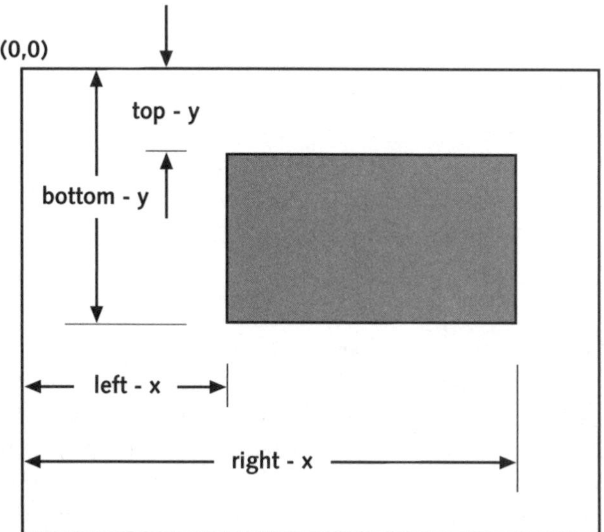

Figure 10-11 Using the <anchor> element

Here is an example of a link that might be associated with a video concerning TLSales revenues for a given year. When encountered, the <video> element automatically links to a specific portion of a speech made by TLSales CEO during the 2002 Annual General Meeting:

```
<video id= "ceorevspk02" region="video_reg1">
       <anchor show="pause"
               href="http://www.TLSales.com/ceo_agm_2002.mpg"
               begin="33s" end="61s" />
</video>
```

Here is another example, where a new motorcycle helmet is shown to protect a crash-test dummy during an impact test. When encountered, the <img> element automatically links to a specific portion of a graphic stored on the local system:

```
<img id= "helmet_test03" region="img_reg1">
       <anchor show="new"
               href="\motor\access\safety\f-face_test03.jpg"
               coords="180,25,225,57" />
</img>
```

VIEWING AND PREPARING SMIL DOCUMENTS

You can use a few browsers to view SMIL 1.0 documents. The two most common SMIL browsers are Apple QuickTime applications and RealPlayer/RealAudio applications. They have proven very popular, with millions of copies installed.

The first commercial SMIL player was RealNetworks' RealPlayer G2. Previous versions of RealPlayer played only RealNetworks' proprietary audio and video file formats. G2 included support for many other media types such as WAV, AVI, JPEG, MPEG, and others. RealNetworks implemented a large subset of the SMIL 1.0 specifications in G2, and intends to continue supporting SMIL with future versions.

Microsoft's IE 5.5 browser includes a useful new feature inspired by the SMIL specification: the TIME module, which is a subset of the SMIL specification. The HTML+TIME implementation is a first version of the SMIL 2.0 profile. As stated earlier, SMIL 2.0 uses modules, and one or more modules can be included in other languages such as XHTML.

Oratrix Development (from the Netherlands) was active in the development of SMIL 1.0—and, later SMIL 2.0—from the start of the SMIL standardization process. Oratrix released the world's first SMIL player in 1998, and the beta versions of the GRiNS/SMIL-2 player (again the world's first!) have been tested by thousands of users worldwide. In addition to custom and enterprise player support, Oratrix also distributes the award-winning series of GRiNS authoring tools for SMIL. Oratrix also offers versions of its GRiNS products that are compatible with nearly all SMIL players (including RealPlayer) and even Microsoft's HTML+TIME.

X-Smiles, a nonprofit project started by the Telecommunications Software and Multimedia Laboratory at Helsinki University of Technology, is a Java-based XML browser. It is intended for both desktop use and embedded network devices and to support multimedia services. The main advantage of the X-Smiles browser is that it supports several XML-related specifications and is still suitable for embedded devices supporting the Java environment. X-Smiles is not an HTML browser, though in the future it may support XHTML.

Helio is a French nonprofit organization based in Melun, France. Their SOJA Cherbourg product is a downloadable Java-based SMIL player.

In 1998, Compaq developed their Hypermedia Presentation and Authoring System (HPAS) to present, integrate, and manage time-based hypermedia documents. HPAS ran as an applet within Netscape Communicator; as a result, an HTML wrapper was needed to call up the applet.

Also about that time, the U.S. National Institute of Standards and Technology (NIST) developed their Streaming Synchronization MultiMedia (S2M2) as a subcomponent of their Streaming Synchronization Multimedia research project. S2M2 is a Java Applet-based SMIL Player (version 1.0). S2M2 1.0 implemented more than 60% of the overall SMIL 1.0 features. Developed under Sun's Java Development Kit 1.1 & JMF 1.0, S2M2 was only an experimental reference prototype.

RealNetworks has recently developed an editor called RealPresenter, which can take a Powerpoint presentation, let you add video and audio to it, transform it into GIF files, and then automatically create a SMIL document that packages and synchronizes all the media elements into a coherent whole. Unfortunately, some of the media objects are occasionally in a format proprietary to RealNetworks, so other SMIL browsers—such as the Quicktime SMIL browser—cannot decode these media object files. The only applications that could properly interpret all the media objects, therefore, would be RealNetworks SMIL browser(s).

Chapter Summary

- Streaming media is a technology for transferring audio, video, and other multimedia data in real time over the Internet or even over private networks, so that it can be processed as a steady and continuous stream. The Synchronized Multimedia Integration Language (SMIL) is an XML-related language that enables authors to create streaming media presentations by combining different types of media.
- The first full specification of SMIL, titled "Synchronized Multimedia Integration Language (SMIL) 1.0 Specification," was endorsed as a W3C Recommendation on June 15, 1998. The second specification, SMIL 2.0, was endorsed as a Recommendation in August 2001.
- An SMIL document, like other XML-related documents, consists of two main parts: a prolog and a <smil> element. The <smil> element consists of the <head> element and the <body> element. The <head> element contains all the layout information for the SMIL document; the <body> element contains all media object and object timing (i.e., synchronization) information.
- In the <head> element, the <root-layout> element contains specifications for the viewport of the SMIL display application; the <region> elements and their attributes specify the number, size and position of separate and discrete regions in the viewport, wherein the media objects are played or displayed. Thus, the region's visual characteristics are defined in the <head> section.

- Child elements in the <body> element specify what media objects are to be rendered in the regions defined in the <head> element. The synchronization elements <seq> and <par> govern whether media objects are displayed or played in sequence or in parallel and for how long. The several kinds of media object elements are all associated with the specific predefined regions Thus, the audiovisual contents are defined in the <body> section.
- A special SMIL element called <switch> makes it possible for you to adapt your presentation according to the capabilities and other properties of your recipient user's system. Using child elements with attributes to conduct Boolean true/false tests, <switch> can determine which characteristics prevail and are executed for optimum bandwidth use and appropriate display.
- Hyperlinking elements provide SMIL documents with the ability to access other SMIL or non-SMIL documents, applications, or plug-ins. The <a> element is used to associate a link with other complete media objects; the <anchor> element facilitates linking to parts of other media objects.
- There are several applications available to create and view SMIL 1.0 documents. The most common are Apple QuickTime applications and RealPlayer/RealAudio applications. However, GRiNS (Oratrix, the Netherlands), X-Smiles (Helsinki University of Technology, Finland), SOJA (Helio, France), HPAS (Compaq, USA) and S2M2 (NIST, U.S.A.) have also produced various SMIL 1.0-compliant applications.

Review Questions

1. ________________ is a technology for transferring audio, video, and other multimedia data in real time over the Internet or even over private networks, so that it can be processed as a steady and continuous stream.
2. What was the two-pronged problem that SMIL was specifically developed to solve?
3. Which of the following are types of streaming technology? (Choose all that apply.)
   a. serverless streaming
   b. clientless streaming
   c. true streaming
   d. HTTP streaming
   e. progressive download streaming
   f. none of the above
4. Controlling the timing, synchronization, and lifecycle of media objects is the same as controlling their ________________ behavior.
   a. corporal
   b. temporal
   c. visual

d. protocol

e. streaming

f. none of the above

5. How many areas of SMIL functionality do the SMIL 2.0 markup modules define semantics and syntax for?

   a. 3

   b. 5

   c. 8

   d. 9

   e. none of the above

6. The most fundamental part of a SMIL document is the <rootl> element. True or false?

7. To fulfill its layout-related duties, the <head> element has to contain:

   a. a <layout> element and a <switch> element, and any number of <meta> elements

   b. one <layout> element, one <switch> element, and one <meta> element

   c. a <layout> element or a <switch> element and any number of <meta> elements

   d. any number and combination of <layout>, <switch>, and <meta> elements

   e. none of the above

8. Why do you have to assign unique id attribute values to each <region> element?

9. Even if you are going to just let the default layout values prevail for *all* the media object elements in your document, you still have to create a <layout> element. It will be an empty element, though. True or false?

10. Inside the <layout> element, the ________________ element determines the size and other attributes of the SMIL 1.0 player's viewport.

11. When defining the left, top, width, and height attributes of a region, you can define the width and height in pixels, but you can define the left and top in pixels and ________________.

    a. percentages

    b. millimeters

    c. inches

    d. all of the above

    e. none of the above

12. Match the following terms:

a. fill; no distortion	1. fit= "scroll"
b. grow; no distortion	2. fit= "meet"
c. scroll; no distortion	3. fit= "slice"
d. fill; distortion	4. fit= "fill"

13. If you want to include additional information (e.g., key words, the author's name, etc.) within the <head> element of your SMIL document, and you don't want to be restricted with respect to the number of such elements you want to include, which element is recommended?
14. What is the name of the unique identifier attribute that can be used in several elements?
    a. base
    b. title
    c. content
    d. type
    e. name
    f. id
15. When planning the sequencing and synchronization of media objects, what diagram comes in handy?
    a. time line
    b. baseline
    c. script
    d. flowchart
16. Which statement makes the most sense?
    a. You can put <seq>s inside <par>s, but not <par>s inside <seq>s.
    b. You can put <par>s inside <seq>s, but not <seq>s inside <par>s.
    c. Don't do either; just put like elements inside one another.
    d. You can put <par>s inside <seq>s, and vice versa.
17. The ________________ and ________________ attributes are the most obvious of the media object lifecycle controls.
18. Which of the media object elements is called the "generic" media element, to be used when an author is in doubt about the category that a media object belongs to?
    a. <ref>
    b. <text>
    c. <meta>
    d. <id>

19. What are the two reasons for adding an alt attribute/value pair to a media object element start tag?
20. Match the following:

a. 4	1.	true color
b. 24	2.	65536 colors
c. 8	3.	16 colors
d. 16	4.	256 colors

21. To the W3C, video and audio files come under the ______________ media category, while text files and graphics files come under the ______________ media category.
22. What is the source to check for language codes, when developing a list to specify with the system-language attribute?
23. SMIL supports those locators currently used in HTML, including name fragment identifiers but not the '#' connector. True or false?
24. Which of the following statements is true?
    a. The <a> element is used to associate a link with a complete media object; the <anchor> element facilitates linking to parts of other media objects.
    b. The <anchor> element is used to associate a link with a complete media object; the <a> element facilitates linking to parts of other media objects.
    c. Both the <a> element and the <anchor> element can be used to associate a link with a complete media object; but only the <anchor> element facilitates linking to parts of other media objects.
    d. none of the above
25. The first commercial SMIL player was:
    a. S2M2
    b. GRiNS
    c. RealPlayer G2
    d. SOJA Cherbourg

10

Hands-on Projects

Project 10-1

In these Hands-on Projects, you create two synchronized multimedia presentations using SMIL 1.0 media object elements. The content and sequence of both presentations are identical, though the technology behind them differs. In the first three projects, you build a presentation that uses Real Networks' RealOne player. RealOne fully supports the SMIL 1.0 specification. The second presentation appears similar, but uses Internet Explorer 5.5 or later and Microsoft's version of SMIL called HTML+TIME.

To set up the project:

1. Use Windows Explorer to create a new folder called **Ch10** in C:\home\<yourname>.
2. Copy the files and directory located in the Ch10\Project_10-1 folder on Data Disk into your C:/home/<yourname>/Ch10 folder.
3. To start XML Spy, click **Start**, point to **Programs** (point to **All Programs** in Windows XP), point to **XML Spy Suite**, and then click **XML Spy IDE**. The XML Spy window opens.
4. To create a SMIL document, click **File** on the menu bar, and then click **New**. The Create new document dialog box opens. Select **smil Sync. Multimedia Integ. Language**, and then click **OK**. The default SMIL document appears in the main window.
5. To save the new document, click **File** on the menu bar, and then click **Save**. In the Save As dialog box, click the **Save in** list arrow to navigate to the C:\home\<yourname>\Ch10 folder. Type **dive.smi** in the File name text box, and then click **Save**.
6. To configure the document, click **View** on the menu bar, and then click **Text view** to view the default SMIL source code.
7. Notice that the default SMIL DOCTYPE declaration references the SMIL dtd and identifies the smil element as the root element of the document. The smil element provided by XML Spy uses the empty element syntax. Replace it with a smil element start and end tag by inserting:

   ```
   <smil>
   </smil>
   ```

   XML Spy automatically inserts the closing tags for many elements, including the smil element.
8. Recall that a SMIL 1.0 document has both a head and a body element. Within the smil element, type the following:

   ```
   <head>
   </head>
   <body>
   </body>
   ```

   The head element contains the presentation information for the document, while the body element contains the media and synchronization information. Your document should resemble Figure 10-12.
9. Click **File** on the menu bar, and then click **Save** to save your work. Leave dive.smi open in XML Spy for the next project.

XML Spy - [dive.smil]

File Edit Project XML DTD/Schema Schema design XSL Document Editor Convert Table View Browser Tools Window Help

Project

```
<?xml version="1.0" encoding="UTF-8"?>
<!-- edited with XML Spy v4.0 U (http://www.xmlspy.com) by David Crewson (Eydeas Technology (www.eydeas.net)) -->
<!DOCTYPE smil PUBLIC "-//W3C//DTD SMIL 1.0//EN" "http://www.w3.org/TR/REC-smil/SMIL10.dtd">
<smil>
    <head>
    </head>
    <body>
    </body>
</smil>
```

Figure 10-12

Project 10-2

Now that you have prepared the SMIL document, you are ready to define the presentation layout. The presentation is a multimedia demonstration of the underwater world. There are two videos, a text document, and a number of digital images that you assemble into a short feature that you are able to view using the Real Networks' RealOne Player.

To create the presentation layout:

1. With the dive.smi file that you created Project 10-1 still open in XML Spy, create a layout element by inserting the following in the document's head element:

   ```
   <layout>
   </layout>
   ```

   The content of the layout element determines how the media in the document's body are positioned. You could also define multiple layouts based upon the display capabilities of the playback computer using the switch statement.

2. Every SMIL application has a viewport window that displays the media. To define the properties of the application's viewport, you need to set the properties of the root-layout element. Within the layout element, type:

   ```
   <root-layout width="600" height="300" />
   ```

   This sets the viewport window to 600 by 300 pixels.

3. Regions are the areas within the viewport that contain the media objects. While there can be only one root-layout, several regions can correspond to different visual media objects. For this presentation document, you need three regions, one for the video, text, and digital images. Directly below the root-layout element, type:

   ```
   <region id="video" left="0" top="0" width="150" height=
   "150" fit="fill" />
   <region id="text" left="0" top="150" width="150" height=
   "130" />
   <region id="image" left="150" top="0" width="450" height=
   "300" />
   ```

   Each region is uniquely identified in the document body by an id value. The left and top attributes define the position of the region, relative to the upper left hand corner of the viewport. The width and height attributes define a region's static size, although the media can be a different size than the region. In this case, the videos need to be resized by stretching them to fit the region using a fill fit. This

10

type of fit does not proportionally increase or decrease the size, so the visual media may look stretched or compressed, but it precisely fills the region.

4. You have finished creating the layout of the document. It should resemble Figure 10-13. At this point, the document does not contain any media. A blank viewport would appear if you attempted to render the document in a SMIL player. Click **File** on the menu bar, and then click **Save** to save your work.

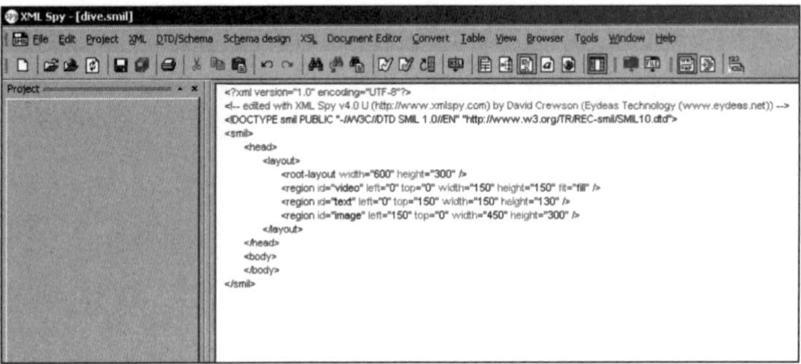

Figure 10-13

Project 10-3

Now that you have created the layout of the presentation, you are ready to add the content and presentation sequence into the body of the document. The presentation begins with a video, text, and a digital image sharing the viewport. The text is a scrolling sequence of phrases contained in a Real Networks' RealText (demo.rt) file and runs in sequence with the video. The digital image remains in place while the video and text are playing, and then transitions into a slideshow.

If you don't have RealOne Player installed on your computer, download a copy of the program from *www.real.com* before performing Project 10-3.

To add the media content to the presentation:

1. Since the viewport requires that three different media pieces are placed into the three regions simultaneously at the beginning of the presentation, you must use a par element to contain the media object elements. The par element renders all child elements at the same time. Directly following the body start tag, <body>, type:

```
<par>
<\/par>
```

2. All media is referenced as external resources in SMIL 1.0. The text for the presentation could have been contained within a text file, HTML document, or any other text-based format. For this presentation, you use the text within a RealText file. RealText is a proprietary format used by the RealOne player. It provides enhanced text window capabilities and allows text markup similar to HTML. To add the RealText file within the par element type:

```
<text region="text" src="demo.rt" dur="indefinite" fill="
freeze" />
```

The text from the demo.rt file is placed in the text region defined in the document head. To prevent the media from disappearing during playback, the duration attribute, dur, is set to indefinite. The fill attribute is initialized to freeze, which keeps the last line of text on the screen after the playback has finished.

3. Two MPEG videos play back-to-back in the video region. The first video begins playing along with the other media when the presentation begins, but the second video must wait for the first video to finish before it begins. Even though the initial presentation of the text, image, and video occur in parallel, the videos themselves are sequential; therefore, they must be synchronized within a sequence element. Directly below the text element, type:

```
<seq>
   <video region="video" src="demo1.mpg" />
   <video region="video" src="demo2.mpg" fill="freeze" />
<\seq>
```

This code indicates that the second video does not start playing until after the first one ends. The browser renders them both in the same region, and freezes the last pane of the second video while the rest of the presentation continues.

4. In the same way that you synchronized the video, you can display the slideshow images in sequence following the end of the video. When the slideshow begins, the browser can show a digital image in a region for three seconds before replacing it with the next image. Directly below the sequence element end tag, </seq>, type the following:

```
<seq>
      <img region="image" src="images/01.jpg" dur="33"/>
      <img region="image" src="images/02.jpg" dur="3"/>
      <img region="image" src="images/03.jpg" dur="3"/>
...
      <img region="image" src="images/17.jpg" dur="3"/>
      <img region="image" src="images/18.jpg" dur="3"/>
      <img region="image" src="images/19.jpg" dur="3" fill
      ="freeze"/>
</seq>
```

Notice that the images are located in a relative directory path called images; there are nineteen images to display in total.

You can synchronize the slideshow to wait for the end of the videos in several ways. The method you used in Step 4 delays the start of the show using the value in the first image's dur attribute. The combined time of the videos is 31 seconds; the second image appears after the first image has appeared for 33 seconds. Each image thereafter is displayed for a duration of three seconds, and the last image freezes in the region following the presentation. Your document should resemble Figure 10-14.

5. Click **File** on the menu bar, and then click **Save** to save your work.

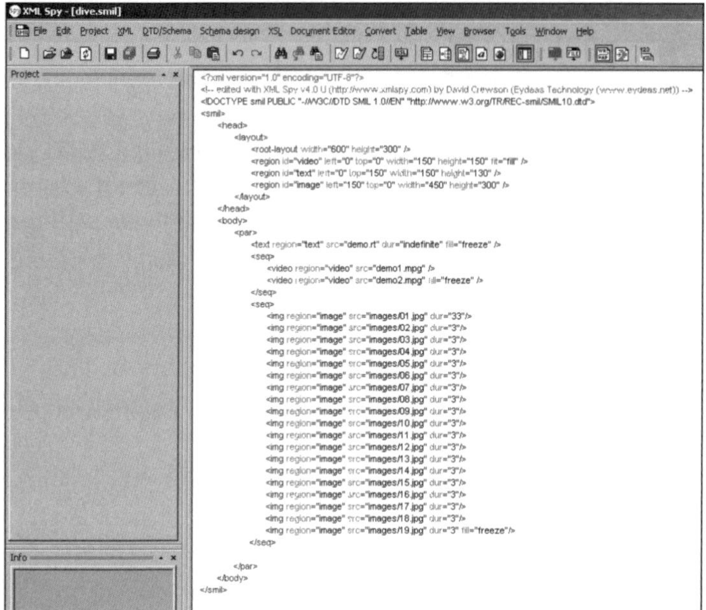

Figure 10-14

6. Click **File** on the menu bar, and then click **Exit** to exit XML Spy.

To view the SMIL document:

1. Click **Start**, point to **Programs** (point to **All Programs** in Windows XP), and then click **RealOne Player**. The Real Networks' RealOne player appears.
2. Close the browser portion of the player by clicking the **Close** button next to the Location text box. The player window resizes and remains active.
3. To play the presentation you completed in this project, click **File** on the menu bar, and then click **Open**. In the Open dialog box, click **Browse**. The Open File dialog appears.
4. Click the **Look in** list arrow, and then navigate to the C:/home/<yourname>/Ch10 folder, if necessary. Select **dive.smi**, and then click **Open**. The RealOne player resizes and loads the presentation.
5. The presentation plays in the viewport. If the presentation does not begin, or if the player posts an error message, return to XML Spy, and ensure that your code matches the document shown in Figure 10-13. Close RealOne Player.

Project 10-4

You now build the same presentation using Microsoft's HTML+TIME. HTML+TIME integrates a subset of SMIL with HTML, and runs as an Internet Explorer default behavior extension, similar to VML. In this project, you will prepare the document for the underwater presentation in Internet Explorer 5.5 and later.

To set up the project:

1. Click **Start**, point to **Programs** (point to **All Programs** in Windows XP), point to **XML Spy Suite**, and click **XML Spy IDE**. The Spy window opens.
2. To create an HTML document, click **File** on the menu bar, and then click **New**. In the Create new document dialog box, select **html HTML Document**, and then click **OK**. The default source code for a new HTML document appears in the main window.
3. To save the HTML document, click **File** on the menu bar, and then click **Save**. In the Save As dialog box, click the **Save in** list arrow, and then navigate to the C:\home\<yourname>\Ch10 folder, if necessary. Type **dive.html** in the File name text box, and then click **Save**.

   Notice that the document is a plain HTML file. In order for the HTML+TIME behavior to process the SMIL instructions, you must configure the document to explicitly declare a SMIL namespace and import the TIME default behavior to implement the SMIL media object elements.
4. To declare the SMIL namespace, replace the html start tag, <html>, with the following:

```
<html xmlns:t ="urn:schemas-microsoft-com:time">
```

10

5. Replace the title of the HTML document within the head element with the following:

```
<title>The Underwater World</title>
```

   There are two ways to identify elements that require processing by the HTML+TIME behavior. For HTML elements (that are not SMIL media object elements), you can synchronize using a style sheet declaration. The style sheet rule associates all elements of a certain class with the HTML+TIME behavior.
6. To declare the internal style sheet, type the following directly below the title element:

```
<style type="text/css">
.time  { behavior: url(#DEFAULT#TIME2); }
</style>
```

   The second method uses the IMPORT processing instruction to map SMIL media object elements using the t namespace to the HTML+TIME behavior. All SMIL media object elements in the HTML document use the t namespace prefix and are processed by the HTML+TIME behavior.
7. Directly below the style element end tag, </style>, type:

```
<?IMPORT namespace="t" implementation="#default#TIME2" ?>
```

   You have now finished creating the framework required to build an HTML document supporting the TIME default behavior in Internet Explorer 5.5+. Your document should resemble Figure 10-15.
8. Click **File** on the menu bar, and then click **Save** to save your work.

```
<html xmlns:t ="urn:schemas-microsoft-com:time">
  <head>
    <title>The Underwater World</title>
    <style>
        .time { behavior: url(#DEFAULT#TIME2); }
    </style>
    <?IMPORT namespace="t" implementation="#default#TIME2" ?>
  </head>
  <body>
    <p>Enter the body text of your HTML document here</p>
  </body>
</html>
```

Figure 10-15

Project 10-5

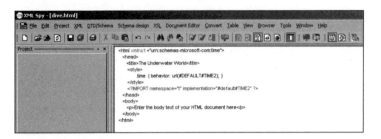

Now that you prepared the framework of the HTML+TIME document, you are ready to define the presentation layout. The presentation is the same multimedia demonstration of the underwater world that you created in Projects 10-1 to 10-3. Notice that Internet Explorer does not use the SMIL dtd; there is no smil element, and no layout element in the HTML document. You define the presentation using style attributes within the SMIL media object elements. Compare the code that you add in the following project with the SMIL document that you created in Projects 10-1 to 10-3.

To create the presentation layout:

1. Recall from Project 10-3 that the presentation requires that the text, video, and digital image are simultaneously placed into the browser at the beginning of the presentation. You use a par element to contain the data and render all child elements at the same time. Replace the default paragraph element with the following:

   ```
   <t:par>
   </t:par>
   ```

   Notice that the par element uses the t namespace prefix. This ensures that the browser forwards the par element data to the TIME behavior for processing.

2. Recall that two videos play sequentially in the presentation. Use a seq element to manage the playback of the videos. Within the par element, type:

   ```
   <t:seq style="position:absolute; top:0; left:0; width:150;
    height:150;" fit="fill">
          <t:video src="demo1.mpg" mute="true" />
          <t:video src="demo2.mpg" mute="true" fill="freeze"/>
   </t:seq>
   ```

   Because HTML+TIME does not use regions or the concept of a layout, each media object element either positions itself within the browser pane, or inherits the layout properties from its parent. The style attribute for the seq element sizes and positions the video object elements in the same position. The default fit for the media objects is fill, and the video objects are resized to 150 by 150 pixels.

3. Instead of managing the text externally as in the last presentation, the text is imbedded in the document, and encapsulated using the HTML div element. Directly below the seq end tag, </t:seq>, type:

```
<t:seq style="position:absolute; top:150; left:0;
     width:150; height:150;">
       <div class="time" dur="3">
             <b>Welcome to the underwater world!</b>
       </div>
       <div class="time" dur="4">
          It's amazing what you can see under the sea...
       </div>
       <div class="time" dur="6">
              Care to soar with an eagle ray...
       </div>
       <div class="time" dur="7">
              Or swim with the sharks.<br/><br/>
              (Better here than in the boardroom!)
       </div>
       <div class="time" dur="3">
              Check out all the cool stuff
       </div>
       <div class="time" dur="3">
              In an octopus' garden
       </div>
       <div class="time" dur="indefinite">
          Under the sea.<br/><br/>
          <a href="http://www.padi.com" target="_blank">
                     Click here to get certified!
             </a>
       </div>
</t:seq>
```

This is the same text you used in the demo.rt RealText file in the previous presentation. Note that each line uses the class attribute time value of the div element to identify that it should be processed by the TIME behavior. This is the style sheet rule that you declared in the style element, and is the method that non-SMIL media object elements use to participate in the timing model. Each line is presented in sequence for a duration specified by the value of the dur attribute.

10

4. The last step towards finishing the document involves adding the slideshow. The slideshow uses the same timing principles as the first presentation. Type the following immediately following the second seq element's end tag, </t: seq>:

```
<t:seq style="position:absolute; top:0; left:150;
    width:450; height:300;">
<t:img dur="32" src="images\01.jpg" />
<t:img dur="3" src="images\02.jpg" />
<t:img dur="3" src="images\03.jpg" />
...
<t:img dur="3" src="images\17.jpg" />
<t:img dur="3" src="images\18.jpg" />
<t:img dur="3" src="images\19.jpg"  fill="freeze"/>
</t:seq>
```

5. Your document should resemble Figure 10-16.

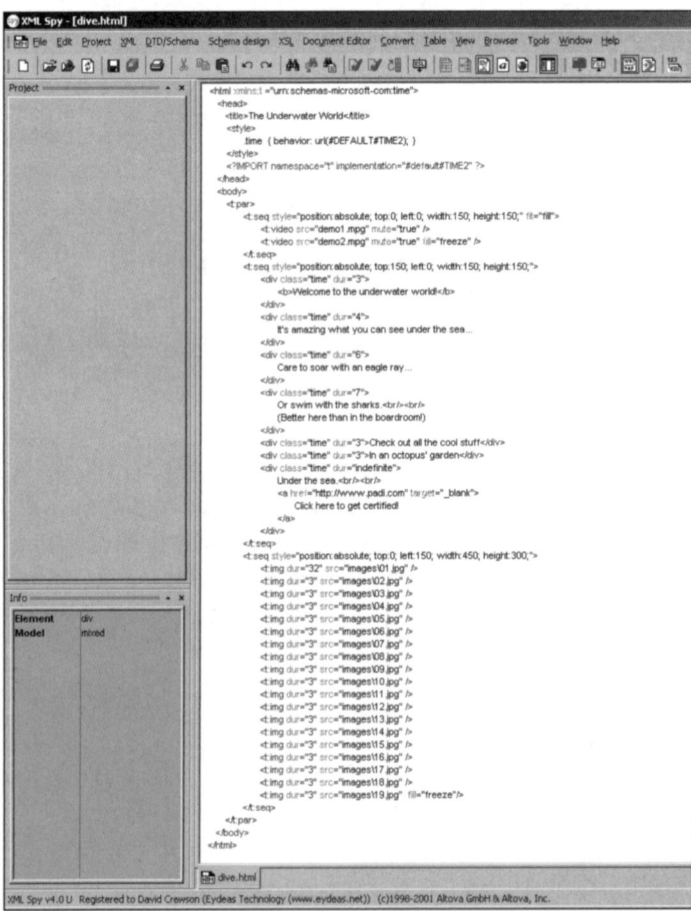

Figure 10-16

6. Click **File** on the menu bar, and then click **Save** to save your work.
7. Click **File** on the menu bar, and then click **Exit** to close XML Spy.

View the SMIL document

1. Click **Start**, point to **Programs** (point to **All Programs** in Windows XP), and then click **Internet Explorer**. The Internet Explorer browser window opens.
2. In the Address text box, type **C:/home/<yourname>/Ch10/dive.html**, and then press **Enter**. The HTML+TIME document begins to play back in the browser. (Substitute your drive letter for C:, if necessary.)

   If the presentation does not begin, or if the browser posts an error message, return to XML Spy, and ensure that your code matches the document in Figure 10-15.
3. Try opening both the **demo.smi** and the **demo.html** files in Internet Explorer 5.5 or later, Netscape Navigator, Real Networks' RealOne, and the Browser view in XML Spy. Note the differences in compatibility and SMIL 1.0 support.

Case Project

The Ch10\Case_Project folder contains html, video, and audio files that you can use to create a SMIL 1.0 sequence. You can either start by creating a new file in XML Spy or by copying an existing file that you know is currently working. Table 10-7 lists the available files.

10

Table 10-7 Available files for case project

Filename and Location	Type
Ch10\Case_Project\promo1.html	XHTML
Ch10\Case_Project\promo2.html	XHTML
Ch10\Case_Project\promo_video.html	XHTML
Ch10\Case_Project\promo_combo.html	XHTML
Ch10\Case_Project\promo_combo2.html	XHTML
Ch10\Case_Project\promo_combo3.html	XHTML
Ch10\Case_Project\promo_combo4.html	XHTML
Ch10\Case_Project\text1.txt	Text
Ch10\Case_Project\text2.txt	Text
Ch10\Case_Project\images*.*	AVI, JPG, MP3, and SMIL

All of these files use the Microsoft Internet Explorer time-sequencing modules. Be sure to modify the paths in these files to reflect the appropriate locations on your computer.

CHAPTER

11

INTRODUCTION TO CASCADING STYLE SHEETS (CSS)

In this chapter, you will learn:

- About Cascading Style Sheets
- How to specify styles for XML documents
- How to create style rules
- How to insert images with CSS style rules
- About other introductory style specifications
- Why style sheets cascade

Developing an XML-related document does not guarantee that it will be displayed the way you want it to appear. This chapter explains how you can control the style elements, such as the fonts, colors, and spacing of your XML Web documents by developing and using Cascading Style Sheets (CSS), a style language that lets you separate content and style as you design Web pages. In this chapter, you learn how to use CSS to achieve the style results you want by specifying styles for your XML documents, creating style rules, inserting images, and adding other style elements such as borders.

An Overview of Cascading Style Sheets

In Chapter 6, you learned that the W3C developed the Extensible Stylesheet Language (XSL) to transform XML data. That is, XSL applies its own type of style sheet to transform one kind of XML-related document into another. By comparison, **Cascading Style Sheets (CSS)** files contain specifications that XML processes to add stylistic control to HTML or XML Web documents. In other words, unlike XSL transformations that change a document's type, CSS specifications control a document's appearance.

The World Wide Web Consortium and Cascading Style Sheets

The W3C originally developed the CSS language to add style to HTML documents, but has since expanded CSS to complement documents pertaining to XML-related languages, such as XHTML, SVG, and SMIL.

Historically, both the CSS Working Group and the XSL Working Group actively but independently developed style controls. Their activities included developing a style sheet language, constructing a test suite, and creating validators and sample style sheets. The W3C now anticipates that the primary future role of the CSS Working Group will be to coordinate the efforts of the XSL, SVG, SYMM, MathML, Xforms, and other Working Groups as they determine how CSS style sheets will be implemented in the future.

Levels of Cascading Style Sheets

Cascading Style Sheets, Level 1 (CSS1) became a W3C Recommendation on December 17, 1996, and was revised on January 11, 1999. Web page developers use CSS1 as a language to create simple style sheets that allow authors and readers to attach simple style controls to HTML documents. To specify its style controls, CSS1 uses terms that are familiar to those who work with common desktop publishing technology.

One of the fundamental features of CSS in general is that it cascades—or combines and coordinates—style-control specifications from various style sheet files. This means, for example, that document authors can attach their preferred style sheets to Web documents, while users can apply their personal style sheets to accommodate their preferences, compensate for human disabilities, or adjust for equipment differences. This cascading nature, including rules for setting priorities and resolving conflicts among different style control sources, are discussed in more detail later in this chapter.

Cascading Style Sheets, Level 2 (CSS2) was endorsed as a W3C Recommendation on May 12, 1998. As an upgrade to CSS1, it includes more sophisticated style-control features such as page-based layout, support for downloadable fonts, and the definition of rectangular regions for displaying different parts of documents. CSS2 also makes it easier to develop media-specific style sheets, so that you can develop documents specifically for visual browsers, printers, handheld devices, aural devices, and Braille devices, for example. The CSS2 specification also supports content positioning, downloadable fonts, table layout, features for internationalization, automatic counters and numbering, and some properties related to the user interface. Finally, because CSS2 is built on CSS1, valid CSS1 style sheets, with few exceptions, are valid CSS2 style sheets.

If you are experienced with CSS1, you may feel that some changes introduced with CSS2 are confusing and even contradictory. If so, check Appendix B of CSS2 at *www.w3.org/TR/REC-CSS2/changes.html#changes-from-css1* where you can find a summary of all CSS1 to CSS2 changes, grouped according to three categories: new functionality, updated descriptions, and semantic changes from CSS1.

At the time of this writing, the **Cascading Style Sheets, Level 3 (CSS3)** specification is in development. Along with all of the features that users and developers have come to expect in their desktop publishing environments, CSS3 will include many new features designed for an international and multimedia Internet.

CSS3 is expected to consist of several separate module specifications that allow developers to incorporate one or more modules at a time into new languages, documents, and Web sites. For example, CSS3 will include a color module to specify more ways to use colors, including a semi-transparency property; a mobile profile module to specify a common set of CSS features for all mobile devices; and a selectors module to select elements based on specified contents, whether they are unique elements or affiliated with certain XML namespaces.

Over a dozen modules are anticipated, and they are ultimately expected to be covered by several Recommendations.

Support for Cascading Style Sheets

Browsers and other programs supporting CSS have been developed by many W3C member companies, nonmember companies, and Open Source projects. There is excellent support for CSS1 and growing support for CSS2.

See *www.w3.org/Style/CSS/* for a discussion of CSS resources, including browsers and authoring tools.

The W3C also provides a CSS Validation Service at *http://jigsaw.w3.org/css-validator/*. You can choose to use the validator to check your CSS specifications at the Jigsaw site in one of four ways:

- You can download the validator and use it on your system.
- You can validate a cascading style sheet by providing a URI at the Jigsaw site.
- You can validate a cascading style sheet by providing your style control text.
- You can validate a cascading style sheet source file by uploading it to the Jigsaw site.

SPECIFYING STYLES FOR XML DOCUMENTS

You may be aware of the three methods of specifying styles in HTML documents: affiliating (i.e., attaching) the HTML document with an external style sheet using a specific declaration, specifying internal style sheets, and using inline style control in element start tags. You can use all three methods to specify styles for XML documents.

Affiliating External Style Sheets With XML Documents

Although you can use methods similar to the three HTML style specification methods listed earlier, for XML-related documents, you should use a declaration to an external style sheet whenever possible. Following are the major reasons for this recommendation:

- An author can change a document's style without having to access and modify the document itself.
- External style sheets can be shared among documents and thereby become the most efficient technique for applying your specified styles to more than one document at a time.

As a result of these features, you can use external style sheets to change the style of an entire Web site just by modifying or replacing one style sheet file.

The syntax for affiliating an external style sheet to an XML document is different from the HTML affiliation syntax, which appears in the <HEAD> element of an HTML document. To affiliate an external style sheet to an XML document, you incorporate the following processing instruction into the prolog of the XML document:

```
<?xml-stylesheet type="text/css"
    href="stylesheetname.css" ?>
```

The first part of the processing instruction—?xml-stylesheet—informs the parser that the XML document should access an external style sheet. The media type specification—type="text/css"—follows next. Whenever an XML document uses an external style sheet, this specification must appear. It tells the parser what type of media to specify in the HTTP data headers when the external style sheet is retrieved. Text/css means that the primary media type (also called the general media type) is text, while the media subtype (also called the specific format) is css.

For further information regarding the text/css media type, please refer to the Request for Comments RFC2318 on the Internet Society's Web site at *www.ietf.org/rfc/rfc2318.txt.*

The last part of the instruction—href="stylesheetname.css"—specifies that the value of the href pseudo-attribute is a URI. In this example, the value is *stylesheetname.css*, a generic filename. In your code, you replace this value with the name of the CSS file you want to use. Because the instruction does not include a directory path to the style sheet's filename, the parser looks for the style sheet file in the same directory as the XML document. If it is not located in the same directory, you should include a path to its directory.

Figure 11-1 shows another example of a CSS processing instruction. In contacts.xml, the third line designates a style sheet file that is found in the root directory of the Web server.

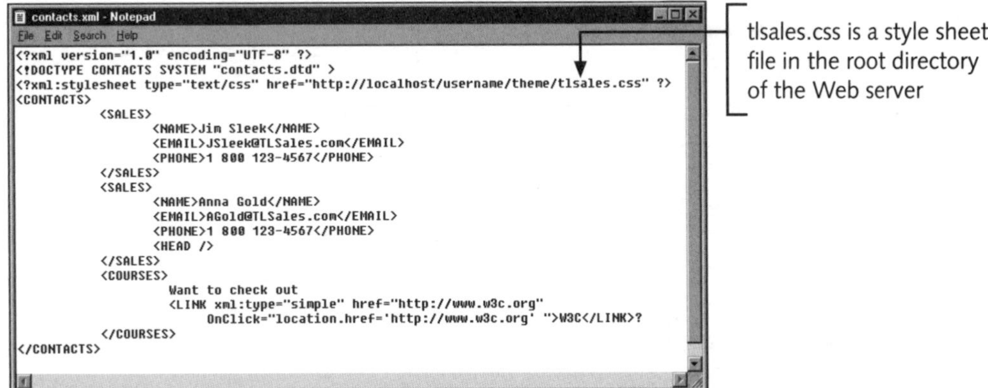

contacts.xml - Notepad

File Edit Search Help

```
<?xml version="1.0" encoding="UTF-8" ?>
<!DOCTYPE CONTACTS SYSTEM "contacts.dtd" >
<?xml:stylesheet type="text/css" href="http://localhost/username/theme/tlsales.css" ?>
<CONTACTS>
        <SALES>
                <NAME>Jim Sleek</NAME>
                <EMAIL>JSleek@TLSales.com</EMAIL>
                <PHONE>1 800 123-4567</PHONE>
        </SALES>
        <SALES>
                <NAME>Anna Gold</NAME>
                <EMAIL>AGold@TLSales.com</EMAIL>
                <PHONE>1 800 123-4567</PHONE>
                <HEAD />
        </SALES>
        <COURSES>
                Want to check out
                <LINK xml:type="simple" href="http://www.w3c.org"
                     OnClick="location.href='http://www.w3c.org' ">W3C</LINK>?
        </COURSES>
</CONTACTS>
```

tlsales.css is a style sheet file in the root directory of the Web server

Figure 11-1 contacts.xml refers to CSS file in the Web server root

Note

You may have noticed that the XML style sheet affiliation syntax has already appeared in several figures in Chapters 3, 4, and 7. Explaining the syntax then would have detracted from the topics then being discussed. Now that you are well-grounded in basic XML concepts, style sheets and their references can be more properly explained.

Figure 11-2 illustrates how XML processes an external CCS style sheet.

In this case, the XHTML file named example.html is passed to an XML parser which reads its prolog, sees that the external style sheet file named stylesheetname.css is required, and retrieves that file. The parser then passes the data from both files to the program (in this case, the program is a browser), which then processes the data and displays the result. In the figure, the style rules have been deliberately simplified to the representative phrase "...*style rule* ...". Actual style rules, including syntax and examples, are discussed later in this chapter.

11

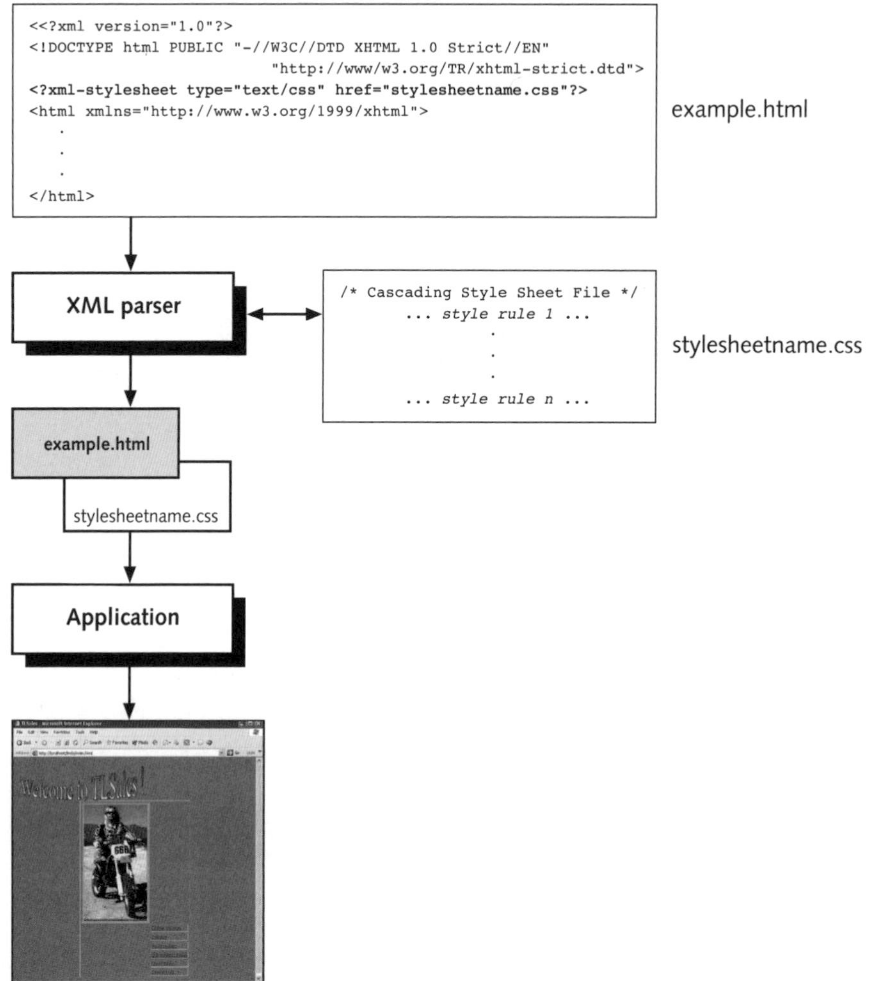

Figure 11-2 Processing with an external style sheet

Specifying an Internal Style Sheet

You also can include style rules in the data document itself. Figure 11-3 shows a simplified example, where the style rules are included in the <head> element of an XHTML file. Again, the style rules have been simplified for this illustration.

Specifying an internal style sheet is practical for small-scale XML projects. However, for large-scale development, an internal style sheet is not recommended because you lose the two major advantages of working with external style sheets—changing a document's style without modifying the document itself, and sharing external style sheets among documents to increase efficiency

```
<<?xml version="1.0"?>
<!DOCTYPE html PUBLIC "-//W3C//DTD XHTML 1.0 Strict//EN"
   "http://www/w3.org/TR/xhtml-strict.dtd">
<html xmlns="http://www.w3.org/1999/xhtml">
   <head>
      <title> Welcome to TLSales, Inc.!</title>
      <style type="text/css">
         ...style rule 1...
                  .
                  .
                  .
         ...style rule n...
      </style>
   </head>
   <body>
      .
      .
      .
   </body>
</html>
```

Figure 11-3 Simplified internal style sheet

The example in Figure 11-3 shows how to apply cascading style sheets to an XHTML document. Remember, in XHTML documents, all element and attribute names must be lowercase. From this point on, however, the cascading style sheet examples concern more generic XML files containing uppercase element and attribute names.

11

Specifying Inline Styles

In addition to using external and internal style sheets, you can also use the STYLE attribute to add styles to individual elements inline (that is, within the XML document, without having to resort to the external style sheet file). Figure 11-4 illustrates a generic syntax for using the STYLE attribute. Remember that, with certain XML-related languages such as XHTML, the attributes must be in lowercase.

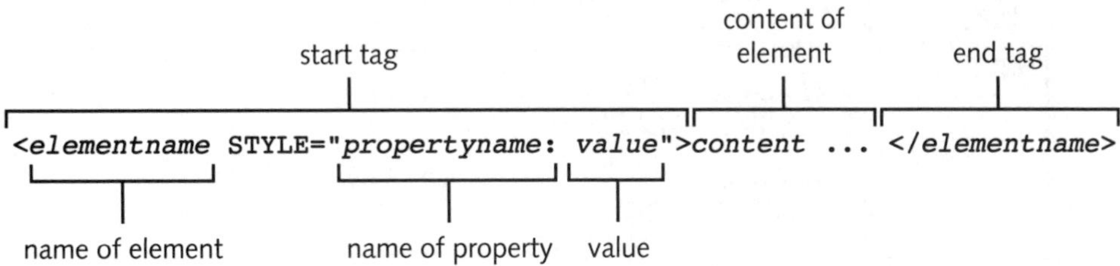

Figure 11-4 Generic inline STYLE syntax

To illustrate how to use an inline display style specification, return to the original contacts.xml file. Consider nesting an element called <LCASE> within each of the <EMAIL> elements, as in the following example:

```
<EMAIL>
     <LCASE STYLE="text-transform: lowercase" >
          JSleek@TLSales.com
     </LCASE>
</EMAIL>
```

Also review the following example:

```
<EMAIL>
     <LCASE STYLE="text-transform: lowercase" >
          AGold@TLSales.com
     </LCASE>
</EMAIL>
```

<LCASE> ensures that the e-mail addresses are lowercase. As in previous examples, so that contacts.xml remains valid, you must add the following declarations to the contacts.dtd file:

```
<!ELEMENT LCASE (PCDATA)* >
<!ATTLIST LCASE STYLE PCDATA #IMPLIED >
```

Creating Style Rules

Before applying styles to the elements in an XML document, review the basic style rule design concepts (recall that Chapter 2 introduced the basic XML components). This chapter uses two simplified files to introduce and illustrate its style rules. The first file is an example XML document file named contacts.xml, shown in Figure 11-5.

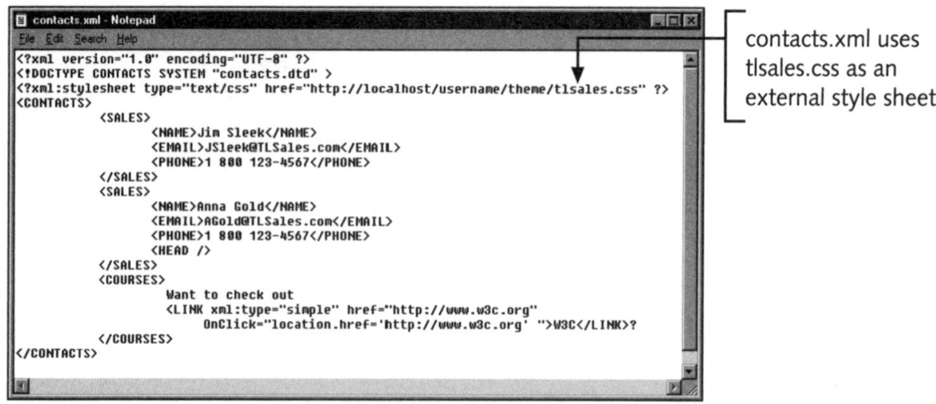


```
<?xml version="1.0" encoding="UTF-8" ?>
<!DOCTYPE CONTACTS SYSTEM "contacts.dtd" >
<?xml:stylesheet type="text/css" href="http://localhost/username/theme/tlsales.css" ?>
<CONTACTS>
        <SALES>
                <NAME>Jim Sleek</NAME>
                <EMAIL>JSleek@TLSales.com</EMAIL>
                <PHONE>1 800 123-4567</PHONE>
        </SALES>
        <SALES>
                <NAME>Anna Gold</NAME>
                <EMAIL>AGold@TLSales.com</EMAIL>
                <PHONE>1 800 123-4567</PHONE>
                <HEAD />
        </SALES>
        <COURSES>
                 Want to check out
                 <LINK xml:type="simple" href="http://www.w3c.org"
                      OnClick="location.href='http://www.w3c.org' ">W3C</LINK>?
        </COURSES>
</CONTACTS>
```

Figure 11-5 contacts.xml, a simple XML data file

The other file used to illustrate the rules and concepts in this chapter is the style sheet file named tlsales.css, shown in Figure 11-6.

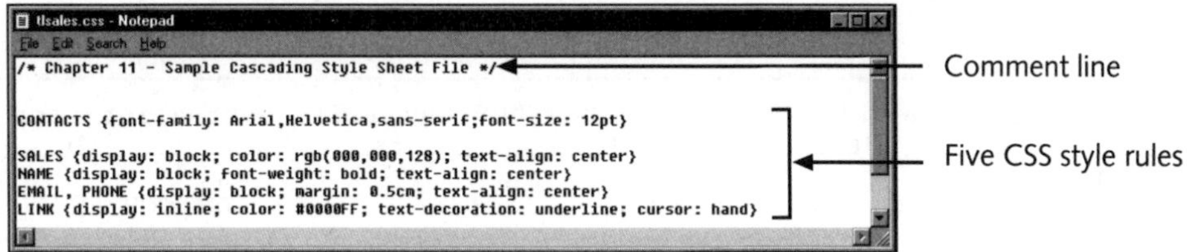

Figure 11-6 tlsales.css, a simple external style sheet file

You also work with files named contacts.xml and tlsales.css in the Hands-on projects at the end of this chapter. Those are different files, and do not resemble the ones shown in Figures 11-5 and 11-6.

In this chapter, when each new style concept or technique is introduced, it is always applied to the *original* data and style sheet files to minimize confusing the techniques and the syntax. However, once you are familiar with the techniques, feel free to combine them to achieve the results you want.

Figure 11-7 shows the result of applying tlsales.css, shown in Figure 11-6, to contacts.xml, the basic XML document.

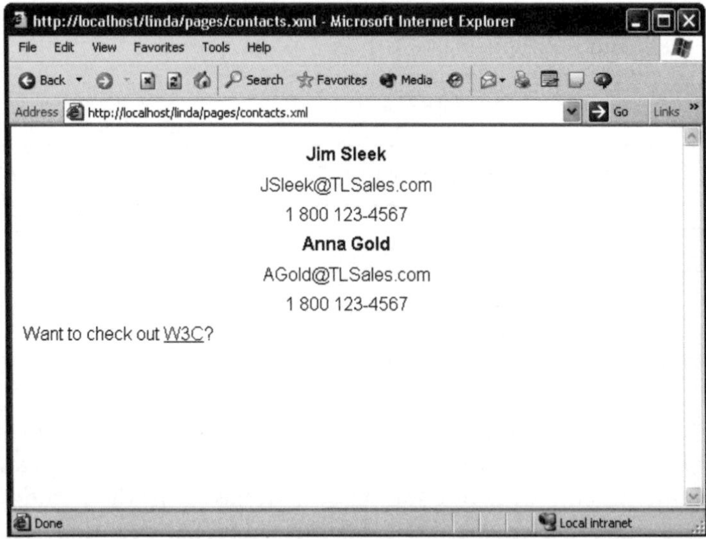

Figure 11-7 contacts.xml rendered in a browser

Recall that tlsales.css contains a comment line at the beginning followed by five simple CSS style rules. From their syntax, you can see that style rules require special, but consistent, notation. Figure 11-8 illustrates the generic syntax for a typical style rule.

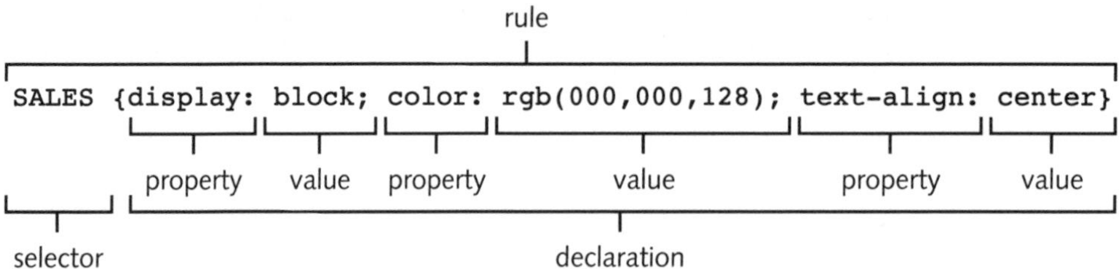

Figure 11-8 Generic syntax for style rule

You can see that a **rule** has two major components: the selector (in this case, SALES) and the **declaration** (in this case, {display: ... center}). Each declaration, in turn, is made up of one or more **property name:value** pairs. For example, in the first pair, "display" is the name of the property being specified, and "block" is the value specified for display.

Understanding Selectors and Inheritance

The **selector** portion of a rule lists the element or elements for which the properties in the declaration are specified. You can use the names of all the elements in an XML document as selectors individually (e.g., the element <SALES> in Figure 11-8) or as part of a **selector group**. For example, the elements <EMAIL> and <PHONE> form a selector group in Figure 11-9. If a selector group is specified, the element names within it must be delimited by commas.

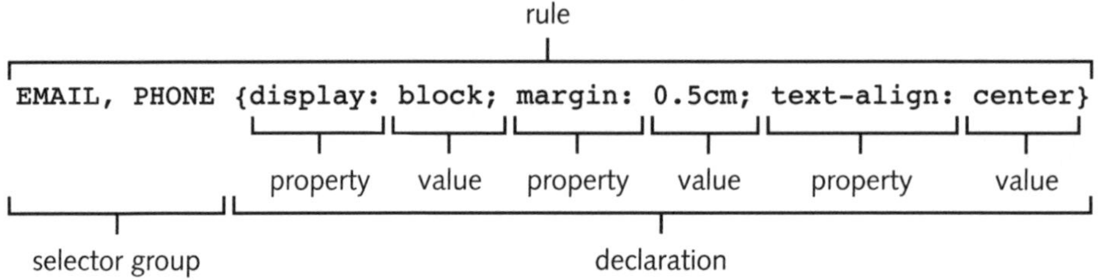

Figure 11-9 Example of selector group syntax

In tlsales.css, the combined selectors provide style rules for all the elements in the contacts.xml file. Every element name may not be explicitly listed (for example, the <COURSES> element name does not appear in tlsales.css), but the name of the parent element for the missing element likely appears. For example, tlsales.css lists the <CONTACTS> element, parent to the <COURSES> element. This illustrates that style rules observe inheritance. In other words, a child element inherits the style rules specified for its parent elements unless a specific rule is created for the child, with the child's name appearing in the selector or selector group.

Using Declarations, Properties, and Values

The declaration forms the second major component of a style rule. The declaration is separated from the selector by curly brackets, { and }. As mentioned earlier, each declaration contains at least one property name: value pair. If there are two or more pairs, you use semicolons to delimit them, as shown earlier in Figures 11-8 and 11-9.

CSS provides for over 50 properties, and as developers continue working with CSS, they periodically add more. Most of the properties available to CSS2 are listed in Table 11-1. A few prominent properties are discussed later in the chapter.

If you want to add properties to a style sheet now, or modify those in a current style sheet, visit the CSS Web sites at *www.w3.org/TR/REC-CSS1* and *www.w3.org/TR/REC-CSS2* to learn more about the syntax and values of CSS properties.

Table 11-1 Cascading style sheet properties

General Category	Property Name	
Font properties	font font-family font-size font-size-adjust	font-stretch font-style font-variant font-weight
Background properties	background background-attachment background-color	background-image background-position background-repeat
Text properties	color direction letter-spacing line-height text-align text-decoration text-indent	text-shadow text-transform unicode-bidi vertical-align white-space word-spacing
Box properties	border border-bottom border-bottom-color border-bottom-style border-bottom-width border-color border-left border-left-color border-left-style border-left-width border-right border-right-color border-right-style border-right-width border-style	border-top border-top-color border-top-style border-top-width border-width margin margin-bottom margin-left margin-right margin-top padding padding-bottom padding-left padding-right padding-top

11

Table 11-1 Cascading style sheet properties (continued)

General Category	Property Name	
Classification properties	clear cursor	display float
Table properties	border-collapse border-spacing column-span	empty-cells row-span table-layout
Visual effects properties	clip overflow	visibility
List properties	list-style list-style-image	list-style-position list-style-type
Element shape and position properties	bottom left position right	top vertical-align z-index
Element dimension properties	height line-height max-height max-width	min-height min-width width

Displaying Inline and Block Elements

In Table 11-1, note that one Classification property is display. The display property has two values, block and inline. In tlsales.css, shown in Figure 11-10, the value of the <NAME> element's display property is block. This means the <NAME> element does not start on the same line as the previous element; it starts on a new line. It also means that the element following <NAME> starts on a new line, too. In other words, the element <NAME> appears in its own block or paragraph. Elements such as <NAME>, which are defined with "display:block", are called **block-level elements**.

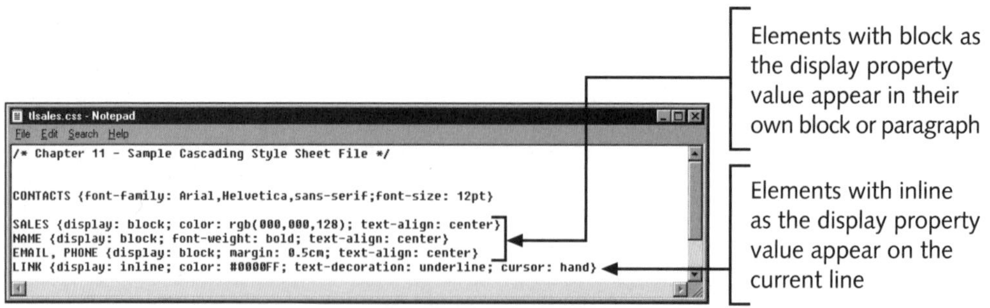

Figure 11-10 Inline and block elements in tlsales.css

In contrast, the display value for <LINK> is inline. That means that the line does not break before or after the <LINK> element. Elements such as <LINK>, which are defined with "display:inline" and so do not appear in their own blocks, are called **inline-level elements**.

The block and inline display values are especially important for XML. HTML has default display property values for predefined HTML elements. For example, the HTML element <H1> is interpreted as display: block by default, so <H1> elements always appear in their own block. However, many XML elements cannot have default values because document authors usually give those elements unique names and definitions. In XML, you must explicitly define how to display elements, including whether they are block or inline.

Using Selectors with Pseudo-Elements

So far, you have seen individual element names or groups of element names used as selectors. You can also use pseudo-elements. You add **pseudo-elements** to style sheets to add specific effects to selectors or parts of selectors. Figure 11-11 shows the generic syntax for pseudo-elements.

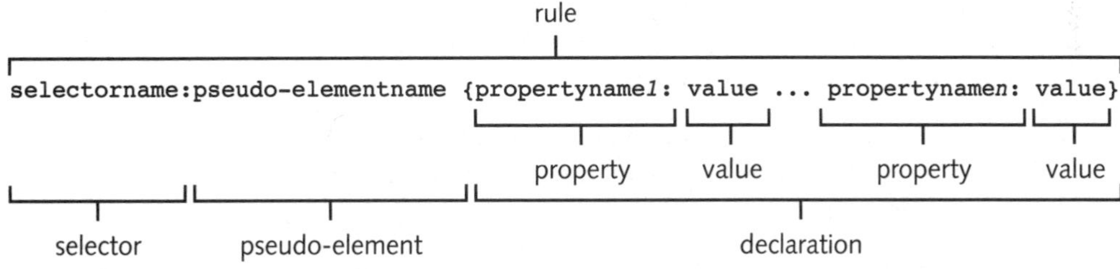

Figure 11-11 Generic pseudo-element syntax

11

Table 11-2 lists the pseudo-elements you can use in CSS.

Table 11-2 Available pseudo-elements

Pseudo-element name	Originated in	Explanation	Use only with
first-line	CSS1	Adds a special style to the first line of text in a selector; the size of the browser window determines the extent of the first line	Block-level elements
first-letter	CSS1	Adds a special style to the first letter of the text in a selector	Block-level elements
before	CSS2	Specifies the location of display-related content to display before an element's data-related content; the value of the content property is the content to insert	content property
after	CSS2	Specifies the location of display-related content to display after an element's data-related content; the value of the content property is the content to insert	content property

Note that you can combine several pseudo-elements in one style rule.

The original tlsales.css style sheet file does not specify any style rules for the <COURSES> element. In the following example, you learn how to use selectors with pseudo-elements to alter the appearance of the text in that element.

Example-Using Selectors With Pseudo-Elements

In the original copy of tlsales.css, you could insert the following code before the line containing the <SALES> element:

```
COURSES {font-size: 12pt}
COURSES:first-line {color: #0000FF}
COURSES:first-letter {color: #000000; font-size: 200%}
```

This code specifies that the first line of characters in the <COURSES> element should be 12 points. The first-line pseudo-element specifies that the first line should be blue (#0000FF), but the first letter of the first line should be black (#000000) and twice the size of the normal 12-point text.

To insert green quotation marks around the <COURSES> element, add the following rules after the three lines you just inserted. This code contains the before and after pseudo-elements.

```
COURSES:before { content: open-quote; color: green }
COURSES:after { content: close-quote; color: green }
```

Figure 11-12 compares the original version of tlsales.css to the modified version.

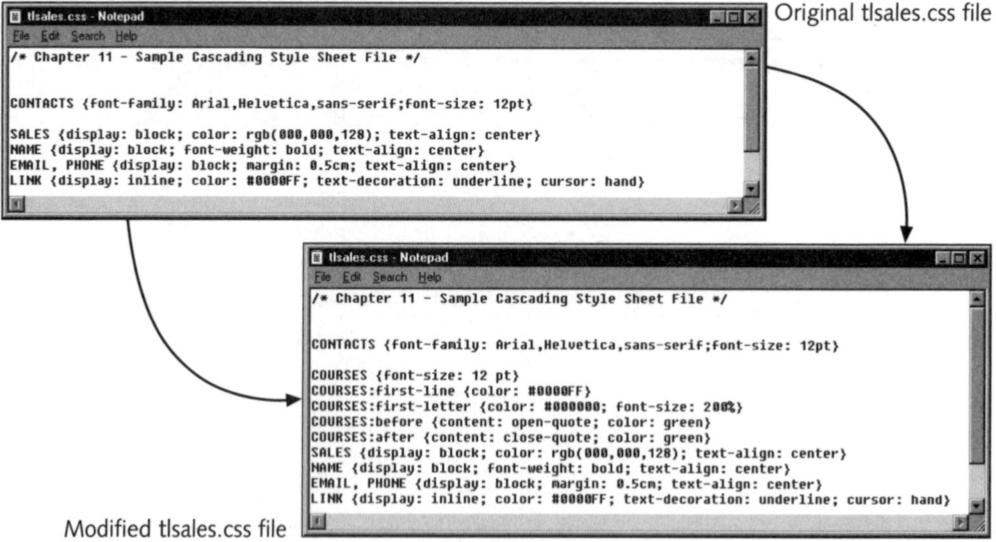

Figure 11-12 Adding pseudo-elements to tlsales.css

Grouping Selectors by Classes

The original tlsales.css style sheet includes the following selector group:

```
EMAIL, PHONE {display: block; margin: 0.5cm;
    text-align: center}
```

Suppose you have more than just two elements that you want to display with these property name:value pairs. An alternative is to create a selector class within the style sheet file; the class would contain the specified property name:value pairs. In the XML documents, you assign the individual elements to the classes by inserting the appropriate attribute/value pair (the attribute must be called CLASS) into the element's start tag. Figure 11-13 illustrates the generic syntax.

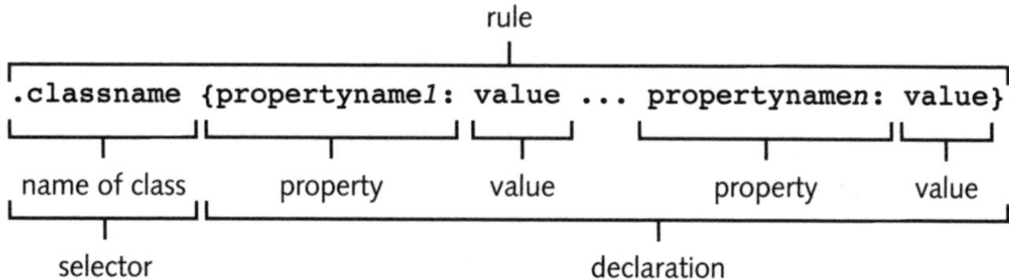

Figure 11-13 Generic selector class syntax

Grouping Selectors by Classes Example

In the following example, you learn how to use the contact list to introduce the basic steps for creating and using a selector class.

In the original copy of tlsales.css, you delete the EMAIL, PHONE group selector and replace it with the following class definition:

```
.CONNECT {display: block; margin: 0.5cm; text-align: center}
```

Be sure to include the period (.) at the beginning of the name of the selector class.

The modified CSS file resembles the one shown in Figure 11-14.

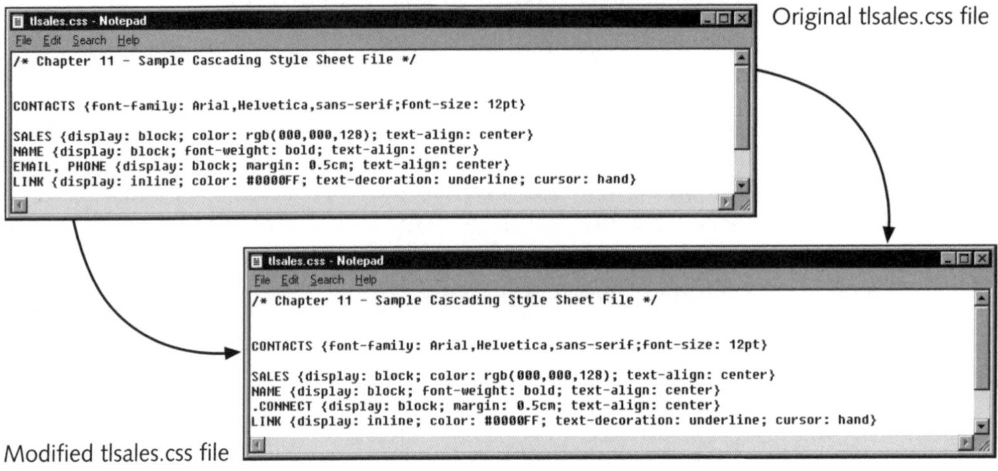

Figure 11-14 Adding a selector class to tlsales.css

To apply the new class definition to the selected element, you open the appropriate XML document, and insert the attribute that refers to the class definition. Modify the following elements:

```
<EMAIL CLASS="CONNECT">JSleek@TLSales.com</EMAIL>
<PHONE CLASS="CONNECT">1 800 123-4567</PHONE>
<EMAIL CLASS="CONNECT">AGold@TLSales.com</EMAIL>
<PHONE CLASS="CONNECT">1 800 123-4567</PHONE>
```

The modified XML file should now resemble the one shown in Figure 11-15.

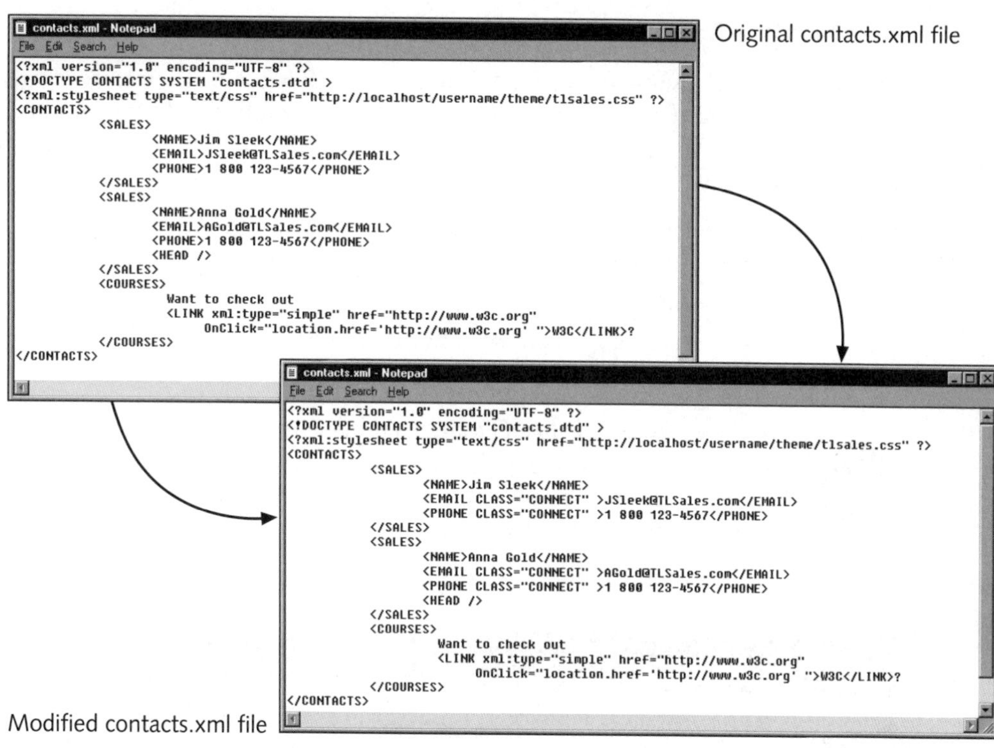

Figure 11-15 Adding selector class attributes to contacts.xml

To ensure that the contacts.xml file is valid, you must declare the new CLASS attribute in the appropriate DTD or schema. In the contacts.dtd file, you insert declarations similar to the following:

```
<!ATTLIST EMAIL CLASS CDATA #IMPLIED >
<!ATTLIST PHONE CLASS CDATA #IMPLIED >
```

So far, you can apply the CONNECT class selector you created in tlsales.css file to any element in the XML document. As a variation on class selectors, you can also create a class that applies only to a certain specified element. The generic syntax for doing so is shown in Figure 11-16.

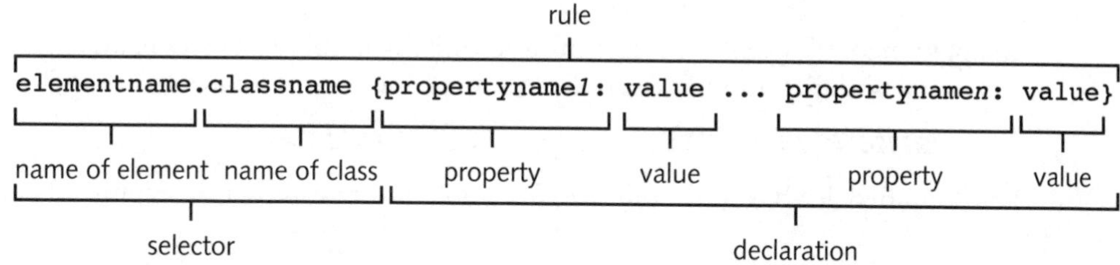

Figure 11-16 Generic specific selector class syntax

11

Applying a Selector Class to a Specific Element Example

In the following example, you learn how to work with the contacts list to alter the appearance of the department head's name (Anna Gold) so it keeps its current display style and appears in red on a black background. To do this, you apply a specific class to that element only.

In the original version of tlsales.css, after the current NAME selector, you could add another selector with the following class definition:

```
NAME.HILITE {display: block; font-weight: bold;
    text-align: center; color: red;
    background-color: black}
```

Previously, placing the period (.) at the beginning of the name of the selector class made it possible to apply the class to all elements. Here, placing a period between a specific element name and the class name ensures that the class applies to that element only.

The modified CSS file should now resemble the one shown in Figure 11-17.

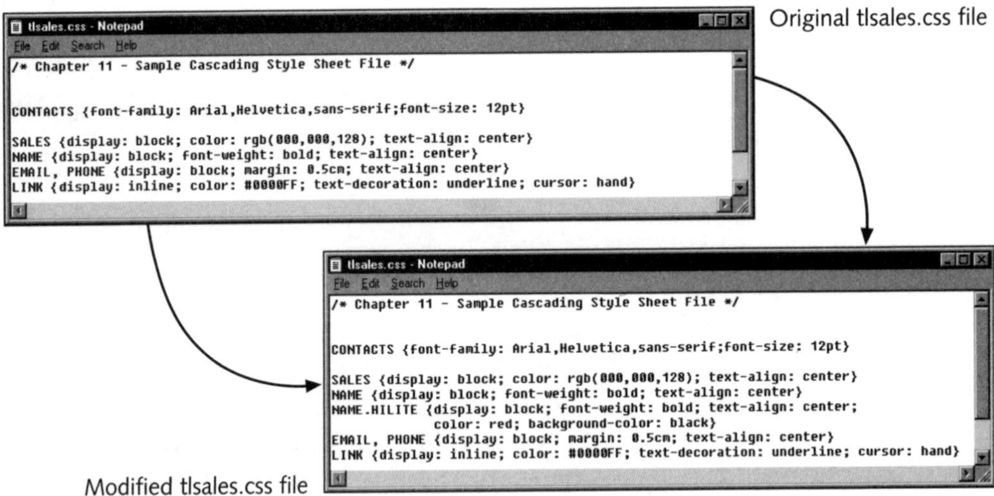

Figure 11-17 Adding a specific selector class to tlsales.css

To apply the new specific class definition to the department head's name, you work with the contacts.xml to modify Anna Gold's name element as follows:

```
<NAME CLASS="HILITE">Anna Gold</NAME>
```

The modified XML file should now resemble the one shown in Figure 11-18.

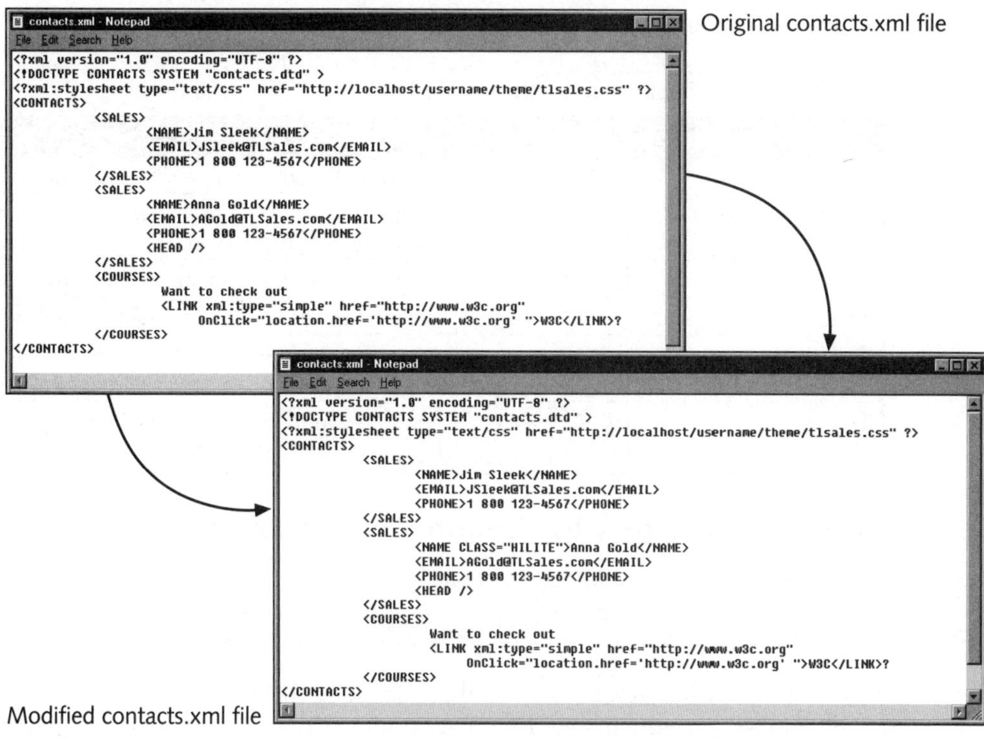

Figure 11-18 Adding a specific class selector definition to contacts.xml

To ensure that the contacts.xml file is valid, you again have to declare the new CLASS attribute in the contacts.dtd file by inserting the following into that file:

```
<!ATTLIST NAME CLASS CDATA #IMPLIED >
```

Grouping Selectors by Pseudo-Classes

Just as you can use pseudo-elements, you can also use pseudo-classes to further customize your selectors. Figure 11-19 illustrates the generic syntax for pseudo-classes. Note that pseudo-class names are not case sensitive.

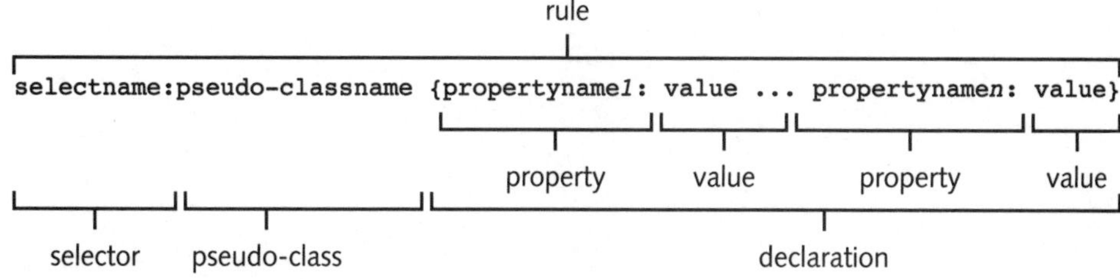

Figure 11-19 Generic syntax for pseudo-classes

Table 11-3 lists and explains the pseudo-classes available in CSS.

Table 11-3 Available pseudo-classes

Name of pseudo-class	Originated in	Explanation
active	CSS1	Adds a specified style to a selected hyperlink
hover	CSS1	Adds a specified style to a hyperlink when the mouse pointer is placed over it
link	CSS1	Adds a specified style to an unvisited hyperlink
visited	CSS1	Adds a specified style to an already visited hyperlink
first-child	CSS2	Adds a specified style to an element that is the first child element of a specified parent element
lang	CSS2	Allows the author to specify a language to be used in a specified element

Grouping Selectors by Pseudo-Classes Example

A common use for pseudo-classes is changing the color of a hyperlink depending on its status. Recall that the contacts list includes a link to the W3C Web site. In the following example, you learn how to change the color of the link depending on several possible states.

You start by modifying the original tlsales.css style sheet file by deleting color: #0000F; in the <LINK> element style rule. The modified rule should appear as follows:

```
LINK {display: inline; text-decoration: underline;
     cursor: hand}
```

After that line, you add the following:

```
LINK:link {color: #0000FF}
     /* hyperlink is blue until selected */
LINK:hover {color: #FF00FF}
     /* hyperlink turns fuchsia when
        mouse pointer is moved over it */
LINK:visited {color: #00FF00}
     /* visited hyperlink turns green */
```

The modified CSS file should now resemble the one shown in Figure 11-20.

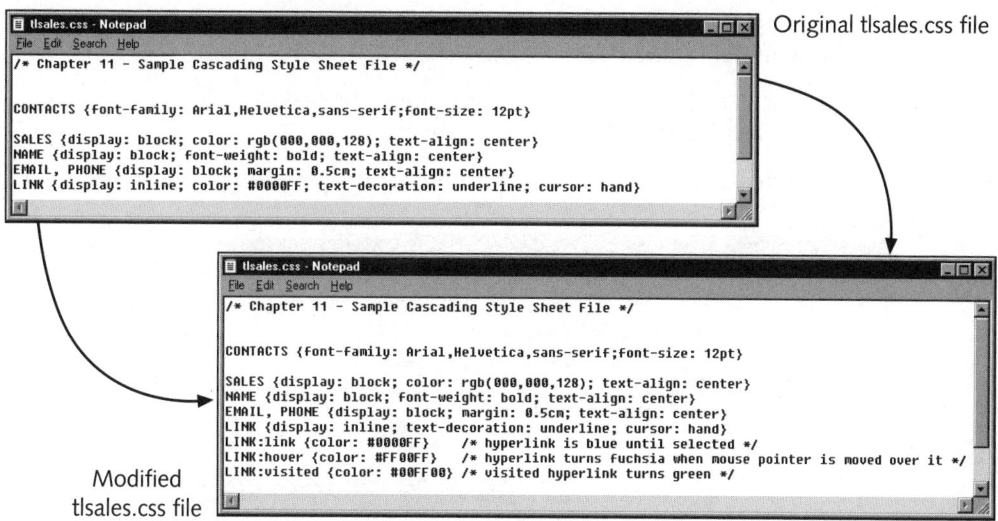

Figure 11-20 Adding pseudo-classes to tlsales.css

Pseudo-classes can also be combined with other CSS classes. The generic syntax is illustrated in Figure 11-21.

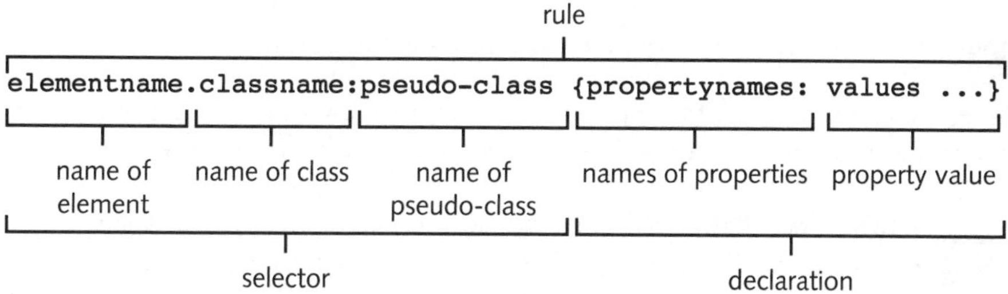

Figure 11-21 Combined class/pseudo-class syntax

Combining Classes and Pseudo-Classes Example

Combining classes and pseudo-classes can save steps. For example, a Web document might contain many links. You could design the document to change the visited display property for all the links at once without having to access individual document files. To do so, you create a pseudo-class called VISITED in the style sheet, and then specify an attribute in each hyperlink element start tag so that the element observes the modified VISITED display behavior.

After the current LINK selector in the original tlsales.css file, add another selector with the following combined pseudo-class/class definition:

```
LINK.VISITED:visited {color: #FFFF00;
    background-color: black}
```

The modified CSS file should now resemble the one shown in Figure 11-22.

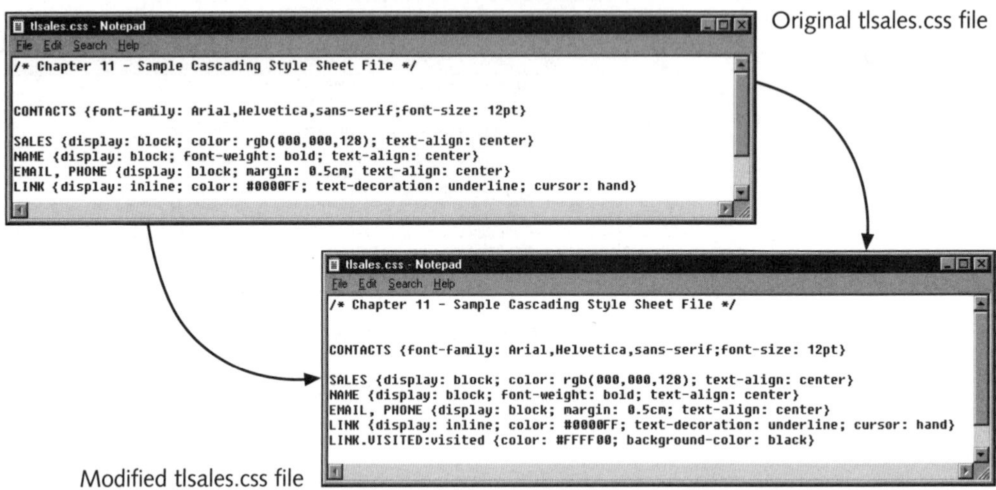

Figure 11-22 Adding a combined class/pseudo-class to tlsales.css

Here, the class name is VISITED and the pseudo-class name used is also "visited." In the meantime, after the hyperlink has been used, its color turns yellow (#FFFF00).

Remember that placing a period between the LINK element name and the class name VISITED ensures that the combination class/pseudo-class applies to that element only.

To apply the new specific class definition to the hyperlink, work with the contacts.xml file to modify the <LINK> element as follows:

```
<LINK CLASS="VISITED" xml:type="simple"
      ref="http://www.w3c.org"
      onClick="location.href='http://www.w3c.org'">
      W3C
</LINK>?
```

The modified XML file should now resemble the one shown in Figure 11-23.

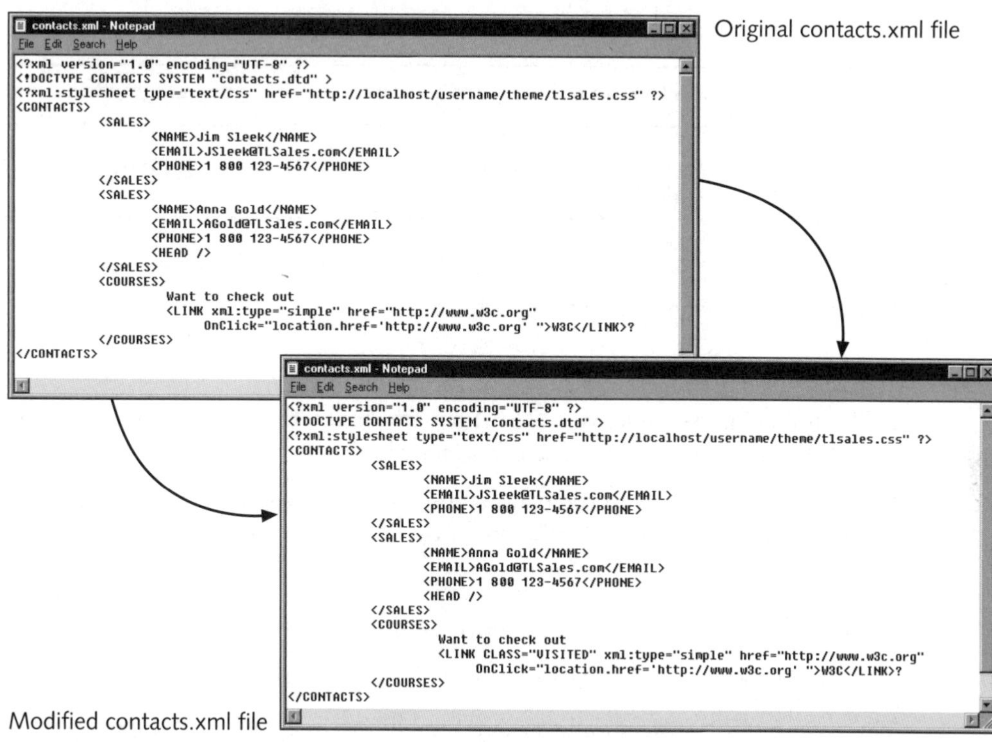


```
<?xml version="1.0" encoding="UTF-8" ?>
<!DOCTYPE CONTACTS SYSTEM "contacts.dtd" >
<?xml:stylesheet type="text/css" href="http://localhost/username/theme/tlsales.css" ?>
<CONTACTS>
	<SALES>
		<NAME>Jim Sleek</NAME>
		<EMAIL>JSleek@TLSales.com</EMAIL>
		<PHONE>1 800 123-4567</PHONE>
	</SALES>
	<SALES>
		<NAME>Anna Gold</NAME>
		<EMAIL>AGold@TLSales.com</EMAIL>
		<PHONE>1 800 123-4567</PHONE>
		<HEAD />
	</SALES>
	<COURSES>
		Want to check out
		<LINK xml:type="simple" href="http://www.w3c.org"
			OnClick="location.href='http://www.w3c.org' ">W3C</LINK>?
	</COURSES>
</CONTACTS>
```

```
<?xml version="1.0" encoding="UTF-8" ?>
<!DOCTYPE CONTACTS SYSTEM "contacts.dtd" >
<?xml:stylesheet type="text/css" href="http://localhost/username/theme/tlsales.css" ?>
<CONTACTS>
	<SALES>
		<NAME>Jim Sleek</NAME>
		<EMAIL>JSleek@TLSales.com</EMAIL>
		<PHONE>1 800 123-4567</PHONE>
	</SALES>
	<SALES>
		<NAME>Anna Gold</NAME>
		<EMAIL>AGold@TLSales.com</EMAIL>
		<PHONE>1 800 123-4567</PHONE>
		<HEAD />
	</SALES>
	<COURSES>
		Want to check out
		<LINK CLASS="VISITED" xml:type="simple" href="http://www.w3c.org"
			OnClick="location.href='http://www.w3c.org' ">W3C</LINK>?
	</COURSES>
</CONTACTS>
```

Figure 11-23 Adding the specific class definition to contacts.xml

11

To ensure that the contacts.xml file is valid, you again have to declare the new CLASS attribute for the element <LINK> in the contacts.dtd file. Insert the following into that file:

```
<!ATTLIST LINK CLASS CDATA #IMPLIED >
```

After changing the <LINK> element, you can change the visited status color on any element with the CLASS="VISITED" attribute/value in its start tag. To do so, you alter the color code in the tlsales.css file. You do not have to visit the individual documents, as long as they are affiliated with style sheet in that file.

Grouping Selectors by ID

You can change the display style for a specific element by using its ID (or id) attribute. Figure 11-24 illustrates the general syntax.

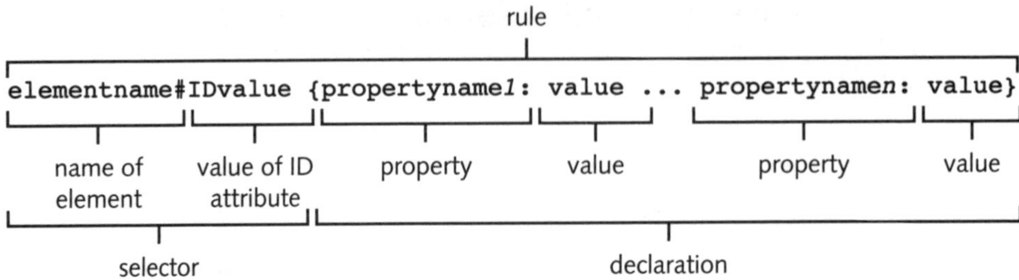

Figure 11-24 Generic ID selector syntax

Grouping Selectors by ID Example

In the following example, you learn how to change the color of the font and the background for the first Sales Department contact in the contacts.xml file (that is, for Mr. Sleek).

In the SALES style rule in the original tlsales.css file, you delete color: rgb(000,000,128); so the SALES line appears as shown in the following code:

```
SALES {display: block; text-align: center}
```

After the current SALES line, insert the following new rule:

```
SALES#FIRST {color: red; background-color: maroon}
```

The modified CSS file should now resemble the one shown in Figure 11-25.

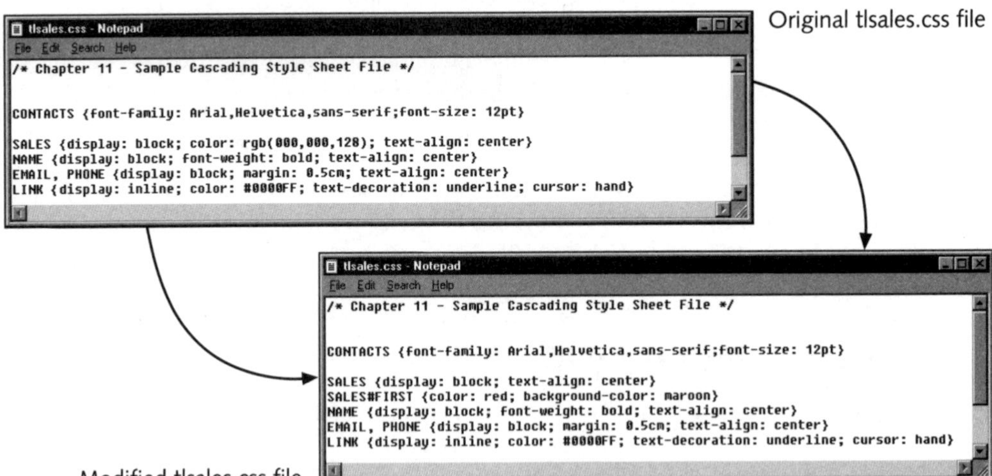

Figure 11-25 Adding an ID selector rule to tlsales.css

To apply the new ID attribute to the first Sales Department contact, work with the contacts.xml to modify the first <SALES> element as follows:

```
<SALES ID="FIRST">
     <NAME>Jim Sleek</NAME>
     <EMAIL>JSleek@TLSales.com</EMAIL>
     <PHONE>1 800 123-4567</PHONE>
</SALES>
```

The modified XML file should now resemble the one shown in Figure 11-26.

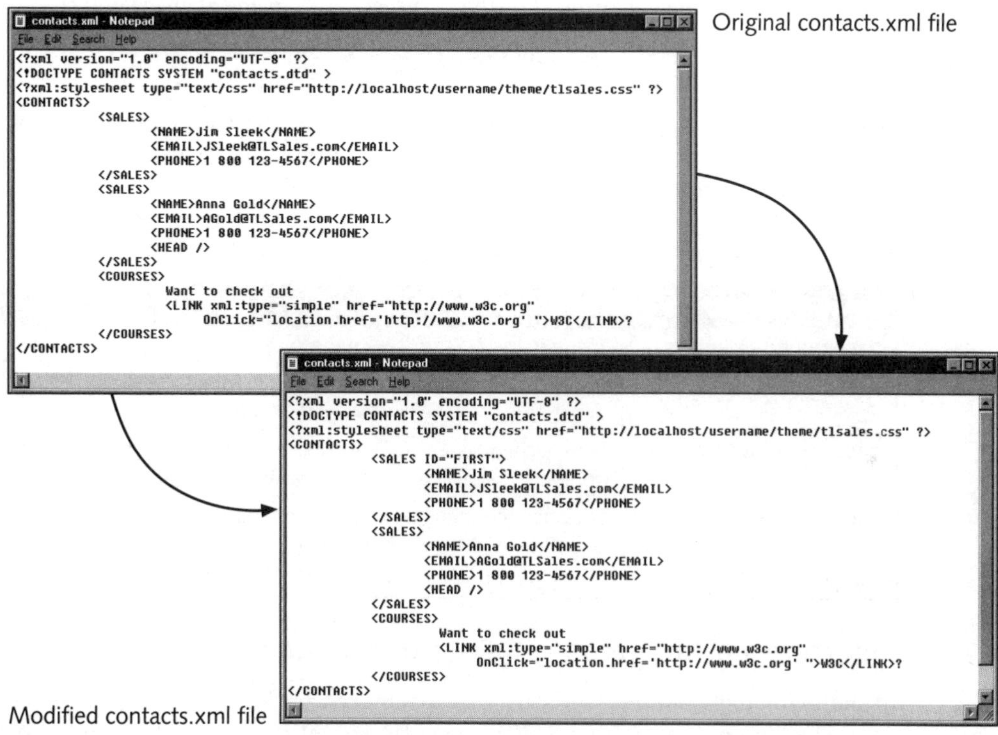

Figure 11-26 Applying ID attribute to an element in contacts.xml

To ensure that the contacts.xml file is valid, you again have to declare the new CLASS attribute for the element <SALES> in the contacts.dtd file. Insert the following into that file:

```
<!ATTLIST SALES ID CDATA #IMPLIED >
```

INSERTING IMAGES WITH CSS STYLE RULES

To make Web sites more visually attractive, page developers sometimes insert images as backgrounds to text and other elements, or as discrete elements in themselves. This section examines both approaches.

Inserting Images as Backgrounds

Figure 11-27 illustrates the generic syntax for inserting a background-image style rule into the style file.

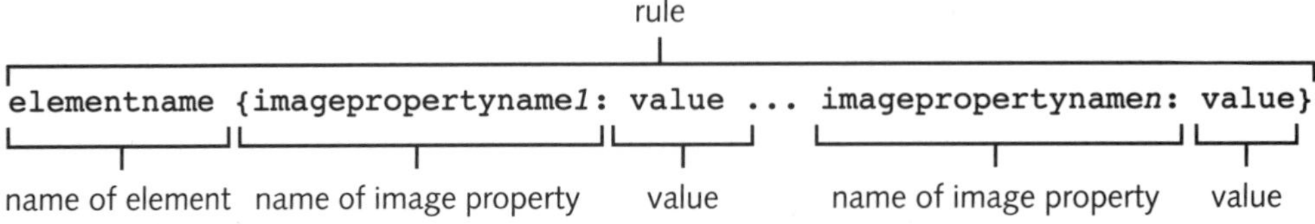

Figure 11-27 Generic image rule syntax

Note that the background image may appear behind the root element—in which case, the root element would be specified—or behind individual elements. Table 11-4 lists the available image property names and their values.

Table 11-4 Available image property names

Image Property Name	Explanation
background-image	Value is the URI of the image file
background-repeat	Values are "repeat", "no-repeat", "repeat-x"(repeat in the horizontal direction), or "repeat-y"(repeat in the vertical direction)
background-attachment	No specific values; if the property name "background-attachment" appears, the background scrolls with the rest of the document
background-position	Specifies the initial position of the image; values are"x" and "y" coordinates in percentages (e.g., "0%" or "100%", etc.) to specify the location of the image's upper-left corner

Inserting an Image as a Background Example

In the following example, you learn how to insert a background logo on the contacts.xml page. The logo indicates that the Web page is in compliance with CSS1 and CSS2 standards

After the CONTACTS line in the original tlsales.css file, insert two new lines as shown in the following code:

```
CONTACTS {font-family: Arial,Helvetica,sans-serif;
            font-size: 12pt;
         background-image: url (w3c_css_compl_logo.tif);
         background-repeat: no-repeat; background-
            position: 0% 0% }
```

The modified CSS file should now resemble the one shown in Figure 11-28.

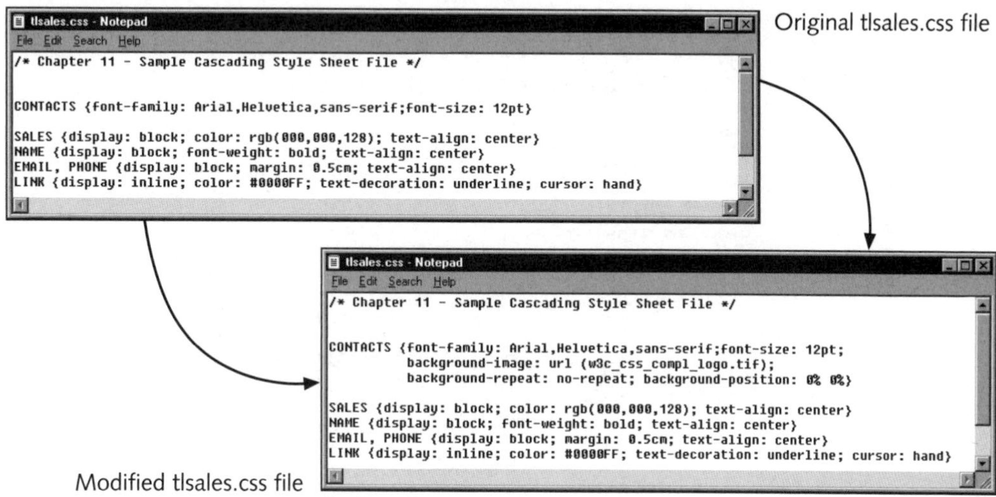

Figure 11-28 Inserting a background logo through tlsales.css

Inserting Images as Discrete Elements

If you want to insert an image by itself, you create a dedicated element just for it in the XML document. In the style sheet file, you specify the image as the background to that dedicated element. Because you are simply building another background image, the syntax you use in the style sheet file is the same as the previous example.

Inserting an Image as a Discrete Element Example

In the following example, you learn how to add a discrete image to the contacts list by nesting an <IMAGE> element within the <CONTACTS> element in the contacts.xml file.

You start by modifying the <CONTACTS> element as follows:

```
<CONTACTS>
     <IMAGE> </IMAGE>
     <SALES>
        <NAME>Jim Sleek .... etc.
</CONTACTS>
```

The modified XML file should now resemble the one shown in Figure 11-29.

In the original copy of tlsales.css, add the following style rule before the SALES line:

```
IMAGE {background: url (w3c_css_compl_logo.tif)
     no-repeat 0% 0%;
     height: 50 px; width: 100 px; float: left}
```

The modified CSS file should now resemble the one shown in Figure 11-30.

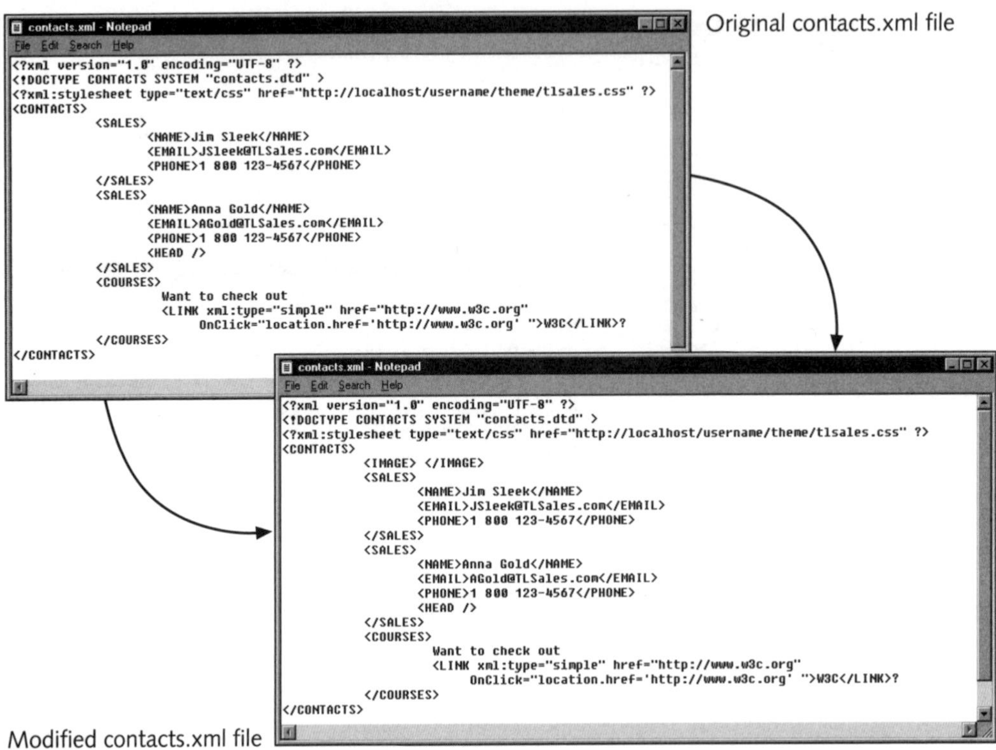

Figure 11-29 Inserting an image element into contacts.xml

Notice how the background image syntax is varied in this example. This is a shorthand treatment that is allowed for situations like this as long as the values are entered in this strict order. When creating these image specifications, it is possible, with some trial and error, to tailor their dimensions to the actual dimensions of the image. Also note how the image is also specified to float at the left side of the browser window.

Other Introductory Style Specifications

So far in this chapter, you have learned several introductory techniques to define and affiliate style specifications and to create style rules (including inserting images). This section introduces you to other fundamental yet valuable style concepts and specifications, including how to emphasize elements by drawing borders around them, how to manipulate text and margins, and how to position elements.

Drawing Borders Around Elements

To make certain elements stand out, you can draw borders around them by adding one or more of the border-related properties found under the Box properties category listed in Table 11-1.

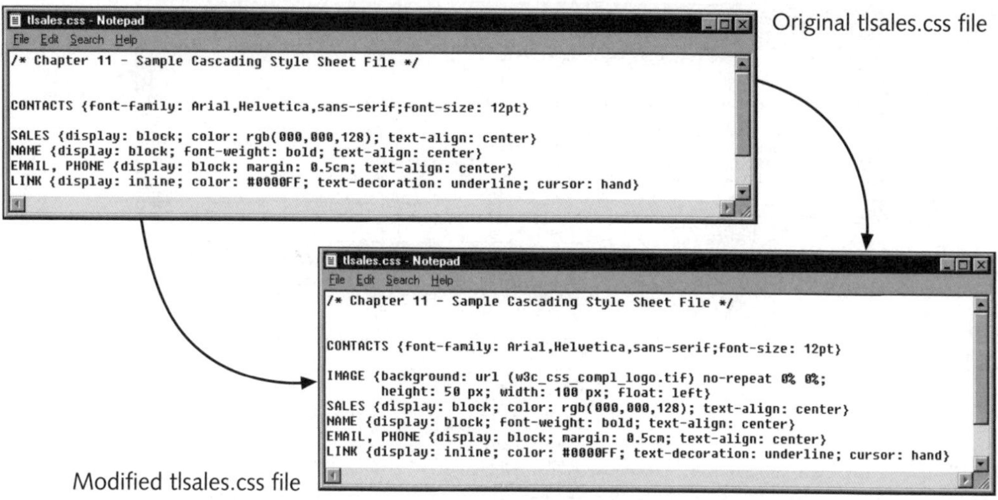

Figure 11-30 Adding an image style rule to tlsales.css

Drawing Borders Around Elements Example

For example, you can draw a green, dashed border of varying thickness around each of the <NAME> elements in the contacts.xml document. The only coding necessary is the modification of the (original) NAME style rule in the tlsales.css file:

```
NAME {display: block; font-weight: bold;
     text-align: center; border-color: green;
     border-style: dashed; border-top-width: 10 px;
     border-bottom-width: 10 px;
     border-left-width: 5 px;
     border-right-width: 5 px }
```

Figure 11-31 shows the modified tlsales.css file.

Text Alignment, Margins, and Indentations

If you design Web sites or related documents, you probably work with text alignment, margins, and indentations frequently. They involve the properties listed under the Text properties and Box properties categories in Table 11-1.

Aligning Text Example

For example, you can alter the alignment of the <NAME> elements in tlsales.css, which are already centeraligned. Make them aligned to the left margin by modifying the (original) NAME style rule in tlsales.css as in the following code:

```
NAME {display: block; font-weight: bold; text-align: left}
```

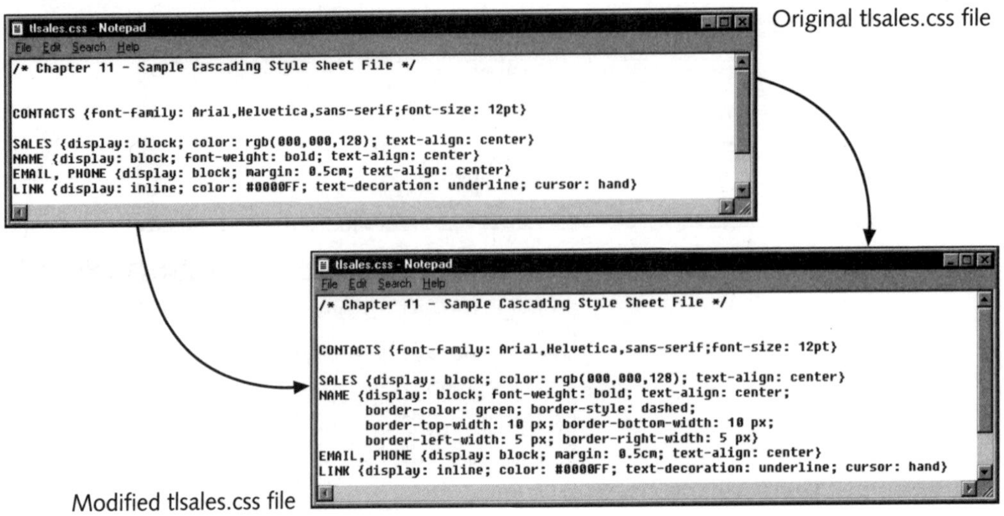

Figure 11-31 Adding a border to the <NAME> element through tlsales.css

Increasing Margins Example

To increase the margin for the <EMAIL> and <PHONE> selector group to 1 centimeter by changing the original EMAIL, PHONE style rule:

```
EMAIL, PHONE {display: block; margin: 1.0cm;
    text-align: center}
```

To insert a 50-pixel indentation to the W3C hyperlink, you can modify the original LINK style rule to look like the following code:

```
LINK {display: inline; color: #0000FF;
     text-decoration: underline;
     text-indent: 50px; cursor:hand}
```

These changes are all shown in the modified tlsales.css file in Figure 11-32.

Absolute and Relative Positioning

You have already been introduced to the concept of absolute and relative positioning in previous chapters, generally with respect to graphics. You can use the Element Shape and Position properties listed in Table 11-1 to position specific elements of any kind, including text.

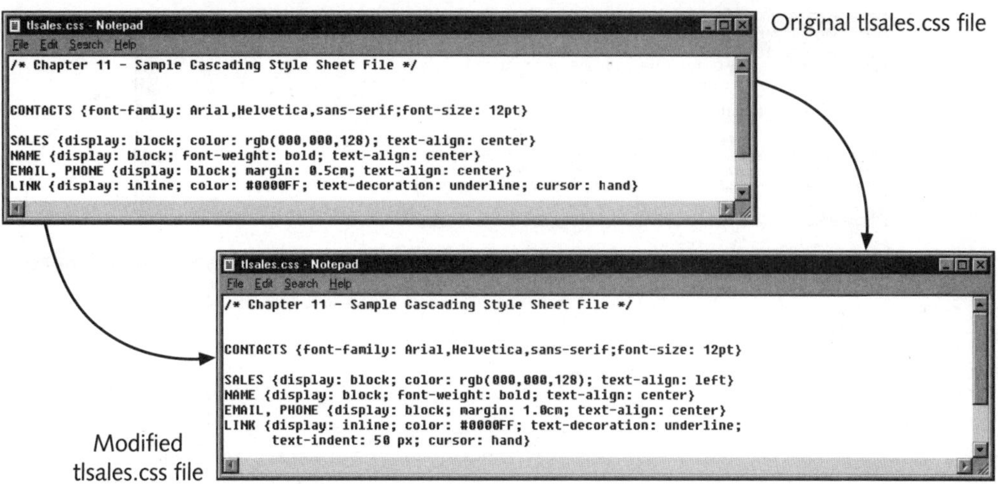

Figure 11-32 Changing alignment, margins, and indentations through tlsales.css

Positioning Examples

For example, recall that you included the <IMAGE> element in contacts.xml to display a background image. This element is illustrated in the following code:

```
<CONTACTS>
  <IMAGE> </IMAGE>
  <SALES>
        <NAME>Jim Sleek .... etc.
</CONTACTS>
```


You can change the tlsales.css style sheet to provide an absolute location within the browser window to display the CSS-compliance logo image. To do so, add the following style rule to tlsales.css:

```
IMAGE {background: url (w3c_css_compl_logo.tif) no-repeat 0% 0%;
       height: 50 px; width: 100 px;
       position: absolute; left:100; top: 125}
```

These changes are all shown in the modified tlsales.css file in Figure 11-33.

You can also use relative positioning to move elements one way or another relative to their normal position in the flow of elements or text. Consequently, relative positioning is often used inline as a form of superscripting and subscripting. For example, use it in the following manner with the original contacts.xml document file to superscript the 1-800 prefix in each of the contact phone numbers:

```
<PHONE>
     <SUP_SCRPT STYLE= "position: relative; top: -5 >
          1 800
     </SUP_SCRPT>
          123-4567
</PHONE>
```

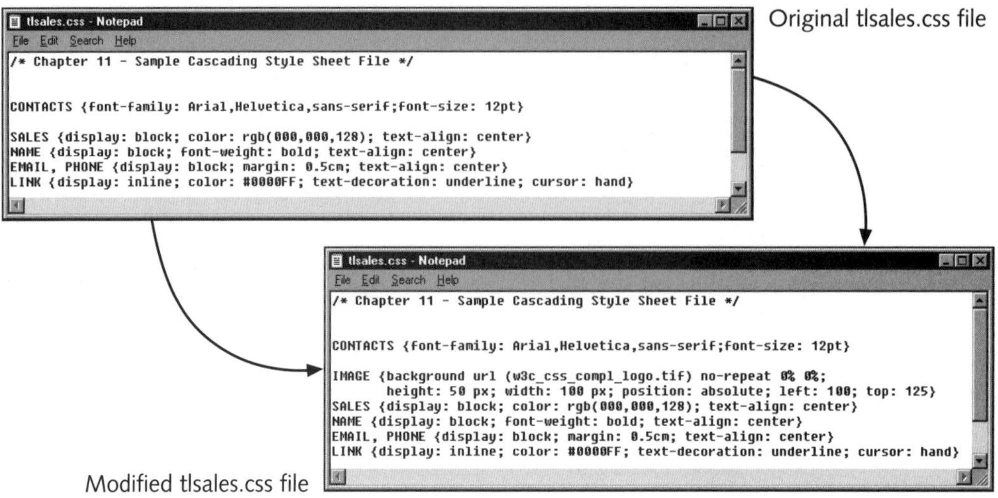

Figure 11-33 Modifying the <IMAGE> element through tlsales.css

WHY AND HOW STYLE SHEETS CASCADE

As you've seen in the preceding sections, style-control information is specified in several ways:

- In one or more external style sheet files
- Inside an internal style sheet within the <HEAD> element of an HTML document or within the <head> element of an XHTML document
- Inline within an element's start tag

But what if you use more than one style-control source? What style specifications prevail? The answer begins with the fact that all the specifications are combined (i.e., are "cascaded") into a single, virtual style sheet. Thereafter, the controls are applied in the following order, from high to low:

1. Inline specifications within element start tags
2. Specifications in internal style sheets
3. Specifications in external style sheets (if there is more than one and there seems to be a contradiction or overlap with respect to their selectors, then the most recent style sheet specification prevails)
4. Styles inherited from parent elements
5. Browser default styles

In addition to the general rules previously listed, there are additional refinements such as:

- Specifications applied by ID prevail over those specified by class
- Class specifications prevail over group selectors
- As of CSS2, the end user's "!Important" rules prevail over the document author's "Important" rules (an advanced technique not covered in this book, but worth noting because, in CSS1, the reverse was true)

- General author rules prevail over general reader rules (reader rules are also considered beyond the scope of this introductory book)

Thus, the final appearance in the browser and on paper results from the interaction of the original XML document, all the style specifications, and the behavior of the browser or other application. Appearance is dictated by the most specific rules over the more general rules.

In general, and to make life easier, you should try to include as many style control specifications as possible in external style sheets. That way, you can change the appearance of one or more XML-related documents by making changes only to the style sheet files; you need not have to visit each XML document.

CHAPTER SUMMARY

- Originally developed to add style to HTML documents, the functionality of Cascading Style Sheets has been expanded to complement XML-related languages and the development of the W3C's Cascading Style Sheet Recommendations.
- CSS has been through several stages of development: CSS1, CSS2, and the anticipated CSS3. Each adds more sophisticated style control features. CSS3 will be modular.
- There is excellent application and utility support for CSS1 and growing support for CSS2. The W3C also has a Web site page listing CSS-compliant applications, tutorials, and utilities.
- Although you can use three methods for implementing style-control specifications with XML documents, it is recommended that, whenever possible, you use a declaration to an external style sheet.
- Style controls are specified in one or more rules, each composed of a selector and a declaration. Each declaration contains at least one property name:value pair. If there are two or more pairs, semicolons are used to delimit them.
- There are over 50 CSS properties, separated into almost a dozen general categories, according to their functionality. Category definitions and boundaries vary according to information source (e.g., the W3C, this book's authors, other developers and experts, etc.) but have no impact on the capability of any property.
- More than ten different selector methods and combinations that provide basic controls over style were introduced in this chapter. The most important concepts to remember are inline as compared to block displays, the use of element names as selector names, the inclusion of images, and positioning concepts.
- If you are introducing new elements or attributes—or modifying existing elements or attributes—to facilitate style controls, ensure that all relevant documents reflect those additions and modifications (e.g., the XML data documents, relevant DTDs or schemas, and the external CSS files).

Review Questions

1. If you try to display an XML document with a browser and the result looks similar to the raw XML data, but not like what you expected, which of the following types of files do you need?
   a. DTD file
   b. CSS file
   c. schema file
   d. XSLT file
   e. none of the above
2. XSL and CSS can both apply versions of style sheets to transform one document into another while simultaneously controlling the new document's appearance. True or false?
3. Match the following terms:

a. CSS3	1. media-specific style sheets
b. CSS2	2. colors, spacing, background images
c. CSS1	3. modular

4. Which of the following are methods for implementing style controls for HTML documents?
   a. inline specifications in element start tags
   b. internal style sheets
   c. affiliating the document to an external style sheet with a specific declaration
   d. all of the above
   e. none of the above
5. Which of the following are methods for implementing style controls for XML documents?
   a. inline specifications in element start tags
   b. internal style sheets
   c. affiliating the document to an external style sheet with a specific declaration
   d. all of the above
   e. none of the above
6. If you are affiliating a document to an external style sheet, you declare it in the prolog. In which statement do you insert the declaration?
   a. XML declaration
   b. processing instruction
   c. attribute declaration
   d. selector
   e. document type declaration
   f. a. or c.
7. How many major components does a style rule have? What are they called?
8. The concept whereby the style rules specified for a parent element are passed to a child element, unless a specific rule is created for the child, is called ________________.

9. If you are specifying values for margins, borders, and padding, then you are dealing with which of the following category of properties?
   a. imaging
   b. element position
   c. text
   d. box
   e. document type declaration
   f. table
   g. none of the above
10. If Element B starts on a different line than the previous Element A, and the element following Element B, in turn, starts on its own new line, then Element B is a block-level element. True or false?
11. Why are there no default inline/block display values for XML elements as there are for HTML elements?
12. Placing a(n) ________________ between an element name and the class name ensures that the combination class/pseudo-class applies to that element only.
13. The term "first-line" refers to a pseudo-________________ property and the term "first-child" refers to a pseudo-________________ property.
14. Which of the following is commonly used to change the color of a hyperlink depending on its status (e.g., not-yet visited versus visited).
   a. pseudo-class
   b. pseudo-element
   c. selector class
   d. selector group
   e. specific selector class
   f. none of the above
15. It is very important to include a period (.) at the beginning of the name of a selector class, so that any element with a start tag that includes a "CLASS" attribute with a value the same as the selector class has the specified style. True or false?
16. To ensure that an XML document remains valid, you must ensure that, whenever you introduce new elements and/or attributes to control style, you also update the ________________ or ________________ file, whichever is applicable.
17. When adding inline styles to element start tags, what is the name of the attribute you use?
   a. DTD
   b. CLASS
   c. STYLE
   d. ID
   e. none of the above
18. To make Web sites more visually attractive, developers are interested in including images in two ways. What are they?
19. If the property name "background-position" appears, then the background scrolls with the rest of the document. True or false?

20. If you want to insert an image by itself, you create a dedicated element just for it in the XML document and then, in the style sheet file, you specify the image as the ________________ to that dedicated element.
21. If you want to move elements one way or another relative to their normal position in the flow of elements and/or text, then you use which of the following types of positioning?
    a. absolute
    b. float
    c. relevant
    d. relative
    e. none of the above
22. If you use more than one style control source, then all the specifications are combined (i.e., are cascaded) into what?
23. If there are conflicts in style rules from the following sources, some prevail over others. Sort them according to pecking order, from highest prevalence to lowest prevalence (to get you started, a. = 2 (second highest)).
    a. specifications in internal style sheets
    b. browser default styles
    c. inline specifications within element start tags
    d. specifications in external style sheets (if there is more than one and there seems to be a contradiction or overlap with respect to their selectors, then the most recent style sheet specification prevails)
    e. styles inherited from parent elements
24. What is the major advantage to the author's recommendation that, if at all possible, you should try to include as many style control specifications as possible in external style sheets?
25. Following are some syntax examples presented earlier in this chapter. Match them to the respective style control techniques.

a. .CONNECT {display: block; ... etc}	1. Group by ID
b. <LCASE STYLE="text-transform: ... etc.>	2. Pseudo-elements
c. SALES#FIRST {color: red; ... etc.}	3. Inline styles
d. COURSES:first-letter {color: ... etc.}	4. Selector group
e. EMAIL, PHONE {display: block ... etc.}	5. Group by classes

HANDS-ON PROJECTS

Project 11-1

In the next three projects, you add style properties to HTML documents using three different methods: inline style attributes, internal style sheets, and external style sheets. The methods of applying the styles are different, but the result is the same. The objective of the projects is to demonstrate the purpose of each method when applying style rules.

In the first project, you add style rules to a small HTML file using the inline method. Note that in the following projects, the drive letter you are using might differ from drive c.

To set up the project:

1. In Windows Explorer, create a new folder called **Ch11** in C:\home\<yourname>.
2. Copy the files located in the Ch11\Project_11-1 folder on your Data Disk into your C:/home/<yourname>/Ch11 folder.
3. Click **Start**, point to **Programs** (point to **All Programs** in Windows XP), point to **XML Spy Suite**, and click **XML Spy IDE**. The XML Spy window opens.
4. Click **Project** on the menu bar, and then click **Open Project**. In the Open dialog box, click the **Look in** list arrow, and then navigate to **C:/home/<yourname>/Ch11**. Click **contacts.spp**, and then click **Open**.
5. Under the HTML Files branch in the Project pane, double-click **contacts1.html** to open the HTML document. The document opens in the main window. Notice that the rendered document looks fairly plain in the XML Spy browser.
6. Click **View** on the menu bar, and then click **Text view** to display the HTML source code.

To add inline style attributes to an element:

1. Inline styles are applied directly to an element using the style attribute. Add an inline style attribute to the body element by typing:
   ```
   style="font-family:Arial; background-color:silver;"
   ```
   The default font value for all text data within the document, including child element data, is inherited from the font-family style property in the body element. All text is rendered as Arial unless a descendent element overrides the style property with another rule containing the font-family property. The background for the body of the document is set to silver.
2. Add the following style attribute to the h1 element:
   ```
   style="font-weight:bold; font-size:18; color:blue;"
   ```
   The text within this h1 element is displayed as blue, bold and 18 points in size.
3. Following the h1 element, add the following style attribute to the div element containing the name Jim Bigman:
   ```
   style= "font-weight:bold; font-size:15; margin-left:15pt;
   ```
   The div element is used as a generic container element and allows properties to be applied to a block of text data. With the above style attribute, the text within the div element appears as 15 point bold and inherits the Arial font from the body element.
4. Add the following style attribute to the anchor element containing the e-mail address Bigman@TLSales.com:
   ```
   style= "font-size:12; margin-left:25pt; color:red;"
   ```
   The data from the a element appears indented 25 points from the left of the page margin. The data appears as 12-point red text.
5. Directly following the a element, add the style attribute to the div element:
   ```
   style="font-size:12; margin-left:25pt;"
   ```
   The XML document should now resemble Figure 11-34

   To view the document, click **View** on the menu bar, and then click **Browser view** to examine the document. The document should look similar to Figure 11-35. Compare the rendered data with the changes that you made to the presentation.

11

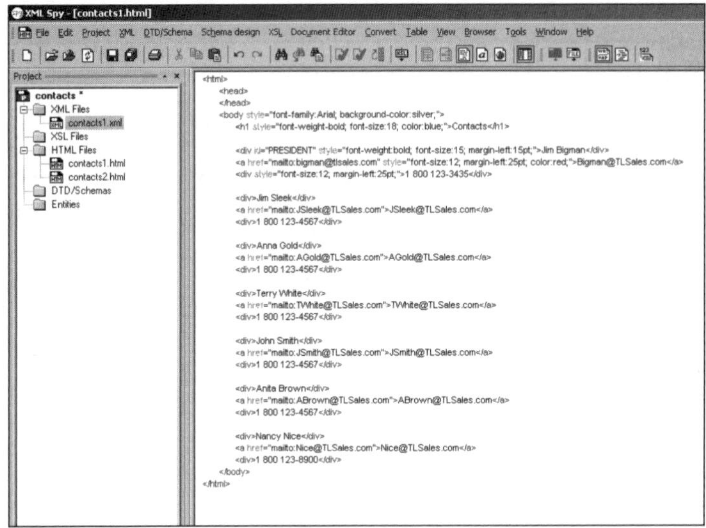

Figure 11-34

6. Click **File** on the menu bar, and then click **Save** to save your work.
7. Click **File** on the menu bar, and then click **Close** to close the document.

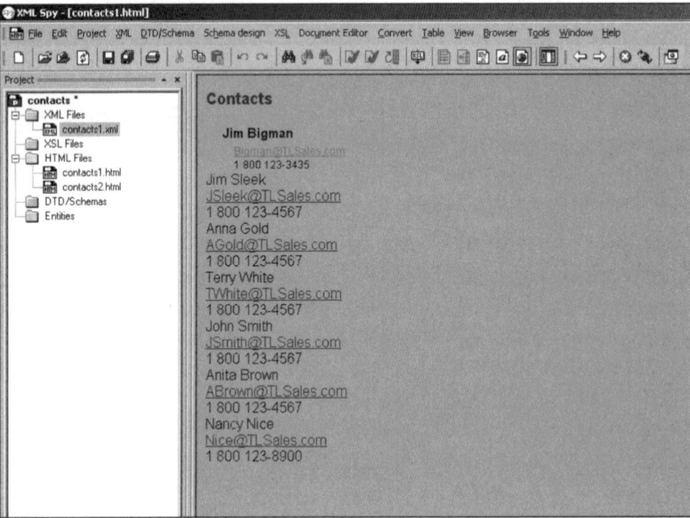

Figure 11-35

Project 11-2

As you saw in Hands-on Project 11-1, a lot of effort is required to define the style attributes for each individual element. The work to apply and maintain style rules increases as the document gets bigger. In this project, you see how styles can be applied to all similar type elements, as well as only specific elements using a class specifier.

To add an internal style sheet:

1. With the contacts.spp project still open in XML Spy, double-click **contacts2.html** under the HTML Files branch in the Project pane to open the HTML document. The document opens in the main window.
2. Click **View** on the menu bar, and then click **Text view** to display the HTML source code.
3. Internal style sheet rules are defined within a style element and are always placed in the head element of an HTML document. On the line after the head element, type the following:

```
<style type="text/css">
        body  {
              font-family: Arial;
              background-color:silver;
              }
        h1    {
              font-weight:bold;
              font-size:18;
              color:blue;
              }
        a     {
              font-size:12;
              margin-left:25pt;
              color:red;
              }
  </style>
```

   Notice that the style element is declared as a Cascading Style Sheet by setting the type attribute to text/css. Within the style sheet, style rules are declared for the body, h1, and a elements. The style rules are the same for the elements in the previous project; the difference is that the style rules are consolidated into a single element and applied to all the participating elements. Within the document, all elements with style rules share the same style properties.
4. Click **View** on the menu bar, and then click **Browser view** to view the document. Notice that all of the h1 and a element data are rendered according to the style rules.

To add class rules:

1. Click **View** on the menu bar, and then click **Text view** to return to the source code.
2. Immediately before the style element end tag, </style>, type the following:

```
   .name      {
              font-weight:bold;
              font-size:15;
              margin-left:15pt;
              }
 .number      {
              font-size:12;
              margin-left:25pt;
              }
```

11

Ensure that a period is placed before each selector class.

3. The class attribute associates a selector class in the style sheet with an element in the document. In all the div elements containing name data, add the attribute:

   class="name"

   Notice that the period is not included in the attribute value.

4. In all the div elements containing the phone number data, add the attribute:

   class= "number"

   Your document should resemble Figure 11-36.

5. Click **View** on the menu bar, and then click **Browser view** to view the document. Notice how all of the styles for the a and h1 elements match, but the two div elements are different from each other due to the distinguishing class attributes. The rendered document should resemble 11-37.

6. Click **File** on the menu bar, and then click **Save** to save your work.

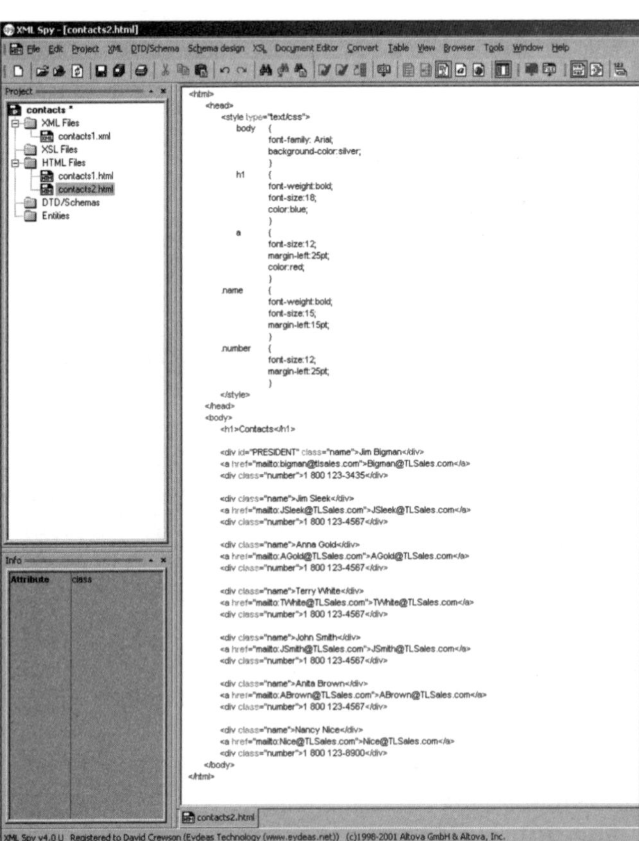

Figure 11-36

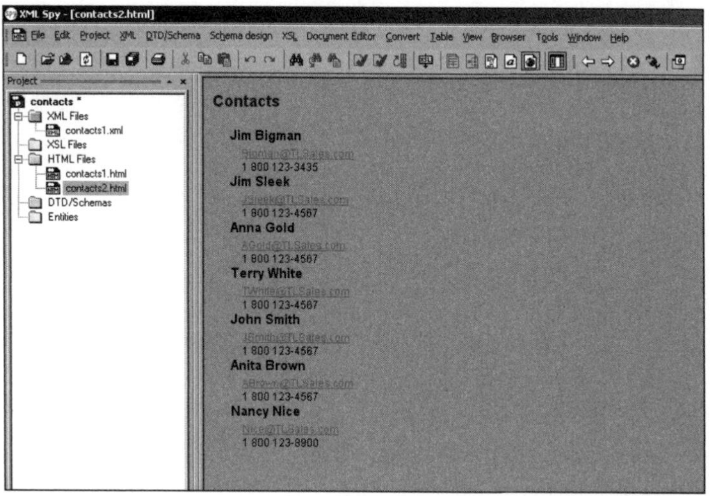

Figure 11-37

Project 11-3

The third and most flexible method of adding style rules to a document is to use an external style sheet. In this project, the style rules are identical to the internal style sheet, but the external sheet provides a method to easily replace the style rules, and share the rules amongst several documents. Since XML Spy 4.3 does not support Cascading Style Sheets, you create the style sheet using Microsoft Notepad.

To create an external style sheet:

1. Click **Start**, point to **Programs** (point to **All Programs** in Windows XP), point to **Accessories**, and then click **Notepad**. The Notepad window opens.
2. Click **File** on the menu bar, and then click **Save As**. In the Save As dialog box, click the **Save in** list arrow, if necessary, to navigate to **C:/home/<yourname>/Ch11**. Type **contacts.css** in the File name text box, and then click **Save**.
3. An external style sheets uses the same syntax as an internal style sheet. In the file that you have just created, type the following:

```
body    {
        font-family: Arial;
        background-color:silver;
        }
h1      {
        font-weight:bold;
        font-size:18;
        color:blue;
        }
a       {
        font-size:12;
        margin-left:25pt;
        color:red;
```

```
            }
.name       {
            font-weight:bold;
            font-size:15;
            margin-left:15pt;
            }
.number     {
            font-size:12;
            margin-left:25pt;
            }
```

The rules that you have added to the style sheet are identical to the rules of the internal style sheet that you created in the previous project.

4. Click **File** on the menu bar, and then **Save** to save your work.

To add an external style sheet reference:

1. Double-click **contacts3.html** under the HTML Files branch in the project pane. The document opens in the main window.
2. Click **View** on the menu bar, and then click **Text view** to display the HTML source code.
3. Within the head element, type the following:

```
<link rel="stylesheet"href= "contacts.css" type="text/css" />
```

The link element defines a document relationship with the external style sheet referenced by the href attribute. The rel attribute defines a style sheet relationship between the current document and the linked document, and the type defines the style sheet as conforming to the Cascading Style Sheet syntax. You can link multiple style sheets to the document in this manner.

4. In all the div elements containing name data, add the attribute:

class= "name"

5. In all the div elements containing the phone number data, add the attribute:

class="number"

Your document should resemble Figure 11-38.

6. To view the document, click **View** on the menu bar, and then click **Browser view** to examine the document. Notice that the document appears identical to the document from Project 11-2 with the internal style sheet. The rendered document should resemble Figure 11-39.
7. Click **File** on the menu bar, and click **Save** to save your work. Then close the contacts.css file.

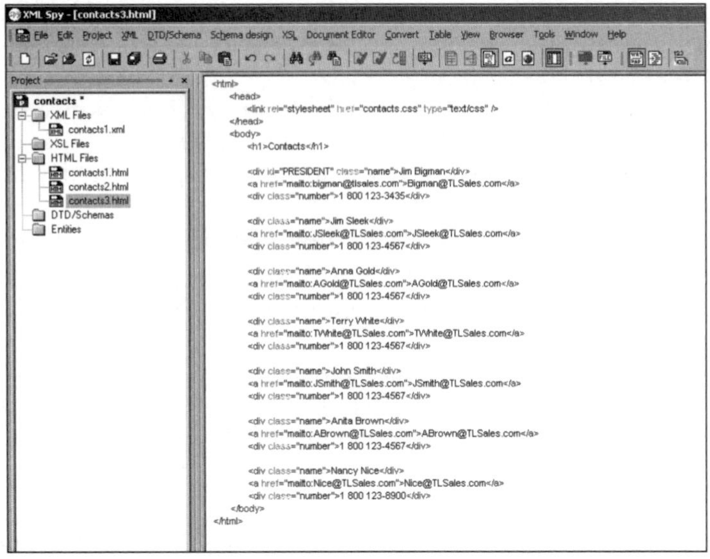

Figure 11-38

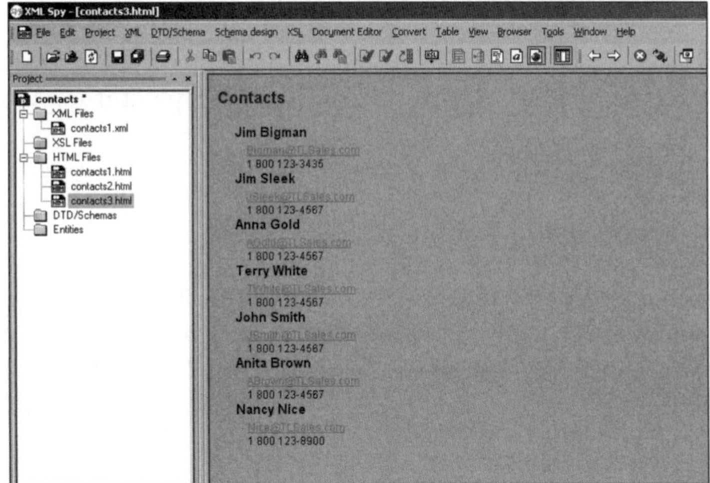

Figure 11-39

Project 11-4

In this project, you change the appearance of the document by making a single change to the document to reference a different style sheet. You then edit the style sheet to examine how to associate styles using IDs, pseudo-elements, and pseudo-classes.

To change the style sheet reference:

1. With the **contacts3.html** document from Project 11-3 open in XML Spy, switch to Text view, and then change the href attribute value in the link element to **contacts2.css**.
2. Click **View** on the menu bar, and then click **Browser view**. Notice that the appearance of the document has changed significantly. The style rules of the new Cascading Style Sheet have been applied simply by changing the document's style sheet reference.
3. Click **View** on the menu bar, and then click **Text view** to return to the source code.
4. To open the style sheet, click **Start**, point to **Programs** (point to **All Programs** in Windows XP), point to **Accessories**, and then click **Notepad**. The Notepad window opens.
5. Click **File** on the menu bar, and then click **Open**. In the Open dialog box, click the **Look in** list arrow, if necessary, to navigate to C:/home/<yourname>/Ch11. Type **contacts2.css** in the File name text box, and then click **Open**. The Cascading Style Sheet opens in the Notepad window.

To update the style sheet:

1. Notice the rules in the style sheet and how they correspond to the changes in the new document appearance. Following the last rule, type the following:
   ```
   h1:first-letter    {
                      font-size:30pt;
                      color:maroon;
                      }
   ```
   This rule specifies a style rule for the pseudo-element first-letter of the h1 element. The first letter of all h1 elements is rendered as 18 point maroon text.
2. Next, type:
   ```
   a:hover {
           color:gray;
           font-weight:bold;
           }
   ```
   The style rule assigned to the pseudo-class hover on the a element renders the text as bold and gray whenever the mouse pointer is over any anchor text.
3. To assign a style to a specific element represented by an ID value, type the following:
   ```
   #PRESIDENT{
                   color:white;
                   background-color:black;
                   }
   ```
   The information for the element with the ID attribute of PRESIDENT appears in reverse text.
4. Click **File** on the menu bar, and then click **Save** to save your work.
5. Click **File** on the menu bar, and then **Exit** to close Notepad.
6. Return to XML Spy and click **View** on the menu bar, and then click **Browser view** to view the rendered document. Notice the changes to the document. Make sure that you pass the cursor over an anchor element to observe the behavior. Notice the information that appears in reverse text.

7. Click **View** on the menu bar, and then click **Text view** to return to the source code. Examine the document to find the element with the ID value of PRESIDENT. The text within the element was what appeared in reverse text in the browser view of the document.

Project 11-5

In this project, you use Cascading Style Sheets to display an XML document in a browser window. Elements in an XML document have no implicit formatting style; all of the presentation information is obtained from the style rules. You create an external style sheet to display the contact information from the contacts.xml document in a readable fashion and associate the document with the style sheet.

To open the document:

1. Close the contacts.spp project, still open in XML Spy, add the contacts.xml file from the Ch11\Project_11-5 folder to the contacts.spp project. Then double-click **contacts.xml** under the XML Files branch in the Project pane to open the XML document. The document opens in the main window.
2. Notice the xml-style sheet processing instruction on the fourth line. The type attribute value text/css instructs the XML processor to format the document using cascading style sheet syntax and the href attribute associates the contacts3.css style sheet with the document.
3. To create an external style sheet, click **Start**, point to **Programs** (point to **All Programs**), point to **Accessories**, and then click **Notepad**. The Notepad window opens.
4. Click **File** on the menu bar, and then click **Save As** in the Save As dialog box. Click the **Save in** list arrow, if necessary, to navigate to C:/home/<yourname>/Ch11. Type **contacts3.css** in the File name text box, and then click **Save**.

11

To add the style rules:

1. A Cascading Style Sheet for an XML document uses the same syntax as for an HTML document. In the style sheet, type:

```
CONTACTS    {
            font-family:Arial;
            }
```

Similar to style sheets used with HTML documents, style rules are applied to document elements. In this case, the data within the CONTACTS element, including data of any child elements, is rendered using the Arial font.

2. Following the CONTACTS selector, type:

```
PRESIDENT   {
            display:block;
            border-width:1;
            border-style:solid;
            }
```

The PRESIDENT element is declared as a block item. The element is displayed as a discrete unit within the text flow. It starts on a new line and a new line follows the end of the element. The element and all of its children are rendered surrounded with a solid border one pixel wide.

3. Following the PRESIDENT selector, type:
```
SALES, CUSTSRV  {
                display:block;
                }
```
The selectors SALES and CUSTSRV are grouped in order to share the same style rules.
4. To format the NAME element, type the following:
```
NAME            {
                display:block;
                color:navy;
                font-style:italic;
                font-weight:bold;
                font-size:15pt;
                margin-top:15pt;
                }
```
5. To format the E-MAIL and PHONE elements, group the selectors by typing:
```
E-MAIL, PHONE   {
                display:block;
                color:black;
                font-size:12pt;
                margin-left:15pt;
                }
```
6. Click **File** on the menu bar, and then click **Save** to save your work.
7. Click **File** on the menu bar, and then click **Exit** to close Notepad.
8. To view the XML document, click **Start**, point to **Programs** (point to **All Programs** in Windows XP), and then click **Internet Explorer**. The Internet Explorer window opens.
9. In the Address text box, type **C:/home/<yourname>/Ch11/contacts.xml** and then press **Enter**. The XML document appears in the browser window. Examine the document and observe the relationship between the style rules and the rendered document.

CASE PROJECT

Continue to work with the contacts.spp project in XML Spy to add other style properties to the contacts1.html, contacts2.html, and contacts3.html documents. Experiment with inline style attributes, internal style sheets, and external style sheets. Save the HTML documents with the same names in the Ch/Case_Projects folder.

CHAPTER

12

XML DATA BINDING BASICS

In this chapter, you will learn:

- About data binding
- About data consumer elements
- How to integrate XML data with XHTML documents
- How to use data binding agents and table repetition agents
- How to work with data source objects
- How to navigate recordsets

Data binding involves mapping, synchronizing, and moving data from a data source, usually on a remote server, to an end user's local system where the user can manipulate the data.

Using data binding means that after a remote server transmits data, the user can perform some minor data manipulations on their own local system. The remote server does not have to perform all the data manipulations nor repeatedly transmit variations of the same data.

This chapter introduces data binding concepts and illustrates how you can use XML-related documents as data sources and as data retrieval documents. You learn how to use XHTML documents for data binding because, as you learned in Chapter 8, XHTML uses and extends HTML elements while adhering to the stricter grammar and structure rules in XML.

The examples and projects use Microsoft Internet Explorer as the browser application because all versions since IE version 5 support XML data binding.

DATA BINDING FUNDAMENTALS

Simply stated, **data binding** involves mapping and synchronizing data in a data source to a data consumer. For now, consider that data consumers are elements in a Web page that are designated to receive and render data; they are further defined and discussed in the next section. Data binding also involves moving data from a data source to a local system, and then manipulating the data—searching, sorting, and filtering it, for example—on the local system. When you bind data in this way, you do not have to request that the remote server manipulate the data and then retransmit the results; you can perform some data manipulations locally.

Figure 12-1 shows a simplified database architecture diagram. You are probably familiar with the concepts of a data source, which is represented by the cylinder in the upper-left corner of Figure 12-1, and data presentation, represented by the terminal screen in the lower-right corner. The concepts illustrated between the data source and presentation may not be as familiar. Each is explained as the chapter progresses.

In data binding, the data source provides the data, and the appropriate applications retrieve and synchronize the data and present it on the terminal screen. If the data changes, the applications are written so they can alter their presentation to reflect those changes.

You use data binding to reduce traffic on the network and to reduce the work of the Web server (especially for minor data manipulation) while using the resources on the local client system more efficiently. Binding data also separates the task of maintaining data from the tasks of developing and maintaining binding and presentation programs. Separating those tasks allows the database administrator and the Web page designer to work independently, which is especially beneficial on large projects.

You can bind XML elements and attributes that represent data components to presentation models using Java, C++, JavaScript, and HTML, for example. This chapter explains how to use JavaScript and HTML to bind data.

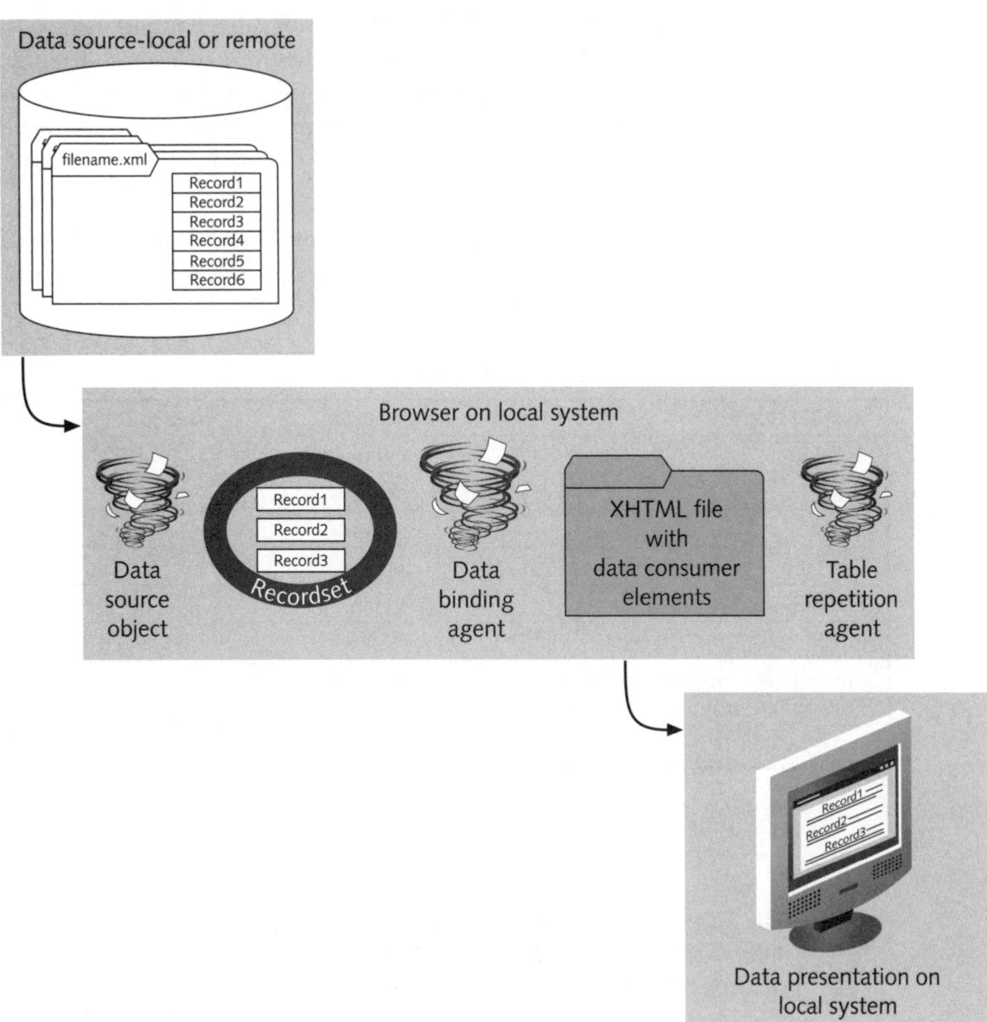

Figure 12-1 Database architecture diagram

12

DATA CONSUMER ELEMENTS

While you are designing your Web site, you identify the information and data that you want to present to the end users on their local systems. After you acquire or develop that data, you create the documents that appear as Web pages. In this chapter, you learn how to create XHTML documents, which contain elements and attributes whose names are written in lowercase. However, they could also be HTML documents, in which case the element names would appear in uppercase. Meanwhile, in addition to text, graphic, and formatting elements, the document can also contain elements that function as data consumers. Recall that

data consumers (also called **bindable elements**) are elements in an XHTML or HTML document that have been predefined so they can receive and render data. You can then use these elements to display the results of data queries, such as when a user accesses a Web page and searches for information about a particular product. For example, later in this chapter, you examine a motorcycle parts list that is updated when the vendor introduces a new part.

XHTML elements that can function as data consumers are shown in Table 12-1. In the table, they are shown in lowercase, which is correct for XHTML. If you use the elements in HTML files, they should be in uppercase.

Table 12-1 XHTML data consumer elements

<a>	<legend>
<applet>	<marquee>
<button>	<object>
<div>	<param>
<frame>	<select>
<iframe>	<span>
<img>	<table>
<input type="button I checkbox I hidden I password I radio I text >	<textarea>
<label>	

Figure 12-2 illustrates an XHTML file that could be used in a data binding scenario. In this figure, <table> and <div> are shown in bold text, and are data consumer elements.

The <div>, <span>, and <table> elements are discussed later in this chapter. Information on the other elements is available at Microsoft's MSDN Web site at *msdn.microsoft.com/library/*.

Besides using HTML elements, you can also bind data using Java applets and ActiveX controls, which are considered advanced techniques. This chapter focuses on the XML data-binding architecture in Internet Explorer.

Data consumer elements can bind two types of data: single-valued or tabular. **Single-valued data consumer elements**, such as the <span> element, bind only with a single value from the records found in the data source. For example, you will learn how to use <span> to select the price for an item *or* to select a part name. On the other hand, **tabular data consumer elements**, such as the <table> element, allow you to insert more than one value—in fact, a whole structured set of records—from the data source. For example, you will learn how to use <table> to select a part name *and* number from an external data file. Inserting more than one value at once is called **set binding**.

```
<html>
  <!-- Filename - parts2.html -->
  <head>
    <title>Parts List</title>
  </head>
  <body>
    <xml id="PList" src="partslist.xml" />
    <p> </p>
    <h1>TLSales</h1>
    <h2>Parts List</h2>
    <p>
      <table cellspacing="1" cellpadding="1" width="75%" border="1" datasrc="#PList">
        <tbody>
         <tr bgcolor="purple">
            <td>Name:</td>
            <td>
              <div dataFld="name" />
            </td>
          </tr>
          <tr>
            <td>Part Number:</td>
            <td>
              <div dataFld="partNo" />
            </td>
          </tr>
          <tr>
            <td>In stock:</td>
            <td>
              <div dataFld="stock" />
            </td>
          </tr>
          <tr>
            <td>Price:</td>
            <td>
              <div dataFld="price" />
            </td>
          </tr>
        </tbody>
      </table>
    </p>
  </body>
</html>
```

Figure 12-2 Data consumer elements

Using Extended Attributes to Retrieve Data

Using data consumer elements to indicate where to insert data is one part of providing data on a Web page. You must also include instructions in your Web page document so the browser knows where to find the data and exactly which data to display. For example, in Figure 12-2, <table> and <div> are bindable elements, and their start tags contain attribute/value pairs. The <table> element includes a datasrc attribute and each <div> element contains a datafld attribute. These are examples of XHTML/HTML extended attributes. The datasrc attribute indicates the name of the data source that the browser should search for (that is, the name assigned to the data source that actually contains the data), and the datafld attribute indicates what to query for and retrieve from the data source. You can use many kinds of data sources, including Oracle, IBM DB2, and other formats. This chapter focuses on XML-related data sources.

The datasrc and datafld attributes are mandatory. Without them, the browser or other application does not know where to find the data, nor what data to retrieve.

You generally find the datasrc and datafld attributes in close proximity to one another in a Web document. Occasionally, you find them in the same element start tag, as indicated earlier in the <span> element example. To bind a single-valued element to data, use both the datasrc and datafld attributes, as in the following example. Otherwise, the browser or other application does not know where to find the data.

```
Price: <span datasrc="#PList" datafld="Price" > </span>
```

This code tells the browser or other application, "immediately after displaying the text string "Price:", insert the value you obtained from the <Price> element (in this case, <Price> can also be considered the equivalent of a field) in the data source identified by the name "PList". Insert the value on the same line as "Price:"; do not start a new line."

Notice that the datasrc attribute includes a hash mark (#) just before the value "PList". The hash mark is mandatory and indicates that the value specified is the name of a data source. The datafld attribute names the field in the data source that is queried, and whose value is returned.

Using the <div> and <span> Elements

The <div> and <span> elements are called **grouping elements**. They provide mechanisms for keeping elements together and adding structure to XML-related documents. The <div> element defines logical divisions in your Web page. Basically, <div> breaks paragraphs by acting as a paragraph end or beginning.

Remember that while you can have paragraphs within a <div>, you can't have a <div> inside a paragraph.

For physical layout and display, however, the <div> tag is limited on its own. Besides using it to break text into paragraphs, you can also use <div> with its align attribute to specify the alignment of a section of data on the page. If you use <div> with style sheet specifications, however, it helps customize the XHTML and the appearance of the resulting Web page.

Although XHTML is not as extensible as other XML-related languages, you can use the <div> and <span> elements to achieve the effect of customizing element names. In Figure 12-3, <div> provides the name of a bicycle part in a table. The <div> element is used inside this table data (<td>) cell because you can bind XML data to <div>. To do so, you specify the data field of the data source. That is why the datafld attribute, the value of which is "name", appears within the element's start tag. Using <div> means that the name appears on a new line following the "Name:" line.

```
<html>
  <!-- Filename - parts1.html -->
  <head>
    <title>Parts List</title>
  </head>
  <body>
    <xml id="PList" src="partslist.xml" />
    <p> </p>
    <h1>TLSales</h1>
    <h2>Parts List</h2>
    <p>Part Name</p>
    <p>
      <div datasrc="#PList" dataFld="name" />
  </p>
... etc.
```

Figure 12-3 The <div> element

Following is a list of <div> attributes that you are most likely to use with XML binding:

- style—specifies style information such as color and font size for the element
- datasrc—specifies the location of the data source
- datafld—specifies the data to look for within the data source
- id—a unique identifier for the element (as discussed in previous chapters, for reference from the XML-related application)
- align (left | center | right | justify)—specifies the horizontal alignment of the <div> element with respect to its surrounding context (deprecated with HTML 4.01)
- name—assigns a control name, similar to an id (deprecated with HTML 4.01 and not recommended; use id instead)

12

Similar to the <div> tag, <span> allows you to specify a text style, but only the style of the inline text it encloses. However, unlike the <div> tag, <span> doesn't provide any default formatting features. While <div> can act as a break between paragraphs and affect a document's logical structure, <span> can only tell the browser to apply a style to the data between the <span> element's start and end tags.

The two primary attributes most often used with the <span> element are style and align; both have the same purpose as when used with the <div> element.

You can use <span> when you want to change the style of an element without naming it in a separate division within the document. For example, if you use a Level 2 Heading (<h2>) that reads "Sale Ends January 15!" and you want the words "January 15" to be colored gold, you use <span> as follows:

```
<h2>

     Sale Ends
```

```
        <span> style="color: gold;">January 15</<span>
        !
    </h2>
```

The sale deadline would still be a part of the <h2> tag, but it would be displayed in gold because of the specification in <span>.

Figure 12-4 illustrates another way you can use the <span> element.

```
<html>
  <!-- Filename - parts1.html -->
  <head>
    <title>Parts List</title>
  </head>
  <body>
    <xml id="PList" src="partslist.xml" />
    <p> </p>
    <h1>TLSales</h1>
    <h2>Parts List</h2>
    <p>
     Part Name: <span datasrc="#PList" dataFld="name" ></span>
    </p>
... etc.
```

Figure 12-4 The <span> element

As in the <div> example in Figure 12-3, <span> causes the browser to search for the name of a bicycle part. This time, however, <span> specifies that the name appears on the same line as "Name:".

When using <span> to display XHTML text, make sure that the text appearing within the <span> element does not include any XHTML block-level elements, such as <h1>. This could lead to unwanted results.

Using the <table> Element for Data Set Binding

Recall that data consumer elements support the binding of two types of data: single-valued or tabular. The data retrieved from a data source often is displayed in a table. So tabular data consumers, such as the <table> element, provide retrieval and display power, allowing you to insert whole sets of records at once, allowing for data set binding.

To achieve this data set binding, you include the datasrc="*value*" attribute/value pair in the start tag of the <table> element. Each child element in <table> can inherit the value of the datasrc attribute, but must specify its own datafld="*value*" attribute/value pair to display data values. For example, in Figure 12-5, <table> specifies that its data comes from the source it calls PList, which was defined in the <xml> element as the external partslist.xml document. The <td> element, a child element of <table>, includes <div> to indicate that the data for the Name cell comes from the <name> element in PList.

```
<html>
  <!-- Filename - parts2.html -->
  <head>
    <title>Parts List</title>
  </head>
  <body>
    <xml id="PList" src="partslist.xml" />
    <p> </p>
    <h1>TLSales</h1>
    <h2>Parts List</h2>
    <p>
      <table cellspacing="1" cellpadding="1" width="75%" border="1" datasrc="#PList">
        <tbody>
          <tr bgcolor="purple">
             <td>Name:</td>
             <td>
               <div dataFld="name" />
             </td>
          </tr>
          <tr>
             <td>Part Number:</td>
... etc.
```

Figure 12-5 The <table> element

If you want an individual child element within the parent <table> element to obtain its data from a different source, the child element can contain its own specific combination of datasrc="*value*" and datafld="*value*". For example, if the <div> element in Figure 12-5 actually got its information from another data source, such as "#PList2", the corresponding portion of code would resemble the following:

```
<p>
   <table cellspacing="1" cellpadding="1" width="75%"
         border="1" datasrc="#PList">
         <tbody>
               <tr bgcolor="purple">
                     <td>Name:</td>
                     <td>
                        <div datafld="name"
                     datasrc="#PList2"/>
... etc.
```

12

Note that Figure 12-5 includes the <tbody> element. <tbody> is considered part of a template for dynamic table behavior, which is discussed later in this chapter.

INTEGRATING XML DATA SOURCES WITH XHTML DOCUMENTS

To display updated data on a Web page, your browser must access the source of the data. As mentioned previously, the data source can be a simple ASCII delimited data file, another XML-related file, such as an XHTML file, or a more complex relational database table.

For simple Web sites, the data might even be stored within the same XHTML file that displays the rest of the Web page. For larger Web sites, however, the data is probably stored remotely, and when users issue requests through their browsers, the data is accessed and transmitted across a network.

Because of the advantages XML offers, its popularity is rapidly growing, and the number of data sources containing XML documents is increasing. When XML documents are used for data storage, the data is stored in distinct elements. Those XML data elements are called **data islands**. If the XML elements are included in the same XHTML document as the rest of the Web page information, the XML data elements create an **internal data island**. If the XML data elements are included in a separate document, they are called **external data islands**. The following sections explain how Internet Explorer 5 and higher integrate internal and external XML data islands.

Using Internal Data Islands

Figure 12-6 shows an XHTML document named parts1.html that contains an element named <xml>, nested within the <body> element. This element contains an internal data island, a parts list defined by a set of XML tags.

```
<html>
  <!-- Filename - parts1.html -->
  <head>
    <title>Parts List</title>
  </head>
  <body>
    <xml id= "PList">
      <partslist>
        <part>
          <name>Seat</name>
          <partNo>1234</partNo>
          <stock>12</stock>
          <Price>$59.99</Price>
        </part>
      </partslist>
    </xml>
    <p> </p>
    <h1>TLSales</h1>
    <h2>Parts List</h2>
    <p>
      <table cellspacing="1" cellpadding="1" width="75%" border="1" datasrc="#PList">
        <tbody>
          <tr bgcolor="purple">
             <td>Name:</td>
             <td>
               <div dataFld="name" />
             </td>
          </tr>
          <tr>
             <td>Part Number:</td>

    ... etc.
```

Figure 12-6 XHTML file containing internal XML data island

The data island is called internal because it is contained in the same XHTML file that presents the rest of the Web page. The data is called an island because it consists of an XML document—with XML, not XHTML or HTML, elements—in an otherwise XHTML/HTML element structure.

The <xml> element's start tag includes id="PList" as an attribute/value pair. The id attribute here indicates that the <xml> element is an XML data island. The value of the attribute specifies the name of the data, such as PList for Parts List. When you are using an *internal* data island, do not include a src="*value*" attribute/value pair in the <xml> element's start tag; src="*value*" indicates that an *external* data island must be accessed (external data islands are discussed in the next section). The browser then knows that the data is found immediately after the <xml> tag in the same XHTML document and is not contained in a separate file.

In summary, you include an <xml> element to embed XML data in an XHTML or HTML page. (If it is embedded in an HTML document, the element must be in uppercase, such as <XML>.) Within the <xml> element is a complete XML document. The first element in the XML document is called the root node or root element. For example, <partslist> is the root element in the XML document contained in parts1.html. The root node is a formal XML element. Nested within it is the actual data, enclosed in XML data elements.

When an <xml> element is wrapped around the other XML data elements, as it is in parts1.html, the structure is called *inline* because the <xml> child elements fall between the <xml> element's start tag and end tag. Note that this is not the same kind of inline concept to which you were introduced earlier. For example, with the <span> element, "inline" applies only to the data on the same line of XHTML/HTML code.

The <XML> element and its XHTML counterpart, <xml>, are also sometimes called unofficial HTML elements because it is not listed within the W3C's HTML Recommendations. However, it is a Microsoft extension to HTML, is included in the HTML Document Object Model—a standard Application Programming Interface (API) for HTML—and is supported by Internet Explorer 5 and later.

Internal data islands are appropriate for small amounts of data. But, if you want to access larger amounts of data, use external data islands.

Using External Data Islands

To use an external data island, you store XML data in an XML file that is separate from the XHTML document that defines the Web page. Then you add the src attribute to the <xml> element tag in the XHTML document. The value of the src attribute is the filename and location of the XML file containing the data. The separate XML file becomes your external data island. It is called external because the data is not contained within the XHTML document that displays the Web page.

Figure 12-7 shows an XHTML file named parts2.html that references an external data island located in an XML file named partslist.html. The parts2.html file is almost identical to parts1.html, the file that contains the internal data island, except for the following differences:

- In parts2.html, the <xml> element is a declared empty element with a syntax of <xml ... />
- In that single <xml> element tag, the id="Plist" attribute/value pair is the same as it was in parts1.html but an additional pair—src="partslist.xml"—is added as the reference to the external data island

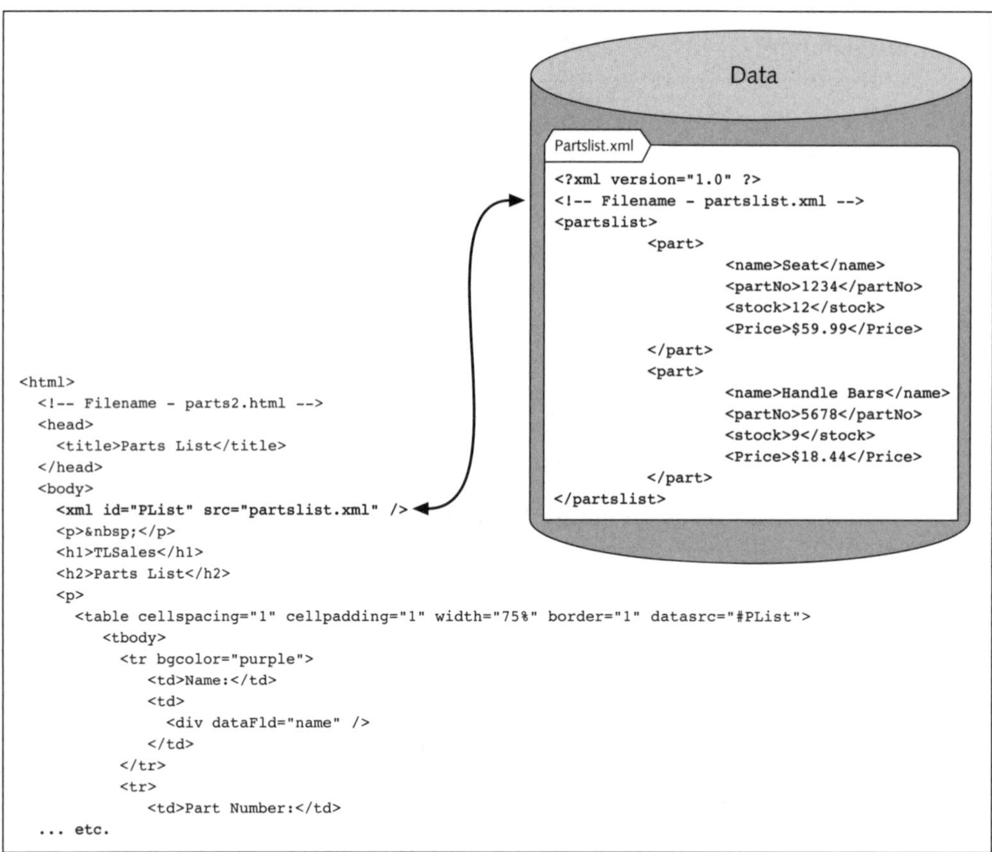

Figure 12-7 XHTML file referencing external XML data island

When you use an external data island, the browser looks for an <xml> element with the id value set to the name of the external file, such as PList. Then it interprets the src= "partslist.xml" attribute/value pair, which indicates that the data is not within the XHTML document, but in a separate document called partslist.xml.

Creating an external data island illustrates a highly recommended best practice: separating data administration from data presentation. The data is kept in one file—an XML file—and the data consumers are kept in the other file—an XHTML file. Using this strategy and file structure, Web page designers and database administrators can work on separate tasks, a particular advantage when working on large projects.

Pairing Data Sources and Data Fields

Refer back to Figures 12-6 and 12-7, and note that an XHTML <table> element follows the </xml> element that closes the data island. The <table> element is used to display the information imported from the data island. The <table> element's start tag contains a number of attribute/value pairs, including datasrc="#Plist". This data source attribute identifies the source of the data that appears in the table. Figure 12-8 shows how to use the datasrc attribute in both internal and external data islands.

In both cases, the datasrc attribute affiliates the XML data island with the id attribute value of PList to the <table> element in the XHTML document. The datasrc attribute points to the <xml> element with the id attribute identical to the value of the datasrc attribute. That <xml> element then points to the XML data island, whether internal or external to the XHTML document. Recall that data binding involves three tasks—locating a data source, retrieving the data, and then displaying the data. You use the datasrc attribute to perform the first task of identifying the data source.

When the browser loads a Web page that references a data source, it scours the XHTML document, looking for data consumers among the elements, such as <table>, <td>, <div>, and <span>. To retrieve and display the appropriate data from the data source, the browser looks for a datafld="*value*" attribute/value pair in the start tags of these data consumer elements. The datafld="*value*" attribute/value pair is also known as the **data field key**. The value of the datafld attribute is the name of the element in the data source that contains the data. In database terms, the value is the name of the field that contains the data. Adding the data field key completes the second step in the data binding task—it binds the XML element data to a position within the XHTML file.

12

In general, the datafld attribute assigns the content of a specific element to a bindable element. The browser then displays that content as specified in the XHTML document.

When you use XML namespaces, you must also declare them in the datafld binding. For example, if you name a targeted field <v:customername> instead of <customername>, the specified datafld value would be "v:customername", and not the unqualified "customername".

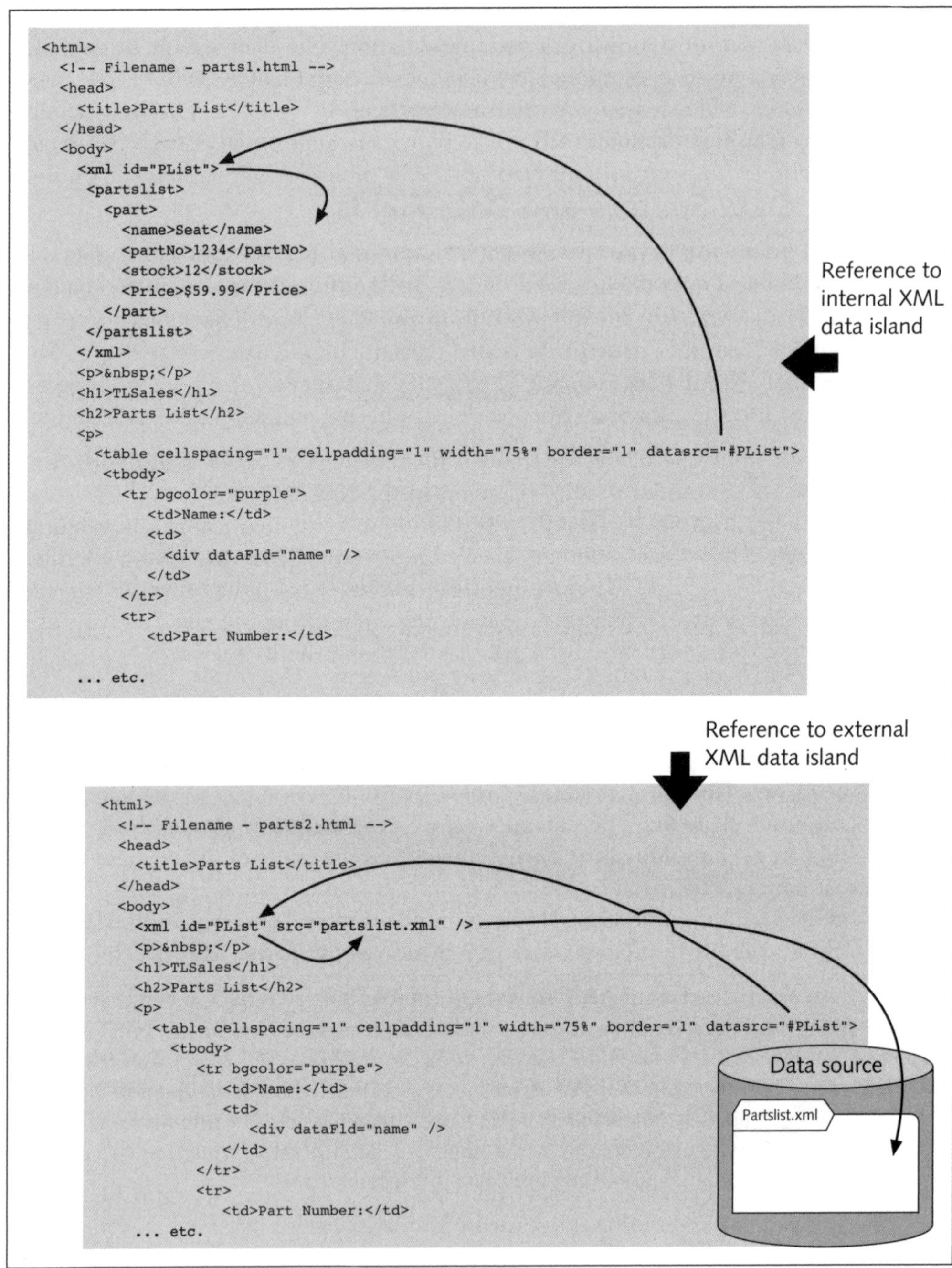
<html>
<!-- Filename - parts1.html -->
<head>
<title>Parts List</title>
</head>
<body>
<xml id="PList">
<partslist>
<part>
<name>Seat</name>
<partNo>1234</partNo>
<stock>12</stock>
<Price>$59.99</Price>
</part>
</partslist>
</xml>
<p> </p>
<h1>TLSales</h1>
<h2>Parts List</h2>
<p>
<table cellspacing="1" cellpadding="1" width="75%" border="1" datasrc="#PList">
<tbody>
<tr bgcolor="purple">
<td>Name:</td>
<td>
<div dataFld="name" />
</td>
</tr>
<tr>
<td>Part Number:</td>
... etc.
Reference to internal XML data island
Reference to external XML data island
<html>
<!-- Filename - parts2.html -->
<head>
<title>Parts List</title>
</head>
<body>
<xml id="PList" src="partslist.xml" />
<p> </p>
<h1>TLSales</h1>
<h2>Parts List</h2>
<p>
<table cellspacing="1" cellpadding="1" width="75%" border="1" datasrc="#PList">
<tbody>
<tr bgcolor="purple">
<td>Name:</td>
<td>
<div dataFld="name" />
</td>
</tr>
<tr>
<td>Part Number:</td>
... etc.
Data source
Partslist.xml

Figure 12-8 The datasrc attribute

USING DATA BINDING AGENTS AND TABLE REPETITION AGENTS

A **data binding agent** utility establishes and maintains the synchronization of the data values to the HTML document. The binding agent and the table repetition agent are implemented by appropriate dynamic link libraries in Internet Explorer, and they operate as background processes. When Internet Explorer loads a page, the binding agent searches it, looking for data consumer elements, and then determines which data source object (DSO) to use, based on the attribute values found in the start tags of certain elements. Once the binding agent recognizes all data consumers and DSOs, it synchronizes the data that flows between them. For example, when the DSO obtains more data from its data source, the binding agent is the process that actually transmits the new data to the consumers. Conversely, when an end user updates a databound element on a Web page, the binding agent should notify the DSO and a display-to-data source process, reverse in nature to the source-to-display process, should be initiated.

The binding agent can also send scriptable signals and messages to alert a developer to changes in the state of the data.

As the Web page receives data from the data source, the **table repetition agent** in the browser works with the XHTML <table> data consumer elements to expand the table rows. This means you do not need to recode the XHTML table to create cells when the Web page receives additional data. This dynamic table behavior is illustrated in Figure 12-9.

The parts list on the left indicates that, at the time the page was originally displayed, its XML data source file contained only one XML <part> element (i.e., the bicycle seat), with its respective child element data fields. The parts list on the right represents the same XHTML page after the XML data file has been updated. It now contains two XML <part> elements—the seat and a set of handle bars. The table repetition agent in the browser expanded the table in the XHTML document and on the Web page to accommodate the second bicycle part. If you added a third XML <part> element to the XML data file, the XHTML table would again expand automatically.

Because the browser expands the table on the client system, you can optimize network bandwidth. The remote Web server is only used to provide the data, not to format it on the page.

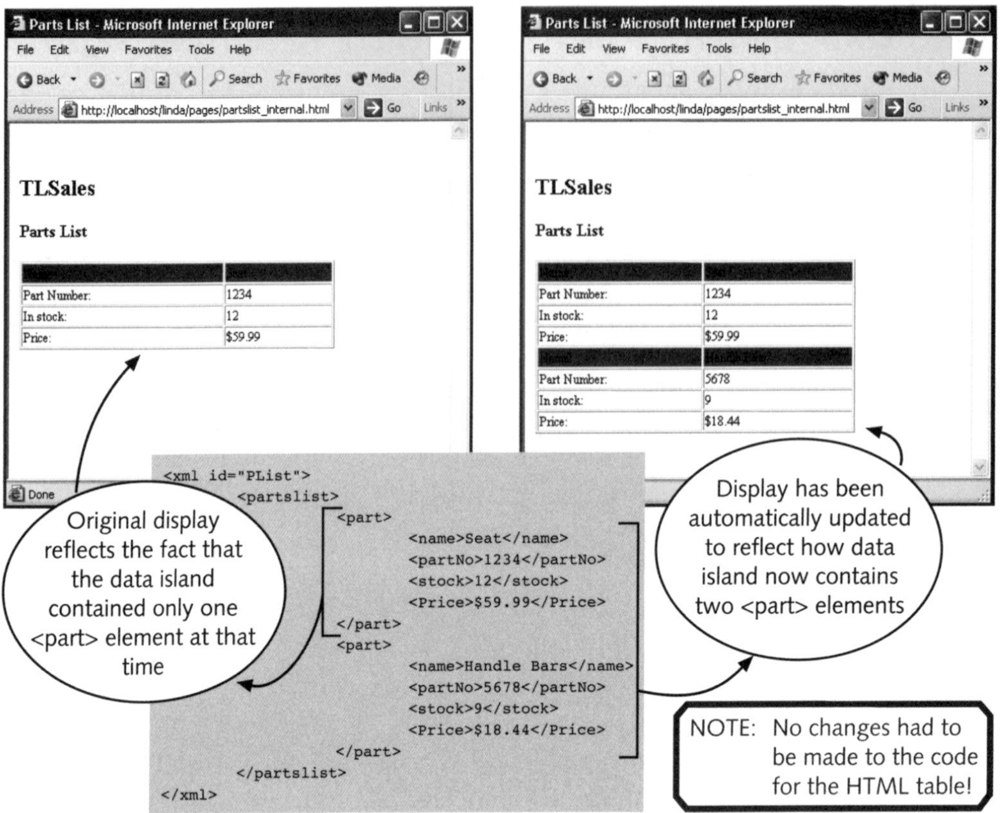


```
<xml id="PList">
      <partslist>
         <part>
               <name>Seat</name>
               <partNo>1234</partNo>
               <stock>12</stock>
               <Price>$59.99</Price>
         </part>
         <part>
               <name>Handle Bars</name>
               <partNo>5678</partNo>
               <stock>9</stock>
               <Price>$18.44</Price>
         </part>
      </partslist>
</xml>
```

Figure 12-9 Dynamic table behavior

Working with Data Source Objects (DSOs)

Versions of Internet Explorer 5 and later use data source objects to implement data binding. Developed along with Dynamic HTML (DHTML), DSOs download the data along with the Web page, and work with the data binding agent and table repetition agent, if necessary, to update data automatically. If the data within the XML data elements changes, the changes are automatically updated the next time the browser accesses the Web page. This adds extra data flexibility that is not offered by other, more static HTML presentations. This ability is particularly useful when you want to display current information in forms, tables, fields, or other compatible objects on your Web site.

Internet Explorer contains several data source objects for use with various kinds of data, including:

- Tabular data control
- Remote data service
- Java Database Connectivity (JDBC) DataSource applet
- Custom data source objects
- MSHTML data source object
- XML data source object

Each DSO gathers data from different sources and has unique methods for manipulating the data. They access the respective data sources, query for specific data, and then return with that data and provide it to the data consumer elements in the XHTML file.

After you create and identify your data, you specify in the XHTML file the DSO that provides the data. You use a particular syntax to add the specification for the DSO to your XHTML file. For example, you could specify the JDBC DSO by including an <applet> element (also called an <applet> object) with appropriate attributes and child elements. To specify the RDS DSO, you include an <object> element with its respective attributes and child elements.

When you are using an internal XML data island, you specify the XML DSO by using the <xml> element with the attribute/value pair id="*value*". When you are using an external data island, you add an src="*filename*.xml" attribute/value pair. The parts1.html document shown in Figures 12-6 and 12-7 specifies the XML DSO.

Understanding How the DSO Returns Data

To understand how the DSO acts during data retrieval and conveyance, start by reviewing the XML data source file usedbikes.xml in Figure 12-10.

The whole data source is contained within the <import> element. It contains three records, each defined within a <row> element. Each record contains five fields: the <desc>, <color>, <mileage>, <aprice>, and <image> elements. Each field contains data. To be a valid XML file, the data file must conform to a DTD or schema.

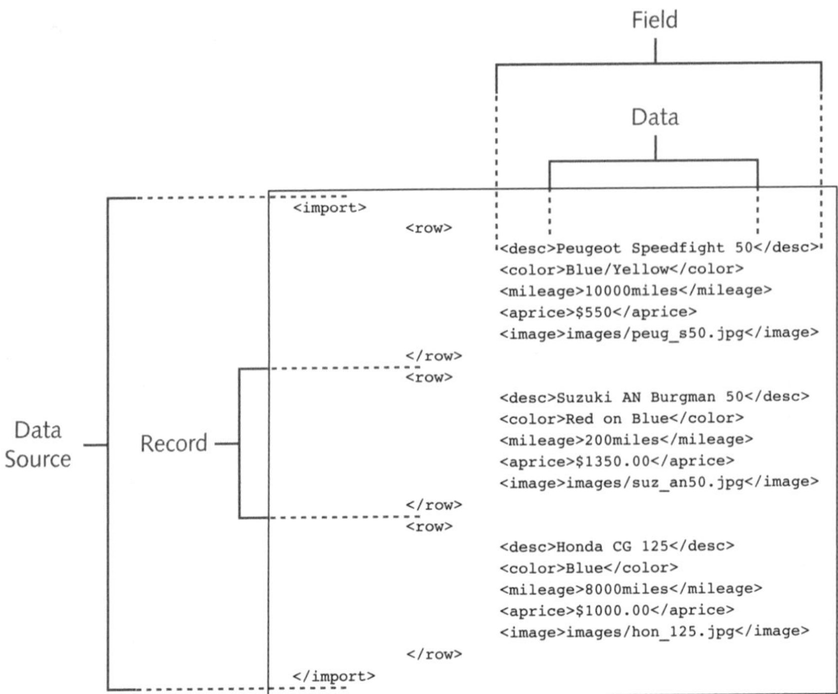
Field
Data
Data Source
Record
<import>
<row>
<desc>Peugeot Speedfight 50</desc>
<color>Blue/Yellow</color>
<mileage>10000miles</mileage>
<aprice>$550</aprice>
<image>images/peug_s50.jpg</image>
</row>
<row>
<desc>Suzuki AN Burgman 50</desc>
<color>Red on Blue</color>
<mileage>200miles</mileage>
<aprice>$1350.00</aprice>
<image>images/suz_an50.jpg</image>
</row>
<row>
<desc>Honda CG 125</desc>
<color>Blue</color>
<mileage>8000miles</mileage>
<aprice>$1000.00</aprice>
<image>images/hon_125.jpg</image>
</row>
</import>

Figure 12-10 Simple data source file—usedbikes.xml

Figure 12-11 shows the Web page document named usedbikes.xml, the XML data source file usedbikes.xml from Figure 12-10, and the data the DSO retrieves from usedbikes.xml. This data, a subset of all the data in usedbikes.xml, is called a **recordset**. The datafld attributes in the XHTML file instruct the DSO to query the data source for mileage and price information. Each time the DSO obtains the data from one mileage field and one price field, it constructs one record. In other words, a single record can be defined as one tabular row of data. The records that the DSO builds are data objects. The data is conveyed to the system's RAM record by record, and the DSO combines them into a recordset that is passed to the binding agent and table repetition agent, if necessary.

The recordset contains records, or objects, that contain data from the two fields that were specified and bound by the datafld attributes in the XHTML file. The recordset does *not* contain data from all of the five fields in the data source records. The DSO recordset is a subrecordset of the data source.

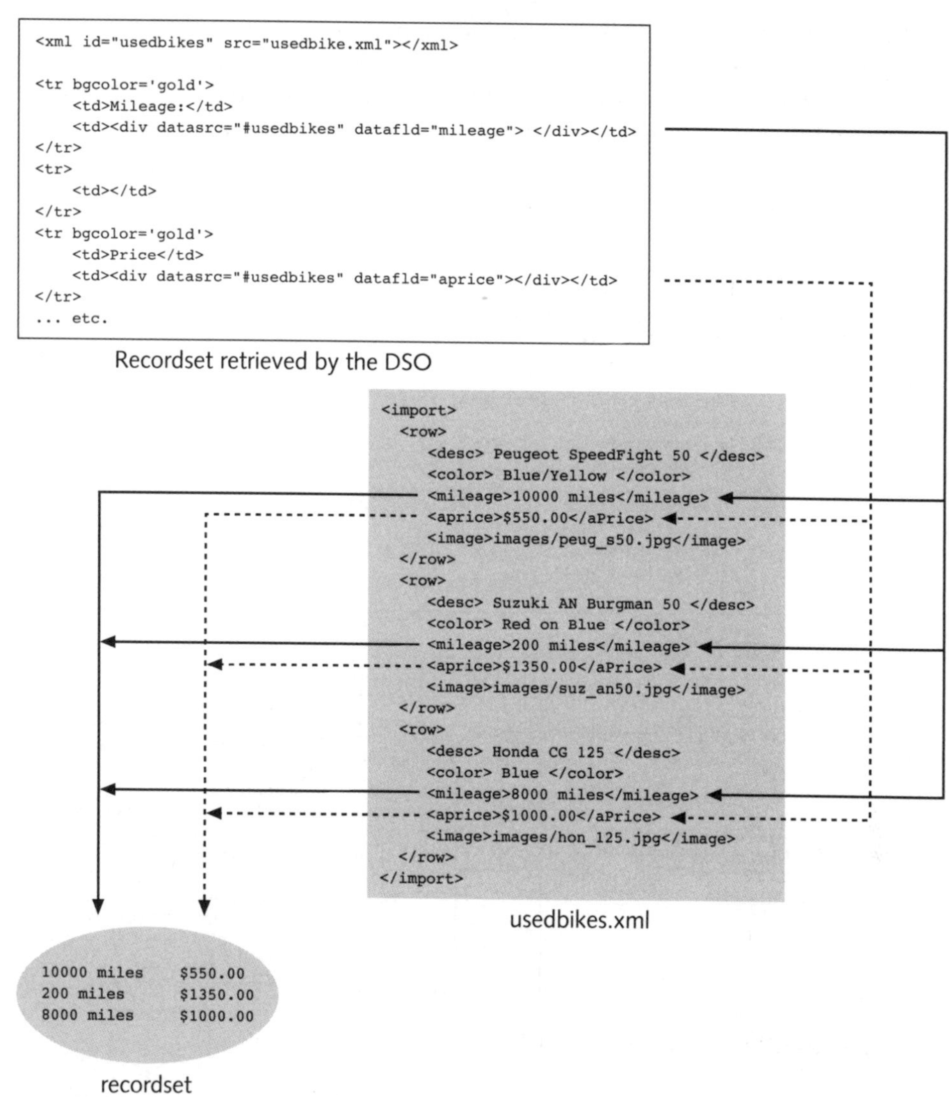

<xml id="usedbikes" src="usedbike.xml"></xml>
<tr bgcolor='gold'>
<td>Mileage:</td>
<td><div datasrc="#usedbikes" datafld="mileage"> </div></td>
</tr>
<tr>
<td></td>
</tr>
<tr bgcolor='gold'>
<td>Price</td>
<td><div datasrc="#usedbikes" datafld="aprice"></div></td>
</tr>
... etc.
Recordset retrieved by the DSO
<import>
<row>
<desc> Peugeot SpeedFight 50 </desc>
<color> Blue/Yellow </color>
<mileage>10000 miles</mileage>
<aprice>$550.00</aPrice>
<image>images/peug_s50.jpg</image>
</row>
<row>
<desc> Suzuki AN Burgman 50 </desc>
<color> Red on Blue </color>
<mileage>200 miles</mileage>
<aprice>$1350.00</aPrice>
<image>images/suz_an50.jpg</image>
</row>
<row>
<desc> Honda CG 125 </desc>
<color> Blue </color>
<mileage>8000 miles</mileage>
<aprice>$1000.00</aPrice>
<image>images/hon_125.jpg</image>
</row>
</import>
usedbikes.xml
10000 miles $550.00
200 miles $1350.00
8000 miles $1000.00
recordset

Figure 12-11 Data copied into recordset

Data Nesting and the Two-Level Rule

So far in this chapter, the data source files have been fairly flat. That is, the records, fields, and data have not been nested deeply, element within element. However, you can nest both <table> elements and XML data elements several layers beneath the root elements of their documents. With data binding, if you nest the data any deeper than two levels from the root element, you must add a datafld="*value*" attribute/value pair to the consumer element start tag. As the value of that datafld attribute, you must also add a full path specification to the parent element of the data fields. Think of this as the Two-Level Rule.

12

In Figure 12-12, the XML source file named custcredit.xml nests up to three levels below the <customer> root element. The corresponding XHTML document also has three levels of nested tables. Some of the datafld attributes for the <table> elements require full path descriptions to enable the DSO to access the data.

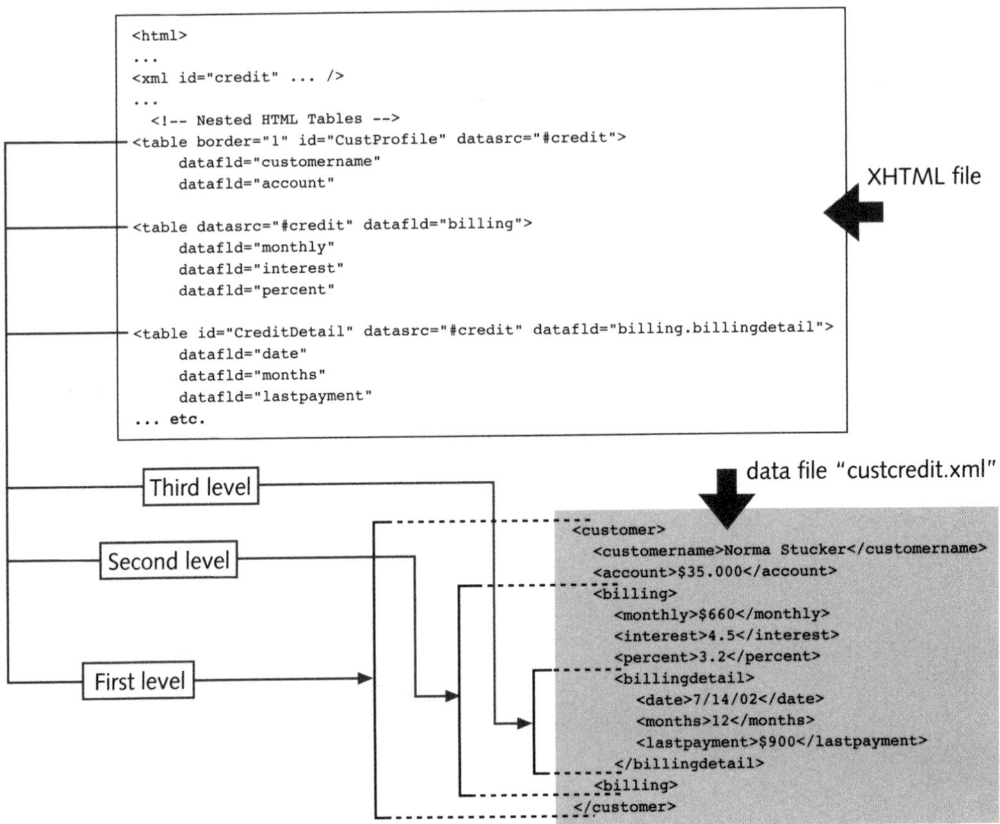

Figure 12-12 The Two-Level Rule

The first level <table> element includes datafld attribute values that specify "customername" and "account". This element does not require a path to bind the datafld attribute because the data in custcredit.xml falls within the Two-Level Rule. The targeted fields in custcredit.xml and their data are listed immediately beneath the root <customer> element.

The second level <table> element includes datafld attribute values that specify "monthly", "interest", and "percent". Again, according to the Two-Level Rule, this element does not require a path because the targeted fields and data are nested only once. However, you can add a path to clarify where the data is stored. In Figure 12-12, a datafld attribute has been added, and its value has been set to "billing" (i.e., datafld="billing"); "billing" is the name of the element that is queried to find the data fields.

The third level <table> element includes datafld attribute values that specify "date", "months", and "lastpayment". To bind <table> element, the value of its datafld attribute must be a full path to the element being queried because the nesting of the "billingdetail" element exceeds the Two-Level Rule. In Figure 12-12, the attribute/value pair "datafld='billing.billingdetail' " has been added to the <table> element. Note that this specification concatenates the names of the parent elements of the targeted fields—in other words, it combines them and uses a period for the delimiter. This is the standard syntax for a full path value that references more than one element.

If you specify the full path of the datafld attribute within a <table> element, you do not need to specify the same path to the subsequent datafld values referenced within the same table (e.g., within the <td> tags). Those elements inherit the full path from their parent elements. However, if an element specifies a different data source and its targeted fields are nested more than two levels deep, they require their own full path specifications.

NAVIGATING RECORDSETS

Recordsets returned by the DSO are separate data objects, and can be navigated or manipulated by any element, function, or program that understands data binding. This provides the following opportunities:

- The users of your Web page can process and manipulate the records in the recordsets, resulting in a more flexible and informative presentation.
- Users navigate and manipulate the recordsets at the client system in the browser. There is no need to send requests back to a Web server to have it do the navigation and manipulation, which saves bandwidth.
- The Web page developer needs to be aware of the information in the recordsets, which enhances development and security.

12

One way to navigate the recordsets is by using simple JavaScript techniques. For example, Figure 12-13 shows an XHTML file called usedbikes.html that has been split into three sections for this discussion. Part A shows JavaScript code contained within a <script> element. That code defines basic JavaScript functions that are explained later in this section. Part B defines an XHTML table.

Part C defines a set of XHTML buttons that are used to execute the JavaScript functions defined in Part A. (Those buttons are also shown later in Figure 12-16.)

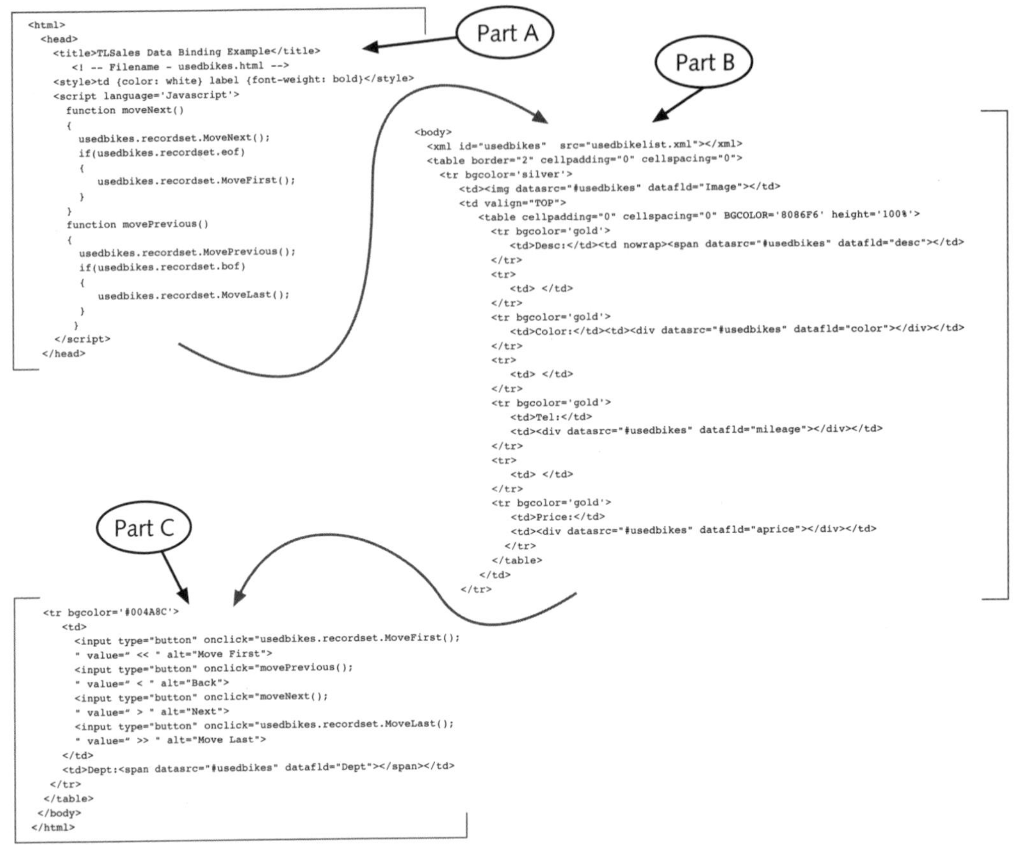


```
<html>
  <head>
    <title>TLSales Data Binding Example</title>
      <! -- Filename - usedbikes.html -->
    <style>td {color: white} label {font-weight: bold}</style>
    <script language='Javascript'>
      function moveNext()
      {
        usedbikes.recordset.MoveNext();
        if(usedbikes.recordset.eof)
        {
           usedbikes.recordset.MoveFirst();
        }
      }
      function movePrevious()
      {
        usedbikes.recordset.MovePrevious();
        if(usedbikes.recordset.bof)
        {
           usedbikes.recordset.MoveLast();
        }
       }
    </script>
  </head>
```

```
<body>
  <xml id="usedbikes"  src="usedbikelist.xml"></xml>
  <table border="2" cellpadding="0" cellspacing="0">
    <tr bgcolor='silver'>
       <td><img datasrc="#usedbikes" datafld="Image"></td>
       <td valign="TOP">
          <table cellpadding="0" cellspacing="0" BGCOLOR='8086F6' height='100%'>
            <tr bgcolor='gold'>
               <td>Desc:</td><td nowrap><span datasrc="#usedbikes" datafld="desc"></td>
            </tr>
            <tr>
               <td> </td>
            </tr>
            <tr bgcolor='gold'>
               <td>Color:</td><td><div datasrc="#usedbikes" datafld="color"></div></td>
            </tr>
            <tr>
               <td> </td>
            </tr>
            <tr bgcolor='gold'>
               <td>Tel:</td>
               <td><div datasrc="#usedbikes" datafld="mileage"></div></td>
            </tr>
            <tr>
               <td> </td>
            </tr>
            <tr bgcolor='gold'>
               <td>Price:</td>
               <td><div datasrc="#usedbikes" datafld="aprice"></div></td>
              </tr>
            </table>
          </td>
       </tr>
```

```
  <tr bgcolor='#004A8C'>
     <td>
       <input type="button" onclick="usedbikes.recordset.MoveFirst();
       " value=" << " alt="Move First">
       <input type="button" onclick="movePrevious();
       " value=" < " alt="Back">
       <input type="button" onclick="moveNext();
       " value=" > " alt="Next">
       <input type="button" onclick="usedbikes.recordset.MoveLast();
       " value=" >> " alt="Move Last">
     </td>
     <td>Dept:<span datasrc="#usedbikes" datafld="Dept"></span></td>
   </tr>
  </table>
 </body>
</html>
```

Figure 12-13 XHTML file with JavaScript—usedbikes.html

Figure 12-14 shows the XML file named usedbikes.xml, which is the external data island for the XHTML file usedbikes.html shown in Figure 12-13. Both files illustrate how you can create and navigate a customized DSO recordset.

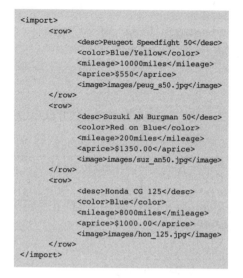

```
<import>
     <row>
          <desc>Peugeot Speedfight 50</desc>
          <color>Blue/Yellow</color>
          <mileage>10000miles</mileage>
          <aprice>$550</aprice>
          <image>images/peug_s50.jpg</image>
     </row>
     <row>
          <desc>Suzuki AN Burgman 50</desc>
          <color>Red on Blue</color>
          <mileage>200miles</mileage>
          <aprice>$1350.00</aprice>
          <image>images/suz_an50.jpg</image>
     </row>
     <row>
          <desc>Honda CG 125</desc>
          <color>Blue</color>
          <mileage>8000miles</mileage>
          <aprice>$1000.00</aprice>
          <image>images/hon_125.jpg</image>
     </row>
</import>
```

Figure 12-14 XML data source file

The XHTML file requires the browser to query the records in usedbikes.xml, and then return the information from all five fields in each record in a recordset. Figure 12-15 shows that recordset. Figure 12-15 also indicates the BOF (beginning of file) and EOF (end of file) positions. When navigating through a recordset, the JavaScript navigation functions always refer to these positions.

12

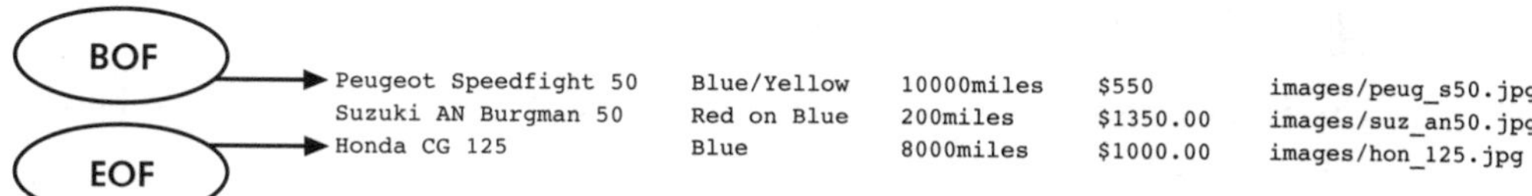

Figure 12-15 Navigating the recordset

The JavaScript function code in the usedbikes.html file in Figure 12-13 defines the following four functions: moveNext, movePrevious, moveFirst, and moveLast. The users of the Web page use the built-in behavior of these functions to navigate through the recordset. They see a rendered XHTML display similar to the one shown in Figure 12-16. The XHTML code at the bottom of usedbikes.html defines the relationships between the functions and the buttons. When users click a button, the Web page runs the corresponding JavaScript function.

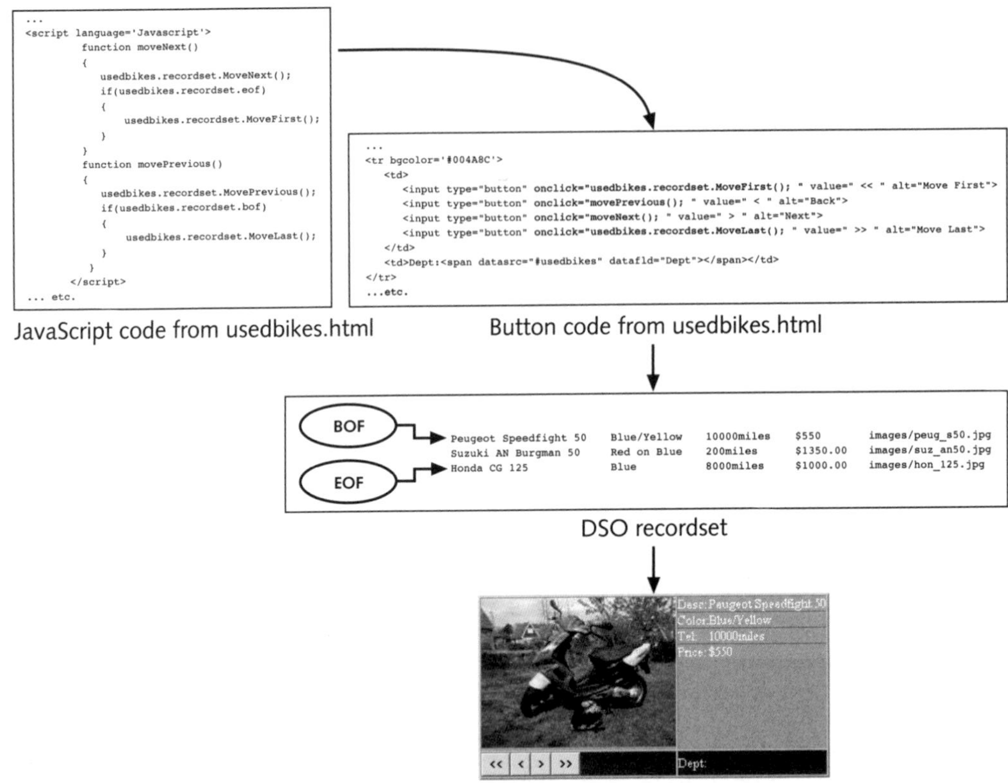

Figure 12-16 Evolution of on-screen navigation

The JavaScript and XHTML code features work together to allow an end user to navigate through the recordset as follows:

- When a user clicks the MoveFirst (<<) button, the MoveFirst() function points to the first record in the recordset, and the XHTML code retrieves information for that record—the information for the Peugeot Speedfight 50—and displays it on the page.
- When a user clicks the Back (<) button, the MovePrevious() function points to the previous record unless it is already at the top (i.e., the BOF position). If it is at BOF, the MoveLast() function is executed and points to the last record in the recordset.
- When a user clicks the Next (>) button, the MoveNext() function points to the next record unless it is already at the bottom (i.e., the EOF position). If it is at EOF, the MoveFirst() function is executed and points to the first record in the recordset.
- When a user clicks the MoveLast button (>>) button, the MoveLast() function points to the last record in the recordset.

Special Situation—Using the dataPageSize Attribute

After you bind data consumer elements, such as a <table> element and its child elements, to a data source, by default, the Web page displays *all* the records obtained by the DSO from the data source. If the recordset is large, the dynamic table behavior might cause a page to grow beyond what is practical to display. In this case, you can include a dataPageSize="*value*" attribute/value pair in the start tag of the data consumer element to specify the maximum number of records that should be displayed at any one time. Use the following syntax:

```
<table border="1" id="CustProfile" datasrc="#credit"
      dataPageSize="10">
```

After that, to enable the user to move to the next and previous pages of records viewed in the table, you could code nextPage( ) and previousPage( ) methods in the XHTML document, in a manner similar to the navigation code shown earlier in Figure 12-13.

Special Situation—Using Single-Valued Elements Instead of Tabular Elements

The <table> element and its child elements can occasionally be too restrictive or exacting for displaying data. If this is the case, but you still want to display data in a table, you can use one or more single-valued consumer elements—those listed in Table 12-1. You can also use these elements in XHTML tables.

An easy to way to display nontabular data is to bind the data to either a <span> or <div> element. Using this technique, you can display the data from a data island anywhere on an XHTML page. Figure 12-17 illustrates two methods for doing this.

```
<html>
  <head>
    <link rel="stylesheet" href="http://localhost/username/theme/tlsales.css" type="text/css" />
       <title>Used Bikes</title>
  </head>
  <body>
    <xml id="UsedBikes" src="usedbikelist.xml" />
    <p> </p>
    <h1>TLSales</h1>
    <h2>List of Used Bikes</h2>
    <br />Description:
       <div datasrc="#UsedBikes" datafld="desc" ></div>
    <br />Color:
       <div datasrc="#UsedBikes" datafld="color" ></div>
    <br />Mileage:
       <div datasrc="#UsedBikes" datafld="mileage" ></div>
  </body>
</html>
```

or

```
<html>
  <head>
    <link rel="stylesheet" href="http://localhost/username/theme/tlsales.css" type="text/css" />
       <title>Used Bikes</title>
  </head>
  <body>
    <xml id="UsedBikes" src="usedbikelist.xml" />
    <p> </p>
    <h1>TLSales</h1>
    <h2>List of Used Bikes</h2>
    <br />Description:
       <span datasrc="#UsedBikes" datafld="desc" ></span>
    <br />Color:
       <span datasrc="#UsedBikes" datafld="color" ></span>
    <br />Mileage:
       <span datasrc="#UsedBikes" datafld="mileage" ></span>
  </body>
</html>
```

Figure 12-17 <span> or <div> as alternatives to <table>

The results resemble a simple table and are identical for either method, as illustrated in Figure 12-18.

With these examples, however, you likely can only see a partial view of your XML data. To navigate to the next line or page of data, you have to add scripting code to your XHTML document to help users navigate the pages.

To quickly display the data from all the fields in an entire XML data source, you can use "$Text" as the value for your datafld attribute, as shown in Figure 12-19.

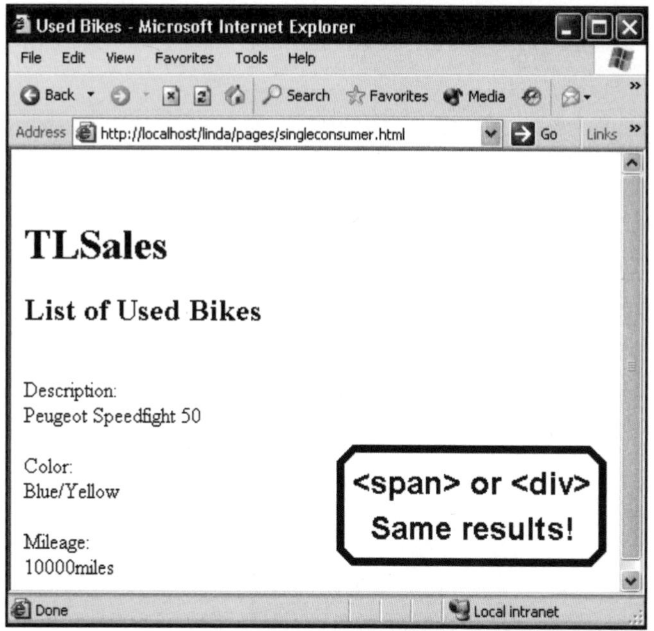

Figure 12-18 <span> or <div> results

```
<html>
  <head>
    <link rel="stylesheet" href="http://localhost/username/theme/tlsales.css" type="text/css" />
    <title>Used Bikes</title>
  </head>
  <body>
    <XML id="UsedBikes" src="usedbikelist.xml" />
    <p> </p>
    <h1>TLSales</h1>
    <h2>List of Used Bikes</h2>
    <br />Full Details :
      <div datasrc="#UsedBikes" datafld="$text" ></div>
  </body>
</html>
```

Figure 12-19 Code for displaying data with $Text

The results resemble Figure 12-20 except that, where Figure 12-20 shows that the information for only *one* record is displayed, *all* the records are displayed uncontrollably. Adding the appropriate JavaScript code to your XHTML Web page file, however helps to control this behavior.

12

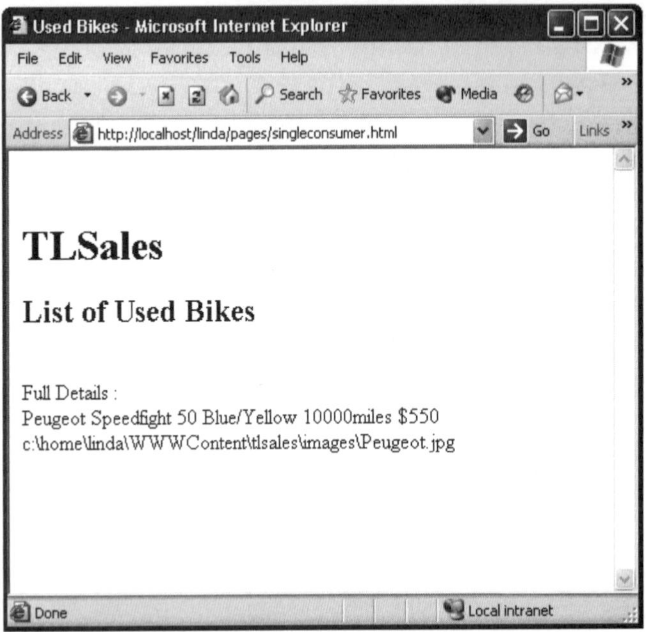

Figure 12-20 Results from using datafld="$Text"

Again, in this example, you can use the <span> and <div> elements instead of tabular data consumers.

Chapter Summary

- Data binding is mapping and synchronizing data to a data consumer. An example of a data consumer is an element on an XHTML or HTML page that is designed to receive and render data. Data binding also involves moving data from a data source, which is often a remote Web server, to a local system, and then manipulating the data.
- Use data binding to reduce the work done on Web servers, to make better use of the resources on local systems, to reduce network (including Web) traffic, and to separate the maintenance of data from the development and maintenance of the binding and presentation program(s).
- You can bind data using two XHTML data consumer element types (single-valued or tabular) plus extended attributes.
- XML data elements and attributes lend themselves to data binding models using Java, C++, JavaScript, and HTML, for example.
- Constructing and using XML internal and external data islands allows you to dynamically integrate data with Web pages and other presentations.

- Binding involves two steps: identifying a data source with datasrc and src attributes, if necessary, and then using datafld to bind XHTML elements to specific fields in the data source.
- Synchronization takes place as a result of interactions among the binding agent, the DSO, and the table repetition agent, if necessary.
- The data source object acts as a data supplier to create and manage recordsets. Web page users can use Internet Explorer and higher to display, manipulate, and navigate the recordsets on their local systems.

Review Questions

1. Currently, data binding is limited to XML elements and HTML pages. True or false?
2. Which of the following languages can you use to bind XML elements to a presentation model?
   a. HTML
   b. XML
   c. C++
   d. JavaScript
   e. Java
   f. all the above
3. Binding XML data to HTML or XHTML documents requires additional software other than an up-to-date Internet Explorer browser. True or false?
4. What does the acronym DSO mean?
5. Which statement best describes a DSO?
   a. an ActiveX control feature that updates automatically
   b. an ActiveX control feature that represents a live connection to the data source that updates automatically
   c. an ActiveX connection to a data file, XML file, or database
6. To display XML elements using a <table> element and specify the name of the data island as the value of the datasrc attribute, you must precede the name of the data island with a(n) ______________.
7. Which statement best describes an internal XML data island?
   a. an internal data island is 100% equivalent to its resulting data set
   b. an internal data island can be in a separate file
   c. an internal data island is contained within a set of XHTML <xml> element tags within the same XHTML file
   d. an internal data island is contained within a set of XML element tags within the same XHTML file

12

8. Based on the following XML code, which of the following XHTML <table> element start tags would properly bind this data to the table?

```
<XML id="PList">
   <partslist>
        <part>
              <name>Seat</name>
              <partNo>1234</partNo>
              <stock>12</stock>
              <Price>$59.99</Price>
        </part>
   </partslist>
</XML>
```

   a. `<table cellspacing="1" cellpadding="2" border="2" src="partslist">`

   b. `<table cellspacing="2" cellpadding="1" border="1" datasrc= "#partslist">`

   c. `<table cellspacing="1" cellpadding="2" border="2" src="#partslist">`

   d. `<table cellspacing="2" cellpadding="1" border="1" datasrc= "partslist">`

9. State two reasons for using external data islands.

10. Given the following XML file called newpart.xml, what would be the correct syntax for the <XML> element tag, inside the XHTML file, to use the newpart.xml file as an external data island?

```
<partslist>
     <part>
           <name>Seat</name>
           <partNo>1234</partNo>
           <stock>12</stock>
           <Price>$59.99</Price>
     </part>
     <part>
           <name>Handle Bars</name>
           <partNo>5678</partNo>
           <stock>9</stock>
           <Price>$18.44</Price>
     </part>
</partslist>
```

   a. `<XML id="partslist" datasrc="newpart.xml" />`

   b. `<XML id="newpart" src="#newpart.xml" />`

   c. `<XML id="newpart" src="newpart.xml" />`

   d. `<XML id="partslist" datasrc="partslist.xml" />`

11. Code a simple XHTML table to display the following information from the usedbikelist.xml file. Use all the elements defined in the example. The final rendering should look like the Web page shown in Figure 12-21.

```
<Import>
<Row>
  <desc>Peugeot Speedfight 50</desc>
  <color>Blue/Yellow</color>
  <mileage>10000miles</mileage>
  <aPrice>$550</aPrice>
  <Image>c:/home/username/WWWContent/tlsales/
                               images/Peugeot.jpg</Image>
</Row>
<Row>
  <desc>Suzuki AN Burgman 50</desc>
  <color>Red on Blue</color>
  <mileage>200miles</mileage>
  <aPrice>$1250.00</aPrice>

<Image>c:/home/username/WWWContent/tlsales/images/suzuki.
jpg</Image>
</Row>
<Row>
  <desc>Honda CG 125 CG125</desc>
  <color>Blue</color>
  <mileage>8000miles</mileage>
  <aPrice>$1000.00</aPrice>

<Image>c:/home/username/WWWContent/tlsales/images/Honda2.
jpg</Image>
</Row>
</Import>
```

TLSales

List of Used Bikes

Description	Color	Miles	Asking Price
Peugeot Speedfight 50	Blue/Yellow	10000miles	$550
Suzuki AN Burgman 50	Red on Blue	200miles	$1250.00
Honda CG 125 CG125	Blue	8000miles	$1000.00

Figure 12-21

12

12. The DSO manages data on a record-by-record basis. When data is added to an XML file, the XHTML data does not necessarily have to change. A new table row is created for every row of data supplied from the DSO. This behavior is provided by the ________________.
    a. recordset
    b. table repetition agent
    c. data source object
    d. supplier agent
13. The <table> element is known as a typical ________________.
    a. data consumer
    b. data supplier
    c. data source consumer
    d. repetition agent
14. Which of the following statements best describes a recordset?
    a. A recordset is the result of querying for all the XML elements that are defined inside the datasrc.
    b. A recordset is the result of querying for only those XML elements that were bound to an XHTML element using the datafld attribute.
    c. A recordset is the result of XHTML output to the browser or output file.
    d. A recordset is the entire XML file that was used as an external data island.
15. A recordset is an implicit object that can be used by an element or function that understands data binding. True or false?
16. What is the mechanism that is used by a JavaScript function such as MoveFirst( ) as a demarcation point to locate the top of the recordset?
    a. EOF
    b. BOF
    c. ONCLICK
    d. moveNext( )
17. Name the four XML DSO/JavaScript functions available to page through data elements.
18. In what situation(s) would a full path to the datafld be required?
    a. when an XML file is too long for data elements to display properly
    b. when an XML element is nested more than two layers deep, including the root element
    c. when the number of XML element's sibling elements exceeds three
    d. when an XML element is nested more than two layers deep, excluding the root element

19. Given the following XML file named inventory4music.xml, code a sample <table> element with the necessary attributes to allow access to the <copies>, <pages>, and <title> elements.

```
<musicroom>
     <roomNo>Norma Stucker</roomNo>
     <stage>$35,000</stage>
        <inventory>
             <horns>$660</horns>
             <drums>4.5</drums>
             <keyboards>3.2</keyboards>
                   <sheetmusic>
                        <copies>34</copies>
                        <pages>12</pages>
                        <title>Hard Day's Night</title>
                   </sheetmusic>
        </inventory>
</musicroom>
```

20. If a recordset bound to a table is too long, what attribute can be set to reduce the amount of rows displayed inside the table?
    a. recordset reduce
    b. dataPageSize
    c. nextPage ( )
    d. previousPage( )
21. Which of the following are not tabular consumers?
    a. <span>
    b. <table>
    c. <input type=button>
    d. <div>
22. The <span> and <div> elements are identical. True or false?
23. A simple way to display all of the fields inside an XML element is to use the ________________ identifier.
24. What would be a situation where you can use a <div> element instead of a <span> element inside your XHTML code?
    a. shorten table output
    b. formatting purposes
    c. display inline data inside of a paragraph
    d. isolate information between the <div> elements

12

25. What would be a situation where you would use a <span> element as opposed to a <div> element inside your XHTML code?
    a. shorten table output
    b. formatting purposes
    c. display inline data inside of a paragraph
    d. isolate information between the <div> elements

Hands-on Projects

Project 12-1

In Projects 12-1, 12-2, and 12-3, you create an inventory report that displays information from internal and external data islands. Recall that a data island is a data source that can exist either within the HTML document or in an external file. This project demonstrates how to include XML structured information within an HTML document by creating an internal data island.

To set up the project:

1. In Windows Explorer, create a new folder called **Ch12** in the C:\home\<yourname> folder. Then copy the files from the Ch12/Project_12-1 folder on your Data Disk into your C:/home/<yourname>/Ch12 folder. Your drive letter may vary.
2. To create an HTML document, start XML Spy. Click **Start**, point to **Programs** (point to **All Programs** in Windows XP), point to **XML Spy Suite**, and then click **XML Spy IDE**. The XML Spy window opens.
3. Click **File** on the menu bar, and then click **New**. The Create new document dialog box opens. Select **html HTML Document** and then click **OK**. A new HTML document appears in the main window.
4. Click **File** on the menu bar, and then click **Save As**. The Save As dialog opens. Click the **Save in** list arrow, and then navigate to the C:/home/<yourname>/Ch12 folder. Type **inventory.html** in the File name text box, and then click **Save**.
5. Replace the title element in the HTML document head with the following:
   ```
   <title>Inventory Summary</title>
   ```
6. Replace the p element in the HTML document body with the following:
   ```
   <h1>Inventory</h1>
   ```

You can place the XML data anywhere in the file as long as it is contained within an XML element. Because the XML element is an HTML extension, meaning that it is not part of the HTML 4.0 standard, browsers that do not support data binding ignore the contents. Browsers such as Internet Explorer 5 or later that support this style of data binding parse the document and locate the references to the XML data islands.

To add the internal data island:

1. Type the following XML data on the line after the end tag of the html element, </html>:

```
<xml id="inventory">
      <store>
            <location>Whistler, BC</location>
            <inventory>
                  <part>
                        <name>Seat</name>
                        <partnum>1234</partnum>
                        <stock>12</stock>
                        <price>$59.99</price>
                  </part>
                  <part>
                        <name>Handle Bars</name>
                        <partnum>2345</partnum>
                        <stock>5</stock>
                        <price>$34.99</price>
                  </part>
            </inventory>
      </store>
</XML>
```

Your HTML document should resemble Figure 12-22.

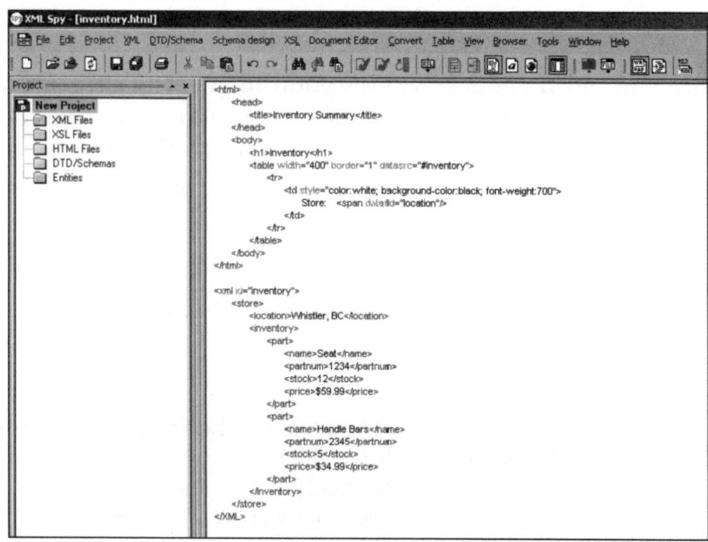

Figure 12-22

2. Click **File** on the menu bar, and then click **Save** to save your work. Leave inventory.html open in XML Spy for the next project.

Project 12-2

In this project, you add a tabular data consumer element to the document to represent the data in the HTML document. Tables are powerful data binding elements that allow you to display a variable number of records without knowing the exact number of records in the recordset. You add a series of tables that display the inventory information contained in the internal data island.

To add a data consumer element:

1. With inventory.html still open in XML Spy from Project 12-1, insert the following code on a new line immediately below the h1 element in the HTML document body:

```
<table width="400" border="1" datasrc="#inventory">
       <tr>
             <td style="color:white;
               background-color:black;
                     font-weight:700">
                     Store: <span datafld="location"/>
             </td>
       </tr>
</table>
```

Notice that the start tag for the table element, <table>, has a datasrc attribute with the same value as the XML element's id value prefixed with a number sign, #. The datasrc attribute references the data island specified at the end of the document.

2. Click **View** on the menu bar, and then click **Browser view** to view the rendered document. Notice that the location element value from the data island appears in the browser window.
3. To add nested data consumers, click **View** on the menu bar, and then click **Text view** to return to the source code.

Nested elements within an XML data source are bound using nested HTML table elements. The table that you added in the previous section allows child elements of the store element to be bound to HTML data consumer elements. To access the values of the name, partnum, stock, and price elements, you must add two additional nested tables.

4. Directly below the table row end tag, </tr>, within the table element, type the following:

```
<tr>
   <td>
     <table  width="100%" datasrc="#inventory"
        datafld="inventory">
       <tr>
         <td>
           <table border="1" style="border-collapse:
             collapse; width: 95%"
             datasrc="#inventory"
               datafld="inventory.part">
           </table>
         </td>
       </tr>
     </table>
   </td>
</tr>
```

Tabular elements, such as the table element, allow you to insert multiple sets of data using the repetition agent. The XML data island that you created in Project 12-1 contains two part elements. Although the table structure that you complete in this project looks like it can only handle a single part element, the repetition agent automatically repeats the code for every instance of the element within the data island.

5. Within the innermost table element, type the following:

```
<thead>
   <tr>
          <th>Name</th>
          <th>Part Number</th>
          <th>In Stock</th>
          <th>Price</th>
   </tr>
</thead>
<tbody>
   <tr>
          <td><div datafld="name" /></td>
          <td><div datafld="partnum" /></td>
          <td><div datafld="stock" /></td>
          <td><div datafld="price" /></td>
   </tr>
</tbody>
```

Notice that some of the table data (td) elements are div elements with dataFld attributes. The values of the attributes reference the elements within the XML data island. For every part element in the internal data island, the values for the name, partnum, stock, and price elements will be rendered within the HTML document. The HTML code should resemble Figure 12-23.

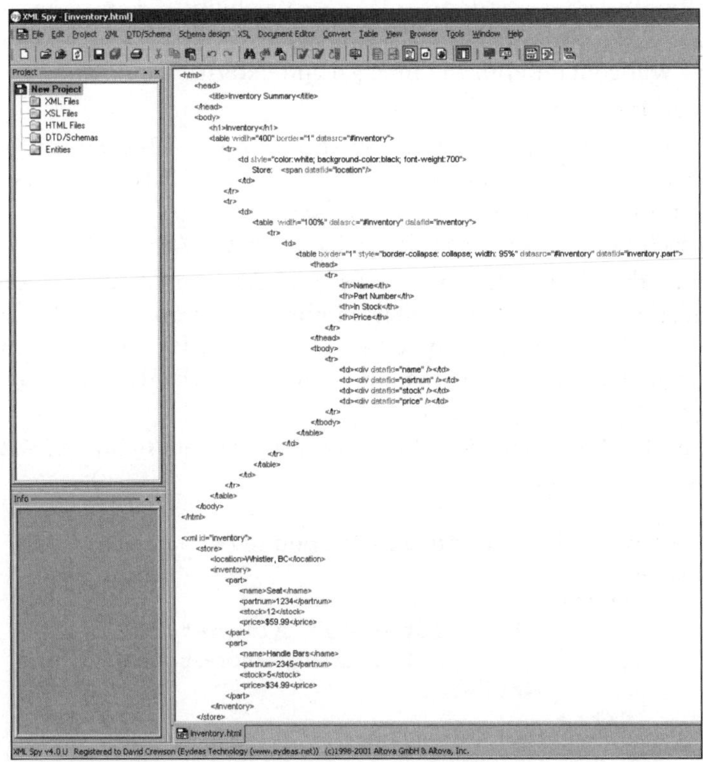

Figure 12-23

12

6. Click **File** on the menu bar, and then click **Save** to save your work.
7. To view the document, click **View** on the menu bar, and then click **Browser view** to examine the document in the XML Spy browser. The document should appear similar to Figure 12-24. Notice that all of the data from the two part elements exist within the table.

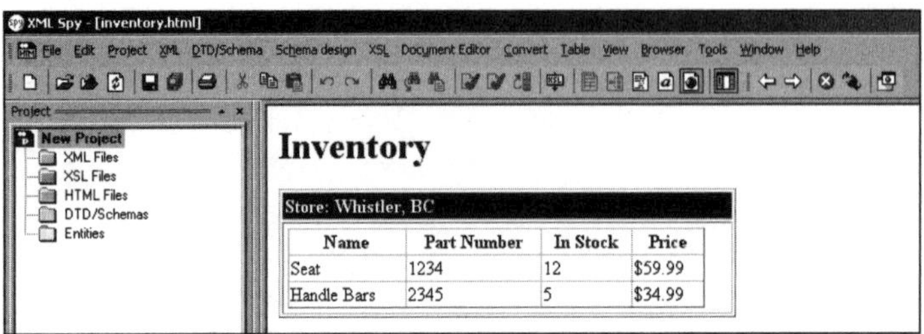

Figure 12-24 Rendered HTML document with tabular data consumer elements

Leave inventory.html open in XML Spy for the next project.

Project 12-3

Internal data islands, like the one used in Project 12-2, are fine for small projects, but moving XML data to an external file (i.e., to an external data island) is better for larger amounts of data. External data islands provide more flexibility and are easier to manage. In this project, you add a data island that references an external XML document. The HTML document will contain both the internal and external data islands.

To add the external data island:

1. With inventory.html still open in XML Spy from Project 12-2, switch to Text view, click between the html end tag, </html>, and the XML inventory data source tag, <xml id="inventory">, and then type:

```
<xml id="specials" src="specials.xml" />
```

In the same way that the HTML document references data source information from the internal data island, the document can reference information from the external XML file identified by the src element. In fact, where the data is located is completely transparent to the document, which allows you to change the source of the data without modification to the HTML code.

2. To add the data-binding, click after the outer table element's end tag, </table>, and then type the following:

```
<br/>
<table width="200" datasrc="#specials">
   <thead>
          <tr>
                <th colspan="2" align="left">
                        Upcoming Promotions
                </th>
          </tr>
   </thead>
```

```
        <tbody>
            <tr>
                <td><div datafld="item"/></td>
                <td><div datafld="price"/></td>
            </tr>
        </tbody>
    </table>
```

Even though the data source is external, the information is bound in the same manner as you saw with the internal data island. Your HTML document should resemble Figure 12-25.

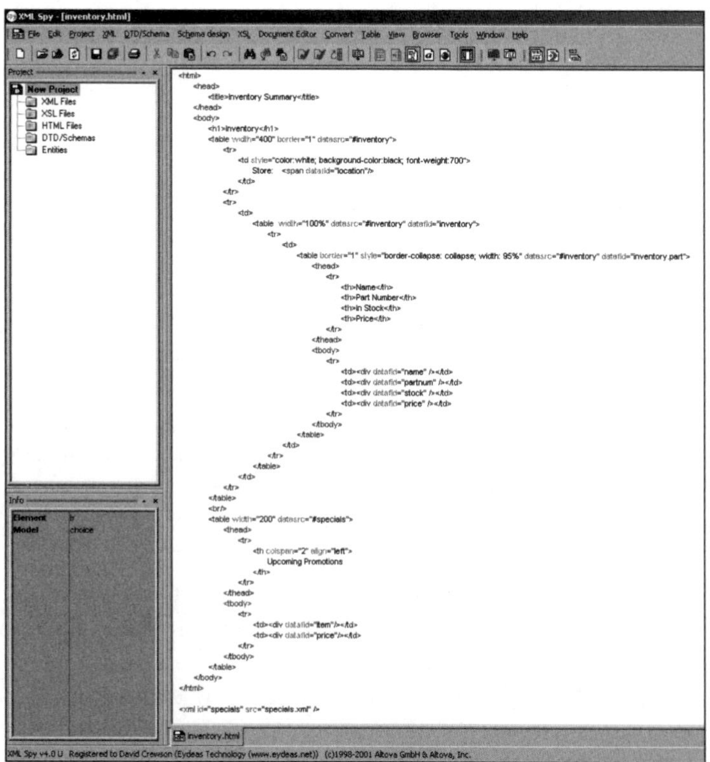

Figure 12-25

3. Click **View** on the menu bar, and then click **Browser view** to display the updated document. The document should resemble Figure 12-26. Examine the new data provided from the external data source. You can open the specials.xml document in the Ch12/Project_12-3 file on your Data Disk to compare the raw xml data with the data bound into the HTML document.

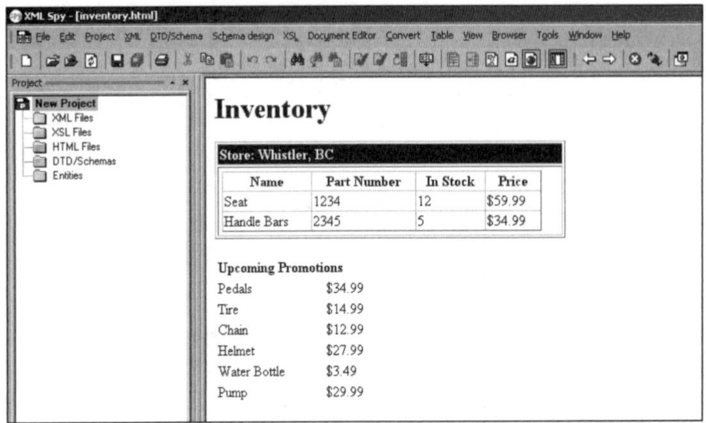

Figure 12-26

4. Click **File** on the menu bar, and then click **Save** to save your work.
5. Click **File** on the menu bar, and then click **Close** to close the document. Leave XML Spy open for the next project.

Project 12-4

In the next two projects, you create an electronic catalog system that displays information about a number of products. The information comes from an external data island, but you will reference the data using single-valued data consumer elements. You can use JavaScript code to have the single-valued data consumer display the data of a single element, or record, at a time. The user can scroll through the information by clicking the navigation buttons. In this project, you create the navigation components using HTML and JavaScript.

To create an HTML document and add navigation buttons:

1. Click **File** on the menu bar, and then click **New**. In the Create new document dialog box, select **html HTML Document**, and then click **OK**. A new HTML document appears in the main window.
2. Click **File** on the menu bar, and then click **Save As**. In the Save As dialog box, click the **Save in** list arrow, if necessary, to navigate to the C:/home/<yourname>/Ch12 folder. (Your drive letter may vary.) Type **catalog.html** in the File name text box, and then click **Save**.
3. Replace the title element in the HTML document head with the following:

```
<title>Catalog</title>
```

4. The user navigates through the catalog using a set of Next and Previous buttons. To add the buttons, replace the p element in the HTML document body with the following:

```
<input type="button" style="width:75;" onclick=
"movePrevious();"
   value="<" alt="Previous Item">
<input type="button" style="width:75;"
    onclick="moveNext();"
   value=">" alt="Next Item">
```

Delete the closing </input> tag as necessary. The HTML input element adds a button that displays the text from the value of the alt attribute. Whenever the user clicks a button, the event handler declared in the onClick attribute is called.

An event handler is a function that is called in response to a user's action. In the next step, you add code so that when a Next or Previous button is clicked, the button calls the function defined in the onClick attribute.

5. To add the event handlers, on the line after the title element in the document header, type the following:

```
<script language="Javascript">
            function moveNext()
            {
                  catalog.recordset.MoveNext();
                  if (catalog.recordset.eof)
                           catalog.recordset.MoveFirst();
            }
            function movePrevious()
            {
                   catalog.recordset.MovePrevious();
                   if (catalog.recordset.bof)
                       catalog.recordset.MoveLast();
            }
   </script>
```

The script element contains two JavaScript functions. Without getting into too much detail, the functions simply operate upon a collection object containing the entire set of item elements from the catalog.xml data source. The moveNext function moves forward in the collection until the end is reached, and then cycles to the first element. The movePrevious function is similar, but moves in the opposite direction. Your HTML document should resemble Figure 12-27.

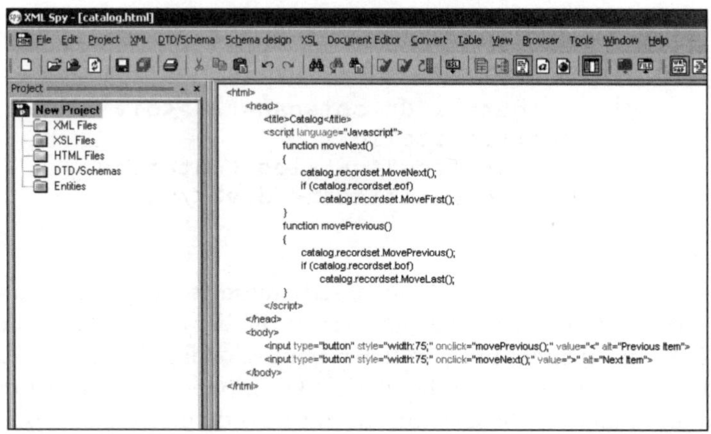

Figure 12-27

6. Click **File** on the menu bar, and then click **Save** to save your work. Leave catalog.html open in XML Spy for the next project.

Project 12-5

Now that you have created the HTML navigation buttons and event handlers, you need to declare the data island and build the catalog presentation. Each item has a picture, manufacturer name, model, price, and brief description. The information is updated every time the user clicks one of the navigation buttons.

To add the external data island and the presentation:

1. With catalog.html open in XML Spy from Project 12-4, click after the html end tag, </html>, and then type:

   ```
   <xml id="catalog" src="catalog.xml" />
   ```

2. An image of the catalog item is presented in the upper-left corner of the table. The manufacturer, model, and price are all positioned in a single cell to the right of the picture, and the description of the item spans the entire lower portion of the table. Directly below the body start tag, type the following:

   ```
   <table width="600" border="1">
      <tr>
             <td>
                   <img width="400" height="250"
                         datasrc="#catalog"
                         datafld="image"/>
             </td>
             <td width="200" align="center">
                    <div datasrc="#catalog" datafld=
                    "manufacturer"></div>
                    <br/>
                    <div datasrc="#catalog" datafld="model">
                    </div>
                    <br/>
                    <div datasrc="#catalog" datafld="price">
                    </div>
             </td>
      </tr>
      <tr>
             <td height="100" colspan="2"><div style=
             "font-style:italic;"
                    datasrc="#catalog" datafld=
                    "description"></div></td>
      </tr>
   </table>
   ```

Delete the src and alt attributes that XML Spy inserts automatically. Notice that the table element does not have a datasrc attribute, but each of the div elements refers to the catalog data source. Each div element binds to the current value for the data source element specified in the datafld attribute. When the user clicks on one of the navigation buttons, and the event handler function changes the current record, then the data bound to the elements is updated. Your HTML document should resemble Figure 12-28.

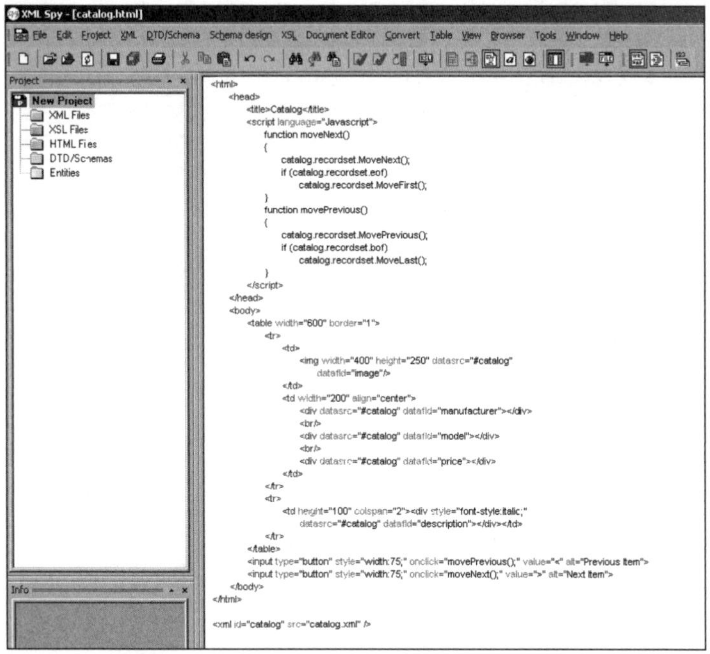

Figure 12-28

3. Click **View** on the menu bar, and then click **Browser view** to view the rendered document. The rendered document should resemble Figure 12-29. Notice the buttons below the table. Click each button a number of times. Notice how the content of the document automatically updates with the content from the new record.

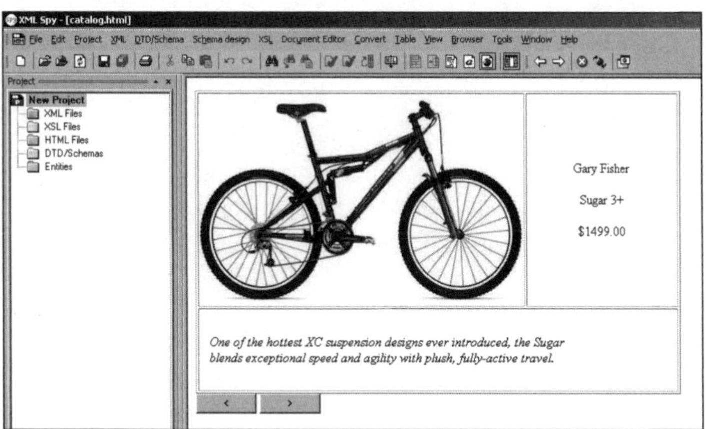

Figure 12-29

4. Click **File** on the menu bar, and then click **Save** to save your work.
5. Click **File** on the menu bar, and then click **Exit** to close XML Spy.

CASE PROJECT

Refer to the Hands-on Projects in this chapter to create an HTML file that will serve as another internal data island that contains sales information for the products listed in inventory.html. Sales information can include product name, part number, stock number, price, and the name of the sales associate. Display the sales data in a series of tables. Then create an external data island that includes product information for a summer special sale.

CHAPTER

13

INTRODUCTION TO MATHML

In this chapter, you will learn:

- About mathematical expression issues
- About MathML
- About considerations for using MathML on Web pages
- How to use tools to create math expression
- About examples of math editors and presenters

Presenting mathematical and scientific expressions in print and on a computer screen, and then communicating them to others in a meaningful way, has presented challenges for many years, starting long before the advent of the Internet with the first math and scientific chronicles.

To share mathematic and scientific expressions, those who write them and those who read them must understand all of the information—the concepts, symbols, data, algorithms and results—that the expressions are intended to convey. In addition, the reader of those expressions often wants to digest, store, reuse, and retransmit that mathematic and scientific information.

The final goal of presenting mathematic information can range from producing printed material in a science textbook to creating calculations for an automated research design or simulation program. In any case, the number and symbol combinations lose their meaning or even mislead the reader if they are not coded or represented accurately.

This chapter explores the challenges faced by those who are striving to make mathematical and scientific notation—the display *and* the underlying meaning—more consistent across the Web. This chapter introduces you to MathML, the W3C's specifications for mathematical expression. It introduces you to some tools for developing math expressions that meet these modern challenges.

Understanding Mathematical Expression Issues

Historically, those who have wanted to communicate mathematical and scientific expressions have faced several challenges. The first problem involves symbol ambiguity. Identical (or nearly identical) symbols are occasionally reused for different functions, especially in different fields of mathematics and science. For example, Figure 13-1 illustrates two common ambiguities in mathematical expressions: confusion about the meaning of symbols and numbers, even if they appear in a familiar context.

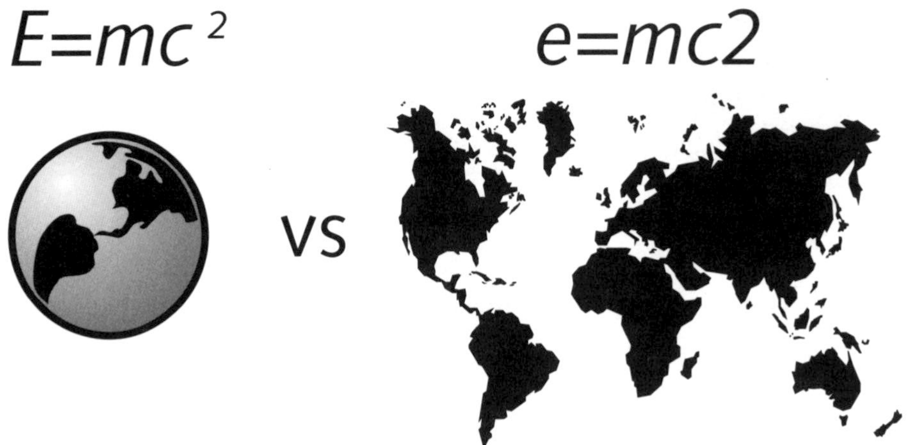

Figure 13-1 Ambiguities can be misleading

In Figure 13-1, the equation on the left ($E=mc^2$) is the venerable Einstein mass-energy equivalence equation, where E represents the internal energy of a substance; m, the mass of the substance; and c, the speed of light.

However, what if you encountered E outside of the context of this equation? What might it mean then? Most people in the English-speaking world consider "E" the uppercase format for the fifth letter of the English alphabet, used with other letters to spell English words. But, in science or mathematics communities, E might represent the internal energy of a substance. Or it might be a Euler number, or the strength of an electric field. So, if someone wants to communicate a concept by mathematical or scientific expression, and they want to include an E in that expression, they must use E as it is accepted by their community or clearly explain what the E means in their context. Otherwise, they risk causing confusion for their readers.

Letters are not the only symbols that can be ambiguous in mathematical contexts. The number 2 in the equation on the left in Figure 13-1 indicates that the speed of light must be squared (multiplied by itself) for the equation to provide a correct answer. However, in other mathematical applications, the number 2 in an expression might mean the addition of 2 units or multiplication by 2.

The Einstein equation on the left is not the same as the equation on the right (e=mc2). The e=mc2 equation does not represent any known scientific or mathematical concept but, oddly, many people—Web site developers among them—often portray this equation as equivalent to Einstein's $E=mc^2$. To verify that claim, use a Web search engine to search for "e=mc2" on the Web, and then examine the results. This variation of the equation appears fairly frequently on the Web, *and* on Web sites that are affiliated with Dr. Einstein and his discoveries.

In terms of appearance, interchanging E with e and omitting the superscript format of the 2 doesn't really do any harm. The two equations look similar enough that a Web document reader who is familiar with Einstein would acknowledge e=mc2 as a substitute for $E=mc^2$ in a document, but would not use e=mc2 literally in research or design. However, if e=mc2 is mistakenly taught instead of $E=mc^2$, or is used instead of $E=mc^2$ in the world of theoretical physics, nuclear power generation, or even space travel, then serious errors and great risk to life and property might occur. As Figure 13-1 illustrates, the world, or certain aspects or regions of the world, could go flat.

In addition to symbol or number ambiguities, the actual syntax for expressions may differ from country to country, even if they use common character sets. The expressions could suffer from dialectical problems: one country's subscripts may be another's superscripts, for example. Or some countries, according to their custom, may substitute different symbols in an expression. Still others may reverse the order of appearance of symbols or numbers within their version of an expression.

Even if you manage to work around ambiguity and dialectical problems, how do you overcome the difficulties of people who have visual disabilities?

These problems have challenged publishers of math and science information ever since the first scientific chronicles were published. The problems are compounded now that the Web has simplified the exchange of information. Over the past two or three generations, the IT world has highlighted two major challenges to the rendering of mathematical expression:

- Similar to previous technologies, the presentation of understandable math and science expressions should be consistent. **Presentation** involves coding, transmitting, and displaying mathematic and scientific information.
- Developers should create "active" documents that not only display mathematical or scientific expressions, but communicate the underlying meaning, or the **semantics**, of the symbols and numbers within the expressions. That is, active documents should facilitate further automatic processing, searching and indexing, and reuse in other mathematical applications and contexts

The development of the Internet and the World Wide Web has exacerbated these issues. The objectives—and, to a great extent so far, the achievement—of the Web has been to make billions of pages of information accessible to billions of people. The Web community clearly needs a way to render mathematical expressions accurately. As more research is conducted and coordinated via the Web, the Web community has also encouraged the development of math and science documents (and other objects) that are active to provide the ability for the automatic processing and manipulation described earlier.

From the earliest development of printed information to the present day, hard-copy publishers have developed tools and techniques to overcome all of the issues—except those highlighted by the World Wide Web, of course—surrounding the rendering of mathematical expression.

Information technology and computer networking industries have also overcome the obstacles of visually presenting mathematical expressions during the past 25 years or more, as indicated in Table 13-1. However, please note that these developments all deal with the visual presentation of math expressions, not with conveying the underlying content.

Table 13-1 Previous math expression publication developments

Development	Explanation
eqn	1975—Developed by B.W. Kernighan and L.L. Cherry of Bell Labs for use with the Unix typesetting system named troff. The features of eqn inspired the approach taken later by EzMath.
TeX	Late 1970s—Developed by D. Knuth (then Professor at Stanford University; now Professor Emeritus). TeX provides more control over typesetting details and relies heavily on macros. Became the most popular method for electronic typesetting of mathematics. Available as freeware or shareware, or from commercial vendors.
LaTeX	1985—developed by L. Lamport; now a common macro package for TeX. Maintained and developed by the LaTeX3 Project. Available for free by anonymous ftp through the LaTeX3 Web site at *www.latex-project.org/ftp.html*.
AMS-TeX	1990s—A set of fonts and macros for mathematical typesetting, above and beyond those available with TeX and LaTeX. Developed by the American Mathematical Society.
ISO12083:1994	1994—ISO 12083:1994 is a DTD for Mathematics; one of four DTDs that comprise ANSI/NISO/ISO 12083, the Electronic Manuscript Preparation and Markup standard.
Various applications	1980s and 1990s—math expressions were created with various word-processing or graphics applications and then converted into images in several formats, such as JPEG, GIF, TIFF, etc.

All the developments listed in Table 13-1, with the exception of the last one, were too complex for the ordinary Web page developer and end user. That's why many opted to use various commercial word-processor and graphics applications to create mathematical expressions as graphic images and then load those into Web pages. That way, the browser was less likely to misinterpret the code and would at least present *something*. This approach, however, has several drawbacks, among which are:

- The pages with the images are slow to load in the end user's browser.

- The equations cannot be manipulated once they have been transmitted and displayed.
- Once presented on the screen, the images may not be satisfactory to look at. Bitmapped images especially are not scalable, and so can become jagged with higher magnification (these principles were discussed previously in Chapter 9).
- You have to manage a number of GIF or other graphic files as well as the Web document files to which they are affiliated.
- The font size for expressions is fixed and may not match the end user's font preferences.
- There is no effective alternative for people who can't see the images.
- The expressions can't be moved to a mathematical manipulation package.

With all those drawbacks, it is clear that using graphic images to render mathematical expressions is not ideal; often, it is unacceptable. When ISO 12083:1994—the Electronic Manuscript Preparation and Markup standard—was developed, there was no consensus on how to describe the math formula content (i.e., semantics), so this DTD only describes declarations for presentation syntax. However, it represented the first major step toward integrating presentation and semantic markup.

The W3C and MathML

The proliferation of the Internet sparked a fundamental change in the storage and transmission of data, a change in which large-scale networking plays a major and central role. It followed that Web developers would try to make information accessible to as many people as possible.

Even in the early days of the Internet, many recognized that the Internet provided an opportunity and a capability to share mathematical information, especially to facilitate research, design, and publishing among distributed computer systems.

They wanted to communicate mathematics in one of the following ways:

- *Using traditional notation and presentation*—To display concepts and calculations for the purpose of transferring knowledge, taking advantage of evolving notational applications, such as word processors, graphics applications and electronic publishing environment
- *Using modern semantics and content*—To facilitate automatic mathematical processing

Web developers encouraged the development of "active" documents that actually communicate the semantics of the symbols and numbers within their expressions, and so can facilitate automated processing. But the successful and consistent exchange of such mathematical expressions proved to be a challenge, and still is today. Even though progress is being made, right now there is no direct way to easily include mathematical expressions in Web pages, for example. It seems that, among other issues, Web browsers do not provide adequate support for equation interpretation in terms of presentation or content.

In the early 1990s, the W3C recognized the issues surrounding the expression of mathematics and the need for better support for scientific communication. In fact, Dave Raggett included a proposal for HTML Math in the HTML 3.0 working draft in 1994. In mid-1996, after approximately two years of discussions, meetings and proposals, the HTML Math Editorial Review Board was formed after a meeting of the Digital Library Initiative brought many interested parties together. The Board grew and, in 1997, became the W3C Math Working Group. Over the years, the membership of the Working Group has included representatives from organizations such as the American Mathematical Society, the Boeing Company, Design Science, Inc., Geometry Technologies, Inc., IBM Corporation, the French National Institute For Research In Computer Science And Control (INRIA), MacKichan Software, Inc, MATH.EDU, Inc., Microsoft Corporation, the Numerical Algorithms Group Ltd. (NAG), Radical Flow Inc., Stilo Technology, Universita di Bologna (Italy), University of Western Ontario (Canada), Waterloo Maple Inc., and Wolfram Research, Inc.

When these organizations began their work, their plan was to extend HTML to support mathematical expression. As their work progressed, it became clear to them that they should extend XML instead.

Their work resulted in the W3C Recommendation titled Mathematical Markup Language (MathML) 1.0 Specification (MathML 1.0), endorsed by the W3C in April 1998. See Figure 13-2.

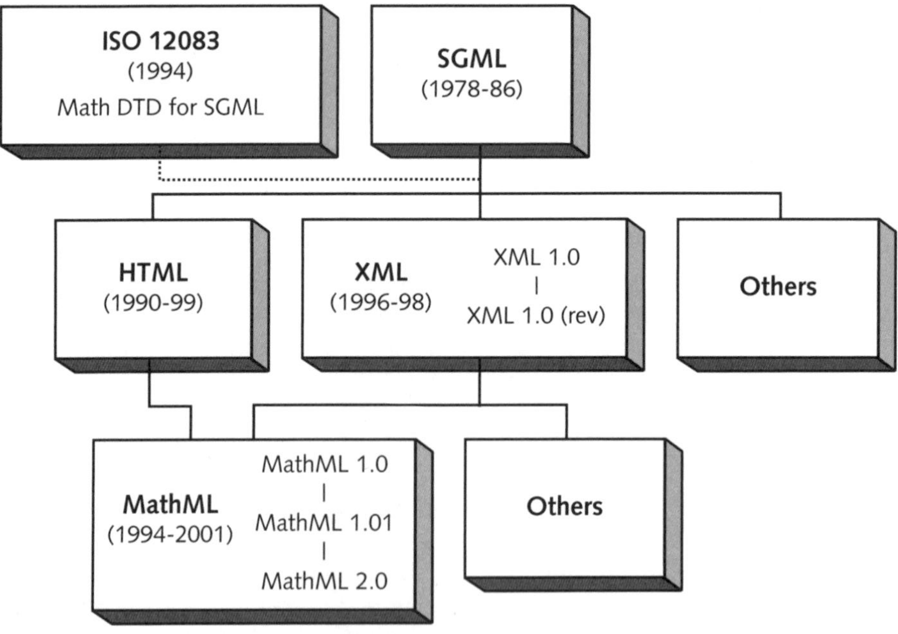

Figure 13-2 Evolution of MathML

Work continued and the W3C Recommendation titled Mathematical Markup Language (MathML) 1.01 Specification was endorsed as a revision of MathML 1.0 in July 1999. They didn't stop there, either. Mathematical Markup Language (MathML) Version 2.0 (MathML 2.0) was endorsed as a W3C Recommendation in February 2001.

MathML Design Goals

As mentioned earlier, the rapid growth of the World Wide Web seemed to call for an extension to languages existing at that time. To the W3C, math expressions represent one of several kinds of structured data which would have to be integrated into the Web using extensions.

Originally, a simple straightforward extension to HTML was envisioned; one that could be easily implemented in browser applications, among others. Although only the first two were official W3C Math Working Group goals, overall design goals included the following:

- The language had to be easy to implement and then easy to use, but still sophisticated enough to meet everyone's requirements.
- The language had to interact with other programs so that expressions did not lose their meaning and did not have to be reentered or reconstructed to work.
- The language still had to produce high-quality rendering in several media.
- Existing mathematical markup languages would have to be easily converted to MathML.
- Existing authoring tools should be easily modified to generate MathML.
- Users should be able to embed MathML markup seamlessly in HTML documents so that they can be accessed by future browsers, search engines, and Web applications.
- Users should be able to render any MathML code already embedded in HTML at the version level of today's Web browsers, even if the results are not perfect.
- Ideally, the language should provide specialized services for input and output, and general services for interchange of information and rendering to multiple media. That is, its user groups would be better served by tailored input and output (for example, existing electronic publishers would likely want a system that allowed for direct entry of their markup languages in Web documents, while students may need simpler methods to enter math expressions.)

MathML as Part of a Layered Software Architecture

The W3C saw that any mathematical expression language that could meet all of these requirements would be fairly complex. The "specific needs" requirement(s), especially, led them to believe that a layered architecture approach might be best. See Figure 13-3.

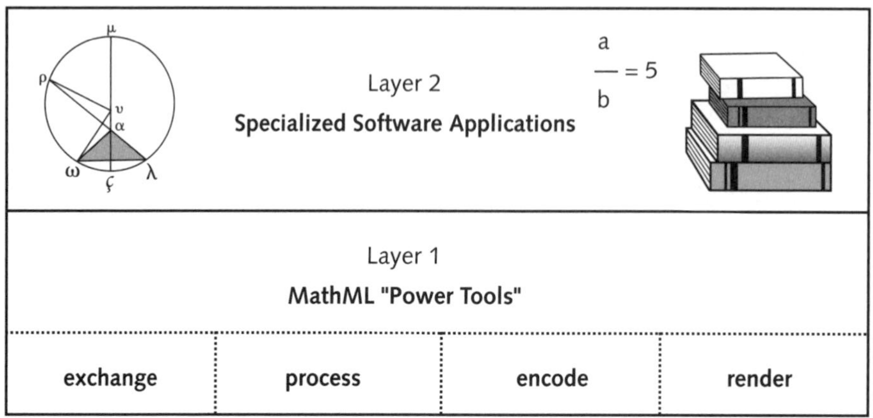

Figure 13-3 Two-layered architecture model

The first (bottom) layer is called Layer 1 and provides a set of common and powerful tools used to exchange, process, encode, and render math expressions. The second (top) layer is called Layer 2 and consists of specialized software tools that can be used to generate coded mathematical data and expressions to meet the needs of specific user groups, but that also can be shared with a more general audience. The following sections explain the layers in more detail.

Layer 1—MathML as a Set of Power Tools

MathML is part of Layer 1, the bottom layer of the layered architecture model, and features interoperability, ease of implementation, ease of processing and rendering, and ease of maintenance. Thus, MathML/Layer 1 is a platform-independent, general yet powerful specification that serves as a model for writing other software and data files, and that facilitates interoperability between and among the different specialized applications proposed in Layer 2. In other words, MathML as part of Layer 1 provides a set of common and powerful tools that Layer 2 applications use to exchange, process, encode, and render presentations.

Consequently, although MathML is legible to humans, it is not primarily intended for direct use by authors. In most cases (especially when you want to combine presentation and content elements), coding MathML is complex and better left to equation editors, conversion programs, and other specialized software tools.

The W3C compares MathML to another low-level, communication format: Adobe's PostScript language. Like PostScript files, MathML documents can be generated in several ways, such as by hand and with word processors or graphics programs. Once you have created or obtained the PostScript file, you can share it widely. Many devices are capable of rendering it almost everywhere.

Layer 2—Authoring and Rendering Software

Layer 2, the top layer of the layered architecture model, consists of all the mathematical-expression authoring and rendering applications developed in industry. This software is specialized and aimed at specific user groups; the authors within those groups have a choice of tools to accomplish their tasks.

Students or newcomers might prefer to use a menu-driven equation editor that can write MathML directly to an HTML document. Researchers might prefer software that can extract mathematical content from a Web page. An electronic publisher might want an application that converts TeX documents, for example. And scientists at the National Aeronautics and Space Administration's Jet Propulsion Laboratory probably have different needs than their counterparts at the **Институт Космических Исследований** (if you prefer the English translation, that's the Space Research Institute (IKI) in Russia).

The W3C expects that MathML might soon be integrated into other mathematical formula applications, such as spreadsheets, statistical packages, and engineering tools. They are currently working with several vendors to facilitate the development of new software. In the meantime, the W3C provides links to a list of several MathML-compliant applications at their *www.w3.org/Math* Web site.

Understanding MathML

13

MathML is a low-level application of XML that is intended to facilitate low-level interoperability between applications and systems. It was designed to stimulate the development of Layer 2 mathematical Web software, and to help coordinate the development of other authoring tools and rendering software.

MathML itself consists of a number of XML tags that can be used to mark up expressions in terms of their presentation and also their semantics. As you see later in this chapter, about 30 of the elements—the presentation elements—describe notational structures, while another 130 or so—the content elements—unambiguously specify the intended meaning of a math expression. Interface elements—most notably, the <math> element—facilitate the embedding of MathML into HTML documents.

MathML can be used to encode the presentation of math expressions for high-quality visual display and for their mathematical content for those applications where semantics play a major role, such as computer algebra and other algorithms, scientific software, and voice synthesis. MathML can also be used as an interface to other documents. MathML was also developed to use mathematical and scientific content on an organization's extranet and over the Internet and World Wide Web.

A properly structured, coded, and supported MathML expression can be searched, indexed, manipulated with a scientific or mathematical application, rendered in a Web browser, edited in your word processor, displayed on your screen or through a projector, and printed on printers or plotters. Thus, MathML fulfills its role in Layer 1 of the layered architecture model of math expression software.

MathML General Markup Specifications

Currently, there are two main presentation markup specifications: one for MathML 1.0 and one for MathML 2.0. The specifications appear to behave similarly to one another when you use them with small, uncomplicated equations. However, their differences become apparent when you deal with more complex applications.

Even with fairly simple expressions, you can see differences between MathML 1.0 and MathML 2.0 specifications. Notice, for example, in Figure 13-4 that all three of the MathML 2.0 variants have a top level <math> element, but that the MathML 1.0 variant does not. This is one of the major improvements of MathML 2.0 over MathML 1.0. MathML 2.0 specifies the single top-level <math> element, which provides a number of improvements: it encapsulates each instance of MathML markup within an HTML page, resolves some presentation issues, and can produce improvements in functionality and interoperability.

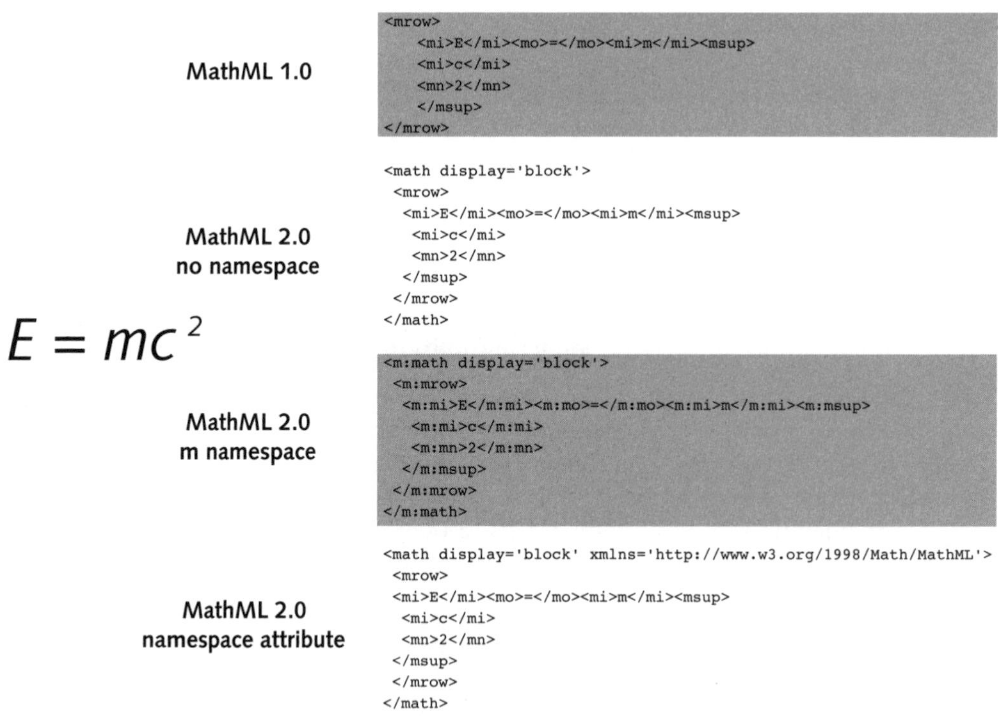

Figure 13-4 Differences in MathML presentation coding

The math element must always be the outermost element in a MathML expression. However, it is an error for one <math> element to contain another. No nesting of this sort is allowed.

Figure 13-4 also shows that the <math> element can contain attribute/value pairs, like display="block", that are specific to style. The **<math>** element also provides an attachment point for information, which affects a MathML expression as a whole. For example, the **<math>** element is the logical place to attach style sheet or macro information when these facilities become available for MathML.

If the MathML document is used by an application that conforms to the Namespaces in XML Recommendation, you place a MathML namespace declaration in the <math> element start tag because the <math> element is the interface element. The syntax resembles the following:

```
<math xmlns="http://www.w3.org/1998/Math/MathML">
  . . .
```

The attributes of the <math> element affect all the elements nested within the <math> element. They are therefore called **inward-looking attributes**.

Here are the inward-looking attributes:

- class="*value*"—provided for CSS support
- style="*value*"—also provided for CSS support
- id="*value*"—also provided for CSS support
- macros="*URL...*"—Provides a way of pointing to external macro definition files. Macros are not part of the MathML specification, but a macro mechanism is anticipated as a future extension to MathML.
- mode="display | inline"—(Deprecated in MathML 2.0) Specifies whether the enclosed MathML expression should be rendered in a display style or an inline style. The default is mode="inline".
- display="block | inline"—Replaces the deprecated mode attribute. Specifies whether the enclosed MathML expression should be rendered in a display style or an inline style. Allowed values are block and inline (default).
- xref="*URI*"—Along with id, provided for use with XSL processing

Because implementation levels vary among user agents, some attributes have also been developed to integrate with third-party rendering software, especially to render MathML-compliant expressions properly in a browser, and to integrate them into XHTML documents. The W3C calls these the **outward-looking attributes**.

Here are the outward-looking attributes:

- overflow="scroll | elide | truncate | scale"—If size negotiation is not possible or fails (e.g., a long equation), overflow can be used to suggest an alternative processing method to the rendering application. Scroll means that the window provides a viewport into the display of the expression. Horizontal or vertical scrollbars are used to look through the viewport. Elide means that the expression is abbreviated by removing enough of it so that the remainder

13

fits into the window (e.g., a large expression might have only the first and last terms displayed, with + ... + between them). Truncate means the expression is abbreviated by simply cutting remainders off at the right and bottom borders. And scale means that, if the expression is too large, the fonts used to display the mathematical expression are chosen so that the full expression fits in the window.

- altimg="*URL*"—Provides a fallback for browsers that do not support embedded elements.
- alttext= "*text string*"—Another kind of fallback for browsers that do not support embedded elements or images. Always provide an alttext attribute so that your users can point to an object and read a label if there has been a MathML malfunction.

When providing values for any MathML attributes, consult with the W3C's MathML Web site, because the values are required to be in a particular format.

The final piece of MathML syntax to understand is how the actual text and symbol characters needed for mathematical formulas are encoded. Consider the dissected Einstein equation in Figure 13-5 as an example.

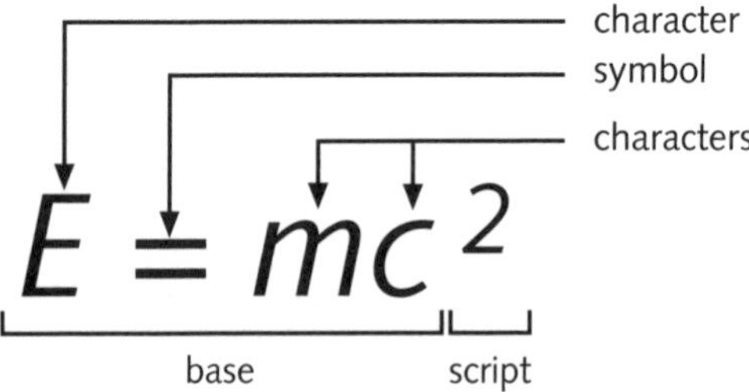

Figure 13-5 Dissected math expression

The expression consists of a base, which is E = mc, and a script, which is the single character 2. The base also contains a sequence of three characters—E, m, and c—and one symbol, the equal sign (=).

The characters and symbols can only appear inside a handful of special MathML elements called token elements, which are discussed in more detail in the next section.

MathML Presentation Markup Specifications

Presentation markup element tag names generally begin with the "m" character, which is followed by additional characters that indicate the content of the element. For example, <mo> indicates that the content is an operator; <mi> indicates its content is an identifier; <mn> indicates a number, and so on. Similarly, <mrow> elements indicate that the expression appears in horizontal groups.

The MathML presentation encoding for the Einstein equation is shown in Figure 13-6.

$$E = mc^2$$

```
<mrow>
    <mi>E</mi><mo>=</mo><mi>m</mi>
 <msup>
    <mi>c</mi>
    <mn>2</mn>
 </msup>
</mrow>
```

Figure 13-6 Example of presentation markup

The top-level structure in this figure starts with a general layout schemata element named <mrow> that instructs the parser to format the expression horizontally. The base E, m, c characters are each inside a <mi> token element; this element means these should be displayed as identifiers. The equal sign (=) is inside a <mo> token element, meaning the contents should be displayed as an operator. Finally, the character 2 is inside a <mn> token element, which specifies that the 2 is a number (or value). This number is a superscript to the token element c, because the MathML markup shows that the <msup> and </msup> tags surround the variable c and its power value 2.

As mentioned previously, MathML provides 31 presentation elements and more than 50 atrributes. Those elements, organized into five categories, are listed in Table 13-2. If you need to use more than a few presentation elements and attributes in an expression, do not attempt to code the expression manually. Instead, use an equation editor. (Several are discussed later in this chapter). There are several reasons for doing so. For example, token elements and general layout elements are governed by rules defined in the specific MathML DTDs (also discussed later). General layout MathML elements, like the outer <mrow> element, expect to *only* find token elements in their content. By contrast, the <mi> and <mo> elements are tokens, and their content consists only of characters and symbols. Finally and perhaps most importantly, the equation editors automatically create and nest the appropriate elements for the characters you want to include in the expression.

13

Table 13-2 MathML presentation elements

Element Name	Explanation
Token elements	
<mi>	Identifier
<mn>	Number
<mo>	Operator, fence, or separator
<mtext>	Text
<mspace/>	Space
<ms>	String literal
<mglyph>	Add new character glyphs to MathML

Table 13-2 MathML presentation elements (continued)

Element Name	Explanation
General layout elements	
<mrow>	Group any number of subexpressions horizontally
<mfrac>	Form a fraction from two subexpressions
<msqrt>	Form a square root sign (radical without an index)
<mroot>	Form a radical with specified index
<mstyle>	Change style
<merror>	Enclose a syntax error message from a preprocessor
<mpadded>	Adjust space around content
<mphantom>	Make content invisible but preserve its size
<mfenced>	Surround content with a pair of fences
<menclose>	Enclose content with a stretching symbol (e.g., a long division sign)
Script and limit elements	
<msub>	Attach a subscript to a base
<msup>	Attach a superscript to a base
<msubsup>	Attach a subscript-superscript pair to a base
<munder>	Attach an underscript to a base
<mover>	Attach an overscript to a base
<munderover>	Attach an underscript-overscript pair to a base
<mmultiscripts>	Attach prescripts and tensor indices to a base
Table elements	
<mtable>	Table or matrix
<mlabeledtr>	A row in a table or matrix with a label or equation number
<mtr>	Row in a table or matrix
<mtd>	One entry in a table or matrix
<maligngroup/>	Alignment group marker
<malignmark/>	Alignment point marker
Enlivening expression element	
<maction>	Bind actions to a subexpression

This list, although comprehensive at the time of publication, may be slightly out of date by the time you read it. Therefore, for the latest list of elements, plus detailed instructions and examples, please check *web3.w3.org/TR/MathML2/chapter3.html#presm_summary*.

MathML Content Markup Specifications

Content markup (also called semantic markup) is intended to define characters and expressions so that they can be used as input for computer applications that perform calculations. Where presentation markup prescribes how to display information, content markup prescribes how to manipulate the information mathematically. For this reason, the content markup specification uses a different set of over 131 elements and their attributes to identify the same expression. For example, Figure 13-7 shows the equivalent content markup for E = mc^2.

$$E = mc^2$$

```
<apply>
 <eq/>
 <ci>E</ci>
 <apply>
  <times/>
  <ci>m</ci>
  <apply>
   <power/>
   <ci>c</ci>
   <ci>2</ci>
  </apply>
 </apply>
</apply>
```

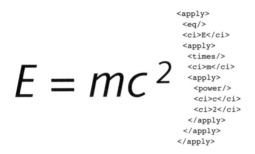

Figure 13-7 Example of content markup

The top-level structure in this figure starts with an application marker. This is encoded with the outermost <apply> and </apply> tags. This element explicitly applies a function to its argument(s), so <apply> is followed by the function or operator (in this case, the equal sign), and then by its argument (the variable named e). The next set of nested tags are the inner <apply> and </apply> tags that denote the m times function. These are followed by another set of nested <apply> and </apply> tags that denote the c squared function. The e, m, c, and 2 characters are placed inside <ci> elements, which indicates that they are content identifiers. The empty <power /> tag defines the squared relationship between the c and the 2. The set of <apply> and </apply> tags in which the <times /> element, the <ci>m</ci> element, and the c squared elements are nested indicates that the relationship between the m variable and the c squared variable is multiplication. Outside of both of these tags is a content identifier element the contents of which consist of the e character. Just before that <ci>E</ci> element is the declared empty <eq /> element. The combination of the <ci> and <eq> elements is equal to the E variable.

13

Note that the code in Figure 13-7 uses a deliberate element nesting scheme instead of parentheses. This scheme for ordering MathML content markup is called **prefix notation (PN)**, because it places the operators (the equal sign, the multiplication sign, the power notation) *before* the respective operands (the E, m, and c) within their elements. If they were in the opposite order (for example, <ci>E</ci><eq />, instead of <eq /> <ci>E</ci>), that would be **postfix notation**. Most people use an **infix notation** scheme, in which the operands and operators are mixed. In fact, the normal E=mc^2 is an example of infix notation.

Prefix notation is also known as **Polish Notation** and is named in honor of Jan Lukasiewicz, who was a prominent academic, mathematician, and even politician in Poland—and elsewhere in Europe—in the early to mid-twentieth century. In the 1920s, Professor Lukasiewicz introduced the prefix notation scheme, which allows mathematical expressions to be written unambiguously without the use of brackets. Later,

Hewlett-Packard adapted the postfix variation of this notation for their calculator keyboards; if you use an HP calculator, for example, you enter "2, Enter, 2, plus sign" to calculate the answer to 2+2. HP dubbed their system Reverse Polish Notation (RPN), also in honor of Professor Lukasiewicz.

The keys to reading MathML content markup are understanding that the elements are nested and using a basic PN strategy. Figure 13-8 shows how the content markup for $E=mc^2$ might be processed by an application. Parentheses, and shorthand forms for <eq />, <times />, and <power />, are used for simplicity and clarity.

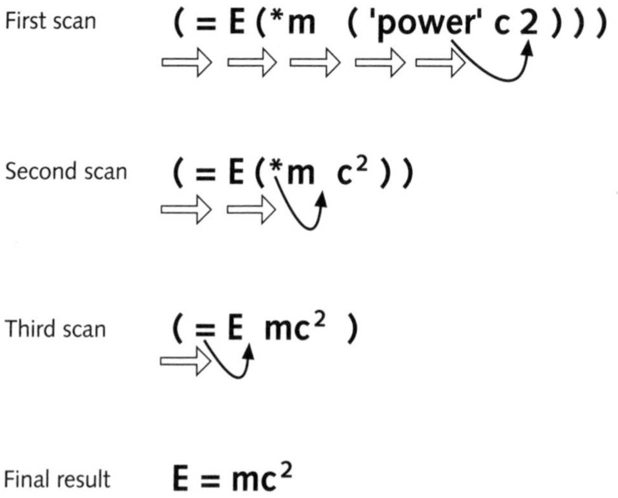

First scan (= E (*m ('power' c 2)))

Second scan (= E (*m c^2))

Third scan (= E mc^2)

Final result $E = mc^2$

Figure 13-8 Example of prefix notation processing

You can also consider the PN processing algorithm as a series of scans from left to right. The first scan travels until it has passed the last operator: the power function. It then applies that function to the subsequent operands to get c^2. On the next scan, the last operator is the multiplication sign, which is applied to the m variable and the c^2. On the third scan, the equality relation element is applied to the E and the mc^2 combination to obtain the final result.

This general notation structure for content markup is comprised of about 75 elements and a dozen attributes. Again, use an equation editor to code equations instead of inserting these elements manually. To preserve the meaning of the math, check your coding by constructing an abstract tree. (The technique for doing so, plus an example using $E=mc^2$, is shown later in this chapter.) The MathML content markup elements available with MathML 2.0 are listed in Table 13-3.

Table 13-3 MathML content elements

Element Name	Explanation
Token elements	
<cn>	Content number
<ci>	Content identifier
<csymbol>	Element with semantics that are not defined in core MathML content (i.e., element is defined externally) (deprecated in MathML 2.0)
Basic content elements	
<apply>	Explicitly applies a function to its argument(s); the first thing after <apply> should be the function or operator, followed by the arguments
<interval>	Interval constructor
<inverse/>	Generic inverse
<sep/>	Separator in numeric values
<condition>	Domain constructor
<declare>	Declaration
<lambda>	Function construction from an expression
<compose>	Function composition operator
<ident>	Identity operator
<domain>	Domain of a function
<codomain>	Codomain of a function (also called the range of a function)
<image>	Image of a given function (i.e., the set of values taken by the function); every point in the image results from application of the function to a point in the domain
<domainofapplication>	Specifies a domain over which a function is to be applied (often used with integrals to specify a domain of integration); alternative to limits.
<piecewise>	Supports piecewise function declarations
<piece>	Indicates a piece of a piecewise function
<otherwise>	Default specification for a piecewise function
<fn>	User-defined function (deprecated in MathML 2.0)
<reln>	Indicates the operator is an equation or a relation; analogous to <apply> (deprecated in MathML 2.0)
Arithmetic, algebra and logic elements	
<idiv/>	Division modulo base; replaced by <quotient> (deprecated in MathML 2.0)
<quotient>	Quotient of an integer division
<exp/>	Exponentiation
<factorial/>	Factorial
<divide/>	Division
<max/>	Maximum
<min/>	Minimum
<minus/>	Subtraction
<plus/>	Addition
<power/>	To the power of
<rem/>	Remainder modulo base

Table 13-3 MathML content elements (continued)

Element Name	Explanation
<times/>	Multiplication
<root/>	Nth root
<gcd/>	Greatest common denominator
<and/>	Boolean and
<or/>	Boolean or
<xor/>	Boolean exclusive or
<not/>	Boolean not
<forall/>	Universal logic quantifier; used with specific restrictions
<exists/>	Existential logic quantifier; used with specific restrictions
<abs/>	Absolute value of a real quantity or the modulus of a complex quantity
<conjugate/>	Complex conjugate of a complex quantity
<arg/>	Arithmetic operator that provides the argument of a complex number (i.e., the angle it makes with a positive real axis)
<real/>	Arithmetic operator that provides the real part of a complex number (i.e., the x in x + iy)
<imaginary/>	Arithmetic operator that provides the imaginary part of a complex number (i.e., the y in x + iy)
<lcm/>	Operator used to indicate the lowest common multiple of its arguments
<floor/>	Operator used to indicate a round-down operator
<ceiling/>	Operator used to indicate a round-up operator
Relation elements	
<eq/>	Equality relation (i.e., equal to)
<neq/>	Not equal
<gt/>	Greater than
<lt/>	Less than
<geq/>	Greater than or equal
<leq/>	Less than or equal
<implies/>	Boolean implies
<equivalent/>	An equivalence relational operator
<approx/>	Binary relational operator meaning "approximately equal"; it is a generic relational operator that does not imply arithmetic precision
<factorof>	Binary relational operator that works with two integers and indicates if one is an integer factor of the other
Elements related to calculus	
<ln/>	Natural logarithm
<log/>	Logarithm to base
<int/>	Integral
<diff/>	Derivative, differentiation
<partialdiff/>	Partial derivative
<lowlimit>	Lower limit (of integral, sum, etc.)
<uplimit>	Upper limit (of integral, sum, etc.)
<bvar>	Bound variable (e.g., for integral)
<degree>	Holds the n in "nth derivative"

Table 13-3 MathML content elements (continued)

Element Name	Explanation
<divergence/>	Vector calculus divergence operator also known as div
<grad/>	Vector calculus gradient operator also known as grad
<curl/>	Vector calculus curl operator
<laplacian/>	Vector calculus laplacian operator
<exp/>	Arithmetic operator; the exponential function associated with the inverse of the natural logarithm of a number (e.g., exp(1) is 2.718281828...)
Elements related to set theory	
<set>	Container element used to construct a set of elements
<list>	Container element used to construct a list of elements
<union/>	Union or meet
<intersect/>	Intersection or join
<in/>	Is in, is a member
<notin/>	Is not in, is not a member
<subset/>	Is a subset
<prsubset/>	Is a proper subset
<notsubset/>	Is not a subset
<notprsubset/>	Is not a proper subset
<setdiff/>	Set difference
<card/>	Unary set operator that specifies the size or cardinality of a set
<cartesianproduct>	Set operator for the Cartesian product of two or more sets
Elements related to sequences and series	
<sum/>	Sum terms of a sequence
<product/>	Multiply terms in a sequence
<limit/>	Limiting value of a sequence
<tendsto/>	Relation on sequences

Elements related to standard trigonometry			
<sin/>	<sinh/>	<arcsin/>	<arcsinh/>
<cos/>	<cosh/>	<arccos/>	<arccosh/>
<tan/>	<tanh/>	<arctan/>	<arctanh/>
<sec/>	<sech/>	<arcsec/>	<arcsech/>
<cosec/>	<csch/>	<arccsc/>	<arccsch/>
<cotan/>	<coth/>	<arccot/>	<arccoth/>

Elements related to statistics	
<mean/>	Mean or average
<sdev/>	Standard deviation from the mean
<variance/>	Variance from the mean
<median/>	Median of data
<mode/>	Mode of data
<moment/>	Statistical moment
<momentabout/>	Qualifier element used with <moment> to represent statistical moments

Table 13-3 MathML content elements (continued)

Element Name	Explanation
Elements related to linear algebra	
<vector>	Vector
<matrix>	Matrix
<matrixrow>	Matrix row
<determinant/>	Determinant
<transpose/>	Transpose
<selector/>	Sequence of elements
<vectorproduct/>	Binary vector operator for creating a vector product from two vectors
<scalarproduct/>	Binary vector operator for creating a scalar product from two vectors
<outerproduct/>	Binary vector operator for creating an outer product from two vectors
Semantic mapping elements	
<semantics>	Container element that associates MathML constructs with other annotations
<annotation>	Container element for non-XML annotation (e.g., TeX annotation)
<annotation-xml>	Contains XML-based representations; always used with <semantics>

These elements are undergoing constant change: additions, deletions, and function modification. This list, although comprehensive at the time of publication, may be slightly out of date by the time you read it. Therefore, for the latest list of elements, plus detailed instructions and examples, please check *www.w3.org/TR/REC-MathML/chap4_4.html#sec4.4* for MathML 1.0 elements, and *http://web3.w3.org/TR/MathML2/chapter4.html#contm_elem* for MathML 2.0 elements.

Considerations for Using MathML on Web Pages

When you work with an application that uses MathML to help you create and display mathematical expressions, you must consider how to use namespaces and DTDs and how to validate the MathML code. The following sections explain how to declare a namespace in an XML document, which DTDs are available, and tools you can use to validate the code.

MathML and Namespaces

If an application that conforms to the Namespaces in XML Recommendation uses MathML, the following namespace should be used:

```
http://www.w3.org/1998/Math/MathML
```

Typical syntax resembles the following; note the use of the <math> element for the MathML namespace declaration.

```
<math xmlns="http://www.w3.org/1998/Math/MathML">
. . .
```

As with other XML-related languages that observe it, the XML Namespaces Recommendation does not require the existence of any real accessible resource at the URI used for a namespace name. The declaration is used solely to create unique element names.

MathML DTDs and Validation

Two MathML.DTDs are available: MathML1.01.DTD and MathML2.DTD. You can download both from the *www.w3c.org/Math* Web site. The MathML elements are listed earlier in Tables 13-2 and 13-3; their attributes and other entities are declared inside the DTD files. The elements all have specific rules for usage and structure, from the token elements to the general layout schemata of the math in the document files.

A MathML validation service is also available at *www.w3.org/Math/validator/*. This validation service is currently considered experimental support, but if the editor you are using does not validate the code on its own, the MathML validation service offers a way to validate your code prior to publication. If you use this service, the MathML Web site informs you that you can also validate MathML files at the W3C Validator Web site at *http://validator.w3.org/*.

Using Tools to Create Math Expressions

Before examining math editors, you should become familiar with techniques or concepts that can aid you in the creation of math expressions, regardless of the kind of markup structure or editor you use. Math editors often use abstract trees and layout boxes for creating math expressions. The following sections describe these tools.

Abstract Expression Trees

The first tool is **abstract expression trees**. Constructing these diagrams, which are similar to directory/folder diagrams, helps you see if a math editor is handling your equation correctly. Figure 13-9 shows an abstract expression tree.

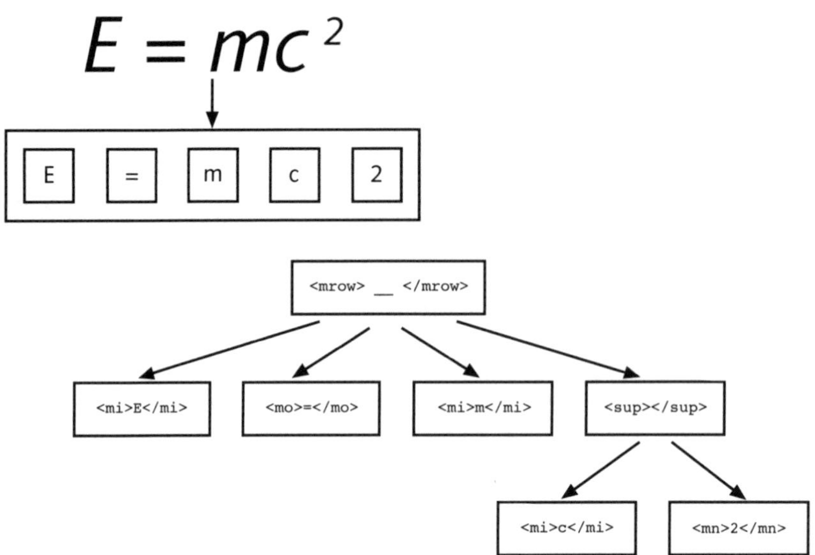

Figure 13-9 Example of an abstract expression tree

This abstract expression tree uses presentation markup elements instead of content markup elements, but it can use either. To organize presentation, the math expression is segmented according to the <mrow> presentation markup element(s). To organize content, the <apply> elements provide the logical places to divide the math expression.

Layout Boxes

The second concept that is handy to understand before you create MathML presentation markup is the **layout box**, a device several math editors provide to help you compose math expressions. See Figure 13-10. You can think of a layout box as an abstract bounding box for a particular kind of mathematical notation. The layout boxes represent and provide specific combinations of MathML elements and attributes. Layout boxes are categorized according to their contents. Simple layout boxes contain individual characters, and their dimensions depend only on the character font. More complicated layout boxes arrange child boxes (like collections of child elements) according to predefined configurations you can select on the math editor's symbol grid. Design Science, Inc.'s popular math editor, MathType, provides at least three rows of layouts that appear as symbols in its symbol grid. In Figure 13-10, the working area of the MathType window shows a fraction box beneath a square root sign. MathType anticipates that the author of this equation will create a fraction because the fraction symbol button on the symbol grid is selected and has activated a widget (i.e., a programming subroutine) that helps to create the fraction. Choosing the fraction box widget automatically adds two child boxes that are stacked vertically with a line between them, and centered horizontally. When the button is selected and the layout boxes appear, the author clicks in the correct box and types a number. MathType creates the appropriate elements and attributes, and then inserts the character the author typed.

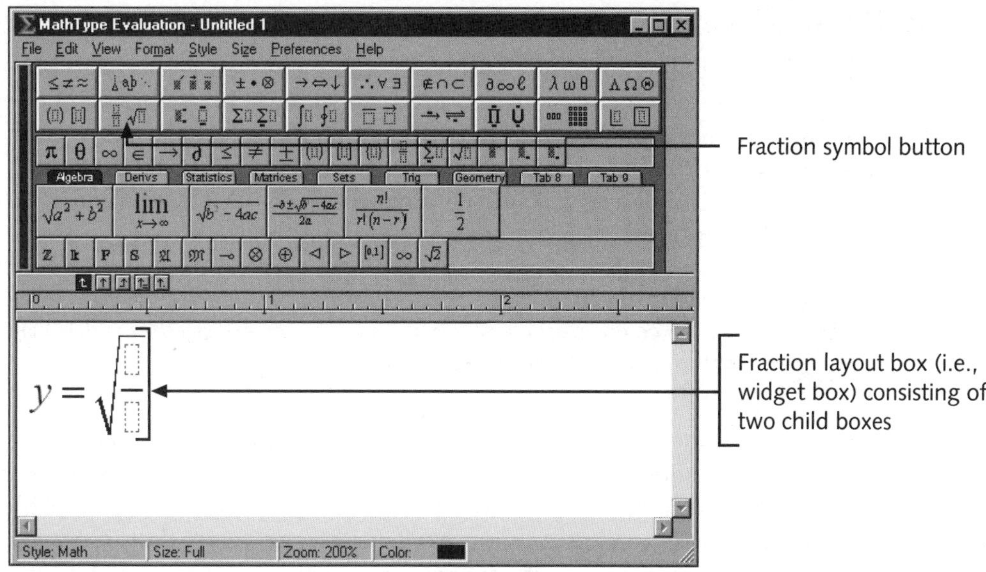

Figure 13-10 Equation editor with activated layout boxes

Layout boxes are often difficult for the beginner, especially because you must select them in the proper order to create the expressions you want. Be prepared to practice with layout boxes until they become more natural to you. Once they do, you may find them a handy, logical tool. Meanwhile, if you would like more information about the Design Science MathType editor, visit their Web site at *www.mathtype.com/*.

Exploring Examples of Math Editors and Presenters

The following sections explain how to use two applications—EzMath and MathType—to create and edit mathematical expressions, and another application, MathPlayer, to display expressions in Internet Explorer. EzMath is designed to create MathML code for HTML pages, and specializes in rendering math equations in HTML documents for display on a Web page. MathType is a more complex math editor than EzMath, and can be used as a stand-alone math editor or integrated with Microsoft Word.

When you use MathPlayer, Internet Explorer detects any <math> elements in an HTML document and then uses MathPlayer to display the expressions.

Exploring EzMath

This section demonstrates a multiple-step rendering process with a MathML-compliant math editor called EzMath. EzMath was developed by Dave Raggett and Davy Batsalle with support from Hewlett-Packard Laboratories. Raggett, formerly with Hewlett-Packard Labs, in Bristol, England, is now on assignment with the W3C for Openwave Systems Inc. At the time of EzMath development, Batsalle was affiliated with the Ecole Nationale Supérieure des Télécommunications, in Paris, France.

Although it is a proprietary application, EzMath is freeware and a Windows 95/NT version can be downloaded from *www.w3.org/People/Raggett/ezmath1_1.zip*. Support for other platforms is expected in the future.

EzMath is a good editor to explore first, because it helps to demonstrate and explain the syntax and methodology used to create MathML code for HTML pages. EzMath specializes in rendering math equations inside of HTML pages for display. EzMath generates explicit content markup, but not explicit presentation markup. However, it creates a special code that the proprietary dynamic link library called npezm32.dll, which comes with the EzMath editor code, can interpret and then translate as though presentation markup were used. In that way, the npezm32.dll acts as a "black box" presentation markup solution.

Quickly summarized, the two-stage process is as follows:

- Take a mathematical expression and create a proper rendering of it in EzMath's WYSIWYG Editor window.
- Display the rendered expression in a browser by generating the appropriate code and inserting it into an HTML file.

The following sections discuss the process in more detail. You have an opportunity to conduct this exercise in Hands-on Project 13-2 at the end of this chapter.

Rendering a Mathematical Expression

In this first stage, EzMath requests that you enter an expression into its Expression Editor window. Enter an expression similar to the spoken version of the expression. For example, type "E equals mc squared." This is straightforward for simple expressions, but can be more involved when translating complex expressions. After you enter the expression and click OK, EzMath displays its translation results in the Editor window, as shown in Figure 13-11.

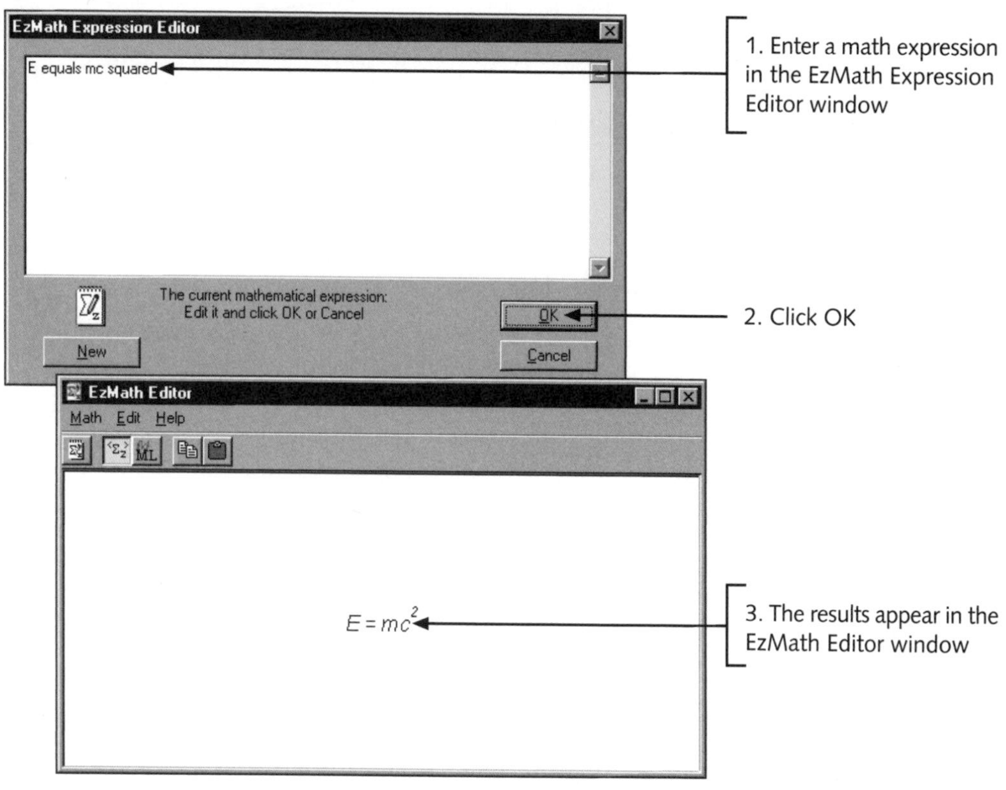
EzMath Expression Editor
E equals mc squared
The current mathematical expression:
Edit it and click OK or Cancel
New
OK
Cancel
EzMath Editor
Math Edit Help
E = mc2
1. Enter a math expression in the EzMath Expression Editor window
2. Click OK
3. The results appear in the EzMath Editor window

Figure 13-11 Rendering a math expression with the EzMath editor

If your results aren't acceptable at first, you can close the Editor window, return to the Expression Editor, and try again. In fact, you can continue to switch between the Expression Editor and Editor windows until you see the desired results in the Editor window. Converting from quasi spoken text to mathematical expression is helpful and impressive.

Note

You could also enter E = mc squared—that is, substitute the equal sign for the word equal—into the Expression Editor and obtain the same results.

Figure 13-12 lists other examples that EzMath can render. EzMath interprets the verbal expressions on the left to produce the math expressions on the right.

EzMath Expression Editor Display	EzMath Editor (WYSIWYG) Display
4x^3 minus 6x^2 plus 12x	$4x^3 - 6x^2 + 12x = 0$
square root (75 over a^6)	$\sqrt{\frac{75}{a^6}}$
(8x^6 over y^- 3)^(2/3)	$\left(\frac{8x^6}{y^{-3}}\right)^{\left(\frac{2}{3}\right)}$

Figure 13-12 Additional math expressions that EzMath can render

To become proficient using MathML coding, keep in mind that you should be familiar with the concept of layout boxes, and the order in which you use them. Once you develop an understanding of how layout boxes relate to elements and subelements, you can use them to code and translate quickly and reliably.

Displaying the Rendered Expression in a Browser Window

The second stage of creating the Einstein expression is translating the rendered mathematical expression into appropriate code so that a Web browser can display the expression without accessing a graphic image of the expression.

You can see the resulting expression from the previous phase in the EzMath Editor window in the upper-left corner of Figure 13-13. At that point in the process, you would use the EzMath menus to specify the data type (perhaps to a MathML or MathML format) for data you store on and retrieve from the Clipboard. When you paste the data, you insert the code for the successfully rendered math expression, as illustrated in the Clipboard window in the lower-right corner of Figure 13-13.

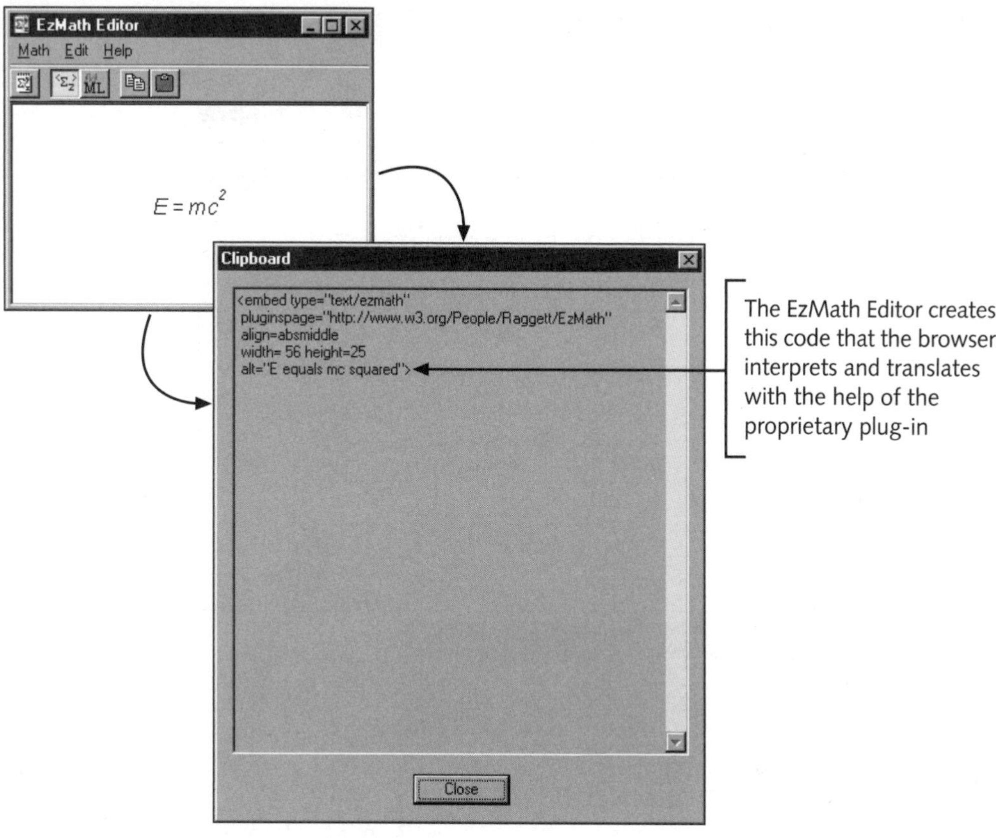

Figure 13-13 Displaying the rendered expression

This code must now be inserted into an HTML file and then refined—for example, all attribute values must be double quoted, not just a few, and the <embed> tag must be altered to reflect its declared empty status—to make it browser-ready. Figure 13-14 illustrates the effects of the touched up code in an HTML file that has been accessed by the Netscape browser.

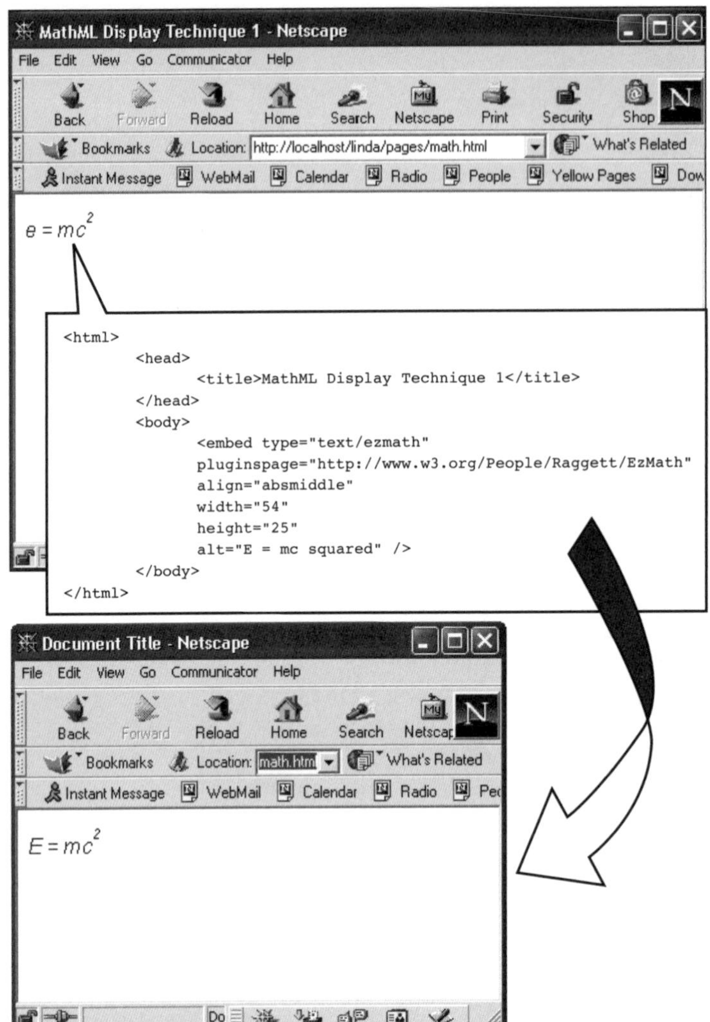

Figure 13-14 Inserting the code

The Web browser needs a plug-in to understand these human-readable expressions. The EzMath editor generates the necessary code for your HTML page, and includes the reference to the required plug-in—in this case, the npezm32.dll file must be copied to the Plug-ins folder prior to viewing. Thus, the code within the <embed> element tag depends on the npezm32.dll that came with the EzMath editor code. The npezm32.dll has essentially the same rendering functionality that EzMath itself has.

With the value for the alt attribute set to the final version of the expression that was originally coded into the EzMath Expression Editor, the code inserted into the HTML file yields the final—and correct—browser view of the math expression, as shown in the browser window in Figure 13-14.

This is one example of how a browser can display math expressions. A math editor such as EzMath can really ease the pain of rendering the presentation of math expressions. The EzMath editor also provides support for marking up expressions in the MathML content tags. To accomplish that, you have to change the Clipboard format to MathML.

Exploring MathType

You were given a brief introduction to Design Science, Inc.'s MathType math editor previously in the Layout Boxes section. MathType is a slightly more complex editor that you can use as a stand-alone application, as illustrated in Figure 13-15, or integrated as an add-in feature with Microsoft Word. Integrating with Word makes it easier to use and to integrate math expressions with document creation.

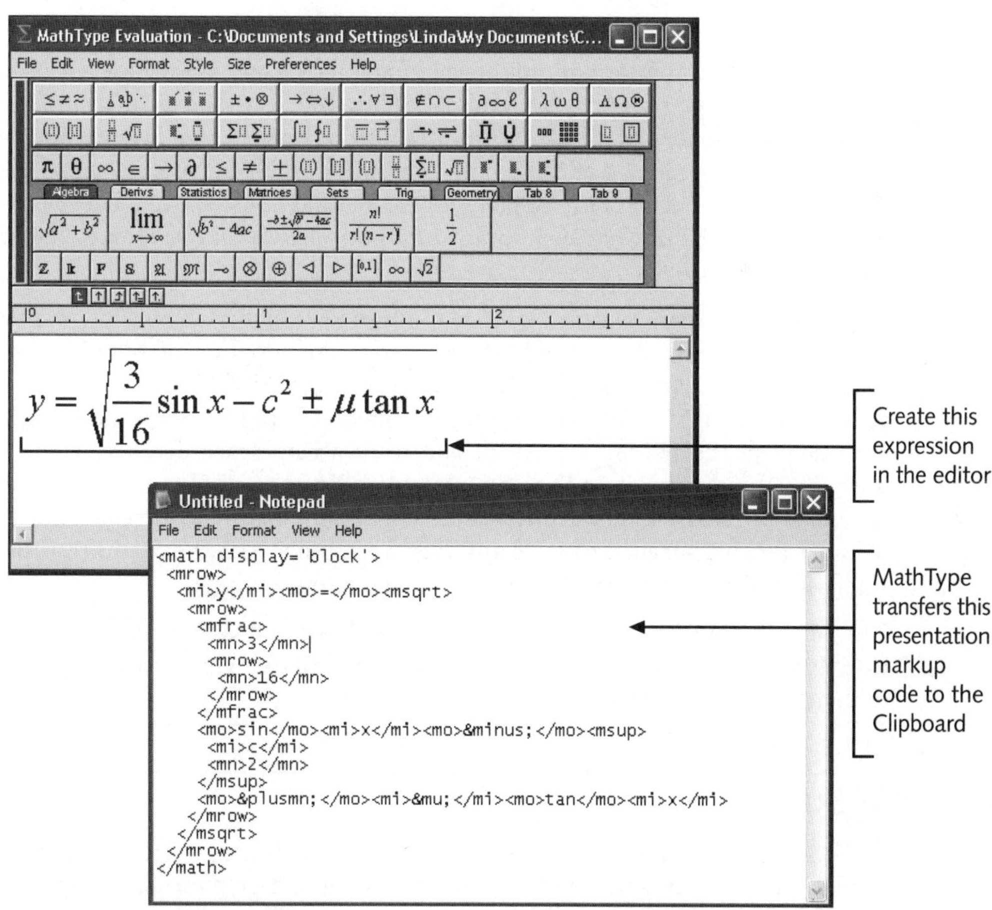

Figure 13-15 Example of math expression created with MathType 5

The MathType 5 editor automatically created the presentation markup shown in the Notepad window in Figure 13-15. The code complies with the MathML 2.0 specifications.

Exploring MathPlayer

Most of the browser-support solutions developed so far (that is, most of the applications that allow you to see and manipulate the MathML expressions at various Web sites) are also proprietary and require very specific programs that are not designed to interoperate well.

In addition to those proprietary applications, there are downloadable plug-in programs (i.e., programs you can download from the Internet and integrate with your browser applications) to help you see and manipulate MathML expressions. However, currently, the only functional plug-ins available are for Netscape and early versions of Internet Explorer. The npezm32.dll plug-in is distributed with Dave Raggett's EzMath math editor software. This plug-in also works with Netscape and earlier versions of Internet Explorer (those released before version 5.5 with service pack 2).

By the time Microsoft introduced Internet Explorer version 5.5 with service pack 2, however, it had dropped support for MathML. Thus, later versions of Internet Explorer cannot be used to render MathML. However, at this writing, Design Science, Inc. has released a beta (i.e., test) version of their new MathML-compliant display engine for Internet Explorer 5.5 and later. That display engine is called MathPlayer. The beta version of MathPlayer can be downloaded from *www.dessci.com/webmath/mathplayer*. Then follow the appropriate links.

According to Design Science, Inc., "MathPlayer is a high-performance MathML display engine...available for free in order to accelerate the adoption of MathML in the math, science, and education communities." After you install MathPlayer, when you visit a Web page that contains MathML math expression, Internet Explorer detects the <math> elements embedded in the HTML document and reads a namespace declaration in the HTML document header. Internet Explorer uses MathPlayer to display and print the MathML islands, if necessary. Because Internet Explorer only loads and executes the MathPlayer software on an as-needed basis, MathPlayer works only with the MathML islands and lets Internet Explorer interpret the rest of the coding on the page.

The MathPlayer Web site includes a link to the Microsoft Web site where you can download Internet Explorer and access the MSDN library, which explains behaviors that Internet Explorer depends on to use MathPlayer.

Chapter Summary

- Coding math and scientific expressions has been a challenge since the first basic books were printed. Computer and network technologies have presented opportunities, and additional challenges, for mathematical expressions. The proliferation of the Internet and the World Wide Web has almost demanded a solution.

- There are two aspects to mathematical expressions: presentation/display and content/semantics. Early solutions focused on presentation and not on content. Many authors have used bitmaps and other images of expression, which are cumbersome, an administrative burden, and convey no content information for further processing.
- In the beginning, MathML's developers perceived that MathML would be an extension to HTML. Ultimately, it became an extension to XML. There have been two major W3C MathML Recommendations. Each has its own DTD.
- MathML had to meet demanding design goals. MathML forms the base of a two-layer architecture model: as an XML application and specification, it facilitates interoperability and communication among Layer 1 software applications.
- MathML consists of about 30 presentation elements, 150 or so content elements, and a few interface elements (the <math> element and attributes that connect various other structure elements).
- MathML has two types of markup specifications: one for presentation and one for content. Combining them can be complex. Content processing is done by prefix notation (also called Polish Notation).
- If you are designing or creating math expressions, it is worthwhile to be familiar with two concepts: abstract expression trees and layout boxes.
- Because creating MathML expressions by hand can be a complex procedure, the more convenient editing solutions, although proprietary, are recommended. There are several listed at the W3C MathML Web site.
- Browsers generally require plug-ins to display MathML-compliant expressions.

REVIEW QUESTIONS

1. What two recent events have made it necessary to revisit the issue of coding mathematical expressions for presentation?
2. Currently, browsers have difficulty consistently displaying math expressions. True or false?
3. List five design goals that MathML had to meet.
4. Which statement best describes the two-layer architecture?
   a. Layer 1 is a proprietary set of instructions that is used to convert all software and application software to conform to the current company's specifications.
   b. Layer 1 is a set of common power tools that Layer 2 applications use to exchange, process, encode, and render presentations.
   c. Layer 2 is a set of common power tools that Layer 1 applications have to use to exchange, process, encode, and render presentations.
   d. Layer 1 is a power tool that was created by the W3C Working Group and is used to create application software to conform to the specifications.

5. Where can you find a current list of equation editors that comply with the new MathML 2.0 specifications?
6. Using a typical math editor such as EzMath, how can you type an expression to look like the one in Figure 13-16?

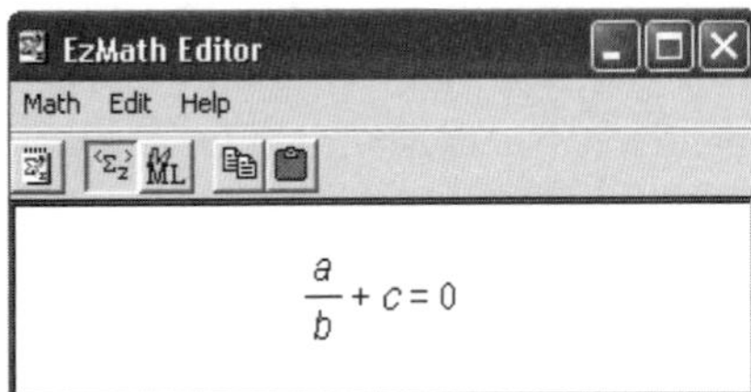

Figure 13-16

7. What does the following expression "x equals the square root of 9" look like when converted in an editor such as EzMath?
8. What does the presentation markup for the equation in Figure 13-16 look like?
9. What does the content markup for the equation in Figure 13-16 look like?
10. What is the one biggest difference between MathML 1.0 and MathML 2.0?
    a. the ability to use fractions
    b. the ability to render university level math
    c. the addition of the <math> element for formatting and embedding
    d. the ability to use namespaces
11. Which attribute should always be included with a <math> element so that users can point to an object and read a label if there has been a MathML malfunction?
12. What are two ways to validate MathML code?
13. Which statement best describes the primary difference between presentation markup and content markup?
    a. Presentation markup is to calculations as content markup is to display.
    b. Content markup is exclusive to alternative displays such as braille and sound files.
    c. Presentation markup is suitable for uncomplicated math calculations.
    d. Content markup is to calculations as presentation markup is to display.
14. Both presentation markup and content markup use the same markup elements and tags. True or false?

15. The use of ________________ is a common way for some presentational math editors to draw layout schemata on a page.
    a. tokens
    b. tables
    c. boxes
    d. symbols
16. The <mrow> element is a ________________ element.
    a. container
    b. token
    c. layout
    d. schemata
    e. none of the above
17. A letter that is to be displayed as an identifier should be within an ________________ element.
    a. <mi>
    b. <mo>
    c. <mn>
    d. <ms>
18. A plus sign (+) that is to be displayed as an operator should be within an ________________ element.
    a. <mi>
    b. <mo>
    c. <mn>
    d. <ma>
19. The secret to being able to read content markup is ________________.
    a. to be able to read right to left
    b. work with the equation using basic PN
    c. draw an abstract tree to expose subelements
    d. work out the inline relationships first
20. MathML uses ________________ type of notation for creating content markup.
21. The only two token elements used for content markup are ________________ and ________________.

22. The following content represents what famous equation?

```
<reln>
      <eq/>
      <apply>
            <plus/>
            <apply>
                  <power/>
                  <ci>a</ci>
                  <ci>2</ci>
            </apply>
            <apply>
                  <power/>
                  <ci>b</ci>
                  <ci>2</ci>
            </apply>
      </apply>
      <apply>
            <power/>
            <ci>c</ci>
            <ci>2</ci>
      </apply>
</reln>
```

23. Create an abstract tree for the equation in the previous question.
24. Which numbers in the equation in Figure 13-17 should be coded as a <cn> content element?

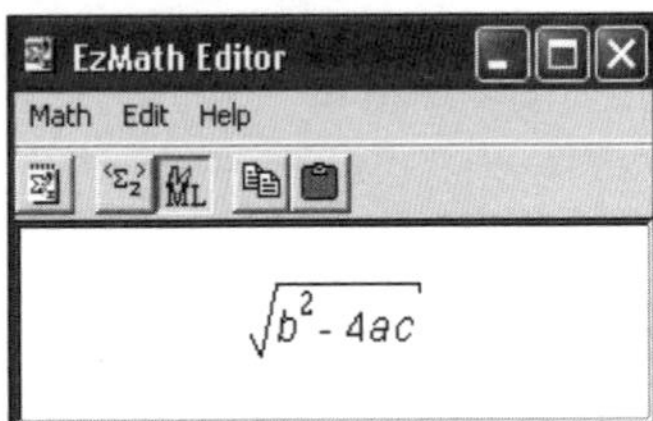

Figure 13-17

25. The following code segment is an example of ______________.
    a. MathML 1.0
    b. MathML 2.0 (m namespace)
    c. MathML 2.0 (namespace attr)
    d. MathML 2.0 (no namespace)

```
<m:math display='block'>
     <m:mrow>
          <m:mi>a</m:mi><m:mo>=</m:mo><m:mi>b</m:mi>
     </m:mrow>
</m:math>
```

HANDS-ON PROJECTS

Before performing the Hands-on Projects for this chapter, you must download MathType 5 and EzMath to create and edit MathML equations. If WinZip or PKZip is not installed on your computer, you must also download one of those programs. Download the software from the following Web sites:

- *MathType 5*—www.dessci.com (download the 30-day free trial)
- *EzMath*—www.w3.org/People/Raggett/ezmath1_1.zip
- *WinZip*—www.winzip.com

or

- *PKZip*—www.pkware.com

13

Project 13-1

In this project, you set up a popular MathML equation editor called MathType 5. You then use MathType to create a math equation and convert it to presentation markup MathML code.

To install MathType 5 and create a basic math equation:

1. Using Windows Explorer, create a folder named **ch13** in the home*yourname* folder on your hard disk. Then browse to the folder where you downloaded MathType 5, and then double-click the **mtw50.exe** file.
2. Accept all of the defaults while installing the software.
3. To start MathType, click **Start**, point to **Programs** (point to **All Programs** in Windows XP), point to **MathType 5**, and then click **MathType**. The MathType editor window opens, as shown in Figure 13-18.

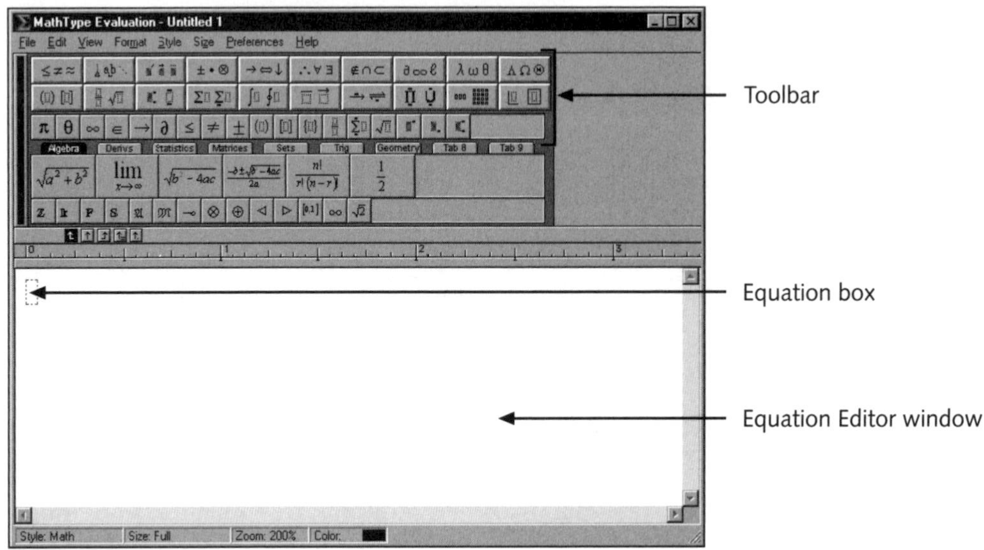

Figure 13-18

You will use MathType 5 to create the equation shown in Figure 13-19.

$$4x^3 - 6x^2 + 12x$$

Figure 13-19

4. In the Equation Editor window, type **4x** in the equation box. Notice that the x character appears in italics, indicating it is a variable.
5. To indicate that the next number (3) should be a superscript, you use a widget template in the toolbar. When you point to a button on the toolbar, its name appears in the status bar. Click the **Superscript and subscript templates** button on the toolbar to open a symbol grid, as shown in Figure 13-20. Then click the **Superscript** symbol. A superscript widget box appears in the Equation Editor window.

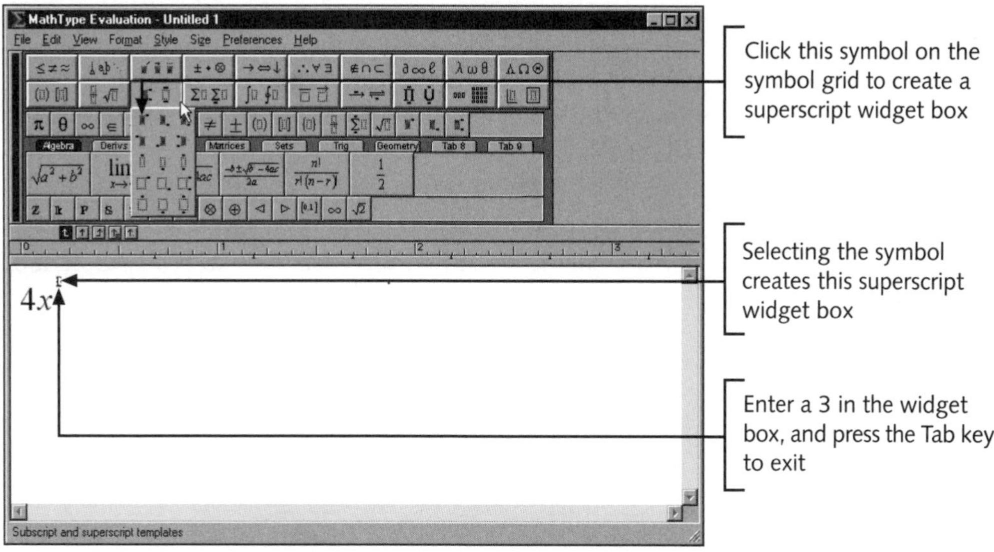

Figure 13-20

6. Type **3**, and then press the **Tab** key to exit the widget box. If you make a mistake, press the **Backspace** key to delete the number and start again.
7. Type a **minus sign** (**-**) after the number 3.
8. Using Steps 4–7 as a reference, type the **6x**. Enter **2** as a superscript. Then type **+12x**. The completed equation should look like Figure 13-21.

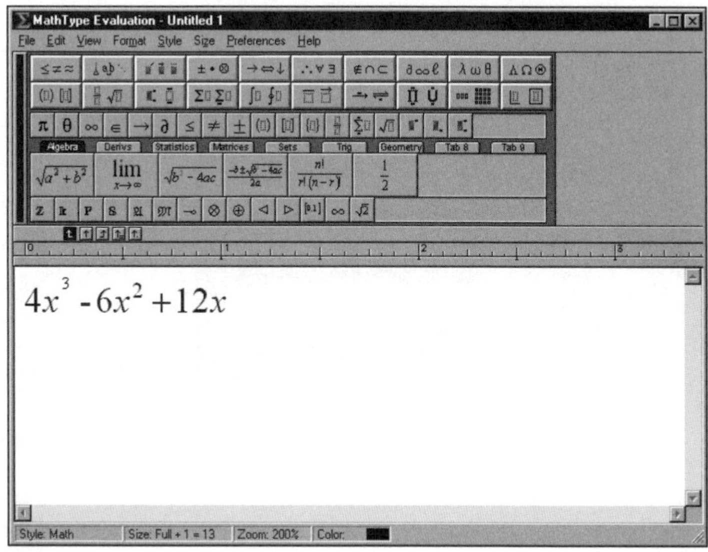

Figure 13-21

9. Click **File** on the menu bar, and then click **Save** to save the file as **Eq1.wmf** in the \home*yourname*\Ch13 folder. A .wmf file is a Windows Metafile Format graphic file. When creating a Web page that shows this equation, you reference the Eql.wmf file in the HTML code. Leave Eql.wmf open in MathType 5 for the next steps.

After you create an equation in MathType and save it as a graphics file, you can convert the equation to presentation markup MathML code. You start by setting the translator type, and then you copy and paste the equation from MathType to Notepad or another editor.

To convert a math equation to presentation markup MathML code:

1. In MathType 5, set the translator type by clicking **Preferences** on the menu bar, and then clicking **Translators**. In the Translators dialog box, click the **Translation to other language (text)** option button, click the **Translator** list arrow, and then click **MathML 2.0 (no namespace)** as shown in Figure 13-22.

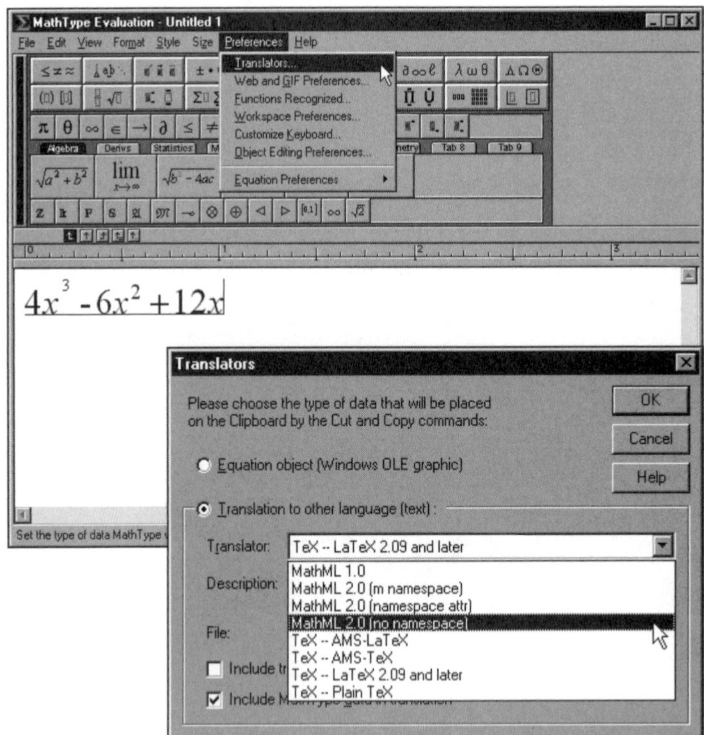

Figure 13-22

2. Click **OK** to set the type of translation you want to perform. To see the code, you have to copy the equation to the Clipboard. Drag to select the entire equation in the Equation Editor window, right-click the equation, and then click **Copy** on the shortcut menu, as shown in Figure 13-23.

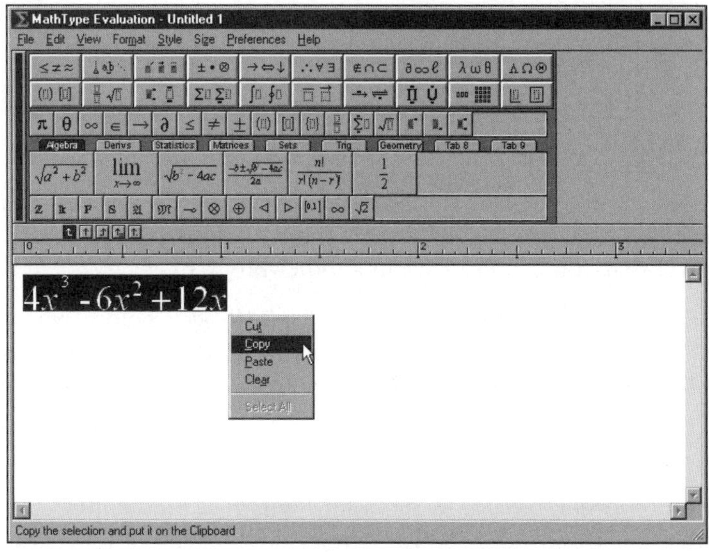

Figure 13-23

3. Next, you paste the code into a text editor such as Notepad or other program to view the results. Start Notepad as you usually do. Click **Edit** on the menu bar, and then click **Paste** to paste the equation into a new document, as shown in Figure 13-24.

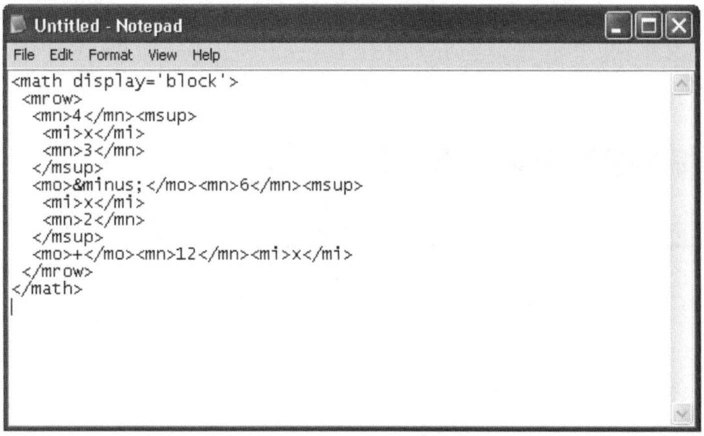

Untitled - Notepad

File Edit Format View Help

```
<math display='block'>
 <mrow>
  <mn>4</mn><msup>
   <mi>x</mi>
   <mn>3</mn>
  </msup>
  <mo>&minus;</mo><mn>6</mn><msup>
   <mi>x</mi>
   <mn>2</mn>
  </msup>
  <mo>+</mo><mn>12</mn><mi>x</mi>
 </mrow>
</math>
```

Figure 13-24

4. The equation appears as presentation markup MathML code. Save the file as **eq1pm.txt** in the \home*yourname*\Ch13 folder. Close Notepad and MathType 5.

MathType 5 specializes in presentation markup code for math equations, and does not generate content markup code.

Project 13-2

In this project you use another equation editor called EzMath to create the same equation you created in Project 13-1. Instead of presentation markup code, EzMath generates content markup code that you can use later in another program.

Be sure to download EzMath from *www.w3.org/People/Raggett* before performing this project. A copy of WinZip or PKZip should also be installed on your computer. In this project, you install EzMath and then use the npezm32.dll file as a plug-in for Netscape Navigator.

To install the EzMath software:

1. Using Windows Explorer, browse to the folder where you downloaded EzMath, and then double-click **ezmath1_1.zip**. Extract the files into a folder called EzMath on your hard disk.
2. To install the EzMath browser plug-in, copy the **npezm32.dll** file from the EzMath\EzMath folder to the folder where the Netscape plug-ins are stored. By default, this is C:\Program Files\Netscape\Communicator\Program\Plug-ins if you are using Netscape Communicator, or C:\Program Files\Netscape 6\Plug-ins if you are using Netscape 6.
3. To open the EzMath equation editor using Windows Explorer, browse to the EzMath\EzMath folder on your hard disk, and then double-click the **EZMATH.EXE** file. The EzMath Editor window opens, as shown in Figure 13-25.

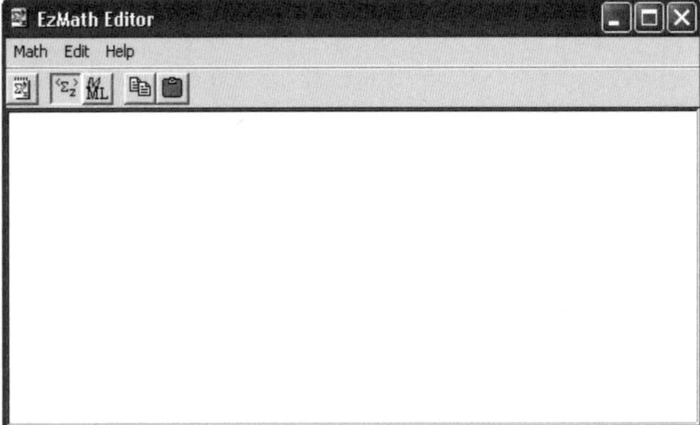

Figure 13-25

You are ready to create the same equation you created in Project 13-1 and shown again in Figure 13-26.

$$4x^3 - 6x^2 + 12x$$

Figure 13-26

To create an equation in EzMath, you enter a mathematical expression as text. Then you can copy the equation to the Clipboard, where it appears as an <embed> element with appropriate plug-in attributes. You can then paste this content markup MathML code into an HTML document and later display the page in a browser.

To create an equation and convert it to content markup MathML code:

1. On the EzMath Editor toolbar, click the **EzMath Expression Editor** button (the first button on the left) on the toolbar to open the EzMath Expression Editor window, as shown in Figure 13-27.

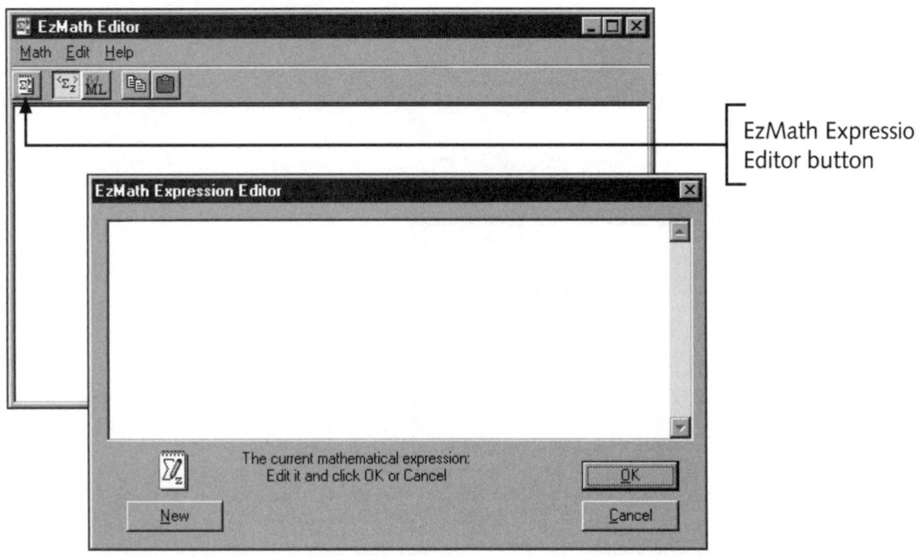

Figure 13-27

13

2. Click in the EzMath Expression Editor window and type the following text.

   4x to the power of 3 minus 6x to the power of 2 plus 12x

   See Figure 13-28.

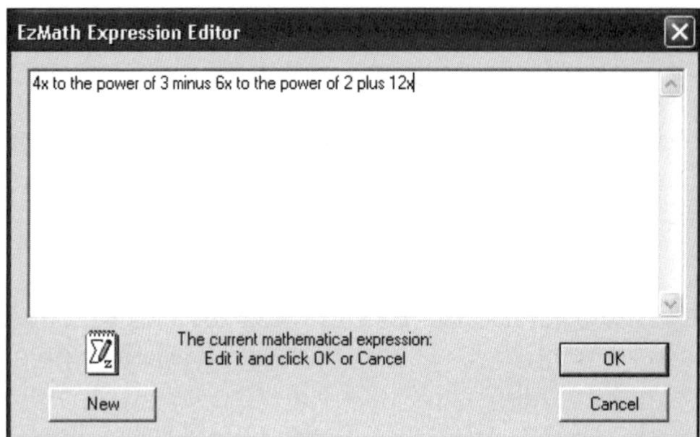

Figure 13-28

3. Click **OK**. The equation appears in the EzMath Editor window, as shown in Figure 13-29.

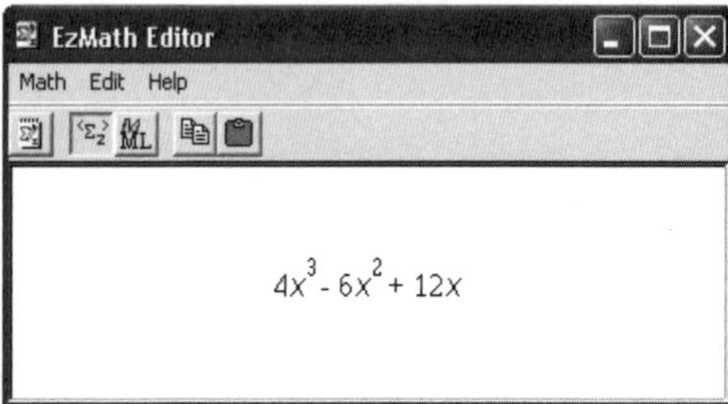

Figure 13-29

4. Next, you create code that the browser can display. Make sure the **Set clipboard format to EzMath** button is selected, as shown in Figure 13-30.

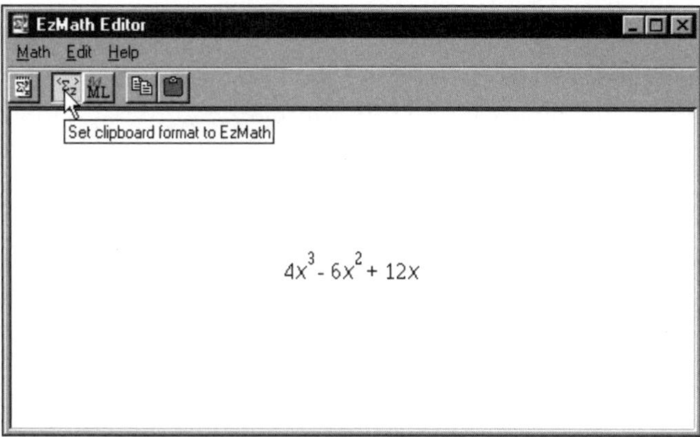

Figure 13-30

5. To copy the equation to the Clipboard, click the **Copy to Clipboard** button on the toolbar.
6. To view the equation set as MathML code, click the **View Clipboard** button on the toolbar. The Clipboard window opens, showing the code for the <embed> element with its plug-in attributes. See Figure 13-31.

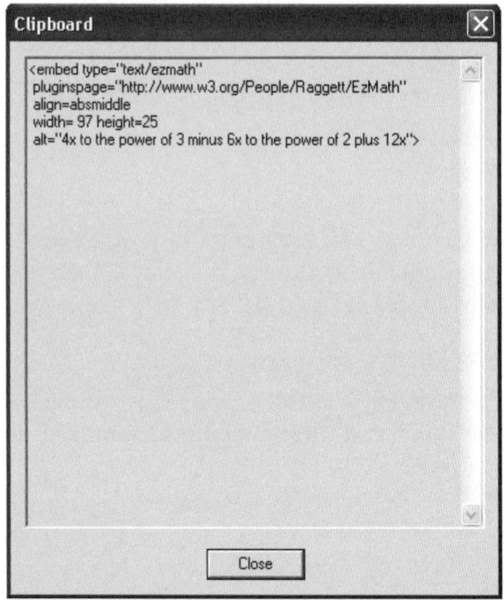

Figure 13-31

Leave the Clipboard window open in EzMath for the next project.

To view the code on a Web page using Netscape:

1. Start XML Spy as you usually do. Click **File** on the menu bar, and then click **New**. The Create new document dialog box opens. Select **html HTML Document** and then click **OK**. A new HTML document appears in the main window.
2. Select the code in the Clipboard window, right-click the selection, and then click **Copy** on the shortcut menu. Click the XML Spy window to make it the active window, right-click in the HTML document, and then click **Paste** on the shortcut menu. Save the file as **EzEq1.html** in the C:\home*yourname*/Ch13 folder.
3. Before you view the file, you must fix the syntax. First, add double quotes around the attributes inside the <embed> element, and then add the missing "17" to close the element, as shown in the following code:

```
<html>
  <head>
  <title>Enter the title of your HTML document
         here</title>
  </head>
  <body>
    <embed type="text/ezmath"
    plug-inspage="http://www.w3.org/People/Raggett/EzMath"
    align="absmiddle"
    width="97" height="25"
    alt="4x to the power of 3 minus 6x to the power of
         2 plus 12x" />
  </body>
</html>
```

You cannot view this document using XML Spy because XML Spy is an Internet Explorer equivalent, and does not have the npezm32.dll file installed, which is a plug-in only for Netscape Navigator. XML Spy, therefore, cannot interpret the plug-in code.

4. Test the view with the Netscape browser. Start Netscape as you usually do. Then open by clicking **File** on the menu bar and then clicking **Open File**. The equation appears, as shown in Figure 13-32.

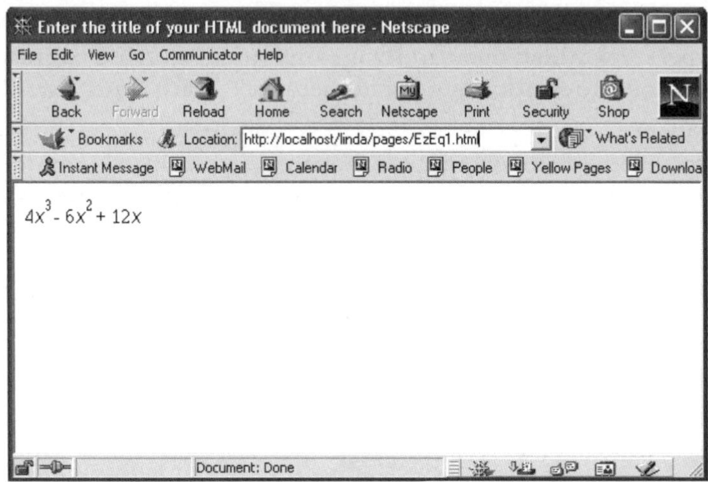

Figure 13-32

If the Plug-in Not Loaded dialog box appears, as shown in Figure 13-33, you might need to copy the npezm32.dll file into the correct plug-ins folder.

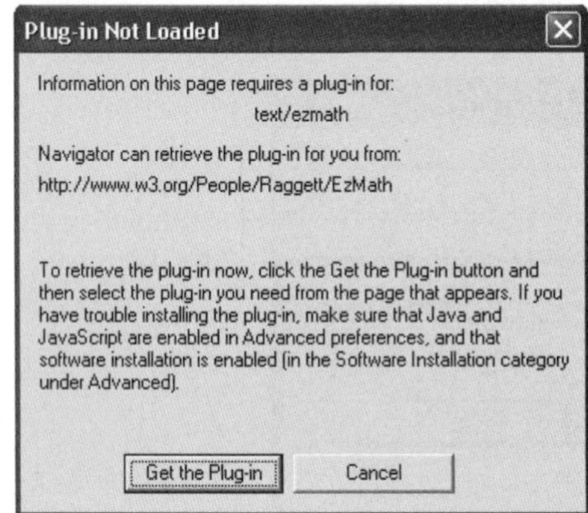

Figure 13-33

5. Save EzEq1.html. Close all open windows.

Project 13-3

In this project you use the MathType 5 editor to create a more complex algebraic equation to calculate a loan payment. This useful equation also introduces you to other widgets available on the MathType toolbar.

To create a complex equation in MathType 5:

1. Start MathType. Click **Start**, point to **Programs** (point to **All Programs** in Windows XP), point to **MathType 5**, and then click **MathType**. The MathType window opens.

   The loan payment equation you create is shown in Figure 13-34. This formula calculates the monthly payment *m*, on a loan of *L* dollars, paid back over *N* months at an annual interest rate of *p*.

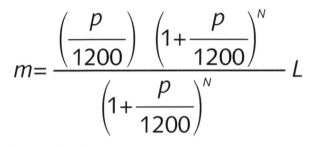

$$m=\frac{\left(\frac{p}{1200}\right)\left(1+\frac{p}{1200}\right)^{N}}{\left(1+\frac{p}{1200}\right)^{N}}L$$

Figure 13-34

2. To create the new equation, type **m=**. To type the rest of the equation, you need a new template. Click the **Fraction and radical templates** button on the toolbar, and then click **Full-size fraction**. (Recall that you can point to a button to see its name on the status bar.) See Figure 13-35.

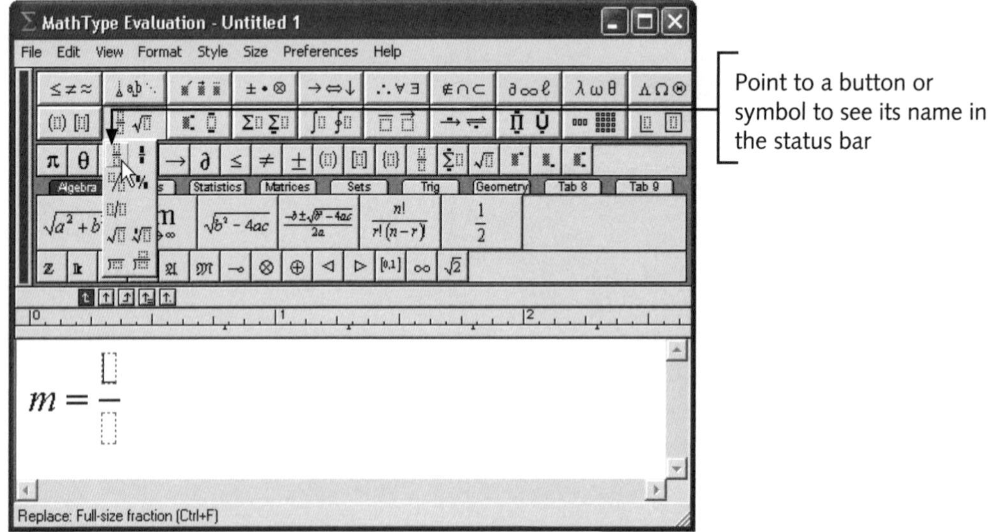

Figure 13-35

3. Click the **Fence templates** button on the toolbar, and then click **Parentheses or round brackets** to enter parentheses in the upper box of the fraction.

4. To enter the top fraction, click the **Fraction and radical templates** button on the toolbar, and then click **Full-size fraction**. In the upper box, type **p** and in the lower box type **1200**. Your equation should now look like Fig 13-36.

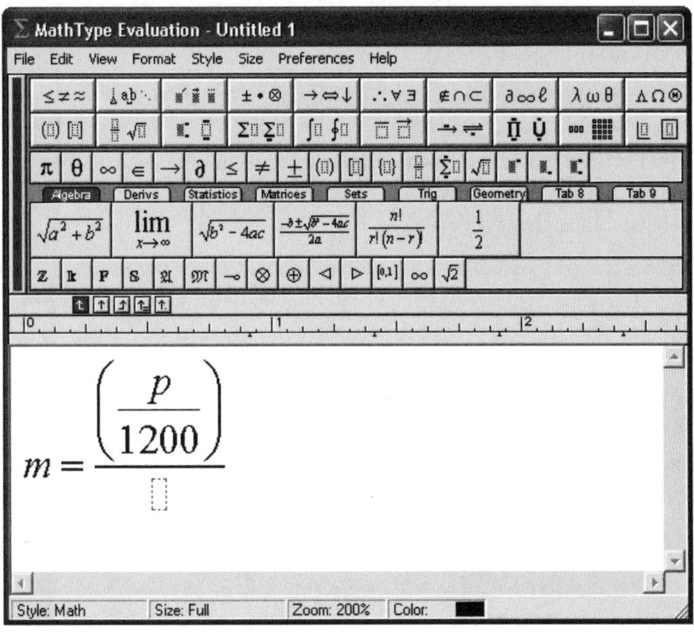

Figure 13-36

5. Click the **Tab** key until you move the insertion point outside the parentheses, click the **Fence templates** button on the toolbar, and then click **Parentheses**. Within the parentheses, type **1+**.
6. To enter the top fraction, click the **Fraction and radical templates** button on the toolbar, and then click **Full-size fraction**. In the upper box, type **p** and in the lower box type **1200**. Press the **Tab** key until you move the insertion point outside of the parentheses.
7. Click the **Expression 16: (Template) superscript** button on the toolbar, and then type **N**.
8. The lower part of the equation contains a partial expression from the upper part of the equation. As in most editors, MathType allows you to copy and paste recurring expressions. Drag to select the second bracketed equation, including the exponent, copy, and then paste it into the lower box.
9. Press the **Tab** key, and then type **L** to complete the equation.
10. Click **File** on the menu bar, and then click **Save** to save the file as **eq13-3mt.wmf** in the \home*yourname*\Ch13 folder. Close MathType.

Project 13-4

In this project you use EzMath to create the same loan payment equation you created in Project 13-3. This time, however, you create and save the content markup to describe this equation.

To create a complex equation in EzMath:

1. Using Windows Explorer, browse to the EzMath\EzMath folder on your hard disk, and then double-click the **EZMATH.EXE** file. The EzMath Editor window opens. Click the **EzMath Expression Editor** button on the toolbar to open the EzMath Expression Editor window. If an equation appears in this window, click the **New** button to clear the window.
2. Click in the EzMath Expression Editor window and type **m equals p over 1200**. Then press **Enter**. The EzMath Expression Editor window closes, and the equation appears in the EzMath Editor window, as shown in Figure 13-37.

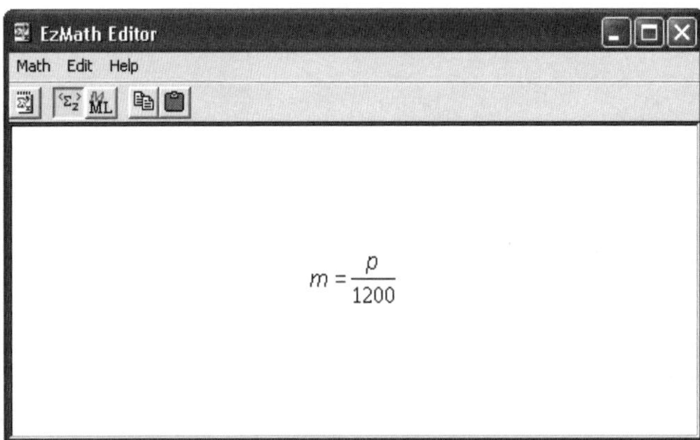

Figure 13-37

3. Click the **EzMath Expression Editor** button on the toolbar to return to your formula in the EzMath Expression Editor window. The EzMath program works with both plain language and mathematical symbols. Revise the expression so it appears as:

   m equals **(**p over 1200**) (1+p/1200) to the power of N**

   Press **Enter** to verify the equation in the EzMath Editor window, shown in Figure 13-38.

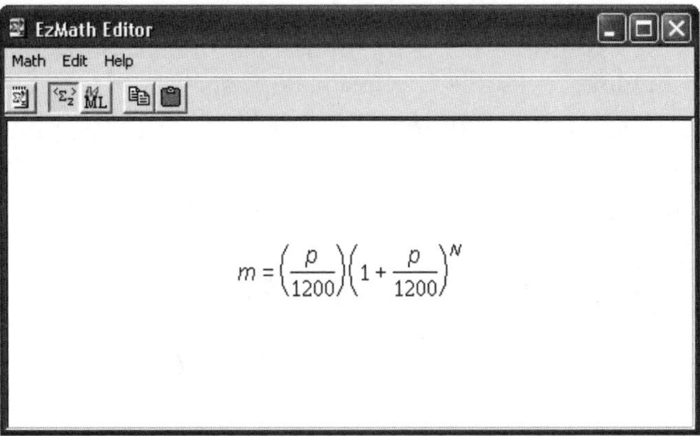

Figure 13-38

4. To create the denominator of the fraction, click the **EzMath Expression Editor** button to open the EzMath Expression Editor window. Revise the expression so it appears as:

   m equals (p over 1200) (1+p/1200) to the power of N **over (1 + p/1200)^N**

   To create the "to the power of" character (^), press **Shift+6**.
5. Press **Enter** and review your work in the EzMath Editor window.
6. The final step is to multiply your rate by the loan (L) itself. Return to the Expression Editor window and type **times L** at the end of the expression. Press **Enter** to verify the result, as shown in Figure 13-39.

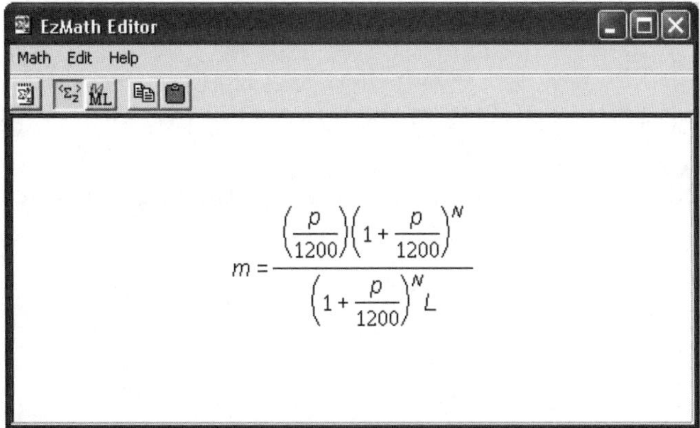

EzMath Editor
Math Edit Help
$m = \frac{\left(\frac{p}{1200}\right)\left(1 + \frac{p}{1200}\right)^N}{\left(1 + \frac{p}{1200}\right)^N L}$

Figure 13-39

7. The loan variable (L) should not appear as part of the denominator. To fix this problem, surround the expression being multiplied with brackets. In the EzMath Expression Editor window, revise the expression so it appears as:

   m equals **(** (p over 1200) (1+p/1200) to the power of N over (1 + p/1200)^N **)** times L

   Press **Enter** and verify your expression, as shown in Figure 13-40.

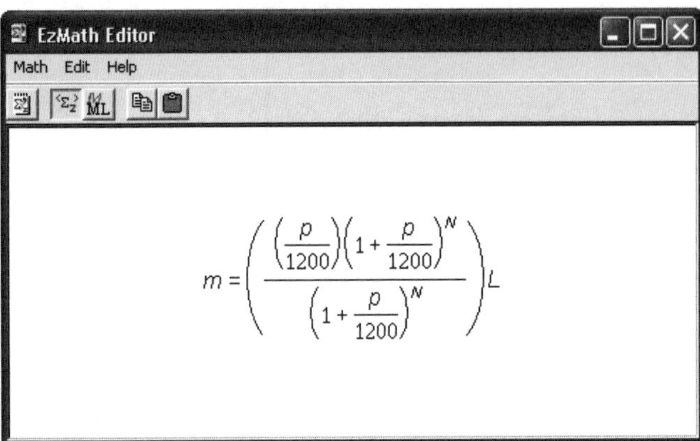

Figure 13-40

   Although the expression is mathematically correct, it doesn't precisely match the equation shown in Project 13-3, which does not include the parentheses around the fraction. If you use a pair of curly brackets around the expression instead of parentheses, you logically group the fraction, but do not show the parentheses.

8. Return to the EzMath Expression Editor window and modify the expression so it appears as:

   m equals **{** (p over 1200) (1+p/1200) to the power of N over (1 + p/1200)^N **}** times L

   Press **Enter** and confirm that your equation matches the one shown in Figure 13-41.

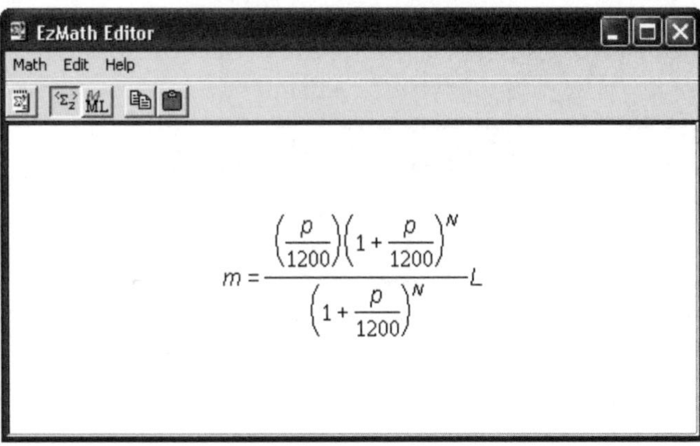

Figure 13-41

9. To save the expression as an XML file containing the content markup, click the **Set clipboard format to EzMath** button on the toolbar to select it, if necessary. Then click the **Copy to Clipboard** button on the toolbar.
10. Start Notepad as you usually do. Paste your content markup in Notepad by clicking **Edit** on the menu bar, and then clicking **Paste**. Click **File** on the menu bar, and then click **Save** to save the file as **eqA_ez.xml** in the \home*yourname*\Ch13 folder. Close Notepad and EzMath.

Project 13-5

In this project, you create simple calculus equations using the MathType 5 editor.

To create a calculus equation:

1. Start MathType. In the following steps, you create the equation shown in Figure 13-42.

$$\int_{0}^{2\pi} \frac{\cos x}{x^2}\,dx$$

Figure 13-42

2. Click the **Integral templates** button on the toolbar, and then click the **Definite integral with superscript and subscript limits**, as shown in Figure 13-43.

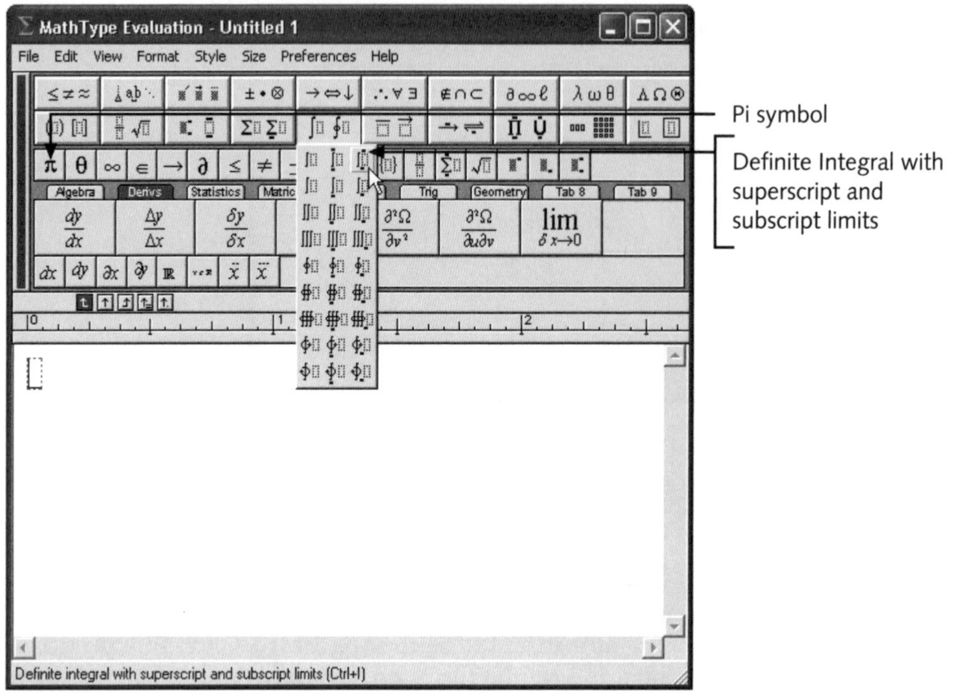

Figure 13-43

3. Click in the superscript box and type **2**. Click the **Pi** (π) button on the toolbar. Click in the subscript box and type the number **0**.
4. Now that the integral is complete, you can create the function. Click the **Fraction and radical templates** button on the toolbar, and then click **Full-size fraction**. In the upper box, type **cosx** and in the lower box type **x**. Click in the remaining box, click the **Expression 16: (Template) Superscript** button on the toolbar, and then type **2**.
5. Your final step is to place the equation into context with respect to *x*. Press the **Right Arrow** key until you move to the end of the equation. Click the **Derivs** tab on the toolbar and click the **dx** button. Compare the equation to the one shown in Figure 13-42.
6. Save the file as **eqB_mt.wmf** in the \home*yourname*\Ch13 folder.

   Next, you can create the equation shown in Figure 13-44, which uses other derivative symbols.

$$\frac{d^2y}{dx^2} = 2\cos\theta$$

Figure 13-44

7. Click **File** on the menu bar, and then click **New**. Close the MathType window containing eqB_mt.wmf. In the new MathType window, click the **Derivative** symbol on the toolbar, as shown in Figure 13-45.

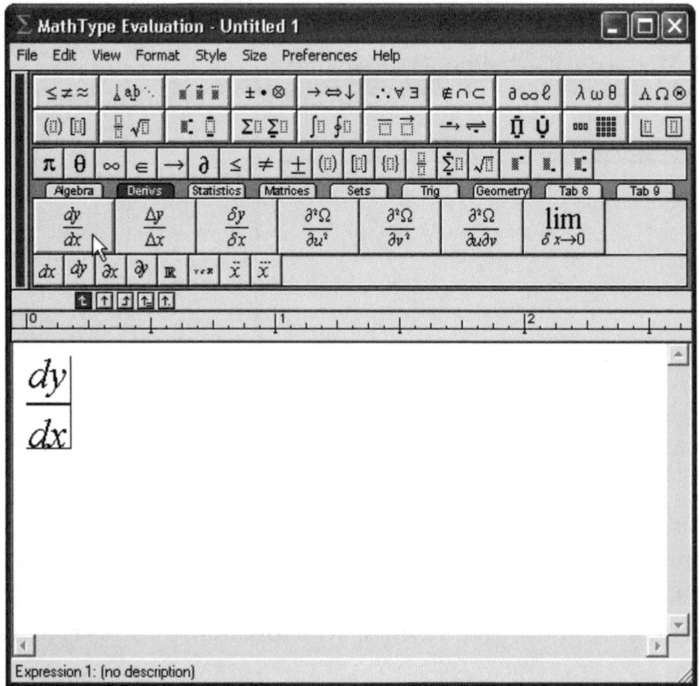

Figure 13-45

8. Click between the d and y in the *dy* expression. Using the **Superscript** button, add a superscripted **2** to create a second derivative. Do the same to add a superscripted 2 to the x in the *dx* expression.
9. Press the **Right Arrow** key twice to move to the end of the equation, and type **= 2 cos**.
10. As a final step, locate and click the **theta** symbol (θ) on the toolbar. The completed equation should now match the one shown earlier in Figure 13-42.
11. Save the equation as **eqC_mt.wmf** in the \home*yourname*\Ch13 folder. Close MathType 5.

13

Project 13-6

In this project, you use EzMath to recreate the calculus equations you created in Project 13-5.

To create calculus equations in EzMath:

1. Start EzMath. Open the EzMath Expression Editor window, and then click the **New** button, if necessary, to clear the window. You are ready to create the calculus expression shown earlier in Figure 13-42.
2. Click in the EzMath Expression Editor window, type **{cos x over 2x squared}**, and then press **Enter** to confirm your results, shown in Figure 13-46.

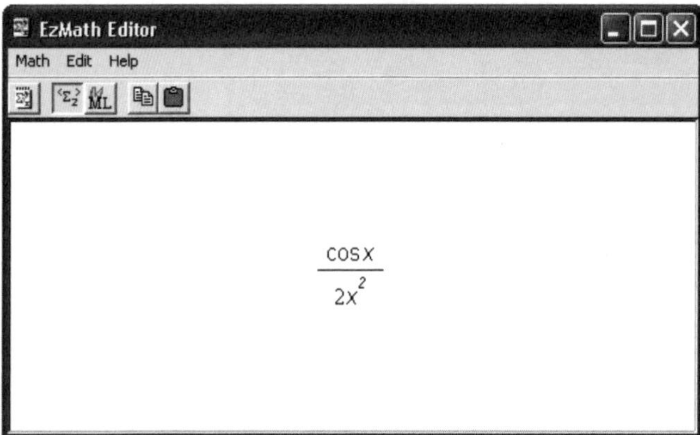

Figure 13-46

3. To integrate this equation, return to the EzMath Expression Editor window, and then type **integral of** in front of the bracketed expression.
4. To specify the definite limits, type **from 0 to 2 pi** after the bracketed expression.
5. The final step is to define the context of the integral. The expression is being integrated with respect to *x*. To represent this in EzMath, type **wrt x** at the end of the equation.
6. Press **Enter** and confirm that your equation matches that shown in Figure 13-47.
7. Copy the content markup to the Clipboard. View the Clipboard, and then copy and paste the code into a new Notepad document. Save the content markup as **eqB_ez.xml** in the \home*yourname*\Ch13 folder.

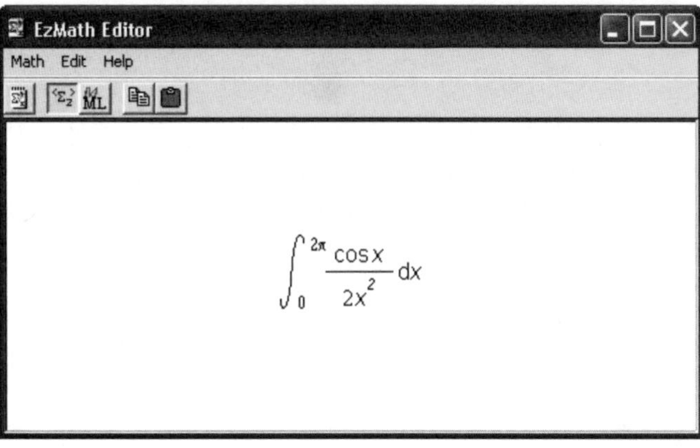

Figure 13-47

8. To create the second derivative equation, open the EzMath Expression Editor window, and then clear your previous work. The second derivative is taken from variable *y* with respect to *x*. In the EzMath Expression Editor window, type **2nd derivative of y wrt x**.
9. Create the equality expression by typing **equals 2 cos theta**.
10. Confirm that your completed equation matches the one shown in Figure 13-48.

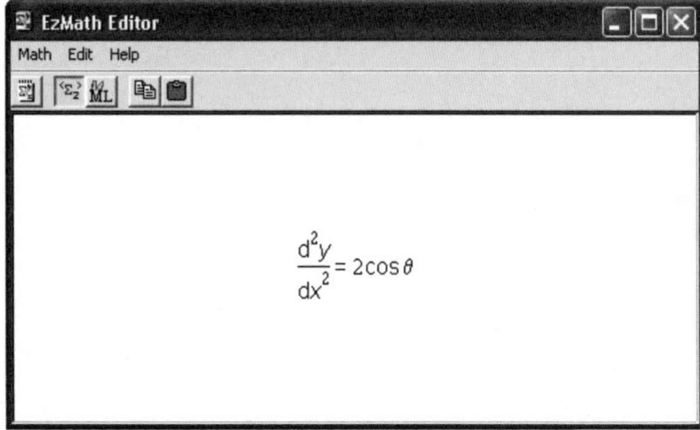

Figure 13-48

11. Save the content markup to the Clipboard. View the Clipboard, and then cut and paste the code into a new Notepad document named **eqC_ez.xml** in the \home*yourname*\Ch13 folder.
12. Close all open windows.

Case Projects

Case Project 13-1

Using MathType, enter the equation shown in Figure 13-49, and display the presentation markup upon completion. You will have to make extensive use of the symbols provided in the MathType toolbar.

$$\sigma_{\bar{X}}^{2} = \frac{1}{n}\left\{\sum_{i=1}^{n} X_{i}^{2} = n\bar{X}^{2}\right\}$$

Figure 13-49

Case Project 13-2

Use EzMath to create the equation shown in Figure 13-50, and then display the content markup upon completion. Use the Netscape 6 browser to view the results.

$$y = \sqrt{\frac{3}{16}}\,\sin x - c^{2} \pm \mu \tan x$$

Figure 13-50

CHAPTER

14

INTRODUCTION TO THE CHANNEL DEFINITION FORMAT

In this chapter, you will learn:

- About push, pull, and webcasting technologies
- About the Channel Definition Format (CDF)
- How to use channels
- How to create a CDF channel
- How to create a CDF file
- About CDF resources

This chapter explains an XML-related language known as Channel Definition Format (CDF). Instead of creating new documents and inserting new data into them so users can access them on demand, such as previous XML-related languages discussed in this book, CDF provides the capability to manipulate and condense existing collections of documents and combines them with specific new data, and then deliver the modified data to subscribers on a regular schedule. CDF was developed by Microsoft Corporation as part of their refinement of their webcasting technology, and was first introduced with Internet Explorer 4 in 1997. CDF differs from most XML-related languages in two major ways: it has no universal DTD, so its documents need only be well-formed and not necessarily valid (individual developers can create and impose their own validity tests, however); and the CDF specification is currently only a W3C Note, with no realistic prospect of becoming a W3C Recommendation. Nevertheless, Microsoft continues to develop and refine CDF, just as it continues to develop the successive versions of IE.

PUSHING, PULLING, AND WEBCASTING

The concept of a channel comes from traditional mass communication media concepts. For instance, the concept of **push technology**, where data is broadcast without regard to whether anyone is connected to the medium, is the backbone of radio and television. Sending e-mail across the Internet is identical, and is the pioneer of IT push technology, because messages are sent to individuals whether they are online or not. As illustrated in Figure 14-1, the sender transmits a message to a designated receiver, and then counts on that receiver to log on, download messages, and reply in a timely fashion. This is similar to radio and television broadcasters relying on listeners and viewers to periodically tune into their channels. But, whether it's radio, TV, or e-mail, the sender recognizes that the message may not be received immediately.

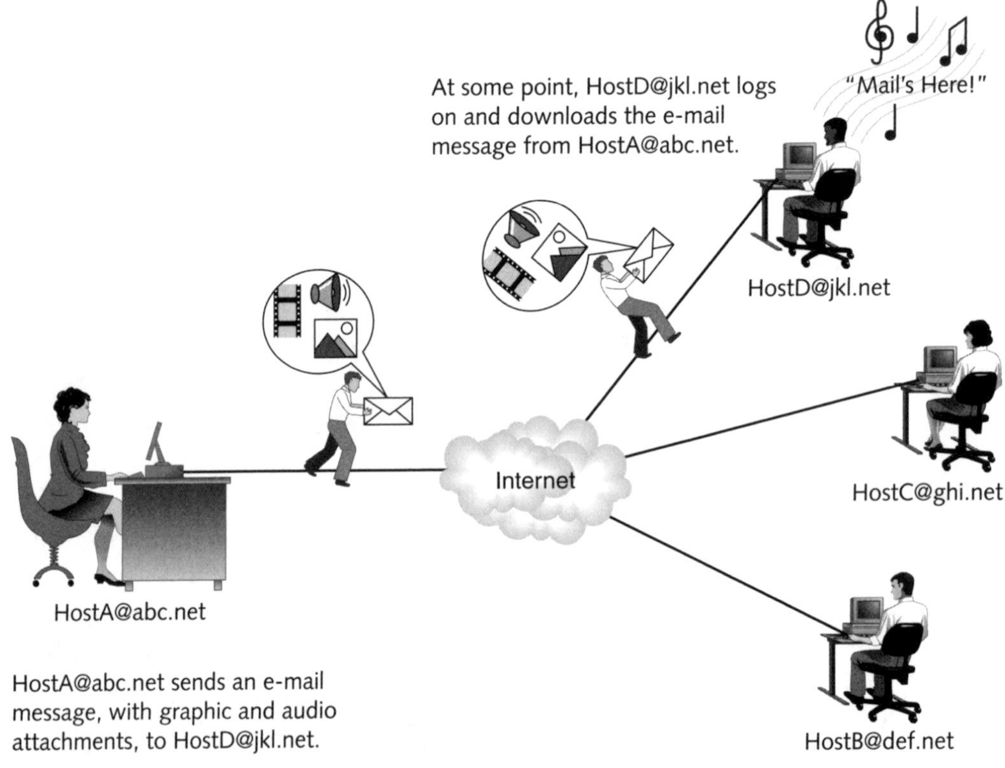
At some point, HostD@jkl.net logs on and downloads the e-mail message from HostA@abc.net.
"Mail's Here!"
HostD@jkl.net
Internet
HostC@ghi.net
HostA@abc.net
HostA@abc.net sends an e-mail message, with graphic and audio attachments, to HostD@jkl.net.
HostB@def.net

Figure 14-1 E-mail as a pioneer of push technology

General Web surfing, on the other hand, reflects **pull technology,** as illustrated in Figure 14-2: an end user with a browser application requests information from a specific location by entering its URL in the browser location bar.

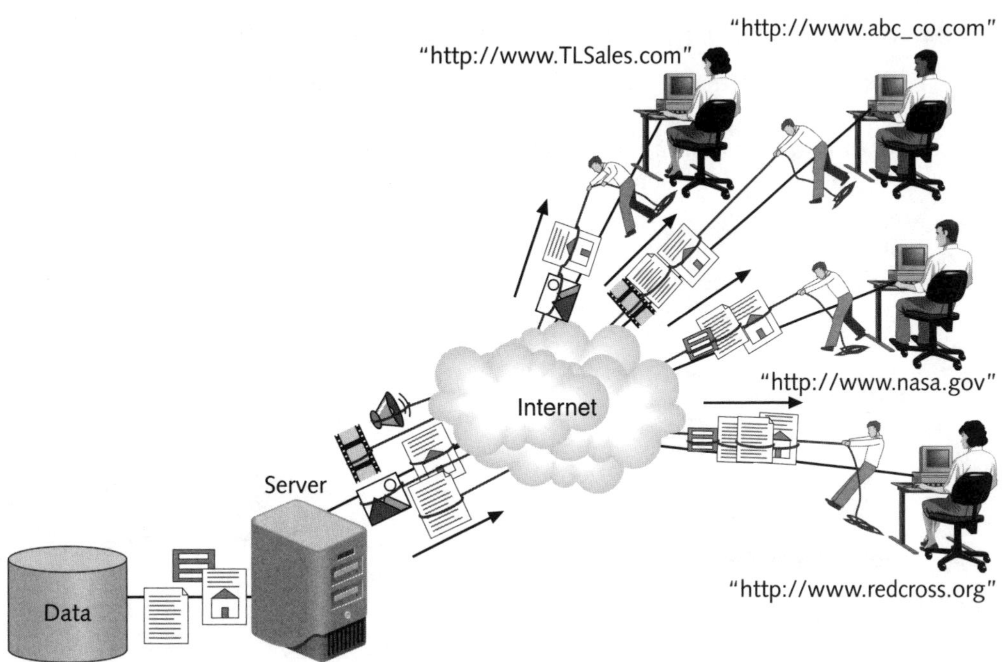

Figure 14-2 Web surfing as basic pull technology

Web surfing, thus, is like a telephone call: when you dial a certain code, you are requesting someone to answer at the other end, and then provide you with information.

The mid-1990s saw the birth of **webcasting**, which is another application of push technology over the Internet, especially to the World Wide Web. After the introduction of e-mail, push technology quickly expanded, as organizations realized they could use a similar approach for mass delivery of information, services, and advertising. With webcasting, end users were spared some of their content-searching effort. Instead, they could subscribe to their favorite information suppliers who, in turn, would distribute content to them directly and automatically. (Subscribing to online information providers is discussed later in this chapter.)

Many organizations are using webcasting over the Internet to deliver information, and many developers see it as "the future of the Net." They see webcasting as a welcome development, and providers and subscribers have begun to depend on it. If you have configured your home page—the page that first is displayed when you start your browser—to be msn.com, yahoo.com, a stock ticker, weather channel, or your favorite sports or entertainment Web site, you are also depending on webcasting technology.

Basic Webcasting, Managed Webcasting, and Active Channels

Basic webcasting—early Microsoft webcasting technology, available with Internet Explorer 3—used what is called a sitecrawler. Basically, a **sitecrawler** is a configurable set of dynamic link libraries that the browser accesses and uses to examine information on Web pages to which the user has subscribed. The browser then compares the information to similar information already stored on the user's system for that Web site and decides whether to import the data from the Web site. This basic webcasting was innovative at the time, but had several drawbacks which had the potential for creating the chaos depicted in Figure 14-3.

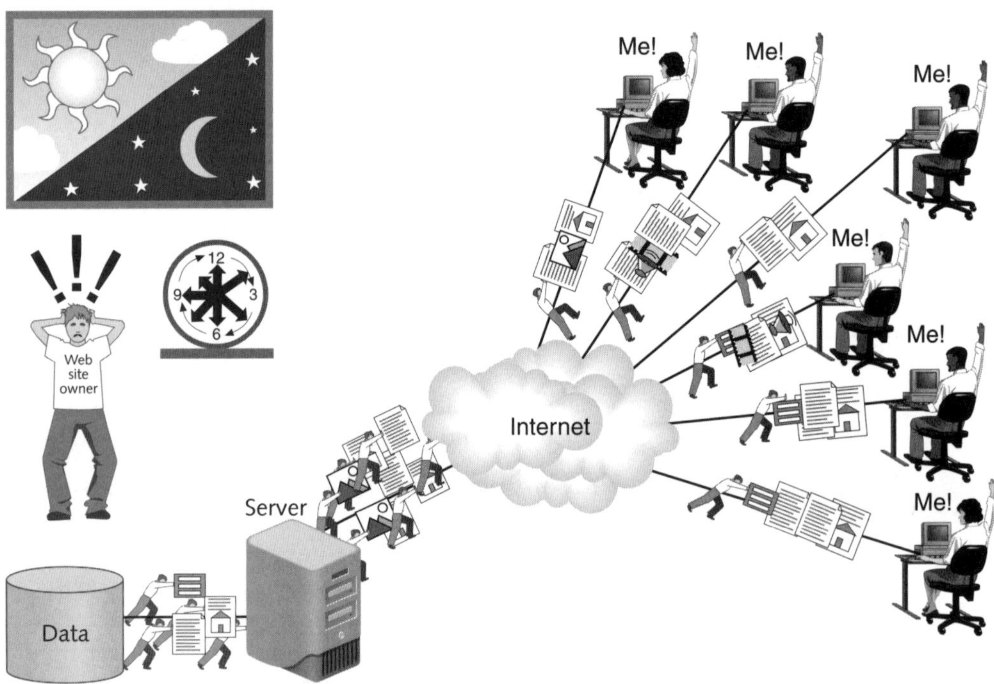

Figure 14-3 Potential chaos from basic webcasting issues

Following are the drawbacks of the early webcasting technology:

- Configuration, although simple in concept, was complex and confusing for the average user.
- All the information, sometimes including the lower-level documents the user wanted, such as Web pages, would be downloaded from the Web site. Thus, too much information was usually downloaded.
- Users could not specify the actual *types* of information they wanted; the sitecrawler grabbed *all* the new and updated information.

- The Web site owner had no way to offer organized groups of information to users.
- The Web site could not instruct the user's system when to schedule updates, so a user might always be a step behind—unless update times were advertised on the Web site.
- Some Web sites disabled site crawling, because it could put a strain on their Web server(s).
- Web site owners had limited control over site subscriptions and updating, because the end users did the subscribing and scheduling. Thus, the organizations might have difficulty scheduling maintenance or otherwise optimizing their own intranet performance.

To help overcome these issues, Microsoft introduced Active Channel and Active Desktop items with Internet Explorer 4 to create "managed webcasting." To incorporate these concepts into IE 4, Microsoft also developed the Channel Definition Format (CDF).

Managed webcasting—that is, managed by the Web site owner—provides the following advantages over basic webcasting:

- The Web site owner can specify which pages on their Web site are available for a user to subscribe to and monitor for changes. This reduces network traffic. If subscribers choose to view Web pages offline, managed webcasting also means fewer pages are downloaded and cached on the subscriber's systems, conserving hard disk space. (See "Making a Channel Available for Offline Viewing" later in this chapter for more information about offline viewing.)
- The owner can provide a structured view of Web site content to make navigation easier and faster.
- Web site owners can schedule updates to coincide with Web site content updates, or to take place during times of lower network loading.
- A Web site owner can convert an existing Web site to managed webcasting without having to completely overhaul the Web site. The only new requirement would be the addition of a CDF file.

From a user's standpoint, the benefits of managed webcasting through the use of channels include the ability to keep track of favorite sites, receive notification when their channels or favorites have been updated, and receive content directly on their system for on- or offline examination. See Figure 14-4.

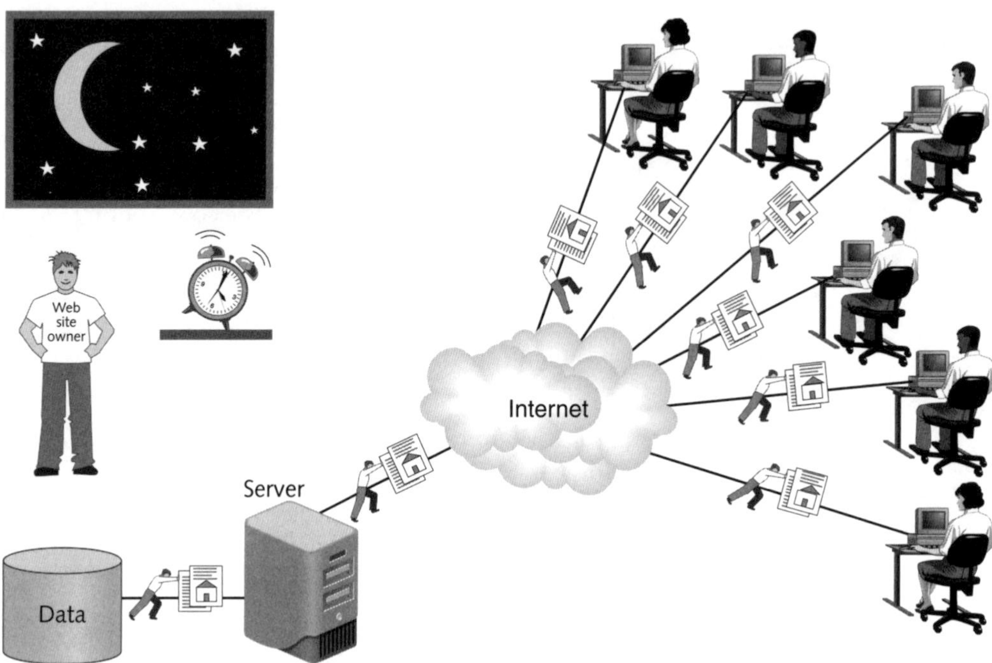

Figure 14-4 Advantages of managed webcasting

Understanding the Channel Definition Format

This section discusses two aspects of the CDF: the features of the XML-related language itself and the specification proposal submitted to the W3C by Microsoft in March 1997 related to that language.

CDF As an XML-Related Language

Channel Definition Format is an XML-related language that allows Web site developers to deliver all or part of a Web site's frequently updated information automatically to client browsers. These browsers include Microsoft Internet Explorer 4 and later and others that may be compliant with CDF. Although CDF is most prominent in push webcasting, it also supports pull webcasting and other data operations, such as searching, indexing, profiling, filtering, and personalizing content. Mostly, CDF allows information to be delivered in the form of **channels**, which are specifically defined documents or other logical groupings of information, and which can be served from any Web server that supports the HTTP protocol. A channel can be designed to represent a single page, multiple pages, or the content of a whole Web site. A Web site owner can create a channel that informs IE and other CDF-compliant browsers about what Web site information the end user can access, and then provide for a regular and periodic automatic download of Web site information or software updates. As defined by Microsoft, **automatic** means that the user only has to select and configure a channel once. After that, information is delivered according to the specified schedule, without any more intervention by the user, unless the user chooses to cancel or otherwise modify the subscription information.

A Web site developer uses CDF's specialized XML data files to define the groupings and to allow subscribers to configure the scheduling for its channels. Once the channels are created, the user only needs to click an icon to subscribe to the owner's Web site and, thereafter, download the information prescribed in the CDF file that defines the channel. As mentioned in the introduction to this chapter, CDF also enables automatic user notification when Web site content changes. CDF's abilities to search, index, profile, filter, and personalize content are facilitated by CDF's XML-related heritage.

When downloaded to an end user's browser, CDF channels resemble a local index to a remote resource. In this case, they are index entries that can take you to the source if you are online (i.e., if you are connected to the Web). If you have already selected an offline viewing option, your channels can be configured to display their content whenever you want to, even if you are not connected to the Web, as long as your system has had an opportunity to go on online beforehand and download the information to your hard disk.

CDF, the W3C, and RDF

In March 1997, Microsoft submitted their proposal for an open Channel Definition Format specification to the W3C. The CDF specification document defined the language of CDF by specifying definitions for CDF's elements and attributes, as well as DTD declarations for those components.

The specification document was intended for review, discussion, and comment by W3C members, and continues to be subject to change.

The W3C received other push technology proposals in 1997, most notably the following:

- The Open Software Description Format (OSD), related to software distribution, was submitted in mid-August.
- The HTTP Distribution and Replication Protocol (DRP), a competitor to CDF, was submitted in late August.

The W3C held a Push Technology Workshop in September 1997, at which these proposals were discussed. The W3C recognized that the proposals shared common themes: the use of channels, the use of metadata, and multicasting over the IP protocol, among others. The results from the proposal submissions and the Workshop were:

- All the proposals were given W3C Note status.

- Subsequent W3C Metadata Activity would focus on a common framework approach to address the combined needs of all of the proponent groups, and to find a single, interoperable format that might ultimately increase the success of push technology.

W3C Notes were previously discussed in Chapter 9, with respect to the Visual Markup Language (VML). Recall that Notes are dated, public records of ideas, comments, or documents. They contain proposals for specifications and, as such, are published at the director's discretion. As the W3C states, a Note does not represent any commitment by the W3C to pursue work related to it. Neither does its Note status indicate any endorsement of its content, nor any present or future allocation of resources to the issues addressed by it.

Ultimately, the W3C Metadata Activity, illustrated in Figure 14-5, produced the Resource Description Framework Model and Syntax Specification (RDF), which provides a more general treatment of metadata, and which achieved W3C Recommendation status in February 1999. (An RDF Schema Specification became a W3C Recommendation later, in March 2000.)

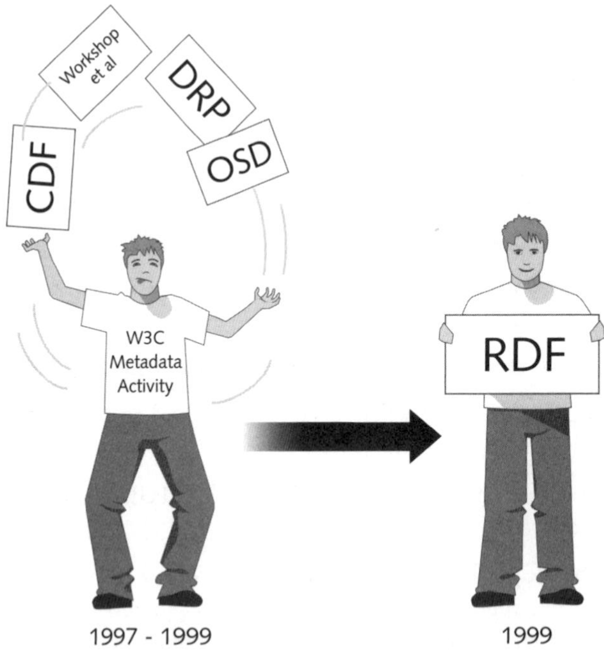

Figure 14-5 Evolution of RDF from CDF, et al

The CDF specification never attained W3C Recommendation status, despite Microsoft's continued development (more elements and attributes have been added to the set described in the original submission) and the popularity of Internet Explorer, which supports CDF and other XML languages. CDF remains a W3C Note, as shown in Figure 14-6.

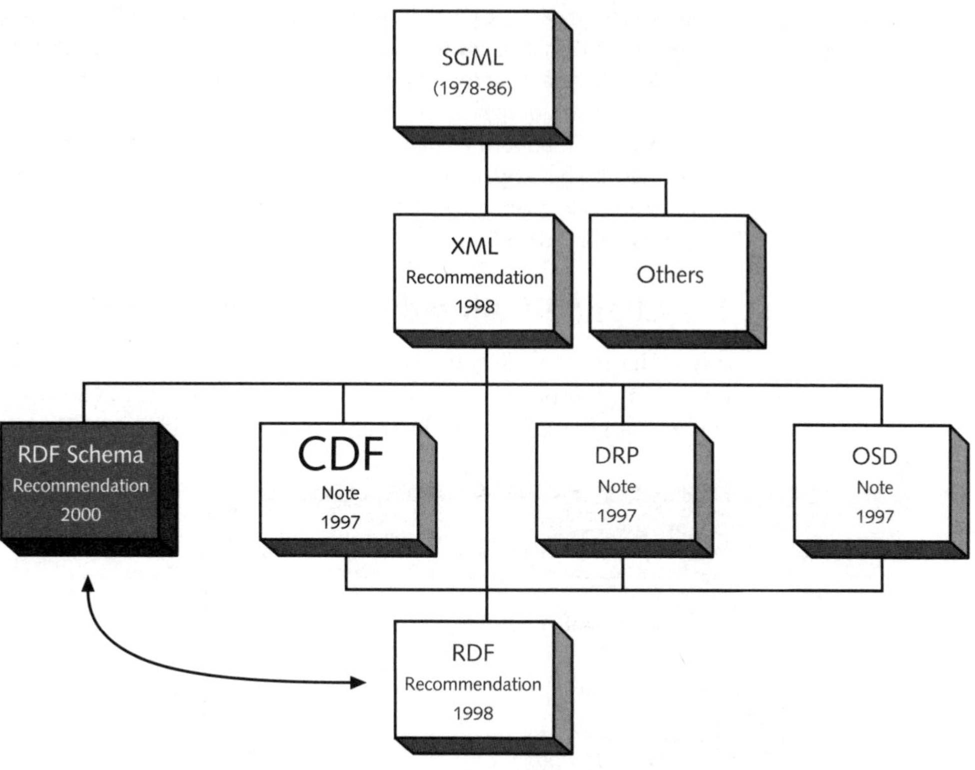

Figure 14-6 Relation of CDF and RDF to XML

The CDF Note was overtaken and passed by the development of RDF, in the same way that VML and its rivals were overtaken by Scalable Vector Graphics development. CDF is similar to RDF, but it is geared toward Microsoft Internet Explorer functionality.

The CDF specification is listed as an Acknowledged Member Submission at *www.w3.org/TR/*, among the other W3C Notes.

Using Channels

As a quick and practical introduction to channels, you can examine how to perform two simple procedures: investigating what channels are currently available to you in Microsoft Internet Explorer, and adding a channel to your list of channels.

The following sections describe procedures performed with Internet Explorer 5.5, the latest version of IE that clearly refers to channels by name. As this book goes to press, the latest available version of Internet Explorer is IE 6.0, which groups channels with Favorites, despite their differences, and no longer refers to them as channels. IE 6.0 still supports channels and CDF, but you manage channels as you do Favorites. If you upgrade to IE 6.0, it preserves any channels you have created. To create new channels with IE 6.0, refer to the following procedures and to the Help tools in IE 6.0.

Investigating the Channels Already Available to You

To discover which channels you can use, you can click Favorites on the Internet Explorer menu bar, and then point to Channels to open a submenu. Click a channel or point to a channel category to select a channel, as shown in Figure 14-7.

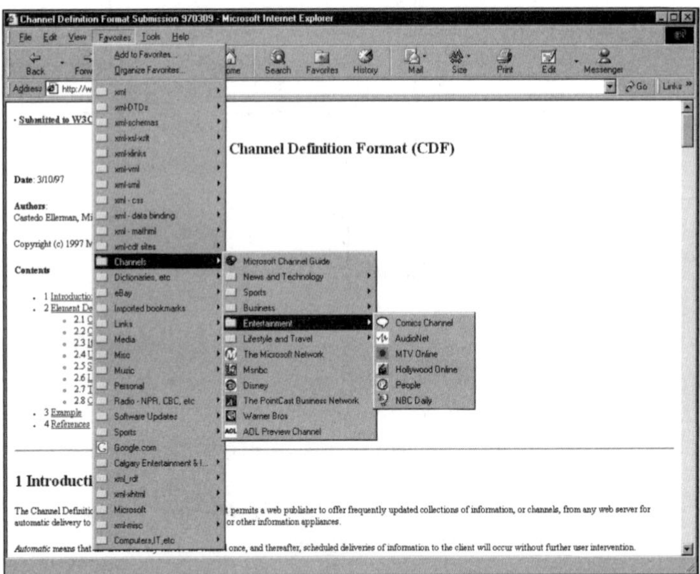

Figure 14-7 Investigating available channels—option 1

You can also use other methods to display the channels you can access. One way is to use the Favorites pane in Internet Explorer. To open the Favorites pane, you click View on the Internet Explorer menu bar, point to Explorer Bar, and then click Favorites, as shown in Figure 14-8.

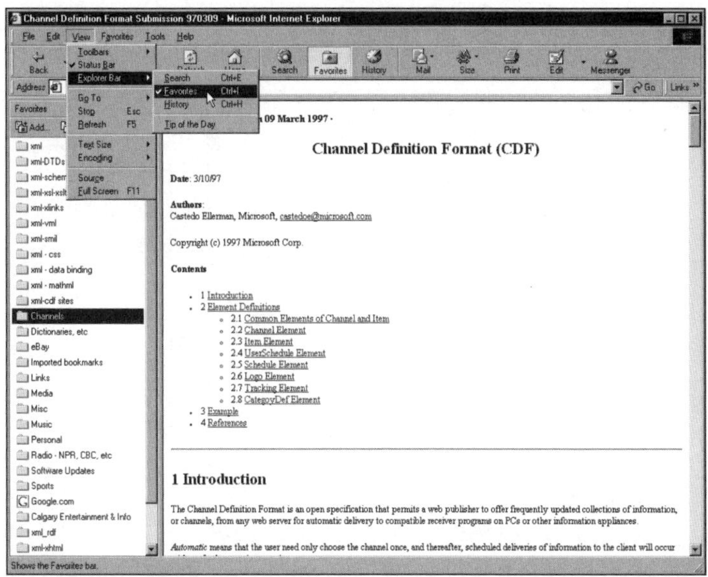

Figure 14-8 Investigating available channels—option 2

In the Favorites pane, or Channel bar (also called the Channels Explorer bar), you click Channels to display the channels available to you. Click the channel of your choice. You can also click the Favorites button on the Standard Buttons toolbar to open the Channel bar and access channels. To close the Channel bar, click its Close button.

No matter which method you use to investigate your channels, a typical result is shown in Figure 14-9.

Remember that a single channel can represent a single page, multiple pages, or the content of a whole Web site. Once you click your selected channel, at least one document from the corresponding Web site downloads to your system.

14

In addition to downloading channels on demand, you can also download them according to a schedule you specify. You also can configure the channels to download while you are online, so that you can view them later when you are offline.

Adding a Web Site to Your Channel List

Despite the similarity in terms, adding a channel is different from adding a Web page to your Favorites list. When you add a Web page as a Favorite, you simply add its URL as a shortcut to your browser to make it easy to access the page; Internet Explorer does not notify you of new content, nor does it regularly download information to your system. When you add a channel to the Channel bar, however, you usually add a reference to more than one document at the same Web site, enable your system to display the Web pages when you are offline, and set a schedule for updating those Web site pages.

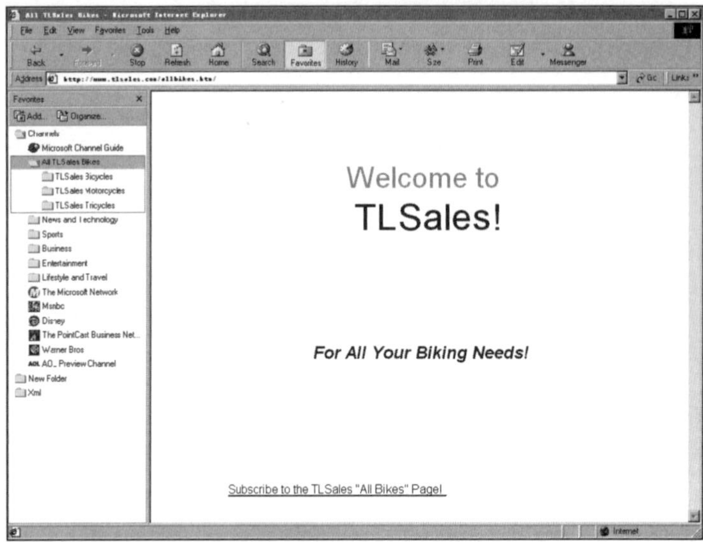

Figure 14-9 Typical channel browser

Adding a Web Site without CDF

Adding a new channel to your channel list when the Web site owner doesn't use CDF is more involved than if the Web site owner uses CDF. For example, suppose you want to create a channel for the Web site of the British Broadcasting Corporation (BBC). First, you access the BBC Web site, shown in Figure 14-10.

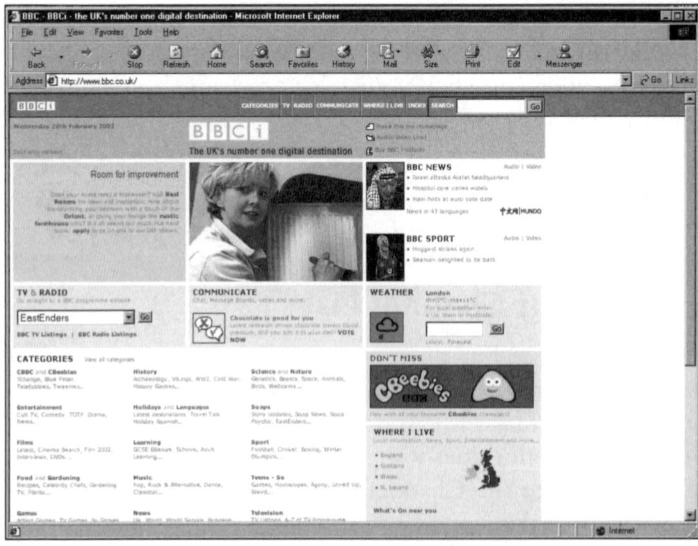

Figure 14-10 Initial BBC home page

Figure 14-11 depicts the next three steps. With a Web page open in your browser, you click Favorites on the menu bar, and then click Add to Favorites. When the Add Favorite dialog box opens, you can set the following options:

- *Make available offline*—Select this check box to make the channel available offline.
- *Name*—Enter a name for the channel, or accept the Web site's default name, such as "BBC - BBCi - the UK's number one digital destination."
- *Create in*—Select the favorites folder to which the channel should be added, such as News and Technologies.

In the third step, you set options for using the Web site offline by clicking the Customize button to start the Offline Favorite Wizard. You use this wizard to specify how much content you want to make available offline and to set a schedule for updating, or synchronizing, the offline pages with the pages on the Web site.

Figure 14-12 shows the next stage of the process. Click Next to open the next dialog box in the wizard, where you determine whether you want to download any pages linked to the current page. Click the Yes option button to do so. You can also set how many linked pages to download. Figure 14-12 shows that the "links to other pages" was chosen with a level of 2 (although that value was chosen here, if you are adding a news, sports, entertainment, or other channel with their numerous links, it is not recommended to go higher than 1). Click Next to configure a synchronization schedule. For example, you can update the pages every five days at 3:30 AM.

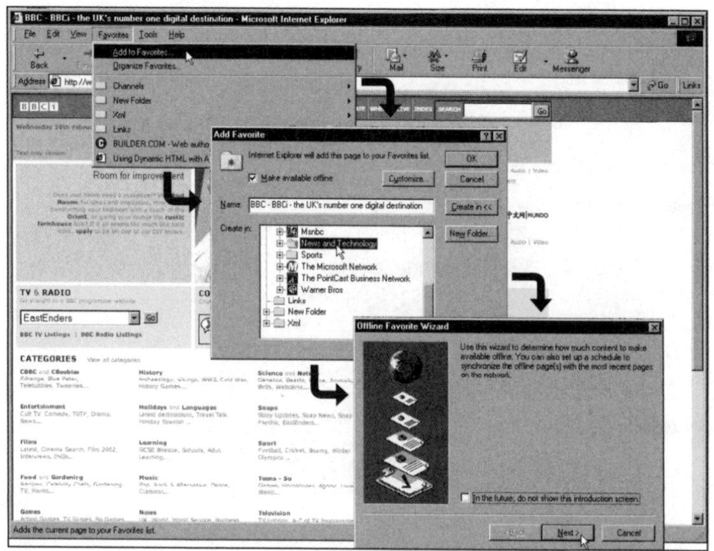

Figure 14-11 Adding a new channel without CDF—steps 1 to 3

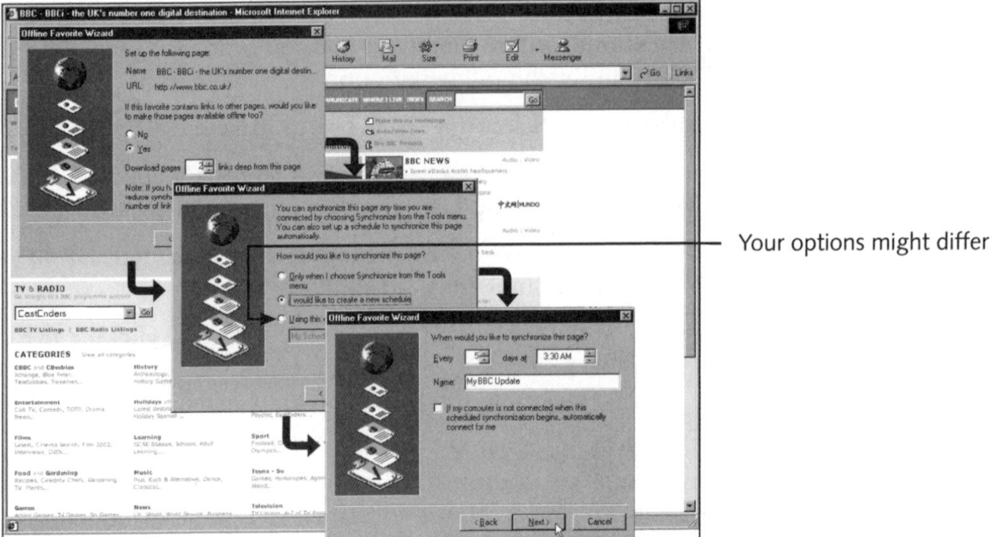

Figure 14-12 Adding a new channel without CDF—steps 4 to 6

The first step shown in Figure 14-13 follows immediately after the last step in Figure 14-12. At this point, you can enter authentication information, if necessary. If you click the No option button, you can click Finish to return to the Add Favorite dialog box. After you click OK, you can verify the name and location of the channel, and then the browser begins to synchronize for the first time.

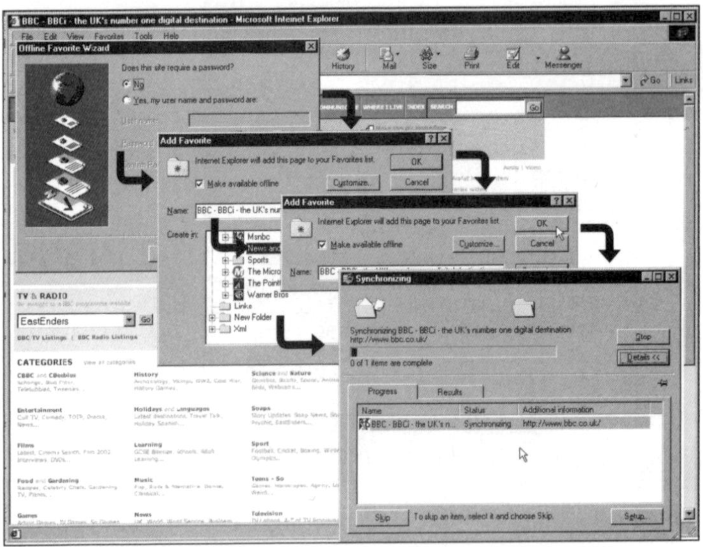

Figure 14-13 Adding a new channel without CDF—steps 7 to 10

Once you are notified that the synchronization is complete, you return to the Web page.

You can delete a channel later by removing it from the Favorites bar. To do so, highlight the name of the channel, right-click it, and then select Delete.

If you have used or added channels while using a previous version of Internet Explorer on the same system, those channels are still listed in the Channels folder in your Favorites list in the upgraded IE version.

Adding a Web Site Already Equipped with CDF

Adding a new channel to your Channel bar when the Web site owner uses CDF is less complicated than when the owner does not use CDF. For example, suppose you want to create a channel for the TLSales Web site. First, you access the TLSales home page, shown in Figure 14-14.

Figure 14-14 Initial TLSales home page, with CDF-related link

Assume that the "Subscribe to the TLSales "All Bikes" Page!" link comes from an <A> tag that refers to a CDF file. Just by clicking the link, you accomplish what it took several wizard and other dialog boxes to do in the previous section. If you click the link, Internet Explorer adds the TLSales home page to the Channel bar, as in Figure 14-15.

14

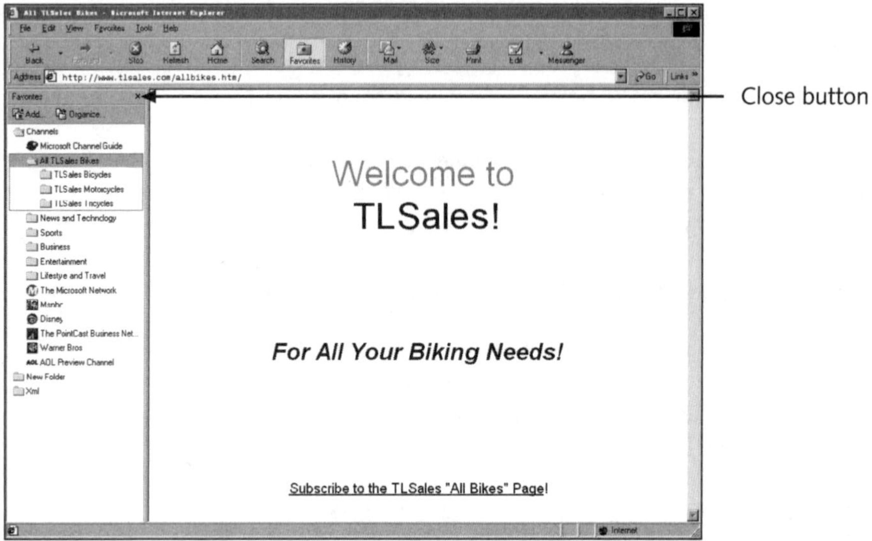

Figure 14-15 Adding new channel by clicking CDF-related link

Further, Internet Explorer also opens the Channel bar on the left. If you don't want the Channel bar to appear, click the Close button (i.e., click the X) in its upper-right corner.

When the Channel bar automatically appears on the left, it is not a frame. That sort of action is something that you might expect of frames on Web pages, but no frame has been created here. The Channel bar is simply a way of constantly displaying the Favorites, channels, and other links.

Making a Channel Available for Offline Viewing

Although the actual procedure was discussed in the previous section, when you elect to make a Web channel and its pages available for offline viewing, you allow the latest version of the channel to be downloaded to your hard disk, or synchronized, so you can access it and read its content when your computer is not connected to the Internet. That can facilitate entertainment or research, especially if you do not want to tie up a phone line by continually being online.

Although downloadable content depends on how the Web site manager has configured the Web site, you saw how you can specify how much content you want to download: from a single page to a page with all its links. You can also select synchronization frequency.

If it is your intent to view material offline, it is often best to manually synchronize the Web site to the channel prior to going offline. The first part of the procedure for doing so is shown in Figure 14-16. Click Tools on the Internet Explorer menu bar, and then click Synchronize. The Items to Synchronize dialog box appears. You select the Web channel(s) you wish to synchronize and either click the Synchronize button if you have already set the synchronization options, or click the Setup button to set the options. Figure 14-16 shows the process of setting the options.

In Figure 14-16, the new BBC channel reference appears alongside another item, a previously configured CNN channel item.

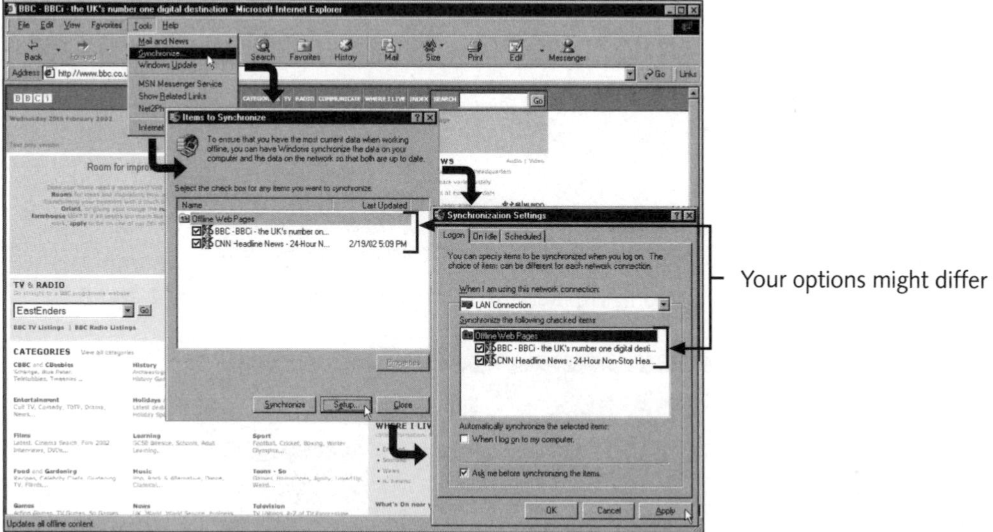

Figure 14-16 Synchronizing a channel for offline viewing—steps 1 to 3

In the next three synchronization dialog boxes shown in Figure 14-17, you log on, if necessary, change the schedule, and complete other setup tasks. Once the setup is finished, you return to the Items to Synchronize dialog box so you can select the items you want to synchronize, and then click the Synchronize button to initiate the synchronization process.

When the process is complete, you receive a Synchronization Complete notification message. At that point, you can shut down the browser, if you like. Later, you can work offline and still view the version of the channel that you just finished downloading.

Viewing a Channel Offline

In order to view your offline version of the channel, you start Internet Explorer and select its Work Offline command. Figure 14-18 shows you how to get started.

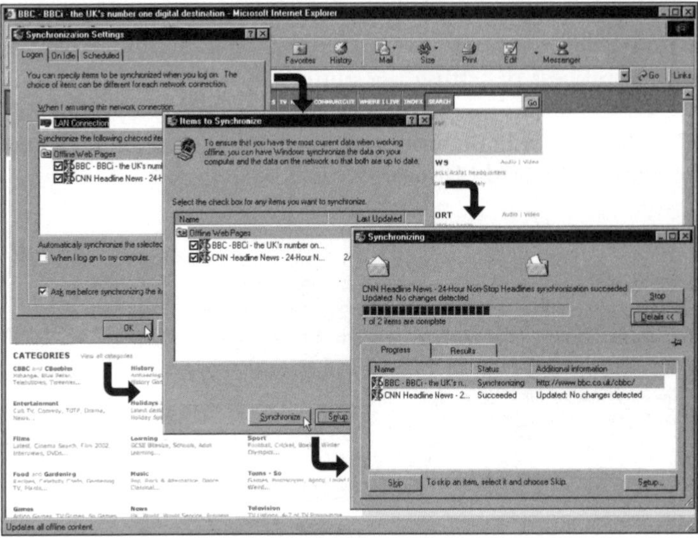

Figure 14-17 Synchronizing a channel for offline viewing—steps 4 and 5

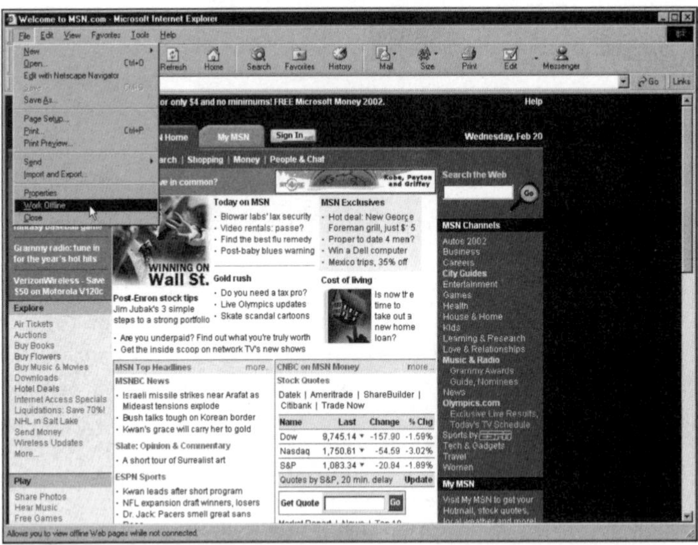

Figure 14-18 Viewing a channel offline—step 1

Click File on the menu bar, and then click Work Offline. Then, as shown in Figure 14-19, click Favorites on the menu bar, point to Channels, and then point to the folder in which you saved the channel when you subscribed to it, such as News and Technology.

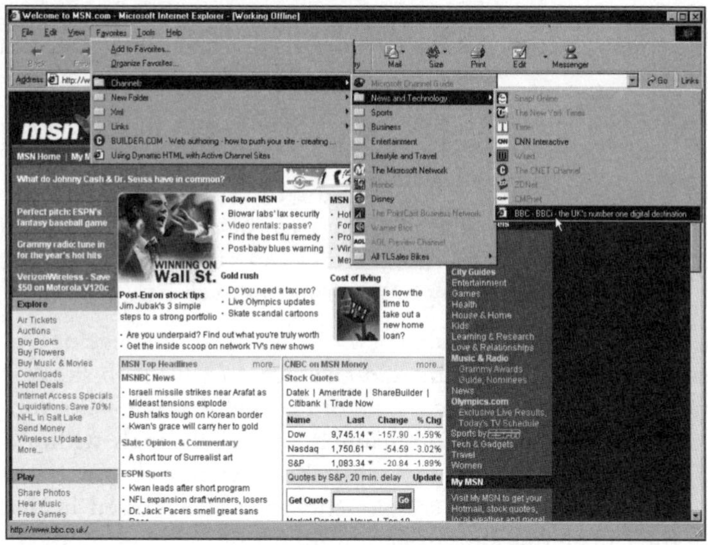

Figure 14-19 Viewing a channel offline—step 2

In the channel folder submenu, click the channel you want to view. The channel appears in the browser window. Depending on your configuration preferences and those of the Web site owner, you may have all, or only some of the linking functionality available to you.

Remember, now that you have selected the Work Offline feature in your browser, it maintains that setting until you switch it off manually, or until you try to access an online Web site, at which point the browser asks you whether you wish to go online.

In previous versions of Internet Explorer, "subscribing" only referred to the process that was used to configure offline viewing. In this chapter, subscribing refers to the act of an end user adding a new channel to their browser configuration, with no assumptions about online or offline viewing.

Creating a CDF Channel

As mentioned previously, a channel is one or more Web pages specified within a channel definition format file, which is an XML-related document that indexes those Web pages. The CDF file also enables end users to subscribe to a channel, and provides a means for a Web site developer to specify the titles, URLs, content, description, browser and desktop icons, some additional functionality (a screen saver, for example), user-traffic logging, and the creation of a schedule for updating and synchronization. CDF files are capable of housing more functions, such as authentication and other personalization features, but those are beyond the introductory scope of this text. These channel specifications listed above are stored in a CDF document, which is separate from their related Web pages, but usually linked to one of them.

So far, you have examined channels from a user's standpoint. In those examples, the channel content was downloaded on demand. The user has only to start the CDF file, usually by clicking a hyperlink such as a "Subscribe to this page" link to establish the channel in Internet Explorer. When activated, the page or pages that a channel is configured to represent are downloaded so that the user can view them without having to repeatedly request (or pull) the remaining pages from the Web site.

For the rest of the chapter, adopt the point of view of a Web site developer or content provider to see how to create, specify, and add channels to your Web site. You discover how you can create one CDF file for each type of channel that you want for your Web site, or how you can create hierarchies of channels and subchannels within one document. The CDF file can allow end users to subscribe to your Web site as a channel or also as a desktop component (desktop components are not discussed in detail in this chapter, because of their operating system ramifications).

If you intend to create channels, you complete the following general steps:

1. Design the channel.
2. If you want to use your own customized logo images instead of the default images, create the logo images now.
3. Create the CDF file.
4. Post the CDF file so that it is publicly accessible.
5. Offer the channel to the user community.

Design the Channel

When creating a Channel Definition Format file, the first and most important step is to determine the structure of the channel and its hierarchy of channels, items, and other functions. The channel can be designed to mirror the structure of an existing Web site, or it can be a subset of the Web site's content, but with a different hierarchy.

Figure 14-20 depicts a channel that does not contain all the documents found on its Web site. The CDF file is shown on top. Its top-level channel calls for one document, and its three items each call for one document. However, the middle of the figure shows a portion of the Web site file systems. The documents being used by the channel and its elements are shaded for illustration. Notice that, once the relevant documents have been specified in the CDF file, other documents remain. They are displayed on the Web site, but do not form part of the channel definition. The bottom of the figure shows a browser window belonging to a user who has subscribed to the channel. In the channel browser on the left, you can see how the channel and the items are referenced.

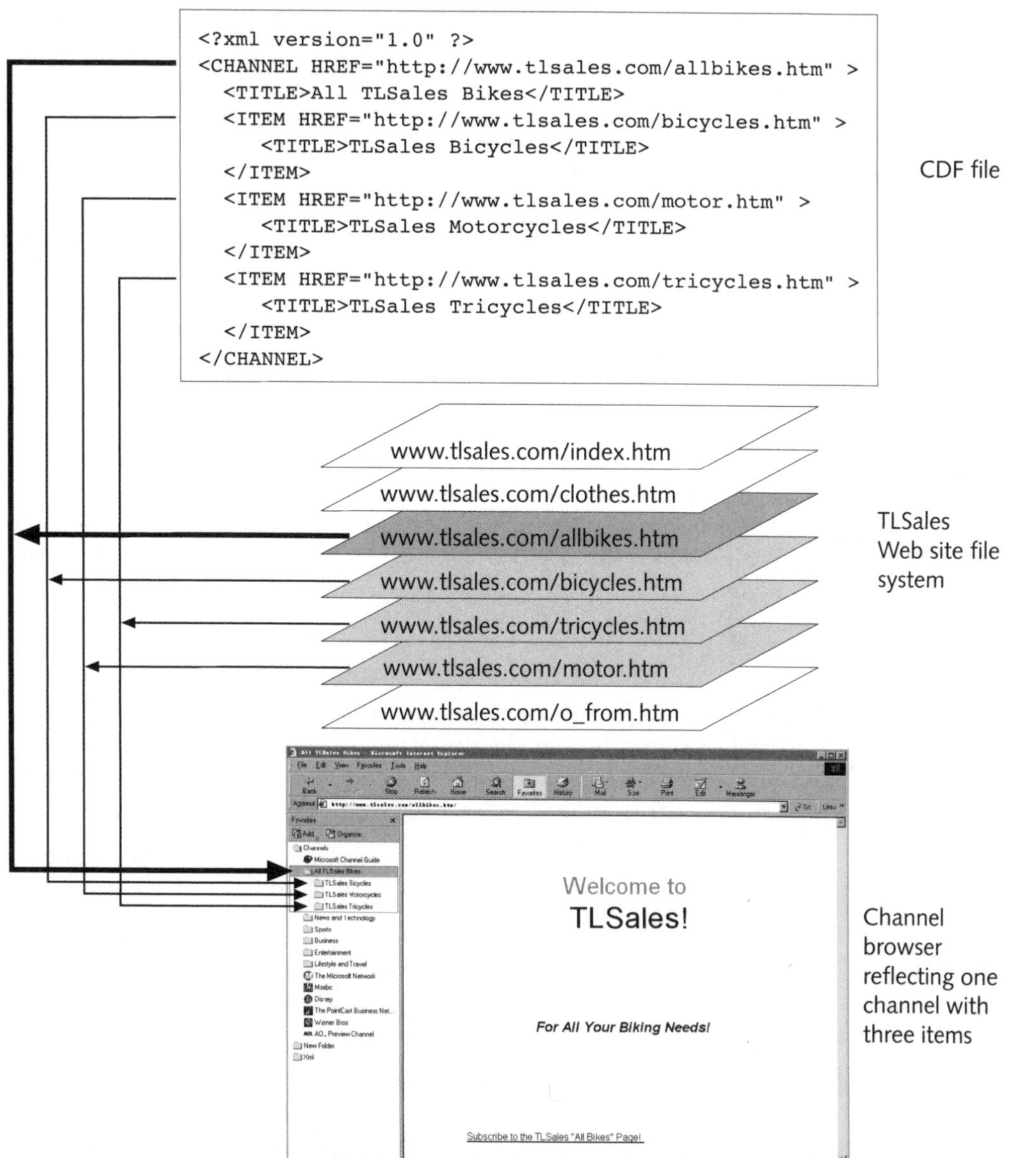
<?xml version="1.0" ?>
<CHANNEL HREF="http://www.tlsales.com/allbikes.htm" >
<TITLE>All TLSales Bikes</TITLE>
<ITEM HREF="http://www.tlsales.com/bicycles.htm" >
<TITLE>TLSales Bicycles</TITLE>
</ITEM>
<ITEM HREF="http://www.tlsales.com/motor.htm" >
<TITLE>TLSales Motorcycles</TITLE>
</ITEM>
<ITEM HREF="http://www.tlsales.com/tricycles.htm" >
<TITLE>TLSales Tricycles</TITLE>
</ITEM>
</CHANNEL>
CDF file
www.tlsales.com/index.htm
www.tlsales.com/clothes.htm
www.tlsales.com/allbikes.htm
www.tlsales.com/bicycles.htm
www.tlsales.com/tricycles.htm
www.tlsales.com/motor.htm
www.tlsales.com/o_from.htm
TLSales Web site file system
Welcome to
TLSales!
For All Your Biking Needs!
Subscribe to the TLSales "All Bikes" Page!
Channel browser reflecting one channel with three items

Figure 14-20 Channels need not contain all your Web site documents

The structure of the channel is created in the CDF file using one or more <channel> elements that represent the major segments, and usually more <item> elements that make up the hierarchy within the <channel> element(s). To prevent users from being overwhelmed with information and images, to provide a uniform design among channels, and to conserve bandwidth and minimize download delays, observe the following guidelines:

- Microsoft recommends that a channel should have no more than eight subitems in the first level.
- As a channel publisher, you should provide all the logo images to be used with the channels and items. In later versions of Microsoft IE, default logos are provided, as you see later in the chapter. But, default logos should be replaced by logos more appropriate to the Web site and channel.

Even though the CDF document in Figure 14-20 doesn't show one, consider inserting a <schedule> element in the file, so that as the Web site owner, you maintain control over updates and synchronization.

For additional information, see the discussion of the <channel>, <item>, and <schedule> elements, as well as the explanation of the sample CDF file, later in this chapter. Also, consult the Microsoft Developers Network library and search for "CDF."

Create the Logo Images

You can place various icon images in several locations in the channel's user interface (that is, in the Channel bar, in the Favorites or Channels menus, and on the Active Desktop). However, to do so, you must observe Microsoft's strict dimension and other requirements. For instance, here are the dimensions you must observe:

- In the Active Desktop Channel bar, the icon images must be displayed at 32 pixels high by 80 pixels wide (i.e., 32H × 80W).
- In the Channel bar, the images must be 32H × 194W. Microsoft Internet Explorer 4.0 was the first to allow logos to be displayed in the Channel bar. Logos were allowed in the Favorites/Channel bar with Internet Explorer 5 and later.
- Icons for items must be 16H × 16W.

For more information, refer to the article "Creating Active Channel Logo Images" at *msdn.microsoft.com/workshop/delivery/channel/tutorials/images.asp* to investigate all the requirements.

With respect to logos for channels and items, you should be prepared to create and provide the appropriate images. However, Internet Explorer 4.0 and later provide default images wherever necessary.

Create the CDF File

Once you have examined the channel hierarchy and created the logo images, you can begin work on the CDF file. Creating the file is discussed later in this chapter. Remember, however, that the CDF file, because CDF is related to XML, is subject to the stringent XML vocabulary and structure rules.

Post the CDF File to Your Web Server

After creating the CDF file, you handle it like any other Web entity. Post it to the appropriate Web site. That is, place it in the defined limits of the document root directory on the Web site's HTTP server. If in doubt, consult your system and security administrator(s).

Provide Access to the Channel

Finally, as a Web site developer, you have to consider how your users can access the channel. One way to start the channel subscription process is by inserting an HREF attribute whose value is the location of the CDF file, in the start tag of an <A> element which, in turn, is nested within the <BODY> element. This is illustrated in Figure 14-21.

Nesting the <A> element within the <BODY> element in the HTML document is preferred, although some suggest putting it in the <HEAD> element.

For better functionality, Microsoft suggests that your HTML page should include the Add Active Channel or Add to Active Desktop logo buttons. That means, of course, that you would also have to store the following button logos with your other images and make them accessible to the page(s):

and/or

To use these buttons, you must agree to the terms of the Active Channel Logo Agreement. Then you have to place JavaScript elements in the <HEAD> element plus add other specific HTML coding in the <BODY> element. When users click these buttons, they provide a more visible, consistent, and easily recognizable method for adding Active Channel sites and Active Desktop items. They also perform the proper behavior in any browser.

For further information regarding these buttons and how to install them, visit *msdn.microsoft.com/workshop/delivery/cdf/tutorials/generic.asp*.

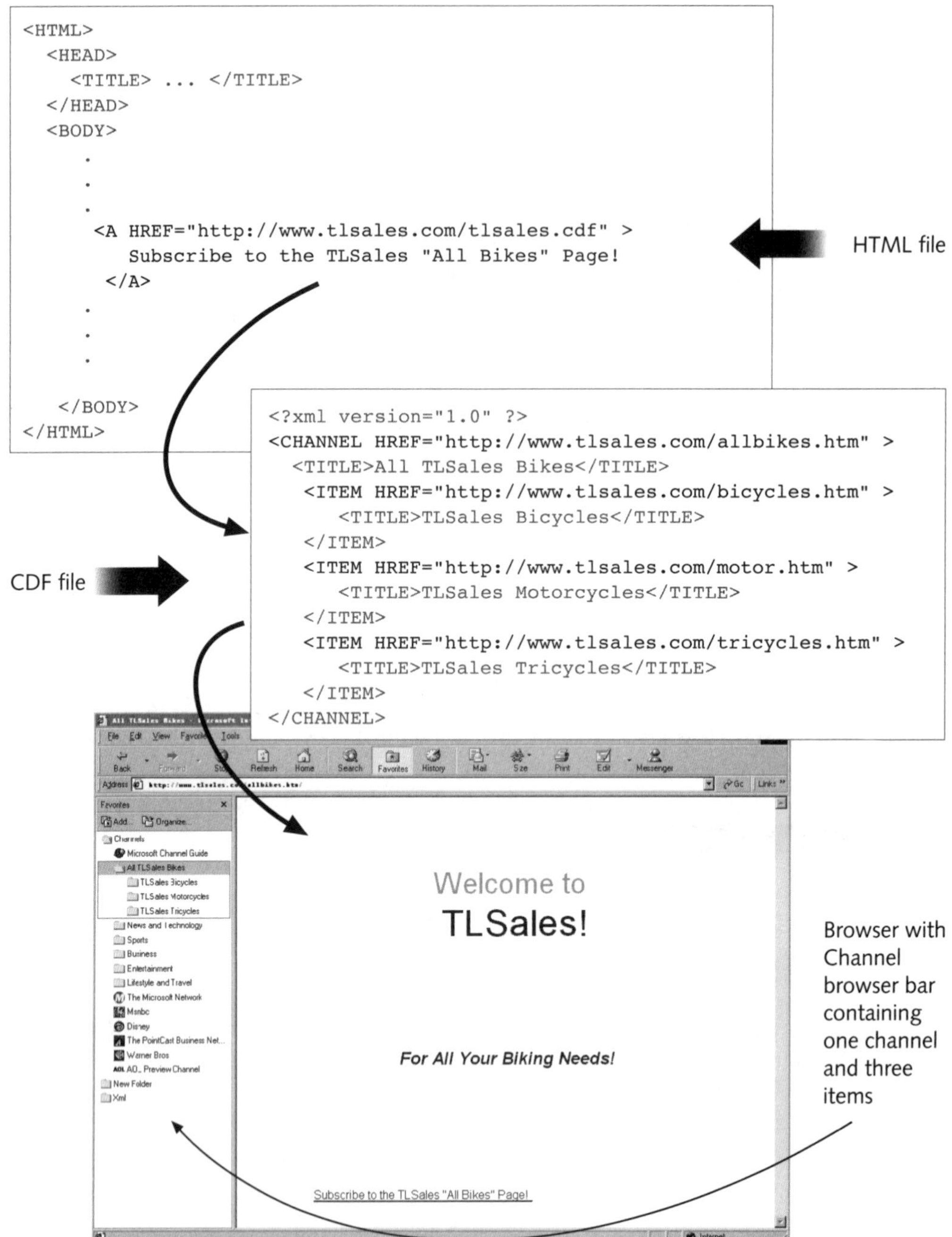
<HTML>
<HEAD>
<TITLE> ... </TITLE>
</HEAD>
<BODY>
<A HREF="http://www.tlsales.com/tlsales.cdf" >
Subscribe to the TLSales "All Bikes" Page!
</A>
</BODY>
</HTML>
HTML file
<?xml version="1.0" ?>
<CHANNEL HREF="http://www.tlsales.com/allbikes.htm" >
<TITLE>All TLSales Bikes</TITLE>
<ITEM HREF="http://www.tlsales.com/bicycles.htm" >
<TITLE>TLSales Bicycles</TITLE>
</ITEM>
<ITEM HREF="http://www.tlsales.com/motor.htm" >
<TITLE>TLSales Motorcycles</TITLE>
</ITEM>
<ITEM HREF="http://www.tlsales.com/tricycles.htm" >
<TITLE>TLSales Tricycles</TITLE>
</ITEM>
</CHANNEL>
CDF file
Welcome to
TLSales!
For All Your Biking Needs!
Subscribe to the TLSales "All Bikes" Page!
Browser with Channel browser bar containing one channel and three items

Figure 14-21 CDF file is referenced from <A> element in HTML document

Now that the general procedure has been briefly discussed, you can focus on the details of creating a CDF file.

CREATING A CDF FILE

Because CDF files are related to XML, they resemble XML and HTML. CDF files contain a prolog and a root element called <channel>. The other elements in the CDF file are nested within that top-level <channel> element.

The code examples in this chapter range from using HTML syntax, where elements and attributes are uppercase, to XHTML syntax, where they are lowercase. Meanwhile, the W3C's CDF Note contains elements and attributes of mixed case. Feel free to adopt any convention as long as you are consistent. However, the authors suggest the XHTML syntax.

The Prolog

It is mandatory to include a prolog in a CDF document. The prolog could be as simple as a one-line XML declaration or it could contain the XML declaration, a document type declaration, and one or more comments. The document type declaration may also contain a reference to an XML DTD or schema.

The <channel> Element: Root Element and Channel Identifier

The <channel> element performs two duties in a CDF document. First, a <channel> element forms the top-level element of the body of the document, and immediately follows the prolog. Second, each channel definition must be contained within a <channel> element; that is, the full definition of the channel—the channel title, description, and schedule information—plus its associated items must fall between <channel> start and end tags.

Further, one CDF document can contain one or more channel definitions. If a CDF document contains more than one channel definition, then each channel definition must be enclosed within its own <channel> element. Channels nested within other channels are called subchannels and are subordinate to the channel in which they are nested. They are also displayed in a position subordinate to their higher-level channel. Channel elements contained within higher-level <channel> elements can create a hierarchy of channel items. Thus, each top-level <channel> element in a CDF document has no parent element, but each subchannel <channel> element has a <channel> element as a parent.

A <channel>'s child element can be one of two varieties:

- The type that can occur a maximum of one time only, such as <A>, <abstract>, <log>, <login>, <logo>, <logtarget>, <schedule>, and <title>
- The type that can occur one or more times, such as <channel>, <item>, and <softpkg>

Figure 14-22 illustrates the syntax and hierarchical structure for two different scenarios. The simplified CDF document on top contains one top-level channel that contains two <item> elements. The CDF document on the bottom contains one top-level channel that, in turn, contains two subchannels. The first subchannel contains two items; the second contains only one.

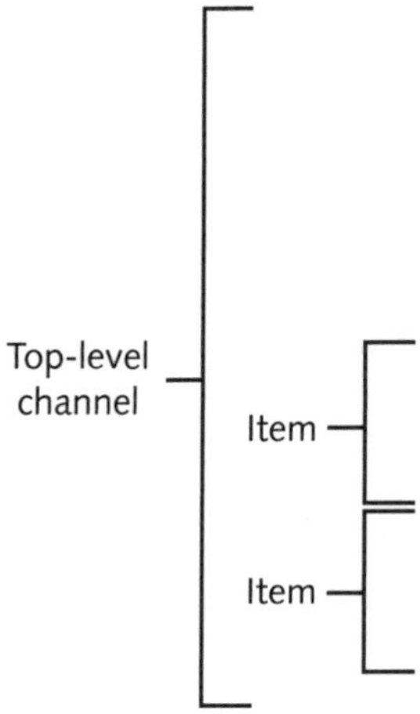

Top-level channel
Item
Item

```
<?xml version="1.0"?>
<!DOCTYPE Channel SYSTEM "http://www.TLSales.com/dtds/cdf_sample.dtd" >
<!-- Comment - Example CDF Document -->
<channel HREF=" ... " BASE=" ... " >
  <title> ... </title>
  <abstract> ... </abstract>
  <logo HREF=" ... " STYLE=" ... " />
  <logo HREF=" ... " STYLE=" ... " />
  <schedule STARTDATE=" ...  >
    <intervaltime ... />
    <earliesttime ... />
    <latesttime ... />
  </schedule>
  <item HREF=" ... " >
     <logo HREF=" ... " STYLE=" ... " />
     <title> ... </title>
     <abstract> ... </abstract>
  </item>
  <item HREF=" ... " >
    <logo HREF=" ... " STYLE=" ... " />
    <title> ... </title>
    <abstract> ... </abstract>
  </item>
</channel>
```

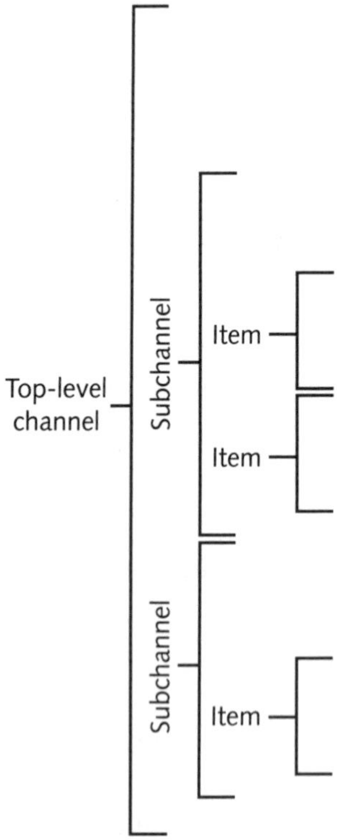

Top-level channel
Subchannel
Item
Item
Subchannel
Item

```
<?xml version="1.0"?>
<!DOCTYPE Channel SYSTEM "http://www.TLSales.com/dtds/cdf_sample.dtd" >
<!-- Comment - Example CDF Document -->
<channel>
  <logo HREF=" ... " STYLE=" ... " />
  <schedule STARTDATE=" ...  >
    <intervaltime ... />
    <earliesttime ... />
    <latesttime ... />
  </schedule>
  <channel HREF=" ... " BASE=" ... " >
    <title> ... </title>
    <abstract> ... </abstract>
    <logo HREF=" ... " STYLE=" ... " />
    <item HREF=" ... " >
       <logo HREF=" ... " STYLE=" ... " />
       <title> ... </title>
       <abstract> ... </abstract>
    </item>
    <item HREF=" ... " >
       <logo HREF=" ... " STYLE=" ... " />
       <title> ... </title>
       <abstract> ... </abstract>
    </item>
  </channel>
  <channel HREF=" ... " BASE=" ... " >
    <title> ... </title>
    <abstract> ... </abstract>
    <logo HREF=" ... " STYLE=" ... " />
    <logo HREF=" ... " STYLE=" ... " />
    <item HREF=" ... " >
       <logo HREF=" ... " STYLE=" ... " />
       <title> ... </title>
       <abstract> ... </abstract>
    </item>
  </channel>
</channel>
```

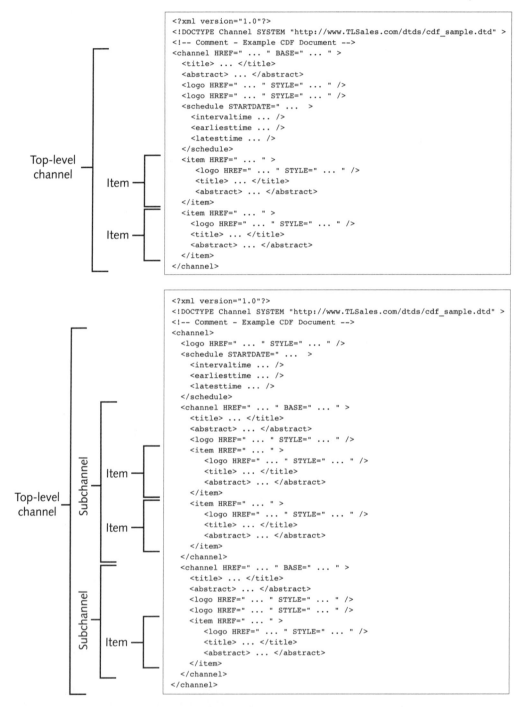

Figure 14-22 Two different CDF documents

Figure 14-23 depicts what you would see in the Internet Explorer Channel bar if you created a top-level channel called TLSales that contained three subchannels. Figure 14-23 also shows three items that would be displayed if you highlighted the subchannel called All TLSales Clothing.

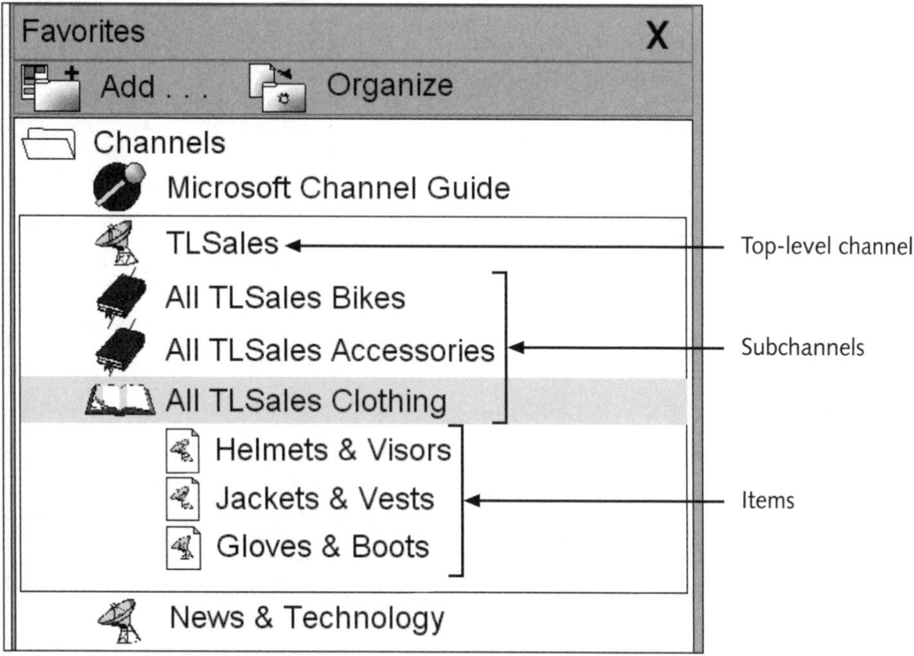

Figure 14-23 Top-level channel with three subchannels

<channel> Element Attributes

You can include several attributes in the start tag of a <channel> element. The first is the attribute called BASE, which specifies the base URL for the channel. It is an optional attribute that is used to resolve the subsequent relative URLs specified in <item> and <channel> elements contained within this channel. This means that the BASE attribute specifies the URL of the location where the channel's resources, such as document files, graphics, and audio files, are stored. Once you define the base URL, you can specify other URLs in the channel with respect to the base, using only the relative paths from the base. The BASE attribute then applies to all the child elements of the channel or subchannel in which it is specified. Thus, inheritance is downward only, not across to other sibling subchannels, nor upward to parent channels. In fact, if another BASE attribute has been specified in a parent channel, the presence of the BASE attribute in a subchannel of that parent channel supersedes the BASE value(s) previously defined within the parent <channel> element(s). When specifying the URL, ensure that it ends with a trailing "/", or the last word is removed and the path becomes inaccurate.

The next significant attribute is the optional HREF attribute, which also uses a URL as a value. It specifies which Web page is displayed in the browser when the channel is selected. Although HREF appears in the overwhelming number of examples presented in this chapter, it really *is* an optional attribute, because the same URL could also be specified in a child <A> element instead. If a BASE attribute specification has been specified in a parent element, it is inherited, and then the HREF need only be a relative path. If no BASE has been specified, the HREF URL has to be an absolute address.

If you use more than one mechanism to specify a URL for a channel and the URLs contradict one another, IE recognizes the URLs in the following order of precedence:

1. The HREF attribute found in the start tag of the <channel> element
2. The HREF attribute specified in the start tag of an <A> (i.e., anchor) element that has been inserted as an immediate child of the <channel> element, if one has been inserted

This means that as the CDF document author, you must be aware of these options and should be precise when you select a location of the HREF attribute. If you want to use an <A> element, the HREF specification should not appear in the parent <channel> element.

The next attribute is LASTMOD, which is also optional and provides the date and time, in terms of Greenwich Mean Time (GMT), that the page referenced by the HREF attribute was last modified. Thus, the LASTMOD date and time is not necessarily local time. This attribute allows the end user of the channel to determine whether the content has changed since the last time it was downloaded. The item is downloaded only if the date associated with the cached information is older than the LASTMOD value in the Channel Definition Format (CDF) file. The date format used in the LASTMOD attribute is *yyyy-mm-ddThh:mm*. Be sure to insert the capital T between the date and the time.

The optional attribute LEVEL specifies the number of levels (or links, if you prefer) deep that the client should "site crawl" and precache the HTML content from the URL specified in the HREF attribute. The default is zero, which means that the end user can only precache the data found at the URL specified in the <channel> along with any images it uses. If the URL contains frames, the client also retrieves all content inside the frames. By default, the maximum number of levels that can be specified for site crawling is three. Keep in mind the type of Web site you have here. If it has many links, even lower numbers can create excessive traffic and cause download times to be unacceptably long.

The optional PRECACHE attribute specifies whether content is downloaded. Values are: No, content is not downloaded into the cache, and the value of the LEVEL attribute is subsequently ignored; Yes, the default value, whereby content is downloaded only if the user has also specified that channel content should be downloaded; and a value actually called Default, which specifies that whatever the end user has specified is acceptable.

An optional SELF attribute can also be added to the top-level channel to indicate the location of the CDF file to use for creating a channel subscription. Note that this attribute is deprecated and unnecessary, so it is only supported by newer versions in case of backward compatibility.

All attribute values must be enclosed in quotation marks, even if the value is a number.

Other CDF Elements

This section describes several other elements and their associated attributes that are valuable when creating CDF files. Depending on your intentions for the CDF file, you include some elements and exclude others. Some CDF files, for example, may be geared toward the other types of Microsoft-related webcasting, such as Active Desktop items and Software Update Channels, which are not covered in this introductory chapter. The elements you insert also depend on the value you specify for the <usage> element. For each of these elements, the respective attributes and child elements are mentioned, along with other pertinent information.

For a complete list of other CDF elements, refer to the Web sites listed under "CDF References" near the end of this chapter. Examples of several of the following elements are presented later in this chapter, when a single CDF file is discussed.

<?XML ... ?>

Contrary to the belief of some who use CDF, <?XML...?> is not an element. It is the XML declaration that must appear on the first line of the CDF document. However, some refer to it as an element and use it like one in a CDF document.

<A>

14

The anchor element <A> defines the presence of a hyperlink. Its attribute is the mandatory HREF, whose value is the URL to be associated with the parent element. Its parent elements are <channel> and <item>, and it has no child elements.

The anchor element also plays a significant role in the HTML document that starts the CDF file to begin with. In the <BODY> element of the Web page, the CDF file is specified as the value of an HREF attribute in the (HTML-related) <A> element.

<abstract>

When the mouse pointer points to a <channel> or <item> title, Internet Explorer displays the content you specified for the <abstract> element text in a ScreenTip located in the Channel bar. Figure 14-24 illustrates the result of including an <abstract>-style element in an IE browser window, as the mouse pointer hovers over the Microsoft

Channel Guide channel. You see another example of an <abstract> element in the sample CDF file discussed later in this chapter.

Figure 14-24 ScreenTip resulting from <abstract> element

The <abstract>'s parent elements are <channel>, <implementation>, <item>, and <softpkg> (an element used for software updating via CDF file specifications). <abstract> is not allowed any child elements. <abstract> was once just an attribute of <channel>, but is now its own separate element. A significant attribute for <abstract> is the optional XML-SPACE, the value of which specifies how white space is to be treated in the ScreenTip. Possible values for XML-SPACE are: "Default", which permits white space to be filtered out during file processing; and "Preserve", which ensures all white space characters are retained.

<schedule>

The <schedule> element defines an update schedule by indicating, with the help of other related elements (to be discussed next), how often and during what time period its channel should be updated. The parent element of <schedule> is <channel>; its child elements are <start>, <end>, <intervaltime>, <earliesttime>, and <latesttime>.

<schedule> has three optional schedule-oriented attributes: STARTDATE (the date on which the schedule is to take effect; specified in yyyy-mm-dd), STOPDATE (the date on which the schedule is no longer in effect; also specified in yyyy-mm-dd), and TIMEZONE (specified as +/- zzzz, where the z is an offset from GMT in hhmm. For TIMEZONE—which, incidentally, impacts the child elements <earliesttime> and <latesttime>—the plus or minus sign indicates whether the time specified is ahead (+) or behind (-) GMT.

<intervaltime>

<intervaltime> specifies the length of time between channel updates. Its parent element is <schedule> and it has no child elements, although it is commonly coordinated with the sibling elements <earliesttime> and <latesttime>.

Its attributes are all optional and include DAY, a nonzero number specifying the day between updates; HOUR, a nonzero number based on a 24 hour clock, specifying the number of additional hours that one must wait before updating is allowed; and MIN, a nonzero number specifying the additional minutes that one must wait before updating is allowed. Thus, the effects of the attributes are additive. For example, examine the following code:

```
<intervaltime DAY="5" HOUR="7" MIN="30" />
```

This code means "the interval between updates will be 5 days, 7 hours, and 30 minutes".

<earliesttime>

<earliesttime> specifies the *beginning* of a valid range of time within which channel updates are allowed. Its parent element is <schedule> and it has no child elements.

Its attributes are all optional and include: DAY, a nonzero number specifying the day within the specified <intervaltime> that updates are allowed; HOUR, a nonzero number based on a 24-hour clock, specifying the first hour within the <intervaltime> during which updates can take place; and MIN, a nonzero number specifying the first minute within the <intervaltime> during which updates can take place.

<latesttime>

Similar to <earliesttime>, <latesttime> specifies the *end* of a valid range of time within which channel updates are allowed. Its parent element is also <schedule>, and it also has no child elements.

Its attributes are identical to those for <earliesttime>.

<item>

The versatile and powerful <item> element defines a channel item—an additional, often supplementary Web page document that forms a section of the channel. <item> elements allow you to populate a hierarchical structure and provide further choices of information to end users. By structuring the <channel> element properly with <item> elements—although the additional information might be limited—a balance should be struck between information provided and network traffic generated.

Ultimately, the items are each listed in the end user's Channel bars and Favorites menus. They appear along with their icons, as specified in their <logo> child elements, and in order according to the Web site owner's designed channel-item hierarchy.

<item> has only one parent element: <channel>. But, <item> has the following child elements: <A>, <abstract>, <channel>, <log>, <logo>, <title>, and <usage>. However, in any one <item> element, those child elements can only occur once.

The <item> element has four attributes. The first is HREF, which is mandatory (with one exception) and specifies the URL for the Web page accessed by the item. The only exception is when a child <A> element is nested within the <item> element that contains the URL. If traffic logging is desired, the URL cannot contain more than 255 characters. (If this limitation causes a problem, consider adjusting the <channel> element's BASE attribute.)

The next important attribute for <item> is the optional LASTMOD. Similar to its role with <channel>, this attribute specifies the last date and time, in terms of GMT, that the file specified by the HREF attribute was modified. Similar to <channel>, this affects whether the URL referenced by the HREF attribute is downloaded. Again, the format for the LASTMOD specification is *yyyy-mm-ddThh-mm*.

The next attribute is the optional LEVEL, which specifies the number of levels (or links) deep that a client should site crawl to obtain and precache Web site content from the specified URL. The default is zero, which specifies that the client browser can precache only the page specified by the URL *and* the images it references, but no linked documents. However, if the URL contains frames, the client may also retrieve the content in those frames.

The last <item> element attribute is the optional PRECACHE, which specifies whether content is downloaded. Like the <channel> element discussed previously, the available values are No, meaning content is not downloaded into the cache, and the value of the LEVEL attribute is ignored; Yes, the default value, meaning content is downloaded only if the user has also specified that channel content should be downloaded; and a value called Default, meaning that whatever the end user has specified is acceptable.

If you want to prevent an item from appearing in a Channel bar, such as when you want the item to be downloaded and used as a link from another page, include a <usage> element as a child element of the <item> element, and then insert the VALUE attribute in the <usage> element's start tag and specify a value of "none" for the VALUE attribute.

Several <item> elements are discussed with respect to the sample CDF file dissected near the end of this chapter.

The <item> and <usage> elements can also be used to define an HTML page as an Active Desktop item and to define a Web page as a screen saver. For more information, consult the CDF References listed near the end of this chapter.

<title>

The <title> element specifies a text string that eventually appears as the title of its respective <channel>, <item>, or <softpkg> element. Use of <title> is fairly straightforward; the only cautions are those against improper coding of special characters and the treatment of white space, such as spaces, tabs, or blank lines.

As mentioned earlier, the parent elements are <channel>, <item>, and <softpkg>. <title> does not have any child elements. However, it has the one optional, white space-related attribute XML-SPACE, the possible values of which are Default, which specifies to the parser that white space doesn't matter, and Preserve, which specifies that the white space should be preserved during processing and display.

When used as an attribute of a parent element, the value specified for the XML-SPACE attribute applies to all child elements unless it is specifically overridden with a different XML-SPACE attribute.

When applied to the top-level <channel> element, the <title> element should appear near the top of the CDF file, before any <item> elements or nested <channel> elements are inserted.

<logo>

The <logo> element specifies the image used to represent the respective <channel>, <item>, and <softpkg> elements. Those are its parent elements; it does not have child elements.

The <logo> element has two required attributes: HREF and STYLE. The value specified for HREF is the URL of the image file. There are three possible values for the STYLE attribute: icon, image-wide, and image.

When the value "icon" is specified for the STYLE attribute value for a <channel> element, the image specified by the HREF URL appears in the Favorites menu and Channel bar in the browser, and is 16-pixels high by 16-pixels wide. See Figure 14-25, which illustrates the syntax for the <logo> element as well as the effect on the Favorites menu and Channel bar.

If the value "image-wide" is specified for the STYLE attribute, the image appears in the Channel bar and is 32-pixels high by 194-pixels wide. This is also illustrated in Figure 14-25.

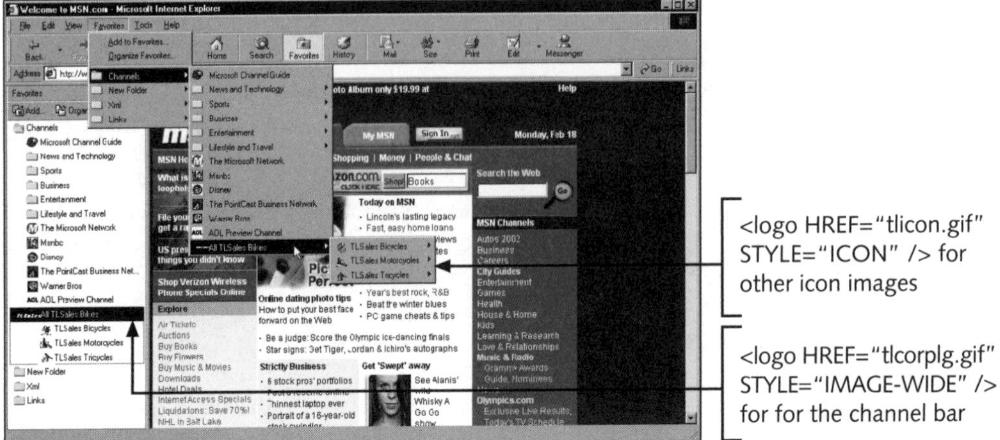

Figure 14-25 Image-wide and Icon-style logo's

If the value "image" is specified for STYLE, the image appears in the Active Desktop channel bar, is 32-pixels high by 80-pixels wide, and appears to pop up when the mouse pointer passes over it. Figure 14-26 illustrates the syntax and the effect.

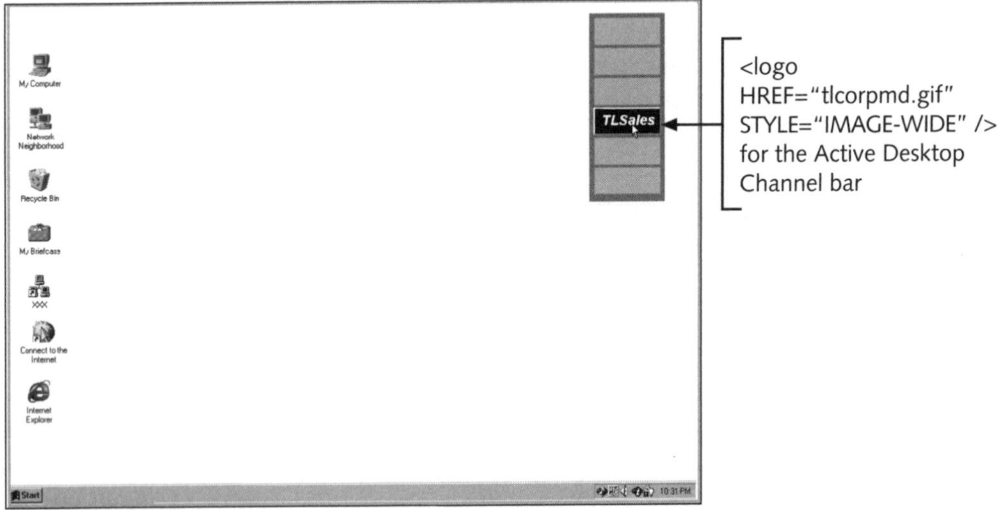

Figure 14-26 IMAGE-style logo on Active Desktop

GIF, JPEG, and other standard graphic image formats are supported for logo images. However, animated GIF files are not supported with the <logo> element. Be aware that image formats and styles are subject to change.

The top-level <channel> element should include three <logo> child elements, one for each type of style attribute, as follows:

```
<CHANNEL HREF="http://sample.microsoft.com/
    mainchannel.htm">
<!-- For the Browser Channel Bar -->
   <LOGO HREF="tlcorplg.gif" STYLE="IMAGE-WIDE"/>
<!-- For the Channels/Favorites Explorer Bar -->
   <LOGO HREF="tlcorpmd.gif" STYLE="IMAGE"/>
<!-- For the Active Desktop Channel Bar -->
   <LOGO HREF="tlicon.gif" STYLE="ICON"/>
  .
  .
  .
</CHANNEL>
```

Many users can install Active Desktop on their system. So it is recommended that the STYLE="icon" attribute/value pair be included in the top-level <channel> element. The channel then appears on the desktop in the appropriate location. Other Active Desktop considerations are beyond the scope of this chapter.

All other <channel> and <item> elements in the CDF file should include only one <logo> element, and the value specified for the STYLE attribute should be "icon".

Microsoft provides other advice regarding <logo> specifications. For more information, see the article "Creating Active Channel Logo Images" at *msdn.microsoft.com/workshop/delivery/channel/tutorials/images.asp*.

<log>

14

If you want to monitor the number of times a page is accessed on your site (called page-hit traffic), you can use a <log> element to log information about both online and offline hits to an item within a channel. Each time the <log> element's parent <item>'s URL is viewed by the end user, its URL is recorded in the page-hit log file. If you want to monitor traffic to more than one URL, you must insert a <log> element into each <item> element.

If you *do* log this information, be aware that large log files can quickly result, especially if the URL specified in the <item> element is popular. Include a <log> element in only those <item> elements for which you need to track traffic.

The <log> element's only parent element is <item> and it has no child elements. Once you specify <log>, you must include its VALUE attribute and specify the value "document:view" for it. (That is the only value supported by IE.)

Only items in the same domain as the Channel Definition Format file can be logged. For example, only items in *www.tlsales.com* can be logged by the tlsales.com developers; they can't log traffic in anyone else's domain or Web site. This prevents one provider from tracking the client's use of other provider's sites.

<logtarget>

Once you decide to log page hits, use the <logtarget> element to specify where you want the log information sent. <logtarget> specifies the URL of the log file to which the information, which is really just the URL of the parent <item> element every time it is accessed, should be recorded. Again, be aware that this activity can produce large log files quickly.

<logtarget>'s only parent is the <channel> element, but it can have two child elements: <http-equiv> and <purgetime>. Each of those, however, can only occur once per channel. <logtarget> has two mandatory attributes, HREF and METHOD, and one optional attribute: SCOPE. The value of HREF is a URL that specifies where the log information is to be sent. The values for METHOD are either "POST" or "PUT", two different methods of storing data depending on what additional processing the data is expected to undergo.

The values for the optional SCOPE attribute are "offline" (meaning that traffic to those pages downloaded to the system during a synchronization and then read from the local cache during offline work are to be logged), "online" (meaning that offline work traffic is to be ignored, but online work traffic is to be logged),) or "all" (hits from both online and offline work are to be logged).

The log file is stored in the user's local cache in the %userprofile%\history\log folder. This file is cleared after it is successfully posted to the HTTP server during the Channel Definition Format update. That's why offline logging can take place and the data can eventually reach the Web site. The log information is in the form of a record of URLs.

In any CDF file, the <logtarget> element must occur before any <item> elements.

Similar to the stipulation for the <log> element, the <logtarget> element's domain must be the same as the CDF file's domain. The log file can only be sent back to the domain that served the channel. This is to prevent providers from tracking the client's use of other provider's sites.

<http-equiv>

This element is one that supplies information to the parser using HTTP response headers as the transmission medium. As files are sent using the HTTP protocol through the

<logtarget> element, <http-equiv> indicates that an HTTP header parameter should be added, based on the information in the <http-equiv> element. The parent element of <http-equiv> is <logtarget> and <http-equiv> has no child elements. Once specified, <http-equiv> has two mandatory attributes: NAME, a string value which names the HTTP protocol header parameter sent with the traffic log file, and VALUE, a string value of the corresponding parameter.

Following is code the TLSales Web manager might use to specify how a compressed log file should be sent back to the TLSales Web site HTTP server:

```
<logtarget HREF="http://www.tlsales.com/traf_log/"
     METHOD="POST">
      <HTTP-EQUIV NAME="encoding-type" VALUE="gzip" />
</LOGTARGET>
```

<purgetime>

The <purgetime> element specifies the maximum age of valid page hits when the log file is being uploaded. This element indicates that the Web site owner has set an age or time limit on the data he trusts.

Usually, the <purgetime> and the <http-equiv> elements are nested within a <logtarget> element. In fact, <purgetime> is a child element of <logtarget>, but has no child elements of its own. The only attribute for <purgetime> is HOUR; its value must be a positive integer.

Recall that the log file is stored in the user's local cache in the %userprofile%\history\log folder. That file is cleared after it is successfully posted to the HTTP server during a Channel Definition Format update.

Here's an example:

```
<purgetime HOUR="36" />
```


This code means that as the traffic information is uploaded, any information older that 36 hours is purged.

<usage>

The <usage> element specifies how its parent element should be used. First, its parent elements are <item> and <softpkg>; it has no child elements of its own. It has one mandatory attribute, VALUE, which can have one of several values specified for it:

- *"Channel"*—This item appears in the browser channel pane. This is the default behavior when no <usage> element appears under an <item>.
- *"DesktopComponent"*—This item is displayed in a frame located on the Microsoft Active Desktop. Attributes assigned this value can only be used in the context of an Active Desktop item.

- *"Email"*—The parent element is an e-mail message that is sent when the channel content is updated (only one of these can be inserted per CDF document).
- *"NONE"*—This item does not appear in the Channel bar.
- *"ScreenSaver"*—This item is displayed in the special Microsoft Internet Explorer screen saver (one per CDF).
- *"SoftwareUpdate"*—Indicates that the CDF file is being used for an automatic Software Update channel. This value is only valid for the top-level channel.

Like the element <abstract>, the <usage> element deprecates an older attribute that used to appear in the start tag of a parent element. In this case, the <usage> element replaces the older SHOW attribute that used to be inserted in the <item> element. In other words, some older implementations of CDF clients look for a SHOW attribute instead of a <usage> child element inside the <item> element.

The sample CDF file that is presented and discussed later in this chapter includes as an example of <usage> the classic designation of an <item> element as a screen saver for an Active Desktop. Its code resembles the following:

```
<item HREF="tlscrn01.htm">
  <usage VALUE="ScreenSaver"></usage>
```

<login />

The declared empty element <login /> specifies that the channel requires authentication before the channel is subscribed to. This element is found within the top-level <channel> element, but has no child elements of its own, nor any attributes.

A Channel Definition Format file containing the <login /> element causes the end user to be prompted for a name and password during the channel subscription process. The actual authentication attempt is often validated against a separate third-party authentication, authorization, and accounting application.

No Official DTD for CDF

Recall that CDF has no public DTD or schema, as other XML-related languages often do. So Integrated Development Environments and other editors are not likely to be able to automatically validate CDF files.

However, if you want to check your CDF files for validation, declarations for the early elements and attributes are included in the original specification submission to the W3C, which can be found at *www.w3.org/TR/NOTE-CDFsubmit.html*. You can adopt those declarations into your own DTD file and add more of your own for your own custom elements or attributes.

Special Characters and Character Encoding

Recall from Chapters 2, 4, and 5 that when inserting content between an element's start and end tags, you must use a special code for special characters to prevent CDF parsing errors. Table 14-1 lists the five special characters for your review.

Table 14-1 Coding for special characters

Character to insert	Coding to use
< (i.e., "less than")	<
> (i.e., "greater than")	>
' (i.e., an apostrophe)	'
" (i.e., a double quotation mark)	"
& (i.e., an ampersand, to mean "and")	&

For example, in Figure 14-27, each of the three items within the subchannel called "All TLSales Clothing" contained ampersands in their text. Those items have been reproduced in Figure 14-27.

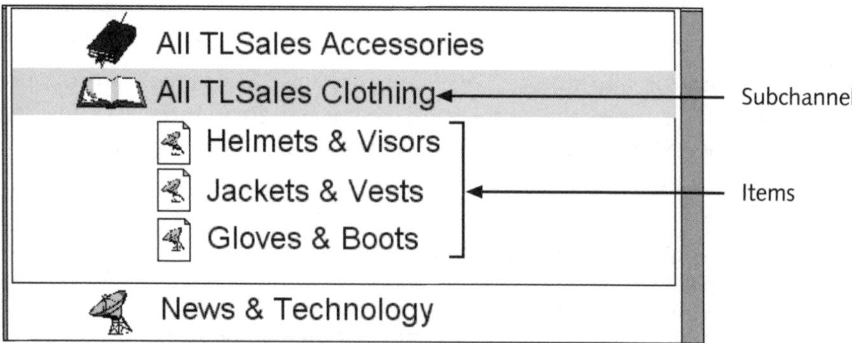

Figure 14-27 Special characters in <item> element data

Figure 14-28 illustrates the coding you must insert into the <title> elements of each respective <item> element so that the ampersand appears correctly and is not misinterpreted by the parser.

14

```
. . .

<channel HREF="http://www.tlsales.com/allclothing.htm" >
  <title>All TLSales Clothing</title>
  <item HREF="http://www.tlsales.com/helmets_visors.htm" >
     <title>Helmets &amp; Visors</title>
  </item>
  <item HREF="http://www.tlsales.com/jackets_vests.htm" >
     <title>TLSales Jackets &amp; Vests</title>
  </item>
  <item HREF="http://www.tlsales.com/gloves_boots.htm" >
     <title>TLSales Gloves &amp; Boots</title>
  </item>
</channel>

. . .
```

Figure 14-28 Coding for the special ampersand character

For a complete list of other named character set entities, see the documentation on Microsoft's HTML Character Set Web site at *msdn.microsoft.com/library/default.asp?url=/workshop/author/dhtml/reference/charsets/charsets.asp.*

The CDF specification also supports encoding for any ASCII character that uses the format &#nnn. For example, the ampersand characters in Figures 14-28 could also be encoded with the ASCII decimal value of 38; thus, you would encode the string & instead of & in the CDF document.

Sample CDF File and Description

Figure 14-29 illustrates a simple CDF file consisting of a top-level channel with two items and a subchannel with three items. A description of the coding in the file follows the figure.

Lines 1 through 3 of the sample file form its prolog. Line 1 is the mandatory XML declaration statement, which indicates that the current version of XML being utilized in the file is Version 1.0. Line 2 is the document type declaration statement. Normally, with a CDF, that statement is optional. However, in this case, it indicates the location of a validating DTD (perhaps it serves as a validity-related quality control check by the document developer). The comment statement, line 3, simply introduces the top-level <channel> element, which begins on line 4.

```
<?XML version="1.0" ?>
<!DOCTYPE Channels SYSTEM "http://www.TLSales.com/dtds/tl_cdf.dtd" >
<!-- Top-level channel - Corporate Info -->
<channel HREF="http://www.tlsales.com/channels/index.htm"
   BASE="http://www.tlsales.com/channels/"
   LASTMOD="2005-09-21T10:59:59" >
   <logo HREF="images/tlcorplg.gif" STYLE="IMAGE-WIDE"/>
   <logo HREF="images/tlcorpmd.gif" STYLE="IMAGE"/>
   <logo HREF="images/tlcorpicon.gif" STYLE="ICON"/>
   <title>TLSales Main Channel</title>
   <abstract>TLSales! For all your biking needs!</abstract>
<!-- Scheduling Updates -->
   <schedule  STARTDATE="2002-09-30" STOPDATE="2004-09-30">
      <intervaltime DAY="7" />
      <earliesttime HOUR="2" TIMEZONE="-0500" />
      <latesttime HOUR="4" TIMEZONE="-0500" />
   </schedule>
<!-- Storing Logs of End User Traffic -->
   <logtarget HREF="http://www.tlsales.com/cgi-bin/hitlog.cgi"
                                         METHOD="POST" SCOPE="All" />
   <purgetime HOUR="24" />
<!-- Item - Corporate Info -->
   <item HREF="corp/tlsales1.htm">
      <logo HREF="images/tls_sml1.gif" STYLE="ICON"/>
      <title>TLSales, Inc. Info</title>
      <abstract>This is TLSales!</abstract>
<!-- Logging End User Hits to the Corporate Info Page -->
   <log VALUE="document:view" />
   </item>
<!-- Item - Screensaver -->
   <item HREF="tlscrn01.htm">
      <usage VALUE="ScreenSaver"></usage>
   </item>
<!-- Subchannel - Product Info -->
   <channel HREF="products/tlprod01.htm" >
      <title>TLSales Products</title>
      <abstract>Looking for a new bike? We&apos;ve got them!</abstract>
      <logo HREF="images/tlsales_bikes_large.gif" STYLE="IMAGE-WIDE"/>
      <logo HREF="images/tlsales_bikes_medium.gif" STYLE="IMAGE"/>
      <logo HREF="images/tlbikes_icon.gif" STYLE="ICON"/>
<!-- Item - Bike Info -->
      <item HREF="products/bikes01.htm">
          <logo HREF="images/bike_sml.gif" STYLE="ICON"/>
          <title>TLSales Bikes!</title>
          <abstract>Have a look at our newest wheels!</abstract>
      </item>
<!-- Item - Accessory Info -->
      <item HREF="products/access01.htm">
    <logo HREF="images/acc_sml.gif" STYLE="ICON"/>
    <title>TLSales Accessories!</title>
    <abstract>Accessories for your bike and for you!</abstract>
  </item>
<!-- Item - Clothing Info -->
  <item HREF="products/clothz01.htm">
    <logo HREF="images/boot_sml.gif" STYLE="ICON"/>
    <title>Cycle Clothing!</title>
    <abstract>For biking and for &apos;apres-biking&apos;!</abstract>
  </item>
<!-- End of subchannel -->
 </channel>
<!-- End of Top-level channel -->
</channel>
```

Figure 14-29 Sample CDF file

The top-level <channel> element start tag appears on line 4. The value of its HREF attribute indicates that, when the top-level channel is downloaded, a copy of the Web site's home page (that is, a copy of its index.html document) is displayed. The value of the BASE attribute, on line 5, indicates that the Web site's channels directory is at the top of the file system hierarchy that houses the documents to be used by the channels and their respective items. Figure 14-30 illustrates the file directory structure of the Web site.

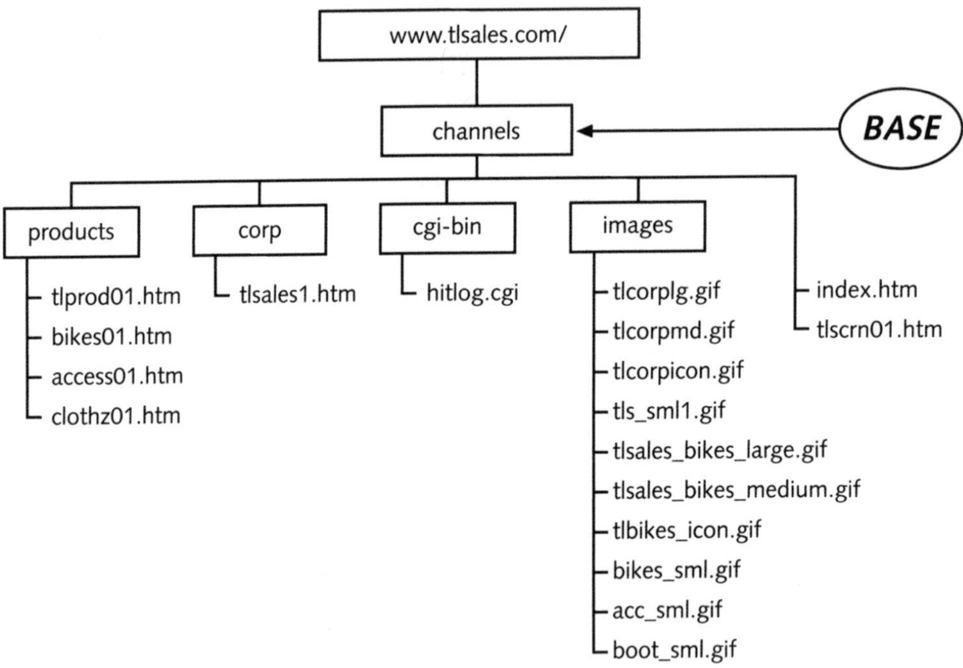

Figure 14-30 File directory for sample CDF file

The <channel> element's LASTMOD attribute, in line 6, indicates that this sample CDF file was last updated on September 21, 2005, just before 11 a.m.

The <logo> elements in lines 7 through 9, shown in Figure 14-31, address the locations of logos to be used when displaying the channel, and also the STYLE to use when displaying.

```
7.    <logo HREF="images/tlcorplg.gif" STYLE="IMAGE-WIDE"/>
8.    <logo HREF="images/tlcorpmd.gif" STYLE="IMAGE"/>
9.    <logo HREF="images/tlcorpicon.gif" STYLE="ICON"/>
```

Figure 14-31 Lines 7 through 9 of the sample CDF file

All three logo files are found within the BASE *channels* directory. The logo to be used for the style="IMAGE-WIDE" attribute value (that is, for the logo to be located in the channel browser bar to the right in Figure 14-25) is tlcorplg.gif. The one to be used for the ICON style (the one to be displayed in the Favorites menu, also shown in Figure 14-25) is tlicon.gif. If an end user has configured the Microsoft Active Desktop, then the tlcorpmd.gif would be displayed on it.

The <title> element on line 10 specifies the text "TLSales Main Channel" that is associated with this channel, and that is displayed in the browser's Channel bar and on the Favorites menu. The <abstract> element on line 11 defines the text string "TLSales! For all your biking needs!" that is displayed in a ScreenTip when the mouse pointer hovers over the channel. (Refer back to Figure 14-24.)

Lines 12 through 17, shown in Figure 14-32, define the channel's delivery schedule, which determines when the latest updated information is pushed to the subscriber systems.

```
12.  <!-- Scheduling Updates -->
13.      <schedule  STARTDATE="2005-09-30" STOPDATE="2007-09-30">
14.        <intervaltime DAY="7" />
15.        <earliesttime HOUR="2" TIMEZONE="-0500" />
16.        <latesttime HOUR="4" TIMEZONE="-0500" />
17.      </schedule>
```

Figure 14-32 Lines 12 through 17 of the sample CDF file

According to its STARTDATE and STOPDATE attributes, the schedule is effective from September 30, 2005, to the same date in 2007. Every seven days the channel information is to be updated (i.e., "pushed" to the subscribers), between 2 a.m. and 4 a.m. Eastern (North American) time, which is Greenwich Mean Time minus five hours, as shown in the TIMEZONE attribute.

Lines 18 through 20, shown in Figure 14-33, specify where any end user traffic log information is to be sent. Log information is gathered per item, not per channel, but the target is specified per channel. In this case, all (online and offline) user traffic log information is, at the time of a channel update, posted to a file named hitlog.cgi in the cgi-bin directory at the TLSales Web site. After it is posted, it is manipulated with CGI scripts.

```
18.  <!-- Storing Logs of End User Traffic -->
19.     <logtarget HREF="http://www.tlsales.com/cgi-bin/hitlog.cgi"
20.                                       METHOD="POST" SCOPE="All" />
21.     <purgetime HOUR="24" />
```

Figure 14-33 Lines 18 through 21 of the sample CDF file

Line 21's <purgetime> specifies that no user traffic information older than 24 hours should be sent to the target.

Lines 22 through 29, shown in Figure 14-34, define the first item within the top-level channel. When the item is displayed in the Channel bar or Favorites menu, the logo named tls_sml1.gif is displayed next to the title. When the mouse pointer hovers over the item, a ScreenTip with "This is TLSales!" appears.

```
22. <!-- Item - Corporate Info -->
23.     <item HREF="corp/tlsales1.htm">
24.        <logo HREF="images/tls_sml1.gif" STYLE="ICON"/>
25.        <title>TLSales, Inc. Info</title>
26.        <abstract>This is TLSales!</abstract>
27. <!-- Logging End User Hits to the Corporate Info Page -->
28.     <log VALUE="document:view" />
29.     </item>
```

Figure 14-34 Lines 22 through 29 of the sample CDF file

When selected, the Web page document named tlsales1.htm is displayed. This page contains information about TLSales, Inc. as a company, and not about their products. Information regarding the number of times an end user accesses this page is recorded. That information is eventually sent back to the Web site developer according to the specifications in lines 19 through 21 discussed previously.

Lines 30 through 33, shown in Figure 14-35, define another item under the top-level channel. This <item> element, when a value "ScreenSaver" is specified for its USAGE attribute, provides the end user with an opportunity to use the document specified as the value for the HREF attribute—namely, tlscrn01.htm—as a screen saver on their system.

```
30. <!-- Item - Screensaver -->
31.     <item HREF="tlscrn01.htm">
32.        <usage VALUE="ScreenSaver"></usage>
33.     </item>
```

Figure 14-35 Lines 30 through 33 of the sample CDF file

The subchannel, which provides access to TLSales products, is defined in lines 34 through 40, shown in Figure 14-36.

```
34. <!-- Subchannel - Product Info -->
35.     <channel HREF="products/tlprod01.htm" >
36.       <title>TLSales Products</title>
37.       <abstract>Looking for a new bike? We&apos;ve got them!</abstract>
38.       <logo HREF="images/tlsales_bikes_large.gif" STYLE="IMAGE-WIDE"/>
39.       <logo HREF="images/tlsales_bikes_medium.gif" STYLE="IMAGE"/>
40.       <logo HREF="images/tlbikes_icon.gif" STYLE="ICON"/>
```

Figure 14-36 Lines 34 through 40 of the sample CDF file

When the channel is selected, the tlprod01.htm, stored within the products directory within the BASE, is displayed. As indicated in the <title> element, the title of the channel is "TLSales Products".

The various logos, listed under their <logo> elements, are displayed according to the code in lines 7 through 9. Within the <abstract> element, note that "'" had to be used instead of the special apostrophe character in "We've got them!"

Figure 14-37 shows a Channel bar created from the sample code.

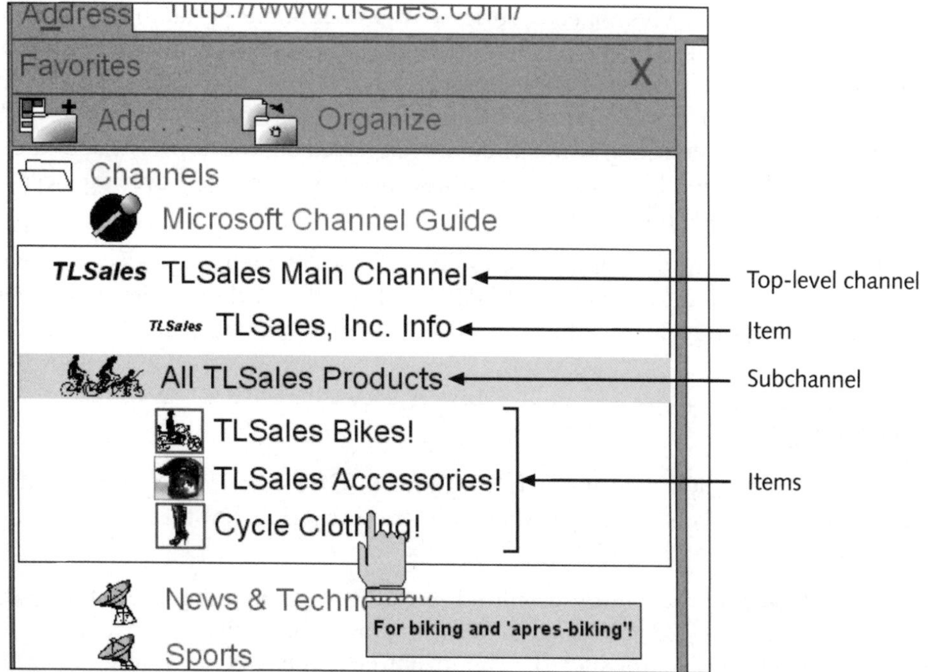

Figure 14-37 Inserting TLSales logos

Because the three items within the subchannel are so similar, they are discussed at one time. Lines 41 through 58 define the three items; those lines are illustrated in Figure 14-38.

```
41. <!-- Item - Bike Info -->
42.        <item HREF="products/bikes01.htm">
43.           <logo HREF="images/bike_sml.gif" STYLE="ICON"/>
44.           <title>TLSales Bikes!</title>
45.           <abstract>Have a look at our newest wheels!</abstract>
46.        </item>
47. <!-- Item - Accessory Info -->
48.        <item HREF="products/access01.htm">
49.      <logo HREF="images/acc_sml.gif" STYLE="ICON"/>
50.      <title>TLSales Accessories!</title>
51.      <abstract>Accessories for your bike and for you!</abstract>
52.    </item>
53. <!-- Item - Clothing Info -->
54.    <item HREF="products/clothz01.htm">
55.      <logo HREF="images/boot_sml.gif" STYLE="ICON"/>
56.      <title>Cycle Clothing!</title>
57.      <abstract>For biking and for &apos;apres-biking&apos;!</abstract>
58.     </item>
```

Figure 14-38 Lines 41 through 58 of the sample CDF file

The item elements, when selected, display Web documents pertaining to the three major product groups: bikes (products/bikes01.htm), accessories (products/access01.htm), and clothing (products/clothz01.htm), respectively. Each <item> element contains three child elements which address the respective logos that are displayed, the titles of the items when they are listed and when they are displayed in the browser, and the text that appears in the Tool Tips when the mouse pointer/cursor is hovering over the titles. Again, Figure 14-37 illustrates the result of this coding.

Finally, according to the comments on lines 57 and 59, the two </channel> end tags on lines 58 and 60 indicate the end of the subchannel and the top-level channel, respectively. At this point, the specification of the channels and their items is complete.

CDF Resources

This section lists and describes a few significant CDF resources. You can find others on the World Wide Web, including some very good tutorials, but these are the most fundamental to understanding CDF.

1. The Microsoft note submitted to the W3C, containing the CDF specification: *www.w3.org/TR/NOTE-CDFsubmit.html.* This is the site that also contains the DTD declarations for the significant elements and attributes.
2. Another W3C site, *www.w3.org/submission/1997/2/Overview.html*, contains a copy of the Microsoft submission of CDF to the W3C, and their request that the submission be adopted as a W3C standard.

3. CDF version 0.4, which is Microsoft's suggested revision to Channel Definition Format, is found at *msdn.microsoft.com/workshop/delivery/cdf/reference/channels.asp*. The Web site has a comprehensive list of elements for the various Microsoft CDF applications—Microsoft Active Channels, Microsoft Active Desktop items, and Software Update Channels.
4. A downloadable automatic CDF generator is available at *msdn.microsoft.com/downloads/samples/internet/default.asp?url=/Downloads/samples/Internet/browsertools/cdfgen/default.asp*. The Microsoft CDF Generator is an easy-to-use tool for creating Channel Definition Format files. It has a graphical interface that does not require previous knowledge of channels. It supports all CDF tags and UTF-8 encoding and can also be used for testing because it parses the CDF files and detects the errors. Also, there is a tutorial and reference for the CDF generator at *msdn.microsoft.com/library/default.asp?url=/workshop/delivery/cdf/reference/CDF.asp*.

Chapter Summary

- Developed by Microsoft Corporation as part of their refinement of their webcasting technology, CDF provides you with the capability to manipulate and condense collections of documents and combine them with specific new data to deliver the modified data to subscribers on a regular schedule.
- With push technology, data is broadcast without regard to whether anyone is connected to the Internet at the time. E-mail was a pioneer IT application of push technology. Webcasting is push technology on a large scale.
- Web surfing is an IT application of pull technology: an end user with a browser requests information from specific locations by entering a URL in a browser's location bar.
- Managed webcasting provides several advantages over basic webcasting, including the ability to specify which Web site documents can be subscribed to, plus easier navigation, easier content updating, and a simple approach to Web site conversion.
- CDF allows information to be delivered in the form of channels, which are specifically defined documents or other logical groupings of information, and which can be served from any Web server that supports the HTTP protocol. They are similar to specialized TV or radio channels.
- Microsoft submitted CDF to the W3C as a specification proposal in 1997. Although it remains a W3C Note, CDF contributed to the development of the W3C's RDF Recommendation. Meanwhile, Microsoft has continued CDF development.
- Adding a new channel to your browser's channel list when the Web site owner doesn't use CDF requires more steps than if the Web site was equipped with CDF.

- To create channels, first design the channel, then create and store your logo images, create the CDF file, post the CDF file so that it is publicly accessible, and finally offer the channel to the user community.
- CDF files are XML-related documents, so they follow XML rules. They need a prolog and a root element (in CDF's case, the root element is called <channel>). You may define channels, subchannels, and items in a CDF file. They must be well-formed, but validation—although recommended—is left to the Web site developer or owner. There is no publicly available DTD or schema.

Review Questions

1. Which of the following are examples of push technology? Select all that apply.
   a. telephone
   b. e-mail
   c. television
   d. CDF
   e. Web surfing
   f. webcasting
   g. all of the above
2. A(n) ________________ is a configurable set of dynamic link libraries that is started by a browser and then examines information on Web pages that the user has subscribed to, compares the information to similar information already stored on the end user's system for that Web site, and then decides whether to import the data from the Web site.
3. Channels are specifically defined documents or other logical groupings of information that can be served from any Web server that supports the HTTP protocol. True or false?
4. Which of the following is not an advantage of managed webcasting?
   a. The Web site owner can specify which pages on their Web site are available for a user to subscribe to.
   b. The Web site owner can provide a structured view of Web site content.
   c. Updates can be scheduled to coincide with Web site content updates, or to take place during times of lower network loading.
   d. All of a Web site's information may have to be downloaded from the Web site.
   e. The Web site owner can convert an existing Web site without having to completely overhaul the Web site.

5. Which of the following were competing metadata specification proposals filed with the W3C in 1997? Select all that apply.
   a. DRP
   b. CDF
   c. OSD
   d. VML
   e. RDF
   f. all of the above
6. When a Channel bar is activated, it acts like a frame. True or false?
7. Downloading the latest version of a channel to your hard disk so you can access it and read its content later when your computer is not connected to the Internet is called:
   a. synchronizing
   b. webcasting
   c. synthesizing
   d. pulling
   e. none of the above
8. Conceptually, there is no difference between adding a new Favorite or a new channel to your browser. They are all equivalent terms. True or false?
9. Which of the following cannot be specified through a CDF file?
   a. titles, URLs, content, description, and browser window and desktop icons
   b. screen savers
   c. user-traffic logging
   d. the creation of a schedule for updating and synchronization
   e. authentication
   f. none of the above
10. Following are the basic steps for creating a channel. Please place them in the recommended order:
    a. Create and store your logo images.
    b. Design the channel.
    c. Create the CDF file.
    d. Offer the channel to the user community.
    e. Post the CDF file so that it is publicly accessible.
11. Like all XML-related documents, CDF files must be well-formed and valid. True or false?

12. Microsoft recommends that a channel should have no more than ________________ subitems in the first level.
    a. four
    b. six
    c. eight
    d. unlimited
    e. none of the above
13. Which two of the following elements are the major building blocks in a CDF file?
    a. <logo>
    b. <channel>
    c. <subchannel>
    d. <item>
    e. <href>
14. With CDF, you can begin the channel subscription process by inserting ________________, the value of which is the location of the CDF file in the start tag of an <A> element which, in turn, is nested within the <BODY> element of an HTML document.
15. Which of the following statements about the BASE attribute in a <channel> element start tag is false? Select all that apply.
    a. It specifies the URL of the location where the channel's resources (e.g., document files, graphic and audio files, etc.) are stored.
    b. Once it has been defined, Web developers can then specify other URLs in the <channel> element with respect to the base, using just the relative paths from the base.
    c. The BASE attribute value applies to all the child elements of the channel or subchannel in which it is specified. The inheritance also applies to sibling subchannels, but not to parent channels.
    d. When specifying the URL, ensure that it ends with a trailing "/", or subsequent path references become confused.
16. If a HREF attribute is inserted into the start tag of a <channel> element to indicate the URL of the channel document and the developer has inadvertently added a child <A> element with a contradicting HREF attribute value, what is the order of precedence observed by Microsoft Internet Explorer?
    a. The latest HREF attribute value specification, i.e., the one given in the <A> element
    b. The HREF attribute value from the start tag of the <channel> element
    c. Neither is observed and a "404 Page Error" is displayed in the end user's browser whenever they try to subscribe to the Web site
    d. none of the above

17. If the value specified for the attribute LEVEL is zero, then a client can only site crawl to and precache the page specified by the URL and the affiliated images, but not its frames. True or false?
18. When the mouse pointer pauses over a <channel> or <item> title, Internet Explorer displays the content you specified for the ________ element as text in a ScreenTip in the Channel bar.
19. How would you express the following statement, using the appropriate child element within the <schedule> element?

    "The interval between updates will be 10 days and 12 hours."
20. Match the following:

a. STYLE="ICON"	i. browser Channel bar	A. 32 × 194
b. STYLE="IMAGE-WIDE"	ii. Active Desktop	B. 16 × 16
c. STYLE= "IMAGE"	iii. Favorites menu	C. 32 × 80

21. What can you do if you do not want an item to be listed in the Channel bar?
22. A Web site owner cannot monitor the number of times a channel subscriber accesses an <item> Web page when the subscriber is viewing the page offline. True or false?
23. What do the <usage> and <abstract> elements have in common with respect to their respective development histories?
24. When used as an attribute of a parent element, the value specified for the XML-SPACE attribute applies to all child elements unless it is specifically overridden in a child element with a different XML-SPACE attribute. True or false?
25. A CDF file containing the ________ element causes the end user to be prompted for a name and password during the channel subscription process.

14

HANDS-ON PROJECTS

To complete the projects in this chapter, you must use Internet Information Server (IIS) or Personal Web Server (PWS) to set up a default Web site on your computer. The default Web site should be set to the following path: localhost/yourname/Ch14. See your instructor or technical support person for more information about installing IIS or PWS and setting up a default Web site.

Project 14-1

In this project, you replace an ordinary HTML link with a CDF file to enhance communication with any user who visits your site. The CDF file is then used to automatically prompt users to add the "Catalog" link as a new Favorite in their browsers. In the following steps, substitute the drive letter of your hard disk for C, if necessary.

To set up the project and create a CDF file:

1. In Windows Explorer, create a new folder called **Ch14** in the C:\home*yourname* folder. Then copy the files and the images folder from the Ch14/Project_14-1 folder on your Data Disk into your C:/home/*yourname*/Ch14 folder. Your drive letter may vary.
2. Start XML Spy. Click **Start**, point to **Programs** (point to **All Programs** in Windows XP), point to **XML Spy Suite**, and then click **XML Spy IDE**. The XML Spy window opens.
3. Make sure the contacts project is open ("contacts" should appear at the top of the Project pane). If it is not, click **Project** on the menu bar, and then click **Open Project**. Navigate to the C:/home/*yourname*/Ch14 folder, and then double-click **contacts.spp** to open the project.
4. Add the main.html and coupon2.html files to the contacts project. Click **Project** on the menu bar, and then click **Add Files to Project**. Navigate to the C:/home/*yourname*/Ch14 folder, if necessary, select **All Files** in the Files of Type list box, select the **main.html** and **coupon2.html**, and then click **Open** to add them to the project.
5. Use the same technique as in Step 4 to add the image files from the C:/home/*yourname*/Ch14/images folder to the project.
6. Create a new CDF file. Click **File** on the menu bar, and then click **New**. Select **xml Extensible Markup Language** in the Create new document dialog box, if necessary, and then click **OK**.
7. To switch to text view, click **View** on the menu bar, and then click **Text view**. Create a <CHANNEL> element with an HREF attribute that links to your product.xml file. Note that in the following code, "yourname" is the name for your personal Web server. In the middle pane of the XML Spy window, type the following bold code. Note that XML Spy inserts the closing </CHANNEL> tag for you.

```
<?xml version="1.0" encoding="UTF-8"?>
<CHANNEL HREF="http://localhost/yourname/Ch14/
    product.xml">
</CHANNEL>
```

8. Save the XML file as **catalog.cdf** in the C:/home/*yourname*/Ch14 folder.
9. Save the **catalog.cdf** file in the project. Click **Project** on the menu bar, and then click **Save Project**.

To connect the CDF file to the Web page:

1. Edit the Catalog link in the main.html file so that it points to the catalog.cdf file instead of the products.xml file. In the Project pane of the XML Spy window, double-click **main.html**. Switch to Text view, if necessary, and then change product.xml to **catalog.cdf**.

The link should now point to the CDF file and should look like the following code:

```
<a href="Ch14/catalog.cdf">Catalog</a>
```

2. Save the main.html file, and leave XML Spy open for the next project.
3. Test the results using Internet Explorer. Go to:

   http://localhost/yourname/Ch14/main.html

   Then click the **Catalog** link.

To avoid confusion with any pages that may be cached on your system, be sure to exit the browser between changes. Then you can retry the HTML link that represents the CDF file.

The Add Favorite dialog box opens, shown in Figure 14-39.

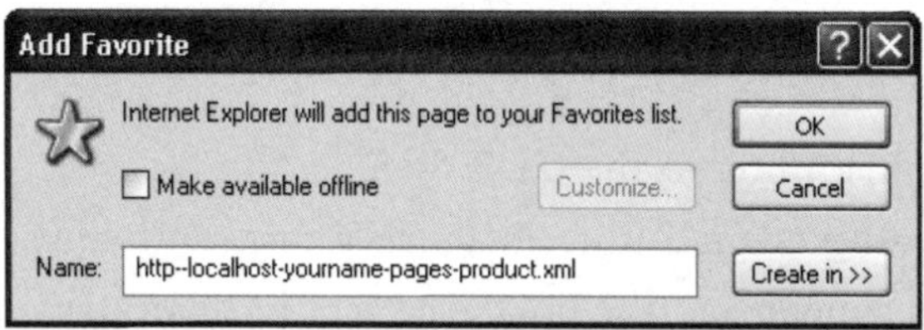

Figure 14-39

Users can work with this dialog box to add your main.html Web page to their Favorites list.

4. Close Internet Explorer.

Project 14-2

In this project, you modify the CDF file created in Project 14-1 to include a description of your Web page in the Add Favorites dialog box that Internet Explorer opens when users visit your Web site.

To add title information to the catalog.cdf file:

1. In XML Spy, click the **catalog.cdf** tab, if necessary, to return to this file. Modify the file by adding the following code shown in bold:

```
<?xml version="1.0" encoding="UTF-8"?>
<CHANNEL HREF="http://localhost/yourname/Ch14/
     product.xml">
    <TITLE>TLSales Spring Summer Catalog</TITLE>
</CHANNEL>
```

2. Save the catalog.cdf file, and leave XML Spy open.

3. Test the results using Internet Explorer. Go to:

   http://localhost/yourname/Ch14/main.html

   Then click the **Catalog** link.

   A modified Add Favorite dialog box opens, as shown in Figure 14-40.

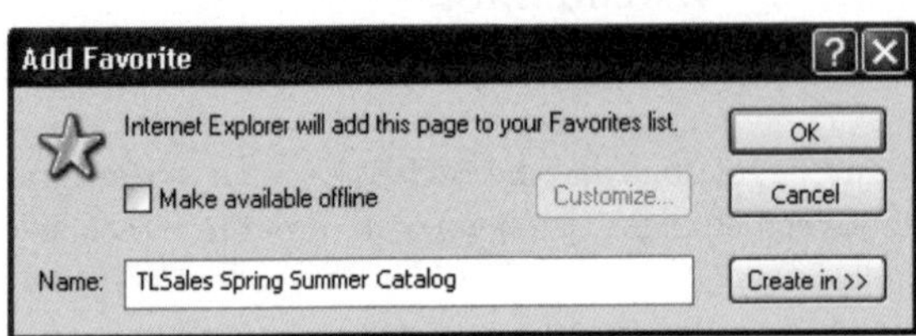

Figure 14-40

This dialog box now shows the title of your main Web page.

4. Close Internet Explorer.

To add a child page for the Coupon link to the CDF file:

1. In XML Spy, click the **catalog.cdf** tab, if necessary, to return to the file.
2. On the line after the title element, add the boldfaced text in the following code:

```
      <TITLE>TLSales Spring Summer Catalog</TITLE>
  <ITEM HREF="http://localhost/yourname/Ch14/coupon2.html">
    <TITLE>TLSales Spring Summer Coupon</TITLE>
  </ITEM>
```

2. Save catalog.cdf. In XML Spy open **product.xml** and edit the path names to match the local folders on your hard disk. Then save product.xml.
3. Test the results using Internet Explorer. Go to:

   http://localhost/yourname/Ch14/main.html

   Then click the **Catalog** link.

   An additional child object for the coupon link appears when the browser opens.
4. Test the coupon link. Click **TLSales Spring Summer Coupon**. The page showing the coupon information opens. See Figure 14-41.
5. Close Internet Explorer.

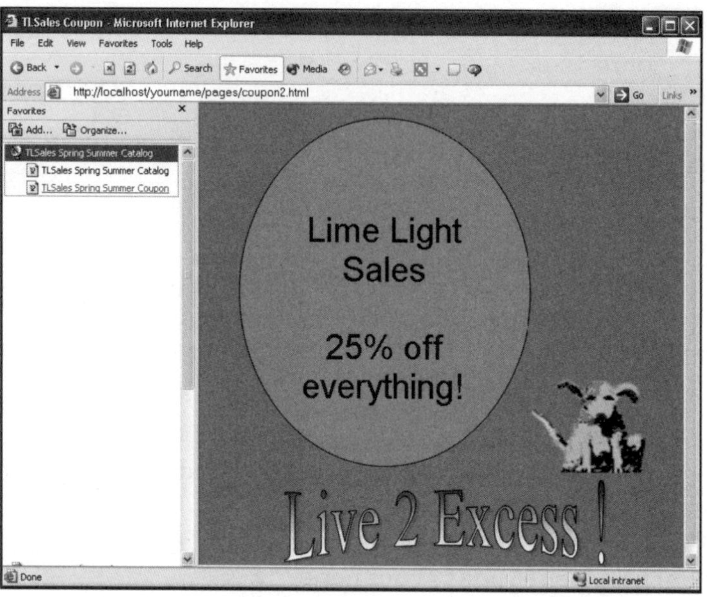

Figure 14-41

Project 14-3

In this project, you replace the generic icons used on the channel links with customized icons. You also add a logo element to the catalog.cdf file.

To use customized icons for channels:

1. In XML Spy, click the **catalog.cdf** tab, if necessary, to return to the file in Text view.
2. On the line after the item element, add the following line of code to the catalog.cdf file.

```
<ITEM HREF="http://localhost/yourname/Ch14/coupon2.html">
  <LOGO HREF="http://localhost/yourname/Ch14/images/
        saddle.gif"STYLE="ICON" />
  <TITLE> TLSales Spring Summer Coupon </TITLE>
```

3. Save catalog.cdf, and leave it open in XML Spy for the next project.
4. Test the results using Internet Explorer. Go to:

   http://localhost/yourname/main.html

The icons should appear as cycle seats, like those in Figure 14-42.

14

Figure 14-42

5. Close Internet Explorer.

Project 14-4

In this project, you continue to enhance the TLSales channel. This includes adding features for the user and maintaining readable code. You improve code readability by adding a BASE attribute and then inserting comments. Then you provide additional channel images and contextual tips for the user.

To improve code readability:

1. With catalog.cdf open in XML Spy from Project 14-3, add a BASE attribute to the root channel element, as in the following code:

```
<CHANNEL HREF="http://localhost/yourname/Ch14/product.xml"
  BASE="http://localhost/yourname/">
  <TITLE>TLSales Spring Summer Catalog</TITLE>
```

2. In the ITEM and LOGO elements, delete the base part (the http://localhost/yourname/) of the URL to make the code easier to read. These elements should match the following code. Also add the comments shown in bold in the following code. Comments are valuable for others who work with your code. As a rule, you should comment each element that has children.

```
<?xml version="1.0" encoding="UTF-8"?>
<!-- Top Level - The TLSales web channel -->
<CHANNEL HREF="http://localhost/yourname/Ch14/
     product.xml"
  BASE="http://localhost/yourname/">
    <TITLE>TLSales Spring Summer Catalog</TITLE>
<!-- Item - Our Coupon Offering -->
  <ITEM HREF="Ch14/coupon2.html">
    <LOGO HREF="images/saddle.gif" STYLE="ICON" />
    <TITLE>TLSales Spring Summer Coupon</TITLE>
  </ITEM>
</CHANNEL>
```

3. You can make the code easier for users by placing the following code on the line after the BASE element of the root channel. Including the following three LOGO elements supports all the ways the logos can be used, and is considered a best practice.

```
BASE="http://localhost/yourname/">
<LOGO HREF="images/saddle-image.gif" STYLE="IMAGE" />
<LOGO HREF="images/saddle-wide.gif" STYLE="IMAGE-WIDE" />
<LOGO HREF="images/saddle.gif" STYLE="ICON" />
```

4. On the line after each title element, add ABSTRACT elements for both the channel and item elements, as shown in the following code. The ABSTRACT elements provide the ScreenTip text to show when a user points to the title.

```
    <TITLE>TLSales Spring Summer Catalog</TITLE>
    <ABSTRACT>Browse our spring and summer line!</ABSTRACT>
  !-- Item - Our Coupon Offering -->
    <ITEM HREF="Ch14/coupon2.html">
      <LOGO HREF="Ch14/images/saddle.gif" STYLE="ICON" />
      <TITLE>TLSales Spring Summer Coupon</TITLE>
      <ABSTRACT>Save money now!</ABSTRACT>
```

5. Save catalog.cdf, and leave it open in XML Spy for the next project.
6. Test the results using Internet Explorer. Go to:

   http://localhost/yourname/Ch14/main.html

Point to the **TLSales Spring Summer Catalog** title. The ScreenTip appears, as in Figure 14-43.

If the ScreenTip does not appear when you point to the title, check to be sure that you have provided coding for special characters and the xml-space attribute where necessary.

7. Close Internet Explorer.

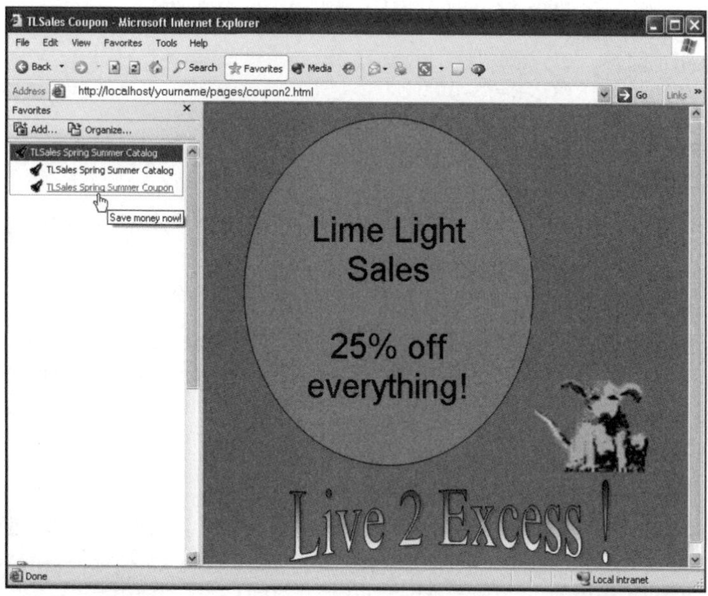

Figure 14-43

14

Project 14-5

In this project, you continue to enhance the TLSales channel by using the scheduling features of the channel to avoid synchronizations between 1:15 AM and 2:45 AM.

To schedule synchronizations:

1. With catalog.cdf open in XML Spy from Project 14-4, insert a SCHEDULE element on the line before the item comment, as in the following code. The schedule is a function of the channel and therefore will reside at that level.

```
    <ABSTRACT>Browse our spring and summer line!</ABSTRACT>
         <SCHEDULE >
  <!-- Item - Our Coupon Offering -->
```

2. Suppose that your host is located in California, placing them in the Pacific Time Zone, which is seven hours behind GMT. Add the TIMEZONE attribute to the SCHEDULE element to compensate for this difference. Insert the boldface text in the following code:

```
<SCHEDULE TIMEZONE="-0700" >
```

3. Now add the EARLIESTTIME and LATESTTIME elements to avoid synchronizations during service hours. On the line before the SCHEDULE element, insert the comment shown in bold in the following code. On the lines after the schedule element, add the EARLIESTTIME and LATESTTIME elements and add the closing tag for the schedule element.

```
     <ABSTRACT>Browse our spring and summer line!
     </ABSTRACT>
<!-- Scheduling to avoid service hours -->
  <SCHEDULE TIMEZONE="-0700" >
    <EARLIESTTIME HOUR="2" MIN="45" />
    <LATESTTIME HOUR="1" MIN="15" />
  </SCHEDULE>
```

4. Save your changes to catalog.cdf, and leave XML Spy open for the next project.

Project 14-6

In this project you make further enhancements to the TLSales channel. Suppose that you want to know more about site activity. The Web site uses a separate software package to gather site statistics, and you need to integrate the information collected for the Web coupon. To do so, you can set up logging on your channel.

To set up logging on a channel:

1. A fellow developer has provided you with the following address to a statistics program on the site: http://localhost/Ch14/cgi-bin/counter.cgi. Use Windows Explorer to create a folder in the Ch14 folder named **cgi-bin**. Copy the counter.cgi file from the Ch14 folder on your Data Disk to the cgi-bin folder.

With catalog.cdf open in XML Spy from Project 14-5, add a comment and the LOGTARGET element on the line after the closing SCHEDULE tag. Place this element as a child of the root channel element, as shown in the following code:

```
     </SCHEDULE>
<!-- Logging Activity -->
<LOGTARGET HREF="http://localhost/Ch14/cgi-bin/
     counter.cgi" />
```

Notice that the path does not extend from the BASE element you have specified. For a LOGTARGET element, you must enter the full path into your href attribute.

2. To capture visits to the site while the user is offline, add the scope attribute with the logical value "offline". Your inserted code should appear as follows:

```
!-- Logging Activity -->
<LOGTARGET HREF="http://localhost/username/Ch14/cgi-bin/
     counter.cgi" SCOPE="offline" />
```

3. Now you must specify what log information to collect. In the TLSales site, you want to monitor your users' traffic on the coupon page. Within the ITEM element, add a LOG element on the line after the abstract element to specify that you are tracking the item's page. Also add a VALUE attribute with the value "document:view".

```
<ITEM HREF="Ch14/coupon2.html">
 <LOGO HREF="images/saddle.gif" STYLE="ICON" />
 <TITLE>TLSales Spring Summer Coupon</TITLE>
 <ABSTRACT>Save money now!</ABSTRACT>
 <LOG VALUE="document:view" />
 </ITEM>
```

4. The TLSales Web channel is complete. Confirm that the contents of your file resemble the following code, and then save the catalog.cdf file.

```
<?xml version="1.0" encoding="UTF-8"?>
<!-- Top Level - The TLSales web channel -->
<CHANNEL HREF="http://localhost/yourname/Ch14/
     product.xml"
  BASE="http://localhost/yourname/Ch14">
  <LOGO HREF="images/saddle-image.gif" STYLE="IMAGE" />
  <LOGO HREF="images/saddle-wide.gif"
     STYLE="IMAGE-WIDE" />
  <LOGO HREF="images/saddle.gif" STYLE="ICON" />
  <TITLE>TLSales Spring Summer Catalog</TITLE>
  <ABSTRACT>Browse our spring and summer line!</ABSTRACT>
<!-- Scheduling to avoid service hours -->
  <SCHEDULE TIMEZONE="-0700" >
     <EARLIESTTIME HOUR="2" MIN="45" />
     <LATESTTIME HOUR="1" MIN="15" />
  </SCHEDULE>
<!-- Logging Activity -->
```

```
    <LOGTARGET HREF="http://localhost/username/Ch14/
      cgi-bin/counter.cgi" SCOPE="offline" />
<!-- Item - Our Coupon Offering -->
      <ITEM HREF="pages/coupon2.html">
      <LOGO HREF="images/saddle.gif" STYLE="ICON" />
      <TITLE>TLSales Spring Summer Coupon</TITLE>
      <ABSTRACT>Save money now!</ABSTRACT>
      <LOG VALUE="document:view" />
    </ITEM>
</CHANNEL>
```

CASE PROJECTS

Case Project 14-1

You are adding a Web page to the TLSales Web site that lists the salespeople users can contact for more information about TLSales. The new page is called contacts3.html and uses the contacts2.css file. If necessary, add these files to the contacts project from the Ch14/Case_Project folder on your Data Disk. Then add code to the catalog.cdf file to reference the HTML file. The title for this item is "Contact salespeople at TLSales". The logo for this page is saddle.gif. Include a comment to identify this section of code as the contacts page. Test the results in Internet Explorer.

Case Project 14-2

Now you can revise the catalog.cdf file so that a new reminder appears when users point to the title of the product.xml page. Revise the catalog.cdf file from Case Project 14-1 to have the following ScreenTip appear when users point to the "TLSales Spring Summer Catalog" "Be sure to visit our Contacts page" title.

Also add code so that the following ScreenTip appears when users point to the "Contact salespeople at TLSales" title: "Contact a salesperson now to participate in our Internet auction next Wednesday. All of last year's inventory will be auctioned off starting at 9:00 AM, ending at 6:00 PM. Everything must go! Hope to see you there." Test the results in Internet Explorer.

Index

* (asterisks), 119–120
| (pipes), 119
+ (plus sign), 119, 145

A

ActiveX controls for data binding, 474
Adobe FrameMaker + SGML, 76
agents, data binding, 485
Air Transport Association (ATA) language, 9
aligning text with style rules, 453
all compositors, 170
Amaya, 308–309, 318–319
American National Standards Institute (ANSI), 8
anyURI type, 172
Apple SimpleText editor, 70
application profiles of SGML, 10
application software, 30
Arbortext Epic Editor, 86–87
archetypes, 174, 178
arcs, 240
asterisks (*), 119–120
ATA (Air Transport Association) language, 9
attribute list declarations
  CDATA type, 124
  default value specifications, 125–126
  defined, 107, 123
  ENTITIES type, 124
  ENTITY type, 124
  ENUMERATED type, 125
  example project, 147–148
  #FIXED "value," 125
  IDREFS type, 125
  IDREF type, 124
  ID type, 124
  #IMPLIED, 125
  NMTOKEN(S) type, 125
  NOTATION type, 125
  #REQUIRED, 125
  syntax, 123
  types, table of, 124–125
  "value," 125
  XML:space attribute, 126
attributes
  adding to DTDs. *See* attribute list declarations
  child elements, compared to, 47
  converting elements to, 232–234
  declaring in DTDs. *See* attribute list declarations
  default values, 109
  defined, 46
  example project, 65–66
  language specification, 126–127
  naming, 47
  restriction inheritance in schemas, 176–177
  schema, 170–171, 195
  syntax, 46
  value assignment to, 47–48
  value normalization, 127
  XHTML, 301–303
audio
  FlowML, 17
  intrinsic duration objects, 400
  notation declarations, 130–132
  SMIL. *See* Synchronized Multimedia Integration Language (SMIL)
authoring compliance, DTDs for, 109–110
authoring tools. *See* editors, XML
automatic structure checking, 72–73

B

Berners-Lee, Tim, 19, 289
binary type, 172
bindable elements. *See* data binding, data consumers
bitmap graphics, 326–328. *See also* images
boolean type, 172, 195
borders, adding, 452–453
Bray, Tim, 13
browsers
  Amaya, 308–309
  Cascading Style Sheets (CSS) support, 427
  data binding, support for, 471
  MathML support, 541–545
  Microsoft. *See* Internet Explorer, Microsoft
  Netscape. *See* Netscape Navigator
  SMIL support, 408–409
  Vector Markup Language (VML) support, 331, 338

C

cardinality of elements, 119, 145, 171
Cascading Style Sheets (CSS)
  absolute positioning, 455
  aligning text, 453
  background color, 461
  background image properties, 449–452
  background properties, 435
  block-level elements, 436

bolding text, 461
borders, adding, 452–453
box properties, 435
browser support for, 427
cascading nature of, 426, 456–457
child elements, 444
classes, adding to HTML, 466
classification properties, 436
class rules, adding, 439–442, 463–464
coloring elements, 461
creating style rules, 432–433
creating style sheets, 465
declarations, 434–435
delimiters, 435
display property, 436
DTDs for classes, 441, 447
element properties, 436
external style sheets, affiliating, 465–469
first item, modifying, 447–449, 468
font properties, 461
hovering, 444
hyperlinks, 444–447
id attributes, 447–449
images as backgrounds, 450–451
images, inserting, 451–452
!Important rules, 456
inheritance of style rules, 434, 456
inline-level elements, 436–437
inline styles with STYLE attribute, 431–432, 460–462
internal style sheets, 463–464
language specification, 444
Levels of, 426–427
links, 444–447
list properties, 436
margins, setting, 454
positioning elements, 454–456
priority of style sheet application, 456–457
properties, 434–437
property name:value pairs, 434
pseudo-elements, 437–438
purpose of, 425–426
references to, 428–429, 466–467
relative positioning, 455
rules, 434
selectors. *See* selectors, CSS
specifications, 426–427
specifying style sheets, 428–432
STYLE attribute syntax, 431–432
style rule syntax, 433–434
syntax for style rules, 433–434
table properties, 436
text/css media type, 463
text properties, 435
validation service, W3C, 427
values, 434–435
visual effects properties, 436
VML with, 332
W3C role in, 426
XHTML strict variant with, 294
XML documents, displaying with, 468–470
?xml-stylesheet instruction, 428
case sensitivity
XHTML, 299, 301, 305
XML, 115
CDATA
PCDATA, 43, 115–116
sections, 53
type attributes, 124
CDF (Channel Definition Format). *See* Channel Definition Format (CDF)
CERN (European Organization for Nuclear Research), 11
chameleon namespaces, 167
Channel Definition Format (CDF)
& (ampersands), 609–610, 615
abstract elements, 599–600, 613, 615, 626
access, client, 593
Active Channel Logo Agreement, 593
Active Desktop Channel bar, 602–605
Active Desktop items, 602
Add Active Channel buttons, 593
Add Favorites dialog box, 622–623
adding to Channel lists, 581–586, 622–623
attributes of channels, 597–599
attributes of item elements, 602
automatic downloading, 577
BASE attributes, 597, 612, 625
Channel bars, 592, 597, 602–605, 615
channel concept, 572, 576
channel definitions, 595–599
channel elements, 591–592, 595–599, 610–612, 622
character encoding, 609–610
child elements, 595, 602
child pages, 624
comments, adding, 625–626
creating CDF files, 593–595, 621–623
creating channels, 589–594, 621–622
defined, 13, 16
deleting channels, 585
designing channels, 590–592
discovering availability of channels, 580–581
DTDs, 608, 610
earliesttime elements, 601, 627–628
A (anchor) elements, 599
file creation, 593–595, 621–622
guidelines, 591–592
headers, adding, 606–607
hierarchies, 590–591
hits, measuring, 605–607
HREF attributes, 598, 602, 603, 612, 622
http-equiv elements, 606–607
icons for logos, 592, 625

IMAGE-WIDE attributes, 613
index-like nature of, 577
Internet Explorer 6.0, 580
Internet Explorer channels, using, 579–586
intervaltime elements, 601
item elements, 591–592, 601–602, 614–616, 624
LASTMOD attributes, 598, 602, 612
latesttime elements, 601, 627–628
LEVEL attributes, 598, 602
levels of links to crawl, 598
linking of channels, 585–586, 593, 622–624
linking, offline, 589
log elements, 605–606, 628–629
login elements, 608
logos, 592, 603–605, 612–615, 625–626
logtarget elements, 606, 613, 628–629
Make available offline option, 583
managed webcasting, 575
manual synchronization, 586–587
Microsoft as sponsor of, 571
Microsoft CDF Generator, 617
modification dates, 598
offline viewing, 586–589
origins of, 571, 574
posting CDF files to servers, 593, 622
PRECACHE attributes, 598, 602
prologs, 595, 610
pull technology, 572–573
purgetime elements, 607, 614
push technology, 572, 573
RDF Recommendation, 578–579
resources on Web, 616–617
schedule elements, 592, 600, 613, 627–629
screen savers, 602, 614
ScreenTips, adding, 626, 630
SELF attributes, 598–599
SHOW attributes, 608
sitecrawlers, 574
softpkg elements, 603
Software Update channels, 608
special characters, 609–610, 615
STARTDATE attributes, 613
STOPDATE attributes, 613
structure of documents, 596
STYLE attributes, 603, 612
subchannels, 595, 610, 614
summary, 617–618
synchronization, 586–587, 613
syntax, 596
timezones, 598, 600, 613, 627
title elements, 603, 613, 623–624
top-level elements, 595–599, 610–612
traffic, measuring, 605–607
update intervals, 601, 613
URL specification, 597–598
USAGE attributes, 614
usage elements, 602, 607–608
VALUE attributes, 602, 607–608
viewing offline, 587–589
W3C Note on, 577–579
webcasting, 573–575
Work Offline command, 587–588
XML basis of, 576–577
XML declarations, 599, 610
character data
CDATA. *See* CDATA
parsed, 171
PCDATA, 43, 115–116
characters
CDF, encoding in, 609–610, 615
passing markup characters, 53
references, numeric, 51–52
reserved, 49
set encodings, 33–34
UCS, 33–34
UNICODE, 33, 51–52
Chemical Markup Language (CML), 16
child elements
adding to schemas, 190–191
attributes, compared to, 47
attributes, converting to, 65–66
child axes, XPointer, 262
defined, 40
example project declarations, 145–146
syntax for in DTDs, 116
choice compositors, 170
classes
CSS, 439–443
schema, 161
clientless streaming, 384
closed captioning, 402
closing tags, 41
CML (Chemical Markup Language), 16
comments, 36–37
complex type declarations, 175–177
complex type elements, 169
components of XML documents
attributes. *See* attributes
CDATA sections, 53
comments, 36–37
declarations, XML. *See* XML declarations
document type declarations. *See* DOCTYPE keyword
elements. *See* elements
entities, 31
major, list of, 31
physical structure, 31
processing instructions, 35–36
prologs. *See* prologs
types, 31
compositors, 170
Conglomerate, 77
constraints, 161, 182
content attributes, 178
content elements, simple, 176

content model constraints, 161
content models
  any content, 118
  creating, example project, 144–146
  defined, 107, 115, 139
  element content only, 116
  empty elements, 117–118
  mixed, 116–117
  operators for, 118–120
  parsed data only, 115–116
  #PCDATA keyword, 115–116
  sequenced child elements, 116
content of elements, 43–46
content separators, 6
content type elements, 169
continuous media, 400
conversion to XHTML, 205–209, 314–318
conversion to XML systems
  accounting considerations, 90
  benefits, 89–90
  cost-benefit spreadsheets, 90
  cost considerations, 89–90
  general considerations, 87–88
  initial considerations, 88
  non-XML converters, 81
converters, 81
converting DTDs to schemas, 186–187
creating XML documents
  Notepad for, 62–64
  XML Spy for, 64–65
customer list schema example, 188–189

D

database architecture, 472–473
databases. *See* data binding
data binding
  # (hash marks), 476, 506
  ActiveX controls for, 474
  agents, 485
  applet elements, 487
  architecture, database, 472–473
  BOF (beginning of file), 493
  browser support for, 471
  buttons, creating, 510–511
  customizing element names, 476
  data consumers, 472–475, 506
  data field keys, 483
  datafld attribute, 475–477, 483, 489–491
  data islands, 480–483, 495–496
  dataPageSize attributes, 495
  data sources, 472
  datasrc attribute, 475–477, 483–484, 506
  defined, 471–472
  div elements, 475, 476–478, 507
  DSOs, 485–491
  dynamic table behavior, 485
  EOF (end of file), 493
  event handlers, 511
  extended attributes, 475
  external data islands, 480, 481–483, 508–514
  goals of, 498
  grouping elements, 476–478
  id attributes, 481
  internal data islands, 480–481, 504–508
  Internet Explorer data source objects, 487
  Java applets for, 474
  JavaScript with, 491–493, 510–514
  location of data, specifying, 481–482
  name attribute of div, 477
  namespace declarations, 483
  navigating recordsets, 491–498
  nested elements of data sources, 488–491, 506
  paragraph structure, 476
  recordsets, 488, 491–498
  referencing external data, 481–482, 508
  repetition agents, 485, 506–507
  set binding, 474, 478–479
  single-valued consumer elements, 474, 476, 495–498, 510–514
  sources for data, 479–480
  span elements, 476–478
  src attribute, 481, 508
  styling elements, 477
  synchronization of data, 485
  syntax to bind single-valued elements, 476
  table elements, 475, 478–479, 505–508, 512–513
  table repetition agents, 485, 506–507
  tabular data consumer elements, 474
  Two-Level Rule, 489–491
data content, 43
data islands, 480–483
data source objects (DSOs)
  applet elements, 487
  data objects, 488
  dataPageSize attributes, 495
  defined, 485
  navigating recordsets, 491–498
  nested elements, 488–491
  purpose of, 486
  recordsets, 488
  returning of data process, 487–488
  single-valued consumer elements, 495–498
  Two-Level Rule, 489–491
  types of, 487
  updating of data consumers by, 486
datatype constraints, 161
date type, 172
data type elements, 169
decimal type, 172

declarations
  attributes in DTDs. *See* attribute list declarations
  elements in DTDs. *See* element declarations
  XML. *See* XML declarations
declared empty elements, 44–46, 117–118
default attribute values, 125
default namespace declarations, 135–136
definition of XML, 2
definition of XML documents, 31
delimiters
  CSS, 435
  defined, 6
  tags, of, 31, 41
  VML, 346
depicting structures, 37–38
deploying XML files, 66–67
development of XML, 13–15
DHTML, 486
digital imaging technologies, 326–328
disadvantages of XML, 18
Distribution and Replication Protocol (DRP), 577
DOCTYPE keyword
  internal DTDs, 110
  syntax, 34–35
  vs. DTDs, 149
  XHTML, 298, 314–315
document analysis process, 137–138
documentation of DTDs, 138
document modeling, 106. *See also* document type definitions (DTDs)
documents, XML
  adding data to, 150–152
  components of. *See* components of XML documents
  creating based on schemas, 192
  creating from DTDs, 148–149
  defined, 30
  logical structure, 31
  physical structure, 31
  structure of, 39–40
  validity, 55–57
  well-formed, 53–55, 57
document type declarations, 34–35. *See also* DOCTYPE keyword
document type definitions (DTDs)
  * (asterisk), 119–120
  | (pipes), 119
  + (plus sign), 119, 145
  advantages over schemas, 159
  attribute declaration function, 107
  attribute declarations. *See* attribute list declarations
  authoring compliance, 109–110
  Channel Definition Format (CDF), 608, 610
  class declarations, CSS, 441
  complex element declarations, 120–123
  content model function, 107
  converting to XML schemas, 186–187
  creating, 143–148
  creating XML documents from, 148–149
  CSSs, 441, 447
  declaration identifiers, 108–109
  default attribute values, 109
  disadvantages of, 106, 158
  DOCTYPE. *See* DOCTYPE keyword
  document analysis process, 137–138
  documentation, 138
  elements, declaring. *See* element declarations
  empty element declarations, 45
  entity declarations, 127–130
  external. *See* external DTDs
  goals for, 138
  history, 106
  internal, 110, 113–114, 152–154
  language specification, 126–127
  local storage of, 296
  MathML, 535
  metainformation, 108
  miscellaneous functions, 108
  namespace declarations, 132–137
  notation declarations, 130–132
  operators for element declarations, 118–120
  overview of, 107–108
  prefix namespace declarations, 136–137
  prologs, as component of, 34–35
  purpose of, 109–110
  rootnames, 34
  schematic, basic, 108
  SGML, 9–10
  SMIL, 386–388
  standalone attributes, 34, 110
  Strict variant, 294–295
  syntax for declarations, 109
  syntax for declaring, 34
  testing, 137–138
  Transitional XHTML, 303–304
  types of, 139
  variants of XHTML, 293–296
  viewing with XML Spy, 144
  vocabulary definition function, 107
  white space handling with, 109, 126
  XHTML, for, 293–294, 303–304, 324
  XLink, 249–255
  XML:space attribute, 126
  XSLT, using with, 201–207
DrawML Specification, 335
DRP (Distribution and Replication Protocol), 577
DSOs. *See* data source objects (DSOs)
DTDs. *See* document type definitions (DTDs)
duration facet, 181
Dynamic HTML, 486

E

EBNF (Extended Backus-Naur Form), 260
editors, XML
  Adobe FrameMaker + SGML, 76
  Conglomerate, 77
  Emacs, 70–72, 74
  Epic Editor, 86–87
  graphical. *See* graphical text editors
  IDEs. *See* integrated development environments (IDEs)
  installing, 95–100
  Komodo, 86
  Notepad. *See* Notepad, document creation with
  Peter's XML Editor, 75, 97–98
  SimpleText editor, 70
  simple text editors, 69–72
  test environments, advantages of, 102
  Turbo XML, 85–86
  types of, 69
  vi, 70
  Word, Microsoft, 77–81
  WordPad, Microsoft, 70
  XAE, 74
  Xeena, 83–84, 100
  XMetal, 77
  XML Notepad, 73–74, 95–96
  XML Pro, 74–75, 98–99
  XML Spy. *See* XML Spy
EIL (Extensible Indexing Language), 16
Electronic Thesis & Dissertation Markup Language (ETD-ML), 17
element content, 116
element declarations
  * (asterisk), 119–120
  | (pipes), 119
  + (plus sign), 119, 145
  ANY keyword, 118
  child element syntax, 116
  complex example, 120–123
  content models. *See* content models
  defined, 114
  EMPTY keyword, 117–118
  example project, 145–146
  naming elements, 114–115
  operators for, 118–120
  #PCDATA keyword, 115–116
  syntax, 114
elementFormDefault attribute, 167–169
elements
  adding to DTDs. *See* element declarations
  attributes of. *See* attributes
  cardinality, 119, 145, 171
  child. *See* child elements
  complex type, 169
  content, 43–46. *See also* content models
  converting to attributes, 232–234
  data content, 43
  declarations in DTDs. *See* element declarations
  defined, 31
  delimiters, 31
  empty, 41, 44–46
  example project, 62–65
  extent of, 42–43
  hierarchy of, 37–39
  mixed content of, 43–44
  names, 41–42, 114–115
  no content in, 45
  #PCDATA contents, 43
  prefixes to names. *See* namespace declarations
  representations of, 37–39
  root. *See* root elements
  SGML, 9
  siblings, 40
  summary of rules, 58
  syntax of generic, 41
  tags for, 41–42
  types, 42, 169
element types
  defined, 42
  table of, 172
  XML Schema specification of, 169
Emacs, 70–72, 74
empty elements
  content model for, 117–118
  schema declarations of, 179
  syntax for, 41, 44–46
  XHTML, 300–301
encoding attribute, 33–34
end-of-line markers, 126
end tags, 41
entities
  character references, 51–52
  declaring. *See* entity declarations
  defined, 31, 49
  ENTITY type, 124, 172
  external, 49
  general, 49, 127–128
  internal, 49
  parameter, 50, 51, 128–130
  parsed, 31, 49
  predefined, 49
  referencing, 49, 128–130
  text, 49
  unparsed, 49, 131
  uses of, 59
entity declarations
  character references in, 51–52
  defined, 49, 127
  external parameter, 130
  general, 49, 127–128
  internal parameter, 128–130
  parameter, 50, 128–130
  syntax, 50
entity references, 49
enumerated type, 125, 177, 195

Epic E-Content Engine (E3), 81
Epic Editor, 86–87
ETD-ML (Electronic Thesis & Dissertation Markup Language), 17
European Organization for Nuclear Research (CERN), 11
evolution of XML. *See* history
exposing namespaces, 168
Extended Backus-Naur Form (EBNF), 260
extended links, XLink, 238–239
Extensible Hypertext Markup Language (XHTML)
  advantages of, 292–293
  alt attributes, 317
  Amaya, 308–309, 318–319
  attribute errors, fixing, 316–318
  attribute ids, 302–303
  attribute syntax, 301–303
  attribute values, quotation marks for, 301, 305
  case sensitivity, 299, 301, 305
  closure of elements requirement, 299–303
  compatibility, 293, 305
  converting HTML sites to, 305–309, 314–318
  core modules, predefined, 291
  creating using Amaya, 318–319
  CSS with, 294, 304
  data binding with. *See* data binding
  data consumer elements, 473–474
  DOCTYPE definitions, 298, 314–315
  DTDs, 293–294, 303–304, 324
  editing using Amaya, 320–323
  elements, syntax for, 299–303
  empty elements, 300–301
  errors, fixing, 316–318
  extending documents, 303–304
  extensibility of, 292–293
  Frameset variant, 296
  graphics, adding, 323
  history of development, 289–291
  horizontal rules, 301
  HTML compatibility of, 288–289, 292
  HTML TIDY, 307–308, 314–316
  line breaks, 301
  links, adding, 321–322
  minimized attributes, 302
  modularization, 290, 293
  namespace declarations, 298, 303–304
  naming elements, 299, 305
  nesting requirement, 298
  portability, 293
  prologs, 297–298, 305
  purpose of, 288
  root elements, 298
  Ruby Annotation, 291
  specifications, 291
  structure compared to HTML, 296–297
  summary attributes, 317
  tables, 291, 320–321, 324
  Tidy, 307–308, 314–316
  Transitional variant, 295–296, 303
  validation, 305–307
  variants, 293–296
  Vector Markup Language (VML) compatibility, 339–440
  W3C Recommendation, 289–291
  W3C's validation service, 306–307
  well formed requirement, 297–299
  XML data islands in, 480–481
  XML validity of, 288, 292
Extensible Indexing Language (EIL), 16
Extensible Stylesheet Language (XSL), 199–203. *See also* XML Path Language (XPath); XSL Transformation (XSLT)
extension, 176
extents of elements, 42–43
external DTDs
  creating with XML Spy, 143–148
  designating, 110
  external URLs, 111–112
  FPIs, 112–113
  internal DTDs with, 113–114
  private, 110–111
  public access to, 112–113
  PUBLIC keyword, 112
  SYSTEM keyword, 110
external identifiers, table of, 131
external parameter entity declarations, 130
external style sheets, affiliating, 428–430
EzMath editor, 538–543, 554–559, 562–565

F

facets, 177, 179–182
fatal errors, 30, 55
files, organizing, 100–102
#FIXED keyword, 125
flat catalog approach, 172–175
FlowML, 17
formal public identifiers (FPIs), 112–113
formatting XML documents. *See* Cascading Style Sheets (CSS)
FORMEX (Formalized Exchange of Electronic Publications), 9
FPIs (formal public identifiers), 112–113
fractionDigits facet, 181
fragment identifiers, 258
freeform XML, 55

G

GCA (Graphic Communications Association), 5
general entities, 50, 127–128

Generalized Markup Language. *See* GML (Generalized Markup Language)
generic identifiers (GIs). *See* types
globally declared elements, 167, 168, 193–194
global references, 174
GML (Generalized Markup Language), 5–8
goals for XML, 19–20
Goldfarb, Charles, 8
graphical text editors
  Adobe FrameMaker + SGML, 76
  advantages of, 72–73
  automatic structure checking, 72–73
  Conglomerate, 77
  defined, 69
  features of, 73
  Peter's XML Editor, 75, 97–98
  Word, Microsoft, 77–81
  XAE, 74
  XMetal, 77
  XML Notepad, 73–74, 95–96
  XML Pro, 74–75, 98–99
graphics. *See also* images
  bitmaps, 326–328
  notation declarations, 130–132
  vector, markup language for. *See* Vector Markup Language (VML)
  XHTML, adding in, 323

H

headers. *See* XML declarations
hexadecimal references, 52
history
  Document Type Definitions (DTDs), 106, 289
  HTML, of, 10–13, 289–291
  markup, pre-GML, 4–5
  SGML, of, 8–10
  Text Description Language, 5
  Vector Markup Language (VML), 332–333
  XHTML, of, 289–291
  XML, of, 1, 13–15
hovering, CSSs for, 444
HTML. *See* Hypertext Markup Language (HTML)
HTML+, 289
HTML+TIME, 408
hypertext, 11
Hypertext Markup Language (HTML)
  converting to XHTML, 305–309, 314–318
  data consumer elements, 473–474
  defined, 10
  history of, 10–13, 289–291
  SGML, as subset of, 10
  specifying style sheets, 428–432
  Tidy, 307–308
  W3C extensions of, 15
  weaknesses of, 287–288
  XHTML. *See* Extensible Hypertext Markup Language (XHTML)
  XML compared to, 14–15
  XML data islands in, 480–481
Hypertext Transfer Protocol (HTTP) streaming, 384

I

IBM
  GML, creation of, 5
  Xeena editor, 83–84
IDEs (integrated development environments). *See* integrated development environments (IDEs)
ID type, 124, 172
IEC (International Electrotechnical Commission), 33
IIS Web service, creating, 66
images
  backgrounds, CSS-set, 450–451
  bitmap graphics, 326–328
  bitmaps, adding in VML, 374
  CDF IMAGE-WIDE attributes, 613
  inserting with CSS, 451–452
  vector. *See* Vector Markup Language (VML)
  VML bitmap references, 332, 360–361, 365
#IMPLIED, 125
importance of XML, 16–18
Information Technology Markup Language (ITML), 17
inheritance
  extension, 176
  restriction, 176–177, 180
inline styles, 431–432
installation script example, 25–26
instance documents, 161
instantiation, 216
integer type, 172
integrated development environments (IDEs)
  defined, 69, 81, 91
  Epic Editor, 86–87
  features of, 81
  Komodo, 86
  multi-user, 81
  project cycles, 82
  resemblance to text editors, 69
  test environments, advantages of, 102
  Turbo XML, 85–86
  versioning, 82
  Xeena, 83–84, 100
  XML Spy. *See* XML Spy
integrating XML with existing systems. *See* conversion to XML systems
internal DTDs, 110, 113–114, 152–154

internal style sheets, 430–431
internal subsets. *See* internal DTDs
International Electrotechnical Commission (IEC), 33
International Organization for Standardization (ISO), 8
Internet Explorer, Microsoft
  behaviors, 341–342
  channels, using. *See* Channel Definition Format (CDF)
  data binding, support for, 471
  MathML support, 541–545
  SMIL support, 408
  SVG support, 336
  viewing XML with, 63
  VML support, 331, 337–338
  Work Offline command, 587–588
ISBNs, 181
ISO (International Organization for Standardization), 8
ITML (Information Technology Markup Language), 17

J

J2 SDK JDE, 98
Java applets for data binding, 474
Java Development Environment, installing, 98
JavaScript
  Add Active Channel buttons, 593
  buttons, creating, 510–511
  event handlers, 511
  function code, 492–493, 511–512
  navigating recordsets with, 491–493
  single-valued consumer elements, 495–498, 510–514
Java servelets example, 26–28

K

Komodo, 86

L

language encoding. *See* characters
languages based on XML. *See* XML-based languages
language specification, 126–127
language type, 172
Length facet, 181
libxml, 270
linking
  CDF, 585–586, 589, 593, 622–624
  overview, 235
  XLink. *See* XML Linking Language (XLink)
  XPointer. *See* XML Pointer Language (XPointer)
local elements of schemas, 167–169
locator attributes, 204
logical structure of XML documents, 31
logon resource example, 26

M

Macintosh computers, SimpleText editor, 70
margins, setting with style rules, 454
markup declarations. *See* document type definitions (DTDs)
markup language
  advantages of, 6–7
  defined, 2, 3
  examples of, non-XML, 3
  GML, 5–8
  history of, pre-XML, 4–13
  HTML, 10–13
  standards development, 7–8
  tags, 4
  XML as, 2–4
  XML-based, 18
markup specification language. *See* markup language
MathML (Mathematical Markup Language)
  1.0 *vs.* 2.0, 524
  abstract expression trees, 535–536
  algebra elements, table of, 531–532, 534
  algebraic expressions, creating, 550–552, 554–565
  alttext attribute, 525
  ambiguity of symbols, 516–517
  application software using, 523
  apply elements, 529
  arithmetic elements, table of, 531–532
  basic elements, table of, 531
  browsers, displaying in, 541–545, 558–559
  calculus elements, table of, 532–533
  calculus equations, 565–570
  components of expressions, 526
  content elements, table of, 531–534
  content markup code generation, 554–559
  content markup specifications, 528–534
  CSS support attributes, 525
  defined, 17, 523
  derivatives, 567, 569
  design goals, 521
  display attribute, 525
  displaying expressions in browsers, 540–543
  downloading editors, 549
  DTDs, 535
  editors, 537–544, 549. *See also* EzMath editor; MathType editor
  embedded elements, attributes for, 526
  equation editors, 527
  expressions, entering in EzMath, 538–540

EzMath editor, 538–543, 554–559, 562–565
fractions, 560–561
general markup specifications, 524–526
glyphs, 527
goals of MathML development, 519–521
graphic images, drawbacks of, 517–518
history, 518–520
identifiers, 527
integrals, 565–566, 568
inward-looking attributes, 525
Layer 1, 522
Layer 2, 523
layered architecture approach, 521–522
layout boxes, 536–537
layout elements, table of, 528
linear algebra elements, table of, 534
loan payment equation examples, 559–565
localization issues, 517
math element, 524–525
MathPlayer, 544
MathType editor, 536, 543–544, 549–554, 559–561
"m" elements, 526–528
mrow elements, 526–527
namespace declarations, 525, 535
need for math expression, 515
numbers, 527
operators, 527
outward-looking attributes, 525–526
overflow attributes, 525–526
Polish notation, 529
prefix notation (PN), 529–530
presentation issues, 517
presentation markup specifications, 526–528
presenters, 537
purpose of, 523
reading content markup, 530
relational elements, table of, 532
script elements, table of, 528
semantic issues, 517
semantic markup specifications, 528–534
sequence elements, table of, 533
set theory elements, table of, 533
space, 527
statistics elements, table of, 533
string literals, 527
subscripts, 528
superscripts, 528, 550–551, 561
syntax, fixing, 558
table elements, table of, 528
text, 527
token elements, 527, 531
top-level elements, 524
trigonometry elements, table of, 533
validation service, 535
W3C Recommendation for, 520–521
Web page design considerations, 534–535
Word, Microsoft, 543
xref attribute, 525
MathType editor, 536, 543–544, 549–554, 559–561
maxExclusive facet, 181
maxInclusive attribute, 191
maxLength facet, 181
maxOccurs attribute, 171, 188, 190
metainformation, DTDs. *See* document type definitions (DTDs), metainformation
metalanguage, XML as, 2–3
Microsoft
CDF Generator, 617
Channel Definition Format (CDF), 13, 16
Internet Explorer. *See* Internet Explorer, Microsoft
MSXML Parser, 224
Notepad, 62–64
Word, 77–81, 91, 380–381
XML Notepad, 73–74, 95–96
minExclusive facet, 181
minInclusive attribute, 180
minLength facet, 181
minOccurs attribute, 171, 190
mixed content elements in XML schemas, 178–179
mixed content of elements, 43–44
Mozilla, XLink support, 270
MS Word. *See* Microsoft, Word
MSXML Parser, 224
multimedia. *See* Synchronized Multimedia Integration Language (SMIL)
Murray-Rust, Peter, 13
music, FlowML, 17. *See also* audio

N

namespace declarations
abbreviations, 164–165
chameleon namespaces, 167
data binding, XHTML, 483
defaults, 165
DTDs with, 132–137
exposing namespaces, 168
MathML, 525, 535
purpose of, 163–164
qualifying elements, 168
schemas with, 163–167
SMIL, 389
support namespaces, 167
target namespaces, 165–167, 189
URL's role in, 164
Vector Markup Language (VML), 339–340, 369
W3C Namespace Recommendation, 163–164

XHTML, 303–304
XLink, 241, 245
XSLT, 207
XSL Transformation (XSLT), 207
names, specifying, 114–115
navigating recordsets, 491–498
NCNames, 242
N-converters, 81
nesting, 39, 54
nesting doll structures, 172–175
Netscape Navigator
MathML support, 541–545
SVG support, 336
viewing XML with, 63
NMTOKEN(S) type, 125, 177
non-XML converters, 81
notation declarations, 130–132
NOTATION type, 125
Notepad, document creation with, 62–64

O

object-oriented graphics. *See* Vector Markup Language (VML)
opening tags, 41
Open Software Description Format (OSD), 577
operators, element declarations, 118–120
Oratrix Development, SMIL support, 408
organizing files, 100–102
OSD (Open Software Description Format), 577

P

parameter entities, 50, 51, 128–130
parent elements, 39–40
parsed character data, 171
parsed entities, 31
parsers
XML, 30, 224
XSL, 203, 224–225
PATH variable, 98
pattern facet, 180–181
#PCDATA, 43, 115–116
Personal Web server, 102
Peter's XML Editor, 75, 97–98
PGML. *See* Precision Graphics Markup Language (PGML)
physical structure, 31
pipes (|), 119
PIs (processing instructions), 35–36
pixels, 326
plus sign (+), 119, 145
points, XPointer, 263, 266–268
positioning elements with style rules, 454–456
PowerPoint data, converting to SMIL, 409
Precision Graphics Markup Language (PGML), 334–335
prefix namespace declarations, 135, 163–165
processing instructions (PIs), 35–36
prologs
Channel Definition Format (CDF), 595, 610
comments, 36–37
components of, list, 32
defined, 31–32
document type declarations, 34–35
external style sheets, affiliating with XML, 428–430
optional nature of components, 32
processing instructions, 35–36
schema, 162
SMIL, 387–388
Vector Markup Language (VML), 338–339
white space in, 32
XHTML, 297–298
XML declarations, 33–34
pseudo-attributes, 204
PUBLIC identifier, 131
pull technology, 572–573
push technology, 572, 573

Q

qname type, 172
qualifying elements of schemas, 168
QuickTime, SMIL support, 408

R

ranges, XPointer, 267
raster graphic files, 326
RDF (Resource Description Framework Model and Syntax Specification), 578
RealPlayer, SMIL support, 408–409
Recommendations of the W3C
Cascading Style Sheets, 426–427
CDF note, 578–579
MathML, 520–521
Namespace Recommendation, 163–164
Schema Recommendation, 157, 159–160
SVG, 335–336
VML note, 332–333
well-formed documents, 54
XHTML, 289–291
XLink, 236
XML, 19–20, 28
XPointer, 256
recordsets
advantages of, 491
BOF (beginning of file), 493
dataPageSize attributes, 495
defined, 488
EOF (end of file), 493
functions, navigation, 493–494
JavaScript for navigating, 491–494
navigation example, 510–514
nested elements, 489–491
single-valued consumer elements, 495–498
references to external CSSs, 428–429, 466–467
referencing entities, 128–130
ref keyword, 173–175

#REQUIRED keyword, 125
reserved characters, 49
Resource Description Framework Model and Syntax Specification (RDF), 578
restriction, 176–177, 180
root elements
  creating, example project, 145
  defined, 39
  element content, 43
  schema elements, 163–169
  smil elements, 387–389
  XSLT stylesheet elements, 207–208
rootnames, 34
Russian doll structures, 172–175

S

Scalable Vector Graphics (SVG), 325, 333, 335–336
schema elements
  elementFormDefault attribute, 167–169
  globally declared elements, 167, 168
  local elements, 167–169
  namespace declarations in, 163–167
  root elements, equivalent to, 163
schemas. *See* XML schemas
scientific expressions. *See* MathML (Mathematical Markup Language)
scoped language, 174
selectors, CSS
  after elements, 437–438
  classes with, 439–443, 464
  defined, 434
  DTDs for classes, 441, 447
  before elements, 437–438
  elements, classes with specific, 442–443
  first item, modifying, 447–449
  first-letter elements, 437
  first-line elements, 437
  grouping by id attributes, 447–449
  grouping by pseudo-classes, 443–447
  hyperlinks, 444–447
  id attributes, grouping by, 447–449
  links, 444–447
  pseudo-classes, 443–447
  pseudo-elements with, 437–438
  selector groups, 439
  XML elements with, 469–470
sequence compositors, 170
set binding, 474, 478–479
SGML (Standardized General Markup Language)
  Adobe FrameMaker + SGML editor, 76
  disadvantages for Web use, 10
  document type declarations, 107
  DTDs, 9–10
  elements, 9
  Epic Editor, 86–87
  history of, 8–10
  HTML as subset of, 10
  languages based on, 8–9
  XML compared to, 14
  XML defined as subset of, 2, 13
siblings, 40
simple content elements, 176
SimpleText editor, 70
simple text editors
  characteristics of, 70
  defined, 69
  Emacs, GNU, 70–72
  Notepad, 62–64, 70
  SimpleText editor, 70
  vi, 70
simple types
  elements, 169
  globally referenced, 178
  table of, 172
single-valued data consumer elements, 474
SMIL. *See* Synchronized Multimedia Integration Language (SMIL)
SoftQuad XMetal, 77
specifications. *See* Recommendations of the W3C
specifying style sheets, 428–432
Sperberg-McQueen, C.M., 13
standalone attributes, 34, 110
Standardized General Markup Language. *See* SGML (Standardized General Markup Language)
standards development, 7–8
start tags, 41
store archive tools example, 25–26
streaming media, 383–384. *See also* Synchronized Multimedia Integration Language (SMIL)
string type, 172
structure of XML documents, 39–40
STYLE attribute syntax, 431–432
styling XML documents. *See* Cascading Style Sheets (CSS)
subelements. *See also* child elements
  adding to schemas, 190–191
  attributes, 170–171
  defined, 163
  sequencing, 170
Sun Microsystems J2 SDK installation, 98
support namespaces, 167
SVG (Scalable Vector Graphics), 325
Synchronized Multimedia Integration Language (SMIL)
  anchor elements, 401, 404–407
  animation elements, 399
  attributes of anchor elements, 406–407
  attributes of an element, 405–406
  attributes of media object elements, 400–401

attributes, seq elements, 397–398
audio elements, 399
bandwidth determination, 402
begin attributes, 398, 401
body elements, 387, 388, 395–396, 414
browser support for, 408–409
child elements, 395
clients, testing capabilities of, 395, 402–403
closed captioning, 402
components of, 409–410
content, adding to presentations, 416–420
continuous media, 400
creating documents, 387, 408–409, 413–414
defined, 384
discrete media, 400
div elements, 421
DOCTYPE definitions, 387–388
DTDs for, 386–388, 414
a elements, 404–407
elements of, 409–410
end attributes, 398, 401
features of, 384–385
filling regions, 393–394
fragment parts, 405
growing objects into regions, 393–394
head elements, 387–389, 414
HTML documents, linking to, 404–407
HTML+TIME, 408, 418–423
hyperlinks, 401, 404–407
id attributes, 388–389, 391, 401
img elements, 391, 399, 400, 417, 422
IMPORT instruction with, 419
Internet Explorer with, 418–423
intrinsic duration objects, 400
language selection, 402–403
layout elements, 389–390, 415–416
lifecycle control, 398
links, 401, 404–407
location bars, 390
markup modules, 386
media object elements, 399–403
meta elements, 394
namespace declarations, 389, 419
Oratrix Development, 408
overlap priority, 392
parallel operations, 395–396, 398–399, 416, 420
players, 390
positioning, 390–394
PowerPoint, converting to SMIL, 409
progress bars, 390
prologs, 387–388
purpose of, 17, 383–384
RealNetworks support for, 408–409, 416–418
RealText files, 416–417
ref elements, 399, 400
region attributes, 400, 417
region elements, 391–394, 400, 415–416
root-layout elements, 390–391, 415–416
scrollable objects, 394
sequential operations, 395–398, 417, 420–422
slide shows, 417, 422
SMIL 2.0, 384, 385–386
smil elements, 387–389
specifications, W3C, 385–386
status bars, 390
stream separation, 384
stylesheet declaration, 419
switch elements, 395, 402–403
synchronization elements, 395–396
temporal sequences, 396–398
text elements, 399
textstream elements, 399
title attributes, 394
video elements, 399, 417, 420
viewing documents, 408–409
viewports, 390–394
XML declarations, 387
z-index values, 392
SYSTEM identifiers, 131

T

tabular data consumer elements, 474
tags. *See also* elements
attributes in, 46–48
delimiters, 41
end, 41
GML, 6
HTML, limitations of, 11
markup language, 4
names, rules for, 41–42
opening, 41
start, 41
syntax of, 41
TEI (Text Encoding Initiative), 9
Telecommunications Industry Markup (TIM), 9
test environments, advantages of, 102
text/css media type, 463
Text Description Language, 5
Tidy, 314–316
TIM (Telecommunications Industry Markup), 9
time type, 172
totalDigits facet, 181
transforming XML documents
DTD interpretation, 205–207
grammar conversion, 232–234
HTML, converting to, example, 224–230
matching elements, 213–214
phases of process, 198–199
process, basic steps, 198–199
pseudo-attributes, 204
purpose of, 198
source trees, 203, 212–213

styling for HTML, 217–220
XPath, 201
XSL, 199–201
XSLT, 201–202, 207–214
transportableness of documents, 6
traversing links, 240
tree diagrams, 38–39
true streaming, 384
Tunnicliffe, William, 5
Turbo XML, 85–86
Two-Level Rule, 489–491
types
complex type declarations, 175–177
defined, 31
simple types, table of, 172

U

UCS (Universal Multiple-Octet Coded Character Set), 33–34
Unicode
character references, 51–52
encoding attribute, 33
Uniform Resource Identifiers (URIs)
(hash symbol), 257
| (pipes), 257
anyURI type, 172
connectors, 257
defined, 134
fragment identifiers, 258
locations, 258–259
paths, location, 258–259
steps, location, 258–259
syntax for, 260
Web site address portion, 257
XPointer addressing of, 257–259
xpointer keyword, 258
Universal Multiple-Octet Coded Character Set (UCS), 33–34
UNIX Emacs editor, 70–72
unparsed data notation declarations, 130–132
unparsed entities, 31, 131
unqualified local elements, 169
UPCs (Universal Product Codes), 180
upgrading systems to XML. *See* conversion to XML systems
URIs (Uniform Resource Identifiers). *See* Uniform Resource Identifiers (URIs)
use attribute, 177

V

validation
Cascading Style Sheets, 427
criteria for, 55–57
DTDs for, 114
MathML, 535
XHTML, 305–307
XLink, 249–255
XML Spy to check for, 153–154
values of attributes, assigning, 47–48
vector graphic images, 328–331. *See also* Vector Markup Language (VML)
Vector Markup Language (VML)
absolute positioning, 352–353
advantages, 330, 336–337
arcs, 348
attributes for predefined shapes, table of, 350
attributes of fill elements, 358–361
attributes, shape elements, 344
behavior declarations, 341–342, 370
Bézier curves, 345
bitmap references in, 332, 360–361, 365
body elements, 338–339
boxes, block level, 343
browser support for, 331, 338
circles, 348
color, adding to shapes, 357–358, 375
combining elements, 362–364
coordinate systems, 343, 349
coupon example, 371–379
creating documents, 337–338, 369–370
CSS with, 332
curved lines, 348
default templates, 343, 350
defined, 331
delimiters, 346
design requirements from W3C, 333
disadvantages of vector graphics, 330–331
element categories, 343
examples, finding on Web, 338
fillcolor attributes, 344, 350, 351
fill elements, 358–361, 376
flipping images, 354–355
gradient fills, 359, 376
grouping elements, 362–364, 378–379
head elements, 338–339
history, 332–333
HTML integration of, 332
id attribute, 350, 351
imagedata elements, 360–361
images, bitmap, adding, 374
lines, 348
Microsoft Office 2000 support for, 337, 340, 342, 380–381
mirror images, 356–357
namespace declarations, 339–340, 369
ovals, 348
overlap control, 353–354, 373
path attributes, 344–346
path elements, 344, 346–347, 374–375
pattern fills, 360
pen commands, 345

PGML, compared to, 334–335
picture fills, 360–361
placement on Web pages, 351–357
polylines, 348
positioning attributes, 343
predefined shapes, 343, 347–351
Primary category, 343
primitive graphic objects, 342
prologs, 338–339
proprietary motives for, 334
purpose of, 325–326
rectangles, 348, 371–372
relative positioning, 353
reusing figures, 351, 377–378
rotation, 354–355
scaling, 362
shadows, 372
.shape, 342
shape elements, 343–344, 374–375
shapetype elements, 351, 377–378
squares, drawing with paths, 345–346
start tags, 352
static positioning, 352
stroke attributes, 350
style attributes, 344, 356
style elements, 338–339, 341–342
Subelements category, 343
SVG to supersede, 333
text boxes, 371–372, 376
title elements, 339
Top-level category, 343
vector graphic image fundamentals, 328–331
VML Generator, Microsoft, 338
W3C note on, 332
Word, Microsoft, creating with, 380–381
XHTML syntax compatibility, 339–440
XML basis of, 331
XML Spy support for, 338
z-index, 353–354, 373
Venn diagrams, 38–39
versioning, 82
vi, 70
video. *See also* Synchronized Multimedia Integration Language (SMIL)
intrinsic duration objects, 400
notation declarations, 130–132
visual web content. *See* Vector Markup Language (VML)
VML. *See* Vector Markup Language (VML)
VML Generator, Microsoft, 338
vocabularies, XML. *See* XML vocabularies
Voice Extensible Markup Language (VXML), 17
VXML (Voice Extensible Markup Language), 17

W

W3C. *See* Recommendations of the W3C; World Wide Web Consortium (W3C)
W3C Notes
CDF, 578–579
VML, 332–333
WARNING tags, 44
weaknesses of XML, 18
webcasting, 573–575
Web Schematics proposal, 335
Web service, creating, 66
well-formed documents, 53–55, 57, 66
white space
CDATA sections for, 53
DTDs for handling, 109, 126
interpretation of, 48–49
preservation of, 49
prologs with, 32
whiteSpace facet, 181
XSLT, 212
whiteSpace facet, 181
Word, Microsoft
VML generation, 380–381
XML generation, 77–81, 91
World Wide Web Consortium (W3C)
hosts, 19
HTML development by, 15
notes. *See* W3C Notes
purpose of, 19
Recommendations. *See* Recommendations of the W3C
Web site, 28
XML defined by, 2
XML development by, 13, 19–20

X

XAE (XML Authoring Environment for Emacs), 74
Xeena, 83–84, 100
XHTML. *See* Extensible Hypertext Markup Language (XHTML)
XLink. *See* XML Linking Language (XLink)
XLL. *See* XML Linking Language (XLink)
XMetal, 77
XML applications, 18, 30
XML Authoring Environment for Emacs, 74
XML-based languages
defined, 18
table of examples, 16–17
XML declarations
attributes of, 33
defined, 33–34
encoding attribute, 33
standalone attribute, 34, 110
syntax, 33
XML schemas, 162
XML documents. *See* documents, XML
XML:lang attribute, 126–127

XML Linking. *See* XML Linking Language (XLink)
XML Linking Language (XLink)
- actuate attributes, 242–243
- advantages over HTML, 236
- arcrole attributes, 241
- arcs, 240, 247–248, 281
- attributes, 241–244
- creating extended links, 280–281
- creating links in XML with, 240–248, 277–279
- declaring links, 245–248
- defined, 236
- DTDs for, 249–255
- elements, 240–241, 243–244
- ending resources, 240
- extended links, 238–239, 246–248, 280–284
- extended-type elements, 246–248, 250–255
- formatting links with style rules, 277
- from attributes, 242, 281
- global attributes, 244
- href attributes, 241, 281
- hyperlinks, 237
- implementations available, 270–271
- inbound arcs, 240, 250
- label attributes, 242, 249
- links, defined, 237
- local resources, 240
- locator-type linking elements, 249–250
- multidirectional links, 240
- multiple channels feature, 236
- namespace declaration, 241, 245, 281
- NCNames, 242
- Netscape Navigator 6.2 support for, 277–279
- outbound arcs, 240, 250–251
- parent/child attribute restrictions, 244
- Recommendations of the W3C, 236
- relationships, encapsulating, 251
- remote resources, 240
- resources, 239–240, 247–249, 281
- resource-type linking elements, 249
- role attributes, 241, 249, 281
- show attributes, 242, 281
- simple links, 237–239, 245, 255
- starting resources, 240
- third-party arcs, 240
- title attributes, 241, 249, 281
- to attributes, 242, 281
- traversing links, 240
- type/attribute restrictions, 244
- type attributes, 241, 243–244, 281
- unidirectional links, 240
- validation, 249–255
- viewing with XML Spy, 276
- well-formed requirement, 249

XML Notepad, 73–74, 95–96
XML parsers, 30, 224
XML Path Language (XPath)
- axes, 260–262
- defined, 200
- purpose of, 201
- XPointer, basis for, 256

XML Pointer Language (XPointer)
- :: (defined by symbol), 260
- abbreviations for references, 269–270
- axes, 260–262
- booleans, 263
- character-points, 267–268
- child nodes, 267
- counting elements, 263
- EBNF, 260
- features of, 256–257
- fragment identifiers, 258
- functions, 263
- here() function, 263
- id() function, 263, 269
- implementations available, 270
- indexes, 267, 284
- location paths, 258–259, 283–284
- locations, 258–259
- node-points, 267–268
- node sets, 263
- node tests, 260, 262–263
- numbers predicates, 263
- origin() function, 263
- points, 263, 266–268, 284–285
- predicates, 260, 263
- purpose of, 255–256
- ranges, 263, 267, 268–269, 284–285
- references, 265, 269–270, 283–284
- result tree fragments predicates, 263
- root() function, 263
- simple links with, 256
- start-point() function, 268
- steps, location, 258–259
- strings predicates, 263
- syntax for URIs, 260
- Universal Resource Identifiers (URIs), 257–259
- viewing, 282–283
- W3C Recommendation, 256
- XPath basis of, 256

XML Pro, 74–75, 98–99
XML processors, 30
XML Schema. *See* XML schemas
XML Schema Definition Language (XSD), 159, 162. *See also* XML schemas
XML schemas
- abbreviations, namespace, 164–165
- adding elements to, 189–191
- advantages of, 159–160
- archetypes, 174, 178
- attributes of elements, 170–171, 195
- based on XML, 159
- cardinality of elements, 170
- classes, 161

complex type declarations, 169, 175–177
compositors, 170
constraints, 161
content attributes, 178
content model constraints, 161
content type, 169
creating documents based on, 192
creating, example project, 188–189
data type, 169
datatype constraints, 161
defined, 159–161
disadvantages *vs.* DTDs, 159
DTD's, converting from, 186–187
elementFormDefault attribute, 167–169
empty element declarations, 179
enumerated type, 177, 195
facets, 179–182
flat structures, 172–175
globally declared elements, 167, 168, 193–194
global references, 174, 178
grammar, 161
headers, 162
instance documents, 161
local elements, 167–169
maxInclusive attribute, 180, 191
maxOccurs attribute, 171, 188, 190
minInclusive attribute, 180
minOccurs attribute, 171, 190
mixed content elements, 178–179
modeling languages, list of, 158
namespace declarations, 163–167
nesting doll structures, 172–175
pattern facet, 180–181
prologs, 162
purpose of, 161
qualifying elements, 168
referencing element declarations, 173–175
restricting data selection, 195
restriction, inheritance, 176–177, 180
schema elements, 163–169
sequence elements, 170
simple content elements, 176
simple types, table of, 172
subelements, 163, 170–175
type attributes, 170
types, 169
use attribute, 177
vocabularies, 161
W3C Schema Recommendation, 157, 159–160
XML declarations, 162
.xsd files, 162

XML:space attribute, 49, 126

XML Spy
adding data to documents, 150–152
configuring file sharing with server, 102
converting DTDs to schemas, 186–187
creating documents from DTDs, 148–149
DTDs, creating, 143–148
features of, 84–85
Intelligent Editing feature, 145
namespace abbreviation default, 164
organizing files with, 100–102
schema creation, 187–189
SMIL file creation, 414
style sheets, opening, 101
validating XML, 153–154
viewing XML with, 64–65
VML, support for, 338
well-formedness, checking, 66
XSL parsers for, 203, 224–225

?xml-stylesheet instruction, 428

XML vocabularies
advantages to creating, 105–106
creating, example projects, 143–148
defined, 18
XML schemas to establish, 161

xmnls. *See* namespace declarations

XPath
context setting, 213
template rules in XSLT, 213

XSchema. *See* XML schemas

XSD. *See* XML Schema Definition Language (XSD)

.xsd files, 162

XSL. *See* Extensible Stylesheet Language (XSL)

XSL parsers, 202–203

XSL Transformation (XSLT)
applying transformations, 226–227
attribute-set elements, 209
choose statements, 230–232
conditional processing elements, 230–232
context setting, 213
current template rules, 216
decimal format elements, 209
defined, 200
displaying output, 218
document elements, 207
DTDs with, 201–207
encoding for output method, 212
for-each elements, 217–220, 226
formatting output, 218
grammar conversion, 232–234
headers, 207
HTML, converting to, 224–230
HTML document templates, 215–216
if statements, 230–232
import elements, 209–210
include elements, 209–210
key elements, 209
looping, 217–220
matching to nodes, 213–214
modes, 229–230
namespace-alias elements, 209–210

namespace declarations, 207
nodes, table for matching, 214
output attributes, 211–212, 225, 232
output elements, 209–211
param elements, 209
preserve-space elements, 209
process of transformation by, 202–203
purpose of, 201–202
query context, 212–213
result trees, 203, 212–213, 221
sorting, 217, 228–229
source trees, 203, 212–213, 221
strip-space elements, 209
style sheets, 207–212
tags, 207
template elements, 209, 213, 225, 229–230
template rules, 213
top-level elements, 208–209
variable elements, 209, 230–232
version for output method, 212
viewing files, 225–226
white space, 212
XPath expressions in, 213
XSL code, adding, 227
XSL parsers with, 202–203
xsl: prefixes, 207